Television
and Radio

❖ AN INTRODUCTION ❖

By

GIRAUD CHESTER

General Programming Executive
National Broadcasting Company

AND

GARNET R. GARRISON

Professor of Speech
Director of Television
University of Michigan

Second  Edition

APPLETON-CENTURY-CROFTS, Inc.

New York

TELEVISION AND RADIO

PREFACE

WHEN the first edition of this book was published in 1950, about 100 television stations were broadcasting programs several hours a day and about 5,000,000 television sets had been installed in American homes. In 1956, on the publication of this second edition, about 450 television stations are on the air—many of them broadcasting programs 18 hours a day. About 37,000,000 television sets are now in use an average of about 6 hours a day. From morning through the late evening hours, television now commands the "strongest sustained attention" of many millions of American families. In competition with television, radio has continued to maintain a place as a major mass communications medium, but its hold on the American public has lessened markedly, especially in the evening hours, and its programming has undergone vital changes.

These facts, together with increased student interest in television, have induced us, in preparing this new edition, to make important changes in content and emphasis to reflect the new facts and new interests. Our basic intention, however, remains the same: to provide a comprehensive, up-to-date textbook for introductory courses in broadcasting. These courses are now offered in several hundred colleges and universities. Many of these courses have been created in answer to student demands; others have resulted from the acquisition by educational institutions of FM radio broadcasting licenses, television broadcasting licenses, or closed-circuit studio equipment; still others have been organized by faculty members who perceive the value of training in television and radio and the social significance of the entire broadcasting enterprise.

Faced with the problem of training students in the broadcasting skills and supplying them with a body of knowledge about the field, many teachers find it difficult to organize and present effective courses without the aid of a comprehensive textbook and adequate practice materials. It has been a matter of real gratification to us that the first edition of this text won such wide acceptance from college teachers and students throughout the country. It is our belief that this second edition, prepared on the basis of our experience in teaching college courses, in educational broadcasting, and in commercial broadcasting, contains all the basic materials essential to a first course in broadcasting.

For courses concerned primarily with the social aspects of broadcasting, Part I, supplemented by such chapters from Part II as time will allow, may suffice. For courses concentrated on training in fundamental broadcasting skills, Part II, which introduces the student to television and radio studio practices and techniques, may be used alone or together with chapters chosen from Part I. Thus the text may cover two semesters of study in the order preferred by the individual instructor. Or the book may be utilized in one semester by concurrent assignments in Parts I and II; for example, in the same week, students may be asked to read Chapters 1 and 15. In our own teaching we have preferred to link content and skills in this manner.

Knowing how hard it often is to obtain good exercise material for classroom use, we have provided ample broadcast copy for the various skills discussed in Part II, so that the text may be used as a working handbook. Most of the script excerpts included in the first edition have been replaced with more recent examples of broadcast copy. We have also increased the range of exercise material with many entirely new and different script illustrations. We have obtained clearance for the use of these selections in the classroom, *but we are obliged to caution all readers that these scripts are fully protected by copyright and common law and may not be broadcast without permission in writing from the individual authors or copyright holders, as the case may be.*

We have chosen to deal with television and radio concurrently because we believe that study of the nature and influence of the two communications media can most profitably proceed in this way. In the presentation of programming and production skills, we have tended to relate the two media by comparison and contrast. To satisfy the needs of those instructors who prefer not to teach both television and radio at the same time, we have provided separate chapters and sections for matters that pertain to one medium but not to the other. We have also provided separate practice material for production exercises in television and in radio. Where institutions lack the equipment necessary for direct instruction in television, this text should at least help to orient students to the field of television and to prepare them for what they must later learn in the television studio. We believe that those instructors who want to combine instruction in television and radio will find in this book a reasonably adequate treatment of both.

In order to provide additional space for the treatment of television without seriously reducing the space given to radio, we have increased the length of the book by about 100 pages. While the format and approach of this revision are not fundamentally different than those used in the first edition, certain chapters ("Programming" and "Educational Radio and Television") have been completely rewritten, other chapters have been extensively revised and enlarged to incorporate more recent information, and two entirely new chapters have been added—"Elements of Television Production" and "Film in Television."

Although in conception and execution this volume has been a joint project throughout, we have found it expedient to divide our primary responsibilities for authorship as follows: Part I plus the chapters on "Elements of Television Production," "News Programs," and "Discussion Programs"—Chester; all the other chapters—Garrison. One co-author is an executive of a national television network; the other is a professor and director of television at a state university. In this book, however, each of us speaks in his own right; the views we express are not to be ascribed to the company or institution with which we are affiliated.

We voice our thanks to the following for the assistance they gave us in obtaining useful materials for this book: Helen Borsum, Fred Buckner, Jack Drees, Paul Dudeck, Rodney Erickson, Bill Fleming, Ben Greer, Alan Handley, Lou Hazam, Frank LaTourette, Karl Lohmann, Merrill Mc-Clatchey, Tom McCray, Jack McGiffert, Robert Newman, Dick Osgood, Lynn Poole, Fred Remley, G. F. Roll, Howard Sacher, Hazen Schumacher, John Rich, John Turner, Josephine Wenk, Ed Wheeler, and L. H. Woodman. Our appreciation is also expressed to the numerous individuals, stations, networks, advertising agencies, publishers, and manufacturers who have permitted us to reproduce their materials, charts, and photographs. We also thank Mr. Howard Monderer, of the National Broadcasting Company, who read most of this book in galley proof and advanced many wise suggestions.

We are also greatly indebted to the many good people from whom we have learned much of what we now propose to teach. A complete accounting of this debt cannot be made here, and a long list of the names of our intellectual creditors would be pointless. There are some, however, whose names we choose to designate because our outstanding obligations are so large: Messrs. Julian Bercovici, Warren Burrmeister, Joseph Cunneff. Michael Dann, Samuel C. Fuller, John J. Heywood, Harold Kemp, Carl Lindemann, Jr., Tom Loeb, Stewart MacGregory, Thomas A. McAvity, Sidney Piermont, Richard A. R. Pinkham, Morris Rittenberg, William V. Sargent, Robert W. Sarnoff, Edward J. Stegeman, Sylvester L. Weaver, and Mort Werner.

G. C.

G. R. G.

CONTENTS

ix

CONTENTS

SCRIPTS

ILLUSTRATIONS

PHOTOGRAPHS

xiii

Studio Scene, Television Network Drama
Courtesy of National Broadcasting Company

Production Scene, "Medic"
Courtesy of National Broadcasting Company

RCA Color Vidicon Film Camera
Courtesy of Radio Corporation of America

FIGURES

Part I

TELEVISION AND RADIO
IN SOCIETY

Social Aspects of Broadcasting

IT HAS BEEN said that of all the peoples in the world, Americans, with their millions of television and radio sets, apparently stand most in fear of a moment of silence. It has also been said that the development of television and radio is the most significant technical advance in human communications since the invention of movable type. It is surely true that no student of the twentieth century can fail to observe how television and radio have succeeded in permeating everyday life in America, changing social habits and creating new ones, upsetting staid political practices, affecting tastes in all forms of entertainment, building unprecedented demand for products and services never before so widely distributed, and providing the individual at home with an eye and ear to the world outside.

The full social impact of television and radio has not yet been fully gauged or charted, but all preliminary evidence indicates that they represent a major new force in American society.

So useful have these new media of communication become that our whole society has become geared to them, and our daily lives are shaped by the messages they bear. Yet, less than two-score years ago, hardly more than a moment in the span of human history, broadcasting was little understood as a science and even less as an art. It was of no concern to the public, and was bereft of any social impact whatever. The change that has come over our society in these years can be described as nothing less than revolutionary. To the responsible citizen of today, it becomes significant to ask what is the full story of broadcasting's impact on our way of life and what social problems derive from its influence upon us?

This chapter will try to answer these questions by presenting a general outline of the role of television and radio in America. In doing so, it seems wise to discuss the following points: (1) the nature of the broadcasting media; (2) the dimensions of television and radio; (3) what television and radio convey to the American people; and (4) their effects on us and our ways of doing things.

· BROADCASTING DEFINED ·

For the sake of convenience in this discussion, we may define broadcasting as the transmission through space, by means of radio frequencies, of signals capable of being received either aurally or visually or both aurally and visually by the general public.

There are several types of broadcasting: Standard or AM (amplitude modulation) broadcasting of sound; FM (frequency modulation) broadcasting, a higher fidelity form of sound transmission; television, the transmission of moving pictures and sound; facsimile, the transmission of still pictures and writing, with or without sound, to be received on photographic paper; and numerous other types of broadcasting, including short-wave transmissions overseas, police radio, Army and Navy radio, microwave relays, and highly specialized forms of broadcasting such as radar. When we use the term "broadcasting" in this volume, it should be understood to include only AM and FM radio, and television.

· TRANSMISSION OF BROADCASTING ·

One way to gauge the scope of American broadcasting is to note how much effort and money go into the operation of our broadcasting system. In 1956, there were in operation four national radio networks, more than 2,800 individual AM radio stations, and more than 500 FM radio stations. There were three national television networks and more than 450 individual television stations, with additional stations in the offing.

Most of these stations transmit programs from sunup to sunset, and many continue until midnight and beyond. To produce income, they sell programs and time to advertisers. In 1954, according to the Federal Communications Commission, the revenues of the broadcasting industry, comprising revenues derived from the sale of time, talent, and program materials to advertisers, were reported as follows: radio $449 million, television $593 million, making a total of over $1 billion. That year industry profits from television (before federal income taxes) amounted to $90 million; the profits from radio that year were $42 million.

Of the $593 million total revenues of the television broadcast industry in 1954, $452 million (76 per cent) were derived from the sale of time on the air and $141 million (24 per cent) from sales of talent, program material, and production. Radio's total revenues of $449 million consisted of $404 million (90 per cent) from the sale of time and $45 million (10 per cent) from talent and program sales. In addition to these expenditures, $133 million were paid in commissions to advertising agencies and station representatives in connection with the sale of time and programming, and an estimated $193 million were paid by advertisers for talent and program production costs to organizations which do not operate networks and stations. Thus, the total advertising expenditures for television and radio in 1954 are estimated at $1.4 billion. In 1955, the advertising investment in television alone is estimated at over $1 billion.

· RECEPTION OF BROADCASTING ·

Television. From 1949 to 1956, the number of television sets installed in U. S. homes increased from 1 million to 36,900,000, the latter figure representing 70 per cent coverage of all U. S. households. By 1956, better than two out of three homes in America had a television set, representing a public investment of more than $15 billion for equipment, servicing, and repair, or nearly $100 for every man, woman, and child in the country, whether they own and enjoy television or not. Television set owners pay out an estimated $80 million each year solely to replace burned-out tubes with new ones, and close to half a billion dollars a year for electric power to operate their sets.

According to the A. C. Nielsen Co., these television sets were viewed in 1956 on the average of 6 hours and 2 minutes per day in each home! It is clear that, as Frank Stanton, President of the Columbia Broadcasting System, has said, "The strongest sustained attention of America is now, daily and nightly, bestowed on television as it is bestowed on nothing else."

Radio. Family ownership of radio sets in America has reached the point of approximately total saturation. More than 98 per cent of American homes have at least one radio set in working condition. More than 110 million radio sets are now in use, with 75 million installed in various rooms in U. S. homes: 25 million in living rooms, 22 million in bedrooms, 16 million in kitchens, 4 million in dining rooms, and 7 million in other places in the home. More than 35 million automobiles have radio installations, and 10 million sets are available in restaurants, offices, stores, and other places away from home.

In homes that have both radio and television receivers, the people listen to their radios an average of 1 hour and 45 minutes per day *in addition* to their television viewing; in homes without television, people listen to the radio an average of 4 hours and 5 minutes per day. Radio, with its unique ability to entertain and inform individuals while they are engaged in some other activity, has become the "companion" of the American individual, following him from room to room, to public places, and on the highway.

It has been said, with much truth, that listening to the radio and looking at television are the great common denominators of the American people. They dominate all leisure-time activity, with television viewing clearly assuming the role of America's favorite leisure-time pursuit.

• TELEVISION AND RADIO AS
SOCIAL FORCES •

With an audience as broad in scope as the American community itself, television and radio have become singularly powerful media to do good or evil in society. Their program offerings usually reflect the desires and values of our society, while their persistent command of our attention tends also to make them important creators of our values, desires, and tensions.

It is on those occasions when television and radio have turned America into a single thinking and feeling unit that the social force of these media has been made most evident. The power of radio was first indicated as early as 1933 when Franklin D. Roosevelt delivered his first inaugural address to an audience of many millions, assuring them that "the only thing they had to fear was fear itself." Roosevelt's fireside chats to audiences of 62 million people suggested the amazing potential of the radio medium—one individual, in a moment of time, bringing to bear upon a nation at large the full force of his vocal persuasiveness. In 1956, when President Dwight D. Eisenhower announced over all television and radio networks his intention to seek a second term, the total audience hearing his voice was estimated at 70 million.

The power of television to direct public attention to a single event was first demonstrated dramatically in March, 1951, when the telecast of the Kefauver Crime Committee hearings brought daytime business operations to a practical standstill as millions of people sat glued to television receivers at homes and in public places. This power to produce "peak" audiences is uniquely characteristic of television today, and it extends to the full range of nighttime entertainment programming. Mary Martin's performance in a telecast version of *Peter Pan* in March, 1955 was viewed simultaneously by 67 million people—doubtless the largest audience ever to witness a musical play at the same time.

Three television programs produced by Walt Disney dramatizing the life of Davy Crockett turned young America overnight into a mass of admiring and imitative fans of the coonskin-capped mountaineer.

Television and radio coverage of real happenings of importance throughout the world have made the American people direct eye and ear witnesses to events they could otherwise know only at second-hand—such events as the Coronation of Queen Elizabeth II, Presidential nominating conventions, meetings of the United Nations Security Council, Congressional committee hearings, atomic bomb test explosions, and numerous others. In this way, television and radio encompass the press, the public platform, the theater, the music hall, and the "real world" outside, and communicate them to an eager and attentive audience comfortably situated at home.

The significance of television and radio as forces in our society can be more fully understood by an examination of the several major areas of

belief and action in which their effects can be observed. These include
(1) politics; (2) economics; (3) education; (4) culture; and (5) social
behavior.

· TELEVISION, RADIO, AND POLITICS ·

Of all the facts that make television and radio important institutions in
our society, probably the most imposing is the opening of private homes for
the purpose of conveying political messages, either directly in the form of
political talks, or indirectly through the coverage of political events.
Political programs are important because it is clear beyond all doubt that
listeners and viewers at home are influenced by what they see and hear.

It has been demonstrated experimentally, for example, that even a single
fifteen-minute radio talk can significantly influence our attitudes on political
issues, and these shifts in attitude can still be observed two weeks after the
talk.[1] Our first dramatic evidence of the political effectiveness of radio came
in the 1930's when it was a common broadcasting practice to allow the air
to be used for political exhortation. The effectiveness of radio in inducing
specific political action was demonstrated on an extraordinary scale in 1935
when Father Charles E. Coughlin, a Detroit priest, denounced the World
Court in a radio talk and 200,000 telegrams tied up the wires of Western
Union. Again in 1938, Father Coughlin, in opposing a bill pending in
Congress, appealed to his listeners by saying, "The immediacy of the danger
insists that before tomorrow noon your telegram is in the hands of your
senator." By the next day, 100,000 telegrams had piled up on Congressional
desks, and thousands were still pouring in when the time came for a vote.

The great effectiveness of television and radio in election campaigning
has caused the major political parties to stage their political conventions
with a primary concern for broadcast coverage and to devote the lion's
share of their campaign budgets for the purchase of television and radio
time. These broadcasts offer the campaigner an unparalleled means to speak
directly and personally to the voters. In the Presidential campaign of 1952,
the first to be fully covered by both television and radio, Dwight D. Eisenhower and Adlai E. Stevenson turned to the broadcast media to reach the
voting public. Stevenson, a relatively new figure on the national political
scene, won millions of adherents through his television addresses. Eisenhower's saturation campaign of spot announcements on television and radio,
and the Republican Party's election eve telecast were considered by many
to be vital factors in influencing the outcome of the election. Both candidates
spent $6 million on television and radio during the campaign. "Never
before," stated the *New York Times* in an editorial, "has the voter had
such widespread opportunity to get the 'feel' of the man he may or may not

[1] John Dietrich, "The Relative Effectiveness of Two Modes of Radio Delivery in
Influencing Attitudes," *Speech Monographs*, XIII, No. 1 (1946).

vote for to sit in the White House. Never before has he been able, with his own eyes, to take measure repeatedly of the sincerity, the goodwill, and the intelligence of a candidate for high office."

In many local and state-wide campaigns, the use of all-day and all-night appearances over local television and radio stations have put more than one candidate into office; in New York State, Governor Thomas E. Dewey found that the extended personal appearance on television in a twenty-four-hour period was one of his most successful campaign devices. The use of television and radio for special "get-out-the-vote" campaigns has generally been credited with much of the responsibility for the increase in the number of voters casting their ballots in recent elections.

The wide use of television and radio in campaigning has also forced candidates to change the nature of their talks to meet the requirements of effective broadcast presentation. A greater emphasis has been placed on brevity in sustained speaking, greater informality of delivery, and an extreme concern for personal appearance. Interviews and discussions have been widely substituted for the formal address. Political leaders draw up convention schedules with a view toward best exposure on television and radio.

Outside of formal campaign periods, television and radio are used to foster political causes and personalities. Congressmen use television and radio to "tell the folks back home" how matters stand in Washington. Government administrators broadcast reports to the public, and parties out of power just as frequently seek air time to reply, when controversial matters are at stake. Labor and management spokesmen make regular use of the air to win support for particular legislative programs. Some politicians who appear on discussion programs claim that a supposedly nonpolitical appearance before a camera can be just as effective in winning friends, if not more so, than a straight political appearance. The numerous news summaries broadcast throughout the day with their news reports of important political statements and addresses also serve as vehicles for political messages to the public. Indeed, most experienced politicians release copies of their addresses for news coverage prior to the actual delivery of the speeches. Thus we often hear in an early evening newscast what a politician is scheduled to say to an audience later in the evening; several hours later newscasts repeat what he did say. In this way many politicians obtain double news coverage of addresses that are actually delivered before an audience of only a few hundred people.

The political uses of television and radio extend beyond that of election campaigning and building up political causes and personalities. Broadcasting has also been used as an instrument of war and violence. Germany's "strategy of terror" by radio, in its prewar campaign against Czechoslovakia and Poland in 1938 and 1939, laid the foundation for the acceptance of radio as a weapon of war. Broadcasts of a steady stream of distortions and lies, in the hands of skillful propagandists such as Hitler's minister, Joseph

Goebbels, were used to enslave the minds and corrupt the morals of whole populations. During World War II, the Allies, as well as Germany and Japan, tried to use radio to encourage dissension among the enemy. In a cold war, when the antagonists close their borders to travel, it is primarily through the airwaves that political information can be conveyed to foreign publics.

Knowing how vital a role broadcasting plays in America, the government has devised a means by which we can maintain our broadcasts even during enemy air attacks, without enabling the enemy planes to use the broadcast signals as beacons to guide them toward their bombing objectives.

Under a program known as "Conelrad" (CONtrol of ELectro-magnetic RADiation), announced by the United States in 1952, domestic FM radio and television stations will be silenced during emergency alerts, but designated AM stations will use 640 or 1240 kilocycles to broadcast essential news, information, and civil defense instructions. This operation will be juggled so as to confuse the enemy regarding the location of the participating stations.

• TELEVISION, RADIO, AND ECONOMICS •

The economic significance of television and radio extends far beyond the dollar volume of their business alone. Their full significance is measured by their importance as advertising media for the distribution and sale of all forms of consumer goods. Television has established itself as the most effective advertising and selling medium ever developed, while radio's ability to persuade listeners to buy certain goods is indicated by the fact that advertisers spend roughly half a billion dollars a year to use radio for this purpose.

A few examples will demonstrate the advertising effectiveness of television. The first example is the experience of the Dow Chemical Company which used television to advertise Saran Wrap, a consumer product that had been gathering dust on grocery shelves for eight years. In November, 1953, when Dow Chemical decided to promote Saran Wrap on network television, only 20,000 cases of the product were being sold each month. With television support, sales jumped to 110,000 cases in January, to 169,000 cases in February, and to more than 600,000 by October of the following year.[2]

The story of the Hazel Bishop lipstick company is another example of the amazing effectiveness of television advertising. In 1950, when the company came under new management, its gross annual business was $50,000. Thereafter, its sales campaigns were supported almost entirely (90 per cent) by television advertising. Its sales rose to $4,500,000 in 1952, to $10 million in 1953, and to $12 million in 1954, by which time it was spending $6

[2] *Advertising Age*, March 29, 1954.

million a year on television advertising and doing 25 per cent of the nation's lipstick business.

Another outstanding example of the remarkable effectiveness of television advertising was the experience of the Sunbeam Corporation which, through one season of network television advertising, succeeded in selling 1 million electric frying pans at $24.95 each, more than double their original expectation.

The immediate and phenomenal success of "The $64,000 Question," premiered on CBS television in 1955, within a few weeks sold out the entire stock of a new cosmetic advertised on the show; for months thereafter, the sponsor, the Revlon Company, had difficulty maintaining production at the level of the runaway sales. This episode, perhaps more than any other, dramatized a new fact of television programming and advertising: A major network television program success can affect not only the competitive positions of the networks themselves, but the competitive positions of the big consumer-product manufacturing companies in the nation, even to the extent of creating new industrial giants.

A special two-year study of the impact of television on the people of Fort Wayne, Indiana, was financed by the National Broadcasting Company. The research project was undertaken to determine what people did before television, how they spent their time, how they reacted to brand names, ideas and products—and what they did after television. The results of the study, entitled *Strangers into Customers,* were as follows:

1. After getting TV, people became more conscious of advertising. Television accounted for 7 out of 10 advertising impressions people absorbed. Television became a greater advertising source than newspapers, magazines, and radio combined were before the family acquired its set. (85 per cent *vs.* 80 per cent.)
2. TV made people aware of a brand name (average brand awareness increased 45 per cent), taught them what a product is and does (average brand-product association went up 59 per cent), increased their ability to recognize a trademark (average trademark recognition increased 68 per cent), taught consumers to identify a slogan or copy-point and made the housewife rate a brand more favorably (average brand rating went up 41 per cent).
3. TV presold durable goods, yielded great public-relation benefits and brought out the advertised brand as a make people would consider and buy. After TV, a washing machine manufacturer was thought of 44 per cent more often as "making the best," and 38 per cent more housewives would "consider buying" a brand-name refrigerator.
4. TV increased the number of customers. TV brands usually increased at the expense of their non-TV competitors (a brand-name evaporated milk won 51 per cent more buyers, while a competitor lost 14 per cent). More nonbuyers changed to product buyers among the housewives who had sets. TV also brought its advertisers a bigger share of the market. (In the whole of Fort Wayne, TV brands increased their share of purchases by 19 per cent in the typical package-goods field, while non-TV brands fell off 11 per cent).

5. The more a product was advertised on TV, the more buyer increase it got. The most advertised brands increased 48 per cent among set owners, while the brands with small TV schedules increased only 28 per cent.
6. TV worked fast and continued working. Those who had owned their sets longest, averaging a year or more, showed the highest buying levels for TV brands.
7. The effects of TV advertising were reflected sharply at the retailer level. Four dealers out of 10 stocked new brands as a result of TV advertising. TV advertising topped all other media in causing the dealer to give a brand more shelf space and special displays. On "doing the best job of moving goods in your store," dealers favored TV over newspapers almost 3 to 1, over magazines almost 10 to 1.[3]

No wonder television is referred to by advertisers as a selling machine.

• TELEVISION, RADIO, AND ENLIGHTENMENT •

Television and radio also serve as major sources of information and enlightenment for the American public. News broadcasts have long been among the public's favorite types of radio programs. During World War II, radio's ability to broadcast news bulletins a few moments after the actual events gave it a decided advantage over newspapers which had to contend with the delays of typesetting. For most people, radio has supplanted the press as the main and most trusted source of news. Although not to as great an extent as radio, television has also developed the news program as an integral element of its program fare. In the public mind both media are established sources for the first word of unexpected news developments.

The coverage of special events, including natural disasters such as floods and hurricanes, and events of public importance such as a Presidential inauguration or the announcement of the Salk polio vaccine, offers the public an opportunity to be present at the unfolding of history. Well-known programs, like "Meet the Press" and "See It Now," use the broadcast media to ventilate controversy on public matters and to probe deeply into issues of current importance. Programs of agricultural and consumer information and market and weather reports have come to play a vital role in the commerce of the nation. American farmers, especially, have become dependent on farm broadcasts for essential planting and marketing information. Formal and informal education programs have been presented by networks as well as by local commercial and noncommercial stations, and many of these have been successful. Broadcasts prepared for reception in schoolrooms have converted television and radio into schools-of-the-air in many cities and states. In the primary grades especially, television and radio have been markedly effective in beaming lesson material to the classroom where teachers and pupils may benefit by the greater facilities and skill at the

[3] *Strangers into Customers* (New York, National Broadcasting Company, 1955).

command of the studio instructor. In addition, networks have undertaken campaigns of what Sylvester L. Weaver, Chairman of the Board of the National Broadcasting Company, calls "enlightenment through exposure," in which elements of educational value are worked into the popular entertainment programs.

• TELEVISION, RADIO, AND CULTURE •

The ways in which people choose to entertain themselves or to be entertained, their levels of taste, the place they assign to creative works of art, are all matters of cultural significance. The fact that watching television and listening to the radio represent the favorite leisure-time activities of the American people makes both television and radio objects of cultural concern. What kinds of programs do people watch and listen to so eagerly? What levels of taste do these programs represent? What place is assigned to works of artistic quality? To what extent do television and radio develop cultural patterns of their own? To what extent do they create their own materials of entertainment and art? Or do they serve simply as a showcase for art and entertainment created elsewhere? To what extent has the public absorption in television and radio affected their interests and activities in other leisure-time pursuits, such as reading, conversation, sports, movie attendance, music study, painting, arts and crafts, etc.?

These are questions that deserve serious consideration if we are fully to understand the relationship between television, radio, and American culture. Answers to the questions, however, must remain tentative for the moment. We know that by and large the kinds of programs that people watch and listen to in greatest numbers are those that combine the broadest elements of audience appeal in comedy, variety, drama, personality shows, and programs involving audience participation. We know that unlike other fields of communication such as magazine and book publishing, which are able to publish all kinds of magazines and books ranging from those with very specialized appeal, and therefore limited readership, to those with broad appeal and mass readership, the television and radio media have tended, especially during the evening hours, to broadcast only those programs that are likely to attract the largest audiences. The reason for this is simple: a program with limited appeal set into an evening network program schedule makes it difficult to regain the audience for the following program because most people tend to stay with the station to which they are tuned rather than change stations at the end of each program. Nevertheless, programs of superior artistic taste have been produced at great cost by national television and radio networks in the hope that the public will turn to what is worth while rather than adhering to habitual tuning patterns. The concept of the "Spectacular" program developed by Sylvester L. Weaver, of the National Broadcasting Company, is based upon the idea that a program of superior quality, of whatever length necessary to do justice to its program material, will overcome habit patterns and attract an audience of substantial size. The best demonstrations of the truth of this concept appeared in the great success of the telecasts of *Peter Pan* and *Petrified Forest,* which drew larger audiences than their competition on another network—the regularly scheduled "I Love Lucy" program which at the time was the most popular weekly program on television.

By and large, both television and radio in the past have depended on the legitimate theater, the music hall, and the night clubs to provide them with performers and program material. Within less than ten years of its beginning, the television industry has discovered that its program demands can no longer be satisfied by turning to other entertainment media; as a result, the broadcast media have undertaken to develop performers and writers of their own in large-scale talent and writer development plans. The success of some of the best television dramatic writers, like Paddy Chayefsky, Reginald Rose, Robert Alan Aurthur, N. Richard Nash, and Rod Serling in transferring their scripts (such as *Marty* and *The Rainmaker*) to the legitimate theater or to motion pictures indicates that television already is developing substantial cultural resources of its own, that it may indeed become, in the field of drama especially, the main source of new talent development in the country. The broadcasting media will always continue to serve as a showcase for the best entertainment created elsewhere, but it is very likely that, because of the huge economic resources of television as well as its great program needs, television networks will eventually underwrite in part or in whole artistic ventures on the legitimate stages throughout the country. By 1956, there were already several instances in which both the National Broadcasting Company and the Columbia Broadcasting System participated in theatrical ventures on Broadway.

That the public's concentration on television has affected the nature of its interest and the extent of its participation in other leisure-time acivities can hardly be doubted. Elmo Roper reported in one of his public opinion surveys that 78 per cent of us regularly seek ready-made forms of sparetime activity and that chief among these are television and radio.[4]

At first it was feared that popular fascination with television would cause people to stop reading books and newspapers, going to movies or the theater, conversing with others, or participating in sports. When movie attendance dropped markedly in 1949 and 1950, many motion-picture executives rushed to the conclusion that television was the primary cause of the loss at the box office. In time it was learned that the box office for quality motion pictures remained as good as ever, but that many people preferred to watch television rather than pay admission to see a mediocre movie. Many motion-picture houses that specialized in the exhibition of Grade B films went out of business (almost 6,500 in the first three years

[4] *Broadcasting-Telecasting,* August 6, 1951, p. 30.

of television), but by 1955, Hollywood motion-picture production for theatrical exhibition was back in full swing, with the emphasis on the production of better films.

The effect of televising football games has been a matter of great concern to colleges and universities which fear a loss in attendance for their own games. A study made by the National Opinion Research Center of the University of Chicago stated that live television coverage of college football games cut attendance by over a fourth without doing anything to create new fans for the sport. The study concluded that "watching the telecasts of games breaks the habit of attendance and becomes a new habit itself." [5]

The effect of television on reading newspapers and magazines appears to be little, but its effect on reading books remains highly speculative. Unfortunately, only a minority of adult Americans are regular book readers. Those who gain great pleasure from reading books are not likely to forsake reading for television; those for whom reading is a marginal pleasure are probably wooed away. The greater concern has been the effect of television on the development of reading habits in children, because we know that children have been almost wholly captivated by television. Professor Paul Witty, of Northwestern University, in his fifth annual study of television viewing by elementary and high school students in the Chicago and Evanston, Illinois, areas, discovered that elementary school children averaged 21½ hours of viewing per week, while high school students averaged 17 hours. [6]

Another question of genuine concern is whether television tends to make people passive observers rather than active participators in the cultural pursuits of our time. Only as we gain greater perspective with the passage of time will we be able to reckon the full effects of television in this regard. It may be noted, however, that, at the very least, many people who always have been observers have been given an opportunity through television to observe cultural undertakings of real quality which they otherwise would never have experienced.

We know that the themes and values of television programs do have some effect on many viewers, although no comprehensive analysis and evaluation of these effects has yet been made. We know, for example, that in the popularizing of a song, radio and television tend to form our tastes for us. A popular song becomes a success by being dinned into our ears through constant repetition. Special studies have shown that the sales of sheet music regularly follow the peak of performances of the song on the air. As a result of this intense repetition, even successful songs are short-lived. In broadcasting classical music, radio undoubtedly has stimulated greater inter-

[5] "Fifth Annual Report of the Effects of Television on College Football Attendance," quoted in *Broadcasting-Telecasting*, June 14, 1954, p. 34.

[6] Paul Witty, "Televiewing by Pupils, Parents, and Teachers," in *School and Society*, LXXIX (May 15, 1954), pp. 150-152.

est in the buying of records for home listening. We also know that on specific matters like modes of dress and speech, large segments of the public are quick to imitate what they see and hear on the air.

• SOCIAL EFFECTS OF TELEVISION AND RADIO •

The social effects of television and radio are many and varied. For one thing, television and radio influence our daily living and buying habits. Group viewing at home, some say, has strengthened the family unit. Listeners and viewers are perceptibly and imperceptibly affected by the programs they hear each day. While broadcast stations try to adjust their schedules to popular living habits, the public in turn often adjusts its habits to the broadcast schedule. Farmers with radios in their homes stay up later at night than farmers without them. Topflight network television programs cause people to make a practice of staying home on certain nights. Refashioning of the living room to accommodate the television set has been the experience of many people. And, needless to say, the advertising we are exposed to on the air influences our buying habits. On the Kraft Television Theater (a one-hour network drama program) broadcast in 1953, the commercial time on one program was devoted to a cake frosting recipe made with cream cheese. The next day's mail brought 79,000 requests for the recipe. In following weeks, better than half a million more requests were received. Nor is the effect of commercial exhortation limited to adults only. In 1955, NBC made a study of children's influence on buying as a result of their watching television with the following results:

1. Children frequently pay as much attention to television commercials as to the program itself. This is particularly true for the animated cartoon type, jingles, and gift offers.
2. Children not only like to watch the commercials—they remember them well enough to repeat them, and to both recognize and request the advertised products.
3. Nine out of ten mothers have been asked by their children to buy a TV advertised product; 89 per cent of these requests resulted in purchase. The highest request rate is among the 5- to 8-year-olds.
4. Children influence brand switching. Three out of five mothers have bought another brand of a product in addition to their regular brand, to satisfy the children's requests.[7]

Television and radio have also demonstrated an exceptional ability to induce mass social action along lines of generosity. This was proved repeatedly during World War II. One network quiz show asked listeners to send a penny to a Staten Island mother to buy War Bonds for her young

[7] National Broadcasting Company, Research Division, "Children's Influence on Buying" (mimeo), February 17, 1955.

son in the Marines. Two hundred clerks were needed to shake out the 300,157 pennies that came from every state in letters that filled 112 sacks of mail. The announcement that prompted this almost fantastic outpouring of popular generosity took only twenty seconds of radio time! [8]

Another outstanding example of radio's influence on mass behavior during the war were the marathon broadcasts of Kate Smith in her War Bond drives. On February 1, 1944, in a round-the-clock appeal on almost every program of the CBS network, Kate Smith begged, cajoled, and demanded that her listeners buy War Bonds. By the end of her all-day drive, she had brought in a total of $105,392,700 in War Bond purchases, marking the greatest single radio bond-selling exploit during the war, an outstanding feat from every point of view. [9]

In a round-the-clock television marathon in 1950, comedian Milton Berle persuaded viewers to donate more than $1,500,000 to the Damon Runyon Memorial Fund. In 1955, viewers of the "This Is Your Life" television program were moved to send in half a million dollars to support an educational venture described by Ralph Edwards on one program devoted to dramatizing the life of a Mississippi educator.

Broadcasting also has a peculiar power to induce panic in insecure and suggestible listeners. This was demonstrated early in the history of radio, at the nervous expense of the public, in three fateful dramatizations of H. G. Wells' fantasy, *The War of the Worlds*. On Halloween week end of 1938, which happened to fall in the period of the unsettling Munich war crisis, Orson Welles produced an adaptation of the fantasy which had hordes of Martians invading New Jersey. The program, done in a seminews style, created a panic on the East Coast, despite frequent announcements during and after the program that the story was fictional. The panic did not subside until the next morning. Several persons were reported to have died of heart attacks and many people prayed in the streets or fled into the country to seek refuge; hardier individuals seized arms and prepared to fight for their lives. [10]

In 1944, an adaptation of the same script was broadcast over a radio station in Chile with the scene of imaginary destruction laid near Santiago. Simulated news flashes had the city's civic center destroyed, the armed forces defeated, and the roads crowded with refugees. For the week before the broadcast, frequent announcements both in the press and on the air had been made, warning the public that the program was to be all in fun. Less than an hour after the broadcast began, thousands of people were panic-stricken and hundreds were having hysterical fits.

[8] Charles N. Winslow, "Sympathetic Pennies: A Radio Case Study" *Journal of Abnormal and Social Psychology,* XXXIX (April, 1944), pp. 174-179.

[9] See Robert K. Merton, *Mass Persuasion* (New York, 1946), for a penetrating analysis of another of Kate Smith's marathon campaigns.

[10] Hadley Cantril, *The Invasion from Mars* (Princeton, 1940); John Houseman, "The Men from Mars," *Harper's,* CXLVIII (December, 1948), pp. 74-82.

In 1949, the country of Ecuador experienced an even more fatal reign of terror induced by another broadcast adaptation of the same story. This time the Martians were heading for Quito. When the people learned it was all a hoax, an enraged mob, hurling gasoline and flaming balls of paper, burned down the radio station, killed at least six persons, and injured fifteen others. Army troops and tanks had to be called out before order could be restored.

Just as radio can induce panic through scare broadcasts, so it can often quell panic stemming from other sources, although the episodes described above suggest its limitations. During earthquakes, floods, and wartime aerial bombings, firm and confident voices carried by radio have calmed, reassured, and directed populaces into controlled and reasoned behavior. We have every reason to believe that radio and television will continue to serve this function in crises to come.

As television and radio have won the acceptance of the American people, they have tended to establish or support certain social values and to accentuate various social trends. Television and radio programs, in their direct advertising messages and in the implicit suggestions and appeals of dramatic shows, tend to convey to the listener and the viewer the social values played up in the continuity and scripts. Together with the press and the movies, television and radio in this way define "success" for us, and give us many of our social values.

Television and radio also have accentuated the standardizing and simplifying of the English language, which continues a social trend first noted in the last century. Mass communication media, including newspapers, magazines, digests, and comic books, as well as television and radio, emphasize brief and completely simple communication to the exclusion of more complex styles of expression and argument. It is now very difficult to get an audience to follow a line of argument for more than fifteen minutes, whereas in former years, it was not unusual for a skillful speaker to hold an audience rapt for hours, as he wound his way through a long argument. Since many issues of great social importance do not lend themselves to brief presentation without the danger of oversimplification and distortion of basic issues and meanings, some observers look askance upon this social influence of broadcasting.

Television and radio also have a great influence on society by conferring status on issues, persons, organizations, and movements to which broadcast time is made available. A broadcast discussion of an issue makes that issue more important in the public mind, just as the television or radio appearance of a relatively unimportant individual boosts that person's prestige in the eyes of the community. As Professors Lazarsfeld and Merton have pointed out, "The mass media bestow prestige and enhance the authority of individuals and groups by *legitimizing their status.*" Television and radio audiences seem to subscribe to the circular belief: "If you really matter, you will be at the focus of mass attention and, if you *are* at the focus of mass attention, then surely you must really matter." [11]

Carried over to the realm of fictional presentations, some persons have feared that programs characterized by extreme violence, sadism, and other forms of antisocial behavior may constitute a contributing factor toward the spread of juvenile delinquency. Although no conclusive evidence has been found to support this view, one television network (NBC) has established a special committee to advise it on the subject of children's programs.

· SUMMARY ·

It should be clear by now that we are dealing with a mass communication industry which has won wide public acceptance. Since it deals with the communication of ideas, it assumes vital social significance. Before we can intelligently appraise its operations, we must find out how our system of broadcasting originated and finally reached its present shape. Historical forces grow out of social needs and desires; the structure and operational scheme of any social institution will reflect the real pressures with which it had to contend throughout its period of growth. We shall review the programming of American television and radio because the final test of any broadcast operation depends upon what appears on the television screen or comes out of the loud speaker. Since the social effects of broadcasting vary directly with the system of ownership and control, we shall turn to that question and describe our present broadcasting structure and the tangled problems of public policy it poses. From there we shall turn to a review of comparative broadcast systems and consider television and radio in a world framework. This will provide us with a large view which we may then use to evaluate all programming operations. Finally, we shall discuss the special problems of educational radio and television and we shall conclude Part I with an analysis of critical standards.

In our treatment of television and radio, we shall be proceeding throughout with the philosophy so ably expressed to the Third Annual Radio Conference in 1924 by Herbert Hoover, then Secretary of Commerce. Referring to the emergence of radio, Mr. Hoover said:

> We may well be proud of this wonderful development, but in our self congratulation let us not forget that the value of this great system does not lie primarily in its extent or even in its efficiency. Its worth depends on the use that is made of it. It is not the ability to transmit, but the character of what is transmitted that really counts. Our telephone and telegraph systems are valuable only in so far as the messages sent from them contribute to the business and social intercourse of our people.

[11] Paul F. Lazarsfeld and Robert K. Merton, "Mass Communication, Popular Taste, and Organized Social Action," in Lyman Bryson (ed.), *The Communication of Ideas* (New York, 1948), pp. 101-102.

For the first time in history we have available to us the ability to communicate simultaneously with millions of our fellow men, to furnish entertainment, instruction, widening vision of national problems, and national events. An obligation rests upon us to see that it is devoted to real service and to develop the material that is transmitted into that which is really worth while. For it is only by this that the mission of this latest blessing of science to humanity may be rightfully fulfilled.

Questions for Discussion

1. In what ways can you justify the statement that "broadcasting can now be identified with American life itself?"
2. How do television and radio compare in influence with other social institutions such as schools, the family, and the church?
3. To what extent has your life been influenced by radio and television?
4. Has broadcasting tended to depress the artistic standards of our society?
5. What should be the ultimate mission of radio and television?
6. Is television making us a nation of spectators rather than participants? If so, is this a healthy development?
7. What should be the responsibility of television and radio to the American public?
8. "If you could use television once every six months, it would be a great amenity. But the world would have been a happier place if television had never been discovered. It contributes to the uneasiness of life today."— statement of the ARCHBISHOP OF CANTERBURY after seeing television in the United States. Do you agree or disagree with this statement? Why?
9. "While it is true that a great man, a modern Pericles, with television can be a thousand times more effective, it is also true that a slippery demagogue, a modern Alcibiades, can also be a thousand times more effective. . . . It is useless and foolish to deny that this medium offers certain dangers to civilization. It adds a tremendous premium to personality as distinguished from intellectuality. . . . I know that this thing is social dynamite that in the hands of a fool or a knave is capable of doing a vast amount of damage."—GERALD W. JOHNSON. Discuss the implications of this statement.
10. "In all it is and seemingly ever hopes to be, television is simply a menace to America's cultural and social life. It is a menace just because there it sits, a constant temptation, gratification, time killer, solace; you have it, why not use it? Your book's a wee bit boring, why not shut it and turn on TV? . . . But it is perhaps most a menace in the sense that the better it is the worse it must be; that the more skill it exhibits, the more big news it conveys, the more big names it can boast, the more druglike must be its hold on vast numbers of people."—From *Company Manners* by LOUIS KRONENBERGER, copyright © 1951, used by special permission of the publishers, The Bobbs-Merrill Company, Inc. Do you agree or disagree with this statement? Why?

❊ 2 ❊

The Growth of American Radio

THE GROWTH of American radio is a dramatic chapter in the history of communications and the shaping of modern American life. The rise of broadcasting is the story of a struggle for control of inventions worth a king's ransom. It is a story of failure on the part of scientists and industrial leaders to recognize what we now accept as obvious: that radio's usefulness as a public broadcast medium is its virtue. It is a story of fumbling to find a sound means of financing a privately operated radio system; a story of governmental intervention in radio, at the request of both industry and the public, to replace chaos and piracy with order and stability; a story of great achievement by a mass communications medium that advanced in twenty years from fledgling status to an important role in American social life.

· SCIENTIFIC ORIGINS AND DEVELOPMENT ·

Although the invention of radio was a natural consequence of scientific advances made in the fields of electricity and magnetism, the path of radio's advance was uneven. The idea of broadcasting without wires of any sort, making use of some unseen waves in the ether, did not come easily to the mind of man. Early inventors found it difficult to obtain financial support for their experiments. They ran into opposition from scientists and editors who could prove, on paper, the impossibility of effective radio broadcasting. The final scientific achievement of radio and television cannot be attributed to any single man or nation. It was made possible by the research of scientists in many nations: the United States, Italy, Denmark, Canada, Great Britain, and others. The early period of scientific development is clouded with controversy. Rival scientists worked independently to produce similar solutions to the same technical problems. It would be risky indeed for the historian to try to unravel the morass of conflicting claims which

20

the patent courts could not clear up to the satisfaction of competing litigants.

In 1864, the British scientist James C. Maxwell laid down the theory of electromagnetism and predicted the existence of the electric waves that are now used in radio. Twenty years later, Thomas Edison worked out a system of communication between railway stations and moving trains without using connecting wires. In 1887, Heinrich Hertz, a German, showed that rapid variations in electric current could be projected into space in the form of radio waves similar to light waves. Hertz thus founded the theory upon which modern radio is based.

By 1894, the investigations of Guglielmo Marconi, a twenty-year-old Italian, led him to the conclusion that Hertzian waves could be used for telegraphing without wires. The next year he secured a patent for wireless telegraphy in Great Britain. In 1901, Marconi's achievement was told to the American people in a front page story in the *New York Times* head-lined, "WIRELESS SPANS THE OCEAN." Marconi, working in New-foundland, had picked up the Morse letter "s" transmitted by wireless telegraphy from England.

Marconi's discoveries stimulated the work of other scientists and the next few years saw the refinement of wireless transmission. The main technical hurdle remaining in the way of wireless voice-broadcasting seemed to be the discovery of a means of high-frequency alternating transmission. Three prominent scientists worked independently on this problem. The result was the invention of the vacuum tube in 1904 by the Britisher John Ambrose Fleming, and its refinement by the Canadian Reginald Fessenden and the American Dr. Lee De Forest. The animosity that developed between Fessenden and De Forest makes it difficult to draw an accurate picture of the sequence of scientific events. Both men took out numerous patents on their inventions. De Forest, using his audion tube, projected speech by radio on December 31, 1906, five days after Fessenden accomplished the same thing with his heterodyne system. In 1908, De Forest broadcast recorded music from the top of the Eiffel Tower in Paris and was heard five hundred miles away.

· THE STRUGGLE FOR CONTROL ·

Marconi was among the first to realize that the future of radio as a point-to-point broadcasting medium depended upon finding commercial applications for it and protecting patent rights. In 1897, the British Marconi Company was formed to acquire title to all of Marconi's patents. A subsidiary of the British company, known as American Marconi, was incorporated in the United States in 1899 and soon came to control almost all of our commercial wireless communications, then limited to ship-to-shore transmissions and special point-to-point broadcasts. That such application of radio was to have commercial usefulness was made abundantly clear in

1910 when Congress passed a law requiring most passenger ships to have radio equipment and operators. This law amply justified itself when, two years later, the *Titanic,* on her maiden voyage, struck an iceberg and sank, but, owing to the prompt wireless call for aid, more than seven hundred passengers were saved. It is an interesting historical note that young David Sarnoff, later to be a major figure in the development of American broadcasting, was the wireless operator who received the distress calls from the sinking *Titanic.*

Although American Marconi dominated the field, a number of American-controlled companies undertook research in radio in order to cut in on the broadcasting business. They won several important radio patents and began to manufacture radio apparatus. Among these companies were General Electric, Westinghouse, and the Western Electric Company, the manufacturing subsidiary of the American Telephone and Telegraph Company. But the further development of radio got snagged in a confused patent situation which brought almost all manufacturing to a halt. Each manufacturer needed patents controlled by his competitors; each refused to license one another or to exchange patents; therefore, if each company continued with its operations, it became vulnerable to patent-infringement suits.

This tangle was still unresolved when the government took over all wireless stations in World War I and asked all the companies to pool their inventions in the hope of devising practical radio-telephone transmitters needed by the Army and Navy. In return, the government assured the companies legal protection against patent suits.

When the war came to an end and wireless stations were returned to their owners, the confused patent situation once again prevented any extensive radio manufacturing. The situation was further complicated by a conflict of interests between the United States and Britain which, through the American Marconi Company, still controlled a substantial part of the wireless industry here. In early 1919, British Marconi undertook negotiations with General Electric for the exclusive rights to the Alexanderson alternator, a device considered of critical importance in long-distance radio transmission. The negotiations were virtually concluded when Rear Admiral W. H. G. Bullard, Director of Naval Communications for the U. S. Navy, appealed to General Electric not to sell the alternator to British Marconi because the British would then hold a practical monopoly on world-wide communications for an indefinite period.

Negotiations were dropped, and General Electric found itself without an outlet for the invention in which it had made a very heavy investment. Under Admiral Bullard's guidance, General Electric evolved a plan by which a new company, controlled entirely by American capital and holding major radio patents, would be organized. The new company, formed in 1919, was the Radio Corporation of America. RCA bought all the patents and assets of American Marconi and entered into cross-licensing agreements with General Electric, Westinghouse, and Western Electric, and thus took a commanding position in the American radio field.

These agreements gave General Electric and Westinghouse the exclusive right to manufacture radio receiving sets and RCA the sole right to sell the sets. A.T.&T. was granted the exclusive right to make, lease, and sell broadcast transmitters, a monopoly of which the telephone company made much use in the next few years. In return these companies were assigned substantial stock holdings in RCA which they did not dispose of for some time. During its first two years of existence, RCA was concerned with ship-to-shore communications, transoceanic point-to-point radio service, and selling radio parts to amateurs for the construction of crystal receivers.

• THE DAWN OF MODERN RADIO BROADCASTING •

The early development of radio, therefore, centered around the perfection of point-to-point broadcasting as a substitute for transmission by cable or telephone lines. The main commercial criticism of radio was its lack of secrecy, making it unsuitable for private service since unauthorized persons could overhear a broadcast conversation. How, then, it was asked, could this invention be turned into a money-making proposition? Efforts were directed toward developing radio as a confidential means of radio-telephony, with controls against eavesdroppers.

Just who it was who first realized the now obvious fact that radio's lack of secrecy is its great commercial strength is not definitely known, but in this failure of many people associated with the rise of radio to realize its best public applications, we have a clear demonstration of how important it is for ideas of social utilization to keep abreast of discoveries in the scientific world. Of all the people connected with radio at this stage, Lee De Forest seems outstanding in his grasp of the possible use of radio as a *public* broadcast medium. He is reported to have said as early as 1909, "I look forward to the day when by the means of radio, opera may be brought into every home. Some day the news, and even advertising, will be sent out to the public on the wireless telephone."

In 1916, David Sarnoff, then an engineer with American Marconi and later the chief executive of RCA, also foresaw the public usefulness of the new communications medium. Sarnoff described a "plan of development" that would make radio a "household utility in the same sense as the piano or phonograph." Not only could radio be used to transmit and receive music, according to Sarnoff, but also to broadcast lectures, special public events, baseball scores, and various other subjects of popular interest.

De Forest's and Sarnoff's notion was not widely entertained, however, and by 1920, there were still only a few individuals who shared their grasp of radio's real future. At the University of Wisconsin, an experimental station (later called WHA) was operated by the University's Physics Department to broadcast weather and market reports. William E. Scripps, of the *Detroit News,* also appreciated the real virtues of broadcasting and started his experimental station, now WWJ, in the summer of 1920. In Pittsburgh, H. P. Davis, a Westinghouse vice-president, and Dr. Frank Conrad, a research engineer, opened the first commercially licensed radio station, KDKA, in November, 1920, broadcasting the returns of the Harding-Cox Presidential election as its first program.

• THE FIRST FLUSH OF BROADCASTING •

The new idea of radio as a public broadcast medium caught the imagination of the American people and spread like wildfire. From three stations in 1920, the number rose to over five hundred in 1923, and the sales of radio receivers rose from $2 million to $136 million in the same three-year period.

Many of these stations were owned and operated by concerns primarily interested in manufacturing and selling radio apparatus. These companies engaged in broadcasting for an obvious reason: unless there were stations to send out programs, the business of selling radio receivers would face collapse. The profit in radio had to be made on the sale of the radio set while the broadcast program had to be supplied to the listener without charge. Westinghouse, RCA, and General Electric all opened up radio stations. Retail department stores then got interested in radio as a means of winning good will: Bamberger, Wanamaker, Gimbels and the Shepard Stores set up stations. Newspapers, encouraged by the success of the *Detroit News* station, began broadcasting as a means of publicizing their papers. Colleges and universities plunged into broadcasting to provide experimental facilities for physics departments and to investigate the possibilities of educational radio. Numerous individuals afflicted with the radio fever rushed to open their own stations with whatever money they could scrape together. They used tiny 5-watt transmitters which could be housed in small cabinets resembling ordinary receivers. Unofficial estimates of the number of these two-by-four stations ran as high as 1,400 in 1924.

Still no way had been found to raise the necessary money to pay for the operating expenses of the stations. Some people, like David Sarnoff, then general manager of RCA and now Chairman of its Board of Directors, believed that the manufacturers and distributors of radio receivers and parts should contribute to the cost of running broadcasting stations as a service to the buyers of sets and in order to stimulate sales. Others felt that radio stations should be operated by the government, or supported by endowment funds contributed by public-spirited citizens. Not yet born was the idea of selling radio time for advertising messages which is the foundation stone of modern commercial broadcasting.

But in the first flush of broadcasting, the financial problem had not yet assumed urgent proportions. Radio required very little by way of programming to attract an audience still thrilled by the very novelty of wireless communication. The main desire of many listeners was to be able to pick up on their battery-operated crystal headphone receivers the call letters of distant stations. Programs at first were really excuses for many stations to go on the air so that they might fulfill their true mission of announcing their call letters. Phonograph records were played and replayed to fill in the time between station identifications.

The broadcast quality of the primitive transmitting and receiving equipment of the early 20's, was indeed poor, judged by present standards, but it was quite satisfactory to the audience of that day. One excited woman wrote to H. V. Kaltenborn, then beginning his commentary career, "You came in last night just as clear as if you were talking over the telephone."

In these circumstances, broadcasters found themselves for the first two or three years under no great pressure to offer topnotch performers. Instead they relied on the phonograph and on the seemingly endless supply of free talent that came to the studio. Even the staff personnel of many stations could be had at virtually no cost. Good, bad, and indifferent musical artists were coaxed to the microphone with the promise of publicity. This was the period of the "great plague of mediocre sopranos badly transmitted and worse received." [1] After a time, however, performers became reluctant to give their services in exchange for publicity only and a more sophisticated public began to demand higher-grade offerings. Entertainers, announcers, and engineers had cooled off from the early thrills and wanted to be paid for their work. But stations earned nothing. Where was the money to come from? One station was operating on an annual budget of $100,000 without tangible earnings of any kind. Westinghouse, having been amply repaid with publicity for its initial expenses, was seriously wondering whether there was a way out.

• RADIO GOES COMMERCIAL •

The solution eventually adopted came about through WEAF (now WRCA), the high-powered A.T.&T. station in New York City. The telephone company had set up WEAF to be operated as a "toll" station, available for hire to those wishing to reach the public by radio. The first sponsored program occurred on August 28, 1922, when WEAF broadcast a ten-minute talk delivered under the auspices of the Queensboro Corporation, a Long Island realty company.

[1] Alfred N. Goldsmith and Austin C. Lescarboura, *This Thing Called Broadcasting* (New York, 1930), p. 146.

The telephone company established a stringent broadcast policy which permitted only a conservative courtesy announcement to identify the sponsor. A.T.&T. ruled out the broadcast of direct advertising messages as being in poor taste for a communications medium that entered the privacy of the home with no forewarning as to the nature of the messages that would follow. Advertising was limited, therefore, to the simple statement of the sponsor's name, the intention being to maintain the dignity of radio and to prevent it from taking on the character of "huckstering."

The telephone company's attitude also reflected a fairly widespread belief, voiced by some newspapers which were apparently indulging in wishful thinking, that the radio medium was incapable of selling products through direct commercial announcements. The emphasis throughout this early period was on the use of radio by commercial companies solely to create public good will. This policy was emphatically approved by the then Secretary of Commerce, Herbert Hoover, who said in 1922, "It is inconceivable that we should allow so great a possibility for service, for news, for entertainment, for education, and for vital commercial purposes to be drowned in advertising chatter." The First Annual Radio Conference held that year recommended "that direct advertising in radio broadcast service be absolutely prohibited and that indirect advertising be limited to the announcements of the call letters of the station and of the name of the concern responsible for the matter broadcasted [sic]."

From 1922 to 1924, even limited goodwill type commercial broadcasting was restricted almost entirely to WEAF. The telephone company claimed the sole right to sell radio time, and because of its control over patents, transmission lines, and radio equipment, it was able to enforce its will on other stations and to prevent them from carrying advertising. It was not until April 18, 1924, when A.T.&T. allowed independent stations to engage in sponsored broadcasting, that widespread advertising support for radio developed, and the system we know today began to take shape.

Advertising on the air soon increased markedly, and the distinction between direct and indirect commercial appeals began to wear thin.

Advertisers and advertising agencies learned that radio campaigns were very effective ways to marketing commercial products and they turned over to radio stations a larger percentage of their advertising budgets. Whereas, in 1922, WEAF's total advertising income for the whole year was about $5,000, in 1930 the same station (which had been sold by the telephone company to RCA) was charging $750 for just one hour of evening radio time.[2] With this advertising money, it became possible to hire high-priced entertainers to put on top-notch comedy, variety, and musical programs. Radio became "show business." Stars like Rudy Vallee expanded the dance-band formula by introducing radio "personalities" in 1929, the

[2] *Ibid.*, pp. 279-281.

same year that "Amos 'n' Andy" and "The Goldbergs" began their long radio tenure. The continual improvement in the technical end of broadcasting persuaded renowned musical artists who had previously refused to risk their reputations on crude microphones and faulty amplifiers to break down and accept radio as a legitimate medium for their art. Opera singers like John McCormack and Lucrezia Bori led the musical flock to radio in 1926 and by the next year, most of the big name musical artists in the country appeared on program logs.

The better radio programs made possible by money obtained from radio advertising were undoubtedly welcomed by the listening audience, but opposition to the pressures which aimed to turn broadcasting into a carry-all for various commercial appeals was still being voiced in responsible industrial and listener circles. The 1929 Code of the National Association of Broadcasters, for example, provided that after 6:00 P.M. commercial programs only of the "goodwill type" were to be broadcast, and between the hours of 7:00 and 11:00 P.M., no commercial announcements of any sort were to be aired!

Industry and public attitudes soon changed, however. If listening to a commercial message was going to make possible the broadcast of better entertainment programs, the public, with certain exceptions and within limitations, was willing to pay this price. The rules against direct advertising were at first relaxed and then gradually they disappeared altogether.

Having established itself as the sole support of radio, advertising progressively took command of the entire broadcast operation. Programs began to stress more popular appeal in order to reach the type of audience desired by various advertisers. The standards for writing and presenting commercial messages on the air were guided almost entirely by considerations of effective selling. The earlier reservations placed upon the use of radio as an advertising medium because of the special way it gains access to our homes were no longer to be heard in broadcasting circles. The new trend was to reach its climax twenty years later when, in 1943, one station broadcast 2,215 commercial announcements in one week, or an average of 16.7 announcements every hour.[3]

• FORMATION OF NATIONAL RADIO NETWORKS •

If advertising was to become one foundation stone of American broadcasting, the national radio network was soon to become the other. The linking of two or more stations by land lines to carry the same program simultaneously was an essential aspect of the science, business, and art of radio. Single stations could not afford to produce elaborate shows to be transmitted to the audience in only one community; listeners in various

[3] *Public Service Responsibility of Broadcast Licensees* (Washington, Federal Communications Commission, 1946), p. 44.

parts of the country wanted to hear the best New York shows; advertisers with regionally or nationally marketed products wanted to launch their promotional campaigns simultaneously throughout the country. All of these desires combined to form the basis for the establishment of the national radio networks.

The A.T.&T. Network. Network broadcasting was inaugurated on January 4, 1923, when A.T.&T. broadcast a program simultaneously over WEAF and WNAC, a Boston station. Later that year, the telephone company set up a station in Washington, D.C., which it frequently linked with WEAF for network broadcasting, forming the nucleus of a network that rapidly expanded in the following years. By the fall of 1924, A.T.&T. was able to furnish a coast-to-coast network of twenty-three stations to carry a speech by President Coolidge.

The National Broadcasting Company. Meanwhile, RCA was making a start in network broadcasting. This was done despite the opposition of A.T.&T. which refused to furnish its telephone lines for use by competing networks and would not permit RCA to sell broadcast time to advertisers. RCA was compelled, therefore, to use inferior telegraph wires for "networking" and to make no charge for the use of radio time. Because of these obstacles, the RCA network did not grow as rapidly as did A.T.&T.'s. In March, 1925, when the telephone company network broadcast the Presidential inauguration over a transcontinental network of twenty-two stations, the RCA network carried it over only four eastern stations.

This situation abruptly changed in 1926, when A.T.&T. decided to withdraw entirely from the radio broadcasting business, sold WEAF to RCA for $1 million, and transferred most of its radio properties to the so-called "Radio Group," made up of RCA, Westinghouse, and General Electric. These transactions cleared the way for the sale of radio time by the "Radio Group," and A.T.&T. agreed to make its telephone lines available to RCA.

On September 9, 1926, RCA formed the National Broadcasting Company as a subsidiary corporation to take over its network broadcasting business and the station properties it had arranged to buy from A.T.&T. NBC thus had control of the only two networks in the country at that time. NBC continued to hold the dominant position in chain broadcasting for almost twenty years until, following a government order, it was forced to sell its second network in 1943.

The Columbia Broadcasting System. The network we now know as the Columbia Broadcasting System came into being on January 27, 1927, under the name of United Independent Broadcasters, Inc. United's purpose was to contract time for a network of sixteen radio stations, to sell time to advertisers, and to furnish programs for broadcasting. Before United actually got under way, the Columbia Phonograph Company became interested in the venture through the Columbia Phonograph Broadcasting System.

which was organized in April, 1927, to function as the sales agency of United. United contracted to pay each of its sixteen stations $500 per week for ten hours of radio time. It soon developed, however, that the sales agency could not sell enough time to sponsors to carry United under this arrangement, and the new network stood near the brink of collapse only a few months after its birth.

The Columbia Phonograph Company withdrew from the project, and all of the capital stock of the sales company was thereupon acquired by United, which took over the name of the Columbia Broadcasting System after dissolving the sales agency. William S. Paley and his family purchased a majority of CBS stock, the network began to thrive, and Paley assumed a role of leadership in broadcasting which, as Chairman of the Board of CBS, he continues to hold to this day.

The Mutual Broadcasting System. The Mutual Broadcasting System, organized along radically different lines from NBC or CBS, did not come into being until 1934 when four stations, WGN, Chicago, WLW, Cincinnati, WXYZ, Detroit, and WOR, New York, agreed to work jointly to get advertising business for themselves. The network drummed up sales to advertisers and made arrangements with A.T.&T. for land-line connections between the four stations. Ultimate control of the new network, through ownership of its capital stock, lay with the *Chicago Tribune* and R. H. Macy & Co., but has since come under the ownership of the General Tire and Rubber Company which also purchased the RKO motion picture studios and, in 1955, set up RKO Teleradio Pictures, Inc., as a subsidiary company in charge of its radio, television, and motion picture activities. Until 1936, only four stations regularly carried Mutual programs, but Mutual now has contract affiliations with more than five hundred different stations.[4]

The American Broadcasting Company. The American Broadcasting Company came into being under its present name in 1945, after purchasing RCA's second network two years before. In 1953, ABC merged with United Paramount Theaters, Inc., to form a new corporation, American Broadcasting-Paramount Theaters, with assets of about $150 million.

· PUBLIC POLICY TOWARD RADIO ·

To make matters more difficult during broadcasting's first decade, the federal government was very slow to make its position clear in its radio laws. Under international agreements, governments had assumed the responsibility to use certain radio frequencies and to provide protection for frequencies used by other countries. But radio's rapid growth quickly outdated the means by which these agreements were to be observed.

[4] Much of this discussion is taken from Federal Communications Commission, *Report on Chain Broadcasting* (Washington, 1941), pp. 9-28 *passim.*

Early Radio Policy. Federal regulation of radio began with the Wireless Ship Act of 1910 which forbade any sizeable passenger ship to leave this country unless it was equipped with radio communication apparatus and a skilled radio operator. It was not until 1912, however, when the United States ratified the first international radio treaty, that the need for general regulation of radio became urgent. In order to carry out our treaty obligations, Congress enacted the Radio Act of 1912. This statute forbade any person to operate a radio station without a license from the Secretary of Commerce.

Enforcement of the Radio Act of 1912 presented no serious problems until radio's value as a public broadcast medium was realized and there was a rush to get on the air. The Act of 1912 had not set aside any particular frequencies for privately operated broadcast stations, so the Secretary of Commerce selected two frequencies, 750 kilocycles and 833 kilocycles, and licensed all stations to operate on one or the other of these channels. The number of stations increased so rapidly, however, that the situation became extremely confused as radio signals overlapped and stations interfered with each other. On the recommendation of the National Radio Conference, which met annually from 1922 through 1925, Secretary of Commerce Hoover established a policy of assigning a specific frequency to each station.

But the increase in the number of frequencies made available was still not enough to take care of all the new stations that wanted to go on the air. The Secretary of Commerce tried to find room for all of them by limiting the power and hours of operation of some stations, so that several stations might use the same frequency. But the number of stations multiplied so rapidly that by 1925, there were almost 600 in the country and 175 applications on file for new stations. Every frequency in the standard broadcast band was by then already occupied by at least one station, and many by several. The new stations could be accommodated only by extending the standard broadcast band, at the expense of the other types of radio services, or by imposing still greater limitations upon time and power. The 1925 National Radio Conference opposed both of these methods and called upon Congress to remedy the situation through legislation.

Until Congress passed a new radio law, the Secretary of Commerce was powerless to deal with this trying situation. He could not simply refuse to issue any more broadcast licenses on the grounds that existing stations would be interfered with, because a court ruling denied him this authority. And, in April, 1926, an Illinois federal district court further tied his hands by holding that he had no power to impose any restrictions whatsoever as to frequency, power, or hours of station operations. A station's use of a frequency not assigned to it was ruled *not* a violation of the 1912 Radio Act, so there was nothing Hoover could do under then existing laws to prevent one station from jumping its frequency to that of its neighbor. This court decision was followed in July, 1926, by an opinion of the Attorney General that the Secretary had no power to issue regulations preventing interference between broadcast stations. Completely frustrated, Secretary of Commerce Hoover issued a public statement abandoning all his efforts to regulate radio and urging that the stations undertake, through gentlemen's agreements, to regulate themselves.

The Period of Chaos. But Hoover's plea went unheeded. From July, 1926 to February, 1927, when Congress enacted new radio legislation, almost two hundred new stations went on the air. "These new stations used any frequencies they desired, regardless of the interference thereby caused to others. Existing stations changed to other frequencies and increased their power and hours of operation at will. The result was confusion and chaos. With everybody on the air, nobody could be heard." [5] The situation became so intolerable that the President in his message of December 7, 1926, appealed to Congress to enact a comprehensive radio law. This time Congress took heed and legislation was enacted.

The Radio Act of 1927. The plight into which radio fell prior to 1927 could be attributed to a basic fact about radio as a means of communication—the radio spectrum simply was not large enough to accommodate every person who wanted to set up a broadcasting station. Regulation of radio by government was, therefore, as necessary to the development of radio "as traffic control was to the development of the automobile," according to the Supreme Court.[6] The Radio Act of 1927 proclaimed that the airwaves belonged to the people of the United States and were to be used by individuals only with the authority of short-term licenses granted by the government when the "public interest, convenience, or necessity" would be served thereby. A temporary Federal Radio Commission was created to administer the law.

The new law automatically revoked the license of every radio station then operating, and allowed sixty days for applications for new licenses to be filed with the Federal Radio Commission. The Commission was given the authority to assign any power, frequency, or time limitations to the stations whose applications it approved. Meanwhile, temporary licenses were issued to most broadcasters so that they might continue in operation while the Commission worked out the jig-saw puzzle of fitting together all the broadcasters into the standard broadcast band, without interference between stations. The Commission required first of all that each station equip itself with frequency control devices to prevent it from wobbling off

---

[5] *National Broadcasting Company* v. *United States,* 319 United States Reports at 212 (1943). This account is based largely on the historical review of public policy included in the majority opinion of the Supreme Court in this case.

[6] *Ibid.,* at 213.

its assigned frequency. After making extensive investigations, the Commission then issued regular licenses good for six months to all but about 150 odd stations for which it felt there was no room on the air.

In 1934, after reviewing seven years of temporary federal radio regulation, Congress was ready to write a permanent law embodying the "public interest, convenience, or necessity" approach which had been tried and found successful. The Communications Act of 1934 created the Federal Communications Commission with substantially the same powers and responsibilities as the earlier Radio Commission, except that it was also given jurisdiction over wire communications. The development of radio broadcasting was turned over to competitive private enterprise, with limited government regulation. The 1934 statute, with certain amendments, remains on the books as the governing law of modern broadcasting.

Thus, anarchy of the airwaves became a thing of the past and order was established. Responsible broadcasters could feel confident that their assigned frequencies would be protected from radio pirates and listeners were able to turn on their radio sets without being greeted by a melee of sounds from overlapping stations. Having bridged this critical period of its growth, radio was now prepared to step forward with its programming, to demonstrate the full artistic, communicative, and business capacities of the broadcast medium.

• THE DEVELOPMENT OF RADIO PROGRAMMING •

The period radio now entered saw the development and refinement of program types and the rise to stardom of entertainers who, in many cases, had won earlier recognition on the stage or in vaudeville. Jack Benny, Eddie Cantor, Fred Allen, Ed Wynn, Bing Crosby, Burns and Allen, Jimmy Durante, Edgar Bergen, Phil Baker, Bob Hope, and Fibber McGee and Molly won their places on the air in the 30's and set a pattern for comedy and variety that was maintained with little change over a score of years. The "Jack Benny Show" held forth Sunday evenings at 7:00 P.M. for more than twenty years without interruption.

In the programming of classical music, this period saw the start of Dr. Walter Damrosch's "Music Appreciation Hour," which held a loyal audience of children and adults for a decade of Saturday mornings; the Sunday afternoon concerts of the New York Philharmonic Symphony Orchestra, and the Saturday afternoon broadcasts from the stage of the Metropolitan Opera House. Some years later the National Broadcasting Company formed its own symphony orchestra, under the leadership of Arturo Toscanini. The "Horn and Hardart Children's Amateur Hour," "Uncle Don," "Let's Pretend," and other children's programs became regular features. These were the years, too, of the amateur-hour programs, which were made famous at first by Major Bowes and which brought to the air a copious supply of one-man bands.

Powerful personalities who won their followings through the effective use of the broadcast word also stand out in this period. They ranged from Franklin D. Roosevelt, whose fireside chats, delivered in a personal and intimate manner, captured the imagination and loyalty of most Americans, to men like the famous Dr. Brinkley, the patent-medicine man who advertised his goat-gland pills over the air to distraught men anxious to regain their lost youth. In between came firebrands like Louisiana's Huey Long and Father Charles E. Coughlin, the Detroit priest who became a storm center when he tried to build up a political movement through his radio broadcasts.

There were, too, the famous individual broadcasts that created momentary sensations. The broadcast reports of the trial and execution of Bruno Hauptmann, kidnaper of the Lindbergh baby, brought fame and fortune to Gabriel Heatter and Boake Carter. Actress Mae West won a permanent niche for herself in the annals of radio when, in reading a seemingly innocent script about Adam and Eve on an Edgar Bergen comedy show in 1937, she introduced an unexpectedly suggestive innuendo that, though it titillated some listeners, caused a flood of protests from offended listeners to swamp the network and the Federal Communications Commission.

In the broadcast of drama, radio at first found itself unable to surmount the limitations of a communications medium in which the audience could hear words, sound effects, and music, but could see nothing. Early dramatic broadcasts picked up Broadway stage plays by putting microphones over the actors' heads or in the footlights. These efforts to transplant stage plays to the air without any adaptation to the limitations of the radio medium resulted in programs little short of the grotesque. The effect on the listener was simply that of sitting in the theater blindfolded. Broadcasters soon realized that if radio drama was to win an audience, original material would have to be written and stage plays would have to be adapted especially for broadcast performance.

The first strictly dramatic radio program was "First Nighter," launched in 1930. It was soon followed by the "Lux Radio Theater." From this point it was only a step to the dramatization of mystery and adventure stories, such as "The Shadow," "The Lone Ranger," and "Bulldog Drummond." The "stream-of-consciousness" technique to take the radio audience into the mind of a character, trick devices like echo chambers, and filters to change vocal quality and perspective, and sound effects to intensify mood and to carry action, were made vital elements of radio dramatic techniques. In 1937, Archibald MacLeish wrote *The Fall of the City,* the first verse drama written especially for radio. Writer-producers Norman Corwin, Arch Oboler, and Orson Welles won national fame for a succession of highly imaginative productions. Poet Stephen Vincent Benét contributed several original scripts that demonstrated the immense artistic possibilities of the radio medium.

These years also encompassed the period of "stunt broadcasting," when radio called the attention of the world to its great feats of wireless communication. Of especial fascination were the broadcasts from great heights and great depths or from widely separated points. Programs might be picked up from a glider in the air or from a bathysphere hundreds of feet under Bermuda waters. NBC broadcast two-way conversations between an aerial balloon flying high over the East Coast and an airplane off the Pacific Coast, between London and the balloon, and a four-way conversation between Chicago, New York, Washington, and the balloon. Like a child playing with a new toy, networks used their new short-wave equipment to broadcast a singer from New York accompanied by an orchestra in Buenos Aires or to pick up a piano concert from a dirigible in mid-Atlantic.

Such freakish broadcasts admittedly made small contribution to radio art, but they unquestionably prepared broadcasters for the more imposing tasks of covering important public events in different parts of the world. The hook-up of nineteen widely separated broadcasting centers around the world in 1931 for a program dedicated to Marconi marked a great step forward in the science of broadcasting. Between 1933 and 1935, there were numerous broadcasts from Admiral Byrd's Antarctic Expedition. In 1934, a sensational on-the-spot description of the burning of the vessel *Morro Castle* off the New Jersey coast, was brought to the public by radio. The dramatic farewell address of King Edward VIII who abdicated his throne for "the woman I love," and the impressive coronation of King George VI in 1937 were covered in the most elaborate overseas broadcast arrangements to that date.

The 30's also saw the rise of news broadcasting. Radio's capacities as a news medium were barely appreciated by the pioneer broadcasters of the 20's who did little more than read over the air newspaper headlines and the front pages of late editions. Several newspapermen, like H. V. Kaltenborn of the *Brooklyn Eagle,* broadcast weekly news talks, but nothing like present-day news summaries was regularly scheduled in the 20's. In 1932, the Associated Press furnished Presidential election bulletins to the networks and the following year saw the new policy of interrupting broadcast programs with news flashes. But the advancement of radio as an effective news medium was temporarily brought to a halt by the pressure of powerful newspaper interests who feared the rivalry of broadcast news and therefore hoped to restrict radio's ability to compete with the press in the field of news dissemination.

There ensued, from 1933 to 1935, the "press-radio war," during which time radio news bulletins were limited by agreement to thirty words and a time schedule that prohibited the airing of news while it was hot off the wires. The agreement finally broke down, and radio was free once again to broadcast news supplied by news agencies. Networks built up their own news staffs and sent correspondents to the important capitals and news centers of the world. Kaltenborn broadcast over CBS the actual sounds of battle in the Spanish Civil War and NBC's Max Jordan broadcast an eye-witness account of Hitler's march into Austria and his reception in Vienna. During the Munich crisis in 1938, when for seemingly endless hours the nation turned to its radios to keep pace with the rapidly unfolding political events, the networks took leadership in supplying continual news bulletins and round-ups of informed opinion in Europe. The voices of the chief actors in the international political scene, Hitler, Chamberlain, and Mus-solini, were brought to American listeners with commentaries by network news analysts. Radio gave the mounting war crisis in 1939 sustained and comprehensive news coverage, establishing itself in the public mind as the primary source of news.

· RADIO AND WORLD WAR II ·

From the outbreak of World War II through its conclusion, it was a well-organized, technically proficient, and confident radio system that brought to the American people the great speeches of Winston Churchill, news of the fall of France, the attack on the Soviet Union, and the flash reports of the Japanese attack on Pearl Harbor.

Even as the American military forces mobilized their strength, the radio industry made all its resources available to the federal government for war service. In contrast with World War I, however, when the government took over the operation of all wireless stations, World War II saw the basic radio organization left intact. The government merely enlisted the co-operation of the industry to publicize important morale and public-service announce-ments. Planned scheduling of war-information messages, bond-purchase appeals, and conservation campaigns were coupled with the systematic use of radio for instruction in civilian defense and responsibilities. All show business pitched in wholeheartedly and the "win-the-war" theme permeated radio's offerings. The Office of War Information co-ordinated the govern-ment's wartime propaganda and information services. For the entertainment and information of soldiers and sailors overseas, the Army and Navy set up the Armed Forces Radio Service, with a network of stations in the Pacific and European war theaters. Entertainment programs at home were broad-cast as usual, with the stars and formats of the 30's maintaining their popularity in the 40's. Indeed, few new talents came to the fore; the war took its toll of the lives and energies of many young artists. Perhaps the most notable change in programming was the increase in news and one-man commentaries. The scheduling of news every hour became common; use began to be made of tape recorders to transcribe actual events for airing at subsequent hours. Radio documentaries, casting the factual matter of the war into dramatic and semidramatic programs, were hailed as powerful new art forms.

In the field of special events, radio again scored its greatest triumphs, demonstrating anew its power to bring actual events into our homes and to make the world conflagration meaningful in terms of individual persons. From the broadcast of President Roosevelt's war message to Congress, to the eye-witness description of the signing of the surrender documents aboard the battleship *U.S.S. Missouri* in Tokyo Bay, there was a succession of outstanding programs. On D-Day in 1944, radio reporters were heard from invasion barges in the English Channel and on the Normandy beaches as the greatest military operation in history got under way. George Hicks' running narration from an amphibious ship under aerial attack provided a broadcast that few who heard it will ever forget.

But the war was more than a great programming challenge to American radio. It also brought to the radio industry a period of unprecedented economic prosperity. The 900 odd stations then in existence enjoyed a lush advertising market protected from new competition by the government's refusal to license new stations for the duration. Although the shortage of consumers' goods created a sellers' market, many large manufacturing companies, mindful of the experience of World War I when some companies discontinued advertising and lost out in the public mind, continued their promotional work on a lavish scale. The wartime newsprint shortage which cut down advertising space in newspapers also served to drive more advertising money into radio. Institutional, or name advertising was stimulated by the high wartime income taxes which gave many corporations the alternative of spending large sums on advertising or turning the money over to the government in taxes.

The upshot of all this was that AM radio flourished. From 1938 to 1948, the advertising volume of the four networks more than doubled. From 1937 to 1944, broadcast profits of all networks and stations rose from $23 million to $90 million.

With income figures of such proportions, radio could not escape being viewed primarily as a money-making business rather than as a public-service enterprise. Entrepreneurs anxious to break into radio's magic circle could do so only by purchasing established stations. Radio property therefore acquired a high scarcity value and some stations changed hands at fantastic prices. Many realized from four to ten times the value of their assets. "In one instance the sales price was more than thirty times the original cost. In another, a station sold for 1,534 times its net income." [7]

[7] Charles Siepmann, *Radio's Second Chance* (Boston, 1946), p. 165.

• THE CHANGING FORTUNES OF AM RADIO •

When World War II ended, 950 AM stations were on the air. When the lid was taken off new radio construction, the attractions of the industry's wartime profits brought on a horde of new broadcasters. Refined directional antennas which prevented station interference made it possible to license many new local stations operating on low power. The number of AM stations soon grew like Topsy. Five hundred new stations went on the air in 1946. Another four hundred were authorized in 1947. By the end of 1948, 1,900 AM stations were on the air producing an income of $145 million, compared to the $8,700,000 earned by the fifty television stations then in existence. By 1949, however, when the nation's economy suffered a temporary setback and the inroads from television first began to be felt by AM radio, total network radio billings slipped for the first time in radio history. One metropolitan AM station that was purchased for $250,000 in 1944, was resold for only $150,000 in 1949. Another station dropped in sales value from a wartime $1,500,000 to $512,000 in 1949.[8]

Thereafter, as television continued its rapid expansion, the future of AM radio became clouded with uncertainty. It was clear that network radio had suffered great damage from the competitive inroads of television, especially during the evening hours, as shown in the following table:

DECLINE IN SIZE OF EVENING NETWORK RADIO AUDIENCES

	Highest Evening Nielsen Rating	Number of Homes	Average Evening Nielsen Rating *	Number of Homes
1949 **	27.4	10,700,000	12.6	4,900,000
1950	24.2	9,900,000	10.8	4,400,000
1951	21.5	9,100,000	8.7	3,700,000
1952	16.4	7,200,000	7.5	3,300,000
1953	15.6	6,900,000	6.3	2,800,000
1954	9.2	4,100,000	4.5	2,000,000
1955	6.9	3,200,000	2.6	1,200,000
		TELEVISION		
1955	55.0	16,500,000	24.4	6,600,000

* Once-a-week evening programs.
** Average Audience Rating.
Month of January used for each year.

Reflecting this decline in evening audiences for radio, CBS in 1951 reduced its nighttime advertising rates 10 to 15 per cent. The following year CBS reduced its nighttime rates another 25 per cent, although, at the request of its affiliates, it increased its rates for daytime radio which was

[8] See *Broadcasting-Telecasting*, October 16, 1950, pp. 67-168, for an excellent historical account of radio from 1930 to 1950.

faring more successfully against the competition of television. The average network daytime show now reached larger audiences than the average evening show, a complete reversal from listening habits in radio before the advent of television. The loss by radio to television of the "peak" evening audiences forced the radio industry into a period of intensive self-study. From this study emerged new programming and selling patterns that more accurately reflected the new role radio had come to play in America: emphasis on programs of news and music, developing popular disc jockeys, departing from the strict half-hour program format, increasing the use of remote pick-ups, and flexibility in attracting advertisers who could not afford television. Under the competition of television, AM radio was forced to give up much of its glamour, but industry leaders believed that they had found a successful formula for both AM network and station operation that would hold good for the future. Confidence was further reflected in the continued expansion of AM radio holdings which rose from 2,006 stations on the air in 1949 to 2,800 stations in 1956, with more than 200 applications pending before the Federal Communications Commission for new authorizations.

• FREQUENCY MODULATION (FM) RADIO •

Although FM radio did not come to public attention until the end of the war, it had been known to the radio industry since its development during the previous ten years by Major E. H. Armstrong of Columbia University. Using a much higher band of frequencies than AM radio (from 88 to 108 megacycles), FM has many advantages over standard radio. It is ordinarily free from static, fading, and interference noises. All stations within reception range come in with equal strength. Sound is transmitted with much greater fidelity than over AM radio. Because its coverage is usually limited to the line of sight from the top of the transmitter, FM is better suited for community and metropolitan centers than for rural areas. This limitation in coverage makes it possible for many FM stations, situated not very far apart geographically, to share the same frequency.

FM held high hopes to broadcast aspirants, critics, and educators because the construction and operating costs of an FM station were much less than the costs of an AM station. Schools and community organizations, as well as commercial entrepreneurs, might now consider entering the broadcasting business. Moreover, low-powered FM stations might hope to compete with high-powered stations on the basis of program quality only, since all signals in listening range would be heard equally well. In AM radio, low-powered stations were at a great disadvantage because many listeners made their dial choices primarily on the basis of signal strength, seeking the station they could hear with the least interference, regardless of program quality.

The Federal Communications Commission authorized commercial operation of FM radio in 1941, but the war held back further development until 1945 when the Commission shifted FM to its present frequency band and gave it the go-ahead. So high were hopes for FM that the Chairman of the Commission predicted in 1946 that FM would replace AM radio in two or three years. By 1947, nearly 1,000 FM stations had been licensed, or more than the total number of AM stations before the war.

But FM ran into a number of major stumbling blocks. First, it could not be heard on AM radio receivers without special converters, and AM programs could not be received on FM sets. This meant that FM's audience was limited to the number of people who invested in new-type radio sets. In 1947, the first inexpensive FM attachment for AM sets came on the market and this problem was partially solved. Second, there was the problem of FM programming and advertising support. FM could not attract large audiences unless it offered distinctive programs; it could not get advertising to finance such programs unless it already had the audience. Some broadcasters skirted this dilemma by duplicating their AM programs over their FM outlets, but independent FM broadcasters without AM stations to lean on, objected that such practices would hold back the development of FM, making it a stepchild of AM. Stations that had great investments in AM often looked on their FM licenses as a form of insurance and made little attempt to promote FM vigorously. Third, the absence of automatic tuning controls and the poor quality of cheap FM sets disappointed many listeners who did not find FM tone quality markedly superior to AM. Fourth, FM ran into heavy competition from the well-established AM field, now twice its prewar size, and from television, which hit the market almost simultaneously with FM radio.

In 1948, 300 new FM stations were constructed, but 125 applicants, in an unprecedented demonstration of pessimism in broadcasting, turned back their construction permits to the Federal Communications Commission. In 1949, the trend picked up steam, with licenses of even established stations being turned back. Whereas in 1948 the Federal Communications Commission was besieged with 17 competing applications for 5 remaining FM channels in the New York City area, in 1949 the license of one of the successful applicants practically went begging on the open market. In that year, only 3 of 114 FM-only stations did not suffer losses.

From 1949 through 1952, over 350 other FM station authorizations were returned to the Commission. In 1956, 536 commercial FM stations were on the air. Most of these were owned by AM licensees who simply duplicated on FM their AM program offerings. For many other AM licensees who were unable to obtain permission to broadcast on AM during evening hours, an FM license provided a nighttime outlet. The high-fidelity capabilities of FM have belatedly obtained increasing recognition. A number of FM stations specialize in programming good music to devoted listening audiences. In 1954, one new FM station proposed to broadcast 100 per cent good music programming, and another proposed over 98 per cent.

In order to help FM stations commercially and to make for more efficient utilization of FM frequencies, the Federal Communications Commission has authorized FM stations to engage in such additional services as "functional music," which has many variations including, for example, restaurant, factory, and other background music; also "storecasting," background music in stores; and "transit radio," on passenger-carrying vehicles. These services are made possible on a "simplex" basis during nonbroadcast hours and on a "multiplex" basis during regular broadcast hours. In simplex operation, a supersonic "beep" signal is broadcast along with the music to activate special receivers owned or rented by commercial and industrial establishments for this purpose. A multiplex operation involves the transmission on a broadcast frequency of a second program which can be received only by individuals and organizations having the necessary multiplexing receiving equipment.

• NONCOMMERCIAL EDUCATIONAL FM RADIO •

When the Federal Communications Commission authorized FM broadcasting, it set aside one portion of the band (88 megacycles to 92 megacycles) for use by noncommercial educational stations. In contrast to the decrease in the number of authorizations for commercial FM stations, noncommercial educational FM broadcast service has continually expanded during the last few years, until now more than 100 such educational stations are in operation. More than 40 of these operate low-powered transmitters of 10 watts or less, which provides satisfactory coverage of a college campus and the small towns in which many are located. These can later be built into higher-powered stations if the necessary financial resources are made available.

• SUMMARY •

American radio grew from a fledgling enterprise to a great mass communications medium in less than twenty years. Radio's amazing growth involved a struggle for control of important patents and early failures to realize the true nature of the broadcast medium. The decision to finance broadcasting by the sale of time to advertisers, the formation of national networks, and the intervention of the federal government to establish order after radio had fallen into helpless chaos were each important landmarks in the advancement of radio. AM radio reach a pinnacle of financial success and service to the nation during World War II, but following the advent of television it has been obliged to accept a secondary position. FM radio made its entry on the broadcasting scene after the war, but despite its superior technical quality to AM radio it seems destined to play only a small role on the American broadcasting scene.

Questions for Discussion

1. How does the history of American radio help one to understand present-day broadcasting?
2. Of what significance was the decision in the 1920's to turn to advertising revenue as the financial support for radio?
3. How do you explain the change in public attitudes toward advertising on the air?
4. What role did the national networks play in the development of radio?
5. What events led to the Radio Act of 1927, and what changes in public policy were reflected in this law as compared to the Act of 1912?
6. What have been some of the leading programming changes in the last twenty years of radio?
7. What were the main stumbling blocks to the development of FM?
8. What course can we reasonably expect AM and FM radio to take in the next ten years?

❊ 3 ❊

The Rise of Television

TELEVISION had its coming-out party at the New York World's Fair in 1939 and soon became the talk of the town. Television covered the opening of the fair and featured as its star attraction an address by President Roosevelt. Despite the significance of the event, only a few hundred receivers were able to tune it in. The communications industry had not yet gone into production of TV receivers, and most of those in existence were homemade or special instruments developed for field testing.

Television actually has a longer history than its sudden presentation to the American people in 1939 suggests. Its origins can be traced back to 1884 when the German scientist Paul Nipkow invented the scanning disc which made television possible, and to 1923, when Dr. V. K. Zworykin patented the iconoscope, the television camera that preceded the present-day image-orthicon camera. Experimentation continued throughout the 30's, with RCA, CBS, and the DuMont laboratories working unceasingly on the refinement of television for commercial uses.

Shortly after the 1939 World's Fair, television's progress was interrupted by a series of governmental orders and then by World War II. In 1940, the Federal Communications Commission ordered a halt in the expansion of TV pending completion of an investigation to determine the best technical standards for TV transmission. In 1941, six months before we went to war, the Commission authorized full commercial television on the black-and-white, 525-line basis now in use, in contrast to the 441 lines previously used. The few TV stations then in existence began televising programs two to three hours a day, but there were only 4,700 television sets in the entire New York area. When war came, the production of television sets stopped completely, and telecasting settled down to a skeleton schedule for the duration, with only six commercial television stations on the air.

Television ran into still another obstacle when controversies developed over which band it should be assigned in the broadcast spectrum and whether transmission should be in color as opposed to black-and-white. In

March, 1947, the Federal Communications Commission finally ruled out color television for the immediate future and authorized black-and-white television over thirteen channels between 54 and 216 megacycles in the very-high-frequency (VHF) band. (Channel 1 was subsequently assigned by the Commission to fixed and mobile services instead of television.)

The effect of the Commission's action was swift. Within a year, the number of applications for TV stations jumped from less than 75 to more than 300. Almost a million television sets were sold in 1948, and several hundred advertisers were already buying time over television stations in 16 different cities. The American public had welcomed television with open arms.

• THE PERIOD OF THE FREEZE •

The rush to get into television was now so great that the twelve channels were no longer adequate. It became apparent during 1947 and 1948, as more and more television stations took to the air, that serious signal interference was occurring in the service areas of some stations. Accordingly, in September, 1948, with 36 stations on the air in nineteen cities having approximately one-third the population of the United States, the Commission imposed a freeze on all new television assignments. The freeze applied to new applications only; 70 odd applicants who had received construction permits prior to September, 1948, were permitted to proceed with the construction of their stations.

The freeze imposed upon television was not lifted by the Commission for almost four years during which time the Commission investigated two important questions: (1) What frequency allocation plan would best provide a competitive and nation-wide system of television free from signal interference; and (2) what policy should the Commission take regarding the development of color television?

Meanwhile, within the limitations of the freeze, television grew by leaps and bounds far beyond the expectation of its most ardent supporters. Although television sets cost as much as $750 to $1,000 at first, the public investment in receivers was headlong. Those who could not afford their own sets visited neighbors or taverns that had sets. Programming at first was limited to evening hours, but as the public demand increased, it was extended into the daytime. Many of the early programs were crude presentations— "simulcasts" of radio programs, and a seemingly endless succession of wrestling matches, roller-skating derbies, panel-quizzes, parlor games, dog acts, and acrobats. The first major television variety program was "The Milton Berle Show" on NBC, and it proved such a huge success that in 1948 and 1949 Tuesday night was known as "Berle Night" in New York City. The Berle show probably did more to stimulate television-set buying in the first years of television than any other single sales factor.

For television networks and stations, these first two or three years were extremely costly as well as exciting years. CBS and NBC plunged into television on a big scale. ABC found that it lacked the financial resources to undertake television network programming on a full scale and was forced to proceed cautiously in television while it sought new investment capital. The Mutual Broadcasting System did not attempt to develop a television network, but the Allen B. DuMont Laboratories, manufacturers of television sets without experience in radio broadcasting, went into the business of network programming and sales for several years along with CBS, NBC, and ABC. In 1955, DuMont ceased operating as a television network after numerous difficulties including inadequate station line-ups and lack of top-quality programming. Television program production costs proved to be many times greater than had been known in radio, and because of the relatively small audience at first, as compared with the nation-wide radio audience, the networks were unable to recover a good part of their program costs from advertisers. Some television stations lost as much as $1,000 a day during this period. For the three years 1948-1950, the aggregate operating losses reported to the Federal Communications Commission by television networks and stations were $48 million. Of these losses, $27,500,000 were sustained by the four networks including their fourteen owned and operated stations. Earnings from radio were poured into television, an ironic situation in which one communications medium financed the development of its competitor. Part of the loss in television was caused by the freeze which prevented the networks from adding stations and increasing market coverage. For example, the city of Denver, Colorado, an important advertising market, had no television whatever during the four years of the freeze. In cities like Pittsburgh, only one station (owned by DuMont) was in operation, and the four networks had to share time over the single outlet. (However, this proved very fortunate for the station which was able to profit greatly from its noncompetitive position. After the freeze DuMont sold the station to Westinghouse for $9,500,000.) The installation of coaxial cable and microwave radio relay facilities, necessary to link the stations into a network operation, was a very costly and time-consuming operation. Not until September, 1951, did A.T.&T. complete the network hook-up to the West Coast. Stations not connected by the cable or radio relay were furnished film recordings ("kinescopes") of network shows for local showing. By 1951, many stations had passed the point of loss in television and were starting to show handsome profits from their operation. Public enthusiasm for the new medium continued unabated. Special events coverage by television of baseball and football games, of the World Series, of the important meetings of the United Nations Security Council over the Korean War, the Kefauver Committee hearings, and the Presidential conventions and campaigns of 1952 provided tremendous continuing promotion for television. By the time the freeze came to an end in July, 1952, there were 108 stations on the air in sixty-three cities having two-thirds the population of the country. The number of television sets in the public's hands had risen from 1 million in 1948 to 17 million only four years later!

· THE END OF THE FREEZE ·

On April 14, 1952, the Commission issued its final television allocation plan, known as the "Sixth Report and Order." This plan assigned to television, in addition to channels 2 through 13 in the VHF band, channels 14 through 83 in the ultrahigh frequency band (UHF) which ranged from 470 to 890 megacycles. Utilization of UHF frequencies in addition to VHF, according to the Commission, was the only way to make possible the establishment of more than 2,000 television stations on a nation-wide and competitive basis. The Commission announced that it would resume accepting applications for new television assignments on July 1, 1952.

In the next six months, 175 new television stations were authorized and more than 900 applications were submitted. By May 1, 1954, a total of 377 stations (250 VHF and 127 UHF) were on the air. By 1956, over 450 stations were on the air. The increase in stations made it possible for the networks to increase their station line-ups and provide about 70 per cent national coverage. Television set ownership rose to 37 million. By the end of 1955, television had become a billion-dollar-a-year industry. The networks undertook television programming on a larger scale than ever previously envisaged, with top Broadway and motion-picture talent appearing in major productions. "Spectaculars" costing the advertiser as much as $250,000 for a ninety-minute program, plus another $100,000 for broadcast time, were considered excellent advertising investments in the growing television medium. The public, meanwhile, gained from the improvement in quality of the programs. By 1955, the Hollywood motion-picture industry was ready to co-operate with television, and major studios produced program series for television. Television was established as the dominant medium for show business, for in that year, for the first time, a feature motion picture received a public showing on television prior to release in movie houses. Television had established itself, less than a decade after its start, as the dominant mass communications medium of our time.

· EDUCATIONAL NONCOMMERCIAL
TV STATIONS ·

In the Commission's Sixth Report and Order, special provision was made for educational noncommercial television stations. Following the precedent set in its special allocation plan for FM radio stations, the Commission set aside 242 channel assignments for application by educational noncommercial television stations. This number, since raised to 252, represented over 11 per cent of the total number of allocations made by the Commission. As a result of these allocations, educational television stations affiliated with universities and community educational groups have been established in Houston, Chicago, San Francisco, Boston, Pittsburgh, St. Louis, Madison, Seattle, East Lansing and Detroit, and in Alabama, Oklahoma, Nebraska, and other states. These stations will devote themselves primarily to programming of educational and cultural materials.

· THE UHF PROBLEM ·

Although there was a great increase in the number of television stations with the end of the freeze, this expansion was accompanied by some very serious problems, notably that of new UHF stations. By May, 1954, 132 communities had only VHF stations, 35 had both VHF and UHF stations, and 70 had only UHF stations. In the two years from 1952 to 1954, 29 UHF stations that went on the air were forced to cease operations and 89 others turned in their permits. By way of contrast, only 4 new VHF stations went off the air during the period, and 16 others surrendered their permits.[1]

The numerous failures of new UHF stations became a matter of great concern not only to the investors who lost their money, but to the Federal Communications Commission and to Congress, which held hearings to determine whether the Commission's allocation plan should be changed. It was clear that the main reason for the difficulty experienced by many new UHF stations was the fact that all the television receivers in the hands of the public at the end of the freeze could receive VHF signals only and were unable to receive UHF stations without the owners spending various sums of money, often as much as $100, to convert them. The problem appeared to be much smaller when the new UHF station went up in a city which previously had no television reception, or where only one VHF station had established itself; but where a city already had two or more VHF stations, the new UHF station ran into overpowering competitive obstacles, related not only to the technical problem of reception, but also to the difficulty of obtaining a network affiliation and adequate local advertising support. For example, KCTY, a new UHF station in Kansas City, Missouri, faced competition from three established VHF stations. KCTY went on the air in June, 1953, after investing approximately $750,000. The station expended more money in an attempt to win an audience, but the public was not willing to invest in converters to receive the station when it could obtain most of the top-rated network and syndicated programs from the existing

[1] *Status of UHF and Multiple Ownership of TV Stations. Hearings Before the Subcommittee on Communication of the Committee on Interstate and Foreign Commerce,* U.S. Senate, 83rd Congress, 2nd Session (Washington, 1954), pp. 165-167. Also Harry M. Plotkin, *Television Network Regulation and the UHF Problem, Committee on Interstate and Foreign Commerce Memorandum,* U.S. Senate, 84th Congress, 1st Session (Washington, 1955), p. 5.

BROADCAST REVENUES, EXPENSES, AND INCOME OF
4 TELEVISION NETWORKS AND 410 TV STATIONS

1952—1953—1954

($ Millions)

	1954	1953 [2]	1952 [1]
	Broadcast Revenues		
4 Networks (including 16 owned and operated stations)	$306.7	$231.7	$180.2
92 Pre-Freeze television stations	200.9	174.5	143.4
Subtotal	$507.6	$406.2	$323.6
Post-Freeze television stations:			
177 VHF stations	60.0	16.1	0.6
125 UHF stations	25.4	10.4	
Industry total	$593.0	$432.7	$324.2
	Broadcast Expenses		
4 Networks (including 16 owned and operated stations)	$270.2	$213.7	$170.3
92 Pre-Freeze television stations	133.3	114.0	97.6
Subtotal	$403.5	$327.7	$267.9
Post-Freeze television stations:			
177 VHF stations	63.8	20.3	0.8
125 UHF stations	35.4	16.7	
Industry total	$502.7	$364.7	$268.7
	Broadcast Income		
	(Before Federal Income Tax)		
4 Networks (including 16 owned and operated stations)	$ 36.5	$ 18.0	$ 9.9
92 Pre-Freeze television stations	67.6	60.5	45.8
Subtotal	$104.1	$ 78.5	$ 55.7
Post-Freeze television stations:			
177 VHF stations	(3.8)	(4.2)	(0.2)
125 UHF stations	(10.0)	(6.3)	
Industry total	$ 90.3	$ 68.0	$ 55.5

SOURCE: Federal Communications Commission.

( ) Denotes loss.

[1] 1952 data covers 4 networks and 15 owned and operated stations; 93 pre-freeze and 14 post-freeze TV stations.

[2] 1953 data covers 4 networks and 16 owned and operated stations; 92 pre-freeze and 226 post-freeze stations (114 VHF and 112 UHF).

VHF stations. Within six months after it went on the air, the station was offered for sale for $750,000, then $400,000, finally $300,000, but there were no takers. The owners finally disposed of the station for $1.00! [2]

Other UHF stations, in less competitive markets, have succeeded in establishing themselves successfully. Both NBC and CBS have purchased UHF stations of their own and include UHF stations among their affiliates. Nevertheless, the future of many UHF stations in difficult competitive situations remains very cloudy. Congress and the Federal Communications Commission have studied the problem at length; various proposals have been suggested as possible solutions, including the following: (1) make television all UHF, by transferring all present VHF assignments to the upper band of frequencies; (2) make television all VHF, by adding several additional VHF channels to the current allocations and discontinuing UHF except in the areas where it has succeeded; and (3) reallocate VHF and UHF assignments in cities where they are intermixed in order to make individual cities either all VHF or all UHF, but not a combination of the two.

• COLOR TELEVISION •

The development of color television first presented itself as an issue before the Federal Communications Commission as early as 1940, when it was decided that the quality and method of color transmission was not yet satisfactory. The Commission decided to authorize color television as early as possible in order to avoid a situation wherein many black-and-white receivers would be rendered obsolete by the development of color. Again in 1945 and in 1947, the Commission re-examined the question of color television, and decided that color picture transmission and reception was not yet technically satisfactory. The Commission nevertheless gave continued attention to the prospect of early approval of color television, and manufacturers in the television industry continued their research. CBS, which had developed a field sequential system of color television, proposed that the Commission approve its system. In October, 1950, after extended hearings, the Commission officially approved the CBS system after finding that "of the systems then before it only this system produced an acceptable color picture." One of the other systems had been developed and proposed by the Radio Corporation of America. The RCA system was an electronic system; it also was "compatible," i.e., the color pictures could be received in black and white over existing receivers. The CBS system, on the other hand, used a mechanical device attached to the receiver and was "incompatible"—the pictures could be received only over new color receivers.

[2] Address of FCC Commissioner George Sterling, before the Institute of Radio Engineers, Boston, February 2, 1954. The purchaser also assumed certain of the station's liabilities.

Despite the Commission's ruling in favor of CBS, no television manufacturers except CBS-Columbia appeared willing to invest in the manufacture of color television sets using the CBS system. CBS itself was soon prevented from manufacturing color sets by a government order restricting the use of certain necessary materials that were in short supply during the Korean war. Finally, CBS itself appeared to lose interest in its own system for which it had been unable to obtain industry support, while RCA continued experimentation on its electronic system with a view to perfecting it. The National Television System Committee, an association of engineers and scientists including representatives of many companies engaged in the manufacture of television equipment, also commenced studies looking toward the development of a commercially practicable system of color television. In January, 1953, after conducting numerous field tests, the committee adopted specifications for color television which it recommended to the Commission. RCA, NBC, Philco, Motorola, General Electric, and other companies petitioned the Commission to approve the new color specifications. CBS also signified its approval of the new system. In December, 1953, after renewed consideration, the Commission issued a new set of rules for the electronic and compatible system of color television that is now in use.[3] NBC immediately undertook extensive color television programming in the season 1953-1954, constructing new studios especially designed for color broadcasting and putting every major program on its network schedule into color at least once. The following season NBC launched a major color programming schedule, with many ninety-minute "Spectaculars" telecast in color. CBS also constructed color facilities and began a limited schedule of color programming. The manufacture of color television receivers, however, lagged behind the color programming. Not until the summer of 1955 did color television sets appear for sale in quantity, and these cost about $800. It was expected that prices would drop as soon as the manufacturers engaged in quantity production, and that color would come increasingly to dominate television. For color, unlike a simple increase in picture size, adds another important dimension to television communication, one that enables it to transmit reality far more effectively than ever before. Color is a vital element of perception and identification, and its addition to television transmission meant progress of major proportions.

• "SUBSCRIPTION TELEVISION" •

Another question that went to the Federal Communications Commission in 1955 was a proposal to utilize television frequencies for various systems of "subscription television," also referred to as "pay as you go tele-

[3] "FCC Report and Order Approving Compatible Color Television" (mimeo), December 17, 1953. (Docket No. 10637).

vision" and "toll television." The underlying theory of these proposals is to make certain programs available only to those viewers willing to pay directly for them.

The method of subscription television is to broadcast a program together with a signal that scrambles the picture at the receiving end unless the viewer possesses a decoding device. Three systems have been developed commercially for this purpose: (1) "Phonevision," developed by the Zenith Radio Corporation, uses a coding device attached to the television receiver and a special card with code numbers to be inserted in the device. Viewers would receive a bill for subscription programs which they have watched, as recorded on the special card which they must mail in to the company in order to receive another card. (2) "Skiatron," developed by Skiatron TV, Inc., uses a system similar to Phonevision, but utilizes a standard IBM card on which is imposed a printed electronic circuit. This circuit acts as an "unscrambler" when a button on the device is pressed. Pressing the button would automatically punch the card and make a record of the shows seen. (3) "Telemeter," proposed by International Telemeter Corporation, a subsidiary of Paramount Pictures, proposed to transmit two images on one television channel. One image, which could be seen on all television sets, consists of an advertisement of the subscription program. The second image is the main attraction and this program could be seen only on sets equipped with a Telemeter attachment. The attachment is basically a coin machine that collects the money before each show is seen. The coin machines would be emptied periodically, as in the case of pay telephones.

That subscription television clearly represents a departure from established broadcasting practices cannot be disputed. When the Commission invited public statements on the issue in 1955, it received more than 25,000 communications, mostly opposed to the proposal. The immediate responsibility for deciding this issue will rest with the Commission, although the question as to whether subscription television is in the public interest may ultimately be decided by Congress, the Supreme Court, or by the people themselves.

• SUMMARY •

Despite the problems of the UHF stations, the late start in color television, and the proposals for subscription television, television has risen in less than a decade to the place of dominance over all mass communication media in America. Television has become the foremost advertising medium in the country, the first choice of the people for leisure-time activity, the main source of popular entertainment, the primary means by which most people maintain direct contact with governmental processes: a social, political, economic, cultural, and educational force of the first order; in short, the primary communications medium of the twentieth century.

Questions for Discussion

1. Why did the Federal Communications Commission impose a freeze on the construction of new television stations from 1948 to 1952? What were the effects of the freeze?
2. What caused television to expand so rapidly after the freeze was lifted?
3. How has television changed since its early days in 1947 and 1948, with especial reference to programming and business investments?
4. What kinds of problems did UHF stations run into? Could these have been prevented?
5. What was the course of development of color television? What is its future likely to be?
6. What place in our television system is there for educational stations? Why should they be established separately?
7. What are the pros and cons of subscription television?
8. What is the future of television likely to be? What do you think television will be like five years from now? Ten years from now?

* 4 *

Programming

THE KEY FACTOR in determining public acceptance of television and radio is programming—the determination of what programs to put on the air and at what points in the program schedule. Only through successful programming that wins large audiences do television and radio become attractive to advertisers seeking mass circulation, and it is only through income obtained from these advertisers that commercial station program operations are financed. The production, technical, and sales staffs of networks and stations work to little avail if they do not have effective programming leadership.

· THE PROGRAMMING FUNCTION ·

To understand television and radio programming, we must first have some insight into its scope and nature.

First, the programming function in both television and radio is of such vast proportions that it is difficult to convey its size accurately. Each of the more than 2,800 AM radio stations and 450 television stations plans a program schedule for every day of the week; many stations program fifteen to eighteen hours per day, and some more. The national television and radio networks program from nine to fifteen hours a day and offer these programs to affiliated stations which are then relieved of the necessity to produce programs for those hours. A single television network presents more than 6,500 different programs in the course of a single season. Counting both network and local station offerings in both television and radio, literally tens of thousands of different programs are broadcast each day throughout the country.

Second, the programming function is continuous. Stations do not go on the air to broadcast only one or two programs at a time. Once they sign on in the morning, with few exceptions they program without interruption until sign-off. Networks normally program in three-hour blocks, with affiliated stations programming the intervening hours, although the NBC radio network has broadcast forty consecutive hours on week ends. It is the fact that programming is continuous that develops audience flow from one program to the next. Adult viewers and listeners tend to remain tuned to the same station unless they positively dislike the succeeding program or they know of a program more to their liking on another station. A very popular program on a station or network schedule provides an audience-in-being for the program that follows it. Similarly, a program with small appeal forces the following program to build its audience from scratch. This program adjacency factor plays a great role in the preparation of program schedules. Programs are usually scheduled in blocks in order to build and hold audiences throughout the day and evening.

Third, the programming function is extremely competitive—it is, indeed, the most competitive aspect of television and radio. In the constant search to find and to develop "hit" programs, each network is in vigorous competition with other networks, and every station competes with other stations in the same geographic area. Not only does the competition extend to programming effectively against the competitive programming of the other networks and stations, since they are seeking to attract the same audience, but also to the finding of new hit programs. Thus, a new hit on one network may have a devastating effect on the program broadcast at the same time by a rival network, as well as on adjacent programs. The big networks, always under the pressure to win a majority of the available audience, usually try to meet program strength with program strength, which explains why two big hour variety shows or hour dramas may be scheduled at the same time over rival networks. Failure to compete in this fashion may cause the network to lose out competitively throughout the rest of the evening because of the effect of the failure on adjacent programs. Individual stations which can operate profitably if they attract only a minority of the audience often choose to schedule programs with specialized or local appeal against network hit shows, and this often proves very effective.

Fourth, the programming function, especially in television, is a very costly one in time, effort, money, and creative ability. Frank Stanton, President of CBS, has stated that a typical CBS half-hour television dramatic program is the product of 1,374 man-hours, involving 154 people exclusive of the services of advertising, publicity, traffic and sales personnel. For this one half-hour seven members of the program staff spend 280 man-hours, thirteen stagehands spend 195 man-hours, ten cameramen operating three cameras spend 90 man-hours.[1] The cost to the advertiser of an hour network television dramatic program in 1955 ranged from $35,000 to $60,000, exclusive of about $85,000 for agency commission and network time.

[1] *Testimony of Dr. Frank Stanton before Subcommittee on Communications of the Committee on Interstate and Foreign Commerce, U.S. Senate, 83rd Congress, 2nd Session, Status of UHF and Multiple Ownership of TV Stations* (Washington, 1954), pp. 990-991.

A half-hour filmed situation comedy program costs the advertiser about $35,000, a half-hour audience participation show $15,000 to $20,000, and a major hour comedy variety show costs as much as $130,000. These costs are solely for the entertainment portions of the program and do not include the cost of network time, commercial production, and agency commissions. To make filmed or kinescoped auditions of new programs for television costs from $5,000 to $25,000. A ninety-minute television "Spectacular" can cost well over $200,000 to produce. The two-hour television production of *Peter Pan* required 10,000 man hours of work from 100 professional show people, including actors, musicians, dancers, and other performing talent who rehearsed for four weeks prior to the telecast. Five full days of studio rehearsal with four television cameras and special engineering and lighting effects were required. The labor involved in handling scenery, props, art work, costumes, and makeup required the services of 107 craftsmen, including 26 engineers and 30 stagehands for a total of 8,000 man hours. The total cost of producing *Peter Pan* for a single telecast was reported to be approximately $400,000.

Fifth, the programming function, especially in networks, is extremely complex, because it is interrelated with almost all the other functions and operating processes of television—the simultaneous availability of performing, writing, and production talent, production facilities, including studios, lighting and camera equipment, scenery, costumes, technical crews, network coaxial cables, and the advertising schedules and budgets of network clients, as well as the clearance of the same air time by affiliated stations in different time zones across the country.

Sixth, the programming function tends to seek stability in program schedules that will develop viewing and listening habits with the public, in order to be able to make long-term sales to advertisers, and to obtain relief from the relentless pressure of building new programs. The need to recover from damage caused by program failures induces most networks and stations to leave successful shows undisturbed until they weaken noticeably. Networks plan their schedules on a 39 and 52 weeks basis, and rarely on less than 13 weeks except for summer replacement or tryout purposes.

Seventh, the programming function draws its creative ideas, materials, and talent from all possible sources: professional television and radio performers, and professional program packagers, talent bureaus, Broadway, Hollywood, night clubs, writers, singers, dancers, musicians, community theatrical groups, colleges, journalism, studio audiences, local-station talent, and auditions. The programming function must continually seek new program ideas and develop new program forms if television and radio are to maintain their hold on the public imagination.

Eighth, the programming function is highly speculative. There are no sure rules for predicting which program ideas will result in programs the public will like or which new performers will develop into star talent. If certainty of prediction were possible, there would be fewer failures in all theatrical ventures—Broadway and Hollywood, as well as television and radio! Programming deals with indefinable and intangible aspects of audience appeal.

The best programming executives possess an uncanny ability to evaluate the indefinable and intangible aspects of audience appeal, a thorough knowledge of program sources and show business in general, an acquaintance with program costs that will enable them to evaluate the risks involved in any program venture, and a high degree of boldness and courage.

• RADIO PROGRAMMING •

Let us turn now to an examination of radio programming—what its traditional patterns have been, what new forms have been developed, and how it is handled.

Until the advent of television, radio programming had become fairly well stabilized in content and pattern. The networks concentrated during evening hours on half-hour weekly program series in news, commentary, comedy-variety, situation comedy, mystery, audience participation, music, "personality," and dramatic shows. Programs like "Jack Benny," "Lux Radio Theater," and the "Bob Hope Show" occupied the same time period week after week for years on end. Most of the big network shows were actually produced by advertising agencies with the network supplying only the studio facilities, engineers, and musicians. The networks themselves produced few commercial programs other than news shows. Although radio presented enormous demands on writers for new material, top performers seemed to have an unending welcome in the American home (in contrast, as we shall see, to the experience of programming in television).

In the daytime hours, networks concentrated on audience participation shows and the soap operas—serial dramas with continuing characters and slow moving action that were broadcast fifteen minutes every day of the week.[2] NBC and CBS broadcast as many as 11 to 14 different soap operas each day, practically all of which were produced by agencies and independent program packagers. It was generally understood that the major advertising agencies controlled the production of programs on the networks.

Local radio stations affiliated with the networks rounded out their schedules with local audience participation shows, local newscasts, and programs of recorded and transcribed music. Only the larger local stations and the networks maintained staff orchestras for live music shows. Independent

---

[2] "A soap opera is a kind of sandwich, whose recipe is simple enough, although it took years to compound. Between thick slices of advertising, spread twelve minutes of dialogue, add predicament, villainy, and female suffering in equal measure, throw in a dash of nobility, sprinkle with tears, season with organ music, cover with a rich announcer sauce, and serve five times a week." JAMES THURBER, "Onward and Upward with the Arts," *The New Yorker*, XXIV (May 15, 1948), pp. 34 ff.

radio stations without network affiliations tended to rely more on "disc jockey" personalities who played records and talked informally for three or four hours at a stretch. Local stations also programmed transcribed dramatic and musical programs supplied to them by advertising agencies in behalf of commercial sponsors. Stations with more aggressive program departments tried to develop local talent to be used on their own shows, or sent newsmen out in the city with tape recorders to obtain on-the-scene interviews to be used on news programs.

Under the competitive inroads of television, especially since 1952, network radio programming has undergone substantial changes. Having lost most of the big-name performers to television, the radio networks often have had to content themselves with playing sound-tape recording of some of the popular television comedy shows, like Groucho Marx in "You Bet Your Life," or "People Are Funny." As major advertisers plunged into television, less money was available for producing big radio shows. Networks were forced to seek more flexible program forms that would lend themselves to sale to smaller advertisers. The regular half-hour weekly show began to be abandoned as radio's leading program form. By late 1954, there were only 35 commercial half-hour shows on the program schedules of the four radio networks, out of 216 half-hour units available during nighttime hours. Replacing the traditional half-hour program sponsored by a single advertiser were fifteen- and five-minute programs and half-hour shows with several different "participating" sponsors.[3]

In 1955, the NBC radio network introduced "Monitor," a new program form developed by Sylvester Weaver. This was a forty-hour program scheduled for broadcast without interruption from Saturday morning until Sunday midnight. It was programmed when millions of Americans were listening to their automobile radios. It broke loose completely from traditional programming patterns of radio. It was completely flexible to the needs of advertisers. Its program content ranged over all subjects, and several personalities, designated "Communicators," spelled each other in presiding over the show. "Monitor" enlisted the full technical resources of the network to arrange remote pick-ups from practically any place in the United States and from important points overseas. "Monitor" capitalized on its own formlessness, allowing its subject matter at all times to determine the amount of program time allotted to it. On a continuous basis throughout the weekend "Monitor" provided listeners with an ear on the world—something the television networks were not equipped to do. Soon after "Monitor" came "Weekday," a program broadcast daily through the rest of the week. Thus, in an effort to establish a permanent basis for network radio in competition with television, a new network program form was created.

The new program forms in local radio stations tend more and more to be

[3] *Variety,* December 15, 1954, p. 33.

programs of recorded music and news, with disc-jockeys and local personalities to provide program identification and to develop listener loyalty. It
is a much looser program form than radio has known before, but to most
station managers and observers it provides radio with its best programming
in competition with television. It is also a type of programming that is better
on radio than on television. In addition, there are numerous service programs providing a wide range of current information ranging from sports
to farm news and ladies' fashions.

• TELEVISION PROGRAMMING •

When television programming started in 1948, it was hampered by the
fact that only limited funds were available for programming purposes; even
more seriously it suffered from a wide misunderstanding of the nature of
the television medium. The fact that early network shows were "simulcasts"
of radio programs (cameras placed in front of the radio performers) could
be explained then by the lack of facilities for television's own use and by
the lack of money for television program production. Far more difficult to
justify, however, was the persistent if unthinking view that television programs were a simple extension of radio shows—in other words, hearing
plus sight. This was, of course, true of a number of radio program forms,
notably the audience participation, panel, and quiz shows, provided the
questions and answers were changed to emphasize visual interest. But it
was certainly not true of comedy, variety, and drama, the main staples of
network program fare. Nor could television handle music programming
easily—not records, certainly, and even orchestral concerts presented television with problems that radio never had to face. Moreover, the half-hour
program form, so firmly established in network radio, was transferred to
television intact, and the evils that followed this transfer were numerous.
Certain aesthetic forms like radio drama lent themselves to the half-hour
form: the radio drama, utilizing the imagination to the fullest, was very
successful in establishing characters, plot, and mood in a few moments, and
then developing and resolving the story within thirty minutes. In live television drama, however, the half-hour form proved weak, with the writer
rarely able to establish real characters or to develop his plot adequately. On
the other hand, the full-hour live drama in television immediately demonstrated the soundness of its form, and produced a quality of drama rarely
achieved in the history of radio. Producers and directors such as Fred Coe,
Worthington Miner, Robert Montgomery, Martin Manulis, Albert Mc-
Cleery, Felix Jackson, Herbert Brodkin, Alex Segal, Franklin Schaffner,
Delbert Mann, Vincent Donohue, and others acquired outstanding reputations for presenting topflight original dramatic productions on television.
By the end of 1955, more than 13 full-hour live dramas were scheduled by

the networks every week, with a full-hour live drama scheduled every afternoon by NBC, a new development in daytime programming.

• THE "SPECTACULAR" CONCEPT •

The regularity of the radio program schedule was also transferred to television, although the time and effort required to produce a television show was at least five to ten times as great as that required for radio. Moreover, in contrast to radio, the television audience begins to lose interest in performers, especially comedians, who appear on the air very frequently. As a result, many programs that had been broadcast successfully on radio for many years often failed after a season or two in television. Performers complained of the lack of time to prepare for a weekly television show.

The regular weekly shows also tended to have a sameness about them that caused much of the early excitement in television programming to disappear. In the season 1954-1955, network television broke loose from this pattern with the concept of the "Spectacular" developed at NBC by Sylvester L. ("Pat") Weaver, who has probably influenced the development of television programming more than any other single individual. The Spectacular concept meant a departure from traditional programming practices; it meant big programs, an hour, ninety minutes, or two hours in length, depending upon the needs of the subject matter, and it meant scheduling these programs once a month or sometimes as a "single shot." The forerunners of the Spectaculars were the two-hour Ford show in 1953 that starred Mary Martin and Ethel Merman and the two-hour Rodgers and Hammerstein show in 1954. The hour-long "Bob Hope Show," scheduled every fourth week, also demonstrated the effectiveness of the big, nonweekly program. The largest program budgets in broadcasting history were assigned to the Spectaculars to make it possible to obtain the highest-priced stars, the most elaborate production, and the best scripts. These programs, it was hoped, would break habitual weekly viewing patterns and obtain large audiences through their outstanding quality and special promotional campaigns. In their first season, the Spectaculars recaptured to television the public excitement that had previously made the new medium a "conversation piece."

By the next season, both NBC and CBS were expanding the Spectacular concept with additional series of ninety-minute programs. With aggressive program leadership, television had broken the half-hour bond it inherited from radio, and demonstrated that it was to be a medium for show business on a scale never dreamed of in radio. The thirty-minute show was, of course, still the most common program form used in television for filmed situation comedies, dramatic anthologies, audience participation, and panel shows. But, with a few notable exceptions, the program leaders in public and critical attention were the full hour and ninety-minute shows.

• THE "MAGAZINE" CONCEPT OF PROGRAM SALES •

Another legacy from radio that was to be overthrown before television found its own programming forms was the conventional program sales method of single sponsors for each weekly program series. This method was favored in radio by large advertisers because they were able to obtain complete program and talent identification with their products. It also made it possible for them, either directly or through their advertising agency, to control the show. The program usually belonged to the sponsor or the agency. As television program costs rose, becoming five and ten times as expensive as radio shows, few advertisers could afford a single show, or felt it wise to allocate so large a slice of their advertising budget to one. Thus there developed the pattern of alternate-week sponsorships of the same program by two advertisers. From this it was but one more step to the development of the "Magazine" concept of program sales in which programs were offered for sale to multiple sponsors on an insertion or participating basis. A prospective sponsor might purchase one or a hundred insertions, depending upon his resources and his needs, but in any event he would have no control over the content of the program. No one advertiser would dominate, and many small advertisers, previously excluded from television network advertising, were able to participate in the sponsorship of big network shows that gave their advertising messages a national circulation previously obtained only by a small number of advertisers. Programs like "Today," "Home," "Tonight," "NBC Matinee Theater," and the Sunday night Spectaculars were sold on this basis. One result of this concept was the restoration of control over the programs to the network.

• TELEVISION PROGRAM PACKAGERS •

It should not be thought, however, that as a result of the Magazine concept, the television networks dominate all network programming. There are many sources of television talent and program materials, and many ways in which programs are put together. Two of the most important television program sources are the Music Corporation of America (MCA) and the William Morris Agency, the two largest talent bureaus in the United States. These two companies operate in direct competition with each other and represent most of the star talent in the country. Other bureaus like General Artists Corporation, which represent many prominent singers, and smaller agencies, like Ashley-Steiner, Inc., and James Saphier Agency, represent individual stars, but it is virtually impossible to put together a major variety show without calling upon talent represented by either MCA or William Morris. Both MCA and William Morris represent talent in the night club, hotel, theatrical, motion picture, and literary fields, as well as in radio and

television. Both of these talent bureaus also arrange with independent producing companies to "package" programs, usually with talent they represent,
and they sell these programs either to the networks or directly to sponsors
who have or can get time on the networks and are looking for new shows.
In one season, one talent bureau produced a regular weekly variety show
on one network and also booked the talent for the show competing against
it on another network. The following season it supervised the production
of both rival shows.

Other program packagers, like Goodson-Todman Productions, Lou
Cowan, and Walt Framer Productions, produce network programs like
"What's My Line?," "I've Got a Secret," "The $64,000 Question," and
"Strike It Rich." In the field of television drama, several important program
packagers have been established: Neptune Productions, which produces
"Robert Montgomery Presents"; Talent Associates, which produces "Arm-
strong Circle Theater," and used to produce "Television Playhouse" and
"Mr. Peepers"; and Showcase Productions, Inc., which produces a weekly
drama program and a series of Spectaculars.

Advertising agencies, however, still continue very active in the business
of television program packaging, although not as active as in radio. The J.
Walter Thompson Agency has been a leader in program packaging with the
"Kraft Television Theater" and the "Lux Video Theater" among its many
program packages. Many agencies refrain from entering the program packaging field because of the great expense involved; others believe it is better
to buy programs for their clients on the open market rather than commit
themselves on a long-term basis to any one program.

Because of the operations of the federal income-tax law, many performers
find it desirable to form program-producing companies of their own to
produce one or more different shows, rather than simply to perform as an
actor. Some of these companies have been very successful and have produced many program series on the air.

· FILM *vs*. LIVE SHOWS ·

The place of film programs in television has been a question of continuing
interest to many. Out of 133 network shows in the season 1954-1955, 74
were live shows, 53 were film, and 6 were live and film. Television, of course,
with its enormous demands for program material, has made extensive use
of film programming of two kinds: (1) the feature-length Hollywood or
British film that is released to television after its motion-picture, box-office
possibilities have been exhausted, and (2) half-hour film series especially
produced for television.

The old feature-length films are in many ways television's equivalent to
the recorded and transcribed music programs that fill up so many radio
hours. They add no luster to television network and station programming,

but they fill a program void on local stations. ABC has made extensive use, however, of British feature films for both afternoon and evening network programming. The Hollywood motion-picture industry at first resisted all efforts on television to obtain fairly recent motion pictures for showing on the air. By 1954-1955, this resistance had begun to weaken, and some important studios, like RKO, anxious to produce some quick income, sold whole blocs of their films to television. British motion picture producers were much more ready to co-operate with television, since their old films did not have much remaining potential for additional box-office earnings. In 1955, Alexander Korda, a major British producer, was the first to sell to network television the première showing of a new feature-length film prior to its theatrical exhibition. In contrast with the prevailing views of Hollywood producers, he believed that the single network showing would stimulate, rather than hurt, box-office receipts for the film on its regular theatrical exhibition.

The major Hollywood studios began to look upon television as a means to publicize their new films and their performing stars; they willingly supplied brief excerpts from new releases and personal appearances of movie stars in order to whet the public appetite for the film, and thus build up the box-office in motion-picture houses.

The production of special film series for television has become a major activity in Hollywood, with more than 250 companies in the business. Each half-hour situation comedy- or adventure-film series involves the production of 30 or 39 half-hour films, the equivalent of about 12 feature-length motion pictures. Each half-hour film is usually shot in three days, or two a week. Alternate weeks no films are shot in order to give the performers a rest and a chance to study scripts. In this way 4 half-hour films are turned out each month. The films usually are offered for sale to networks for $30,000 to $35,000 each, which is more than a half-hour live network dramatic show costs. However, the films may be reshown repeatedly at reduced costs, while kinescopes of live television shows may not be reshown on television without special permission of several unions and, with certain exceptions, they also involve full payment again to all performing, music, writing, and directing talent. (In 1956, the television and radio actors union (AFTRA) agreed to accept reduced payments (50 to 75 per cent) for repeat showings of kinescopes.) If no network sale is made, half-hour film series are put up for sale on a syndication basis and thus become available to local stations. Successful films are syndicated repeatedly, so that each film may be shown three or four times in the course of several years. Network film series are often syndicated under different names some time after the individual films have been shown on the network. Thus "Dragnet" went into syndication under the name "Badge 714" while the "Dragnet" series itself continued on the network.

PROFILE OF LOCAL RADIO PROGRAMMING IN
1954 AND 1955

	% Total Respondents	
	1954	1955
Daytime stations—sunrise to sunset	33% *	29% *
Stations on air to midnight	51% *	54% *
Stations programming past midnight	18% *	17% *
Stations on air 24 hours per day	5% *	5% *
Stations affiliated with national networks	50%	50%
Independent stations	50%	50%
Stations programming popular music	88%	92%
Pop music specialists (75 wkly hrs or more)	8%	12%
Stations programming concert music	61%	78%
Concert music specialists (10 wkly hrs or more)	9%	23%
Stations programming folk music	66%	77%
Folk music specialists (10 wkly hrs or more)	14%	16%
Stations scheduling religious programs	54%	83%
Religious specialists (10 wkly hrs or more)	6%	17%
Stations scheduling local farm programs	64%	70%
Farm specialists (5 wkly hrs or more)	41%	31%
Stations scheduling homemaking programs	46%	61%
Stations programming to a Mexican-American audience	7%	7%
Stations programming to other foreign language audiences	19%	17%
Stations programming to a Negro audience	25% *	29% *
Stations offering play-by-play sports	55%	59%
Stations scheduling daily newscasts	92%	98%
Stations subscribing to a national news service	82%	96%
Stations subscribing to a transcription library service	67%	81%

* Totals exclude Canadian respondents

1954: based on questionnaires from 1568 stations: 55% of U. S. stations and 35% of Canadian stations on the air as of April 1, 1954.

1955: based on questionnaires from 2172 stations: 77% of U. S. stations and 66% of Canadian stations on the air as of April 1, 1955.

PROFILE OF LOCAL TELEVISION PROGRAMMING IN
1955

Programming	No. of Stations Responding	% Total Respondents
Stations offering daily local newscasts......	364	96%
Stations offering local newsreel coverage....	191	50%
Stations offering daily sportscasts..........	319	85%
Stations offering play-by-play sports coverage	130	34%
Stations offering local homemaking programs	319	96%
Stations offering local children's programs..	351	92%
Stations offering variety shows............	265	70%
Stations featuring hillbilly-western variety...	134	36%
Stations offering farm service programming .	207	56%
Stations offering syndicated films..........	312	82%
Stations offering daily feature films	361	95%
Stations scheduling morning films	61	16%
Stations scheduling afternoon films	228	60%
Stations scheduling early evening films......	125	33%
Stations scheduling late evening films	318	83%
Stations programming (at least partly) for a specialized audience	35	9%
Stations affiliated with national networks....	424 *	94% *
Stations affiliated with national sales representatives	446 *	99% *
Stations with vhf channel allocations.......	326 *	72% *
Stations with uhf channel allocations.......	125 *	28% *

* Based on total of 451 stations on air as of April 1, 1955

* Based on *Sponsor* Magazine's "Buyers' Guide" Study, appearing in *Sponsor*, July 11, 1955. By permission of *Sponsor*.

THE EXTENT FILM IS USED IN TELEVISION *

1. What percentage of all programming does local TV film represent?

SOURCE: *Film Manual, 1955* of NARTB. Based on survey of U. S. TV stations.

Stations in Group 1	Stations in Group 2	Stations in Group 3	Stations in Group 4	Stations in Group 5
41.3%	40.6%	26.5%	26.1%	32.1%

Explanation of station groupings is under chart below.

2. How many hours per week of local station programming are on film?

SOURCE: See question 1 above.

Average Hours Per Week

	Group 1	Group 2	Group 3	Group 4	Group 5	All-station average
Network hours	21:17	32:58	57:36	60:23	55:04	50:35
Local hours	42:40	42:56	45:58	53:52	60:12	47:50
Live	16:17	12:07	18:34	24:00	23:15	18:26
Film	26:23	30:49	27:24	29:52	36:57	29:24
Total operating hours	63:57	75:54	103:34	114:15	115:16	98:25

Two charts above are from 1955 survey by NARTB to which 106 TV outlets in all parts of the U. S. replied. Stations are grouped as follows: *Group* 1: up to 50,000 TV families; *Group* 2: 50-150,000; *Group* 3: 150-500,000; *Group* 4: 500-1,000,000; *Group* 5: over 1,000,000 TV families. First chart shows clearly that TV films (syndicated shows, features) are an important segment of the total programing, network and local, that stations carry; the average for all stations is almost exactly 30 per cent. Second chart shows that number of hours of local TV film programing at stations in large or small TV markets tops amount of local live programs.

3. What type of TV films do stations use (by weekly hours)?

SOURCE: See question 1.

	Group 1	Group 2	Group 3	Group 4	Group 5	All stations
Feature film						
Morning	—	.9	1.8	1.5	2.0	1.4
Afternoon	6.0	5.3	5.7	7.7	7.1	6.1
Evening	8.4	7.4	6.5	11.1	11.5	7.9
Total	14.4	13.6	14.0	20.3	20.6	15.4
Syndicated film						
Morning	—	.2	.2	.4	.4	.3
Afternoon	.4	1.6	1.6	1.8	2.3	1.6
Evening	5.5	7.4	6.1	5.0	6.2	6.2
Total	5.9	9.2	7.9	7.2	8.9	8.1

* Reprinted from *Sponsor,* February 7, 1955. By permission of *Sponsor.*

Short subjects

Morning	—	—	.5	.7	.9	.4
Afternoon	1.1	1.9	1.0	1.1	3.3	1.4
Evening	.7	.9	.5	.2	.9	.6
Total	1.8	2.8	2.0	2.0	5.1	2.4

Film produced by station

Morning	—	—	—	.1	.2	—
Afternoon	.1	—	.1	—	—	.1
Evening	.8	.4	.2	.3	.5	.3
Total	.9	.4	.3	.4	.7	.4

Free film

Morning	.1	.2	.6	1.0	.1	.5
Afternoon	1.3	1.6	1.3	1.0	.8	1.3
Evening	1.4	1.3	.5	.3	.5	.7
Total	2.8	3.1	2.4	2.3	1.4	2.5

Total Film Hours

Morning	.1	1.3	3.1	3.7	3.6	2.6
Afternoon	8.9	10.4	9.7	11.6	13.5	10.5
Evening	16.8	17.4	13.8	16.9	19.6	15.7
Total	25.8	29.1	26.6	32.2	36.7	28.8

The ultimate place film shows will occupy in television as opposed to live shows remains a matter of conjecture. Most observers believe, however, that film will never displace live television completely. As Frank Stanton, President of CBS, has said,

> I will not deny the entertainment and informative qualities of film programs. Some programs as a matter of fact require film and are better because of it. But good as they are, it is the live quality, the sense of seeing the event or the play, at the same time that it takes place, in front of your eyes as you sit in your living room which is the real magic of television. Take the live quality out of television and you have diluted its excitement and impact.[4]

• PUBLIC-AFFAIRS AND SERVICE PROGRAMMING •

Public-affairs and service programs most clearly demonstrate the use of broadcasting to serve the public interest. In a variety of forms, these programs provide information and understanding about the real world in which we live: they report information and news about activities as different as

[4] Testimony of Dr. Frank Stanton, *loc. cit.*, p. 992.

agricultural marketing and the major league baseball contests; they present direct coverage of important events; they provide a public platform for speeches, press conferences, and discussions of public issues; they dramatize, through documentary techniques, historical events and current social and political problems; they provide a pulpit for religious services; they broadcast practical information for use in homekeeping, shopping, family health, and child raising.

Some of these programs, such as religious programs, are broadcast as "sustaining" shows by stations and networks and are not offered for sale to possible advertisers. Other public-affairs programs, such as sports and news, are among the most popular of program types and are usually sponsored. Network television newscasts are far more involved and expensive to produce than most viewers realize. In the programming of a regular fifteen-minute television news program, CBS calls on the services of 259 people, including 94 staff members and 165 foreign and domestic camera correspondents, not counting operations, engineering, reference, and other network departments.[5]

Network television programs like "See It Now," "Omnibus," "Victory at Sea," "Wide, Wide World," "The Search," the Presidential conventions, have all won much public and critical acclaim. Programs such as these require large production staffs and the expenditure of huge sums of money. According to CBS, the production of "The Search," a half-hour series of twenty-six film programs delineating research done in colleges and universities, cost $500,000. To cover the Presidential conventions of 1952 in 118 hours and 11 minutes of programs required 41,750 man-hours of effort at one network.[6] "Home," a network television service program for women, broadcast an hour each day Monday through Friday, costs about $45,000 a week to produce. But there are many public affairs and service programs that achieve excellent results that are relatively inexpensive. Interview programs with various authorities, local cooking and shopping programs, simple news and feature programs on radio, discussion and debate programs with exponents of conflicting points of view, and other program forms are produced locally as well as on networks with good public acceptance.

• CHILDREN'S PROGRAMS •

No area of television and radio programming is more sensitive to public criticism than children's programs. Special concern has frequently been voiced about the effect on children of programs dramatizing crime and violence. This concern is often expressed by parents who, in what seems to some to be an abdication of parental responsibility, have turned over their television sets for indiscriminate and unlimited viewing by their children.

[5] *Ibid.*
[6] *Ibid.*

We know that children watch television on the average of more than 20 hours a week, and that their viewing is not limited to programs intended for children, but extends in the early evening hours to the popular comedy and variety shows. Regardless of parental responsibility, television and radio stations and networks would seem to have positive responsibility for the quality of the programs they broadcast. Programs like "Ding Dong School" and "Disneyland" have won considerable parental and educational acclaim. As a matter of policy, the national networks usually do not carry mystery and crime programs before 9 o'clock in the evening, in order to avoid viewing by children who will have been sent to bed by that hour; the difference in time zones across the country works against this policy, however, for 9 o'clock in the East is 8 o'clock in the Midwest and 7 o'clock in Rocky Mountain time. Each network and most stations have established programming codes that formulate standards for children's programs and forbid the use of certain materials and appeals.

· SUMMARY ·

The key function in television and radio is programming. The programming function is characterized by its vastness in scope, its continuous nature, its competitiveness and costliness, its complexity, its tendency to seek stability, its variety of sources, and its speculative quality. Radio programming has changed its program forms under the competitive impact of television, while television had to unburden itself of program forms it inherited from radio before it found its own program strength. The Spectacular and Magazine concepts also played important roles in shaping the development of television programming. Film programs and live programs fill the schedules of both network and local station programming. Public-affairs and service programming constitutes the program areas in which networks and stations most directly serve the public interest. Children's programming has been especially subject to public criticism.

Questions for Discussion

1. What are the special characteristics of the programming function?
2. What have been the traditional patterns of radio programming? Why were these patterns changed and what new forms were developed?
3. Compare network radio programming with local radio programming.
4. What is the meaning and significance of the "Spectacular" concept in television programming?
5. In what ways is the "Magazine" concept of program sales different from traditional program sales practices? What is the significance of this development?
6. Compare the relative roles of film and live shows in television programming.

7. What is the function of public affairs and service programming? How have radio and television handled such programming?

8. How do you explain the popular appeal of contest and give-away programs?

9. What role do drama, comedy, and variety play in radio and television programming? What are the relative strengths of each in a program schedule?

10. "TV is the biggest economic revolution in America since the cotton gin, but its monopoly is mediocrity. Look at it this way. Motion pictures produce 500 hours of entertainment a year; TV, I figure, will produce 21,000. There isn't the creative manpower even to make 300 good pictures a year. Maybe five good novels are written; the stage produces at most ten hits. Where is the talent to come from in TV to feed that gigantic whale?"— statement in 1952 of JERRY WALD, Production Chief of Columbia Pictures. Do you agree or disagree with this point of view? Why?

❋ 5 ❋

The Federal
Communications
Commission

ONLY ON RARE OCCASIONS, such as when it lifted the freeze on television or when it authorized color television, does the Federal Communications Commission come directly to the attention of the general public through front-page newspaper stories reporting the Commission's actions. Most of the time, actions of the FCC are reported only in broadcasting trade journals, and the general public has little knowledge of the Commission's authority and responsibility in the field of television and radio.[1] Yet the FCC is one of the four pillars supporting the structure of American broadcasting: (1) The Federal Communications Commission; (2) stations and networks; (3) advertisers and agencies; and (4) the listening and viewing public.

The FCC is the agency of the federal government authorized to carry out the law of radio and television. In this chapter we shall discuss (1) the Communications Act of 1934 which is the basic statute on broadcasting, and (2) the composition and functioning of the Federal Communications Commission.

· THE COMMUNICATIONS ACT OF 1934 ·

In Chapter 2 we related how the federal government stepped into radio in 1927 in response to calls for action by the public and the radio industry. Unregulated radio had fallen into a state of chaos and only Congress, under its Constitutional power to regulate interstate commerce, could do anything about it. Congress passed the Radio Act of 1927 and, seven years later,

[1] See Paul F. Lazarsfeld and Harry Field, *The People Look at Radio* (Chapel Hill, 1946), p. 115.

incorporated the law in the Communications Act of 1934. That statute, with certain amendments, still remains on the books. As defined by the Act, the word "radio" is construed to mean television as well as sound broadcasting.

The Communications Act sets forth as its purpose

> to maintain the control of the United States over all the channels of interstate and foreign radio transmission; and to provide for the *use* of such channels, *but not the ownership thereof,* by persons *for limited periods of time, under licenses granted by Federal authority,* and no such license shall be construed to create any right, beyond the terms, conditions, and periods of the license. No person shall use or operate any apparatus for the transmission of energy or communications or signals by radio . . . except under and in accordance with this Act and with a license in that behalf granted under the provisions of this Act.[2]

In order to leave no doubt about the matter of ownership of radio frequencies and the right of the government to regulate broadcasting, the law states that no license may be granted "until the applicant therefor shall have signed a waiver of any claim to the use of any particular frequency or of the ether as against the regulatory power of the United States." [3]

The yardstick for issuing or renewing radio licenses shall be the "public convenience, interest, or necessity." [4] The FCC is specifically directed to "encourage the larger and more effective use of radio in the public interest." [5] Congressional judgment that radio must be developed as a medium for free expression of opinion without censorship by the FCC is set forth in Section 326 which states:

> Nothing in this Act shall be understood or construed to give the Commission the power of censorship over the radio communications or signals transmitted by any radio station, and no regulation or condition shall be promulgated or fixed by the Commission which shall interfere with the right of free speech by means of radio communication.

From these provisions we can see that American public policy toward radio and television involves the following key ideas:

1. The airwaves belong to the people.
2. The federal government shall maintain control over all broadcasting channels.
3. Use of these channels is limited to persons licensed by the federal government.
4. Licenses may be issued to persons only when the "public interest, convenience, or necessity" will be served thereby.
5. Licenses are good for limited periods of time only.
6. Radio and television shall be maintained as media for free speech.

[2] Section 301. [Italics added.]
[3] Section 304.
[4] Section 307.
[5] Section 303 (g).

7. Use of a radio or television frequency in no way creates an ownership right to that frequency.
8. The regulatory power of the federal government supersedes the right of any individual to the use of a radio or television frequency.

The Act of 1934 created the Federal Communications Commission to carry out the law. The FCC is an independent regulatory commission, quasi judicial in many of its functions, but primarily administrative and policy-making in its day-to-day operations.

• COMPOSITION OF THE FCC •

The FCC is composed of seven Commissioners appointed by the President by and with the advice and consent of the Senate. The President designates one of the Commissioners to be chairman. The Commission functions as a unit, although it often delegates responsibility to boards or committees of Commissioners, individual Commissioners, or the staff of the Commission. Policy decisions are made by the Commission as a whole.

Each member of the FCC must be a United States citizen with no financial interest of any sort in the communications business. Not more than four Commissioners out of the seven may be members of the same political party. Usually the President appoints one or two Commissioners with engineering backgrounds; the others are lawyers or other professional men. Each Commissioner is provided with a personal staff of assistants. The Commission maintains its central offices in Washington and fifty-eight field offices. The Commission's staff is organized in five bureaus: Engineering, Accounting, Law, Secretary, and Administration. The annual budget of the Commission amounted in 1954-1955 to $6,900,000; a total of 1,094 persons, one-third of whom were assigned to field operations, worked for the Commission that year.

• FUNCTIONS OF THE FCC •

The FCC has the following general functions pertaining to radio and television:

1. It advises the State Department in negotiating international radio agreements and it acts as the agent of the United States in carrying out our end of such treaties. Radio waves cross international borders and therefore there must be co-ordination and agreement in a master allocation plan on a world-wide basis to prevent mutual interference. Furthermore, nations must agree on which bands to assign airplane communications, distress signals, ship-to-shore radio, etc.
2. It allocates bands of frequencies to various radio and television services. Examples of this allocating function were the decisions, previously mentioned, to use the 88 to 108 megacycle band for FM radio and to add channels 14 to 83 to the television band.

3. It licenses television and radio stations and broadcast operators. The power to issue licenses is supplemented by the power to revoke or renew licenses and to approve or disapprove transfers of licenses. In carrying out these functions, the FCC holds hearings, conducts investigations, and issues decisions in individual cases involving license applications. It also promulgates regulations binding directly or indirectly on the entire television and radio industry.

4. It classifies television and radio stations and prescribes "the nature of the service to be rendered by each class of licensed stations and each station within any class."

5. It assigns bands of frequencies to the various classes of stations, and assigns frequencies for each individual station, determining the power which each station shall use and the time during which it may operate.

6. It determines the location of stations and regulates the kind of apparatus television and radio stations may use.

7. It makes regulations "necessary to prevent interference between stations and to carry out the provisions" of the Act.

8. It is authorized to make special regulations applicable to stations engaged in network broadcasting.

9. It requires stations "to keep such records of programs, transmissions of energy, communications, or signals as it may deem desirable."

10. It designates call letters of all stations.

11. It polices the ether to make sure that broadcasters stay on their assigned frequencies and that no unauthorized persons use the airwaves. In 1954, the FCC investigated more than 18,000 interference cases.

12. It encourages new uses of radio, particularly those that will promote safety of life and property.

13. It supervises all common carrier telephone, cable, and telegraph services. The American Telephone and Telegraph Company, whose microwave equipment and telephone lines are used in network broadcasting, is regulated by the FCC.

14. In wartime, the FCC co-ordinates the use of television and radio with the national security program. During World War II, the FCC set up a Foreign Broadcast Intelligence Service which monitored enemy propaganda broadcasts.

• LICENSING RADIO AND TELEVISION STATIONS •

In licensing radio and television stations when "the public convenience, interest, or necessity will be served thereby," the FCC must also try to allot stations among the various states and communities of our country so "as to provide a fair, efficient, and equitable distribution of radio service to each of the same."

The period for which licenses are good is limited by law to a maximum of three years. The FCC at first issued six-month licenses for standard radio stations; now AM, FM, and TV stations are licensed for three years.

Applicants for radio or television stations must file written statements describing their citizenship and character, and their financial, technical, and other qualifications to operate broadcast stations. Aliens, foreign corporations, or any corporations "of which any officer or director is an alien or of which more than one-fifth of the capital stock is owned of record or voted by aliens" may not obtain a station license.

An applicant for a license must set forth: (1) the location of the proposed station; (2) the frequency and power he wants to use; (3) the hours of the day during which he proposes to operate the station; (4) the purposes for which the station will be used; and (5) a full statement of his proposed program service.

To preserve competition in radio and television, the law directs the FCC not to grant licenses to applicants when, by doing so, competition would be substantially reduced or commerce restrained. The Commission has ruled that not more than one AM, one FM, and one TV station serving the same listening area may be licensed to the same applicant. This is known as the "duopoly" rule. No more than seven AM, seven FM, and seven TV (five VHF and two UHF) stations serving different areas may be licensed to or controlled by the same persons or corporations.[6]

No charge is made by the government for a broadcast license, although it has been proposed at various times that license fees should be charged that would at least cover the cost of operating the Commission and maintaining its field offices.

The Commission has no direct authority to license or regulate television and radio networks. It does in fact, however, regulate networks through rules directed at stations owned by or affiliated with networks.

Renewal, Revocation, and Transfer of Licenses. At least sixty days before the expiration of a license, a station must file a renewal application with the FCC. In this application, the station is obliged to provide a statement of the program service it has broadcast in the preceding three years. The FCC may take this record of actual program service and compare it with the statement of proposed program service the station made in its original application for a license. If the FCC is satisfied that performance reasonably matches the promises, it will renew the application. If numerous complaints about the station have been made to the FCC or if the comparison between promises and performance does not show a high correlation, the FCC may order a public hearing on the renewal application. In this hearing, the

[6] This limitation was challenged in federal courts in 1955 by the Storer Broadcasting Company.

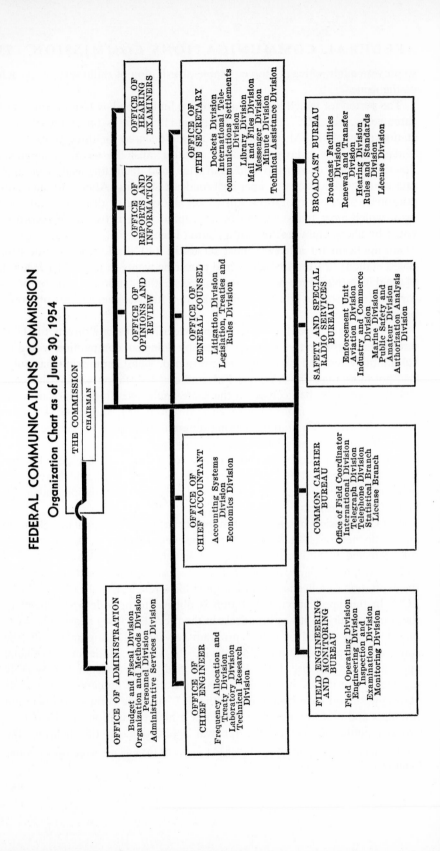

FEDERAL COMMUNICATIONS COMMISSION

Organization Chart as of June 30, 1954

THE COMMISSION

CHAIRMAN

OFFICE OF HEARING EXAMINERS

OFFICE OF REPORTS AND INFORMATION

OFFICE OF OPINIONS AND REVIEW

OFFICE OF ADMINISTRATION

Budget and Fiscal Division
Organization and Methods Division
Personnel Division
Administrative Services Division

OFFICE OF THE SECRETARY

Dockets Division
International Tele-
communications Settlements
Division
Library Division
Mail and Files Division
Messenger Division
Minute Division
Technical Assistance Division

OFFICE OF GENERAL COUNSEL

Litigation Division
Legislation, Treaties and
Rules Division

OFFICE OF CHIEF ACCOUNTANT

Accounting Systems
Division
Economics Division

OFFICE OF CHIEF ENGINEER

Frequency Allocation and
Treaty Division
Laboratory Division
Technical Research
Division

BROADCAST BUREAU

Broadcast Facilities
Division
Renewal and Transfer
Division
Hearing Division
Rules and Standards
Division
License Division

SAFETY AND SPECIAL RADIO SERVICES BUREAU

Enforcement Unit
Aviation Division
Industry and Commerce
Division
Marine Division
Public Safety and
Amateur Division
Authorization Analysis
Division

COMMON CARRIER BUREAU

Office of Field Coordinator
International Division
Telegraph Division
Telephone Division
Statistical Branch
License Branch

FIELD ENGINEERING AND MONITORING BUREAU

Field Operating Division
Engineering Division
Inspection and
Examination Division
Monitoring Division

applicant bears the burden of proving that renewal of his license will serve the public interest.

The FCC has the power to revoke a license when the station fails to operate in accordance with the law or with FCC regulations, or substantially as it said it would in its application. In revocation proceedings, the FCC bears the burden of proving that the station is *not* serving the public interest. The Commission hesitates to use its power of revocation because such extreme action is usually excessive punishment for most violations, and prior to 1952, the Commission usually limited itself to giving a sharp warning to an offending station and waiting until the license-renewal application was submitted before taking further action. In extraordinary cases such as where the licensee concealed the real ownership of his station by deceptive and misleading statements, the FCC took the final step and denied renewal of the station's license.

In 1952, Congress amended the Communications Act to authorize the Commission to issue "cease-and-desist" orders to erring stations. The stations are obliged to reply to the Commission's charges and formal hearings are provided for, with the burden of proof resting on the Commission. Failure by a station to observe a properly issued cease-and-desist order are made legal grounds for revoking the station's license.

• BROADCAST IDENTIFICATION REQUIREMENTS •

The Communications Act states that

All matter broadcast by any radio station for which service, money, or any other valuable consideration is directly or indirectly paid, or promised to or charged or accepted by, the station so broadcasting, from any person, shall, at the time the same is so broadcast, be announced as paid for or furnished, as the case may be, by such person.

FCC regulations require that whenever stations are furnished scripts or transcriptions of political discussion programs, an announcement as to the source of such material must be broadcast. Sponsored programs must carry at least one announcement stating the sponsor's name or the name of his product. This regulation seems a bit whimsical since advertisers seldom need to be pressured into announcing the name of their products; it is designed, however, to prevent deception. Stations are also required to broadcast their call letters and location on the hour and on half- or quarter-hours unless the continuity of longer programs, such as full-hour drama broadcasts, would be interrupted thereby.

• POLITICAL BROADCASTING •

In writing the Communications Act of 1934, Congress made no bones about the power of the federal government to impose upon broadcasting stations, despite the First Amendment to the Constitution, a rigid standard of fairness it has never imposed upon newspapers. Section 315 of the Act provides in part:

> If any licensee shall permit any person who is a legally qualified candidate for any public office to use a broadcasting station, he shall afford equal opportunities to all other such candidates for that office in the use of such broadcasting station, and the Commission shall make rules and regulations to carry this provision into effect: Provided, That such licensee shall have no power of censorship over the material broadcast under the provisions of this section. No obligation is hereby imposed upon any licensee to allow the use of its station by any such candidate.
>
> The charges made for the use of any broadcasting station for any of the purposes set forth in this section shall not exceed the charges made for comparable use of such station for other purposes.

This provision means that television and radio stations must offer free time or sell time on an equal basis (including identical discounts) to all legally qualified candidates for the same office during a political primary or election campaign. Or a station may choose to offer or sell no time at all to any of the candidates, although in this event the FCC would probably request the station to advise the Commission how the station's refusal to make its facilities available for political campaigning served the public interest.

Three problems have arisen in connection with this section of the Communications Act. The first derives from the fact that although we tend to have a two-party system in politics, there are usually, especially in national elections, as many as 18 very small parties that put up legally qualified candidates for office and are therefore entitled to equal opportunity with the candidates of the major parties to obtain air time. If a television station invites the Presidential candidates of the Democratic and Republican parties to appear on one of its programs, it is obligated to extend similar invitations to all other legally qualified candidates for the Presidency. Stations are required to maintain a written record of all broadcast time requested by political candidates and of time sold or given to them.

The second problem stems from the conflict between the ban against censoring political campaign broadcasts and the requirements under state laws that libel shall not be voiced on the air. The FCC has ruled that once a station has agreed to broadcast a political campaign speech, the station must go through with it even though the station manager may consider the speech libelous in part or in whole.[7] The FCC reasoned that fear of libel would

---

[7] *In re Application of Port Huron Broadcasting Company,* FCC Docket No. 6987, decided June 28, 1948.

be a convenient excuse for a station operator to refuse to carry attacks on his political friends. Many state legislatures have now passed laws relieving stations from responsibility for libel contained in speeches delivered under this provision of the Communications Act.

The third problem that arose in connection with Section 315 concerned the practice of some stations to charge more than regular broadcast rates for campaign talks. Following a particularly glaring case of excessive time charges during a Congressional by-election campaign in Pennsylvania in 1949, Congress amended the Communications Act to require stations to charge only standard time rates for political broadcasts.

• SUMMARY •

The federal government, acting through the Federal Communications Commission, plays a vital role in American broadcasting. Through its regulatory powers, the Commission grants temporary and conditional access to the airwaves, without charge, to private broadcasters who pledge to serve the "public interest, convenience, or necessity." Television and radio serve as media of free speech, with the FCC specifically denied any direct power of censorship. The Commission, through license renewal, cease-and-desist orders, revocation proceedings, and its rule-making powers, has supervisory jurisdiction and authority over all broadcasting stations.

Questions for Discussion

1. What role does the federal government play in American broadcasting?
2. What are the key ideas to be found in the Communications Act of 1934?
3. In what ways does the philosophy of the Act of 1912, which required the Secretary of Commerce to grant broadcast licenses to all qualified applicants, differ from the Communications Act of 1934?
4. What provision does the Act of 1934 make to preserve free speech on the air?
5. What are the functions of the FCC?
6. What information are applicants for station licenses required to supply?
7. How has the FCC acted to preserve competition in radio and television?
8. What is the procedure for revoking or failing to renew a station's license?
9. What rule does the Communications Act of 1934 set forth to control political campaign broadcasts and what problems does the rule pose? Should the rule be changed?
10. What authority does the FCC have over a station's program policies?
11. Should fees be charged for broadcasting licenses?
12. Should the FCC be empowered to license networks?

✸ 6 ✸

Networks and Stations

NETWORKS AND STATIONS are the means by which broadcasting becomes possible. When you turn on your radio or television receiver, you must tune in to a particular frequency on the dial in order to hear a program. That program comes from an individual station in your listening area. It may be the same program heard by a listener 2,000 miles away. If so, the explanation is network or chain broadcasting which connects stations by land telephone lines or microwave relays and furnishes the same program simultaneously to all network stations which in turn broadcast the program from their individual transmitters. This is what makes possible the use of Hollywood and New York City as the source of most big-time entertainment programming. Stations and networks are therefore vitally important in the structure of American broadcasting.

We have noted that the FCC has the power to classify stations and to issue licenses. In order to make maximum use of the available channels in the broadcast spectrum and to provide an equitable distribution of these channels throughout the nation, the FCC has divided and subdivided many of these channels as far as engineering and policy considerations have allowed.

• AM RADIO STATIONS •

Generally speaking, AM radio stations are classified in terms of their broadcasting power: (1) small stations—250 watts; (2) medium—500 to 5,000 watts; and (3) large—10,000 to 50,000 watts. The importance of a station depends not only on its wattage, however, but on the population of the area in which it broadcasts; a 250-watt station in Boston may actually have a greater audience than a 5,000-watt station in Montana. The power assigned to a radio station depends upon the frequency channel on which it is licensed to broadcast.

Classification of Channels. A broadcast "channel" is the band of frequencies occupied by a carrier frequency and two side bands of broadcast signals. In AM radio, carrier frequencies begin at 540 kilocycles and follow in successive steps of 10 kilocycles up to 1,600. This allows for 106 channels which the FCC has divided into three classes.

1. CLEAR CHANNELS. A "clear channel" is one in which a station can broadcast over a wide listening area free from interference from other stations. By international agreement, 59 channels have been set apart for clear channel broadcasting in North America and, of these 46 have been assigned to the United States. Of the 46 channels, 24 are occupied by only one station at nighttime (these are the powerful "clear channel stations") and the other 22 have several stations operating at night on each. Under international agreement, the United States is obligated to license at least one high-powered station (a minimum of 50 kilowatts) on each clear channel. As a matter of national policy, the FCC makes the international minimum of 50 kw. the maximum for clear-channel broadcasting, so that no stations in this country may now have more than 50,000 watts power.

2. REGIONAL CHANNELS. A "regional channel" is one on which several stations may operate with power not to exceed 5,000 watts. The primary service area of a station operating on a regional channel may be limited by some interference from other stations.

3. LOCAL CHANNELS. A "local channel" is one on which several stations may operate with power not in excess of 250 watts. The primary service areas of these stations also may be limited by interference from other stations.

Times of Operation. The FCC licenses AM stations to operate according to the following time schedules:

1. UNLIMITED TIME allows broadcasting round-the-clock if the station so desires.

2. LIMITED TIME applies to certain stations operating on clear channels. It permits station operation during the daytime and allows nighttime operation if the dominant station on the same channel is off the air at that time.

3. DAYTIME ONLY permits operation solely between sunrise and sunset.

4. SHARING TIME permits operation during a restricted time schedule required by multiple use of the same channel by several stations.

5. SPECIFIED HOURS means that the exact operating hours of the station are specified in the license.

Call Letters. AM stations east of the Mississippi River have call letters that begin with the letter "W" and stations west of the Mississippi begin with the letter "K." Several old stations like KDKA, Pittsburgh, are exceptions to this rule. Applicants for new AM radio stations may choose any arrangement of four letters beginning with the appropriate "W" or "K" provided they are not identical with the call letters of an existing station. Some stations have used the initials of the owners in choosing their call letters, such as WABC, KRCA, WCBS, WMGM. The state universities of Iowa and Ohio call their stations WSUI and WOSU. Other stations have been given pronounceable combinations like KORN, WREN, and WIND.

Station Operation. The operating function of a station is to produce programs and to sell time to advertisers for its programs or for programs produced elsewhere and made available to the station. The staff and mode of operation of an AM radio station depends upon four factors: its location, its authorized broadcast power, its status as an independent or a network-affiliated station, and its programming and sales concepts.

A 50,000-watt clear-channel station located in a large metropolitan center and operated independently with aggressive programming and sales activity will require a sizeable staff of programming, sales, technical, and administrative personnel, as well as substantial studio and office space. A station that concentrates on local live programs supported by local advertising must have a staff of salesmen to bring in business, a commercial department to handle the administration of all sales orders, a program department to plan and produce programs, and an engineering staff. By way of contrast, a small 250-watt AM station operating in the daytime only, with a programming emphasis on news and recorded music, may manage with a staff of five or six people who double as engineers, announcers, salesmen, and bookkeepers.

Characteristic of many radio stations is the operation of a 1,000-watt daytime-only AM station (WIRC) in Roanoke, Virginia, which operates with a staff of nine. The programming formula of the station calls for 5 special talent programs daily, plus local news coverage in a five-county area 7 days a week. Here is the detailed story of the nine staff jobs on this station, to indicate the nature of local radio station operation: [1]

BUSINESS DEPARTMENT

1. GENERAL MANAGER—In addition to routine business management, he apportions his time mostly to active selling of local advertising, servicing of important accounts, writing spot area news and writing occasional commercial copy. He also handles station promotion, public relations, and supervises programming. News contacts and public relations involve attendance at all major civic or governmental meetings. The overnight spot local newscast each weekday morning is presented by staff announcers, but it requires the General Manager to assemble and write most of the copy between 7-7:45 A.M. The chief engineer, designated as assistant manager, pinch hits in the manager's absence on most of the above activities. He also prepares all FCC technical reports and handles equipment purchases.

2. BOOKKEEPER-RECEPTIONIST—Does all accounting except the annual audit. She supplies monthly statements, handles all commercial billing,

[1] *Broadcasting-Telecasting,* September 10, 1951, p. 46.

shares telephone answering with the program personnel and conducts over-the-counter visitor business. The bookkeeper also types most traffic orders, but does not take dictation for correspondence. WIRC staff members write their own business letters.

PROGRAM DEPARTMENT

1. WOMEN'S EDITOR—Devotes about half her work day to her three air shows—"Woman's World," "Make Believe Time," and "Stork Club." The first is the society-women's news commentary, the second is a children's-story record program, and the third is news of births from three counties. The other half of her day is absorbed mainly by writing spot news for the 12:30 P.M. midday news and for the late afternoon "Home Final"; also by copy writing, script writing, and general program department details. She represents WIRC in the leading women's organizations by active membership and attendance.

2. TRAFFIC-PROGRAM MANAGER—Types the program schedule on the transmitter logs in advance, making several carbon copies for studio use. She also files complete announcer books for every air shift, maintaining the files of all formats, commercial copy, and library scripts. She does her scheduling from traffic orders, but is so skilled at keeping competitive advertising apart that the sales department often leaves it to her to select the best availabilities for short-notice spot schedules. She also keeps the talent mail count, helps answer the telephone, and does her own feminine hillbilly disc jockey half-hour show each afternoon, Monday through Friday. Her work week is 40 hours.

3. STAFF ANNOUNCERS—The two staff announcers are employed on a basis of a 40- to 50-hour work week, including overtime as necessary. They actually average about 41 hours weekly. The relief announcer-salesman is paid a basic salary in the program department for these principal duties: two full relief shifts each week end and copy writing. Otherwise, he is on his own time as an outside commission advertising salesman. All three men earn talent fees paid only by advertisers. WIRC pays no talent fees, but encourages advertisers to pay fees for special shows. Occasionally a staff announcer is allowed a 10 per cent sales commission for personally selling an assigned account which the regular salesmen have repeatedly failed to sell. Thus, all program department personnel, including the traffic-program manager, have inducements in the form of talent fees or commissions for extra initiative.

OPERATING SCHEDULES

4. MORNING SHIFT—The morning man works his announcing shift from sign-on at 6 A.M. until 12:45 P.M., Monday through Saturday. He gets a half-hour break from 8-8:30 A.M. while the salesman-relief announcer

presents the "Swap Shop" talent program personally from the control board. Thus the morning man has 1½ days off each week—all day Sunday and a half-day Saturday. One relief shift is Sunday morning, the other Saturday afternoon.

5. AFTERNOON SHIFT—The afternoon announcer starts on duty at 12 noon. This provides two-voice air work from noon through the midday local news, a fifteen-minute newscast 12:30-12:45 P.M. The afternoon shift varies greatly during the year because of the changing sign-off time. In summer, the announcer's shift lasts from noon until 7:45 P.M., but he gets breaks from 4-4:30 P.M. and 6-6:30 P.M.

The first break is provided by the traffic manager's half-hour hillbilly disc jockey show, during which she operates the control board herself. The late afternoon break is provided by the relief announcer, who also takes part in the home news final, 5:45-6 P.M. In the winter months, when sign-off is as early as 5:15 P.M., he makes up working hours by helping with copy writing and other programming work each morning before lunch. The afternoon announcer's time off is all day Saturday and a half-day Sunday morning.

ENGINEERING DEPARTMENT

1. PERSONNEL—The engineering department consists of only two men, both licensed first-class operators. The only person performing other engineering duties is a part-time remote operator (unlicensed), who handles all Sunday church remotes.

2. OPERATION—The two licensed engineers stand the complete transmitter watch. They make all necessary repairs both to transmitting and studio technical equipment, cut all disc recordings, prepare all engineering reports for the station, and—in the interest of economy—they prepare the yearly proof-of-performance record required by the FCC. The small number of engineering personnel has fostered a friendly attitude of co-operation between the engineers and the other departments.

Since the WIRC transmitter is some 2½ miles from the studios and separate operation is therefore necessary, the engineers normally do no announcing. During their regular transmitter watch, the engineers also maintain the station program log. Keeping the log is made as easy as possible for the engineers by the program department. All information which can be pre-entered on the log is typed in advance at the studios. The work week of each engineer is the hourly equivalent of one-half of the station's operating hours for that week. When one engineer is off, the other works the entire broadcast day without a break. Each engineer has two week days and alternate Sundays off.

· FM RADIO STATIONS ·

Most FM radio stations are operated as adjuncts to AM radio stations. The same operating staff runs both stations. The FM station carries the same program schedule as the AM station; for a single price, advertisers are usually sold time on both the AM and FM stations. In cases where the AM station must sign off at dusk, the FM station may continue on the air through the evening, usually with programs of news and recorded music.

FM radio stations owned and operated independently of AM stations are generally run with very small staffs and low budgets. Such stations often specialize in broadcasting high-fidelity classical music recordings which are transmitted with better quality over FM than over AM radio.

Educational, noncommercial FM radio stations, licensed to operate in the 88 to 92 mc. band, often involve a different mode of operation in accordance with their special programming concepts. These stations are discussed in Chapter 13.

· TELEVISION STATIONS ·

Television stations are authorized by the FCC to operate in either VHF (Channels 2-13) or UHF (14-83). In all general business respects, television stations operate along the patterns established by AM radio stations. The wide difference in programming and production methods between radio and television, however, accounts for the differences to be noted in television station operation. Staff requirements are notably greater in television stations in order to provide cameramen, additional engineers, stagehands and electricians, graphic artists, film technicians, camera directors, floor managers, make-up artists, etc. Space requirements are considerably greater, too, to satisfy television studio needs, construction and storage space for settings, props, and set dressings, film storage, editing, and projection facilities, lighting equipment, cameras, cranes, microphone booms, etc. Some small television stations that draw upon a network affiliation and film features for most of their daily schedule manage to operate with minimal staffs and a single studio for live shows. Large television stations that program aggressively in the local interest have extensive space and personnel requirements and are often housed in several different buildings. In all cases, the establishment and operation of a television station requires much more capital than setting up and running a radio station. For example, the capital investment in WTMJ-TV, Milwaukee, Wisconsin, excluding land and the original building, was $630,000, of which $400,000 was spent for operating equipment such as cameras, projectors, etc. An additional $650,000 was required for improvements in transmission facilities.[2] In an effort to make it financially feasible to operate television stations in small communities, the

[2] *Fortune,* January, 1952, p. 132.

FCC has authorized the establishment of "satellite" television stations which are linked with a television station located in another city and simply reproduce the other station's program schedule. In this way, the only operating costs are the rental of the connecting cable, the television transmitter, and a small engineering staff at the transmitter. A satellite station is unable, however, to serve the special needs of the community in which it is established because it has no facilities to originate its own programs. It simply transmits programs furnished by the station to which it is linked.

· TELEVISION AND RADIO NETWORKS ·

Network (or chain) broadcasting is defined in the Communications Act as the "simultaneous broadcasting of an identical program by two or more connected stations." It is accomplished by transmitting the program by cable, usually leased telephone lines in radio and coaxial cables in television, or by microwave relays, from the point of origin to each of the outlet stations of the network. At various points along the network cable, booster stations are operated to maintain the transmission power of the program signal. The cost of these connecting circuits to a television network is approximately $10 million a year.

Function of Networks. Networks are indispensable to the American system of broadcasting. Networks make it possible for programs to be broadcast throughout the country simultaneously. They are the only way in which live programs can be broadcast nationally, and they are the most efficient way in which recorded and film programs can reach a national audience. Because networks exist, important special events, such as a Presidential inauguration, or a major political address or sporting events, such as football games and boxing bouts, can be broadcast live throughout the country. The excitement and impact of live television on a national basis, therefore, is possible only through networks.

With programming and production headquarters located in New York and Hollywood, the talent centers of the nation, networks are able to provide major entertainment programs to affiliated stations which could never obtain such programs if they were obliged to depend on local resources only. Because network programs can reach national audiences they are especially attractive to national advertisers.

Networks, thus, serve both programming and business functions for stations throughout the country, servicing these stations with programs they cannot produce themselves, and providing income from national advertisers that might otherwise never be spent on television or radio.

National Networks. The National Broadcasting Company, the Columbia Broadcasting System, and the American Broadcasting Company operate national television and radio networks. The Mutual Broadcasting System operates a national radio network, but not a television network. The Allen

B. DuMont Laboratories operated a television network until September, 1955, when the network ceased operations.

Each network owns and operates several radio and television stations (limited by FCC rule to a maximum of seven FM, seven AM, and seven TV), and maintains affiliation agreements with a large number of stations across the country. Under these affiliation agreements (a typical agreement is reproduced at the end of this chapter), the stations give the networks the right to sell certain hours of the stations' broadcast time at established rates to national advertisers and to provide the programs that the stations will broadcast during those hours. In return, the network agrees to provide these programs without charge to the stations and to give them a portion of the money received from the advertiser (roughly one-third of the gross sum). The network pays all advertising agency commissions and incentive discounts and absorbs any costs involved in the production of programs. In addition, networks produce at their own expense cultural, religious, and public service programs which are offered without charge as "sustaining programs" to affiliated stations. Stations supplement their income by the sale of station-break announcements that come at the end, and sometimes in the middle, of network programs.

Some idea of the scope of network operations may be obtained from the following description of the CBS television network, supplied by Dr. Frank Stanton, President of CBS: [3]

> CBS supplies 153 programs for a total of seventy-eight and one-half hours of network programs per week, one-third of which is sustaining. Behind these programs is the work of more than sixty different departments: accounting, business affairs, construction, development of new effects, engineering, executive, graphic arts, network operations, news, press information, sales, special events, sports, station relations, television recording, and wardrobe, to name only a few. CBS television has 28 studios; 116 live black-and-white cameras; 31 black-and-white film chains; 17 live color cameras; and five color film chains. It employs more than 3,700 persons of various crafts and skills, such as writers, directors, producers, singers, actors, announcers, technicians, stagehands, scenic designers, editors, film cutters.

Network programming and sales leadership is a matter of vital interest to affiliated stations, not only because the financial compensation received from the network is directly related to network sales, but because topflight network programming makes it possible for the station to achieve program leadership in its own community and therefore to be able to sell its time periods for local programs preceding and following the network shows. A network affiliation pays dividends to an affiliated station in several important ways: (1) it relieves the station of the cost of producing programs

[3] *Testimony of Frank Stanton before Subcommittee on Communications of the Committee on Interstate and Foreign Commerce, U. S. Senate, 83rd Congress, 2nd Session, on The Status of UHF Television Stations* (1954), pp. 990-991.

for the 9 or more hours each day that the network provides programs; (2) it provides income from national advertisers; and (3) it provides programming leadership that increases the value of their station-break announcements and remaining time periods. For a network it is important to have a good line-up of affiliated stations: a line-up consisting of stations that have good local broadcast coverage and effective local programming, and a line-up large enough to provide effective national coverage. (The failure of many UHF stations has made it impossible to obtain four good network line-ups in television. Failure to obtain a good network line-up was one cause of the demise of the DuMont network, and continues to be a problem for ABC.)

The networks, themselves, are large corporate enterprises and are highly competitive in their operations. They compete among themselves and with other entertainment media for talent and programs. They compete for national advertising money with nonbroadcasting advertising media, such as newspapers and magazines, and with other broadcast sales organizations, such as national spot-sales agencies which place national advertising on local stations without going through a network. These agencies sell station time during nonnetwork hours for film programs and local shows; they also sell spot announcements that are made between network shows and at various other times.

THE NATIONAL BROADCASTING COMPANY. NBC is a wholly owned subsidiary of the Radio Corporation of America, which is one of the largest manufacturers of electronic equipment in the U. S. making transmitters and receivers for all broadcast services. It is also one of the leading producers of phonograph records in the country. It owns and operates AM and FM radio stations in New York, Chicago, San Francisco, Philadelphia, and Washington, D. C. It operates a nation-wide radio network of 200 stations with a broadcast coverage unsurpassed by any of its competitors. NBC also owns VHF television stations in New York, Chicago, Los Angeles, Philadelphia, and Washington, D. C., and a UHF station in Buffalo, and has applied for a UHF station in New Britain, Conn. Its television network in 1956 consisted of 200 stations, of which 55 were basic or "must buy" stations.

THE COLUMBIA BROADCASTING SYSTEM. CBS owns and operates AM and FM radio stations in New York, Chicago, Los Angeles, San Francisco, and Boston, and an AM station in St. Louis. It operates a nation-wide radio network of 206 stations. It owns VHF television stations in New York, Chicago, and Los Angeles, and a UHF station in Milwaukee. It has applied for a VHF station in St. Louis and a UHF station in Hartford. Like RCA, CBS is a leading manufacturer of phonograph records. It also engages in the business of manufacturing tubes, radios, phonographs, and television receivers. Its television network in 1956 consisted of 158 stations, of which 51 were basic stations. Its gross billings from July, 1954, to

July, 1955, were over $165 million, larger than that of any other single advertising medium in the world.

THE AMERICAN BROADCASTING COMPANY. ABC started in the broadcasting business in 1943 when RCA was forced to divest itself of the Blue Network. Until 1953, ABC's sole business was broadcasting, but in that year it merged with United Paramount Theatres, one of the largest owners of theaters in the United States, with combined assets of $150 million. ABC owns AM, FM, and VHF television stations in New York, Chicago, Detroit, Los Angeles, and San Francisco. It operates a nation-wide radio network of 360 stations and a television network of 208 stations, some of which have primary affiliation contracts with NBC and CBS.

THE MUTUAL BROADCASTING SYSTEM. Mutual operates an AM radio network of 563 stations, many of which are low-powered stations. Mutual is owned by RKO-Teleradio Pictures, Inc., a subsidiary of the General Tire and Rubber Co., a manufacturer of automobile tires and other rubber products. Mutual has never engaged in large-scale network program production of the proportions attempted by NBC, CBS, and ABC.

Regional Networks. Regional networks are networks created to link stations within certain geographical and marketing areas. Regional networks are attractive to advertisers who market their products in certain sections of the country but not in others, and therefore cannot make use of the national networks. There are about six regional television networks and almost ninety regional radio networks in existence. The stations in these networks group together primarily for sales purposes; the networks themselves do not engage in programming operations.

Some of the regional radio networks are:

American Pacific Network	Texas Quality Network
Columbia Pacific Network	Rural Radio Network
Don Lee Broadcasting System	Yankee Network
NBC Western Network	Michigan Radio Network
Quality Radio Group	Intermountain Network

· STATION-NETWORK RELATIONS ·

Relations between stations and networks are controlled by the Chain Broadcasting Regulations put into effect by the FCC in 1943. After a lengthy investigation of the networks, the Commission concluded that the system of network broadcasting then in operation was stifling competition and was contrary to the public interest. In 1938, CBS and NBC alone owned or controlled 23 powerful stations out of the 660 stations then on the air, and more than 85 per cent of the total nighttime wattage in the nation. The FCC investigated the contractual arrangements between the networks and their affiliates and concluded that these contracts had "resulted in a grossly inequitable relation between the networks and their outlet stations to the advantage of the networks at the expense of the outlets." [4] Some of these contracts forbade affiliated stations to accept programs from any other network and required the outlet to keep almost all of its time available for the use of the network. In 1939, Mutual obtained the exclusive right to broadcast the World Series and offered the program to stations throughout the country, including NBC and CBS affiliates in communities having no other stations. CBS and NBC immediately invoked the "exclusive affiliation" clauses of their network affiliation contracts and, as a result, thousands of persons were unable to hear the broadcasts. The FCC concluded that competition was being stifled and that outlets were being made the servant of the network rather than an instrument for serving the public interest.

To eliminate these evils, the Commission promulgated the following eight rules which are in effect today:

1. No station-network agreement may be made which prevents the station from broadcasting the programs of any other network.

2. One network affiliate may not prevent another station serving the same listening area (in radio) or the same community (in television) from broadcasting network programs that the first station does not carry; nor may it prevent a station serving a substantially different area or community from broadcasting any of the network's programs. A network affiliate may, however, have "first call" for network programs over other stations in the area or community served by the station.

3. Station-network contracts are limited to 2-year periods.

4. A network must give affiliated stations 56 days' notice if it wants to make use of a station's time for network shows, and it may have an option on no more than 3 hours within each of four segments of the broadcast day. Such arrangements may not prevent the station from selling that time to other networks if the affiliated network does not exercise its option.

5. Stations must be free to refuse to carry network programs which the station "reasonably believes to be unsatisfactory or unsuitable." With respect to network programs already contracted for, stations must be allowed to reject any program "which, in its opinion, is contrary to the public interest," or to substitute "a program of outstanding local or national importance."

6. Networks may not own more than one station in the same listening area or in any locality where network ownership would substantially restrain competition.

7. Networks may not operate more than one network of stations. (This forced NBC to divest itself of the Blue Network, now ABC.)

[4] *Report on Chain Broadcasting* (Washington, Federal Communications Commission, 1941), p. 97.

8. Stations may not enter into contracts with networks which would prevent them from fixing or changing their time rates for nonnetwork shows.

· INDEPENDENT TELEVISION AND
RADIO STATIONS ·

Independent television and radio stations operating without any network affiliation are usually found in cities with more than four radio stations or three television stations. As a rule, stations operate independently only when they are unable to obtain a network affiliation. Some independent radio stations, such as WNEW, New York, and WJBK, Detroit, have succeeded in making a virtue of necessity, and are more successful than some of their network-affiliated competitors. Generally speaking, independent stations which necessarily must draw all their income from local and national spot advertising and must produce all their own programs, compete with network affiliated stations under great handicaps. Those that have been most successful have concentrated on programming emphases usually neglected by affiliated stations: strong local programming with local appeal and programs appealing to specialized interests of substantial minorities.

· SUMMARY ·

Networks and stations constitute the second pillar of American broadcasting. Stations vary in modes of operation depending upon their power, location, and network affiliation, if any. Networks make it possible to broadcast live programs simultaneously throughout the country; they make national markets available to advertisers and offer stations major entertainment and public service programs. Station-network relations are carefully regulated by the FCC in order to preserve competition.

Questions for Discussion

1. What role do networks play in American broadcasting? What would radio and television be like without networks?
2. Describe the operation of a small, independent radio station.
3. What is the difference between clear, regional, and local channel AM stations? Is there any special significance to be found in this difference?
4. Compare the major radio and television networks in terms of size, programming, mode of operation, and influence.
5. What are the advantages of a network affiliation?
6. How are network-station relations governed? For what purpose?
7. What limitations are there on the right of networks to exercise an option on time on affiliated stations? Why are these limitations imposed? May a network-affiliated station refuse to carry an important network cultural or public-affairs program in favor of a local commercial show?

A TYPICAL NETWORK-STATION AFFILIATION CONTRACT

CBS TELEVISION

A Division of Columbia Broadcasting System, Inc.

TELEVISION AFFILIATION AGREEMENT

AGREEMENT made this .... day of ...., 19.... by and between CBS TELEVISION, a division of Columbia Broadcasting System, Inc., 485 Madison Avenue, New York 22, New York (herein called "CBS Television") and .... (herein called "Station") licensed to operate television station at .... full time on a frequency of ...... on Channel number ....

CBS Television is engaged in operating a television broadcasting network and in furnishing programs to affiliated television stations over program transmission facilities leased by CBS Television, by "off-the-tube" TV recordings, or otherwise. Some of such programs, herein called "sponsored programs", are sold by CBS Television for sponsorship by its client-advertisers. All non-sponsored programs are herein called "sustaining programs". "Network sustaining programs", "network sponsored programs" and "network programs" as used herein mean network television programs. Station and CBS Television recognize that the regular audience of Station will be increased, to their mutual benefit, if CBS Television provides Station with television programs not otherwise locally available.

Accordingly, it is mutually agreed as follows:

1. CBS Television will offer to Station for broadcasting by Station network sustaining programs as hereinafter provided, without charge, and CBS Television network sponsored programs for which clients may request broadcasting by Station and which are consistent with CBS Television's sales and program policies. Network sustaining programs made available by CBS Television are for sustaining use only and may not be sold for local sponsorship or used for any other purpose without the written consent of CBS Television in each instance.

2. (a) Station will accept and broadcast all network sponsored programs offered and furnished to it by CBS Television during "network option time" (as hereinafter defined); provided, however, that Station shall be under no obligation to accept or broadcast any such network sponsored program (i) on less than 56 days' notice, or (ii) for broadcasting during a period in which Station is obligated by contract to broadcast a program of another network. Station may, of course, at its election, accept and broadcast network sponsored programs which CBS Television may offer within hours other than network option time.

(b) As used herein, the term "network option time" shall mean the following hours:

(i) if Station is in the Eastern or Central Time Zone, Daily, including Sunday, 10:00 A.M. to 1:00 P.M., 2:00 P.M. to 5:00 P.M. and 7:30 P.M. to 10:30 P.M. (expressed in New York time current on the date of broadcast);

(ii) if Station is in the Mountain or Pacific Time Zone, Daily, including Sunday, 10:00 A.M. to 1:00 P.M., 2:00 P.M. to 5:00 P.M. and 7:30 P.M. to 10:30 P.M. (expressed in local time of Station current on the date of broadcast).

3. Nothing herein shall be construed (i) with respect to network programs

offered pursuant hereto, to prevent or hinder Station from rejecting or refusing network programs which Station reasonably believes to be unsatisfactory or unsuitable, or (ii) with respect to network programs so offered or already contracted for, (A) to prevent Station from rejecting or refusing any program which, in its opinion, is contrary to the public interest, or (B) from substituting a program of outstanding local or national importance. CBS Television may, also, substitute for one or more of the programs offered hereunder other programs, sponsored or sustaining, of outstanding local or national importance, without any obligation to make any payment on account thereof (other than for the substitute program, if the substitute program is sponsored). In the event of any such rejection, refusal or substitution by either party, it will notify the other by private wire or telegram thereof as soon as practicable.

4. Station will not make either aural or visual commercial spot announcements in the "break" occurring in the course of a single network program or between contiguous network sponsored programs for the same sponsor where the usual station break does not occur.

5. CBS Television will pay Station for broadcasting network sponsored programs furnished by CBS Television as specified in Schedule A, attached hereto and hereby in all respects made a part hereof. Payment to Station will be made by CBS Television for network sponsored programs broadcast over Station within twenty (20) days following the termination of CBS Television's four or five week fiscal period, as the case may be, during which such sponsored programs were broadcast.

6. CBS Television will offer to Station for broadcasting such network sustaining programs as CBS Television is able to deliver, or cause to be delivered, to Station over coaxial cable or radio relay program transmission lines under arrangements satisfactory to CBS Television. CBS Television shall not be obligated to offer, or make available to Station hereunder, such network sustaining programs as it may have available in the form of TV recordings, unless CBS Television has the right so to do and Station shall agree to pay CBS Television's charges therefor.

7. When, in the opinion of CBS Television, the transmission of network sponsored programs over coaxial cable or radio relay program transmission lines is, for any reason, impractical or undesirable, CBS Television reserves the right to deliver any such program to Station in the form of TV recordings, or otherwise.

8. Station agrees to observe any limitations CBS Television may place on the use of TV recordings and to return to CBS Television, transportation prepaid by Station, immediately following a single broadcast thereof, at such place as CBS Television may direct, and in the same condition as received by Station, ordinary wear and tear excepted, each print or copy of the TV recording of any network program, together with the reels and containers furnished therewith. Each such TV recording shall be used by Station only for the purpose herein contemplated.

9. Neither party hereto shall be liable to the other for claims by third parties, or for failure to operate facilities or supply programs for broadcasting if such failure is due to failure of equipment or action or claims by network clients, labor dispute or any similar or different cause or reason beyond the party's control.

10. The obligations of the parties hereunder are subject to all applicable laws, rules and regulations, present and future, especially including rules and regulations of the Federal Communications Commission.

11. If Station applies to the Federal Communications Commission for consent to a transfer of its license, or proposes to transfer all or any of its assets without which it would be unable to perform its obligations hereunder, it will procure the agreement of the proposed transferee that, upon the consummation of the transfer, the transferee will assume and perform Station's obligations hereunder, unless CBS Television shall waive this condition in writing.

12. All notices required to be given hereunder shall be given in writing, either by personal delivery or by mail or by telegram or by private wire (except as otherwise expressly herein provided) at the respective addresses of the parties hereto set forth above, or at such other addresses as may be designated in writing by registered mail by either party. Notice given by mail shall be deemed given on the date of mailing thereof. Notice given by telegram shall be deemed given on delivery of such telegram to a telegraph office, charges prepaid or to be billed. Notice given by private wire shall be deemed given on the sending thereof.

13. This Agreement shall be construed in accordance with the laws of the State of New York applicable to contracts fully to be performed therein, and this Agreement cannot be changed or terminated orally.

14. As of the beginning of the term hereof, this Agreement takes the place of, and is substituted for, any and all television affiliation agreements heretofore existing between the parties hereto, subject only to the fulfillment of any accrued obligations thereunder.

15. The term of this Agreement shall begin on   and shall continue for a period of two (2) years from such date; provided, however, that unless either party shall send written notice to the other at least six months prior to the expiration of the then current two-year period that the party sending such notice does not wish to have the term extended beyond such two-year period, the term of this Agreement shall be automatically extended upon the expiration of the original term and each subsequent extension thereof for an additional period of two years; and provided further, that this Agreement may be terminated at any time by CBS Television by sending written notice to Station at least twelve months prior to the effective date of termination specified therein.

IN WITNESS WHEREOF, the parties hereto have executed this Agreement as of the day and year first above written.

CBS TELEVISION,
a Division of Columbia Broadcasting System, Inc.
By . . . .
By . . . .

SCHEDULE A

(Attached to and forming part of the agreement between CBS Television and . . . . This Schedule A contains provisions supplementary to said agreement and in case of any conflict therewith, the provisions of this Schedule A shall govern.)

I. CBS Television will pay Station for broadcasting network sponsored programs furnished by CBS Television during each week of the term hereof, thirty per cent (30%) of the gross time charges for such week, less the "converted hour" deduction and the ASCAP and BMI deduction.

II. The "converted hour" deduction for any week shall be one hundred fifty per cent (150%) of the amount obtained by dividing the gross time charges for such week by the number of "converted hours" (as hereinafter defined) in such week.

III. The ASCAP and BMI deduction for any week shall be the amount obtained by (i) deducting the "converted hour" deduction for such week from thirty per cent (30%) of the gross time charges for such week, and (ii) multiplying the remainder by the ASCAP and BMI percentage.

IV. As used herein, the term "gross time charges" for any week shall mean the aggregate of the gross card rates charged and received by CBS Television for broadcasting time over Station for all network sponsored programs broadcast by Station during such week at the request of CBS Television.

V. As used herein, the term "converted hour" means an aggregate period of one hour during which there shall be broadcast over Station one or more network sponsored programs for which CBS Television shall charge and receive its Class A time card rate for broadcasting time over Station. An aggregate period of one hour during which there shall be broadcast over Station one or more network sponsored programs for which CBS Television shall charge and receive a percentage of its Class A time card rate, such as its Class B time card rate, shall be the equivalent of the same percentage of a converted hour. Fractions of an hour shall be treated for all purposes as their fractional proportions of a full hour within the same time classification.

VI. As used herein, the term "ASCAP and BMI percentage" shall mean the aggregate of the percentages of CBS Television's "net receipts from sponsors after deductions" and of CBS Television's "net receipts from advertisers after deductions" paid or payable, respectively, to American Society of Composers, Authors and Publishers (ASCAP) and Broadcast Music, Inc. (BMI) under CBS Television's network blanket license agreements with ASCAP and BMI. (Currently such percentages are 3.025 and 1.2, respectively, so that the ASCAP and BMI percentage is 4.225%, but such current ASCAP percentage may be reduced by as much as .525 during each calendar year of the term hereof.)

VII. In the event that CBS Television shall have license agreements with ASCAP or BMI which shall provide for the payment of license fees computed on a basis other than a percentage of CBS Television's "net receipts from sponsors after deductions" or "net receipts from advertisers after deductions," as the case may be, CBS Television shall deduct from each payment to Station, in lieu of the ASCAP and BMI deduction, the proportionate share of music license fees paid or payable by CBS Television which is properly allocable to such payment.

VIII. The obligations of CBS Television hereunder are contingent upon its ability to make arrangements satisfactory to it for facilities for transmitting CBS Television network programs to the control board of Station.

❉ 7 ❉

Advertisers and Agencies

EVERY SYSTEM of broadcasting requires a sound means of financial support to keep it going. Unless a station has ample funds to maintain a competent staff and facilities and to hire the best talent, its programming will suffer. Various ways have been devised throughout the world to support broadcasting. These include: (1) annual taxes on receivers, similar to our annual state taxes on automobiles; (2) governmental appropriations; (3) endowments, similar to university endowments; (4) subscription broadcasting, in which the public pays for individual programs; and (5) the sale of broadcast time to advertisers.

American television and radio are supported predominantly by income from advertising. Indeed, advertising revenue from the sale of time is the only source of income for all commercial broadcasting; the sponsors, therefore, support not only their own programs, but indirectly all sustaining programs, too. The United States, however, also makes use of other methods of financial support. There are stations owned by states, municipalities, and state universities which receive their entire support from state or city appropriations. There are stations licensed to private universities, which are supported by the university's endowed funds. There are stations which combine endowed income with advertising support, such as Cornell University's WHCU which was built originally with endowed funds and since has supported itself by accepting advertising.

Constituting the complete support of almost all television and radio stations, advertising is a fundamental element in our broadcasting scheme. This being the case, let us proceed to three questions: (1) What do advertisers expect from television and radio? (2) How are television and radio advertising managed? (3) What effect does the advertising method of financial support have on television and radio programming?

· ADVERTISING AND THE
BROADCASTING MEDIA ·

In evaluating television and radio along with other media of communication, such as newspapers, magazines, billboards, sky writing, weekly supplements, match covers, etc., the advertiser is concerned with the following criteria: (1) circulation; (2) effectiveness of the medium to sell his product; and (3) cost.

Circulation. When advertisers buy time on television or radio, they do so because they are impressed with the wide circulation that television and radio can give to their advertising message. A commercial message delivered on a popular network evening television program usually reaches 20 to 30 million people. Only through magazines such as *Life* or *Reader's Digest,* or the purchase of space in many newspapers throughout the country, can the advertiser otherwise hope to reach an audience of this size. In local advertising, the advertiser compares the circulation offered by the local television and radio stations with that offered by local newspapers.

Circulation relates to the number of people who are exposed to the advertiser's message. In television and radio, circulation is influenced by the potential coverage offered by the station by virtue of its transmitting power, the general programming popularity of the station, the popularity of the program on which the advertising message is presented, the popularity of adjacent programs and the attractiveness of the advertising message itself. In printed media, circulation is influenced by the number of copies sold, the position of the advertisement within the publication, and the attractiveness of the advertisement in terms of its ability to command reader attention.

It is therefore to be expected that advertisers who buy television and radio time will generally seek to sponsor the programs that reach the largest audiences.

Effectiveness. Each advertising medium has its own special characteristics of communication that make advertising on it more or less effective. Some advertising media are better for certain types of advertising than other media. In printed media, for example, four-color advertisements are generally considered more effective in promoting sales than advertisements in black-and-white. Department stores, which desire to list dozens of different items for sale, usually turn to newspapers for this purpose. Brand-name identification is often sought through repeated radio announcements. No advertising medium, however, can show a product to potential buyers as completely or effectively as television. Many advertisers have found that television provides them with an opportunity to demonstrate their product and deliver a sales message to millions of people that otherwise can only be done over-the-counter to a few people at a time.

Moreover, the association of the advertising message with a popular program can give the advertiser additional values: good will engendered by the program itself; identification with the program and the program talent that often is used for point-of-sale merchandising purposes; direct sales appeals by the stars; special attention to his advertising message through lead-ins designed to invite attention; and through strategic placement of the messages.

Cost. In evaluating the cost of advertising in relation to its effectiveness, advertisers are often forced to work with variable factors that make it very difficult to arrive at a scientific judgment. Ideally, the advertiser desires to know which method of advertising produces the greatest number of sales of his products at the smallest cost. Because he usually has several different advertising campaigns proceeding simultaneously and because the effectiveness of his own commercial message is not a controlled factor when different media are compared, the advertiser generally contents himself with taking the simple circulation figures, dividing them by a thousand, and dividing that figure into the cost of buying the broadcast time and the program to arrive at a figure representing how much it costs to reach 1,000 viewers. Thus, a half-hour evening television program that reaches 12 million people and costs $75,000 for time and program would cost about $6.00 for each 1,000 viewers. If the advertiser were entitled to three minutes of commercial messages, the cost per 1,000 viewers per commercial minute would be stated as $2.00.

This yardstick is widely used in advertising; in comparing television with other advertising media, it fails to take into account television's special selling effectiveness which often outweighs simple circulation in influencing the number of purchases made as the result of a commercial message.

· RATE CARDS ·

Every commercial television and radio station and every network prepares a "rate card." These cards state in tabular form the cost of broadcast time over the station or network. On the NBC television network, rates are stated in terms of Class "A" hours (6:00-11:00 P.M., Monday through Friday, 5:00 P.M.-11:00 P.M., Saturday and Sunday), Class "B" hours (5:30 P.M.-6:00 P.M., Monday through Friday, 1:00 P.M.-5:00 P.M., Saturday and Sunday) and Class "C" hours (7:00 A.M.-5:30 P.M., Monday through Friday, 7:00 A.M.-1:00 P.M., Saturday and Sunday). A Class "A" hour over the basic line-up of 55 NBC affiliated stations in 1956 cost $68,275. A Class "B" hour cost 75 per cent of this figure; a Class "C" hour cost 50 per cent. An advertiser who buys a half-hour of time pays 60 per cent of the hourly rate; if he buys only fifteen minutes, he pays 40 per cent of the hourly rate. Regular weekly purchases extending for 26 weeks are subject to frequency discounts; advertisers who sponsor the same program all year round are given an additional annual discount. In addition to the cost of the time, advertisers pay program and production costs for their programs and their commercials, as well as a network cable charge.

A local television or radio station lists its rates for air time not only for program sponsorship, but also for 10- and 20-second station-break announcements. Thus a New York City station that charges $4,500 for a Class "A" hour may charge $1,100 for a 20-second and $565 for a 10-second station-break announcement, exclusive of production costs.

Rate cards also contain the necessary facts concerning a station's power, frequency, ownership, network affiliation if any, sales representatives, and other pertinent information. *Standard Rate and Data Service,* a monthly publication, summarizes the rate cards of all stations and is used by advertisers and agencies in buying television and radio time.

· ADVERTISING AGENCIES ·

The formulation and management of advertising campaigns is distinctively the function of advertising agencies. These agencies are hired by advertisers to advise them on promotional matters and to plan and execute advertising campaigns. The size of an advertising agency depends upon the number and size of accounts it handles. The agency receives its income from the advertising media in which it places its client's advertising. Television and radio stations generally give an advertising agency 15 per cent of the gross amount of the time purchase the agency makes in behalf of its client. The agency is also generally entitled to add 15 per cent for itself to all bills submitted to its client for program and production costs.

Agency Organization. Large advertising agencies are equipped to handle all types of advertising in all the mass communication media. To handle this work, an agency employs a staff of skilled personnel, among whom are found the following:

1. Account executives, who supervise the activities of major advertising accounts and maintain liaison between the agency and the client's advertising manager. The account executive is responsible for the general supervision of all advertising placed by his agency in behalf of his client.

2. Media specialists, including time and space buyers, who are closely acquainted with the availabilities and costs of different advertising media.

3. Television and radio production departments, with producers, directors, etc., to prepare and produce television and radio commercials, and, in the instance of a major agency like J. Walter Thompson Agency, to produce major television and radio shows owned by the agency.

4. Copy writers, who prepare the advertisements seen in newspapers and magazines and the commercials seen on television or heard on the radio.

5. Artists and photographers, to prepare art work and photographs for advertisements.

TOP 30 ADVERTISING AGENCIES MOST ACTIVE IN TV-RADIO IN 1954 [1]

Rank	Agency	Combined Radio-Tv Billings	Radio Only (In Millions)	Tv Only (In Millions)
1.	Young & Rubicam	$60	$15	$45
2.	Batten, Barton, Durstine & Osborn	59	13	46
3.	J. Walter Thompson Co.	50	12	38
4.	McCann-Erickson	46	9	37
5.	Biow Co.	33.4	5.6	27.8
6.	Leo Burnett Co.	33.3	6	27.3
7.	Wm. Esty Co.	31	5	26
8.	Benton & Bowles	29.2	8.4	20.8
9.	Dancer-Fitzgerald-Sample	28.5	15.5	13
10.	Ted Bates & Co.	27.5	7	20.5
11.	Kenyon & Eckhardt	22.5	7.5	15
12.	Compton Adv.	22.3	5.5	16.8
13.	Foote, Cone & Belding	22	5.5	16.5
14.	Lennen & Newell	20	4	16
15.	N. W. Ayer & Sons	18	7.5	10.5
16.	Cunningham & Walsh	16	3.5	12.5
17.	Kudner	14	2.6	11.4
18.	Maxon Inc.	14	3	11
19.	Sullivan, Stauffer, Colwell & Bayles	13.8	3.8	10
20.	Ruthrauff & Ryan	13	4	9
21.	Needham, Lewis & Brorby	11.9	3.6	8.3
22.	Bryan Houston Inc.	11.5	4	7.5
23.	Geoffrey Wade	11	7	4
24.	Campbell-Ewald	10	2.2	7.8
25.	Weiss & Geller	10	2	8
26.	Tatham Laird	9.5	1	8.5
27.	D'Arcy	8	3.5	4.5
28.	Erwin, Wasey	8	3	5
29.	MacManus, John & Adams	7	.5	6.5
30.	Doherty, Clifford, Steers & Shenfield	6	2.2	3.8

[1] *Broadcasting-Telecasting,* December 20, 1954, p. 28.

6. Marketing research experts, to evaluate the effectiveness of advertising campaigns and to assist in the choice of advertising appeals.

Agency Operation. The agency starts with the client's sales problem and the budget assigned to advertising. After deciding that television or radio advertising can help to solve the client's sales problem, the agency recommends, on the basis of an allocation of the budget, the best use to be made of these media, including the following considerations:

1. Whether the money should be spent on a network or spot basis, or a combination of both;

2. Whether the emphasis should be placed on evening hours or daytime;

3. Whether the client should sponsor a program availability of one of the networks or should instead develop its own program or buy one from an independent packager and seek air time on one of the networks.

After buying time and program, the agency must then undertake to supervise the client's interest in the program and to prepare and produce the commercials. The agency, through its own production department, arranges to produce the commercials live at the network or station, or makes a radio recording or television film commercial for distribution to the network or station.

The following list of major network television programs sponsored by clients of J. Walter Thompson in 1955-1956 suggests how great a role the large advertising agency plays in broadcasting:

"Meet the Press" (Pan American and Johns Manville)
"Screen Director's Playhouse" (Eastman Kodak)
"Father Knows Best" (Scott Paper)
"Television Theater"(Kraft)
"Ford Theater" (Ford)
"Lux Video Theater" (Lever Bros.)
"Star Stage" (Pond's Extract)
"Omnibus" (Aluminium, Ltd. and Scott Paper)
"Beat the Clock" (Sylvania)
"Star Jubilee" (Ford)
"Medical Horizons" (Ciba Pharmaceutical)
"Star Tonight" (Brillo)
"Ozzie & Harriet" (Quaker Oats)

The list of evening network programs sponsored by Young & Rubicam clients during the same year is no less impressive:

"Goodyear Playhouse" (Goodyear Rubber)
"Caesar's Hour" (Remington Rand)
"People's Choice" (Borden)
"Life of Riley" (Gulf)
"Alfred Hitchcock Series" (Bristol-Myers)
"Appointment with Adventure" (P. Lorillard)
"What's My Line" (Remington Rand)
"Robin Hood" (Johnson & Johnson)
"Talent Scouts" (Lipton Tea)

"I Love Lucy" (General Foods)
"Front Row Center" (General Electric)
"Four Star Playhouse" (Singer Sewing and Bristol Myers)
"Johnny Carson Show" (General Foods)
"Our Miss Brooks" (General Foods)
"The Lineup" (Procter & Gamble)
"Person to Person" (Elgin Watch)

· NETWORK ADVERTISING ·

Network advertisers in 1954 spent approximately $320 million for network television time and $137,600,000 for network radio time, exclusive of money spent on talent, programs, and commercial production costs. Six major product groups were the big advertisers in both network radio and network television: (1) Food and Food Products; (2) Toiletries and Toilet Goods; (3) Smoking Materials; (4) Soaps, Cleansers, and Polishes; (5) Automobiles, Auto Equipment and Accessories; and (6) Household Equipment and Supplies.

The leading network advertisers in television and radio, with their total expenditures for network time (stated in gross billings, exclusive of program costs) were as follows: [2]

TOP TEN RADIO-TV NETWORK
CLIENTS IN 1954

1.	Procter & Gamble Co.	$36,040,869
2.	Colgate-Palmolive Co.	18,903,507
3.	Gillette Co.	17,102,830
4.	R. J. Reynolds Tobacco Co.	13,599,868
5.	General Foods Corp.	13,028,696
6.	General Motors Corp.	12,085,931
7.	Lever Brothers	11,685,803
8.	General Mills	11,355,087
9.	American Tobacco Co.	11,011,769
10.	Chrysler Corp.	10,688,167

TOP TEN RADIO NETWORK
CLIENTS IN 1954

1.	Procter & Gamble Co.	$12,339,668
2.	Miles Labs	6,172,592
3.	Gillette Co.	5,562,378
4.	Colgate-Palmolive Co.	4,813,770
5.	Lever Brothers	4,471,376
6.	General Motors Co.	3,780,932
7.	General Mills	3,724,388
8.	Sterling Drug Co.	3,518,756
9.	American Home Products Corp.	3,474,699
10.	P. Lorillard Co.	3,300,830

[2] *Broadcasting-Telecasting,* March 14, 1955, pp. 29-30.

TOP TEN TV NETWORK
CLIENTS IN 1954

1.	Procter & Gamble Co.	$23,701,228
2.	Colgate-Palmolive Co.	14,089,737
3.	R. J. Reynolds Tobacco Co.	11,828,928
4.	Gillette Co.	11,540,452
5.	General Foods Corp.	9,728,567
6.	American Tobacco Co.	9,485,152
7.	Chrysler Corp.	8,820,955
8.	General Motors Corp.	8,304,999
9.	General Mills	7,630,699
10.	Lever Brothers	7,214,427

• THE "MAGAZINE" CONCEPT •

As we have said, the great expense of single network sponsorship of weekly half-hour shows as well as the lack of flexibility that single sponsorship provides have contributed to the popularity of the "Magazine" concept—the purchase of one minute and minute-and-a-half participations in network shows. Under the Magazine concept, the network produces the program and the client simply pays for the right to insert his commercial in the program. Whereas over a local radio station, such an insertion might cost as little as $1.00, in network television insertions range from approximately $5,000 on a program like "Today" to almost $75,000 for a minute-and-a-half on NBC's "Sunday Spectacular." An additional advantage of the insertion plan, however, is that advertisers are not required to make long-term commitments, but may buy only one or two participations as they desire. The over-all effect of this type of network advertising is reflected in the number of advertisers now able to use network advertising. Whereas in 1947 only 70 different advertisers used the NBC radio network, in 1954, 187 different advertisers used the NBC television network, and as many as 84 different companies placed their advertising on a single program, "Today." Of these advertisers, 25 had budgets of only $100,000 or less for all advertising media. NBC's new network radio programming concept called "Monitor," introduced in 1955, was keyed to the idea that the Magazine concept was the way new income could be attracted to network radio.

• NATIONAL SPOT ADVERTISING •

National spot advertising, where the advertiser purchases time over selected stations for spot announcements or complete programs, has certain advantages and disadvantages when compared to network advertising. National spot offers the national advertiser the chance to buy time on the best station in every market he wants to reach. He cannot do this in network

TOP 100 ADVERTISERS OF 1954

This tabulation lists the top 100 advertisers in the United States and shows how their budgets are distributed among the major advertising media. The comparison with the 1948 budgets shows that sixty spent more than 50 per

Rank	Advertiser	Total 1954 Billings (000)	Total 1948 Billings (000)	1948 Rank
1	Procter & Gamble	$44,151	$26,620	1
2	General Motors	36,774	11,803	3
3	Colgate-Palmolive	26,727	10,803	7
4	General Foods	25,256	12,990	2
5	Gillette	19,499	8,548	11
6	Chrysler	18,378	5,492	16
7	General Electric	17,860	11,772	4
8	Lever Bros.	17,771	11,470	5
9	R. J. Reynolds	16,706	7,704	12
10	General Mills	16,120	10,426	8
11	American Tobacco	15,937	5,371	10
12	Ford Motor	15,418	5,478	17
13	P. Lorillard	12,752	2,521	40
14	Liggett & Myers	12,344	7,600	13
15	American Home Products	11,328	5,460	18
16	Campbell Soup	11,068	9,771	10
17	National Dairy	10,327	4,931	21
18	Swift	9,099	9,263	9
19	Kellogg	8,077	2,244	48
20	Miles Laboratories	7,922	6,242	14
21	Pillsbury Mills	7,882	3,156	33
22	Quaker Oats	7,725	3,547	30
23	Bristol-Myers	7,599	5,338	20
24	Sterling Drug	7,564	11,316	6
25	Goodyear	6,780	3,872	26
26	Distillers Corp.—Seagrams	6,604	6,018	15
27	Philip Morris	6,448	4,148	22
28	A T & T	6,335	3,878	25
29	S. C. Johnson	6,291	1,662	67
30	R C A	5,888	2,462	42
31	Westinghouse	5,677	4,042	23
32	Philco	5,307	3,859	27
33	Armour	5,150	3,745	29
34	Serutan	5,106	1,514	78
35	Du Pont	4,928	2,730	38
36	Standard Brands	4,912	2,042	50
37	National Distillers Products	4,813	3,020	34
38	Coca-Cola	4,523	3,983	24
39	Johnson & Johnson	4,446	2,853	37
40	Rexall Drug	4,340	1,192	..
41	Firestone	4,194	1,606	69
42	Carnation	4,128	1,652	68
43	Borden	4,089	3,219	32
44	Texas Co.	4,030	2,660	39
45	International Cellucotton	3,873	1,863	58
46	Scott Paper	3,704	993	..
47	Avco	3,630	1,620	..
48	Eastman Kodak	3,585	1,830	62
49	Andrew Jergens	3,557	2,409	44
50	National Biscuit	3,531	2,482	47
51	Helene Curtis	3,517	236	..

cent of their advertising budgets on radio and television in 1954; in 1948
only thirty-three spent more than half on radio and television.[3]

Magazines		Supplements		Network Radio		Network Tv	% to Air Media	
1948	1954	1948	1954	1948	1954	1954	1948	1954
$5,048	$ 6,543	$ 3,372	$1,566	$18,199	$12,339	$23,701	68.3	81.6
9,273	20,560	533	2,129	1,976	3,780	10,304	16.7	38.2
3,692	3,713	2,768	4,109	4,342	4,813	14,089	40.1	70.7
5,782	10,037	443	2,190	6,774	3,300	9,728	52.1	51.5
1,711	1,344	567	1,051	6,267	5,562	11,540	73.3	87.7
4,473	7,276	199	413	819	1,867	8,820	14.9	58.1
7,932	9,558	556	390	3,283	949	6,961	27.8	44.2
3,763	2,561	2,390	3,524	5,317	4,471	7,214	46.3	65.7
3,586	2,799	42	306	4,076	1,770	11,828	52.9	81.3
2,320	3,557	915	1,208	7,190	3,724	7,630	68.9	70.4
2,469	4,028	301	897	2,600	1,526	9,485	48.4	69.0
3,849	7,802	....	869	1,629	774	5,972	29.7	43.7
938	2,781	418	....	1,164	3,300	6,662	46.1	78.1
2,203	2,467	352	823	5,043	2,921	6,131	66.3	73.3
769	2,058	97	260	4,592	3,474	5,534	84.1	79.5
2,846	5,081	105	868	5,819	573	4,546	59.5	46.2
2,129	2,972	926	658	1,875	812	5,884	38.0	64.8
4,532	2,117	11,343	1,032	3,387	3,048	2,900	36.5	65.3
1,191	1,513	5	390	1,048	1,910	4,263	46.7	76.4
265	921	91	132	5,885	6,172	695	94.2	86.6
1,040	1,516	1,126	305	989	2,049	4,010	31.3	76.8
703	2,726	164	1,062	2,679	1,570	2,365	75.5	50.9
3,237	3,040	....	296	2,101	1,484	2,778	39.3	56.0
1,390	1,854	863	1,467	9,063	3,518	723	80.0	56.0
3,266	4,743	64	69	541	333	1,643	13.9	29.1
6,018	6,601	....	3	....	....	....	...	...
221	1,652	83	....	3,844	1,126	3,668	94.3	74.3
3,053	5,498	38	21	786	815	....	20.2	12.8
321	1,007	160	704	1,181	1,865	2,714	71.0	72.7
1,807	2,866	26	248	628	883	1,890	25.5	47.0
2,123	2,056	601	....	1,318	....	3,621	32.6	63.7
1,624	1,200	....	58	2,234	1,316	2,731	57.8	76.2
1,455	2,107	375	1,167	1,916	661	1,214	51.1	36.4
....	3	346	236	1,168	....	4,865	77.1	95.2
2,034	4,154	....	32	695	....	741	25.4	15.0
510	3,048	56	726	1,475	....	1,136	72.2	55.6
3,020	4,808	neg	4	....	....	....	...	...
1,463	1,701	....	....	2,519	459	2,362	63.2	62.3
2,659	3,915	194	329	....	....	200	...	4.4
332	2,231	....	21	859	623	1,464	72.0	48.0
830	1,870	....	....	776	766	1,557	48.3	55.3
687	844	....	232	973	1,887	1,163	58.8	73.8
1,648	1,636	354	469	1,216	....	1,983	37.7	48.4
1,418	2,635	....	34	1,241	881	478	46.6	33.7
1,717	2,557	146	470	....	407	436	...	11.2
953	1,457	33	39	....	....	2,208	...	59.6
1,452	1,623	153	454	14	338	1,214	0.9	42.7
1,830	3,121	....	464	....	....	....	...	...
1,502	1,444	100	446	804	195	1,472	33.3	46.8
1,138	749	194	1,066	1,149	660	1,055	49.9	48.5
236	1,057	....	1,219	....	220	1,019	...	35.2

[3] *Sponsor,* **May 30,** 1955. Courtesy of *Sponsor.*

Rank	Advertiser	Total 1954 Billings (000)	Total 1948 Billings (000)	1948 Rank
52	American Motors	3,476	2,507	36
53	Brown & Williamson	3,446	1,384	88
54	Schenley	3,318	3,831	28
55	Sunbeam	3,221	810	..
56	Nestle	3,147	1,467	82
57	Dow Chemical	3,087	535	..
58	Aluminum Co. of America	3,082	1,017	..
59	B. F. Goodrich	3,020	2,150	49
60	Pabst Brewing	3,010	1,287	95
61	Florida Citrus Commission	2,942	523	..
62	Pet Milk	2,906	1,031	..
63	Joseph Schlitz Brewing	2,902	1,307	94
64	Pepsi-Cola	2,902	360	..
65	Hazel Bishop	2,901	....	..
66	U. S. Steel	2,875	1,701	66
67	Corn Products Refining	2,841	1,315	93
68	Sylvania Electric	2,802	217	..
69	Kaiser Motors	2,774	3,401	45
70	William Wrigley Jr.	2,769	984	..
71	Carter Products	2,766	1,724	65
72	Armstrong Cork	2,718	1,533	75
73	Best Foods	2,604	1,425	86
74	Hallmark Cards	2,575	949	..
75	Lambert	2,517	1,995	52
76	Borg-Warner	2,496	1,479	81
77	Reynolds Metals	2,493	355	..
78	Cluett, Peabody	2,475	1,757	83
79	Schick	2,432	440	..
80	Amer. Dairy Assoc.	2,402	432	..
81	Prudential Ins. of Amer.	2,391	2,489	41
82	Admiral	2,318	793	..
83	California Packing	2,350	1,500	80
84	Wesson Oil & Snowdrift	2,348	905	..
85	Simoniz	2,152	512	..
86	Mutual Benefit Health	2,124	728	..
87	Doubleday	2,091	1,197	100
88	Standard Oil of Indiana	2,084	74	..
89	Remington Rand	2,062	714	..
90	Socony Vacuum Oil	2,046	1,164	..
91	Gulf Oil	2,027	985	..
92	Olin Mathieson Chem.	2,015	1,820	..
93	Minnesota Mining & Mfg.	1,974	423	..
94	Ralston Purina	1,973	1,526	77
95	Longines-Wittnauer	1,966	413	..
96	Amer. Chicle	1,964	287	..
97	Block Drug	1,957	463	..
98	Union Carbide & Carbon	1,951	1,503	79
99	Johns-Manville	1,944	955	..
100	Manhattan Soap	1,939	3,404	31

SOURCE: Publishers Information Bureau. All billings are in thousands. Where no rank is shown for 1948, advertiser was below the top 100 list of that year.

NOTE: In cases of merger or purchase of another company since 1948, dollar figures for 1948 are total of merged or purchased firm together with parent firm. However, 1948 ranking is for that of parent firm alone. Philip Morris billings include Benson & Hedges; Avco billings include Bendix Home Appliances; National Biscuit billings include Hills Bros.; American Motors billings include Nash-Kelvinator and Hudson but 1948 ranking is that of Nash-

Magazines		Supplements		Network Radio		Network Tv	% to Air Media	
1948	1954	1948	1954	1948	1954	1954	1948	1954
1,955	1,958	146	....	775	40	1,478	26.9	43.6
75	1,154	133	60	1,174	132	2,100	84.8	64.7
3,750	3,283	81	34	....	....	....	...	...
810	1,332	....	....	....	18	1,870	...	58.6
431	1,307	447	268	588	146	1,424	40.0	49.8
535	792	....	162	....	....	2,131	...	69.0
1,017	1,762	....	....	....	....	1,320	...	42.8
2,150	2,026	....	....	....	....	994	...	32.9
526	427	....	....	760	32	2,551	59.0	85.8
493	842	30	62	....	1,043	994	...	69.2
....	....	....	....	1,031	769	2,136	100	100
1,307	1,073	....	....	....	....	1,828	...	62.9
360	850	....	882	....	....	1,168	...	40.2
....	39	....	....	....	18	2,843	...	98.6
649	1,470	....	....	1,052	....	1,405	61.8	48.8
1,200	1,716	114	730	....	266	127	...	13.8
217	698	....	361	....	....	1,742	...	62.1
2,184	1,057	260	....	957	1,717	....	40.1	61.8
53	434	60	....	871	1,723	612	88.5	84.3
168	5	1	17	1,554	964	1,779	90.1	99.1
1,103	1,509	....	....	429	....	1,209	27.9	44.4
1,159	1,463	265	393	....	....	747	...	28.6
106	240	....	....	843	556	1,778	88.8	90.6
1,643	1,407	64	202	286	346	561	14.3	36.0
1,479	2,039	....	....	....	....	457	...	18.3
355	751	....	4	....	15	1,722	...	69.6
1,580	2,225	176	250	....	....	....	...	...
440	719	....	....	....	....	1,713	...	70.4
297	761	135	46	....	490	1,104	...	66.3
547	8	....	653	1,942	820	908	78.0	72.2
793	1,182	....	18	....	151	1,028	...	50.8
1,235	2,047	265	302	....	....	....	...	...
243	1,092	....	....	662	....	1,256	73.1	53.4
452	633	60	123	....	....	1,395	...	64.8
....	59	....	710	728	523	831	100	63.7
613	941	547	1,117	36	29	2	3.0	1.4
74	84	....	....	....	1,258	740	...	95.8
714	996	....	23	....	....	1,042	...	50.5
944	1,683	220	....	....	363	....	...	17.7
373	326	....	....	612	....	1,701	62.1	83.9
1,750	1,750	69	....	....	....	264	...	13.1
323	379	100	83	....	674	817	...	75.5
114	870	....	151	1,411	326	625	92.4	48.2
250	71	....	....	163	1,223	671	39.4	96.3
224	94	63	....	....	...	1,869	...	95.1
355	52	108	579	....	75	1,250	...	67.7
1,478	1,780	25	142	....	....	27	...	1.3
111	736	....	....	844	1,208	....	88.3	62.1
423	170	176	74	2,803	1,963	....	82.3	87.3

Kelvinator alone; Kaiser billings include Willys-Overland; Olin Mathieson Chemical billings include Olin Industries, Mathieson Alkali Works and E. R. Squibb.

broadcasting, since no one network has all the best stations. He can choose the station according to the particular audience it has attracted by its programming emphases. Moreover, spot broadcasting enables him to purchase any length of time from brief announcements to a three-hour coverage of a sporting event. He may buy time on one station or five hundred stations, using only those which suit his advertising needs, free from the requirements to buy time on a basic or supplementary network. The time differentials involved in network broadcasting are also eliminated in spot broadcasting. Furthermore, spot broadcasting is very flexible in time availability, and an advertiser suddenly faced with the immediate need to unload merchandise can often have his message on the air in spot broadcasting within an hour after he has made up his mind to buy time.

There are disadvantages to national spot broadcasting that becloud the picture painted above. The network shows occupy some of the best broadcast hours. The national spot advertiser is usually obliged to rely on transcribed or film programs that may lack the prestige, publicity, and entertainment value of network shows. Instead of completing negotiations with a single network representative, spot broadcasting involves making arrangements with each station. Program material must be sent to each outlet. The advertiser must hope that local announcers will do a good job in presenting his message, whereas he can audition the network announcer. This may be overcome by transcribing announcements and supplying the discs or film to individual stations, but then cost becomes a factor.

Generally speaking, advertisers who can afford network advertising attempt first to obtain a good network time period and a popular show. They may also desire to supplement their network advertising with national spot campaigns. Advertisers who are unable to obtain a good network time period may have no alternative than to undertake a national spot campaign if they desire national exposure. In 1954, the radio networks got 40 per cent and national spot got 60 per cent of the total national expenditure on radio advertising.

• LOCAL ADVERTISERS •

Radio time sales to local advertisers now account for a major portion of all radio advertising. Local television advertising is sought by all stations to supplement their income from network advertisers and to strengthen their relations with the local community.

Local advertisers include all types of local retailers ranging from department stores to gasoline stations. Arrangements for local advertising are usually made by the station's salesmen and the local merchant who is persuaded to buy broadcast advertising. Some retailers, in co-operation with the station, may develop their own music, news, or other type of program which, when broadcast regularly, favorably associates the merchant with the program in the listener's mind. Most local advertising, however, consists of direct sales messages describing products and giving details of prices. This is the very kind of advertising feared by early leaders in radio. But it is the way in which many stations, particularly the independent stations which have difficulty attracting national advertising, earn their income.

The "Co-operative" program has come into wide use in recent years as a vehicle for local and regional advertisers. These are nationally featured network programs with different local and regional sponsors over each station. Special cut-in arrangements are made by the network to allow for the insertion of the local commercials.

· PROBLEMS POSED BY ADVERTISING ·

Advertising support of broadcasting poses a number of problems for a system of television and radio in which licensees are pledged by law to serve the "public convenience, interest, or necessity" and where broadcasting the best entertainment, informational and cultural programs available is generally considered to be in the public interest.

Advertising Excesses. One of the most common public criticisms of American broadcasting relates to advertising excesses. Networks and stations have set maximum time limits for commercial messages on television and radio programs, usually three minutes per half-hour in the evening, and four minutes and 15 seconds per half-hour and three minutes per quarter-hour in the daytime, exclusive of opening and closing commercial billboards. These limitations are also exclusive of the two local commercial announcements usually made during the 30-second break for station identification. It therefore sometimes happens that a closing program commercial is followed by a closing commercial billboard, by two station-break commercials, by the opening commercial billboard of the following program, and by the first commercial of the next show.

A total of 21 stations in six cities ranging from one-station markets to those with 7 stations were monitored for one day each, from the time the station went on until it went off, amounting in all to 280 hours and 50 minutes of TV.

In all but one case, network and independent alike, there was found what can only be called abuse of the standards set up by the industry itself to regulate commercials. There were 160 cases of programs exceeding the standard commercial time, ranging from a few seconds to single commercials over 10 minutes long in a 15-minute program. Frequent instances were found of triple-spotting during station breaks. Indeed, one case of five announcements in a 1½ minutes period was logged.[4]

In a poll conducted by *Sponsor* magazine on the question "Is television overcommercialized?" almost 59.5 per cent of the advertising agency execu-

[4] Quoted in *Sponsor,* December 14, 1953, p. 28.

tives, station managers, and other men in the broadcasting business who responded to the poll said "yes." The largest single group of respondents to the survey felt that broadcasters, agencies, and clients were equally responsible for misleading, overlong, silly and furiously-paced TV commercials. However, most advertising men felt that the responsibility for enforcing good television practices rested with the broadcasters.[5]

Control of Programs. In addressing a session of the American Association of Advertising Agencies in April, 1954, Sylvester L. Weaver, then President of NBC, made a plea in behalf of network and station control of programming in contrast to the agency and advertiser control that had characterized network radio operations for many years:

> Television is too great and too powerful to be shackled with chains of custom and usage from radio. We must serve all segments and all interests in our population, and there must be an over-all program control that makes the rules in the interest of public service and all-segment population service. This is the business of the networks. If our service dwindles, you will use less of it, or pay less for it. That's the end of your responsibility. If we cater to the heavy viewers with a flood of trivia, as accused in some quarters, we cannot look to you, or to the advertisers large or small, for your jobs are rightly defined by your interest—the sale of the goods and services of your clients. It is not for you to take the blame if the mission of television is reduced from revolutionizing the individual's understanding of his world, as I believe color television should hold as its mission, to become a living room toy to keep the kids quiet.

Weaver's plea was related to the fact that the advertiser's interest in reaching an audience is not always compatible with the most effective over-all program service. If the airwaves are used only by advertisers seeking the largest possible audience, quality programs of necessarily less appeal will find no place on the air. On the other hand, a network may fail in its commercial responsibility if it permits an advertiser to put on a program with limited appeal simply because the advertiser likes that type of program or because it is an inexpensive program that manages, when combined with effective merchandising, to satisfy the advertiser's needs. The responsibility of stations and networks extends to their entire program schedules; they may not delegate to the advertiser or to the advertising agency final say as to what is acceptable on the airwaves. "Only the network can act in the interest of *all* the advertisers," states Weaver.

To a certain extent, the role of the advertiser in deciding whether a program gets on the air or remains on the air can not be altered. Many seemingly good program series have waited years before getting on the air because they could not obtain a sponsor who was willing to finance the broadcast. On the other hand, some good programs have been withdrawn from the air because the sponsor, for a variety of reasons related to his

[5] *Ibid.*

business needs, has withdrawn his financial support and no other sponsor came forward to replace him.

Because agency- and sponsor-developed programs are so closely related to the client's immediate needs, the responsibility for experimentation and development of programming forms will continue to rest primarily with the networks.

· SUMMARY ·

Advertising constitutes the sole financial support of most American broadcasting. Television and radio offer the advertiser wide circulation and effectiveness at relatively low cost. Advertising agencies, which buy air time for advertisers and often produce their own programs, play a great role in television and radio. Network, national spot, and local advertising are the main ways in which air time is purchased by advertisers. Among the problems posed by advertising support of broadcast, are advertising excesses and the question of control over programs.

Questions for Discussion

1. What are the various ways in which broadcasting is supported financially throughout the world?
2. What are the main advantages of television and radio as advertising media? How do these advantages compare with those of other media, such as newspapers, magazines, billboards, match covers, etc.?
3. What constructive functions do advertising agencies serve? How necessary are they for advertising purposes?
4. What role do the large national advertisers play in television and radio?
5. What are the differences between network advertising and national spot advertising? What functions does each serve?
6. What are some of the problems posed by advertising in television and radio? How can these problems be solved?

❊ 8 ❊

The Public

THE EFFECTIVENESS of television and radio depends ultimately on the willingness of the public to listen to or to view what is broadcast. No broadcasting system, however well-intentioned, can survive without public acceptance of the programs it offers. In American broadcasting, where the federal government formulates public policy, stations and networks do most of the programming, and advertising provides the financial wherewithal, the public is the *raison d'etre* of the entire enterprise.

Listeners and viewers express judgments by tuning in and out of programs. Since these acts of judgment take place privately in millions of homes each day, it is impossible to determine with absolute certainty the over-all attitude of the audience to a particular program. There is no formal expression of opinion as in political elections. There are no box-office or circulation figures, as with magazines and theaters. Eager to know what the public reaction to any program will be, but handicapped by these limitations, program planners and advertisers have been forced to rely on *a priori* speculations and on available audience research methods.

In *a priori* judgments, program planners, like producers of Broadway shows, venture a guess as to what the public will like on the basis of past experience. They may try to confirm their hunches by pretesting programs on small panels of representative or expert people. The numerous flops on Broadway and on the air testify to the limitations of the *a priori* approach, but the great successes prove that there are also acute and sensitive minds in show business who possess a keen sense of audience tastes. *A priori* judgments are usually related to the best available evidence of audience attitude, but it is common knowledge that the American public frequently acts unpredictably in ways contrary to the most expert forecasts of pollsters.

More scientific in approach are the audience research methods of estimating the size of the audience for particular programs, determining the composition of the audience, and describing general listening or viewing habits. Television and radio audience research, while definitely not as re-

110

liable as box-office tallies, constitutes the only scientific means by which we may, with some degree of accuracy, form judgments as to the extent of viewing or listening to any program.

Several caution signs should be erected before we proceed further in this discussion of the role of the public in American broadcasting and the ways devised to ferret out the public's judgments. For one thing, the public does not exercise its judgment independently: television and radio condition the public and establish the scale of values, on the basis of which the public must make its judgments. Furthermore, the so-called *public* is actually made up of many diverse publics, brought together at different times out of common interest. Each such broadcast audience is oriented in terms of the choices offered it now and in the past, as well as in terms of its attitude toward television and radio as a whole. There is evidence, for example, that in some areas where very few AM stations can be heard with clarity, listeners relate their tuning habits not to program quality, but to the comparative strength of the radio signals. Given a choice of four daytime serials at the same time, the audience's judgments can relate only to the comparative merits of the four soap operas, or to soap operas as a group, but it cannot indicate preference for other types of programs. A lover of classical music will very likely be pleased if a local station programs good music half an hour daily if it has never done so before, but he will react differently if the half-hour represents a reduction from a previously greater offering of good music.

· AUDIENCE RESEARCH ·

Fan-mail. From the very start of broadcasting, some effort has been made to determine how many people listen to any one program. In amateur short-wave broadcasting, the radio operator often asks people who receive his signal to let him know by sending him a postcard. In the 20's the same request was commonly made over long-distance commercial stations. A letter received from a listener in Alaska would always stir some excitement in a New York station. But such responses proved only that the station's signal could be heard at a certain place at a certain time. It did not provide any information on the size and distribution of the total audience. To get this information, stations at first relied on the spontaneous "fan-mail" they received; listeners who were pleased or excited about a particular program might sit down and write the station a letter to that effect. This was much more common while radio retained the element of novelty. But such fan-mail often proved very misleading. Upon study many of these letters turned out to be the work of the more vociferous members of the audience whom the psychologists call the "lunatic fringe" of the public. There was no way of knowing how representative the letters were of the size or character of the entire audience, so the results had to be used very cautiously.

Stations then sought to increase the volume and broaden the make-up of fan-mail by offering inducements to every listener who would send in a letter or a card. To determine the popularity of one program, a free offer of flower seeds might be announced. The requests for the free offer would be tallied and tabulated geographically, and would serve as a fairly crude index of program popularity. The ratio between letter writers and the whole listening audience was still not known, but it was possible with this mail to compare different programs in terms of public reaction and to get an idea of the distribution of the radio audience. If the total number of letters received from the county in which a station was located was assigned the absolute figure 100, it was possible to compute the relative response from the neighboring counties, and estimate the general lay-out of the audience. Thus, where a neighboring county to the north sent in 60 per cent as many letters as the home county, its relative importance as a listening area was indicated by the fact that the county to the south had sent in only 40 per cent as many. This type of audience analysis is the least expensive and is still widely used by many stations.

Sampling. The limitations and crudities of the mail response method of audience analysis created a need for more refined techniques of research. Under the stimulus of new discoveries in the field of social psychology, progress in general public opinion research was very marked in the 30's, and it soon became apparent that the technique of sampling opinion might be adapted to radio listening studies. The sampling technique is a common technique all of us use in our daily lives: we need taste only a spoonful of soup in order to know whether the bowlful is too hot or too salty. The assumption, of course, is that the spoonful is just like the rest of the soup in the bowl and almost always it is the same. In public opinion research, the technique involves determining the attitudes of a limited number of people who constitute a sample of the larger public, and then projecting the results of the sample to the whole group. But measuring public opinion is more difficult than tasting soup. Constructing a sample of population that will accurately represent all the economic, social, and cultural strains, as well as sex and age distributions and family backgrounds of the whole group, is a complicated matter. Commonly used are "probability" or random samples of the population in which every person theoretically has an equal chance of being selected for the sample. The technique of getting responses by asking questions also involves the possibility of error: questions may not be worded properly, interviewers may be biased, some people may answer questions dishonestly, and the results may be susceptible to various interpretations. Still other problems are those of definition: How long must one tune in to a program to qualify as a listener or viewer? Can the act of tuning in to a station be equated with listening or viewing to that station? How do you determine how many people are watching a single television set? Should out-of-home radio listening be included in computing the size of the audience, and if so, how can this type of mobile listening be measured with any degree of accuracy?

Students of audience-measurement research have worked constantly to reduce the possibility of errors; as a result, quantitative sampling now is a respected research technique. Many business firms have specialized in audience surveys, but the output of some of them has been criticized by experts because they do not reveal all the data on which their reports are based or they lack the quality of "disinterestedness" demanded by scientific research.

· COMMERCIAL RESEARCH ORGANIZATIONS ·

With the high premium set by advertisers on the size of the broadcast audience their programs and announcements reach, it is not surprising that a number of commercial firms have been organized especially to gather such information. Television and radio audience research, which aims to gauge station coverage, the size and composition of the audience, and program popularity, has been a highly competitive field, with several different companies, using contrasting research techniques, bidding for leadership. National ratings of network programs are the most difficult to compile because of variations between time zones, differences in urban and rural listening habits, variations in the number of stations carrying a network program, and the variety of competing programs in localities throughout the country. Serious efforts were made in the early 30's to devise reliable rating systems to indicate relative popularity of programs. The Crossley Reports (later called the Cooperative Analysis of Broadcasting) were the first of such national rating devices, followed by the Hooperatings issued by C. E. Hooper, Inc., and more recently, by the Nielsen Radio Index and the Nielsen Television Index prepared by the A. C. Nielsen Co., a marketing research firm.

Crossley Ratings. The Crossley Reports were based on telephone calls placed in thirty-three cities. During these short conversations, people were asked what programs they had listened to during preceding hours of the day. The calls were placed to individuals listed in telephone directories who presumably constituted a sample of the urban population of the country. The results of the interview were compiled into national rating reports which indicated the percentage of people called who had listened to specified programs. The primary weaknesses of the Crossley Reports were twofold: (1) the "recall" technique, which depended entirely on the memory of respondents, lent itself to numerous errors, and (2) the urban sample did not represent rural listening. Under the competitive influence of the C. E. Hooper Co., the Cooperative Analysis of Broadcasting was forced to modify its technique, and finally, in 1946, it decided to discontinue its radio rating service.

Hooper. Hooperatings were first published in 1934. They had as their distinctive feature the technique of "coincidental" telephone calls. In thirty-six cities that had outlets of the four national networks, telephone calls were placed to a sample of people during the last thirteen minutes of each quarter-hour broadcast period. Respondents were asked whether they were listening to the radio, to identify the program and station to which they were listening, and to name the advertiser who sponsored the program. From the replies to these telephoned questions, biweekly Hooperatings were compiled which provided three figures: program ratings, "sets-in-use," and "share-of-the-audience." A program with a Hooperating of 22.8 meant that out of every 100 telephone calls placed, 22.8 people replied that they were listening to that program. A sets-in-use figure of 44.7 meant that out of the 100 calls, 44.7 per cent of the people who were telephoned said that they had their radios turned on. The "share-of-the-audience" figure of 50.9 was obtained by dividing the program rating by the sets-in-use figure; this indicated the comparative popularity of programs broadcast over different stations at the same time.

The clear superiority of the Hooperatings over the Crossley Reports was evident. The coincidental telephone interviews eliminated the possibility of memory failures with which Crossley had to contend. Soon the entire industry turned to Hooper to evaluate program popularity; agencies and advertisers began to judge programs on the basis of cost per Hooper point. Yet the Hooperating had numerous shortcomings which reduced its reliability and limited its usefulness. The ratings covered only 36 cities and did not survey rural listening, although independent studies had shown significant differences between rural and urban listening habits. Furthermore, since millions of American families have radios but no telephones, the Hooper sample actually represented only those families with both radios and telephones. Listening to radios in automobiles was not covered, nor was any effort made to measure multiple listening in the same household with radio sets in different rooms of the house. Dishonest replies, busy signals, refusals to co-operate, the foreign language problem, etc., all limited Hooper's effectiveness. A respondent might say he was listening to one program, but the interviewer could hear the sound of a different program coming over the telephone. Some listeners did not like to admit that they listened to certain programs. Hooper's small random sample was another factor that made scientific accuracy difficult. A single quarter-hour rating of a program was based on as few as 90 telephone calls.

Nevertheless, Hooperatings thrived as a measurement device through the war years. It was not until the development of the Nielsen Radio Index and the rise of television that the Hooper system began to lose its acceptance in broadcasting circles. The effect of television on listening in the large eastern cities threw out of kilter some of the basic assumptions underlying Hooper's statistical techniques; it consequently became impossible accurately to estimate listening in cities with TV together with listening in cities without TV. The results between the competing Hooper and Nielsen services often showed embarrassing disparities: in December, 1949, four programs rated in the top 15 by Hooper did not appear in Nielsen's top 20; Hooper's 3rd-rated program was Nielsen's 11th. Numerous stations, feeling that the Hooper system was no longer entirely reliable, discontinued their subscriptions when their ratings fell. Faced with the competition of the A. C. Nielsen Co., whose technique seemed more valid for the new situation, Hooper decided, in March, 1950, that the radio audience-research field was not big enough to support two major organizations and discontinued his national rating service after selling part of his organization to Nielsen. Hooper retained his right to issue Hooperatings for individual cities, but agreed to leave the national network field open to Nielsen for five years.

Nielsen. The Nielsen Radio Index was first issued commercially in 1942, but wartime restrictions held back expansion of the system until the late 40's. The Nielsen system makes use of the "Audimeter," an electronic device inserted in radio and television sets which makes continuous records on paper tape or 16 mm. photographic film of every moment a radio or television set is turned on and the station to which it is tuned. Nielsen uses a sample of homes that is claimed to represent substantially the entire United States, including homes of all significant types—those with telephones and those without, urban, small-town, and farm dwellings—in carefully weighted proportions. In constructing the sample, which consists of 1,500 homes for radio and 900 for television, Nielsen accounts for different age groups, incomes, educational levels, and occupational classifications.

With the co-operation of the families constituting the sample, a Nielsen representative inserts an Audimeter into every radio and television set in a sample home. When any of the sets is turned on, the Audimeter graphically records the time and the station tuned in; in this way, every occasion of dial twisting is noted and made available for analysis. From the recording tapes, it is possible to determine whether particular announcements caused listeners to tune to different stations or at what point in a program most listeners tuned in. Every month, the recording tapes are removed from the receiving sets and taken back to the Nielsen office where they are decoded and interpreted. Since the samples of homes used for the survey remains relatively constant (only 20 per cent change annually), it is also possible to establish trends in listening habits. In addition, Nielsen representatives personally visit the sample homes on a regular basis to get reliable information on the advertised brands and commodities actually purchased by each family.

From this information, the Nielsen Radio Index and the Nielsen Television Index are compiled. The Nielsen total audience rating shows the percentage of sample homes listening to or viewing at least six minutes of a program. Multiplying this rating against the total number of homes in the country yields the number of homes listening to the program. A Nielsen television rating is multiplied against the total number of television homes in the country to produce the number of homes viewing a program. Share-of-audience figures are also determined for competitive programs, as well as the audience rating during the average minute of a program. The average minute rating is of especial interest to the advertiser because it represents the best estimate of the size of the audience for a single commercial message. Each Nielsen report covers two weeks, and two reports are published each month. Nielsen publishes ratings only on commercially sponsored programs. Ratings of sustaining programs must be ordered separately. Nielsen also prepares a regular analysis of the audience ratings in nine key television cities.

The advantages of the Nielsen system are self-evident. It avoids the human errors that Hooper had to cope with, it covers rural and urban dwellings, and it records dial twistings by the minute. But the Nielsen system is not without its limitations. The validity of using a sample of homes in which families know that their habits are under observation and study is open to question. People often behave differently under a spotlight than when they are left to themselves. Moreover, while the tape accurately records all the movements of the dial, it cannot tell whether any one is actually listening to a program or whether, for example, a conversation is in progress at the time. Students of public opinion research will also want to know more about the construction of the Nielsen sample to verify its representativeness. Some broadcasting and advertising executives assert that the Nielsen sample is too small to have much value. Nevertheless, with these limitations, plus the rather large cost of subscribing to the system, Nielsen has become the most widely respected national audience-measurement system. In 1955, Nielsen supplemented its use of the Audimeter with listener and viewer diaries.

American Research Bureau. The American Research Bureau (ARB) uses a national diary sample and, like Nielsen, can be projected to produce percentages of the number of homes reached by a network television program. ARB places diaries for one week each month in 2,200 television homes. One member of each family is asked to keep an accurate record of all quarter-hour periods in which he has watched five minutes or more of a television program. The 2,200 homes are changed for each monthly report. ARB rating figures are on an average quarter-hour basis rather than on the total-homes-reached basis used by Nielsen. The ARB figures cover only the first week of each month. They also cover sustaining programs. ARB also prepares ratings of programs in individual cities. The basic difference between ARB and Nielsen, then, lies in the technique of securing their information. While Nielsen uses completely objective methods of measuring tuning behavior, the ARB diary method relies on the accuracy of the respondents reporting on what they did.

Trendex. Trendex uses the telephone coincidental survey method of a random sample of the population in 15 cities where at least three television stations are in operation. Most of these cities are in the Eastern Time Zone so that Trendex is not by any means a national measurement nor can its ratings measure audience size as do Nielsen and ARB studies. Trendex produces ratings which indicate the relative popularity of competing network programs in the 15 cities, and can be obtained within twelve hours following the telecast.

The Trendex sample is made up of 600 television homes to measure half-hour, once-weekly programs, 1,200 television homes for one hour, once-weekly programs, and 1,500 television homes for quarter-hour, five-times-weekly programs.

Over the telephone, Trendex interviewers ask the following questions: "(1) Was anyone in your home looking at TV just now? (2) What program, please? (3) What station, please? (4) What is advertised? or How many men, women, children are looking (listening)? (5) Do you have a television set?" (Asked when television is not specifically mentioned.) Trendex, like ARB, surveys only in the first week of each month, and thus reflects to a maximum degree radical fluctuations created by weather conditions, holidays, special events, unusual promotion or publicity and so on. Trendex ratings are more volatile than Nielsen or ARB ratings; this is often accounted for by the effect of local program competition in cities like New York or Chicago where a nonnetwork baseball telecast may draw a very large audience away from the network shows.

Pulse. The Pulse, Inc. rating system obtains its figures by using the personal interview "aided-recall" method. Pulse representatives visit individual homes and have members of the household examine a roster which lists, in quarter-hour periods, all the programs broadcast in the time period being studied. These interviews are conducted on a block-by-block basis in various cities; the sample of homes to be visited is drawn up with reference to population figures furnished by the census. The data obtained are broken down by sex, age, income, educational level, telephone and nontelephone homes, and by type of dwelling. Pulse reports provide sets-in-use, program, and station ratings. The Pulse program rating is in terms of the per cent of total homes listening or viewing, by fifteen-minute periods, by programs, and by stations. Pulse issues city radio and television ratings and, in 1954, began national television ratings based upon interviews with 67,000 families in sixty areas. Upon request of clients, Pulse also prepares special reports on qualitative reactions to programs, the impact of a program, and pantry inventories, to determine product usage in the homes of listeners and viewers.

Videodex. Videodex, Inc., issues national television ratings based on diary reports from 9,000 homes in more than 200 markets. The size of the New York City sample is 600 homes. A portion of the sample is rotated each month.

Conlan. Robert S. Conlan & Association uses a combination telephone coincidental and personal interview-roster recall system. This method combines broadcast exposure information obtained by the telephone coincidental method in one sample of homes with information obtained by the roster recall method in another sample of homes. Conlan surveys are prepared on order for any station. Conlan covers the listening or viewing activity to that station for an entire week. The results are based upon many more telephone calls and aided-recall interviews for that station than would be practical in a national survey.

Schwerin. The Schwerin Research Corporation does not measure audiences to broadcast programs. Schwerin tests sample groups of listeners and viewers to make qualitative evaluations of television and radio programs and commercial announcements prior to their use on the air. Schwerin scores are measurements of listener or viewer approval. Using controlled samples ranging as large as 1,000, Schwerin has his sample audience indicate their reactions to proposed programs and commercials on score sheets.

· CRITERIA FOR AUDIENCE RATINGS ·

The conflicts between the various rating systems have frequently caused considerable confusion within the broadcasting industry. For example, an ARB report for the first week in October, 1954, showed CBS with 8 out of the 10 top-rated shows, while the Nielsen report covering the same period gave NBC 7 of the top 10 shows. The Trendex rating for one NBC Spectacular was 17.5; its ARB rating was 26.7, and its Nielsen rating was 38.7. A detailed analysis of these ratings showed less conflict than appeared on the surface because each rating actually measured different things and therefore was not directly comparable. The conflict did point up, however, the great limitations in using rating information to draw conclusions as to audience size or program popularity without thorough analysis of the rating information.[1]

As a result of industry concern over conflicts among the rating systems, the Advertising Research Foundation, a trade group, set up a committee of audience-research specialists to study the problem and formulate criteria by which the industry might judge the various rating systems. The methods examined by the committee included the personal coincidental, personal roster recall diary (ARB and Videodex), the recorder (Nielsen), personal coincidental, personal-roster recall (Pulse), personal-unaided recall, telephone coincidental (Trendex), telephone recall, combination telephone coincidental and telephone recall (Hooper), combination telephone coincidental and diary (Hooper), combination telephone coincidental and personal-roster recall (Conlan). After a two-year study, the committee an-

[1] For critical treatments of rating systems, see Bill Davidson, "Who Knows Who's on Top?" *Collier's,* October 29, 1954, pp. 23-27; and Charles Sinclair, "The Ratings Muddle," in *Sponsor,* November 29, 1954, pp. 31-33, 114 ff.

nounced in 1954 a preliminary set of 22 criteria for audience measurement. These criteria related to the information required from an adequate audience-measurement system, and the desired standards of procedure and accuracy. None of the existing rating systems qualified under all the committee's criteria, although Nielsen scored the highest. According to the committee's evaluation, it seemed clear that a combination of the automatic recording device used by Nielsen plus the use of diaries would be the most reliable method. The committee recommended in favor of unrestricted random samples of the population for use in audience studies and stated that a minimum sample size of 400 households for local audience measurements and 1,200 for national audience measurements for each fifteen-minute program or program segment be used.

• INTERPRETATION OF RATINGS •

Until an audience-measurement system is developed that wins unqualified scientific support for its validity and reliability, it is likely that competitive rating systems will continue to operate in the field of television and radio. These rating systems, despite their limitations, will serve a useful purpose to networks, stations, advertisers, and agencies provided they are interpreted properly. To use ratings to determine the popularity of any program or the size of the audience reached, we must be sure to take into account the following considerations:

1. No program rating can be evaluated without knowing what rating system is used. To state that a program had a rating of 20 without stating whether that is a Nielsen, ARB, or Trendex 20 makes it impossible to evaluate the rating.

2. No program rating can be properly evaluated without knowing the full context of the rating:

(*a*) What was the rating of the program that preceded it? The effect of a strong adjacent program can often mislead people into thinking that a program has strong popular appeal when it really is profiting from its fortunate position in the program schedule. One network program that had a good rating actually was tuned out by more people than any other network program. Its strategic position between two very popular shows nevertheless managed to sustain a sizeable audience that it would never have attracted at another time on the program schedule.

(*b*) Did the program have strong competition on the air from programs on other stations or networks? If two equally good programs are on the air at the same time, each may get only half as high the rating it would get if it had weak competition. On the other hand, a program that achieves a fair rating against one of the highest-rated shows may actually have more popular appeal than one with a higher rating earned against weak competition.

(c) What time of the year was the rating made? Viewing and listening tends to be greater in the fall, winter, and early spring than in the summer. A rating that might not be considered very impressive for a fall show might be judged impressive for a summer show.

(d) What time of the day was the rating made? Audiences for television programs are much greater in the evening than in the daytime. For this reason advertisers are unwilling to spend as much money for time and program in the morning or afternoon as they will in the evening. Daytime ratings must therefore be judged within the context of all daytime ratings.

(e) To what extent did the rating benefit or suffer from regular listening or viewing habits, special program publicity, etc. The rating for a program that is broadcast one time only without advance publicity is practically meaningless in judging the program's popularity, because many potential viewers did not know the show was on the air.

3. Ratings must be used not as an absolute measurement, but mainly as a guide to program popularity. "All of the rating services are used as tools at NBC," says Sylvester L. Weaver, "to temper and reinforce judgment and that is how they should be used. To use them otherwise, or to regard them as the be-all or end-all for distinguishing program success from program failure, is to use them incorrectly."

4. Program ratings must not be confused with advertising effectiveness. Ratings can provide an indication of circulation, but not of sales effectiveness which may be related to the special relationship developed between the audience and the program, the effectiveness of the commercial messages, or the special kind of audience attracted to the program.

5. Very low program ratings tend to be less reliable as a guide to judging audience size than high program ratings. In low ratings probable errors that may occur through the operations of chance have a great effect in upsetting estimates of audience size. A rating system that has a probable error of plus or minus 2 percentage points means that a rating of 8 may actually be a rating ranging from 6 to 10. An advertiser may want to invest in a show when it reaches two million homes with a rating of 8, but the two million may actually have been reached when the rating was 6 or 7, or may not have been reached even when the rating is 9. With program ratings of 20 or 30, the effect of the probable error does not have a comparable effect upon judgments of a program's popularity.

6. Small rating differences should be discounted in judging comparative program popularity, all other factors being equal. Competitive ratings of 26.2 and 25.7 should be interpreted as indications of equal popularity; the rating systems are not fine enough in their measurements to yield more than approximations.

· SUMMARY ·

Public acceptance of television and radio programming is essential to any system of broadcasting. It is difficult to determine with accuracy what listeners and viewers think about particular programs, but numerous commercial audience-research organizations, using sampling techniques, provide program ratings and indications of audience size. Despite the limitations of the rating methods, program ratings can serve a constructive function to networks, stations, advertisers, and agencies when they are properly interpreted and used.

Questions for Discussion

1. How accurately can we determine the popularity of a television or radio program?
2. What is the nature of listening and viewing publics in terms of possible tuning behavior?
3. What are the relative advantages and disadvantages of the various audience-measurement methods currently used in television and radio?
4. How much reliance should be put on ratings in determining whether a program should be maintained on the air?
5. How should ratings be interpreted?
6. What has been the effect of audience research on the broadcasting industry?
7. Could we manage without any rating systems?
8. What kind of program rating would command your complete confidence as to its validity and reliability?

❊ 9 ❊

What Constitutes the Public Interest?

THE "public interest, convenience, or necessity," as stated in the Communications Act of 1934, is the touchstone of American broadcasting. But what is the public interest? How is it to be determined? Who shall make the determination? These are the questions with which we deal in this chapter.

The use of a general phrase like "public interest" to embody basic Congressional policy in some field of government activity is rather common. In writing a law, members of Congress realize that they cannot anticipate every situation that may arise in carrying out the law. It is customary for Congress to lay down the broad general policy and to appoint some authority to execute this policy and to make administrative interpretations of the law. Anglo-Saxon legal tradition has developed the rule of reasonableness; executive authorities, in their interpretations of Congressional policy, must not act arbitrarily or capriciously, but solely in terms of reason. The final decisions as to whether or not they have acted reasonably rests in the hands of appropriate courts to which aggrieved parties may appeal.

This procedural aspect of American government characterizes television and radio regulation. Congress laid down the general policy, with limited specific directives such as equal time for political campaign broadcasts, and it created the Federal Communications Commission to execute the law, to issue administrative rules and regulations, to decide cases, and generally to represent the will of the people. The law contains an elastic clause which says that the FCC "may perform any and all acts, make such rules and regulations, and issue such orders, not inconsistent with this Act, as may be necessary in the execution of its functions."

With this authority, the FCC has sought to regulate television and radio in the public interest. The commission itself has not specifically defined what "public interest" means in all instances, but, in various statements and decisions, it has expressed definite judgments as to what the public interest includes and what it does *not* include. Most of these statements are made *ad hoc,* that is to say, in connection with specific cases that come before the Commission in its exercise of the power to grant, renew, or revoke broadcast licenses. There are also FCC rules and regulations, such as the Chain Broadcasting Regulations, which indicate the Commission's interpretation of public policy, and occasional general reports or opinions issued by the Commission. We may also look to the Communications Act itself and its legislative history and to appellate court cases reviewing FCC decisions to determine the meaning of "public interest."

Wherever we turn for light on this subject, we find that in television and radio regulation, as the FCC itself has pointed out, the

> paramount and controlling consideration [is] the relationship between the American system of broadcasting carried on through a large number of private licensees upon whom devolves the responsibility for the selection and presentation of program material, and the Congressional mandate that this licensee responsibility is to be exercised in the interests of, and as a trustee for the public at large which retains ultimate control over the channels of radio and television communication.[1]

· BASIC THEORY OF THE PUBLIC INTEREST ·

In interpreting the public interest clause, the FCC has at various times set forth the following general principles:

1. The right of the public to broadcast service is superior to the right of any individual to use the ether. The legislative history of the Radio Act of 1927 clearly indicates that "Congress intended that radio stations shall not be used for the private interest, whims, or caprices of the particular persons who have been granted licenses."[2]

2. Broadcasting must be maintained as a medium of free speech for the people as a whole.

3. Television and radio stations have a definite responsibility to provide a reasonable amount of broadcast time for controversial public discussion. In programming such discussions, the broadcaster must avoid one-sidedness and observe over-all fairness. The right of the public to be informed of different opinions in important matters of public controversy is the dominant consideration.

4. Licensees must maintain control over the programming of their own stations, and may not surrender their program responsibility by contract or otherwise to networks, advertising agencies, or other program-producing organizations.

[1] Federal Communications Commission, *Report in the Matter of Editorializing by Broadcast Licensees,* Docket No. 8516, June 2, 1949.

[2] Address by Wayne Coy, former FCC Chairman, at Yale Law School, January 22, 1949.

5. Television and radio stations must be responsive to the needs and interests of the communities in which they are located. To this end, the Commission has often favored local ownership of stations, integration of ownership and management, and local live programs.

6. Television and radio stations may not be used exclusively for commercial purposes. They must use some of their broadcast time for sustaining programs and must avoid advertising excesses which offend good taste.

7. Television and radio stations are expected to abide by their promises of program service unless exceptional circumstances supervene. Since the Commission grants licenses on the basis of these promises, the Commission holds that it has the right to determine whether the promises have been kept. The Commission therefore reserves to itself the right to review the over-all program service of stations when licenses come up for renewal. (This right is disputed by many prominent broadcasting executives and attorneys.)

8. The Commission favors diversity of ownership of television and radio stations. In approving the sale of the Blue Network by RCA, the Commission said, "The mechanism of free speech can operate freely only when the controls of public access to the means for the dissemination of news and issues are in as many responsible ownerships as possible and each exercises its own independent judgment." [3]

9. The Commission may not censor any television or radio program in advance of broadcast.

In carrying out these principles, the FCC has taken punitive action only in rare instances of extreme abuse by licensees; most of the time it has resorted to mild or indirect chidings of errant stations and it has relied on persuasion to achieve most of its objectives. For many years this failure to act decisively was attributed to the reluctance of the Commission to invoke the death penalty for a station for anything less than the most unmitigated misuse of a license. Until Congress authorized the FCC in 1952 to issue "cease-and-desist" orders and to suspend and penalize stations violating its rules, the problem of making the punishment fit the crime was almost impossible of solution. One of the most useful devices of the Commission, however, continues to be a letter from the Commission requesting a licensee to explain, for example, how his action, in failing to broadcast any political campaign talks during an election campaign, served the public interest. The licensee then bears the burden of justifying his action in terms of the concept of public interest held by the FCC.

[3] Federal Communications Commission, "Decision and Order in the Matter of RCA, Transferor and ABC, Inc., Transferee," Docket No. 6536, October 12, 1943 (mimeo).

· GRANTING AND RENEWING LICENSES ·

In granting and renewing broadcast licenses, the FCC is often obliged to refine its interpretation of public interest. When the Commission has two or more financially and technically qualified applicants where only one license may be granted, the Commission may have no alternative but to base its decision on the "public interest, convenience, necessity" as expressed in terms of ownership considerations and programming intentions.

Ownership Preferences.

MISREPRESENTATION OF OWNERSHIP. Misrepresentation of ownership is sufficient cause for the FCC to refuse to grant a broadcast license or, if the fraud is discovered at a later date, to revoke the license. In the *WOKO* case, decided in 1945, the Commission refused to renew the license of WOKO because it had concealed the real ownership of 24 per cent of its stock. The Supreme Court upheld the FCC even though the station's programming service was not held to be unsatisfactory.[3a]

MULTIPLE OWNERSHIP. Seeking to achieve as much diversity of ownership as possible, the Commission has set limitations on the number of stations which may be licensed to the same person or corporation. Seven is the maximum number in FM stations, seven in TV (5 VHF, 2 UHF), and seven in AM.[4] Furthermore, under the FCC's "duopoly" rule, one owner may not have two television or two radio stations serving substantially the same listening or viewing area. This regulation is designed to prevent a recurrence in broadcasting of what is often the case in the newspaper business: the same publisher owning two local dailies and operating without competition.

SPECIAL-INTEREST GROUPS. Before World War II, the FCC was reluctant to issue broadcast licenses to special-interest groups like religious organizations and labor unions. The Commission felt that these groups would tend to use a station to advance their own political, economic, or religious ends. The Commission preferred to issue licenses to applicants whose organizational affiliations would not tend to make them favor any one group. By and large, this remains the Commission's policy. Since the war, however, with the huge increase in the number of AM and FM stations, the Commission has licensed radio stations to special interest groups in some metropolitan areas. Labor unions holding licenses have agreed to program their stations for the general public and not merely for their members.

NEWSPAPER OWNERSHIP. During the late 30's, newspaper publishers in great numbers applied for broadcast licenses. In 1931, less than 15 per

---

[3a] *Federal Communications Commission* v. *WOKO, Inc.,* 329 U.S. 223.

[4] In 1955, the Storer Broadcasting Company successfully challenged this FCC ruling and obtained a United States Court of Appeals decision that the ceiling of seven TV stations, irrespective of other considerations, was an arbitrary rule of the Commission and therefore invalid. The FCC appealed this adverse decision to the Supreme Court.

cent of all radio stations were licensed to publishers, but by 1938, a third of all stations were newspaper-owned. The FCC became disturbed about this situation and in 1941 it ordered an investigation into the propriety of joint ownership of newspapers and radio stations in the same area. After many hearings and deliberations, the Commission dismissed the proceedings and newspapers were authorized to apply for broadcast licenses. Nevertheless, when the FCC is faced with competing applications for licenses, one of which comes from a newspaper, the Commission usually includes in its over-all consideration the wisdom of consolidating control over two media of mass communication in the hands of one party.

TYPES OF OWNERSHIP PREFERRED. The Commission favors local owner-ship and integration of ownership and management over absentee owner-ship. In evaluating the qualifications of an applicant, the Commission considers it in the public interest to investigate the applicant's background and personal and business reputation. If the applicant has had brushes with the law, his standing before the Commission will be less favorable than that of competing applicants without such a record.

CHARACTER OF THE LICENSEE. In the *Edward Lamb* case, on which hear-ings were held in 1954 and 1955, the Commission proposed to deny renewal of a broadcasting license on the ground that the licensee was untrustworthy and ordered a hearing. The specific allegation in support of this charge was that the licensee had knowingly signed a false affidavit to the Commission stating that he had never been a member of the Communist Party when, the Commission charged, he had in fact been a member of the party. The licensee denied the truth of the allegation. After many months of hearings, an FCC trial examiner rejected the charge against the licensee as unfounded and recommended renewal of the broadcasting license. The authority of the Commission to deny a license for material untrustworthiness of the licensee, it established after appropriate hearings, seems beyond dispute.

Programming Intentions.

PUBLIC INTEREST *versus* PRIVATE INTEREST. The FCC has always re-quired applicants for broadcast licenses and renewals of licenses to submit detailed statements of their proposed program policies. The decision to grant or deny the application has been based in part on a determination of whether the proposed programming was or was not in the public interest.

The authority of the Commission to follow this procedure has been upheld by the courts in several important cases. In the *KFKB Broadcasting Association* case, the Commission denied renewal of a license after finding that the station's owner had used his facilities to prescribe treatment for patients whom he had never seen, basing his diagnoses on letters from them.[5] In the *Trinity Methodist Church* case, the station was owned by a minister who used it for sensational broadcasts that contained false and defamatory

[5] *KFKB* v. *Federal Radio Commission* (App. D. C.), 47 F. 2d, 670.

statements and vilified other religious groups. On one occasion the minister announced that he had certain damaging information against a prominent unnamed man whose name he would disclose unless a contribution of $100 was immediately forthcoming. As a result, he received contributions from several persons. The Commission refused to renew the station's license and the decision was upheld by the courts.[6] Both of these cases made the point that "the interest of the listening public is paramount and may not be subordinated to the interests of the station licensee."

PROGRAMMING AND COMMUNITY NEEDS. The Commission has held that an indispensable element of public interest is the rendering of a program service designed to meet the needs and interests of the area in which the station is located. In the *Simmons* case, the fact that the applicant intended to "plug" his station into a network line most of the time and to act merely as a relay station was used as a basis for denying the grant.[7]

PROGRAMMING AND THE SALE OF TIME. The proportionate amount of time a licensee intends to sell for sponsorship and to keep on a sustaining basis is also considered by the Commission in weighing applications. While the FCC recognizes the fine quality of many sponsored programs, it holds that some programs properly should not be sponsored and that a certain amount of sustaining time should be programmed by a station. Such time may be used for experimenting with new program ideas, for community talent, for discussing community problems, and for educational broadcasts. An applicant who states that he intends to sell 100 per cent of his broadcast time to sponsors does not stand a good chance of winning Commission approval of his application.

• TELEVISION AND RADIO AS MEDIA OF FREE SPEECH •

In its concern over maintaining television and radio as media of free speech, the FCC has been required to consider a number of difficult questions involving the nature of free speech and censorship. Freedom of speech for whom? The idea of unlimited freedom of speech, such as we generally think of when we mention the soap box, is impossible in television and radio because of the limitations of frequencies and broadcast time. Since not everyone who wants to speak on the air can be given the chance to do so, someone has to decide who shall speak, when he shall speak, and for how long.

One point of view holds that "The broadcast licensee should be given complete and exclusive control over program content, including the sole

[6] *Trinity Methodist Church, South* v. *Federal Radio Commission* (App. D. C.), 62 F. 2d, 850.
[7] *Allen T. Simmons* v. *Federal Communications Commission*, 169 F. 2d 670 *certiorari denied*, 335 U. S. 846.

right to determine who shall speak, and the right to censor any material intended for broadcast." [8] This position gives rise to several questions. Does freedom of the air mean freedom for the licensee to use his station as he pleases? Or does it mean freedom of expression for the persons who broadcast on his station? Is it an act of censorship to restrict the licensee's freedom to make unfair use of his station? Is it an act of censorship when the licensee reviews in advance scripts intended for broadcast over his station? What constitutes unfairness in denying air time or censoring a script and who shall make the final decision? Should the licensee be permitted to use his station the way a publisher uses his newspaper, broadcasting his own editorials and supporting political causes and candidates? Should he deny time on the air to a point of view because it is a minority and perhaps an unpopular point of view? Should the licensee be required to make time available for political campaign talks in between elections? Should the licensee be required to make time available for the discussion of controversial issues of interest in the community served by the station? Does freedom mean that the licensee is free to run these discussions as he sees fit or must such programs be designed so that the public has a reasonable opportunity to hear different opposition positions?

In a number of important rulings and opinions, the Commission has expressed itself on these questions.

The Mayflower Case. In the *Mayflower* case, the issue before the FCC was whether it is consistent with the public interest for a licensee to utilize his facilities to present his own partisan ideas on vital public issues to the exclusion of all opposing viewpoints. The case came up when Station WAAB, Boston, applied for the renewal of its license. The FCC discovered that it had been the station's policy to broadcast editorials urging the election of various candidates for political office or supporting one side of various questions in public controversy, with no pretense at objective or impartial reporting. "It is clear," the Commission observed, "that the purpose of these editorials was to win public support for some person or view favored by those in control of the station." The Commission renewed the license in 1941, but at the same time it issued a *dictum* prohibiting such editorializing in the future, saying: "A truly free radio cannot be used to advocate the causes of the licensee. It cannot be used to support the candidacies of his friends. It cannot be devoted to the support of principles he happens to regard most favorably. In brief, the broadcaster cannot be an advocate."

The *dictum* did not, however, expressly limit the editorial freedom of commentators whom the station hired.

The Commission's ruling was criticized by groups and individuals who

[8] Hearings before a Subcommittee of the Committee on Interstate and Foreign Commerce, U.S. Senate, 80th Congress, 1st Session, on S. 1333 (1947), p. 314. This was the testimony of a representative of the National Association of Broadcasters.

felt that station licensees were being denied a right newspaper publishers had without restriction; that the increase in number of stations made it possible to allow editorializing without fear that all points of view would not be heard; that licensees would be able to play more active roles in their communities if allowed to editorialize; and that the prohibition was an unconstitutional restraint of the licensee's freedom of speech.

Those who supported the Commission's ruling pointed out that licensees should be umpires of public controversy and not public advocates; that it would be unfair and potentially dangerous to allow licensees to make use of the prestige and good will of their stations for editorial purposes; that no constitutional question was involved since broadcasting was, by its nature, a regulated medium; and that it would be impossible to police all stations to make sure that fair treatment was provided all points of view by a licensee who had already committed himself publicly to one side.

In 1948, the FCC held public hearings on the issue in the *Mayflower* decision and, a year later, it issued a new opinion modifying the earlier one. Licensees are now allowed to editorialize in the name of their station provided they maintain an over-all fairness. The Commission stated that "the identified expression of the licensee's personal viewpoint as part of the more general presentation of views or comments on the various issues" may be broadcast.

> But the opportunity of licensees to present such views as they may have on matters of controversy may not be utilized to achieve a partisan or one-sided presentation of issues. Licensee editorialization is but one aspect of freedom of expression by means of radio. Only insofar as it is exercised in conformity with the paramount right of the public to hear a reasonably balanced presentation of all responsible viewpoints on particular issues can such editorialization be considered to be consistent with the licensee's duty to operate in the public interest. For the licensee is a trustee impressed with the duty of preserving for the public generally radio as a medium of free expression and fair presentation.[9]

The WHKC Case. In the *WHKC* case, in 1945, the issue was whether it is in the public interest for a licensee arbitrarily to limit certain types of organizations from securing time on the station to express their opinions on vital issues, or to restrict the manner or method in which they present their views.

The case developed out of the policy of many stations not to sell radio time to labor unions on the grounds that discussion of labor affairs was inherently controversial and therefore not suitable for broadcast on sponsored programs. The president of a national network testified that he would not sell time to the American Federation of Labor to sponsor a symphony orchestra, but that he would sell the same time to an automobile manufac-

---

[9] Federal Communications Commission, *Report in the Matter of Editorializing by Broadcast Licensees*, Docket No. 8516, June 1, 1949.

turer. Corporations might hire commentators to editorialize on the air, but unions were not permitted to buy time for their commentators.

The situation came to a head when the Congress of Industrial Organizations petitioned the FCC not to renew the license of WHKC, Columbus, Ohio, because the station had stringently censored remarks scheduled to be delivered on a United Automobile Workers program. Upon the request of both parties, the Commission dismissed the action, WHKC having promised the union a reasonable opportunity to be heard. In its order, however, the FCC denounced the policy of refusing to air labor discussions on the basis of their controversial nature. The Commission asserted that the public interest requires licensees, as an "affirmative duty," to make reasonable provision for broadcast discussions of controversial issues of public importance in the community served by the station.[10]

The Scott Case. The *Scott* case, in 1946, presented a crucial test to the Commission because it involved a complaint by a member of a group holding a viewpoint contrary to that shared by a majority of the population, that certain stations had refused to afford him or persons sharing similar views any opportunity to state their position, although time was given to representatives of groups holding contrary positions.

Scott, a self-professed atheist, filed a petition with the FCC to have the licenses of three California stations revoked because they flatly refused to give him any time whatsoever for a discussion of atheism. He claimed that these stations carried many broadcasts of religious services which openly attacked atheism and that therefore he was entitled to time to present an opposite point of view. He also complained that some stations had refused him time on the ground that any broadcast on the subject of atheism was contrary to the public interest.

The Commission denied Scott's petition, but it issued an important opinion which said, in part:

> We recognize that in passing upon requests for time, a station licensee is constantly confronted with most difficult problems. Since the demands for time may far exceed the amount available for broadcasting a licensee must inevitably make a selection among those seeking it for the expression of their views. He may not even be able to grant time to all religious groups who might desire the use of his facilities, much less to all who might want to oppose religion. Admittedly, a very real opportunity exists for him to be arbitrary and unreasonable, to indulge his own preferences, prejudices, or whims; to pursue his own private interest or to favor those who espouse his views, and discriminate against those of opposing views. The indulgence of that opportunity could not conceivably be characterized as an exercise of the broadcaster's right of freedom of speech. Nor could it fairly be said to afford the listening audience that opportunity to hear a diversity and balance of views, which is an inseparable corollary of freedom of expression. In making a selection with fairness, the licensee must, of course, consider the extent of the interest of the

[10] *United Broadcasting Co.* (*WHKC*), 10 FCC. 515.

public in his service area in a particular subject to be discussed, as well as the qualifications of the person selected to discuss it.

Every idea does not rise to the dignity of a "public controversy," and every organization, regardless of membership or the seriousness of purposes, is not *per se* entitled to time on the air. But an organization or idea may be projected into the realm of controversy by virtue of being attacked. The holders of a belief should not be denied the right to answer attacks upon them or their belief solely because they are few in number.

The fact that a licensee's duty to make time available for the presentation of opposing views on current controversial issues of public importance may not extend to all possible differences of opinion within the ambit of human contemplation cannot serve as the basis for any rigid policy that time shall be denied for the presentation of views which may have a high degree of unpopularity. The criterion of the public interest in the field of broadcasting clearly precludes a policy of making radio wholly unavailable as a medium for the expression of any view which falls within the scope of the Constitutional guarantee of freedom of speech.[11]

The Scott decision did *not* say that every time a radio station carries religious broadcasts, atheists are entitled to time for the expression of their views. It did say, however, that the licensee, in exercising his judgment as to what is a controversial issue, should not deny time for the expression of a particular point of view solely because he does not agree with that point of view.

The Morris Case. The *Morris* case, in 1946, raised the issue whether the licensee's obligation for over-all fairness in the discussion of controversy extends to advertising messages for products which some listeners consider detrimental.

Sam Morris, a prohibitionist, asked the FCC not to renew the license of a Dallas station because it sold choice time to beer and wine interests and refused to sell time for abstinence messages. The Commission denied Morris' specific request, but it extended the fairness requirement to cover advertising matter by saying that "the advertising of alcoholic beverages over the radio can raise substantial issues of public importance" inasmuch as the question of the sale and consumption of such beverages is often a matter of controversy.

What is for other individuals merely a routine advertising "plug," extolling the virtues of a beverage, essentially no different from other types of product advertising, is for some individuals the advocacy of a practice which they deem to be detrimental to our society. Whatever the merits of this controversy . . . it is at least clear that it may assume the proportions of a controverted issue of public importance. The fact that the occasion for the controversy happens to be the advertising of a product cannot serve to diminish the duty of the broadcaster to treat it as such an issue.[12]

[11] "In re Petition of Robert Harold Scott, Memorandum Opinion and Order," FCC Release No. 96050, July 19, 1946 (mimeo).
[12] *Petition of Sam Morris,* 3 Pike & Fischer, Radio Regulations, 154.

The Richards Case. In 1950, the FCC held public hearings on the renewal of the licenses of the G. A. Richards radio stations (KMPC, Hollywood, WJR, Detroit, and WGAR, Cleveland) because sworn charges were made by former station employees that Mr. Richards had directed them to "slant" news broadcasts unfairly in support of his political ideas and candidates and against certain political and religious groups. FCC hearings were held to determine whether the charges were true and, if so, whether Mr. Richards was qualified to hold a broadcast license. Mr. Richards replied that the charges were false. During the course of extended hearings, Mr. Richards died and the Commission consequently did not make a final determination of the issue. Instead, it approved the transfer of the stations by Richards' heirs to new licensees. Nevertheless, the *Richards* case made it clear throughout the broadcast industry that licensees may not use their stations for purposes of private propaganda without jeopardizing their licenses.[13]

· THE BLUE BOOK ·

In early 1945, the Federal Communications Commission announced a policy of a more detailed review of broadcast station performance in passing on applications for license renewals. A year later, the Commission issued a lengthy, much-publicized, and much controverted report entitled *Public Service Responsibility of Broadcast Licensees,* commonly referred to as the *Blue Book.*

In the *Blue Book,* the FCC examined the logs of several stations and compared them with the promises the stations had made when they filed their license applications. KIEV, Glendale, California, had devoted 88 per cent of its program time in a sample week to transcribed music and less than 3.7 per cent to local live talent whose availability in the community had been the chief argument made by the station in applying for its license. The station's programs were interspersed with spot announcements on the average of one every five-and-a-half minutes. A total of 1,042 spots were broadcast during the sample week, of which 1,034 were commercial and eight were broadcast as a public service. WSNY, Schenectady, New York, broadcast transcriptions for 78 per cent of its air time, although it had promised a maximum of 20 per cent in competing with another applicant for the same station license. WTOL, Toledo, had been given permission to engage in full-time broadcasting on the ground that local organizations needed to be heard. It promised to devote 84 per cent of its evening time to such broadcasts, but the record showed the actual percentage was 13.7.

The Commission expressed concern over the amount of time devoted to commercials, the undue length of individual announcements, and the

[13] For an interesting discussion of the *Richards* case, see Edmund Laurence, "Radio and the Richards Case," *Harper's,* Vol. 205 (July, 1952), pp. 82-87.

piling up of commercials. In a wistful vein the Commission said, "The listener who has heard one program and wants to hear another has come to expect a commercial plug to intervene. Conversely, the listener who has heard one or more commercial announcements may reasonably expect a program to intervene." But the Commission discovered that there were many occasions when a listener might be obliged to listen to five commercial announcements between two programs. Poor taste and propaganda in commercials, the middle commercial in newscasts, and intermixing programs with advertising also disturbed the Commission. "A listener is entitled to know when the program ends and the advertisement begins," the report asserted.

At the end of the *Blue Book,* the Commission announced its future policy with regard to the public interest aspects of broadcasting:

> While much of the responsibility for improved program service lies with the broadcasting industry and with the public, the Commission has a statutory responsibility for the public interest, of which it cannot divest itself ...
>
> In issuing and in renewing the licenses of broadcast stations the Commission proposes to give particular consideration to four program service factors relevant to the public interest ...
>
> 1. *Sustaining programs.* Sustaining programs ... perform a five-fold function in (a) maintaining an over-all program balance, (b) providing time for programs inappropriate for sponsorship, (c) providing time for programs serving particular minority tastes and interests, (d) providing time for nonprofit organizations—religious, civic, agricultural, labor, educational, etc., and (e) providing time for experiment and for unfettered artistic self-expression.
>
> Accordingly, the Commission concludes that one standard of operation in the public interest is a reasonable proportion of time devoted to sustaining programs.
>
> Moreover, if sustaining programs are to perform their traditional functions in the American system of broadcasting, they must be broadcast at hours when the public is awake and listening. The time devoted to sustaining programs, accordingly, should be reasonably distributed among the various segments of the broadcast day.
>
> 2. *Local live programs.* The Commission has always placed a marked emphasis, and in some cases perhaps an undue emphasis, on the carrying of local live programs as a standard of public interest. The development of network, transcription, and wire news services is such that no sound public interest appears to be served by continuing to stress local live programs exclusively at the expense of these other categories. Nevertheless, reasonable provision for local self-expression still remains an essential function of a station's operation, and will continue to be so regarded by the Commission. In particular, public interest requires that such programs should not be crowded out of the best listening hours.
>
> 3. *Programs devoted to the discussion of public issues.* The crucial need for discussion programs, at the local, national, and international levels alike is universally realized. ... Accordingly, the carrying of such programs in reasonable sufficiency, and during good listening hours, is a factor to be considered in any finding of public interest.

4. *Advertising excesses. . . .* some stations during some or many portions of the broadcast day have engaged in advertising excesses which are incompatible with their public responsibilities, and which threaten the good name of broadcasting itself.

As the broadcasting industry itself has insisted, the public interest clearly requires that the amount of time devoted to advertising matter shall bear a reasonable relationship to the amount of time devoted to programs. Accordingly, in its application forms the Commission will request the applicant to state how much time he proposes to devote to advertising matter in any one hour.

This by itself will not, of course, result in the elimination of some of the particular excesses described herein. . . . This is a matter in which self-regulation by the industry may properly be sought and indeed expected. The Commission has no desire to concern itself with the particular length, content, or irritating qualities of particular commercial plugs.

The Commission thus stated its bases of consideration in renewing broadcast licenses. In evaluating over-all program service, the Commission would also have in mind program "balance during the best listening hours."

While it does not have the force of a formal Commission regulation, the *Blue Book* stands as the most comprehensive FCC interpretation of the "public interest, convenience, or necessity" clause of the Communications Act. No licenses have failed of renewal on programming grounds since the *Blue Book* was issued, but some renewals were held up for hearings and new licenses issued on the basis of *Blue Book* criteria in the years immediately following the issuance of the report.[14] With an almost complete change in the membership of the Commission since 1946, many observers believe that the *Blue Book* has become a dead issue in broadcast regulation, although in 1955 one Commissioner (John C. Doerfer) objected to the renewal of the license of Station WTIX, New Orleans, because the station did not meet minimum program standards and failed to include religious, educational, and discussion programs in its schedule. The Commissioner cited the *Blue Book* dicta in support of his belief that the station had not served the public interest. In 1955, the Commission itself sent formal letters to 17 stations applying for renewal of their licenses pointedly advising them of shortcomings in their public service programming. The FCC also refused to renew the licenses and issued temporary permits to the stations.

Moreover, in its 1955 report to Congress, the FCC said

. . . it is the duty of the individual broadcaster to operate in the public interest. That means, in addition to living up to technical requirements, he should give a well-rounded program service, with opportunity for local expression and discussion of matters of local concern.

[14] *Bay State Beacon* vs. *Federal Communications Commission,* App. D. C., 171 F. 2d, 826; *Kentucky Broadcasting Co.* v. *Federal Communications Commission,* App. D. C. 174 F. 2d, 38; *Johnson Broadcasting Co.* v. *Federal Communications Commission,* App. D. C., 175 F. 2d, 351; *Easton Publishing Co.* v. *Federal Communications Commission,* App. D. C., 175 F. 2d, 344.

The Commission does not prescribe any percentages of time which should be devoted to particular subjects, such as news, education, religion, music, public issue, etc. That is something which can vary with the locality. However, the Commission does periodically review the overall performance of a station —engineeringly [sic] and otherwise—when it applies for renewal of its license, to determine whether it has lived up to its obligations and the promises it made in obtaining permission to use the public's airwaves.

• THE CONSTITUTIONAL QUESTION •

The right of the Federal Communications Commission to engage in any kind of program review, even on an over-all basis, has been frequently challenged in court on the ground that such FCC action violates the censorship section of the Communications Act and constitutes an abridgment of the freedom of speech and press guaranteed by the First Amendment to the Constitution.

The FCC has defended its regulatory acts by arguing that television and radio, as licensed media of communication, are not in the same status as the press. The Commission holds that the purpose of the Communications Act is to maintain the control of the United States over broadcasting and that the law explicitly states that the right of free speech by television and radio shall not be impaired. To suggest that persons who are granted limited rights under licenses to run stations may, by their action, make television and radio unavailable to others as a medium of free speech is, in the opinion of the Commission, contrary to the intention of the law.

Wayne Coy, former chairman of the FCC, once said:

> If freedom of radio means that a licensee is entitled to do as he pleases without regard to the interests of the general public, then it may reasonably be contended that restraints on that freedom constitute acts of censorship. If, however, the freedom of radio means that radio should be available as a medium of freedom of expression for the general public, then it is obvious enough that restraints on the licensee which are designed to insure the preservation of that freedom are not acts of censorship.[15]

It is interesting to note that when the issue of constitutionality of radio regulation was raised twenty-five years ago, Secretary of Commerce Hoover commented, "we can surely agree that no one can raise a cry of deprivation of free speech if he is compelled to prove that there is something more than naked commercial selfishness in his purpose.[16]

These are issues which must ultimately be decided by the Supreme Court. Leading cases so far seem to support the Commission's position. Among the more recent Supreme Court decisions, the *Sanders* and the *Network* cases are perhaps the most important guides for deciding the extent of

---

[15] Address by Wayne Coy at the Yale Law School, January 22, 1949.
[16] Address by Herbert Hoover before the Fourth National Radio Conference, Washington, 1925.

Commission authority to review programming without committing an unlawful act of censorship.

The *Sanders* case, decided in 1940, concerned the question of whether the FCC was obliged to consider the economic injury that might result to existing stations in determining whether it shall grant or withhold a license to a new station. The Supreme Court concluded that there was no such obligation.

> An important element of public interest and convenience affecting the issue of a license is the ability of the licensee to render the best practicable service to the community reached by his broadcasts. That such ability may be assured the [Communications] Act contemplates inquiry by the Commission, *inter alia,* into an applicant's financial qualifications to operate the proposed station. But the Act does not essay to regulate the business of the licensee. The Commission is given no supervisory control of the programs, of business management, or of policy. In short, the broadcasting field is open to anyone, provided there be an available frequency over which he can broadcast without interference to others, if he shows his competency, the adequacy of his equipment, and financial ability to make good use of the assigned channel. . . . Plainly it is not the purpose of the Communications Act to protect a licensee against competition but to protect the public. Congress intended to leave competition in the business of broadcasting where it found it, to permit a licensee who was not interfering electrically with other broadcasters to survive or succumb according to his ability to make his programs attractive to the public.[17]

In the *Network* case CBS and NBC challenged the Commission's authority to issue the Chain Broadcasting Regulations on the ground, among others, that the regulations abridged freedom of speech under the First Amendment. The Supreme Court upheld the Commission's regulations and spoke as follows:

> . . . we are asked to regard the Commission as a kind of traffic officer, policing the wave lengths to prevent stations from interfering with each other. But the Act does not restrict the Commission merely to supervision of the traffic. *It puts upon the Commission the burden of determining the composition of that traffic . . .*
> The Commission's licensing function cannot be discharged . . . merely by finding that there are no technological objections to the granting of a license. If the criterion of "public interest" were limited to such matters, how could the Commission choose between two applicants for the same facilities, each of whom is financially and technically qualified to operate a station? . . .
> We come, finally, to an appeal to the First Amendment. The Regulations, even if valid in all other respects, must fail because they abridge, say the appellants, their right of free speech. If that be so, it would follow that every person whose application for a license to operate a station is denied by the Commission is thereby denied his constitutional right of free speech. Freedom of utterance is abridged to many who wish to use the limited facilities of

[17] *Federal Communications Commission* v. *Sanders Brothers' Radio,* 309 U.S. 470, 475 (1940).

radio. Unlike other modes of expression, radio inherently is not available to all. That is its unique characteristic, and that is why, unlike other modes of expression, it is subject to governmental regulation.[18]

This interpretation by the Supreme Court stands as the ruling case today. In a series of recent decisions in the District of Columbia Circuit Court of Appeals, the right of the Commission to consider various aspects of program policy or plans of the applicants for station licenses has been upheld.[19] The Supreme Court itself has cited, in a related case, its prior decisions in the *Sanders* and *Network* cases in further ruling that "Although the licensee's business as such is not regulated, the qualifications of the licensee and the character of its broadcasts may be weighed in determining whether or not to grant a license." [20] Nevertheless, the view persists among many important leaders in the broadcast industry that the public interest clause of the Communications Act of 1934 cannot constitutionally enlarge the function and authority of the FCC beyond that of being a traffic cop of the airwaves without violating the First Amendment to the Constitution.

· SUMMARY ·

The touchstone of broadcast regulation in the United States is the public interest. The Federal Communications Commission has tended to interpret the public interest in piece-meal fashion, proceeding from case to case, but more recently it has expressed a broader interpretation in such documents as the *Blue Book* and the *Mayflower* opinion. The authority of the Commission to review over-all program service to decide whether the public interest is being served has been upheld by various federal courts.

Questions for Discussion

1. What does freedom of broadcasting mean?
2. How can we decide whether a station is serving the public interest?
3. How has the FCC interpreted the "public interest" clause of the Communications Act?
4. How can we reconcile the prohibition against censorship and the FCC's practice of over-all program review in considering license renewals?
5. Should a fixed limit be maintained on the number of stations controlled by the same licensee?
6. What should be our policy toward newspaper ownership of television and radio stations?
7. Should the owner of a station "be given complete and exclusive control over program content, including the sole right to determine who shall speak and the right to censor any material intended for broadcast?"

[18] *National Broadcasting Company* v. *United States,* 319 U.S. 190 (1943). (Italics added.)

[19] See fn. 14, *supra.*

[20] *Regents of Georgia* v. *Carroll,* 338 U.S. 586, 598.

8. Should a broadcast licensee be permitted to use his station the way a publisher uses his newspaper, broadcasting editorials and supporting political causes and candidates?

9. How much time on the air should be made available to minority viewpoints?

10. What criteria for determining whether the public interest is being served are set forth in the *Blue Book* and what criticisms may be made of them?

11. Should television and radio stations be required to pay a federal tax for their broadcasting licenses?

❉ 10 ❉

Self-Regulation
in Broadcasting

IN ADDITION to formal regulation by the Federal Communications Commission, there exist in television and radio written and unwritten codes of regulation promulgated within the industry itself—the nation-wide television and radio codes of the National Association of Radio and Television Broadcasters, the continuity acceptance regulations of the networks and of various stations, the rules of certain groups of professional broadcasters, and informal but no less effective standards of talent and program acceptability by advertisers, agencies, networks, and stations.

As communications media that deal directly with the public, television and radio are especially sensitive to the currents of public opinion. The fields of book and magazine publishing and motion-picture production similarly are subject to public pressures related to the public ideas of acceptability in tastes, morals, and politics.

Television and radio enter our homes in such a way that we cannot fully anticipate what will come out of the loudspeaker or will appear on the television screen. Subject to the limitations of the Communications Act, stations and networks have the responsibility for deciding what programs may be broadcast in keeping with the public interest and the moral standards and tastes of the community. It is obvious to everyone that some precautions are necessary to prevent libel and breaches of common decency on the air. In areas beyond libel and decency, such as the moral values of television dramas or the political affiliations of actors and writers, there has been great dispute in recent years over the proper use of broadcasting's powers of self-regulation. The principles and practices of self-regulation, however interpreted and applied, play a great role in influencing the content and manner of presentation of television and radio programs.

• THE NARTB •

The main channel of self-regulation in television and radio is the national trade association of the industry—the National Association of Radio and Television Broadcasters (NARTB), which acts as a general clearing house for the broadcasting industry and has formalized a code of self-regulation.

The National Association of Radio and Television Broadcasters was organized in 1922 under the name of National Association of Broadcasters to resist pressures for royalties from the American Society of Composers, Authors, and Publishers (ASCAP) which controls important music copyrights.[1] The association developed during the course of years to service the needs of the broadcasting industry—to provide professional advice to members on employee regulations, to formulate engineering standards, to represent the industry before Congress and the public, to engage in research to show the public and commercial importance of television and radio, and to develop programming and advertising standards of acceptability. In 1954, the membership of the NARTB included 1,133 AM stations, 330 FM stations, and 260 TV stations, plus the national networks and over 100 equipment manufacturers and television film producing firms. Member stations of the NARTB pay annual dues based on their net income; it is estimated that 75 per cent of the NARTB's annual income comes from 25 per cent of its membership. In 1954, the organization's income amounted to about $900,000.

Of greatest interest and importance to the public are the codes of broadcast practice promulgated by the NARTB. In its more than thirty years of existence, the organization, seeking to establish uniform practices throughout the industry, has drawn up several codes of self-regulation. The first "Code of Ethics," in 1929, banned the broadcast of commercial announcements between 7 and 11 P.M. A new code ten years later permitted as much as twenty minutes of commercial announcements during evening hours. The present code for radio stations went into effect in 1948; the first television code was adopted in 1951 and went into effect the following year.

The NARTB has no legal power to enforce its codes, but member stations accept the association's standards if they want to remain in good standing. In an effort to put some teeth into the television code, the NARTB created a code review committee and authorized stations that observed the code to display the NARTB's "Seal of Good Practice." As self-proclaimed sets of principles, the codes serve as bases for criticism themselves as well as for criticism of television and radio programs. The problems discussed by the codes range from proper handling of news, controversy and religion, to children's and mystery programs, advertising standards, and contests. In general the codes represent compromises between the demands of network

---

[1] Llewellyn White, *The American Radio* (Chicago, 1947), p. 48.

and station managers who sought stringent rules to prevent advertising and programming abuses that caused public criticism of radio and television, and those managers who felt that more stringent codes would seriously injure the economic standing of the industry. Some critics believe the codes effected some compromises by linking high aspirations with mild restrictions.

Here, in full, is the television code of the NARTB. A close reading of the code reveals the wide range of problems faced by the industry and the ways in which the NARTB has attempted to meet those problems. The official purpose of the code, as set forth in its regulations and procedures "is cooperatively to maintain a level of television programming which gives full consideration to the educational, informational, cultural, economic, moral and entertainment needs of the American public to the end that more and more people will be better served."

TELEVISION CODE OF THE NARTB

Preamble

Television is seen and heard in every type of American home. These homes include children and adults of all ages, embrace all races and all varieties of religious faith, and reach those of every educational background. It is the responsibility of television to bear constantly in mind that the audience is primarily a home audience, and consequently that television's relationship to the viewers is that between guest and host.

The revenues from advertising support the free, competitive American system of telecasting, and make available to the eyes and ears of the American people the finest programs of information, education, culture and entertainment. By law the television broadcaster is responsible for the programming of his station. He, however, is obligated to bring his positive responsibility for excellence and good taste in programming to bear upon all who have a hand in the production of programs, including networks, sponsors, producers of film and of live programs, advertising agencies, and talent agencies.

The American businesses which utilize television for conveying their advertising messages to the home by pictures with sound, seen free-of-charge on the home screen, are reminded that their responsibilities are not limited to the sale of goods and the creation of a favorable attitude toward the sponsor by the presentation of entertainment. They include, as well, responsibility for utilizing television to bring the best programs, regardless of kind, into American homes.

Television, and all who participate in it are jointly accountable to the American public for respect for the special needs of children, for community responsibility, for the advancement of education and culture, for the acceptability of the program materials chosen, for decency and decorum in production, and for propriety in advertising. This responsibility cannot be discharged by any given group of programs, but can be discharged only through the highest standards of respect for the American home, applied to every moment of every program presented by television.

In order that television programming may best serve the public interest, viewers should be encouraged to make their criticisms and positive suggestions known to the television broadcasters. Parents in particular should be urged to see to it that out of the richness of television fare, the best programs are brought to the attention of their children.

Advancement of Education and Culture

1. Commercial television provides a valuable means of augmenting the educational and cultural influences of schools, institutions of higher learning, the home, the church, museums, foundations, and other institutions devoted to education and culture.
2. It is the responsibility of a television broadcaster to call upon such institutions for counsel and cooperation and to work with them on the best methods of presenting educational and cultural materials by television. It is further the responsibility of stations, networks, advertising agencies and sponsors consciously to seek opportunities for introducing into telecasts factual materials which will aid in the enlightenment of the American public.
3. Education via television may be taken to mean that process by which the individual is brought toward informed adjustment to his society. Television is also responsible for the presentation of overtly instructional and cultural programs, scheduled so as to reach the viewers who are naturally drawn to such programs, and produced so as to attract the largest possible audience.
4. In furthering this realization, the television broadcaster:
   (a) Should be thoroughly conversant with the educational and cultural needs and desires of the community served.
   (b) Should affirmatively seek out responsible and accountable educational and cultural institutions of the community with a view toward providing opportunities for the instruction and enlightenment of the viewers.
   (c) Should provide for reasonable experimentation in the development of programs specifically directed to the advancement of the community's culture and education.

Acceptability of Program Material

Program materials should enlarge the horizons of the viewer, provide him with wholesome entertainment, afford helpful stimulation, and remind him of the responsibilities which the citizen has towards his society. Furthermore:
   (a) (i) Profanity, obscenity, smut and vulgarity are forbidden, even when likely to be understood only by part of the audience. From time to time, words which have been acceptable, acquired undesirable meanings, and telecasters should be alert to eliminate such words.
   (ii) Words (especially slang) derisive of any race, color, creed, nationality or national derivation, except wherein such usage would be for the specific purpose of effective dramatization such as combating prejudice, are forbidden, even when likely to be understood only by part of the audience. From time to time, words which have been acceptable acquire undesirable meanings, and telecasters should be alert to eliminate such words.
   (iii) The Television Code Review Board shall maintain and issue to subscribers, from time to time, a continuing list of specific words and phrases which should not be used in keeping with this subsection. This list, however, shall not be considered as all inclusive.

(*b*) (i) Attacks on religion and religious faiths are not allowed.

(ii) Reverence is to mark any mention of the name of God, His attributes and powers.

(iii) When religious rites are included in other than religious programs the rites are accurately presented and the ministers, priests and rabbis portrayed in their callings are vested with the dignity of their office and under no circumstances are to be held up to ridicule.

(*c*) (i) Contests may not constitute a lottery.

(ii) Any telecasting designed to "buy" the television audience by requiring it to listen and/or view in hope of reward, rather than for the quality of the program, should be avoided.

(*d*) Respect is maintained for the sanctity of marriage and the value of the home. Divorce is not treated casually nor justified as a solution for marital problems.

(*e*) Illicit sex relations are not treated as commendable.

(*f*) Sex crimes and abnormalities are generally unacceptable as program material.

(*g*) Drunkenness and narcotic addiction are never presented as desirable or prevalent.

(*h*) The administration of illegal drugs will not be displayed.

(*i*) The use of liquor in program content shall be de-emphasized. The consumption of liquor in American life, when not required by the plot or for proper characterization, shall not be shown.

(*j*) The use of gambling devices or scenes necessary to the development of plot or as appropriate background is acceptable only when presented with discretion and in moderation, and in a manner which would not excite interest in, or foster, betting nor be instructional in nature. Telecasts of actual sports programs at which on-the-scene betting is permitted by law should be presented in a manner in keeping with Federal, state and local laws, and should concentrate on the subject as a public sporting event.

(*k*) In reference to physical or mental afflictions and deformities, special precautions must be taken to avoid ridiculing sufferers from similar ailments and offending them or members of their families.

(*l*) Exhibitions of fortune-telling, astrology, phrenology, palm-reading, and numerology are acceptable only when required by a plot or the theme of a program, and then the presentation should be developed in a manner designed not to foster superstition or excite interest or belief in these subjects.

(*m*) Televised drama shall not simulate news or special events in such a way as to mislead or alarm (*see News*).

(*n*) Legal, medical and other professional advice, diagnosis and treatment will be permitted only in conformity with law and recognized ethical and professional standards.

(*o*) The presentation of cruelty, greed and selfishness as worthy motivations is to be avoided.

(*p*) Excessive or unfair exploitation of others or of their physical or mental afflictions shall not be presented as praiseworthy.

(*q*) Criminality shall be presented as undesirable and unsympathetic.

The condoning of crime and the treatment of the commission of crime in a frivolous, cynical or callous manner is unacceptable.

(r) The presentation of techniques of crime in such detail as to invite imitation shall be avoided.

(s) The use of horror for its own sake will be eliminated; the use of visual or aural effects which would shock or alarm the viewer, and the detailed presentation of brutality or physical agony by sight or by sound are not permissable.

(t) Law enforcement shall be upheld, and the officers of the law are to be portrayed with respect and dignity.

(u) The presentation of murder or revenge as a motive for murder shall not be presented as justifiable.

(v) Suicide as an acceptable solution for human problems is prohibited.

(w) The exposition of sex crimes will be avoided.

(x) The appearances or dramatization of persons featured in actual crime news will be permitted only in such light as to aid law enforcement or to report the news event.

(y) Treatment of animals. The use of animals, both in the production of television programs and as a part of television program content, shall at all times, be in conformity with accepted standards of humane treatment.

Responsibility Toward Children

1. The education of children involves giving them a sense of the world at large. Crime, violence and sex are a part of the world they will be called upon to meet, and a certain amount of proper presentation of such is helpful in orienting the child to his social surroundings. However, violence and illicit sex shall not be presented in an attractive manner, nor to an extent such as will lead a child to believe that they play a greater part in life than they do. They should not be presented without indications of the resultant retribution and punishment.

2. It is not enough that only those programs which are intended for viewing by children shall be suitable to the young and immature. (*Attention is called to the general items listed under Acceptability of Program Materials.*) Television is responsible for insuring that programs of all sorts which occur during the times of day when children may normally be expected to have the opportunity of viewing television shall exercise care in the following regards:

   (a) In affording opportunities for cultural growth as well as for wholesome entertainment.

   (b) In developing programs to foster and promote the commonly accepted moral, social and ethical ideals characteristic of American life.

   (c) In reflecting respect for parents, for honorable behavior, and for the constituted authorities of the American community.

   (d) In eliminating reference to kidnapping of children or threats of kidnapping.

   (e) In avoiding material which is excessively violent or would create morbid suspense, or other undesirable reactions in children.

   (f) In exercising particular restraint and care in crime or mystery episodes involving children or minors.

Decency and Decorum in Production

1. The costuming of all performers shall be within the bounds of propriety and shall avoid such exposure or such emphasis on anatomical detail as would embarrass or offend home viewers.
2. The movements of dancers, actors, or other performers shall be kept within the bounds of decency, and lewdness and impropriety shall not be suggested in the positions assumed by performers.
3. Camera angles shall avoid such views of performers as to emphasize anatomical details indecently.
4. Racial or nationality types shall not be shown on television in such a manner as to ridicule the race or nationality.
5. The use of locations closely associated with sexual life or with sexual sin must be governed by good taste and delicacy.

Community Responsibility

A television broadcaster and his staff occupy a position of responsibility in the community and should conscientiously endeavor to be acquainted fully with its needs and characteristics in order better to serve the welfare of its citizens.

Treatment of News and Public Events

News

1. A television station's news schedule should be adequate and well-balanced.
2. News reporting should be factual, fair and without bias.
3. Commentary and analysis should be clearly identified as such.
4. Good taste should prevail in the selection and handling of news:
   Morbid, sensational or alarming details not essential to the factual report, especially in connection with stories of crime or sex, should be avoided. News should be telecast in such a manner as to avoid panic and unnecessary alarm.
5. At all times pictorial and verbal material for both news and comment should conform to other sections of these standards, wherever such sections are reasonably applicable.
6. Pictorial material should be chosen with care and not presented in a misleading manner.
7. A television broadcaster should exercise due care in his supervision of content, format, and presentation of newscasts originated by his station, and in his selection of newscasters, commentators, and analysts.
8. A television broadcaster should exercise particular discrimination in the acceptance, placement and presentation of advertising in news programs so that such advertising should be clearly distinguishable from the news content.
9. A television broadcaster should not present fictional events or other non-news material as authentic news telecasts or announcements, nor should he permit dramatizations in any program which would give the false impression that the dramatized material constitutes news. Expletives, (presented aurally or pictorially) such as "flash" or "bulletin" and statements such as "we interrupt this program to bring you . . . " should be reserved

specifically for news room use. However, a television broadcaster may properly exercise discretion in the use in non-news programs of words or phrases which do not necessarily imply that the material following is a news release.

Public Events

1. A television broadcaster has an affirmative responsibility at all times to be informed of public events, and to provide coverage consonant with the ends of an informed and enlightened citizenry.
2. Because of the nature of events open to the public, the treatment of such events by a television broadcaster should be effected in a manner to provide for adequate and informed coverage as well as good taste in presentation.

Controversial Public Issues

1. Television provides a valuable forum for the expression of responsible views or public issues of a controversial nature. In keeping therewith the television broadcaster should seek out and develop with accountable individuals, groups and organizations, programs relating to controversial public issues of import to its fellow citizens and to give fair representation to opposing sides of issues which materially affect the life or welfare of a substantial segment of the public.
2. The provision of time for this purpose should be guided by the following principles:
    (a) Requests by individuals, groups or organizations for time to discuss their views on controversial public issues, should be considered on the basis of their individual merits, and in the light of the contribution which the use requested would make to the public interest, and to a well-balanced program structure.
    (b) Programs devoted to the discussion of controversial public issues should be identified as such, and should not be presented in a manner which would mislead listeners or viewers to believe that the program is purely of an entertainment, news, or other character.

Political Telecasts

Political telecasts should be clearly identified as such, and should not be presented by a television broadcaster in a manner which would mislead listeners or viewers to believe that the program is of any other character.

Religious Programs

1. It is the responsibility of a television broadcaster to make available to the community as part of a well-balanced program schedule adequate opportunity for religious presentations.
2. The following principles should be followed in the treatment of such programs:
    (a) Telecasting which reaches men of all creeds simultaneously should avoid attacks upon religion.

(b) Religious programs should be presented respectfully and accurately and without prejudice or ridicule.

(c) Religious programs should be presented by responsible individuals, groups and organizations.

(d) Religious programs should place emphasis on broad religious truths, excluding the presentation of controversial or partisan views not directly or necessarily related to religion or morality.

3. In the allocation of time for telecasts of religious programs it is recommended that the television station use its best efforts to apportion such time fairly among the representative faith groups of its community.

Presentation of Advertising

1. Ever mindful of the role of television as a guest in the home, a television broadcaster should exercise unceasing care to supervise the form in which advertising material is presented over his facilities. Since television is a developing medium, involving methods and techniques distinct from those of radio, it may be desirable, from time to time, to review and revise the presently suggested practices.

(a) Advertising messages should be presented with courtesy and good taste; disturbing or annoying material should be avoided; every effort should be made to keep the advertising message in harmony with the content and general tone of the program in which it appears.

(b) A sponsor's advertising messages should be confined within the framework of the sponsor's program structure. A television broadcaster should seek to avoid the use of commercial announcements which are divorced from the program either by preceding the introduction of the program (as in the case of so-called "cow-catcher" announcements) or by following the apparent sign-off of the program (as in the case of so-called "trailer" announcements). To this end, the program itself should be announced and clearly identified before the sponsor's advertising material is first used, and should be signed off after the sponsor's advertising material is last used.

(c) Advertising copy should contain no claims intended to disparage competitors, competing products, or other industries, professions or institutions.

(d) Since advertising by television is a dynamic technique, a television broadcaster should keep under surveillance new advertising devices so that the spirit and purpose of these standards are fulfilled.

(e) Television broadcasters should exercise the utmost care and discrimination with regard to advertising material, including content, placement and presentation, near or adjacent to programs designed for children. No considerations of expediency should be permitted to impinge upon the vital responsibility towards children and adolescents, which is inherent in television, and which must be recognized and accepted by all advertisers employing television.

(f) Television advertisers should be encouraged to devote portions of their allotted advertising messages and program time to the support of worthy causes in the public interest in keeping with the highest ideals of the free competitive system.

(*g*) A charge for television time to churches and religious bodies is not recommended.

Acceptability of Advertisers and Products

GENERAL

1. A commercial television broadcaster makes his facilities available for the advertising of products and services and accepts commercial presentations for such advertising. However, a television broadcaster should, in recognition of his responsibility to the public, refuse the facilities of his station to an advertiser where he has good reason to doubt the integrity of the advertiser, the truth of the advertising representations, or the compliance of the advertiser with the spirit and purpose of all applicable legal requirements. Moreover, in consideration of the laws and customs of the communities served, each television broadcaster should refuse his facilities to the advertisement of products and services, or the use of advertising scripts, which the station has good reason to believe would be objectionable to a substantial and responsible segment of the community. The foregoing principles should be applied with judgment and flexibility, taking into consideration the characteristics of the medium and the form and content of the particular presentation. In general, because a television broadcast is designed for the home and the family, including children, the following principles should govern the business classifications listed below:
    (*a*) The advertising of hard liquor should not be accepted.
    (*b*) The advertising of beer and wines is acceptable only when presented in the best of good taste and discretion, and is acceptable subject to federal and local laws.
    (*c*) Advertising by institutions or enterprises which in their offers of instruction imply promises of employment or make exaggerated claims for the opportunities awaiting those who enroll for courses is generally unacceptable.
    (*d*) The advertising of firearms and fireworks is acceptable only subject to federal and local laws.
    (*e*) The advertising of fortune-telling, occultism, spiritualism, astrology, phrenology, palm-reading, numerology, mind-reading or character-reading is not acceptable.
    (*f*) Because all products of a personal nature create special problems, such products, when accepted, should be treated with especial emphasis on ethics and the canons of good taste; however, the advertising of intimately personal products which are generally regarded as unsuitable conversational topics in mixed social groups are not acceptable.
    (*g*) The advertising of tip sheets, race track publications, or organizations seeking to advertise for the purpose of giving odds or promoting betting or lotteries is unacceptable.
2. Diligence should be exercised to the end that advertising copy accepted for telecasting complies with pertinent federal, state and local laws.
3. An advertiser who markets more than one product should not be permitted to use advertising copy devoted to an acceptable product for purposes of publicizing the brand name or other identification of a product which is not acceptable.

Advertising of Medical Products

1. The advertising of medical products presents considerations of intimate and far-reaching importance to the consumer, and the following principles and procedures should apply in the advertising thereof.
   (*a*) A television broadcaster should not accept advertising material which in his opinion offensively describes or dramatizes distress or morbid situations involving ailments, by spoken word, sound or visual effects.
   (*b*) Because of the personal nature of the advertising of medical products, claims that a product will effect a cure and the indiscriminate use of such words as "safe", "without risk", "harmless", or terms of similar meaning should not be accepted in the advertising of medical products on television stations.

Contests

1. Contests should offer the opportunity to all contestants to win on the basis of ability and skill, rather than chance.
2. All contest details, including rules, eligibility requirements, opening and termination dates should be clearly and completely announced and/or shown or easily accessible to the viewing public, and the winners' names should be released and prizes awarded as soon as possible after the close of the contest.
3. When advertising is accepted which requests contestants to submit items of product identification or other evidence of purchase of product, reasonable facsimiles thereof should be made acceptable.
4. All copy pertaining to any contest (except that which is required by law) associated with the exploitation or sale of the sponsor's product or service, and all references to prizes or gifts offered in such connection should be considered a part of and included in the total time allowances as herein provided. (*See Time Standards for Advertising Copy.*)

Premiums and Offers

1. Full details of proposed offers should be required by the television broadcaster for investigation and approval before the first announcement of the offer is made to the public.
2. A final date for the termination of an offer should be announced as far in advance as possible.
3. Before accepting for telecast offers involving a monetary consideration, a television broadcaster should satisfy himself as to the integrity of the advertiser and the advertiser's willingness to honor complaints indicating dissatisfaction with the premium by returning the monetary consideration.
4. There should be no misleading descriptions or visual representations of any premiums or gifts which would distort or enlarge their value in the minds of the listeners.
5. Assurances should be obtained from the advertiser that premiums offered are not harmful to person or property.
6. Premiums should not be approved which appeal to superstition on the basis of "luck-bearing" powers or otherwise.

Time Standards for Advertising Copy

1. In accordance with good telecast advertising practices, the time standards for advertising copy are as follows:

Length of Program (minutes)	News Programs Day and Night	Length of Advertising Message (minutes and seconds)	
		All Other Programs	
		Class "A" Time	All Other Hrs.
5	1:00	1:00	1:15
10	1:45	2:00	2:10
15	2:15	2:30	3:00
25		2:50	4:00
30		3:00	4:15
45		4:30	5:45
60		6:00	7:00

2. Reasonable and limited identification of prize and statement of the donor's name within formats wherein the presentation of contest awards or prizes is a necessary and integral part of program content shall not be included as commercial time within the meaning of paragraph 1. above; however, any oral or visual presentation concerning the product or its donor, over and beyond such identification and statement, shall be included as commercial time within the meaning of paragraph 1. above.

3. The time standards set forth above do not affect the established practice of reserving for station use the last 30 seconds of each program for station break and spot announcements.

4. Announcement programs are designed to accommodate a designated number of individual live or recorded announcements, generally one minute in length, which are carried within the body of the program and are available for sale to individual advertisers. Normally not more than 3 one-minute announcements (which should not exceed approximately 125 words if presented live) should be scheduled within a 15-minute period and not more than six such announcements should be scheduled within a 30-minute period in local announcement programs; however, fewer announcements of greater individual length may be scheduled, provided that the aggregate length of the announcements approximates three minutes in a 15-minute program or six minutes in a 30-minute program. In announcement programs other than 15 minutes or 30 minutes in length, the proportion of one minute of announcement within every five minutes of programming is normally applied. The announcements must be presented within the framework of the program period designated for their use and kept in harmony with the content of the program in which they are placed.

5. Programs presenting women's services, features, shopping guides, market information, and similar material, provide a special service to the listening and viewing public in which advertising material is an informative and integral part of the program content. Because of these special characteristics the time standards set forth above may be waived to a reasonable extent.

6. Even though the commercial time limitations of the Code do not specifi-

cally prohibit back-to-back announcements, such a practice is not recommended for more than two announcements, either at station break or within the framework of a single program.

7. Any casual reference by talent in a program to another's product or service under any trade name or language sufficiently descriptive to identify it should, except for normal guest identifications, be condemned and discouraged.

8. Stationary backdrops or properties in television presentations showing the sponsor's name or product, the name of his product, his trade-mark or slogan may be used only incidentally. They should not obtrude on program interest or entertainment. "On Camera" shots of such materials should be fleeting, not too frequent, and mindful of the need of maintaining a proper program balance.

Dramatized Appeals and Advertising

Appeals to help fictitious characters in television programs by purchasing the advertiser's product or service or sending for a premium should not be permitted, and such fictitious characters should not be introduced into the advertising message for such purposes. When dramatized advertising material involves statements by doctors, dentists, nurses or other professional people, the material should be presented by members of such profession reciting actual experience or it should be made apparent from the presentation itself that the portrayal is dramatized.

Sponsor Identification

Identification of sponsorship must be made in all sponsored programs in accordance with the requirements of the Communications Act of 1934, as amended, and the Rules and Regulations of the Federal Communications Commission.

· TELEVISION CODE REVIEW BOARD ·

The regulations and procedures of the code provide for annual review of the code by the Television Board of Directors of the NARTB and sets up a Television Code Review Board, consisting of five members, with the following authority and responsibilities:

(1) To maintain a continuing review of all television programming, especially that of subscribers to the television code of the NARTB; (2) to receive, screen, and clear complaints concerning television programming; (3) to define and interpret words and phrases in the Television Code; (4) to develop and maintain appropriate liaison with governmental agencies and with responsible and accountable organizations and institutions; (5) to inform, expeditiously and properly, a subscriber to the Television Code of complaints or commendations, as well as to advise all subscribers concerning the attitude and desires program-wise of accountable organizations and institutions, and of the American public in general; (6) to review and monitor, if necessary, any particular series of programs, daily programming, or any

other program presentations of a subscriber, as well as to request recordings, aural or kinescope, or script and copy, with regard to any particular program presented by a subscriber; (7) to reach conclusions, and to make recommendations or prefer charges to the Television Board of Directors concerning violations and breaches of the Television Code by a subscriber; (8) to recommend to the Television Board of Directors amendments to the Television Code.

The work of the Television Code Review Board has been more active than many critics expected. After its first year of operation, the Chairman of the Review Board reported that it had handled hundreds of decisions and that it had conducted its work behind-the-scenes without publicity in an effort to win voluntary compliance with the code by broadcasters.

· THE NARTB RADIO CODE ·

The NARTB standards of practice for radio broadcasters is a much shorter document than the television code, although it covers much the same ground. Advertising time limitations are the same as in the television code, and general program standards reveal an almost identical approach. There is, however, no code review board to supervise the adherence of NARTB members to the radio code.

· NETWORK AND STATION CODES ·

Because the NARTB codes do not go into detail or take a firm stand on many questions that arise in connection with putting programs and commercials on the air, networks and stations have formulated their own standards of broadcast practices that are generally compatible with the NARTB code but spell out network and station policy in specific situations. For example, the NBC *Manual on Radio and Television Broadcast Standards* contains almost fifty pages that set forth network policy on acceptable program and advertising content and operating procedures of the Continuity Acceptance Department which screens all programs for the network. As a general operating practice, compliance is obtained voluntarily through frank discussions with program producers and advertising agencies. Self-regulation normally works quietly and effectively and achieves little or no publicity. Prepared scripts are reviewed in advance of broadcast by the Continuity Acceptance Departments of stations and networks. Statements or words that violate broadcast standards may be removed from all except political campaign talks. If a subject is very controversial, a speaker may be advised of station requirements before he writes his script, and he is checked against the prepared script during broadcast. Advertising copy that breaches the station's rules is returned to the agency for revision. Constructive suggestions are often advanced to show how a script may be changed to conform to policy. Staff announcers and commentators are informed of station policy and then entrusted with observing it in their broadcast remarks. Extemporaneous or ad-lib interviews, quizzes, and forums are checked during broadcast. Although a flip of a switch by an engineer can cut short an off-color remark before its completion, such action is only rarely necessary. It is the unintentional slip of speech or unexpected recalcitrance by a performer or speaker that causes difficulty. In large television variety shows, a representative of Continuity Acceptance often attends dress rehearsals to check on costumes, dances, and physical action that has been indicated in the script. It is interesting to note that the NBC manual states the following procedures to be followed upon the failure of program producers to observe the network's rules for continuity acceptance:

> Where material proposed for radio or television broadcast appears to NBC to be questionable, the matter is promptly referred to the agency or talent concerned and every effort is made to arrive at a satisfactory disposition so that the presentation will avoid offense to the public. If the matter cannot be resolved in this manner, and the talent or agency refuses to delete or revise material which NBC believes objectionable, NBC immediately determines what action is to be taken and explains its position to the senior radio or television executive who is available in the agency concerned. If a satisfactory solution is not obtained by this means, the client is advised of the action which will be taken by NBC.
>
> Under such circumstances, it is NBC's policy to delete objectionable portions of a program during actual broadcast as a matter of last resort and only in instances where the material is clearly offensive and contrary to good broadcasting standards. When such deletion can be accomplished in television programs by the diversion of camera to an unobjectionable portion of the presentation without interrupting the continuity of the program, this practice is followed; where, however, the continuity must be interrupted to delete offensive material in radio or television programs, such material is faded, and the following announcement is presented during the period of the deletion: "The National Broadcasting Company regrets the necessity of interrupting this program in order to delete material which in its opinion would be objectionable to listeners (viewers) in many American homes." [2]

· CHILDREN'S PROGRAMMING ·

Self-regulation is not limited, however, to prohibitions; it also extends to the statement of network policy favoring certain program values. Thus, various executive memoranda at NBC have stressed to all program producers the importance of integrating elements of enlightenment in all entertainment programs. The statement on children's programs prepared by NBC's Children's Program Review Committee, appointed in 1955, is another example of this type of self-regulation. In an effort to obtain an expert evaluation of its own children's programming by leaders in American life, NBC organized a committee consisting of three expert educators and

[2] Quoted by permission of the National Broadcasting Company.

appointed a supervisor of children's programs. After a study of several months, the committee issued a report in part commendatory and in part frankly critical of the network's programming for children. The following excerpts from the committee's report are of especial interest in showing how a network has attempted to regulate its own programming operations:

REPORT OF NBC'S CHILDREN'S PROGRAM REVIEW COMMITTEE

Preliminary Observations

1. The committee recognizes that whatever is planned for children must seem good to them as well as be good for them. The committee believes there is no fundamental conflict between the popular and the healthy and that good shows can be more permanently popular than bad ones.
2. Educational television is here. We mean by this much more than academic instruction. We include in it those programs which enlighten and inform and contribute to the understanding and appreciation of our world and of each other. Such programs have been brought to the public as truly by NBC as by any stations specifically labeled "educational." There are numberless opportunities for enlightenment available to people who select them.
3. The problem of network programming is seriously complicated by time zones. The differential in timing means that legitimate adult programs broadcast at one time from one section of the country may be heard at a less suitable time in another section. We recognize that kinescopes . . . are costly and that until other devices are perfected it will be almost impossible for any network to satisfy the children's requirements everywhere in the country. It will always be wholly impossible to satisfy these requirements unless the networks have the co-operation of parents and others who are responsible for guiding children in the use of television, as in all other areas of their experience. . . .

Concerns

The committee has examined network programs designed for children or for family viewing. We have noted a number of weaknesses on present programs, some occasional, some fairly frequent. We are concerned about the following:

1. EFFECT ON PARENT-CHILD RELATIONSHIPS of suggested or demonstrated action which would be forbidden at home. (Destroying public property, shooting seltzer water and throwing things at each other.)
2. OVER-EXCITEMENT of a solid hour or more of disjointed, sometimes frenetic action.
3. BAD GRAMMAR, POOR PRONUNCIATION, NAME CALLING except for strictly character parts clearly identified.
4. OVERDONE, DESTRUCTIVE AND TOO FREQUENT SLAPSTICK of questionable taste.
5. CRUDENESS. Participants in a few programs are encouraged to do things which we would hope would never happen in normal society. Playing a trombone with a mouth full of watermelon is a sample of so-called humor which is more messy than funny.

6. ACTION, CAMERA SHOTS AND ADMONITION TENDING TO frighten children. (Even good advice warning children against danger can often be terrifying.)
7. EXPLOITATION BY PROGRAM BUILDERS OF CHILDREN ON SHOWS. (Although there is room for good juvenile talent programs, the use of youngsters merely to amuse an adult audience is undesirable. Simulated or forced spontaneous endorsement of commercial products by children is bad.)
8. OVER-EMPHASIS ON MONEY and exorbitant rewards for chance performance. (The something-for-nothing idea on some of these shows seems to be thoroughly bad education.)
9. MISUSE OF COMMERCIALS. (Presenting toys as "educational" when only the manufacturer calls them that, is bad. High pressure on young children to urge parents to buy could complicate family relations.)
10. MISGUIDED ENLIGHTENMENT. (Sincere effort on some programs to inject enlightenment is thwarted when the information is inaccurate or couched in terms which children cannot understand. Advice to children hurried in as an afterthought at the end of a frenzied finale is not apt to be effective.)
11. INSUFFICIENT ENLIGHTENMENT. NBC's excellent policy of integrated enlightenment has not yet been as effectively realized on programs designed for children as on those designed for the family as a whole. We believe that the children's programming should, if anything, have a higher proportion of enlightenment, not only because the early years are formative, but because children want to learn, to grow up and to broaden their vision. In fact, our investigations have shown that even children of seven and eight criticize some programs because of the lack of informative material.
12. GROUP RELATIONS. (There seems to be a need for more positive help to children in understanding people unlike themselves. Races and nationality groups need to be presented intelligently as well as sentimentally.)
13. STEREOTYPES, IN PLOT AND CHARACTER. There are too many stereotypes (Indians and others) in some of the older Western movies. The hero and the villain as symbols of all-good and all-bad tend to suggest black and white distinctions and misrepresent ordinary experience. We also question the emphasis on an unconquerable hero who takes all responsibility, and sometimes the law itself, into his own hands.

Recommendations

The concerns which have been listed in the preceding section call for general correction. In order to accomplish that purpose and to effect some other improvements, the committee submits the following suggestions.

1. THE CODE. It may be desirable to add to the existing code a positive emphasis on the fact that the company expresses its intent to render public service as well as entertainment through its children's programs. The code might include a few specifications of possible educational value such as fostering proper language, correct grammar, and a better understanding of the world in which we live. . . .
2. TEEN-AGE PROGRAMS. While recognizing that teen-agers are apt to prefer family or adult shows, the committee feels that special attention might well be given to this group in preparing programs. They seem to be neglected as compared with the younger children.

3. CHILDREN'S HOUR. The committee feels that the 5:00 to 6:00 P.M. hour on weekdays and on Saturday morning shows might well be geared to the 6-12-year-old groups. Including this older range would seem to contribute to family well-being, since the willingness of older children to listen, at those hours, would help to keep the younger interested and in general contribute to family harmony.

We have assumed that weekday mornings from 9:00 to 11:00 will continue to be good hours for nursery school programs and programs for mothers.

4. CHILDREN AS PARTICIPANTS. We believe that the exploitation of children would be avoided by acceptance of the following standards:

(a) Any children used in commercials should be professional actors and actresses. Neither show guests, nor children from the audience, should be made unwitting endorsers of the sponsor's product. This refers to both audio and visual endorsements such as might occur when a child is asked to hold a product on camera, or is asked to eat, drink, or otherwise use the product and express an opinion or reaction regarding it.

(b) Children may possibly be used in games, contests (including those of the "Amateur Hour" variety), skits, etc., which do not submit them to danger, embarrassment, etc., but they should be selected before air time and instructed as to what will be expected of them. This before-air-time selection of children would prevent embarrassment and unhappiness of being turned down or ignored before a television audience.

(c) A child or children may be used on a show to "participate for the the viewer" (as on "Mr. Wizard"), in receiving explanations and asking questions. The number of children used in this way, however, should never be so great that they cannot actually participate in the discussions or activity. Provision should be made so that they can sit quietly while explanations are being made or directions given.

(d) If audience shots of children are used, they should be simply shots of children as interested spectators with no participation, questions, answers, etc., expected from them, except perhaps for group singing or group reactions. Should other participations, ad libs, etc., arise, they should not be exploited.

(e) In no case should ad lib remarks be definitely elicited in order to make entertainment of them for adults because they are ludicrous, humorous, or possibly off-color. Adult promotion of the "cute" in children can be more harmful when it departs from the simple adult approval which all children need, to become adult pressure to earn favor by acting up beyond one's age. It would seem wise to script and rehearse, insofar as possible, the participation of young children on television shows. This might conceivably eliminate some of the freshness and spontaneity, but at the same time it would go far toward eliminating embarrassing and unfortunate incidents.

5. WESTERNS. The committee recognizes the progress that has been made in Western programs—such as the avoidance of killing, the emphasis on folk-song and scenery, and the hero's responsibility to get the law-breaker to court rather than to punish or kill him out of hand. We do not classify

these programs with out-and-out crime programs, partly because they are far removed in time and often place from a child's life, and we would agree with Professor Sheldon Glueck's statement that on the whole they "serve more as a harmless, vicarious outlet than as a harmful influence." Nevertheless, we have two suggestions to make. First, we wonder if Westerns could be places for a positive program for enlightenment by including nature lore and folklore. Second, we believe there is too much time allocated to Westerns on some of the [NBC] Owned & Operated stations, and we recommend that better balance be achieved through the introduction of other types of adventure programs and other subject matter as outlined in the next paragraph.

6. NEED FOR BALANCE. The schedule of children's programs needs more balance, in order to do fuller justice to our young people's wide range of interests, as well as their exploratory urge. Studies indicate that they would welcome:

   (a) More how-to-do-it shows, including arts and craft and other activities such as gardening, fixing things around the house, and community clean-up programs.
   (b) Field trips and visits to interesting, instructive places such as tunnels under construction, factories, the Post Office.
   (c) More music—particularly folk-music from other lands; introduction to instruments and the classics.
   (d) Greater contact with the people and customs of other countries, as as well as travel to strange and interesting places in the wide, wide world.
   (e) Hobby material, to open the child's eyes to a broad range of activities.
   (f) More storytelling, told and dramatized simply.
   (g) Child-animal series using situations and conveying ideas that can be readily transferred by the child-viewer to his own life.
   (h) Adventure programs other than Westerns and space serials—for example exploration.

7. COMMERCIALS. When commercials are incorporated into shows and performers are used to sponsor any commercial item, the commercial should conform to all the standards desirable for children's programs in general.

8. OVERUSE OF FEATURE. We note a natural tendency to overdo certain popular features and personalities. For example, we know that people like cartoons, but some of the children's programs are using so many that we fear a public reaction against all of them. We would suggest less repetition in order to maintain longer interest. This applies to slapstick as well as to cartoons.

9. EXPERT ADVICE. Sensitive areas of social behavior should be discussed with experts in the specialized fields, preferably by script writers; e.g., mental health, child adoption, religion, social welfare. . . .

• UNWRITTEN CODES AND PRESSURES •

The formal codes and declarations of principles do not, however, tell the full story of self-regulation in broadcasting. Much of the self-regulation in television and radio is conducted in an unofficial and unwritten way. The broadcasters, working in a context of conflicting political, economic, and social forces, are under continual pressure from influential majority and minority groups that want to ban certain speakers, performers, writers, or topics from the air. Religious, racial, professional, political, and trade organizations may request a station or network not to carry programs which, in their opinion, reflect unfavorably on them. Some of these groups hope to bring about social improvement by working for the elimination of unfavorable racial stereotypes or provocative themes and actions. Lawyers, policemen, teachers, and workers in other specialized fields frequently object to the way a member of their profession is portrayed in a dramatic presentation. Some religious groups in certain areas have sufficient influence to persuade a station not to carry discussions of controversial questions although representatives of that religion may have been invited to participate in the discussion.

The desire to avoid becoming the object of public controversy of any sort is possibly the most influential factor in the unwritten codes of self-regulation. Charges have repeatedly been made that advertising agencies and networks have secret blacklists of performers and writers who have been deemed to be "controversial" and therefore unacceptable because of their political or personal associations.[3]

In 1950, the sponsor of a program series in which a well-known actress was to be featured, received a number of protests that she was a Communist. Despite the actress' vigorous denials that she had ever been a Communist or had Communistic leanings, the sponsor withdrew her from the program on the grounds that she had become a "controversial personality" whose presence on the show might adversely affect the sale of the advertiser's products.

Many critics who agree that television and radio performers must be acceptable to the public strongly object to the use of publications like Red Channels or other lists to determine whether a performer is qualified to go on the air without evaluating the accuracy or significance of the charges against the performer or providing even the semblance of a hearing. Thus, Jack Gould, radio-TV critic of the New York Times, has stated: "With Red Channels the business community in broadcasting simply abdicated its citizenship in as dismal an hour as radio and TV ever had."[4] Still others have argued that networks and agencies are not competent to evaluate political affiliations of performers, and that the acceptability of a performer for broadcast work should be related solely to competence in performance. This is a tangled and difficult question and extends beyond the area of politics and Communism and extends to the general moral acceptability of performers and writers. The playwright, George S. Kaufman, was removed at the instance of a sponsor of a CBS panel show in 1952 for quipping on

[3] See Merle Miller, The Judges and the Judged (New York, 1952).
[4] New York Times, June 6, 1954, Section X, p. 11.

a pre-Christmas program "Let's make this one program on which no one sings 'Silent Night.' " Several hundred letters and telephone calls objected to the remark on the ground that it was "antireligious" and in questionable taste. After receiving numerous protests against the removal, CBS restored Mr. Kaufman to the show when it went sustaining a few weeks later, even though the advertiser had been unwilling for the remaining weeks of his sponsorship to allow Mr. Kaufman to return.

The doctrine which holds that a person against whom charges are made, regardless of his actual innocence or the irrevelance of the charges, is thereby made "controversial" and unacceptable for broadcasting purposes has also produced the unintended result of rendering controversial the very people who make the charges or publicly approve the doctrine and actively support it. To a large extent, the problem with which broadcasters, advertisers, and performers contend is a reflection of national tensions in a difficult world situation.

· PROFESSIONAL ASSOCIATIONS ·

Several professional broadcasting associations concerned with the working standards of their members have been established.

These include the Association of Radio News Analysts, the National Association of Radio and Television News Directors, the Radio and Television Directors Guild, the American Federation of Radio and Television Artists, the Writers Guild of America, the Screen Actors Guild, the Screen Directors Guild, and the Sports Broadcasters Association.

· SUMMARY ·

Stations and networks are charged with the responsibility for everything that is transmitted on the air. They guard against libel, obscenity, breaches of good taste, and other matters that will offend the public through established continuity-acceptance procedures. The radio and television codes of the National Association of Radio and Television Broadcasters are influential forces for self-regulation in broadcasting. These codes are supplemented by individual station and network standards of practice. Unwritten codes and pressures toward self-regulation reflect orthodox attitudes and the interests of dominant political, economic, and social groups.

Questions for Discussion

1. Why is there a need for self-regulation in broadcasting?
2. How successful has self-regulation been in maintaining standards of decency and good taste in programming?
3. What are the various ways in which self-regulation is exercised?

4. What are the fundamental values expressed in the television code of the NARTB?

5. In a dispute between a station and a sponsor on the definition of commercial time, who must take the responsibility for the final decision?

6. How widely observed is the NARTB Code? Would it be desirable or possible to maintain a strict enforcement policy?

7. How do private pressure groups act to regulate broadcasting? What is the effect of such pressures?

8. Are the limitations placed on radio and television advertising adequate?

9. Evaluate the recommendations of the 1955 report of NBC's Children's Program Review Committee.

10. What should be the standard for determining whether radio and television performers and writers are acceptable to the public and should be permitted to work in programs?

11. "Television is either an ingenious plaything or an important new means of communication, capable of education and perhaps of art. Which is it to be in Britain? If it is to be more than a childish toy its productions, whether light or serious, must be adult. And if they are adult they will sometimes be disagreeable."—Editorial in the *Sunday Times* of London, following a large number of protests over the BBC's television production of GEORGE ORWELL's *1984*. Do you agree with this position?

⁂ 11 ⁂

Comparative
Broadcasting Systems

BROADCASTING HAS developed in practically every country throughout the world. The structure of each nation's broadcasting system depends on the educational level of the populace, the wealth of the nation, its form of government, and the availability of radio and television frequencies. Other factors are the customs and traditions of the country and the cultural and linguistic differences within its borders. Canada, with a French- and English-speaking citizenry, and the Soviet Union, encompassing more than two hundred different cultural groups, obviously cannot rely on a single broadcast service to appeal to all listeners. Countries suffering from extreme shortages of consumer goods can scarcely expect advertising to support broadcasting.

In poor and illiterate countries, radio receivers are beyond the financial reach of most people. Some European countries use *wire broadcasting* and radio relay exchanges to make radio reception available to people who cannot buy their own receivers. A relay exchange, located in a key point in the community, receives programs through the ether and then, over specially adapted telephone lines and circuits, transmits the programs to loudspeakers in individual homes. Wire broadcasting is much cheaper than using individual receiving sets; moreover, it eliminates much of the static and fading typical of cheap receivers. The programs, however, are limited to the ones the relay exchanges make available. Wire broadcasting is especially useful in mountainous regions and in towns where direct reception is poor; it is widespread in the Soviet Union where the government, for political reasons, favors collective listening. Wire broadcasting has developed in Great Britain, too.[1]

[1] R. H. Coase, "Wire Broadcasting in Great Britain," *Economica,* XV (August, 1948), 194-220. Community television antenna systems in the United States use the same principle.

• INTERNATIONAL ALLOCATION OF FREQUENCIES •

International treaties and multilateral agreements allocate the radio spectrum to various countries and continents in order to prevent mutual interference. Regulations on the assignment of call letters to different countries came out of the International Radio Telegraph Conference in 1906. Subsequent international meetings were held in London (1912), Geneva (1925), Washington (1927), Madrid (1932), Cairo (1938) and Atlantic City (1947). At the Geneva conference, the International Broadcasting Union was established to exchange information and to act as a clearing house for international broadcasting. Under the Madrid and Cairo agreements, the band of frequencies from 540 kilocycles to 1600 kilocycles was allocated to AM broadcasting.

Within the American and European continents, further allocations of frequencies and powers of transmission were necessary to avoid interference between adjacent countries in heavily populated areas. In Europe, the allocation was made by the European Broadcasting Convention of Lucerne (1933) and the Copenhagen Plan of 1948, and in the western hemisphere, by the North American Regional Broadcast Agreement (NARBA), drawn up in Havana in 1937, and revised at a general conference at Montreal in 1949. The International Telecommunications and Radio Conference at Atlantic City in 1947 brought together representatives of seventy-two countries, who after several months of negotiations, replaced the Madrid and Cairo agreements with a postwar allocation scheme.

Within the frequency and power limitations assigned by these agreements, each country is free to use radio and television as it sees fit. In small western European countries, where any radio signal is bound to overlap into neighboring countries and only a few frequencies are available to each, the establishment of competitive radio systems often involves insuperable technical problems. As a result, a governmental monopoly of broadcasting is often resorted to, although, were conditions otherwise, a competitive system might be preferred.

• TYPES OF BROADCASTING SYSTEMS •

Broadly speaking, there are four systems of broadcasting used by countries around the globe:

1. Official ownership and operation of stations by the government which runs broadcasting as a state service. This system, found in all totalitarian states, has proved a convenient means for helping to dominate a nation. The control of broadcasting usually rests with the ministry of education or propaganda which "clears" all broadcasting personnel and censors all program material. Hitler perfected this system of broadcasting as a propaganda

arm of the German government. Prominent present-day examples are the U.S.S.R. and Spain. Government-operated broadcasting is not limited to dictatorships, however. A number of European democracies, including France, Belgium, and the Netherlands, use this system; they rely on a sensitive and free parliament to keep the government-of-the-day from misusing its control over broadcasting. Public tax money appropriated by the government supports the system. In some instances, license fees levied on receiving sets supplement this fund.

2. Private ownership and operation of stations by individual broadcasters or corporations, educational institutions, and religious or labor associations, subjected to limited governmental regulation. This system is financed by the sale of time for advertising, by endowments, or by tax money. American television and radio come under this category.

3. Ownership and operation of stations by public or private corporations given a monopoly of broadcasting by the government. These corporations are subject to limited governmental supervision, making possible a degree of independence in programming. Income is derived from license fees, taxes, or advertising, or a combination of the three. Great Britain, Austria, Italy, and Luxembourg have radio systems that come within this classification.

4. Ownership and operation of some stations by a public nonprofit corporation chartered by the government in conjunction with privately-owned and commercially-operated stations. This system, which combines the features of (2) and (3), is found in Canada, Mexico and Uruguay. A modification of this system is used in Great Britain for television. In these countries, commercial stations supported by advertising are usually located in thickly populated urban areas. Without a nonprofit broadcasting system supported in some way by the government, thinly populated areas which cannot support a profitable commercial system would be entirely deprived of broadcast service.

Of these systems of broadcasting, study of those used in Great Britain and Canada has most value for American students of broadcasting. We shall therefore discuss British and Canadian radio and television in some detail and then briefly decribe interesting systems in use in several European and Latin American countries.

· RADIO AND TELEVISION
IN GREAT BRITAIN ·

The development of radio and television in Great Britain is an especially interesting story. Until September, 1955, radio and television were run as a chartered monopoly, were financed directly by the listeners and viewers, and carried no advertising. The monopoly was held by the British Broadcasting Corporation which was created by a royal charter on January 1,

1927, as a public nonprofit corporation. The operations of the BBC were periodically examined during the next twenty-odd years. In 1949, in connection with renewal of the BBC's charter and following open criticism of the BBC's monopoly, a special Broadcasting Committee (popularly known as the Beveridge Committee) was appointed to study the operation of radio and television in Britain and to recommend future government policy in this field. The Committee held extended hearings and collected almost 1,640,000 words of written and oral evidence. In January, 1951, the Committee submitted its report to Parliament, with the recommendation that the BBC monopoly be continued on radio and television without advertising, but with certain minor alterations in its operating practices and constitutional organization.[2] One member of the committee, Mr. Selwyn Lloyd, Minister of State in the Churchill government, dissented from the committee's views and submitted an effective minority report that called for the introduction of competition in British broadcasting.

After nine months of further consideration, a Cabinet committee recommended in 1952 that the BBC's radio monopoly be extended for another ten years, but that some form of television competition should be introduced in Britain as soon as the BBC completed its own arrangements for national television coverage. After several heated Parliamentary debates, the government's proposals were accepted in the Television Act of 1954 which authorized the establishment of the Independent Television Authority to operate competitively with the BBC in the field of television.

The British Broadcasting Corporation. The BBC is a public nonprofit corporation controlled by a Board of Governors chosen by a bipartisan committee made up of the Prime Minister, the leader of the Opposition, the Lord Chief Justice, and other important officials. A director-general, charged with the administration of the BBC, is its chief executive officer.

The BBC is relatively independent of the government-of-the-day by virtue of its chartered status, but its chain of responsibility to Parliament is maintained through a license and agreement with the Postmaster-General, "who is the ultimate authority for wireless telegraphy in Great Britain." [3] The license lays down regulations governing the building of transmitters, the heights of aerials, the frequencies and power to be used, and other technical requirements. It prohibits the BBC from broadcasting commercial advertisements or sponsored programs, and it retains for the Postmaster-General the right of veto over programs.

The only general restriction imposed by the Postmaster-General through his veto power has been a ban upon the broadcasting by the BBC of its own opinion on current affairs. Government departments can, on request,

---

[2] *Report of the Broadcasting Committee, 1949* (London, H. M. Stationery Office, 1951, Cmd. 8116), pp. 327. This report is a very illuminating document that warrants careful reading.

[3] *BBC Handbook, 1956,* p. 15.

insist that their special announcements be broadcast, but the BBC may tell its listeners that the broadcast was made on demand of the government. The BBC is also directed by the license to "broadcast an impartial account day by day by professional reporters of the proceedings in both Houses of the United Kingdom Parliament." There is provision for government control of radio during national emergencies, but this power has not been invoked, even in wartime.[4]

Radio set owners are taxed one pound ($2.80) annually, payable to the Post Office. The Post Office turns over the net revenue from these taxes (less administrative costs) to the BBC for domestic broadcasting operations. Overseas broadcast services are financed by annual grants from the Treasury, much as the "Voice of America" is supported here by Congressional appropriations.

Structure and Programming. Like U. S. networks, the BBC aims to win mass audiences with good entertainment, but unlike its American counterparts, it has been assigned a definite cultural responsibility, frankly paternalistic in nature, to elevate public tastes and standards. Former Director-General Sir William Haley, in speaking of the responsibilities of broadcasting, described BBC programming as resting on the conception of the community as a broadly based cultural pyramid slowly aspiring upwards. This pyramid is served by three main Programmes, differentiated but broadly overlapping in levels and interests, each Programme leading on to the other, the listener being induced through the years increasingly to discriminate in favor of the things that are more worth while. Each Programme at any given moment must be ahead of its public, but not so much as to lose their confidence. The listener must be led from good to better by curiosity, liking, and a growth of understanding. As the standards of the education and culture of the community rise so should the Programme pyramid rise as a whole.[5]

1. THE LIGHT PROGRAMME. Squarely at the base of the pyramid is the Light Programme which broadcasts a frothy schedule of quiz, audience-participation, variety and comedy shows, light music, children's adventure stories, and serial dramas. Sandwiched in between these programs are cultural and informational items: daily concert hours featuring popular symphonies and concertos, successful stage plays adapted to radio, talks on current affairs, newscasts, documentaries, and a daily review of Parliament. Special events and sports programs are generally heard on this service. The foundation of the Light Programme is entertainment designed "to suit those who require relaxation in their listening." Audible throughout the British Isles, the Light Programme is on the air from 9 A.M. to midnight and captures about 63 per cent of the listening audience. The constant aim of

---

[4] *Ibid.*
[5] Sir William Haley, *The Responsibilities of Broadcasting,* lecture delivered at the University of Bristol, May 11, 1948, BBC Publication No. 2223, p. 11.

the Light Programme is to improve the quality of its entertainment offerings without losing its grip on the listeners.

2. THE HOME SERVICE. The Home Service "aims to appeal to a wide range of tastes and to reflect the life of the community in every sphere." Like the Light Programme, the Home Service offers many comedy and variety shows, but it carries the burden of serious political talks, school broadcasts, and good music and drama. Indeed, the Home Service has presented some of the most popular BBC programs, like "Saturday Night Theatre," "Music Hall," and "World Theatre."

London and various regional stations make up the Home Service. Each regional station takes some program from other regions as well as producing many of its own, thereby serving as an outlet for local talent and program experimentation. Six news bulletins, five weather forecasts, and a nightly report of parliamentary proceedings are scheduled daily on the Home Service. The Home Service draws about 36 per cent of British radio listeners.

3. THE THIRD PROGRAMME. The Third Programme, at the apex of the cultural pyramid, is dedicated to the proposition of broadcasting the best music, literature, and talks under the best possible conditions, free from the demands of mass appeal and the tyranny of rigid time schedules. Since it began operating in September, 1946, the Third Programme has been broadcast every night from 6 P.M. to midnight. More than 50 per cent of its program time is devoted to music; about 15 per cent to drama and poetry; 20 per cent to talks, discussions, and readings; and 10 per cent to feature programs. There are no news bulletins or regular series of programs fixed at particular times. With this flexibility, it is possible to broadcast at good listening hours programs appealing to minority audiences. Many broadcasts are repeated several times: dramas at least three times and talks and recitals usually twice. The BBC itself says:

> The Third Programme is designed for the attentive listener, and it is not expected that anybody will listen to it continuously or use it for background listening. The aim is to include in each category only programs which are of artistic value or serious purpose, and to give them the best available performance ... Although it is doubtful whether the Third Programme appeals to all the listeners even some of the time, or even to some of the listeners all the time, it does appeal not to a minority but to a number of minorities, the sum of which may comprise a considerable proportion of the community.[6]

SCHOOL BROADCASTING. Assisted by a School Broadcasting Council, the BBC School Broadcasting Department, with a staff of eighty people, prepares an average of fifty programs a week for reception in classrooms throughout the United Kingdom. Over 26,000 of Britain's 35,000 schools are registered as listening to one or more broadcast series.[7] These broad-

[6] *BBC Year Book, 1949,* p. 126.
[7] *BBC Handbook 1956,* p. 90.

casts are designed to be an aid to teaching, not a substitute for it, and they are normally listened to under supervision. It is generally agreed that British radio has done outstanding work in utilizing radio as a medium for direct and supplementary teaching.

NEWS AND CONTROVERSIAL DISCUSSION PROGRAMS. BBC news broadcasts, prepared by a large staff of news editors in what is one of the most active radio news rooms in the world, are marked by an impartiality and reserve bordering on dullness. Emotionally-loaded words are stripped from all copy, and announcers are instructed to avoid sensationalism or coloring in delivery. The BBC has won wide recognition for reliability and fairness in the handling of news. During World War II, BBC news became the voice of truth for Europe and had a tremendous and intensely loyal listening audience. Between 80 and 90 news bulletins are broadcast weekly in the Home Service and Light Programme and it is estimated that half the adult population of the United Kingdom listens to one or more every day.[8]

Political broadcasts by party members are handled under an arrangement designed "to remove from the party in power the temptation to use the state's control of broadcasting for its own political ends." Ministers of the government broadcast from time to time on noncontroversial matters, but if a minister is inadvertently controversial, the Opposition has a right to reply. There are twelve official party broadcasts each year, apportioned according to the total votes cast for each party at the last general election. Each week the BBC invites an MP to give a talk on "The Week in Westminster," drawing upon the different parties in roughly the same ratio, but with some representation of independents.

In carrying out its mandate for complete impartiality in dealing with controversial issues, the BBC has not in recent years taken the easy way out by banning the discussion of *all* controversy. In the Home Service, the weekly "Friday Forum" offers an unscripted debate on current affairs by MP's and journalists. "Belief and Unbelief" opens the airwaves regularly to the discussion of religious controversy. A debate on the existence of God between philosopher Bertrand Russell and Father Copleston, a Jesuit priest, was a memorable event in the history of broadcast controversy on the BBC.

BBC documentary programs, emphasizing the "actuality" technique and featuring original scripts by leading poets, have won wide acclaim. Topical inquiries like "Focus on Berlin" and "Progress Reports" on the economic crises, have clarified important social problems by casting factual material into dramatic molds.

Organization of the BBC. To run its radio and television services, including overseas broadcasts (which we will discuss in the next chapter), the BBC has more than 87 radio and five television studios in London and has a staff of 13,000. Employees are *not* on civil service and have no tenure, but employment policies are much like those of government service.

[8] *Ibid.,* p. 64.

The BBC itself is organized in five divisions: Sound Broadcasting, Television Broadcasting, External Broadcasting, Technical Services, and Administration. In terms of programming and production, however, there are two main divisions: (1) the variety, drama, features, music, talks, schools, gramophone and recorded program departments which supply programs; and (2) the Home, Light, Third, and Overseas services which plan schedules and make use of the programs supplied them. Thus, the Talks department supplies the three domestic program services each year with about 5,000 different talks and discussions ranging from five-minute chats to hour-long lectures. Drama and music producers similarly plan and direct shows for the Home Service and the Light and Third Programmes. The BBC is the largest employer of musicians in Britain, maintaining the famous BBC Symphony plus a number of smaller orchestras at London and regional stations.

FM Broadcasting. At the 1950 Copenhagen Conference, AM radio frequencies throughout Europe were reallocated. When stations started to operate on the newly assigned frequencies in 1953, interference developed between English stations and stations on the continent, and AM radio reception greatly deteriorated in quality in Great Britain. To solve this problem, the BBC decided to transfer its operations over to FM broadcasting, and on May 2, 1955, the BBC made the first move in the gradual shift when its first FM station went on the air at Wrotham, near London. Ten more FM stations covering England, Scotland, and Northern Ireland are scheduled to be built by 1957, and eventually all radio operations of the BBC will be transmitted on FM. FM sets and converters have been marketed successfully in Britain because of the obvious superiority of FM reception as compared with the degraded AM signal.

BBC Television. "The BBC offers some of the most superlative television in the world. . . . In really going out and reporting the world, the BBC runs rings around American TV. . . . Its documentaries are exceptionally fine. Its best drama is good indeed and its concern with the educational value of TV is often thoroughly rewarding on the screen itself." Thus wrote Jack Gould, *New York Times* radio and television critic, during a visit to Britain in 1955.[9] The BBC began television operations in 1936 and televised the coronation of George VI less than a year later. After a wartime break of nearly seven years, the television service resumed in 1946. Owners of television receivers pay an annual tax of three pounds ($8.40). BBC television provides a single program service to British viewers, with a maximum of 50 hours a week of programming. Evening programs start at 7 P.M. and end by 11 P.M. No programs are telecast between 6 and 7 P.M. when parents are supposed to feed their children and send them to bed. No programs are broadcast on Sunday before 2 P.M.

[9] *New York Times,* September 22, 1955.

BBC television has a coverage of 92 per cent of the British population, and regional BBC studios, film, and mobile units in Bristol, Birmingham, Manchester, Edinburgh, and Belfast supply more than 250 hours a year of television programs to the BBC television service. BBC television has emphasized "live" television and remote pickups. According to Sir George Barnes, Director of Television Broadcasting for the BBC, 24 per cent of the BBC's program output is taken up with telecasts outside the studio, or more than twice as much as either drama or light entertainment programs. During the 1954 general election, the BBC made television pickups at 20 different points in one night. BBC television took viewers underground, into ships at sea, and even to see aircraft flying on and off a carrier at sea. Cameras have been placed under the sea and up in the air in a series of telecasts from a Royal Air Force plane.[10] In 1955, faced with the loss of 350 technicians and other staff employees to its first television competitor, the BBC indicated that it would pursue a vigorous program service in an effort to maintain its hold on the British audience. It raised salaries for its own employees, increased its emphasis on comedy programming with the purchase, for example, of the filmed "Burns and Allen" program series, and started building a new radio and television center on a twenty-one acre tract in White City, London, which would make 16 television studios available for production. The BBC eventually hopes to set up a second television program service to operate competitively but noncommercially, as do the Home Service and the Light Programme in radio. The real future of the BBC, however, will depend upon the popular reaction to the new commercial television service: if BBC television loses the British audience to commercial television there is little likelihood that a second BBC television network will be approved; indeed, there will be strong pressure to commercialize the BBC, too.

BBC Publications. The BBC's annual income from annual license taxes is approximately $35 million. This income is supplemented by earnings from a number of extraordinarily successful BBC publications. *Radio Times,* which prints the weekly program schedules and carries advertising, has a regular circulation of 8 million and is considered the best commercial advertising medium in Britain. It yields an annual profit of over $3 million. The *Listener,* which publishes outstanding BBC talks, has a more modest circulation of 138,000.

Commercial Television. The Television Act of 1954 created the Independent Television Authority (ITA) to operate competitively with BBC television. The ITA was issued a ten-year charter, and a government loan of $5,500,000. It is governed by a ten-member board of directors appointed by the Postmaster-General, and its Director-General, Sir Robert Fraser, is the chief executive of the authority. Whereas the BBC produces its own programs as well as owning and operating studios and transmitting facilities,

[10] *Radio Times,* September 16, 1955, p. 3.

the ITA owns and operates facilities, but its programs are supplied by privately financed companies known as program contractors with which the ITA has made exclusive broadcasting agreements. The ITA is responsible for seeing that the programs maintain a proper balance and for regulating all commercial aspects of the operation. Advertisers and agencies may not produce programs or be identified as sponsoring programs; they may simply buy spot announcements during various time periods and they may not choose the precise time or program in which their announcement will appear. Advertising is limited to six minutes in an hour; announcements may appear only at the beginning or end of a program or "at natural intervals." The Television Act is very specific in describing acceptable commercial practices:

> Nothing shall be included in any programs broadcast by the Authority whether in an advertisement or not, which states, suggests, or implies, or could reasonably be taken to state, suggest or imply, that any part of any program broadcast by the Authority which is not an advertisement has been supplied or suggested by any advertiser.

The Postmaster-General has the authority to forbid the advertising of any goods or services he may determine to be undesirable and he may also issue instructions against methods of advertising which he does not feel should be employed. The Postmaster-General is also the final authority, in consultation with the ITA, as to rules covering the placement of commercials in shows and as to the types of broadcasts into which advertisements may not be inserted. The Television Act bans commercials by or for any religious or political group or cause and any commercial related to a labor dispute.

Program contractors must submit to the ITA in advance of telecast scripts and particulars of programs, including commercials. The ITA has the power to forbid "the broadcasting of any matter or class or description of matter. Nothing may be broadcast without previous approval of ITA."

Advisory committees on religious and children's programs, similar to committees of this type that work with the BBC, advise the ITA on programming policies in these fields. An advisory committee on advertising provides the ITA and program contractors with a binding code of advertising practices, which excludes such things as misleading statements.

The Postmaster-General or any other Minister of the Crown may order the ITA to broadcast any announcements he feels necessary or expedient "in connection with his functions." The Postmaster-General has the power to prohibit the ITA, program contractors, and the BBC from gaining exclusive rights to important sporting or special events.

When the ITA began telecasting in September, 1955, it had made agreements with several different program contractors. The ITA began its telecasts over a single station in London; by 1957, three other stations would provide outlets for the ITA: one in Staffordshire to cover Birmingham and the Midlands; one in Lancashire to cover Manchester and the northern industrial area; and one in Yorkshire. One program contractor is a company called Associated-Rediffusion, owned by Associated Newspapers, publishers of the *Daily Mail* and the *Evening News*. Associated-Rediffusion was given the contract to produce programs Monday through Friday over the London station. A second program contractor is the Associated TeleVision, Ltd., the principals of which are two theatrical impresarios and two local Birmingham newspapers. Associated TeleVision, Ltd. has the contract to produce programs Saturday and Sunday over the London station, and Monday through Friday over the station in Staffordshire. A third program contractor is the Granada Company, controlled by Sidney Bernstein, a wealthy theatrical entrepreneur. The Granada Company will produce programs Monday through Friday over the station in Lancashire. A fourth program contractor is the Associated British Cinemas, which contracted to provide programs on weekends for Birmingham and Manchester.

The program contractors receive their income from selling spot announcements on their programs. The top charge over the London station during evening hours in 1955 was $2,800 per minute-spot; in Birmingham the top charge was $1,400. One serious competitive obstacle to ITA and the program contractors is the fact that more than two-thirds of the television receivers in London were single-channel receivers and not equipped to receive ITA programs. Multichannel tuning devices cost about $30 to install. Like UHF stations in many American cities, the ITA was saddled with a technical handicap that only very strong programming would overcome. This the program contractors pledged to provide. Associated-Rediffusion arranged for outstanding stars to produce favorite plays of their own choosing for an eight-week stage run in London, to be followed by a filmed telecast over ITA. U. S. television shows, like "I Love Lucy," "Ford Theater," "Person to Person," etc., were bought by program contractors to compete with the BBC. "Sunday at the Palladium" promised to compete effectively with the BBC Sunday night drama show. By general agreement, U. S. programs were to be limited to 20 per cent of the program schedule of ITA, and efforts were made to develop British TV stars.

Television news programs are produced by a single program packager—the Independent Television News Company—which supplies news programs to the other program contractors.

Like BBC television, the ITA is prohibited from telecasting between 6 and 7 P.M. The ITA may not, under its present charter, engage in any radio broadcasting.

• BROADCASTING IN CANADA •

Broadcasting in Canada has taken an unusual form due to the special geographical and cultural make-up of that country. Canada encompasses five different time zones, and is larger than the United States, but it has a population of only 14 million. Most Canadians speak English, but some speak only French. Great distances separate the large metropolitan centers. The cost of a national radio service linked by land lines is prohibitive for independent commercial networks. Advertisers, quite naturally, are interested in reaching heavy concentrations of people and cannot undertake to finance broadcasts that reach only scattered listeners.

When radio got under way in Canada in the 20's, most stations were located in densely populated areas where profitable advertising markets could be tapped, and sparsely populated farming areas were virtually excluded from broadcast reception. It soon became clear that if radio was to be made available to all Canadians, commercial broadcasting could not do the job by itself. Shortly after Congress passed the Radio Act of 1927, the Canadian Parliament appointed the Aird Commission to study Canada's problem and to recommend policies by which a radio service might be established (1) to cover the entire country; (2) to offer an outlet for Canadian talent by not being completely dependent on the United States; and (3) to foster Canada's national consciousness and its cultural growth. After studying the American and British radio systems, the Aird Commission concluded that only "by some form of public ownership, operation, and control behind which is the national power and prestige of the whole public of Canada" could these objectives be achieved.

Broadcasting in Canada operates under the Canadian Broadcasting Act of 1936 which, following the Aird Commission's recommendations, created the Canadian Broadcasting Corporation. The CBC is modeled after the BBC, but there are several substantial differences. The CBC is run by an appointive Board of nine Governors who serve without salary (except the Chairman), and by a General Manager who, like the BBC's Director-General, is responsible for the day-to-day operations of the corporation. The CBC is directed by Parliament to "carry on a national broadcasting service" and is authorized to "maintain and operate broadcasting stations" for that purpose. It may also accept advertising. The CBC now owns and operates 22 radio stations and three networks. It is financed by an annual Treasury grant, excise taxes on broadcast receivers, and advertising revenues. In 1954-1955, the CBC's income for its radio services amounted to $13,459,983, mainly derived from Treasury grants. The CBC takes commercial programs because many listeners want to hear the popular sponsored shows originating in the United States; the income from these programs also provides revenues to improve the CBC's noncommercial offerings.

The Minister of Transport licenses private stations for commercial operation, but only on the advice of the CBC, which supervises the programming and operations of the private stations. The 154 privately owned stations now in existence draw their entire income from advertising, but the law limits commercials to not more than 10 per cent of program time, and bans from the air certain categories of advertising.

The CBC resembles the BBC in that it is relatively free from the party in power, since it is directly responsible to Parliament as a whole, but it differs from the BBC in that (1) it does not have a monopoly over all broadcasting, and (2) it carries advertising. Since the CBC has the authority to regulate the private stations with which it competes for listeners, the stations are put in a rather anomalous position, not comparable to private stations in the United States.[11]

Station and Network Structure. Using its own stations as focal points, the CBC has established three radio networks in Canada.

1. TRANS-CANADA NETWORK. This is a full-time network made up of 26 basic and 18 supplementary stations covering most of Canada. Thirteen of the basic stations are owned by the CBC and the remaining 13 are privately owned. During daytime hours, the Trans-Canada Network carries American daytime serials to its listeners; in the evening, it offers, in addition to its own productions, Hollywood and New York programs piped in from our national networks.

2. THE DOMINION NETWORK. The Dominion Network operates mainly during evening hours. It is made up of 31 basic and 19 supplementary stations. The CBC owns the key station of the network in Toronto, but all the others are privately owned. The Dominion Network, like the Trans-Canada, produces many of its own shows and also relays broadcasts from the United States, such as the "Bob Hope Show" and other top-flight network programs.

3. THE FRENCH NETWORK. This network, designed for listeners in Quebec province, is made up of 4 basic CBC stations and 20 supplementary stations. Most French Network programs originate in CBC's Montreal studios. Programs piped in from the United States use French-speaking commentators.

For special programs of nation-wide import, the facilities of the three networks can be combined to form a national network.

Programming. About 70,000 programs are broadcast over the three networks in the course of a year. In 1954, 86 per cent of the broadcast hours were noncommercial and 14 per cent were sponsored. The CBC itself produced about 70,000 radio programs that year.

The CBC puts its greatest emphasis on public-service and informational programs. It accepts only as many sponsored shows as its financial needs

[11] See the *Report of the Canadian Royal Commission on National Development in the Arts, Letters and Sciences 1949-1951* (Ottawa, 1951), p. 517.

require. It employs over 1,000 staff personnel. Its organization is much like that of the BBC.

NEWS BROADCASTS. The CBC broadcasts morning, noon, and evening news bulletins and a daily CBC News Round-up "designed to illustrate and amplify current news, through descriptive commentaries, reports on national and international developments, eyewitness accounts, interviews, and actuality broadcasts."

TALKS. The CBC runs a very active talks department aiming at "a pattern of coverage which provides balanced and varied information and opinions during each week." Programs like "Capital Report" and "Week-end Review" are regularly scheduled. A weekly "Points of View" presents debates and discussions on controversial questions in the public mind.

MUSIC. Music programs account for more than half of all broadcast hours over the CBC. Canadian music is emphasized; nearly every CBC serious music broadcast includes at least one composition by a Canadian. Leading American orchestras and the Metropolitan Opera are brought to Canadian listeners by arrangements with CBS, ABC, and NBC.

DRAMA. To judge from the number of awards it has won in international competition, Canadian radio has done outstanding work in creative dramatic art. In a single year, the CBC produces as many as 320 dramatic programs. Many of these are original, some are adaptations, but 90 per cent of the scripts are by Canadian writers. Series of full-hour unit dramas have been cited by the Ohio State University Institute for Education by Radio for "courageous and adult radio dramas on serious themes and the high quality of writing, acting, and production." To produce these radio plays, the CBC maintains a repertory company at its Toronto studios.

EDUCATIONAL AND CHILDREN'S PROGRAMS. The CBC co-operates with Canadian provincial departments of education by contributing its production skill, studio facilities, and network lines, while the educational departments pay the writers, actors, and musicians for educational programs. The CBC also presents a weekly series of its own called "National School Broadcasts," discussing current affairs, history, and literature in talks or dramas prepared for in-school listening. A "Kindergarten of the Air" is broadcast for pre-school children.

FARM BROADCASTS. Five regional noon-hour farm programs are broadcast daily in Canada. These broadcasts are designed to meet varying regional needs for weather reports, market prices, and agricultural news. The CBC also runs a "National Farm Radio Forum," which is a listening group project combined with the broadcast. Every Monday night during the winter, farmers get together to discuss topics covered in the weekly broadcast.

CBC WEDNESDAY NIGHT. Since 1947, the CBC has offered "something new in radio on the North American continent—a block of noncommercial programs broadcast for a full evening on a national network, and produced primarily for the discriminating listener." Like the BBC's Third Programme,

"CBC Wednesday Night" offers a variety of high-grade entertainment. The format changes from week to week, but it usually consists of a half-hour of music followed by a play lasting an hour or two, after which come news reports and a final half-hour of music. In 1950, "CBC Wednesday Night" was cited by the Ohio State Institute for Education by Radio "for its courageous experiments with radio themes, techniques and writing, and for the excellence of its music and production."

Canadian Television. After a period of watchful waiting, television was launched in Canada in September, 1952, with a Parliamentary grant of $6,250,000 to the CBC for television programming. The basic plan for the development of Canadian television has been similar to the plan of Canadian radio: a combination of stations owned and operated by the CBC, and private stations regulated by the CBC, with the CBC's income obtained through advertising, license fees, and special grants from Parliament. In 1954, of the 24 television stations in existence in Canada providing 75 per cent national coverage, 6 were owned and operated by the CBC, with 2 stations in Montreal (one English language, one French), and 1 station each in Toronto, Winnipeg, Ottawa, and Vancouver. Eighteen stations were owned by private companies which were obligated to carry at least ten and a half hours of CBC programs each week, thus guaranteeing a national program service in television. The CBC produced a full schedule of drama, variety, music, and news programs at a cost that exceeded the CBC's income from advertising, but considerably less than its total income which included the proceeds from a 15 per cent tax on the sale of television sets, tubes, and other accessories. In the fiscal year ending March, 1955, CBC television received $21,275,805, of which $16,959,965 came from Treasury grants, $4,157,325 from advertising, and $158,515 from other sources. During the same year, expenses amounted to $15,915,901, including $9,016,850 for programs. The television budget of the CBC registered a surplus of $4,479,421 over its total income from all sources.[12]

The desire of the Canadian authorities to retain a special identity for Canadian culture and to avoid being annexed culturally by the United States is an important reason for the CBC's insistence on producing expensive programs of their own rather than carrying more U. S. commercial network shows which would increase its advertising revenues and reduce production costs. According to A. Davidson Dunton, Chairman of the CBC's Board of Governors, there is no early prospect of the CBC's television service becoming self-supporting from advertising revenues alone because of the requirements of this cultural policy.

Evaluation of Canadian Radio and Television. Canadian radio and television have been severely criticized in recent years by the Canadian Association of Broadcasters which represents privately owned stations. The main criticisms of these broadcasters are: (1) the CBC has too much power over

[12] Canadian Broadcasting Corporation, *Annual Report 1954-1955.*

all Canadian radio and television; (2) free speech is endangered by the present system; (3) the law unduly limits the advertising that private stations may carry; and (4) the CBC competes with local stations for local advertising revenue. From 1949 to 1951, a Canadian Royal Commission commonly referred to as the Massey Commission, studied the CBC's mode of operation and evaluated the achievements and shortcomings of Canadian broadcasting against Canada's needs. The Massey Commission, with certain exceptions, supported the CBC's general programming and regulatory policies. The Commission *Report* concluded:

> We believe that Canadian radio broadcasting legislation contemplates and effectively provides for one national system; that the private stations have been licensed only because they can play a useful part within that system; and that the CBC control of network broadcasting, of the issue and renewal of licenses, of advertising and of other matters related to radio broadcasting, is a proper expression of the power of the CBC to exercise control over all radio broadcasting policies and programs in Canada.[13]

The Massey Commission made the following recommendations, among others:

1. That no private radio broadcasting station operate in Canada as part of a network without the permission of the CBC.
2. That licenses for private commercial radio stations continue to be nontransferable and to confer no property right to the licensee, but that they should be issued for five-year terms subject to noncancellation for nonobservance of clearly defined regulations.
3. That the CBC refuse all local commercial business for those stations which it operates directly, except in places where advertising service from private stations is not available.
4. That the CBC refuse all commercial programs not acceptable in content and that it consider the possibility of eliminating some of the less desirable commercial programs carried, and of replacing them with programs more appropriate to Canadian listeners.
5. That the CBC spend more money and effort to obtain informational talk programs presented popularly as well as authoritatively by able broadcasters.

The Massey Commission also recommended that television policy be reviewed every three years. Accordingly, in 1955 a Canadian parliamentary inquiry was begun in the field of television programming and regulation.

• EUROPEAN BROADCASTING SYSTEMS •

There are juxtaposed, within the continent of Europe, many heavily populated countries with varying governmental forms, cultural traditions, and

---

[13] *Report of the Canadian Royal Commission on National Development in the Arts, Letters, and Sciences, 1949-1951* (Ottawa, 1951), p. 283.

national aspirations. Each country faces the problem of making most efficient use of a limited number of wave lengths. In totalitarian states the solution is simple: broadcasting is a government monopoly, operated by a department of the government which uses it as a medium for propaganda to sustain the regime in power. Only government-approved material is broadcast. Some totalitarian states have penalized listening to foreign stations and have distributed special receivers which pick up only government stations. In nontotalitarian countries, various systems of broadcasting have developed. We shall briefly sketch the systems in use in France, Luxembourg, and Italy because they are fairly representative of the different types.

France. Radiodiffusion-Television Française (RTF), which comes under the authority of the Minister of Information, runs broadcasting as a state monopoly. It is financed by an annual license tax on the radio and television receivers in use in France, plus a subsidy from the government. No advertising is carried on the air. RTF has 42 radio stations organized into three networks. The *National* Network sends out a steady diet of news, forums, symphonic and light classical music during morning and evening broadcast periods. The *Parisian* Network concentrates on a light program fare, and the third network, *Paris-inter,* is actually nothing more than a symbolic goodwill station which broadcasts international programs on an exchange basis with other countries.

French television is operated by RTF on a public-service basis. The French use a transmission system with 819-line definition, in contrast to the 525-line definition used in the United States. The French television service has 440 permanent employees and telecasts between thirty and forty hours of programs a week. By the end of 1954, only 125,000 television receivers were in use in France.

Luxembourg. The radio system of the tiny Grand Duchy of Luxembourg has made a reputation for itself by attracting many foreign listeners. The Luxembourg Broadcasting Company, a private company, has a monopoly over all broadcasting in the country. A license fee is assessed on every radio receiver, but the proceeds of this tax go to the state and are not used for programming. Radio-Luxembourg derives its entire revenue from the sale of broadcast time to advertisers and pays the government a tax on its income. Radio-Luxembourg, at the request of the government, broadcasts public-service announcements aimed to attract tourists to the country. Before World War II, the equipment of Radio-Luxembourg was considered among the best in Europe.

Télé-Luxembourg went on the air in January, 1955, as a commercially operated television station owned by the Luxembourg Broadcasting Company. Télé-Luxembourg produces programs from mobile units in France and Belgium as well as in its Luxembourg studios.

Italy. Radio Audizioni Italiana (RAI) holds a monopoly on all broadcasting in Italy. When the RAI was assigned its monopoly in 1927, almost all the shares in the company were owned by the Piedmont Hydroelectric Society, a private group, but since the war, the Italian government has taken over the company. Radio Italiana derives its income from license fees on receivers, from taxes on the manufacture of radio equipment, and from advertising. Programs are supervised by a Parliamentary Commission charged with the responsibility for insuring the political objectivity of all broadcasts. A Cultural Committee, made up of representatives of the governmental ministries concerned with art, social services, and tourists, is responsible for supervising the cultural and educational quality of programs. Not more than 10 per cent of the broadcast schedule may be devoted to commercial announcements, and no advertising may accompany news broadcasts. Radio Italiana is working systematically on the production of school broadcasts; five half-hour programs are broadcast to primary schools each week.

The official inauguration of Italian television service under RAI took place in January, 1954. Owners of television sets pay a yearly tax of $29.00. By the end of 1954, 82,000 television receivers were registered in Italy. RAI established three television production centers: in Turin, Milan, and Rome. Transmitters at various points provided coverage throughout Italy, Sicily, and Sardinia. RAI television provided about 35 hours of programs weekly, including programs for women and children, sports programs, and opera telecasts from Milan and Rome. The Italian government decided to accept advertising on television when the number of registered television receivers exceeds 150,000.

• LATIN-AMERICAN BROADCASTING SYSTEMS •

The broadcasting systems of several Latin-American countries are also of interest for the light they shed on the forms broadcasting service can take. We shall review the systems in use in Mexico, Cuba, and Uruguay.

Mexico. The Mexican Broadcasting System consists of 4 stations controlled and financed by the government, and 196 private stations supported by advertising revenues. No license fees are levied on receiving sets. The Mexican government grants fifty-year broadcast licenses to private companies conditional upon their compliance with official broadcasting regulations. Each station is supervised by an official of the Ministry of Communications and Public Works whose salary the station is required to pay. The supervisor can prohibit broadcasts "affecting the security of the state or harmful to morality or to the economic interests of the country." [14] He is also responsible for insuring that commercial announcements do not violate

[14] UNESCO, *Report of the Commission on Technical Needs in Press, Film, Radio* (Paris, 1948), Publication 214, p. 192.

public-health regulations. Commercial announcements are limited to two minutes in length and interludes of music or other program matter must come between announcements. Sponsored programs, however, do not come under these limitations. Station XEW, Mexico's most powerful station, has sold as much as 96 per cent of its time for sponsored programs. State-owned stations do not carry advertising.

The Mexican government requires all stations simultaneously to relay each Sunday a program called the "National Hour" which one of the government stations originates. All stations are also obliged to carry official communiqués of national importance. A UNESCO survey of radio in 1948 noted that "The Mexican government is waging a vigorous war against illiteracy, but has not yet made intensive use of the radio to that end." [15]

In 1954, the number of television receivers in Mexico was estimated at 100,000. Three television stations are operated in Mexico City, and other stations are located at Tijuana, Juarez, and other cities in Mexico. These stations are privately owned and financed from advertising revenues. Three additional stations have been proposed for Mexico City, one for the Mexican government, one to be operated on an educational basis by the University of Mexico, and another commercially operated station.

Cuba. All Cuban broadcast stations but one are privately owned and operated and supported by advertising revenues. They are organized into two networks with excellent transmitting facilities. The government owns one station which is run by the Ministry of Education. Radio broadcast licenses are issued by the Directorate of Broadcasting which is charged with insuring the reliability of newscasts on all stations, preventing libel and slander from being broadcast, insuring "conformity with the grammatical rules of the language, and even more, with the standards of decency and good taste," and insuring that commercial announcements do not give publicity to any product not licensed by the Cuban Ministry of Health. Maximum limits ranging from 28 to 36 per cent are imposed by law on the amount of broadcast time a station may sell for commercial announcements. On Sundays, only half these amounts is permitted. Stations also broadcast sponsored programs as well as announcements, however, and this increases the proportion of advertising matter while keeping within the letter of the law. News broadcasts are sponsored and political broadcasts are paid for at commercial rates. The government station has less kilowatt power than the large commercial stations and attracts only a small audience.

Television in Cuba is operated entirely by private commercial companies and is financed by advertising. There are nine stations on the air: five in Havana and four in various other cities, providing coverage throughout Cuba for an estimated 135,000 receivers. In September, 1954, through the use of "stratovision," the World Series was relayed from the United States to Cuba by means of a relay transmitter in an airplane circling 9,000

[15] *Ibid.,* p. 193.

feet in the air some fifty miles off the coast of Cuba. In 1955, the "Wide Wide World" program featured live pick-ups from Havana.

Uruguay. In Uruguay, radio is operated by an official broadcasting organization as well as by private broadcasting companies. The state service is set up purely for cultural and informational purposes and receives a subsidy from the government to cover its expenses. It is controlled by a governmental committee and is assigned the responsibility of developing Uruguayan culture. It carries no advertising and no license fees are placed on receivers. Drawing on the experience and assistance of the BBC, the official radio service has undertaken a full program of school broadcasts.

Private stations are licensed for commercial operation by the Directorate of Broadcasting Services which sets forth technical and engineering requirements for broadcasts. The government also reserves the right to use fifteen minutes daily on private stations for important public broadcasts. Regulations specify that not more than 150-word commercial announcements may be made between programs.

No television service had been established in Uruguay by 1955, but a government-operated station was expected to begin telecasting by 1956.

· SUMMARY ·

Practically all nations engage in radio broadcasting. Systems of broadcasting now in use include government-operated radio, monopoly broadcasting by public corporations, combinations of government stations and privately-owned stations, and completely commercial operation of almost all stations with a minimum of governmental intervention. British and Canadian radio and television, different in many respects from American broadcasting, invite study because of the many outstanding features of their program service.

Questions for Discussion

1. Upon what factors does the structure of a country's broadcasting system usually depend?
2. What basic factors must be considered in evaluating a national system of broadcasting?
3. What arrangements have been made to prevent mutual interference between countries using the same frequency bands?
4. What are the different systems of broadcasting used by countries around the globe?
5. How does British broadcasting compare with American broadcasting in terms of structure, programming, and regulation?
6. How does Canadian broadcasting compare with American broadcasting in terms of structure, programming, and regulation?
7. What value, if any, would there be in having an interchange of information and programs between different national broadcasting systems?
8. What is the likely course of events in British radio and television now that a commercial television system has been introduced?

❊ 12 ❊

International Broadcasting

"THE STORY of radio in international affairs is part of the story of power politics," write Professors Childs and Whitton.[1] Broadcasting has no equal as a means of international communication. Instantaneous in transmission, it penetrates national frontiers and spans the walls of censorship that bar the written word. Radio can be used to foster international amity, but it has been used mainly to wage psychological warfare on peoples.

• GROWTH OF INTERNATIONAL BROADCASTING •

As early as World War I, when radio was still in its "wireless" stage, international broadcasting was used for espionage and intelligence. The Allies dropped Marconi senders in enemy territories to get reports from secret agents. Radio was also used to communicate with neutral countries across telegraph and mail blockades; the belligerents themselves used radio to send out "peace feelers" and to conduct preliminary armistice negotiations. It was not until the middle 20's, however, that efforts were made to use international broadcasting to influence public opinion abroad. These early efforts were not systematic and were limited to isolated issues and occasions, such as the "radio war" that broke out between Radio Berlin and the Eiffel tower station in Paris during the invasion of the Ruhr in 1923.

The Bolshevik masters of the newly constituted government of the Soviet Union were among the first to make effective use of radio to spread world revolutionary propaganda. Moscow waged a radio war with Rumania over Bessarabia in 1926 and revolutionary appeals were broadcast to German

[1] Harwood L. Childs and John B. Whitton, *Propaganda by Short Wave* (Princeton, 1942), p. 3.

workers in the critical years preceding Hitler's assumption of power in 1933.

But not all early efforts at international broadcasting were unfriendly in intention. Nations exchanged good broadcast programs and occasionally linked their facilities for programs of common interest. The International Broadcasting Union was formed in 1927 to bring radio's warring parties together and to obtain agreements to abstain from hostile propaganda and to avoid mutual interference. Fear of possible attack, however, caused the nations of Europe to expand their radio "defenses." This meant the construction of more radio transmitters since retaliation or "jamming" operations are the only defense a nation has against enemy broadcasts.

Holland, Britain, France, Belgium, and Portugal used international broadcasting to reach their colonies in the late 20's. The broadcasts were directed not to the natives, but to nationals residing in the colonies, or to the ruling emissaries. With its colonies spread around the globe, Great Britain decided to set up regular Empire broadcasting on a round-the-clock basis in 1932. In the same year, the League of Nations formed its own radio facility in Geneva, to transmit international messages to individual countries and to communicate information to its far-flung representatives.

The first use of radio as a weapon of direct warfare appears to have been made by Japan with its broadcasts to enemy armies and civilians during the Manchurian invasion of 1931. The Japanese were not content with using radio merely to win a speedier victory. After the conquest, "broadcasting was organized in Manchukuo to instill new loyalties among the conquered and cut them off from Chinese influence." [2] To do this, free receivers were distributed among the people. In 1935, Japan began short-wave broadcasting overseas to consolidate her new empire.

Radio was immediately exploited by Hitler when he assumed power in Germany. The Nazi government used short-wave transmissions to reach distant countries and broke into the medium-wave band to attract listeners in neighboring European countries. A thorough radio propaganda campaign helped prepare the people of the Saar basin for German re-entry in 1935. Hitler's next triumph took place in Austria where a combination of military threats, radio propaganda, and conspiracy by secret agents won a reported 99.75 per cent of the total Austrian vote to approve the country's incorporation within the German Reich. In the days that preceded the plebiscite, the Nazis distributed 100,000 radios among the Austrians.[3] The German government's next step was to set up a short-wave broadcast service to spread Nazi doctrine to its friends and potential supporters overseas. Foreign audiences of German birth or ancestry were organized into clubs for group listening.

From 1936 to 1939, during the Spanish Civil War, radio got a dress

---

[2] *Ibid.*, p. 10. This account of the growth of international broadcasting is drawn mainly from Childs' and Whitton's discussion.

[3] *Ibid.*, p. 18.

rehearsal for World War II. Childs and Whitton write that "By virtue of ... diabolically clever propaganda the democracies were split internally from top to bottom and were not only neutralized into 'nonintervention' for the duration of the war, but for years to come were politically paralyzed by the formation of 'appeasement' parties hostile to any action against Fascism." [4] In actual combat, Franco used radio to keep in touch with his fifth column in Madrid and to direct a propaganda barrage against the civilian populace. Advised by German and Italian propaganda experts, Franco used vituperation, threats, sadism, and braggadocio in his radio propaganda campaigns. A weary Spanish republic, split from within by Communist machinations and left without support from friendly democracies, finally succumbed.

Benefiting from its own successes and the Spanish experience, Germany launched a propaganda war against the Czechs before fomenting the Munich crisis of 1938. Radio laid down a "drum-fire barrage of terror and propaganda" which continued even after the crisis was temporarily resolved and did not come to an end until the Czechs surrendered completely the next year. By the time German troops were ready to enter Prague, the Czech radio had capitulated along with the government, announcing the German occupation at five-minute intervals and warning the people not to offer resistance.

In early 1939, the western European democracies awakened to the danger of unanswered German propaganda and began a vigorous radio counter-offensive. An all-out effort was launched to reach European populations in their native tongues. The BBC set up a European service which, by the outbreak of war, was broadcasting in 16 foreign languages. Nazi reaction was violent. The German people were warned not to listen to the "false" foreign radio propaganda maligning German leaders, and heavy penalties were imposed for such listening or for spreading news heard on foreign broadcasts. The German who harbored a short-wave radio receiver in his home did so at grave personal peril.

During these turbulent years, the United States took no official part in international broadcasting. Private organizations—World Wide Broadcasting Foundation, CBS, NBC, Crosley, Westinghouse, and General Electric—had, however, undertaken regular short-wave broadcasting.[5] CBS set up a "Network of the Americas," hoping to build up a profitable operation in Latin America, and NBC joined the international business soon thereafter. By the time of Pearl Harbor, there were only 13 international voice-broadcasting transmitters in the United States.[6] Until 1940, the United States Army paid scant attention to psychological warfare and in the years

[4] *Ibid.*, p. 24.

[5] Forney A. Rankin, *Who Gets the Air?* (Washington, The National Association of Broadcasters, 1949), p. 35.

[6] Charles A. H. Thomson, *Overseas Information Service of the United States Government* (Washington, 1948), p. 3.

from 1925 to 1935, not one full time officer was assigned even to study the subject.[7]

The reasons for such limited activity in international broadcasting and propaganda by this country are clear. The United States was in a period of isolationist thinking, and the failure to use international broadcasting more fully was merely a reflection of the general political outlook. Business interests in radio also opposed government intervention in any broadcasting out of fear that a precedent would be established for state interference in broadcasting at home. Commercial broadcasters had no motivation to undertake short-wave broadcasting themselves on a regular basis because there was no profit to be made from it.

· RADIO IN THE SECOND WORLD WAR ·

The Second World War saw the full flowering of broadcasting, both domestic and international, as a vehicle for propaganda. The objectives of each belligerent were the same: (1) to demoralize enemies by confusing, terrifying, and dividing them; (2) to maintain the friendships of neutral countries by broadcasts justifying war aims and inviting cultural exchanges; (3) to stimulate the morale of its own fighting forces and civilian populace. Nations constructed transmitters to send out their own programs and set up listening posts to monitor enemy broadcasts in an effort to turn up clues to future enemy policy and to provide ammunition for counter-propaganda. By the war's end, there were more than 360 transmitters manned by thousands of skilled linguists and script writers in more than fifty different countries, sending around the world more than 2,000 words a minute in forty-odd languages.[8]

Perfecting what has been called the "strategy of terror," the German government took early leadership in the radio propaganda war. Raising the image of defeat and subjugation, the Nazis followed up their Czech success with an incessant torrent of words against Poland, and later against France, Holland, and Norway. By 1941 Germany was using 88 of its own short-wave transmitters plus those it took over in occupied countries. It created radio personalities like Lord Haw-Haw and Axis Sally to conduct their English broadcast propaganda. At home, the Nazis clamped heavy penalties on short-wave listening and fed the German people a steady list of misinformation, which caused no problem as long as news of military victories continued to roll in, but which began to wear thin as the prospect of defeat loomed.

Operating through the Overseas Service of the BBC, Great Britain relied

---

[7] Paul Linebarger, "Psychological Warfare in World War Two," *Infantry Journal,* LX (1947), 32n.

[8] Llewellyn White and Robert D. Leigh, *Peoples Speaking to Peoples* (Chicago, 1946), p. 11.

on regular newscasts to point out the lies of the German leaders. To the occupied peoples of Europe, the voice of the BBC, broadcast in fifty different langauges, came as a heartening sound in a world of darkness. An old lady in Holland wrote during the Nazi occupation, "Nowadays I believe nothing but the BBC and the Bible." [9] The BBC developed the "V for Victory" slogan which became the most effective propaganda symbol of the war. At home, the British used radio to sustain the morale of factory workers and civilian defense personnel, with "music-while-you-work" programs and "actuality" broadcasts from microphones set up in canteens and air-raid shelters.

The Soviet Union disclosed great technical ability in countering German radio propaganda. Ingenious technicians and quick-witted broadcasters learned how to track down and wreck German "newscasts" by transmitting on the same frequencies as the German stations. Soviet broadcasters heckled the German announcers, filling in pauses between German news bulletins with caustic comments on their probable falsity, and even mimicked Hitler. Within the U.S.S.R., "Russian foreign propaganda concentrated on denigrating the Allies and celebrating Russia's lone role in the war." [10]

Japan used short-wave broadcasting to hold together its scattered empire of islands and primitive populations, and to wage propaganda warfare against American troops and native populations outside its domain. Tokyo Rose broadcast to American troops hoping to make them more homesick and to sap their fighting ambition. Utilizing racist propaganda, Japan sought to weld a binding tie among yellow-skinned peoples and to turn them against the lighter-skinned Occidentals. The fly in the ointment of this propaganda was China, a nation of inhabitants with pigmentation similar to the Japanese, but with different national aspirations.

With the attack on Pearl Harbor, the United States changed its orientation toward international broadcasting. Although, according to Wallace Carroll, President Roosevelt had little interest or understanding of psychological warfare, he authorized the establishment of the Office of War Information under the direction of Elmer Davis to run America's propaganda efforts at home and abroad.[11] The OWI was empowered to "plan, develop, and execute all phases of the federal program of radio, press, publication, and related foreign propaganda activities involving the dissemination of propaganda." Davis was responsible only to the President, but he seldom had access to him.[12]

The OWI, with 11,000 employees, was divided into two main operations: (1) the domestic branch, which channeled governmental information to the American people through press and radio, and co-ordinated the publicity

---

[9] T. O. Beachcroft, *British Broadcasting* (London, 1946), p. 20.
[10] Thomson, *op. cit.*, p. 99.
[11] Wallace Carroll, *Persuade or Perish* (Boston, 1948), pp. 6-7.
[12] *Ibid.*, p. 7.

efforts of official bureaus; and (2) the overseas branch, which waged the "strategy of truth" through the "Voice of America."

During the four years of its operation, the OWI sent out from its New York offices as many as 2,700 broadcasts a week in twenty-five languages and dialects, and an additional 1,200 programs in twenty-two languages from its San Francisco headquarters. About 700 people were employed for this work. News, news features, analyses, and entertainment constituted the main program fare. In the early stages of the war, emphasis was placed on spot military and political news, but later on more use was made of round tables, special events, interviews, and commentaries. Entertainment consisted of drama, music, poetry, and talks on noncontroversial subjects.[13] At the end of the war, the OWI had a world communications system of 36 transmitters in continental United States and 14 overseas.

The OWI overseas branch did not broadcast to Latin-American countries, which were assigned to the Office of Inter-American Affairs headed by Nelson Rockefeller. The OIAA carried on its own schedule of short-wave programs to our Latin-American allies.

To sustain morale among soldiers and sailors overseas, the Army and Navy set up a joint broadcast operation called Armed Forces Radio Service, which provided entertainment and information for troops stationed in Europe and in the Pacific areas. Small stations were built at headquarters or advanced bases to broadcast recorded music, news, transcriptions of the best network shows with the commercials deleted, and especially prepared AFRS shows.

In 1944, the American Broadcasting Station in Europe (ABSIE) was set up in London

> to broadcast both locally originated and New York programs to the people of Europe as required by the immediate necessities of the invasion and the liberation of the continent. One of the great prizes of the European campaign from the propaganda point of view was the capture of Radio Luxembourg practically intact.[14]

In addition, psychological warfare units were established in the Army and Navy to make use of the latest techniques of strategic and combat propaganda. The most notable use of this weapon during the war were the broadcast talks of Navy Captain Zacharias to the people of Japan.[15]

To detect drifts in Germany policy, the Federal Communications Commission established the Foreign Broadcast Intelligence Service, with a staff of 300 linguists and technicians who recorded and transcribed almost a million words a day of Axis propaganda broadcasts. These scripts were carefully studied for clues to enemy thinking, and daily analyses were prepared for State, War, and Navy department officials.

[13] Thomson, op. cit., pp. 55-56.
[14] Ibid., p. 54.
[15] Ellis M. Zacharias, Secret Missions (New York, 1946).

It is hard to evaluate the total effectiveness of all these efforts at radio propaganda and counter-propaganda. Judging by the large sums and effort expended on radio by Germany, Britain, and the Soviet Union, it would seem that the military and diplomatic leaders of those countries firmly believed that radio was playing an important part in the war. Isolated instances of surrenders which were attributed to specific radio broadcasts by the defeated soldiers bolstered the belief in radio's power. From subjected peoples in occupied countries, there came surreptitious but eloquent testimony to the psychological value of international broadcasting, and from underground agents, communicated with by radio, came evidence of specific military value. At the end of World War II, General Eisenhower said:

> ... I am convinced that the expenditure of men and money in wielding the spoken and written word was an important contributing factor in undermining the enemy's will to resist and supporting the fighting morale of our potential Allies in the occupied countries. ... Psychological warfare has proved its right to a place of dignity in our military arsenal.[16]

• THE COLD WAR IN RADIO •

The Voice of America. Shortly after the Japanese surrender was announced in August, 1945, President Truman abolished the domestic bureau of the OWI and transferred the functions and personnel of its overseas branch to the Department of State. There it remained until Congress, feeling that the commercial radio industry should handle overseas broadcasting, divested the State Department almost completely of its authority over the Voice of America by requiring that 75 per cent of the broadcasts be prepared and produced by NBC and CBS on a contractual basis. After a series of embarrassing incidents involving several scripts that irked some Congressmen, this arrangement came to an end in the spring of 1948, much to the relief of the networks, which had not wanted the job. The United States Information and Educational Exchange Act of 1948 effected this change. The law committed the United States for the first time in our history, in time of peace, to engage in international broadcasting, and assigned the Voice of America to the State Department.

In 1953, after another investigation of our overseas information program, the Voice of America was transferred from the State Department to the newly created United States Information Agency, an independent government agency.

The work of the Voice of America is "to submit evidence to the peoples of other nations ... that the objectives and policies of the United States are in harmony with and will advance their legitimate aspirations for freedom,

---

[16] The Psychological Warfare Division, Supreme Headquarters, Allied Expeditionary Force, *An Account of Its Operations in the Western European Campaign, 1944-1945* (Bad Homburg, Germany, 1945), frontispiece.

progress, and peace." The Voice is also committed to combat international communism and expose Soviet imperialism. The Voice has a network of 78 transmitters of which 30 are short-wave stations located in the United States and ranging in power from 25,000 watts to 200,000 watts. VOA relay stations abroad are located at Munich, Salonika, Tangier, Ceylon, Honolulu, the Philippines, and Okinawa. These installations comprise short-wave, medium-wave, and long-wave transmitters, including 1,000,000-watt transmitters—the most powerful in the world—in the Philippines, at Okinawa, and in Munich. Other relay facilities are leased from the BBC in England and through arrangements with broadcasting organizations in various other countries. The Voice also has a floating broadcasting station, the U. S. Coast Guard Cutter *Courier,* which carries high-powered medium- and short-wave transmitters. The *Courier* provides the VOA with a mobile relay station to meet the demands of changing world conditions and to combat Soviet jamming more effectively.

The Voice broadcasts more than 75 separate programs, ranging from five minutes to an hour in length for a total of thirty and a half hours a day in 38 languages. The broadcasts consist of news, news analyses and features, including commentaries, press reviews, documentaries, discussions, and special events. The program content is generally balanced between 50 per cent news and 50 per cent analyses and features. Of the VOA's total output, approximately 77 per cent is directed to Communist China and countries behind the Iron Curtain. In addition to regular short-wave broadcasts, the Voice ships transcribed radio programs to its relay stations and to local radio stations in foreign countries. The annual budget of the VOA is about $17 million and it employs about 1,600 trained people at home and abroad.

It is difficult to assess the effectiveness of the Voice of America, but definite indications of its value are available. Foremost is the attention given to the VOA by the Soviet Union. This attention has taken the form of continuous and vitriolic attacks on the Voice of America by the controlled press of the U.S.S.R. and its satellites, but of even greater significance have been the large-scale Soviet jamming operations designed to keep VOA broadcasts out of eastern Europe. The Russians have put an estimated 1,000 jamming transmitters into operation at 25 major centers, according to Theodore Streibert, Director of the United States Information Agency.[17]

Specific reactions within the Soviet Union produced by individual broadcasts also cast light on the effectiveness of the VOA in piercing the Iron Curtain. In August, 1948, Osana Kasenkina startled the world by leaping to freedom from the Soviet Consulate in New York City. News of her leap was beamed by the Voice of America to the U.S.S.R. in a few minutes and became common knowledge in Moscow within an hour. American officials in the Russian capital learned of the event from embassy servants who in

[17] Address before the Institute for Education by Radio and Television, Columbus, Ohio, April 8, 1954.

turn had been told about it by friends who had heard the broadcast. Other evidence of the VOA's effectiveness has been obtained from reports of travelers returning from eastern Europe, by letters from listeners, by audience surveys in countries outside the Soviet orbit, and by interviews with escapees.

In television, the Voice of America concentrates on acquiring kinescopes and films from domestic television networks and independent producers for distribution abroad. Through this means the Voice services 18 individual television stations in fifteen foreign countries with an hour and a quarter a week of diversified program material, covering news, special events, historical and cultural subjects. The limited television facilities in many countries prevent the VOA's television activities from assuming any of the large-scale proportions of its radio service.

Radio Free Europe. Operating independently of the Voice of America is "Radio Free Europe," a private organization supported by contributions to the "Crusade for Freedom." With its broadcasting headquarters in Munich, Germany, Radio Free Europe uses five radio stations and 29 powerful transmitters to beam radio programs in native tongues to Czechoslovakia, Hungary, Poland, Rumania, and Bulgaria. Most RFE programs are written and presented by exiles from these countries and bring the people in the Soviet satellite countries news and information about the world outside their homeland, as well as news about their own countries that is often suppressed by the governments in power. Satellite listeners often hear important news about Soviet Russia over RFE before they hear it on Radio Moscow, Budapest, Warsaw, or Prague. For instance, the first bulletins on Stalin's death, Beria's purge, and Malenkov's resignation were broadcast by RFE many hours before Communist stations carried the news. As a private organization, RFE operates free from the diplomatic handicaps imposed on the Voice of America. In 1955, RFE had a staff of 1,468 and it broadcast twenty hours of programs a day.

BBC Overseas Service. Ever since Great Britain awakened in 1938 to the needs of regular international broadcasting as an instrument of foreign policy, the BBC Overseas Service has taken leadership and now offers what is clearly the most active short-wave broadcast schedule in the world. It is supported by an annual grant-in-aid of more than £4 million (about $11 million) from the Exchequer, or about half the money spent by the BBC in running its domestic radio services. The Overseas Service beams an elaborate schedule of programs round-the-clock to meet the political, cultural, and geographical needs of different regions and countries throughout the world. Included within the short-wave operations of the BBC are the General Overseas Service (GOS), special regional overseas services, the European services, Arabic, and the North and Latin-American services.

The General Overseas Service is intended for listeners in the British Commonwealth at large, but it is also followed by British people and others who understand English in many countries outside the Commonwealth. The General Overseas Service offers a full schedule of news, talks, music, interviews, and special events. The BBC publishes *London Calling,* which gives advance details of the BBC's short-wave services and is sold everywhere the BBC is heard except in England itself.

The special Regional Overseas Services are prepared for individual members of the Commonwealth, such as the African and West Indian colonies, Australia, Canada, and Newfoundland. The European Services, aimed at 21 different countries on the continent and broadcast in native tongues, has scheduled news, features, talks, and programs of special interest of the area of reception. BBC news broadcasts continue to maintain their wartime hold over listeners throughout Europe, and in countries like Czechoslovakia, the BBC still attracts very large audiences. A listener survey in France showed that about 17 per cent of the adult French population listen to the BBC from time to time, and that as many as a million and a half do so regularly. Broadcasts in Arabic, Turkish, and Iranian languages are beamed to the Near East for one or more hours a day, and to the Far East a daily half-hour of English is broadcast along with foreign language programs. For its coverage of Latin America, Canada, and the United States, BBC depends primarily on arrangements with stations and networks for rebroadcasts of outstanding BBC programs.

CBC International Service. Canada inaugurated the CBC International Service toward the close of World War II. Its purpose is "to present an honest, objective, colorful picture of Canada and Canadian life through information talks, commentaries, news and entertainment programs." The CBC's International Service is now transmitted in thirteen languages to 11 distinct geographical areas in Europe, South America, South Africa and Australia. The International Service is operated by the CBC for the Canadian government and is financed by a Parliamentary grant of funds. An active broadcast exchange arrangement is maintained with Radiodiffusion Française for the benefit of French-Canadian listeners as well as listeners in France. Over 3,000 broadcasts are made each year by the CBC in the Czech, Dutch, German, Danish, Swedish and Norwegian tongues. Relay and rebroadcast arrangements with friendly countries enable wider reception of CBC news commentary, educational, dramatic, and music programs. In one year more than 37,000 letters were received from listeners throughout the world.

WRUL Interamerican Network. The WRUL Interamerican Network, with studio headquarters in New York City and powerful shortwave transmitters in Scituate, Massachusetts, is operated for the purpose of promoting hemispheric understanding by broadcasting programs from New York to Latin-American stations and by supplying international business organizations with an efficient advertising medium. The network is owned by the World Wide Broadcasting System and has been operated commerciaify only since World War II. The network comprises 16 stations in Colombia, 14 in Venezuela, 11 in Cuba, nine in Central America, three in Puerto Rico, and one in the Dominican Republic, reaching an estimated aggregate audience of 2,650,000 listeners on an average evening. Eight stations in Mexico often rebroadcast WRUL network shows. The programs are in Spanish and emphasize news and music. Special events also play an important role in the program schedule of the network which has covered such events as Vice-President Nixon's goodwill tour of Central America and various inter-American conferences. Stations on the WRUL network receive the programs by short-wave and then rebroadcast them locally over the frequencies used in domestic broadcasting. Commercial fees from advertisers are divided roughly 55 per cent to the affiliated stations and 45 per cent to the network, which supplies sustaining programs without charge to the affiliates.

• EUROVISION •

"Eurovision," an experimental television network of eight different countries in Europe, was launched in June, 1954, with programs featuring a personal appearance of the Pope and a tour of St. Peter's Basilica and a pick-up of a flower festival in Switzerland. Eurovision represents the result of tremendous effort by internationally minded Europeans to link their countries together through television. Making Eurovision possible required the solution of enormous problems: eight different governments, six different languages, three different technical transmission standards, union conflicts and 4,000 miles of linkage, including relays over the mountains of Switzerland. Of the eight governments, Great Britain uses a technical television picture definition of 405 lines, France and Belgium use 819 lines, and West Germany, Italy, Holland, Switzerland, and Denmark use 625 lines. A giant transformer installed in northern France converted the three standards into one. About a hundred relay stations, including one 10,000 feet up in the Swiss Alps, feed Eurovision programs to 55 transmitting stations. The programs are mainly special events and artistic presentations that can be comprehended despite differences in language and customs. Initially, Eurovision transmitted three programs a week to the eight countries. Eventually it is hoped that a heavier program schedule will serve to increase international ties throughout western Europe.

• THE UNITED NATIONS AND RADIO •

When the United Nations was established, there were high hopes that international broadcasting might be turned into an instrument of peace and understanding. In October, 1946, the UN Radio Division was set up on a meager basis with one studio and some recording facilities for radio correspondents. The next year the UN asked the CBC and the United States Department of State to make available to it their short-wave transmitters to disseminate programs of the UN. Since those modest beginnings, UN radio "has developed into a world-wide network operating in twenty-seven languages, using short-wave transmitters in the United States, Canada, Great Britain, Switzerland, and Tangier." [18] Its programs are rebroadcast daily in 33 countries and its recorded programs are played on thousands of stations, including more than one thousand in the United States.

UN programs include broadcasts of the proceedings of important meetings of the General Assembly and its agencies, recorded excerpts from the meetings, news, interviews, dramas, and special features. These broadcasts report day-to-day developments in the UN and explain the varied activities of the organization. UN radio programs have been carried by American networks and independent stations on a sustaining basis. English language broadcasts account for only about half of the UN's radio schedule, however. Programs are beamed to Europe and the Middle East, to the Latin-American countries, and Pacific Ocean areas.

UNESCO, a subsidiary organ of the UN, has also indicated a vital interest in broadcasting by financing several surveys of the radio and television facilities of countries throughout the world.[19] In these projects, UNESCO is obliged to concern itself solely with the technical equipment needed for broadcasting, and to assume that peaceful and constructive use will be made of the improved facilities.

· SUMMARY ·

International broadcasting enables nations to communicate information and propaganda across territorial borders instantaneously and without censorship. Propaganda by short-wave was perfected by Nazi Germany as a political weapon of terror, deception, and demoralization. World War II saw the full flowering of radio as a weapon of psychological warfare. Since the war, international broadcasting, as an instrument of foreign policy, has been continued on a large scale through the Voice of America, the BBC Overseas Service, the CBC International Service, and other broadcasting activities.

Questions for Discussion

1. What advantages does international broadcasting have over other means of communication across national frontiers?
2. How was international broadcasting used in the 30's to influence world public opinion?

[18] Rankin, *op. cit.*, p. 30.
[19] See Bibliography for a list of some of these publications.

3. How was radio used to achieve victory in World War II?
4. What should be the programming policy of the Voice of America to promote better understanding of the United States throughout the world?
5. How can international broadcasting be used by the United Nations to foster peace?

❋ 13 ❋

Educational Radio
and Television

OF ALL THE USES to which radio and television have been put, none has commanded more enthusiasm and at times led to as much disappointment as the educational uses of the broadcasting media. No other means of transmitting knowledge broadly, whether by the printed book, the classroom lecture or discussion, or the magazine article, would seem nearly as effective as radio and television which allow a single teacher to address an educational message to audiences of thousands and, at times, of millions of people. Nevertheless, for a variety of reasons, radio and television have not displaced, and probably never will, traditional means of education; instead, radio and television have been used on a limited scale to supplement and enrich traditional modes of education and, in certain instances, where traditional devices have been found seriously wanting, they have served to fill previously untended needs.

• THE EDUCATIONAL PROGRAM •

What makes a radio or television program educational? Few questions have been subject to more dispute in the field of broadcasting than this. Answers have ranged from the extreme view that any broadcast program constitutes an experience in itself and therefore is educational to the listener or viewer, to the opposite extreme that holds that a program is educational only if it is presented by an educational institution. Neither extreme position is tenable. To equate education with all human experiences, without regard to the nature of the experience and the effect it has on the individual, is to ignore the realities of human life; the advances of civilization were made possible only by the classification of knowledge and the interpretation and evaluation of significant human experience. To say that only educational institutions can teach is to ignore another reality; many other social institu-

194

tions participate in the educational process in various ways and with various degrees of effectiveness.

We know that certain programs are educational to some and not to others, depending upon the state of their interests, knowledge, and learning capacities. In other words, a radio or television program, like a book or magazine article or lecture, is educational only to the extent that it has an educational effect upon an audience. This effect may be one of several types: (1) it may involve adding to the significant knowledge of the audience— knowledge that can be applied for constructive individual and social purposes; (2) it may involve training in and understanding of significant skills; (3) it may involve extending the range of the cultural experience of the audience, with a view toward developing an appreciation of artistic expression and a refinement of artistic tastes; (4) it may involve an exploration of the materials and bases of social and political values and human judgments, toward the end that these values and judgments will be in accord with facts and supported by reason.

To achieve any one of these educational effects, the educational program, like the effective lecture or the well-written book, must capture the attention of the intended audience and hold attention throughout the presentation. Although it is obvious to all that a class that is not paying attention is not learning from its teacher, teachers who engage in broadcasting sometimes ignore the equally obvious fact that listeners and viewers whose attention is not captured will turn to another station or turn off their receiver. In radio and television the techniques of commanding attention are referred to as "showmanship," although the process involved is fundamentally identical to that found in the classroom of effective teachers. To qualify as educational, a radio or television program must combine showmanship with the objective of achieving one or more of the educational effects described above. A successful educational program is one that achieves its objectives to a significant extent.

· ADVANTAGES OF THE EDUCATIONAL PROGRAM ·

There are several unique characteristics of radio and television that make these media especially useful for educational purposes. Among these characteristics are the following: (1) ease of communication; (2) a sense of reality; (3) technical assets available through the media; (4) timeliness; (5) special motivation.

Ease of Communication. Through radio, and even more so through television, it is possible to communicate knowledge quickly to large groups of people situated at different points throughout the country or in small geographic areas. Although the distances may be great in terms of the number of miles between the teacher and the audience, the communicative bond between the two always remains intimate and direct. Through radio or television, thousands of students can be brought into intimate contact with great teachers. The general public need not leave their living rooms to make contact with great minds.

A Sense of Reality. Educational radio and television programs may use as their subject matter real people and the materials of life in a way that is beyond the capacity of the classroom teacher or the writer of books. For example, to explain the governmental process, it becomes possible on radio and television to interview public officials, to observe them in debate, to observe public ceremonies; to discuss art, it becomes possible to bring a masterpiece into the classroom via television. Emotional reactions and attitudes toward people and institutions are also conveyed through radio and television. A "feeling with" peoples of other areas and other races and creeds is inspired when students are transferred by sight and sound to distant places and come into contact with strange people through presentations of their music, art, and literature.

Technical Assets. The radio and television media themselves offer certain technical assets to teaching that are not otherwise available except through the use of motion picture film or recordings. For example, closed circuit television demonstrations of surgery have made it possible for large numbers of medical students to obtain a front row view of operations through the use of the camera close-up. Radio and television dramatizations of significant subject matter also contribute to better understanding and learning, as do documentaries that present facts and interpretations in a dramatized fashion.

Timeliness. Textbooks are often behind the sweep of world events. Even magazines are a step or two removed from the actual events. Special events, news programs, and lecture material refreshed with the latest developments in related fields, make it possible for radio and television presentations by experts to keep teachers and students in the classroom up-to-date in various subject fields.

Special Motivation. Because of the special way in which radio and television programming has captured the public imagination, all communication via these media tends to benefit by the public excitement and to motivate the audience more easily than many other forms of communication. This additional element of special motivation on the part of the student often can make the difference between the attentiveness necessary to learn from a presentation and the boredom that forestalls all learning.

• LIMITATIONS OF THE EDUCATIONAL PROGRAM •

Together with these assets one finds a number of important shortcomings in the educational uses of radio and television. These are: (1) lack of a reciprocal relationship; (2) lack of flexibility; (3) lack of regularity and system; (4) limitation in the physical senses utilized.

Lack of a Reciprocal Relationship. Doubtless the gravest shortcoming to the educational use of radio and television is the lack of a reciprocal relationship between the teacher and the student. There is no way for the student at home or in the classroom to ask questions of the studio teacher during the broadcast. Nor is it possible for the teacher to read the faces of his students to determine how well his material is being understood and whether or not another example or analogy is required to clarify any particular point. The unseen, albeit perceived, student remains much of a mystery to the teacher; to the student the broadcaster remains a distant and unapproachable teacher. In an effort to simulate a true reciprocal educational relationship, some educational broadcasters have brought small groups of students into the studio to serve in place of the unseen broadcast audience. It is generally agreed, however, that only the teacher physically present in the classroom or in the personal teaching situation can fully round out the educational experience.

Lack of Flexibility. Instruction via radio or television contends with the problem of a single fixed presentation for an audience that in many ways is heterogeneous in interest, knowledge, and learning capacities. This is especially true in the case of broadcasts directed to the general adult audience, although it is also true that such broadcasts tend by their very nature to draw more homogeneous audiences than programs of pure entertainment.

Lack of Regularity and System. Effective education generally depends upon an organized presentation of subject matter in a graduated and systematic fashion. The transmission of miscellaneous data and information on an irregular basis rarely results in anything approximating genuine education. Except in school broadcasting situations, such as those described later in this chapter, educational radio and television almost always suffer from a lack of regularity and system in the presentation of material to a constantly changing audience some of whom have attended the previous program in the series and others of whom have not. There is no way of insuring attendance at each presentation in a sequence.

Limitation in the Physical Senses Utilized. The ability to command attention and to communicate meaning and emotion is usually closely related to the variety of physical senses through which the meaning and emotion can be reinforced and restated. One of the main handicaps of radio, like the limitation of the printed page, is its use of only a single physical sense to convey meaning. Certain subjects like music suffer much less by this limitation of radio than other subjects such as geography. On the other hand, color television, combining motion, color, and sound, is extremely effective in communicating chemical demonstrations or works of art.

• TYPES OF EDUCATIONAL PROGRAMS •

Several major types of educational programs have been developed that work within the limitations of radio and television and capitalize on the unique characteristics of the media. They are: (1) direct classroom teaching; (2) supplementary classroom teaching; (3) intraschool broadcasting; (4) informal preschool and out-of-school education; (5) formal adult education; (6) informal adult education; and (7) integrated education and entertainment.

Direct Classroom Teaching. Educational programs on radio and television have been used for direct classroom teaching in various public school systems and by United States military organizations. The U. S. Army Signal Corps in 1955 released the results of a study involving 15,000 trainees who received instruction in basic and technical subjects via closed circuit television. Comparison between television and regular instruction under matched conditions showed that television instruction generally was more effective than the regular instruction, particularly effective for individuals with lower aptitudes, and remembered at least as well as regular instruction by trainees of all intelligence ratings, and even better than regular instruction by those with low intelligence ratings. It does not necessarily follow, of course, that these results will obtain in other types of classroom situations outside the military, or in other than basic and technical subjects.

In the use of radio and television for direct classroom teaching, the program is planned as a substitute for instruction by the classroom teacher. In public education, this use of radio and television is generally limited to subjects that most classroom teachers are unable to handle very effectively. Many rural schools where teaching staffs often lack qualified instructors in various subjects make extensive use of direct classroom broadcasts when they are made available.

The use of closed circuit television (nonbroadcast) for direct teaching purposes appears to be gaining the interest of many professional educators. Experiments in this method of instruction have been conducted at Pennsylvania State and New York University. Many national business organizations have used closed circuit television to convey information and sales instructions to their employees throughout the country. The military services have also made use of closed circuit television in troop training.

Supplementary Classroom Teaching. This is a much more common form of instruction by radio or television. In the state of Wisconsin, for example, for the last twenty-five years hundreds of public elementary schools have made a regular practice of incorporating a systematic schedule of educational radio programs into their regular curricula. Through the use of published syllabi, series of programs in music appreciation, art, geography, nature study, social studies, current events, and history have been coordinated with the regular courses of instruction and synchronized with the classroom schedules. To be used effectively as a supplementary teaching device, teachers must prepare their pupils for the important points to be made in broadcast programs. After the program, they must follow up with appropriate classroom discussions of the program. Many school systems, including those in New York City, Cleveland, Philadelphia, Chicago, and other cities, use radio and, in some cases television, for this purpose. For many years the national radio networks broadcast educational programs for supplementary classroom use. Many adults recall that their first regular musical instruction in the 1930's came from Dr. Walter Damrosch's music-appreciation broadcasts over NBC; others can recall the instruction provided by the "Columbia School of the Air" which was broadcast to schools in the morning for many years, and subsequently was shifted to the late afternoon after schools recessed for the day. Because of time zone differences throughout the country, it is extremely difficult to broadcast programs for reception in schools on a national basis.

Intraschool Broadcasting. Schools of all levels have begun intraschool broadcasting, a simulated form of broadcasting which uses public-address sound systems that permit simultaneous reception in all or in a select number of classrooms in the school. This practice provides many opportunities to integrate various class activities. Student interest increases when the "home folks" do the broadcasting. The number and types of intraschool broadcasting activities are practically limitless. A program series such as "Quiz of Two Classes," matches one section of English with another on questions of vocabulary and grammar, or, in Social Studies, on questions of American History. A school "Information, Please" contest is held, with individual classes conducting elimination contests to select representatives for the final program. Students are encouraged to review class assignments in order to prepare the questions to be used, thus securing participation in the activity by more than a board of experts. Even the disc-jockey program has been used to communicate news of school events, public service announcements about school safety and charity drives, and for interviews with teachers and administrators about school traditions and regulations, sandwiched in between the playing of popular music records during lunch or home-room periods.

Informal Preschool and Out-of-School Education. Many educational programs are intended for listening and viewing by youngsters at home—those too young to go to school and the youngsters who have returned home from school. "Ding Dong School," one of the most successful educational television programs, is telecast by NBC every morning Monday through Friday for an audience of preschool children. "The Friendly Giant," telecast over WHA-TV in Madison, Wisconsin, and "The Children's Corner" in Pittsburgh, are other programs of the type broadcast on a local basis. "Let's Take a Trip," a CBS network television program, provides children at home with an opportunity to visit various interesting places through the use of a television mobile unit. "Disneyland," an ABC television network show, effectively combines educational materials with good entertainment for out-of-school viewing. Various educational radio programs, including programs of story-telling and the playing of games, have likewise attracted regular listening by youngsters.

Formal Adult Education. The use of radio and television for transmitting formal adult education has been limited mainly to credit courses given over local broadcasting facilities by the extension division of various universities. These broadcasts are, of course, available for listening or viewing by anyone and cannot be limited to the students who register by mail and pay an enrollment fee for the receipt of study materials, reading lists, syllabi, and a final examination which they must take in person, usually on the university campus. Western Reserve University, Michigan State University, and other institutions have experimented with the telecast of college courses for credit. The University of Houston has telecast regular undergraduate lecture courses which resident students may view in their rooms instead of at the college lecture hall. The state universities of Wisconsin, Ohio, Illinois, and Minnesota have for many years broadcast by radio many university courses, many directly from the college classroom and others from radio studios, which range freely, yet systematically, over the arts and science curriculum. Listeners at home are at liberty, however, to tune in only when they desire to, and there are no certificates of completion of instruction.

Informal Adult Education. The most common type of educational radio and television program is devoted to informal adult education. It seeks a broad appeal, it usually has interesting subject matter, and it generally lacks a systematic and graduated plan of instruction. Each program generally stands by itself and is evaluated independently. In radio, discussion and documentary programs provide informal adult education. In television, programs such as "Dr. Frank Baxter," "Dr. Spock," "Omnibus," "Adventure," "See It Now," "Meet the Press," "March of Medicine," "You Are There," "Wide, Wide World," as well as special one-time-only programs and dramatic series of literary distinction, usually offer informal adult education.

Integrated Education and Entertainment. It has been said that people obtain their greatest satisfaction from programs that not only entertain them but also give them a feeling of having been enriched by the experience. Such is certainly the case with great dramatic and documentary presentations. In many popular entertainment programs a conscious effort is made to integrate items of some educational significance, whether it be an operatic aria in a popular music program or a commentary on college activity in connection with the pick-up of a football game. Such educational efforts, while they reach large audiences, often suffer from the complete lack of system in presentation and represent only a miscellaneous kind of education. With careful treatment, however, integrated education and entertainment on a large scale over a substantial period of time can leaven popular tastes and create demand for better things.

• EDUCATIONAL NONCOMMERCIAL RADIO STATIONS •

Much of the solid work in educational radio programming has been done in a number of separate geographical areas across the country by a group of educational noncommercial radio stations operated by universities, school systems, and municipalities. These stations are financed by allocations of state or municipal tax money and by endowments and special grants from philanthropic organizations. The stations operate modestly but earnestly and often very effectively with a singleness of purpose—the rendering of a public service through the broadcast of programs of education, information, and constructive entertainment. The educational programs consist of the types mentioned above; the informational programs consist mainly of news, consumer and marketing information, public-health guidance, government reports, etc.; the entertainment usually concentrates on wholesome children's programs, classical music recordings and occasionally live performances, and dramatizations of literary works.

During the first decade of radio broadcasting, there were a large number of educational radio stations, but most of them were concerned primarily with experimenting with the physical and engineering aspects of the broadcast medium. During the 1930's and early 1940's, a hard core of some 20-odd educational radio stations broadcast in the AM band. Some of these stations, like those affiliated with the state universities of Wisconsin, Iowa, Minnesota, Illinois, Ohio, and Oklahoma, as well as WNYC, the municipally-owned and -operated station in New York City, competed successfully with the networks in winning awards for superior educational programming. After World War II, with the development of FM radio and the allocation by the FCC of the 88-92 megacycle band for educational use only, it became possible for many other state universities, school systems, and local schools to establish their own FM radio stations, many of them low-powered, with transmission power limited to 10 watts to provide coverage within a small community area. There are now more than 100 educational FM radio stations in operation, along with the more than 20 educational AM stations, with an estimated broadcast coverage of approximately 50 per cent of the American people. Their actual audiences, however, in contrast with the potential audience, are very small in comparison with the audiences attracted to commercial network radio and television offerings, but large in comparison with the size of the publics reached by other educational media.

Most educational stations belong to the National Association of Educational Broadcasters, with headquarters located at the University of Illinois, at Urbana.[1] With the support of grants-in-aid received from various philanthropic groups, including the Fund for Adult Education and the W. K. Kellogg Foundation, the NAEB has operated a "tape network," furnishing tape recordings of superior educational programs to member stations, and has commissioned the production of several important educational program series.

A list of noncommercial AM and FM educational radio stations in the United States appears on the following pages and indicates the broad distribution of these stations.

NONCOMMERCIAL EDUCATIONAL AM RADIO STATIONS *

City	Call	Licensee	Frequency	Power
Urbana, Ill.	WILL	U. of Illinois	580 kc.	5 kw.
Lafayette, Ind.	WBAA	Purdue U.	920 kc.	5 kw.
Ames, Iowa	WOI	Iowa State College	640 kc.	5 kw.
Decorah, Iowa	KWLC	Luther College	1240 kc.	250 w.
Iowa City, Ia.	WSUI	State U. of Iowa	910 kc.	5 kw.
Lawrence, Kan.	KFKU	U. of Kansas	1250 kc.	5 kw.
Manhattan, Kan.	KSAC	Kansas State College	580 kc.	5 kw.
East Lansing, Mich.	WKAR	Michigan State College	870 kc.	5 kw.
Minneapolis, Minn.	KUOM	U. of Minnesota	770 kc.	5 kw.
Northfield, Minn.	WCAL	St. Olaf College	770 kc.	5 kw.
New York, N. Y.	WNYC	City of New York	830 kc.	1 kw.
Troy, N. Y.	WHAZ	Rensselaer Polytechnical Institute	1330 kc.	1 kw.
Grand Forks, N. D.	KFJM	U. of North Dakota	1440 kc.	1 kw. (Day) 500 w. (Night)
Columbus, Ohio	WOSU	Ohio State U.	820 kc.	5 kw.
Norman, Okla.	WNAD	U. of Oklahoma	640 kc.	1 kw.
Stillwater, Okla.	KOAG	Oklahoma A & M College	840 kc.	10 kw.
Corvallis, Ore.	KOAC	Oregon State College	550 kc.	5 kw.
Portland, Ore.	KBPS	Portland Public Schools	1450 kc.	250 w.
Grove City, Pa.	WSAJ	Grove City College	1340 kc.	100 w.
Vermillion, S. D.	KUSD	U. of South Dakota	690 kc.	1 kw.
Pullman, Wash.	KWSC	State College of Washington	1250 kc.	5 kw.
Madison, Wis.	WHA	U. of Wisconsin	970 kc.	5 kw.
San Juan, Puerto Rico	WIPR	Oficina de Radio- emision Publica	940 kc.	10 kw.

* Those listed as members of the NAEB, October 1, 1954.

[1] See Harold E. Hill, *The National Association of Educational Broadcasters: A History.* (Published by the NAEB, 14 Gregory Hall, Urbana, Illinois, 1954), pp. 61 (mimeo.)

NONCOMMERCIAL EDUCATIONAL FM RADIO STATIONS †

(As of November 22, 1954)

City	Call	Licensee	Frequency	Effective Radiated Power
		ALABAMA		
Tuscaloosa	WUOA	U. of Alabama	91.7 mc	4.8 kw
		ARIZONA		
Phoenix	KFCA	Phoenix College	88.5 mc	10 w
		CALIFORNIA		
Berkeley	KPFB	Pacifica Foundation	89.3 mc	150 w
Long Beach	KLON	Board of Education	88.1 mc	10 w
Los Angeles	KUSC	U. of Southern California	91.5 mc	2.9 kw
Oceanside	KOEN	Oceanside-Carlsbad Union High School District	89.7 mc	10 w
San Bernardino	KVCR	San Bernardino Valley Union Junior College District	91.9 mc	770 w
San Diego	KSDS	San Diego Unified School District	88.3 mc	375 w
San Francisco	KALW	San Francisco Unified School District	91.7 mc	3.3 kw
San Mateo	KSCM	San Mateo Junior College	90.9 mc	10 w
Santa Clara	KSCU*	U. of Santa Clara	90.1 mc	2.45 kw
Santa Monica	KCRW	Santa Monica School Board	89.9 mc	400 w
Stockton	KCVN	College of the Pacific	91.3 mc	3.4 kw
		COLORADO		
Colorado Spgs.	KRCC	Colorado College	91.3 mc	165 w
		FLORIDA		
Lakeland	WFSI	Florida Southern College	88.1 mc	10 w
Miami	WTHS	Lindsey Hopkins Vocational School, Dade County Board of Public Instruction	91.7 mc	5 kw
Tallahassee	WFSU-FM	Florida State U.	91.5 mc	10 w
Tampa	WTUN	U. of Tampa	88.9 mc	770 w
Winter Park	WPRK	Rollins College	91.5 mc	650 w 330 w*

† From *1955 Broadcasting Yearbook-Marketbook.*
* Indicates construction permit only

NONCOMMERCIAL EDUCATIONAL FM RADIO
STATIONS (cont.)

City	Call	Licensee	Fre-quency	Effective Radiated Power
GEORGIA				
Atlanta	WABE	Board of Education	90.1 mc	4.8 kw
HAWAII				
Honolulu	KUOH*	U. of Hawaii	90.5	10 w
Honolulu	KVOK	Kamehameha Schools	88.1 mc	10 w
ILLINOIS				
Chicago	WBEZ	Board of Education	91.5 mc	16 kw
De Kalb	WNIC	Northern Ill. State Teachers College	91.1 mc	10 w
Elgin	WEPS	Board of Education Union School District No. 46	88.1 mc	10 w
Evanston	WNUR	Northwestern University	89.3 mc	10 w
Urbana	WILL-FM	U. of Illinois	91.7 mc 90.9 mc*	100 w 300 kw*
INDIANA				
Evansville	WEVC	Evansville College	91.5 mc	1.9 kw
Gary	WGVE	School City of Gary	88.1 mc	10 w
Greencastle	WGRE	DePauw U.	91.7 mc	10 w 7 w*
Hartford City	WHCI*	School City of Hartford City	91.9 mc	10 w
Huntington	WVSH	School City of Huntington	91.9 mc	10 w
Indianapolis	WAJC	Butler U.	91.9 mc	700 w
Indianapolis	WIAN*	Board of School Comrs.	90.1 mc	120 w
Muncie	WWHI	Wilson Junior High School	91.5 mc	10 w
New Albany	WNAS	School City of New Albany	88.1 mc	10 w 800 w*
New Castle	WYSN	New Castle Henry Township Schools	91.1 mc	10 w
Wabash	WSKS	School City of Wabash	91.3 mc	10 w
IOWA				
Ames	WOI-FM	Iowa State College of Agriculture and Mechanical Arts	90.1 mc	16 kw
Des Moines	KDPS	Independent School District	88.1 mc	1.5 kw
Iowa City	KSUI	State U. of Iowa	91.7 mc	17.5 kw
Waverly	KWAR	Wartburg Normal College	89.1 mc	10 w

City	Call	Licensee	Frequency	Effective Radiated Power
		KANSAS		
Emporia	KSTE	Kansas State Teachers College	88.7 mc	350 w
Lawrence	KANU	U. of Kansas	91.5 mc	35 kw
Manhattan	KSDB-FM	Kansas State College	88.1 mc	10 w
Ottawa	KTJO-FM	Ottawa U.	88.1 mc	10 w
Wichita	KMUW	Municipal U. of Wichita	89.1 mc	10 w
		KENTUCKY		
Lexington	WBKY	U. of Kentucky	91.3 mc	2.3 kw
Louisville	WFPL	Free Public Library	89.3 mc	150 w
Louisville	WFPK	Free Public Library	91.9 mc	19.5 kw
Louisville	WSDX	Southern Baptist Theological Seminary	90.3 mc	10 w
		LOUISIANA		
Baton Rouge	WLSU	Louisiana State U.	91.7 mc	1.8 kw
New Orleans	WBEH	P. G. Beauregard School	89.3 mc	10 w
		MARYLAND		
Baltimore	WBJC	Baltimore Junior College	88.1 mc	125 w
		MASSACHUSETTS		
Amherst	WMUA	U. of Massachusetts	91.1 mc	10 w
Boston	WBUR	Boston U	90.9 mc	20 kw
Boston	WERS	Emerson College	88.9 mc	18 kw
Boston	WGBH-FM	WGBU Educational Foundation	89.7 mc	15.5 kw
Springfield	WEDK	School Committee of Springfield	91.7 mc	10 w
		MICHIGAN		
Ann Arbor	WUOM	U. of Michigan	91.7 mc	44 kw 92 kw*
Detroit	WDTR	Board of Education	90.9 mc	2 kw
East Lansing	WKAR-FM	Michigan State College	90.5 mc	9.7 kw
Highland Park	WHPR	School District of City of Highland Park	88.1 mc	10 w
Kalamazoo	WMCR	Western Michigan College of Education	91.1 mc	400 w

NONCOMMERCIAL EDUCATIONAL FM RADIO
STATIONS *(cont.)*

City	Call	Licensee	Fre-quency	Effective Radiated Power
		MINNESOTA		
St. Paul	WNOV	Northwest Vocational Institute	89.1 mc	10 w
		MISSISSIPPI		
Meridian	WMMI	Meridian Municipal Junior College	88.1 mc	10 w
		MISSOURI		
St. Louis	KSLH	Board of Education	91.5 mc	12.5 kw
		NEW JERSEY		
Newark	WBGO	Board of Education	88.3 mc	20 kw
South Orange	WSOU	Seton Hall College	89.5 mc	2 kw
		NEW MEXICO		
Albuquerque	KANW	Board of Education	89.1 mc	350 w
		NEW YORK		
Brooklyn, NYC	WNYE	Board of Education	91.5 mc	20 kw
Floral Park	WSHS	Sewanhaka High School	90.3 mc	350 w
Ithaca	WITJ	Ithaca College	91.7 mc	10 w
New York	WFUV	Fordham U	90.7 mc	3.5 kw
Springville	WSPE	Board of Education Central School District No. 1 of towns of Concord, Sardinia and Collins (Erie County) and Ashford, Yorkshire and East Otto (Cattaraugus County)	88.1 mc	10 w
Syracuse	WAER	Syracuse U	88.1 mc	730 w
		NORTH CAROLINA		
Chapel Hill	WUNC	U. of North Carolina	91.5 mc	1.45 kw
Greensboro	WGPS	Board of Trustees Greensboro City Administrative Unit	88.9 mc	10 w
High Point	WHPS	Board of School Commissioners	89.3 mc	10 w

City	Call	Licensee	Fre-quency	Effective Radiated Power

OHIO

City	Call	Licensee	Frequency	Effective Radiated Power
Athens	WOUI	Ohio U	91.5 mc	10 w
Bowling Green	WBGU	Bowling Green State U	88.1 mc	10 w
Cleveland	WBOE	Board of Education	90.3 mc	10 kw
Columbus	WOSU-FM	Ohio State U	89.7 mc	14 kw
Delaware	WSLN	Ohio Wesleyan U	91.1 mc	10 w
Kent	WKSU-FM	Kent State U	88.1 mc	10 w
Oxford	WMUB	Miami U	88.5 mc	6.7 kw
Toledo	WTDS	Board of Education	91.3 mc	730 w

OKLAHOMA

City	Call	Licensee	Frequency	Effective Radiated Power
Norman	WNAD-FM	State U. of Oklahoma	90.9 mc	7 kw
Oklahoma City	KOKH	Board of Education	88.9 mc	7.6 kw
Shawnee	KBGC	Oklahoma Baptist U	89.9 mc	10 w
Tulsa	KWGS	U. of Tulsa	90.5 mc	1.1 kw / 4.1 kw*

OREGON

City	Call	Licensee	Frequency	Effective Radiated Power
Eugene	KWAX	State Board of Higher Education	91.1 mc	10 w
Eugene	KRVM	School District No. 4, Lane County	91.9 mc	400 w
Oretech	KTEC	Oregon Technical Institute	88.1 mc	10 w

PENNSYLVANIA

City	Call	Licensee	Frequency	Effective Radiated Power
Havertown	WHHS	Haverford Township Senior High School	89.3 mc	10 w
Philadelphia	WHYY	Delaware Valley Educational TV Corp.	90.9 mc	20 kw
Philadelphia	WPWT	Philadelphia Wireless Technical Institute	91.7 mc	125 w
Philadelphia	WRTI-FM	Temple U	90.1 mc	10 w
Pittsburgh	WDUQ	Duquesne U	91.5 mc	2.75 kw
Scranton	WUSV	U. of Scranton	89.9 mc	10 w
State College	WDFM	Pennsylvania State College	91.1 mc	250 w

SOUTH CAROLINA

City	Call	Licensee	Frequency	Effective Radiated Power
Columbia	WUSC-FM	Extension Division, U. of South Carolina	89.9 mc	10 w

NONCOMMERCIAL EDUCATIONAL FM RADIO
STATIONS (*cont.*)

City	Call	Licensee	Fre-quency	Effective Radiated Power
		TENNESSEE		
Knoxville	WKCS	Fulton High School	91.1 mc	310 w
Knoxville	WUOT	U. of Tennessee	91.9 mc	3.4 kw
		TEXAS		
Abilene	KACC-FM	Abilene Christian College	91.9 mc	250 w
Dallas	KSMU-FM	Southern Methodist U. of Texas	89.3 mc	10 w
Dallas	KVTT	Texas Trade School	91.7 mc	780 w
El Paso	KVOF-FM	Texas Western College of U. of Tex.	88.5 mc	10 w
Houston	KUHF	U. of Houston	91.3 mc	9.6 kw 9.8 kw*
Plainview	KHBL	Wayland Baptist College	88.1 mc	10 w
		UTAH		
Ephraim	KEPH	Snow Branch Junior College	88.9 mc	10 w
Logan	KVSC	Utah State Agricultural College	88.1 mc	10 w
		VIRGINIA		
Harrisonburg	WEMC*	Eastern Mennonite College	88.1 mc	10 kw
		WASHINGTON		
Seattle	KUOW	U. of Washington	90.5 mc	3.4 kw
Tacoma	KTOY	Tacoma School District 10	91.7 mc	3.5 kw
		WISCONSIN		
Chilton	WHKW	State Radio Council	89.3 mc	51 kw
Colfax	WHWC	State Radio Council	88.3 mc	50 kw
Delafield	WHAD	State Radio Council	90.7 mc	52 kw
Highland Township	WHSA	State Radio Council	88.9 mc	50 kw
Holman	WHLA	State Radio Council	90.3 mc	39 kw
Iowa County	WHHI	State Radio Council	91.3 mc	50 kw
Madison	WHA-FM	State Radio Council	88.7 mc	9.3 kw
Wausau	WHRM	State Radio Council	91.9 mc	114 kw

• EDUCATIONAL TELEVISION STATIONS •

From 1948 to 1952, during the freeze on new television broadcasting licenses, of the 108 television stations in operation only one, WOI-TV, in Ames, Iowa, was owned by an educational institution (Iowa State College). Because it was then the only station serving a substantial population in Iowa, WOI-TV carried commercial network entertainment programs in addition to its own educational offerings. During the course of FCC hearings on the issuance of a new television allocation plan, support was developed throughout the country in behalf of a reservation for educational use of as many as 10 to 25 per cent of the broadcast channels to be made avaliable for television. In a rare demonstration of co-ordinated educational effort, under the leadership of the NAEB and a new organization called the Joint Committee for Educational Television (JCET), located in Washington, seventy-six important witnesses appeared before the FCC in support of educational reservations and formal statements from 838 colleges, universities, school systems, and public service agencies were filed with the Commission. The New York State Board of Regents filed a voluminous brief in behalf of its request that the FCC allocate 11 television channels in New York State for an educational television network. In the FCC's "Sixth Report and Order" issued in 1952, 242 television channels out of a total of 2,053, or slightly more than 11 per cent, were reserved temporarily for application by educational groups only. The number of reservations for education was later increased to 252, of which 168 were UHF assignments.

Following the favorable Commission action, there was a groundswell of activity in educational circles to bring new educational television stations into being. Supported by grants of money from the Fund for Adult Education of the Ford Foundation and with leadership provided by the JCET, educational television seminars and institutes were convened throughout the country to alert educational leaders to the needs and promise of educational television and to draw up plans for action in various states and communities throughout the country.[2] Some of these plans failed to materialize, others were blocked by political obstruction, others failed for want of proper organization and adequate finances, and others succeeded in putting on the air a number of educational television stations that will probably occupy a permanent and important place in the American system of television.

In New York State, the ambitious plan of the Board of Regents for a state-wide educational television network was blocked by the negative report of a special committee appointed by the state governor. The main

[2] For example, see the following reports on special meetings held during this period: Carroll V. Newsom (ed.), *A Television Policy for Education* (Washington, 1952), pp. 266; Lester W. Ingalls, Jr. (ed.), *The Use of Television in Education* (New York, 1953), pp. 98 (pamphlet); Robert C. Anderson (ed.), *Regional Cooperation in Educational Television* (Atlanta, 1953), pp. 88 (pamphlet).

arguments advanced against educational television stations operated by state educational institutions generally appeared to be the following: (1) Where UHF assignments were involved, it was feared that the stations would be unable to overcome the technical handicaps imposed upon them, especially in metropolitan centers where VHF stations were already in operation. This fear would appear to have been justified in many instances, as evidenced by the difficulty encountered by many new commercial UHF stations in VHF centers. (2) The cost of constructing and operating educational television stations was considered too great to justify the expenditures. While it is true that many enthusiasts underestimated television costs, especially those involved in maintaining an active program schedule, it was also true that in a state like New York, for example, the cost of setting up the entire proposed ten-station network did not involve an expenditure greater than that caused by the construction of one new metropolitan high school. (3) It was argued that state operated educational television stations might result in the "socializing" of education, although it was never clear how this was substantially different from the American system of public education under which the state and local communities finance and control all public instruction. (4) It was argued that adequate broadcast time over commercial television stations could be obtained by educational institutions for the presentation of programs of an educational nature although the record of commercial radio broadcasting in this country indicated clearly that, despite the best intentions, commercial broadcast operations could not allow for direct teaching on the air, or for regular broadcast time periods, or for programs of special educational appeal to publics limited in size.

Although opposition of this type developed in certain states, in other areas educational television was advanced with the co-operation of community, business, and educational leaders. A National Citizen's Commission for Educational Television was organized to mobilize public opinion in behalf of the movement. Positive results were soon observed in cities like Houston, Texas, where the first post-freeze educational television station went on the air; in the state of Oklahoma, where a three-station educational television network was authorized by the state legislature which floated public bonds to finance the enterprise. Despite the failure of one UHF station that went on the air and then returned its license, a total of fifteen educational television stations were on the air three years after the FCC allocated the channels. Some of these were operated by individual universities, as in the case of Michigan State University and the University of Nebraska. Other stations, like those in Chicago, San Francisco, Boston, Pittsburgh and St. Louis, were operated by an association of the main educational and cultural institutions in the cities. Still others, like the stations in Alabama and Oklahoma, were operated as part of a state educational television network.

EDUCATIONAL TELEVISION STATIONS ON THE AIR

(as of July 1, 1955)

City	Call Letters	Licensee	Channel
Ames, Iowa	WOI-TV*	Iowa State College	4
Houston, Texas	KUHT	U. of Houston	8
Columbia, Mo.	KOMU-TV*	U. of Missouri	8
East Lansing, Mich.	WKAR-TV**	Michigan State University	60
Pittsburgh, Pa.	WQED	Metropolitan Pittsburgh Educational Television Station	13
Madison, Wis.	WHA-TV	Wisconsin State Radio Council	21
San Francisco, Cal.	KQED	Bay Area Educational Television Association	9
Cincinnati, Ohio	WCET	Greater Cincinnati Educational Television Foundation	48
St. Louis, Mo.	KETC	St. Louis Educational Television Association	9
Lincoln, Neb.	KUON-TV**	U. of Nebraska	12
Seattle, Wash.	KCTS-TV	U. of Washington	9
Munford, Ala.	WTIQ	Alabama Educational Television Commission	7
Chapel Hill, N. C.	WUNC-TV	Consolidated University of North Carolina	4
Birmingham, Ala.	WBIQ	Alabama Educational Television Commission	10
Boston, Mass.	WGBH-TV	Lowell Institute Cooperative Broadcasting Council	2

The Following Stations Were Under Construction on July 1, 1955

City	Call Letters	Licensee	Channel
Andalusia, Ala.	WAIQ	Alabama Educational Television Commission	2
Miami, Fla.	WTHS-TV	Lindsay Hopkins Vocational School of Dade County Board of Public Instruction	2
Urbana, Ill.	WILL-TV	U. of Illinois	12
Chicago, Ill.	WTTW	Chicago Educational Television Association	11
Detroit, Mich.	WTVS	Detroit Educational Television Foundation	56
Columbus, Ohio	WOSU-TV	Ohio State U.	34
Oklahoma City, Okla.	KETA	Oklahoma Educational Television Authority	13
Tulsa, Okla.	KOED-TV	Oklahoma Educational Television Authority	11

* Educational institution operating semicommercially on a nonreserved channel.
** Educational institution operating noncommercially on a nonreserved channel.

In addition, in 1955 applications were pending for educational television stations in the following communities:

Sacramento, Cal.	Central California Educational Television, Inc.
Jacksonville, Fla.	Educational Television, Inc.
Atlanta, Ga.	Atlanta, Ga., Board of Education
Savannah, Ga.	Savannah, Ga., Board of Education
Lawrence, Kans.	U. of Kansas
Philadelphia, Pa.	Delaware Valley ETV Corporation
Providence, R.I.	Rhode Island Board of Education
Memphis, Tenn.	Memphis Community Television Foundation
Nashville, Tenn.	Nashville Educational Television Foundation
San Antonio, Tex.	San Antonio Council for ETV
Milwaukee, Wis.	Milwaukee Board of Vocational and Adult Education and Wisconsin State Radio Council
Toledo, Ohio	Greater Toledo Educational TV Foundation

Construction permits for educational television stations were held, in 1955, by the Denver, Colorado, Public Schools, the Connecticut State Board of Education, Kansas State College, the University of Michigan, the New Jersey State Department of Education, the Puerto Rico Board of Education, and the New York State Board of Regents.

The following statement of program policy of Station WCET, in Cincinnati, is fairly typical of educational television programming intentions:

PROGRAM POLICY OF STATION WCET, CINCINNATI

WCET believes that the proper and adequate use of television is an important adjunct to existing educational processes. In Cincinnati the Educational Television Foundation through its membership calls upon all educational systems and institutions to use this station as a means of extending the cultural and civic benefits of the community to each and every citizen.

Thus, WCET is the voice of organized education in Greater Cincinnati, and with this in mind the station's program policy has been formulated to carry out the following objectives:

1. Systematic programming for children of preschool age;
2. Programs which will enrich the classroom experiences for children in the elementary and secondary schools;
3. Constructive programs for out-of-school hours for children of all ages;
4. Courses in formal education in high school and college subjects for youths and adults;
5. Programs for the home viewer to improve skills and earning power; to better understand civic and community problems and projects; to demonstrate new developments in science, art and international affairs;
6. Music, drama, and other programs in the field of the arts, that are both entertaining and self-improving;
7. Programs which will add to the store of personal values which may contribute to better family life, and the long range welfare of the community and the country.

The organizational chart of KUON-TV, the University of Nebraska educational television station, is representative of most university-operated television stations:

ORGANIZATIONAL CHART OF KUON-TV, CHANNEL 12
University of Nebraska, Lincoln, Nebraska

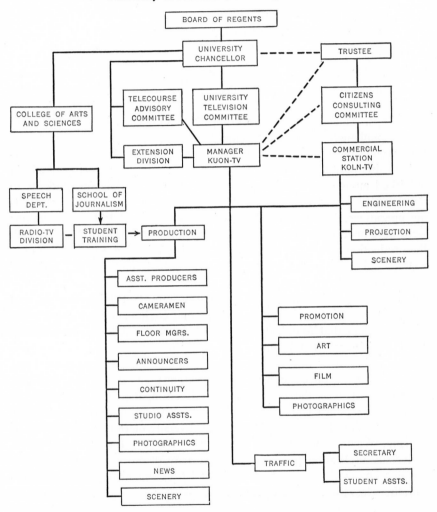

To assist educational television stations with their programming problems, the Educational Television and Radio Center, an organization located in Ann Arbor, Michigan, and financed by a large grant from the Ford Foundation, subsidizes the production of educational program series on kinescope for circulation to all educational stations. In this way the best programs on any one educational station become available to all educational stations. The Center also commissions professional production personnel to prepare special programs to be issued to all educational stations. Various television production centers, like the University of Michigan Television Office which has produced hundreds of television programs over commercial stations in Michigan, and the New York University Television Office, have been utilized by the Center to produce special program series.

• BROADCASTING WORKSHOPS •

The *1954-55 Directory of College Courses in Radio and Television,* issued by the U. S. Office of Education, listed more than 300 colleges that offered at least two courses in broadcasting. Radio workshops on the college level were listed by 269 institutions, while 66 institutions reported television workshops. Many of these workshops are rudimentary, operating with simple public-address systems, tape recorders, home-made sound-effects trucks, and simple manual sound-effects equipment. Their production material consists of student-written scripts supplemented by scripts available in published anthologies. These workshops make it possible for students to develop elementary broadcasting skills and to set up intraschool broadcasting operations. Many of the low-powered educational FM radio stations were developed from simple broadcasting workshops. Often coupled with the production activity of a workshop are simple audience-research studies which familiarize students with research methods and the full range of on-the-air broadcast offerings.

Some broadcasting workshops, located at important universities, have a full complement of professional broadcasting equipment, better and more complete than that found at many small commercial broadcast stations. Their equipment often includes completely outfitted studios and control rooms, with two or three camera chains, motion-picture projectors, kinescope recorders, construction and storage rooms, and other basic facilities. Institutions such as the University of Wisconsin, the State University of Iowa, Northwestern University, University of Michigan, Syracuse University, University of Southern California, University of Illinois, University of Indiana, Wayne University, Ohio State University, Iowa State College, University of Washington, and the University of North Carolina operate broadcasting workshops in both radio and television that provide students with first-class training in the broadcasting skills.

• SUMMARY •

To be successful, educational radio and television must effectively combine showmanship and valid educational content. Despite certain inherent limitations, radio and television possess special characteristics that make them very useful for various educational purposes. Educational programs can be used for direct and supplementary classroom teaching, intraschool broadcasting, education for preschool children, for youngsters out of school, and for adults. Integrated education and entertainment describes the effort of commercial broadcasters to incorporate educational materials into the popular entertainment programs. Noncommercial educational AM, FM, and TV stations serve the special purpose of rendering a public service through the regular scheduling of programs of education, information, and constructive entertainment.

Questions for Discussion

1. How can we best define an educational program?
2. How can radio and television be used effectively by the teacher in the class-room? What is required besides listening to or viewing the program?
3. How do the limitations of radio and television as educational media compare with their advantages as means for conveying information and education?
4. What types of programs are especially useful for educational purposes?
5. What functions, if any, can noncommercial educational stations serve that are not already served by commercial stations?
6. What kinds of programs should an educational station broadcast? How broad an appeal should an educational station make in its effort to win an audience?
7. How do educational programs over commercial outlets compare with educational programs over educational stations? Can you supply examples?
8. To what extent can we hope to develop better discrimination in listening and viewing through the classroom study of broadcast programs?

❋ 14 ❋

Standards of Criticism

ON WHAT BASES should television and radio programs be judged? By their popularity or by their artistic quality? By the amount of useful information they convey or by their effectiveness as vehicles for advertising?

Confusion over standards of criticism is not limited to the field of broadcasting, but is also found in other forms of practical and artistic communication. In the field of literature, for example, the popularity of novels can be measured by the number of copies sold, but judgments of their comparative quality as novels are never made by the yardstick of popularity. These judgments, which often have little or no relationship to matters such as immediate popularity, are made by critics who have read a great many books and who make their evaluations on the basis of criteria involving intrinsic literary merit. In arts like painting, music, and poetry, the enduring judgment is never based upon immediate popularity. Many works of art make an excellent first impression, but soon wear thin due to an essential superficiality; other works, of more enduring if less immediate popularity, encounter initial public and critical resistance, but manage to win increasing favor with the passage of time. In the field of practical communication, the newspaper or magazine with the largest circulation (manifestly the most popular publication) is not necessarily the "best" newspaper or magazine. In the legitimate theater, plays adjudged by professional critics to be of superior quality often fail to win immediate popular appeal, while plays considered by the critics to be inferior, occasionally become box-office hits. It is clear that the standards of immediate popularity and of inherent quality, both of which tend in casual conversation to be assimilated into a single critical concept of "good," are often quite different judgments—one made immediately by the public to which the communication or work of art is addressed, and the other by individuals of professional repute who, through long and discriminating exposure to various forms of communication and works of art, have developed critical standards of judgment. When an immediate popular success is also a critical success, there is general

216

satisfaction. In the course of time, popular and critical judgments are often revised; the ultimate test of quality is usually a single judgment representing enduring popular and critical esteem.

This cleavage in critical standards between immediate popularity and intrinsic quality is probably more evident in television and radio than in most other fields of practical and artistic communication. In broadcasting, the pressure for immediate popularity is overwhelming. Each program competes for an audience with programs broadcast simultaneously over other stations and networks. The elements of immediate enjoyment and breadth of appeal usually determine which program obtains the largest audience. On the other hand, each program, whatever its form—drama, comedy, documentary, or audience-participation—achieves a certain qualitative standard of performance in terms of its form and the potentialities of its material. In the day-to-day judgments of television and radio programs these conflicting considerations often spill over and confusion results. "That was a terrible show," remarks one person, to which another replies " 'Taint so, it had a great rating." Only through an understanding of the broadcasting media and a clarification of the criteria for criticism can we hope to remove some of this confusion.

We have said that television and radio programs in America are used to serve three fundamental purposes: (1) to conduct commerce; (2) to provide entertainment; and (3) to provide public service. Failure to acknowledge the validity of these purposes results, of course, in widely different judgments of an enterprise that involves business, artistic, and educational considerations. The critic who fails to appreciate the financial problems imposed on television and radio by virtue of their competitive nature and their sources of available income is reasoning from faulty premises no less than the broadcaster who looks upon his station solely as a means of making a personal fortune. Proceeding from opposite assumptions, it is easy to see how an advertiser might not be satisfied until his commercial message had been flaunted throughout an entire program, and how a sensitive writer or performer, on the other hand, might be unwilling to have his artistic presentation associated in any way with a commercial product.

• COMMERCIAL STANDARDS •

A common form of criticism of television and radio relates to the number and quality of commercial announcements on broadcast programs. Through long exposure the American people have come to accept commercial messages as the price they pay for programs they like to see or hear. The NARTB code limitation of six minutes of commercials per hour of evening program time appears to be within the tolerance of the American public. Raucous, unduly repetitive, and often stupid commercials do, however,

arouse critical hostility that appears to many persons to be amply war-
ranted. Inasmuch as clever commercials are not only tolerated but often
enjoyed by the public, the question has been raised as to whether advertising
agencies should spend more time, effort, and imagination to improve the
quality of their commercial announcements. The question of whether stations and networks should protect the public not only from misleading and
inaccurate advertising but also from grossly irritating advertising has also
been raised. In order to avoid losing their audience, the broadcasters, who
now pass judgment on the quality of all programs proposed by advertisers,
may eventually be obliged to apply more rigorous standards of quality to
the commercials as well. Clients who mistakenly believe that their commercials are more important than the program must be educated to the truth
that their advertising is wasted without the circulation that can be provided
only by effective programming. Broadcasters who mistakenly believe that
their license to broadcast may be used solely for the production of quick
profit to the exclusion of public service must also be educated to the truth
of their public responsibility. In the long run, however, only those stations
that operate in a successful business manner can provide the financial
resources necessary to program effectively in the public interest.

• ENTERTAINMENT STANDARDS •

In the United States there are many different forms of entertainment that
win substantial popular followings. In the field of sports, there are paying
publics for baseball, football, basketball, hockey, tennis, horse racing, dog
racing, boxing, etc. In the fields of music and dance, there are paying publics
for orchestral concerts, recitals, operas, operettas, jazz concerts, band concerts, dance music, ballet, modern dance, etc. In the theater and motion
pictures, there are publics for musical comedies, serious dramas, light
comedies, Westerns, adventure and mystery dramas, etc. In other words,
there are many levels of taste in the country, in terms of the kinds of entertainment one likes; a single individual may be a member of several different
publics. There are also many levels of performance within each form of
entertainment. Just as it is generally acknowledged that minor league baseball games are less professional (meaning less perfect in performance) than
major league games, it is also generally acknowledged that community
theater or stock company productions are usually less professional than
Broadway productions.

When it comes to commercial television and radio, however, we find that
it is very difficult to accommodate all the levels of public taste or to sustain
a high degree of professionalism in all programs. The very popular and the
less popular forms of entertainment which, outside of television and radio,
compete relatively untroubled for their different publics, must, in television
and radio, compete directly against each other. Since the national networks

are under continual pressure to reach the largest publics possible, they are reluctant to broadcast less popular forms of entertainment in competition with programs of more general appeal. The consequent neglect of certain levels of taste results in unrelenting criticism of television and radio. Networks and stations seek to meet this criticism by broadcasting a limited number of programs of special appeal in marginal-time periods, such as early Sunday afternoon, when program competition is less keen.

The level of professionalism in television and radio entertainment is likewise a subject of much concern. Due to the enormous volume of programs and the great expense of production, it is impossible to assign to every program all the creative talent and the production facilities necessary to produce a top-quality show. In television the rate of production of the finished product has been faster than the rate at which quality raw materials have been developed. Nevertheless, there have been enough demonstrations of first-rate productions in all entertainment and informational forms to establish standards of qualitative judgment. Criticism of program quality must be based, however, on an understanding and acceptance of television and radio as media for the presentation of art forms of their own. It is no more justified to withhold praise from a television drama on the ground that it would not hold up as a two-hour Broadway play, than to withhold praise from a Broadway play on the ground that it would not make a good movie, or to condemn a short story on the ground that it would not make a good novel. The qualitative judgment should always be based on fundamental criteria such as, in the case of a television drama, the following: Did the production excite interest? Was the situation believable? Were the characters real and were their actions adequately motivated? Was the subject matter worthy of the time given to it? Was the production technically competent? Was the total effect emotionally and intellectually satisfying? In the case of informational programs, the criteria would be somewhat different: Was the subject matter worthy of a program? Was the information presented clearly? Was interest sustained? Was the material presented with sufficient effectiveness to cause the audience to remember the main points?

• PUBLIC-SERVICE STANDARDS •

In addressing NBC producers recently, Sylvester Weaver said: "It is not enough that the American people shall be superbly entertained. They must be kept informed. That is not someone else's job. It is yours." In their concern over entertaining the public, many program producers often forget that their audience is made up of human beings and citizens upon whose political and social judgments depends the fate of our country. By virtue of the public license they hold, it seems hard to dispute the fact that broadcasters have an affirmative responsibility to see that the television and radio media are used for purposes of good citizenship through the dissemination of information and opinion on matters of public importance. Criticism of the public-service performance of radio and television is usually related to four aspects: (1) the accuracy of broadcast information and the qualifications of those who comment on the news and express opinions on controversial matters; (2) the balance of fairness in the presentation of controversial points of view; (3) the quantity of public-service programs in relation to the need for them; and (4) the broadcast time allotted to these programs. These are seemingly valid criteria. At CBS the following standards for news and public affairs programs have been established:

> In news programs there is to be no opinion or slanting, the news reporting must be straight and objective. In news analysis there is to be elucidation, illumination, and explanation of the facts and situations, but without bias or editorialization.
>
> Opinion broadcasts must be labeled for what they are. In particular, opinion must be separated from news. The listener is entitled to know what he is receiving, news or opinion, and if it be opinion, whose opinion. When opinion is expressed in any type of information program—excluding news and news analysis where opinion is not allowed—opportunity for reply is given to the person with whom issue has been taken, or to a responsible spokesman representing an opposite viewpoint.
>
> An advertiser who sponsors any type of information program produced by us does not thereby purchase, or in any way gain, any rights to control the contents of the program.[1]

In an effort to break loose from the concentration of public-service programs on Sunday afternoon and their exclusion from other, more desirable places on the broadcast schedule, the national networks have attempted to arrange their commercial sales contracts so that they may from time to time broadcast important public-service programs in prime evening time periods. They have also developed a plan for integrating informational materials into popular entertainment shows.

• THE RESPONSIBILITY FOR LEADERSHIP •

Midst all the concern for programs that will immediately win broad popular appeal, there nevertheless abides with television and radio broadcasters a positive responsibility for leadership in the development of new creative talents and new program forms, in raising popular tastes, eliminating popular ignorance, and advancing public understanding of the world in which we live. To concentrate solely on the immediate problem of giving the public only what the largest single segment of the public currently wants is, in the opinion of some critics, equivalent to engaging in a form of cultural demagoguery that betrays the future of broadcasting and the promise of American life. As Lyman Bryson, formerly CBS Counsellor on Public

---

[1] Address of William S. Paley, Chairman of the Board, CBS, at NARTB convention, Chicago, Ill., May 25, 1954.

Affairs, has said, the broadcaster has a responsibility not only to meet tastes as they are, but constantly to improve them:

> The truth is that as you raise your level of taste in music, drama, literature, or any other art, you find that you demand more, your expectations move up. Your taste gets to be more and more like the preference of listeners who have had more experience and training. This happens, of course, only if you are exposed to good things, to fine music, to drama that is stirring and real, to talk that is logical and thoughtful. If you have a chance to find out what fine things are really like, and you are an average person with average responses, you will demand them for yourself.
>
> If nothing is on the air but what is dull to your ears, because you do not understand it and have not had a chance to get acquainted with it—if, in other words, it is outside your range of tastes, then you do not listen and you do not learn anything. You therefore do not get anything to enjoy. Above all, everybody's tastes in all the arts must depend on his enjoyment.
>
> Since this is so . . . the broadcaster has a clear responsibility to keep music and drama and entertainment of all the decent kinds there are, on the air all the time to meet all the different tastes.[2]

Gilbert Seldes, a television and radio critic, argues in favor of the broadcaster's responsibility for leadership in this way:

> The moment radio took entertainment into the home—which was the great social revolution of our time—a new concept began to take shape, and part of it is the concept of entertainment so copious and familiar that it becomes a necessity of life (as the telephone is). These necessities are not loved, but we cannot live without them. Let the broadcaster be happy that they have joined the other essentials of life—and accept the responsibilities of their position. Let them remember that the telephone company is not satisfied with satisfied customers, and it was not to satisfy public demand that the utility companies switched from direct to alternating current. When you deal with the necessities of life you are obligated to give all the people the best product you can develop, you offer it to them before they ask for it. . . .[3]

To Sylvester L. Weaver, chairman of the board of NBC, the affirmative responsibility of the broadcaster is beyond question. In an address to NBC-TV affiliates in Chicago in December, 1955, Weaver said:

> From the beginning, we have been against the know-nothings, the primitives, because we do not believe that television should be run to give the people what they want. We want to give the people something that will make more of them want more of the better shows.
>
> We believe that every NBC show should serve a purpose beyond diversion, and every time we can increase information, contact, facts, and knowledge, and we deliver a fact somewhere to a mind somewhere in the country, we have added one more tool, one more weapon in the fight against bigotry, stupidity, intolerance and prejudice, and we have taken one more step forward toward sanity, maturity, and adulthood. . . .

[2] Lyman Bryson, *Time for Reason About Radio* (New York, 1948), pp. 41, 46-48. By permission of George W. Stewart, publisher.
[3] Gilbert Seldes, "Satisfaction and/or Enthusiasm," in *The Saturday Review*, October 29, 1955, p. 23. By permission of *The Saturday Review*.

We will certainly continue to integrate cultural and informational themes and material in all of our shows, such as ballets and operas, and doing everything that we can to increase exposure of all the people to those things that we know are good, or fine, or artistic, or cultural. Most people do not like the higher art forms because they have never had the privilege and the time and the money, nor the training and the experience, to know why they are so good. We will show them why they are good, and the people will follow naturally. . . .

We are going to continue to program up, and not down. We will use our showmanship and skill to get great audiences. We will also continue to meet our commercial challenges, and we will do the kind of shows that we know must be done.

Television is far too great an instrument to be degraded into a "home juke-box" to keep the kids quiet.

· PROFESSIONAL CRITICISM ·

While it was true several years ago that there was a "woeful dearth" of professional radio criticism in the United States, the situation has changed considerably since the advent of television. Although publishing media have not yet accorded professional television and radio criticism the same status or space accorded book, theater, or motion-picture reviews, the trend is clearly in that direction. Several important critics like John Crosby, of the *New York Herald-Tribune,* Jack Gould, of the *New York Times,* and George Rosen, of *Variety,* review programs regularly and command the attention of the broadcasting industry. There are many other program reviewers less well-known nationally who write for newspapers in various cities across the country. Unfortunately, some of these writers have no special interest or competence in program evaluation and rely mainly on press handouts or give vent to their personal pique.

Professional criticism of television and radio is also conducted through the issuance of various awards of merit. Among the more esteemed are the Peabody, *Variety,* Sylvania, "Emmy," DuPont, *Look* magazine, and *Billboard* citations.

Still another form of criticism is that offered by organizations and committees specifically created for the purpose of evaluating programs. It is not uncommon for local Parents Associations to set up television committees to review local children's programs. The Wisconsin Association for Better Radio and Television and the National Association for Better Radio and Television in Los Angeles are typical public councils whose stated purpose is, among other things, "to encourage the development of high individual standards of radio and television appreciation both in the schools and in the home, to encourage a co-operative attitude between the radio and television industry and the listening public, and to create and maintain patronage for sponsors who broadcast programs meeting with the standards recommended by the organization."

· SUMMARY ·

Informed and intelligent criticism is essential to the advancement of the broadcasting media. Criticism must take into account the complex operation of television and radio as business enterprises, and as media for the communication of art and public service. The conflict between immediate popularity and broad appeal on the one hand, and inherent program quality on the other, is a fundamental problem in formulating useful standards of criticism. Television and radio programs should be judged in terms of the aesthetics of the broadcast media and the potentialities of the program forms. Broadcasters have an affirmative responsibility for raising public tastes.

Questions for Discussion

1. On what bases should television and radio programs be judged?
2. Compare the practice of literary criticism with the criticism of television and radio programs.
3. Is there any difference between the concepts of "good" and "effective" in evaluating broadcast programs?
4. To what extent can we use audience ratings as a guide to the critical evaluation of programs?
5. Can we reconcile the conflict between artistic and business considerations in broadcasting? How?
6. What is meant by various levels of public taste?
7. How high a level of professionalism do we have a right to expect in television and radio programs?
8. What responsibility, if any, do broadcasters have for raising public tastes?
9. What special problems, if any, are involved in the commercial sponsorship of programs covering political conventions, election results, and official ceremonies, such as the proceedings incidental to a Presidential inauguration?

Part II

TELEVISION AND RADIO IN THE STUDIO

❈ 15 ❈

Inside the Station

THE POWER TO MAKE or break a star, to keep a program on the air or to take it off, to enable a station to operate in the black or in the red, rests with the individual listener or viewer at home and what he decides to do with the tuning devices on his set. Program popularity, station circulation, and sales curves are dependent upon the interest and audience reaction. As a result, what comes out of the loud speaker and is shown on the screen are not there by "happenstance," but by definite planning and organization designed to meet the needs and interests of the audiences.

Let us tune in some stations for a short period of time and observe what is being offered. Then we can draw some conclusions about the people and plans involved, and go behind the program transmission into the stations to learn about the organization and functions of the station personnel.

It is morning. Programs are available to us from clear-channel radio stations across the state; from both a radio and television station owned by the same company in the next county; and a small local radio and television station also under joint ownership in our own community. Several programs we can tell are geared specifically to interest the farmer. Included are complete weather reports, market information, news of exhibitions and demonstrations, Department of Agriculture reports, an on-the-spot interview made via a tape recorder with a nearby farmer who has been particularly successful with crop rotation, films from the state land-grant college on silo construction, and sound film interviews with winners in 4-H Club competition. The people handling the broadcasts are authoritative and experienced farm directors, they present the farm machinery and feed commercials in persuasive manner, the visual devices used are clear and informative, the filmed sequences have a professional touch, commercials between programs are widely varied—from straightforward messages to elaborate filmed cartoons. There is a program of the general "wake-up" type with bright popular music and chatter, five-minute world and local news summaries and weather reports. Here is a program consisting of morning devotions, hymns, and Bible readings. Another program is a relay of a network TV presentation featuring a well-known personality who conducts informal interviews with people in the news or from the entertainment world, together with news summaries and film features from around the nation and world. And another is designed to entertain small children with cartoons and studio banter between announcer and puppet characters.

Later in the morning, we hear a newscast from the nation's capital by a single newscaster who engages in personal expressions of opinion about actions of certain legislators "on the Hill." Western and hillbilly music on records is coming from one of the stations. A film feature popular ten to fifteen years ago has started; a "Breakfast at Home" husband-and-wife interview program has a prominent regional novelist as its guest of the day; household and cooking hints are demonstrated in real kitchens; a telephone quiz on American history is in process; a rebroadcast of an instructional series on the psychology of the child is being projected via kinescope film-recording; radio and television daytime dramatic serials have started; and midmorning variety and participation programs are competing for the attention of listener and viewer.

This listening and viewing during a brief two- or three-hour period is such a simple matter that few people stop to ask what type of organization and planning is necessary to permit the smooth flow for hour after hour, day after day, week after week, on a split-second schedule of programs and announcements, varied in content, style, origination, and personnel.

· STATION ORGANIZATION ·

While the particular organizational details may vary according to the size and type of station, affiliation or nonaffiliation with a network and an active or static program policy, the procedures and jobs to be done are such that the basic functional organization of a station is fairly well standardized throughout the country.

Determination of Station Policy. As has been explained in earlier chapters, each station operates on the basis of a license issued by the Federal Communications Commission. Usually the license is held by a corporation especially formed for the business of operating the station. The Board of Directors of the corporation is the final authority on station policy; it is responsible to the stockholders on the one hand for efficient management and to the FCC on the other hand for operating "in the public interest, convenience or necessity." Stations may also be owned by individuals or partners. In some instances the corporation owning a station may be engaged primarily in other types of business, such as newspaper publishing, insurance, radio and television manufacturing, and motion picture production. Other stations, usually noncommercial, may be owned by colleges or universities, municipalities, trade unions, and religious groups.

General Manager. The person chosen to interpret in detailed fashion station policy as determined in general form by the Board of Directors is called the general manager or station manager. He has supreme authority in running the station. In many instances he is a member of the Board of Directors or an officer in the corporation. The success or failure of the station to operate on a profitable basis depends in large measure on the administrative skill of the manager in selecting and supervising an efficient staff, on the quality of his day-to-day programming judgments, and on his sense of responsibility to the community in fulfilling the obligations laid upon the holders of radio licenses. This is a big order. There are no hard and fast rules for winning public favor. Radio and television combine show business, advertising, and public service. Programs must be interesting and entertaining to get audiences and to sell the goods and services advertised on the station. The manager must be aware of the likes and dislikes of his community; not only the existing likes and dislikes but the potential ones.

Some kind of "station personality" must emerge. For example, to be effective in one area, a station may have to highlight a succession of disc jockeys, another station may find its place in the sun with an active farm schedule, a third may depend chiefly upon sports, a fourth upon feature films, and a fifth upon news and music. The primary responsibility for selecting and developing this station personality and winning acceptance for it in a highly competitive industry is usually in the hands of the general manager.

To carry out the operation of broadcasting, the general manager hires executive assistants to supervise the various departments set up in the station. In the average station these departments are program, engineering, and commercial. Each executive has a staff to carry out the particular duties of the department. In a smaller station the general manager may "double in brass" either as the program director or as the commercial manager. In larger stations the persons who hold these positions are often vice-presidents.

In instances of single ownership of both television and radio stations, management policy may call for separate television and radio departments. However, considerable intermixture of personnel may exist. Other companies may integrate one department and separate others. Considerable variation exists throughout the industry.

Program Department. It is the function of the program director and his staff, the largest department in the matter of personnel, to plan and present the programs in a manner satisfactory to the management, the sponsor, and the audience. The program director supervises the following divisions: announcing, sports, news, film, staging, art, music, transcriptions and records, continuity, production and talent. It is the responsibility of the program director to suggest ideas for sustaining programs; to work with the commercial department in suggesting program ideas for the various advertisers on the station; and to keep a close check on the quality of production and over-all balance of the station's program structure.

ANNOUNCING DIVISION. In a small 250-watt local radio station, three or four announcers may handle the entire day's schedule, relief announcing being taken care of by other members of the staff. As stations grow larger and more complex, the announcing staff may increase to eight or ten and be headed by a chief announcer who has supervision over them. The staff may be supplemented by special announcers handling news and sports. It is desirable, for more effective showmanship, to schedule the announcers so that a man selected to handle a program will fit in with its format and style. A slangy, disc-jockey program conducted by a restrained announcer will annoy listeners.

The program director, aided by the chief announcer, tries to build a staff with different specialties and a range of vocal variety. Alternating announcers for consecutive programming is desirable. In many stations the announcers also handle the studio controls and play the records and transcriptions. When the same management operates both a radio and television station, announcers often are scheduled for assignments on both media.

Recalling the programs mentioned earlier in this chapter, we can note the parts played by the various announcers. They introduce the farm director, broadcast the news, present popular music with a light touch and serious music with a dignified one, chat with the cooking specialists, act as hosts for live introductions to film features, introduce the feature commentators and interviewers, conduct the quizzes with spirit and verve, and during station-breaks and programs, present commercials ranging in subject matter from farm machinery to soap.

As we listened we could draw these conclusions:

An announcer may be classified according to his main duties:

1. Introduction of featured program talent.
2. Master of Ceremonies (MC).
3. Featured personality in his own right.
4. Effective salesman.

NEWS DIVISION. The news has to be prepared in the station's news room for the newscaster or announcer. Preparation of the news may take nothing more than "scissors and paste" as the staff announcer tears off copy from the press association wires. The preferable practice is to have an experienced news editor prepare the copy with the particular area to be served in mind. In small stations, the news editor may also be a part-time staff announcer. In large radio and television stations several writers, still- and motion-picture cameramen, and film editors may be employed to cover local events, to process and rewrite the news dispatches and select and edit newsfilm. Tape recorders, press cameras, and silent- and sound-film cameras are available for on-the-spot coverage.

The men who prepare the news may deliver it themselves. However, the general trend is for trained newsmen to write the news for presentation by announcers with a flair for effective delivery and with an attractive television personality, when that medium is used. "Name" newscasters who prepare their own copy, however, may be featured in their own right. Such persons usually are newsmen with either local or national reputations who acquire personality value for the station.

MUSIC DIVISION. Music is a very important part of the programs presented. Most of it comes from records or transcriptions, but some is performed live by musicians, organists, or small combinations. Television stations do not rely as heavily on music for basic program material as radio stations. In the station's music division we find a music director, who is responsible for selecting the numbers for the various programs, for auditioning talent, and developing standard instrumental and vocal units. If the station is large enough, he may be assisted by a music librarian who maintains a transcription and record library as well as whatever special and stock arrangements are kept on file for use on live music programs. The music staff takes care of clearance and copyright problems and maintains the records necessary to determine payment to special licensing agencies for music actually broadcast.

The musical director in a large station may also be the orchestra leader of whatever staff orchestra is maintained. Some stations keep from six to fourteen men as a basic staff orchestra on an annual or seasonal basis, according to the station's needs and its contract with the American Federation of Musicians. Part of the cost may be directly underwritten by the hiring out of the orchestra on local commercial programs or indirectly by the use of the orchestra on participating commercial programs where higher rates are charged. Even small stations, independent and network affiliated, find it advantageous to keep at least one staff musician. This man is usually a combination pianist and organist and is used as accompanist for variety and talent hours and for local vocalists or instrumentalists. He plays the themes, background and transitional bridge music for children's narrations, women's programs, and feature broadcasts. On some programs he may be given solo assignments. Folk music played by hillbilly or Western ranch-type combinations is essential for many stations. Not only are these musical organizations powerful audience drawing cards, but they can also be useful in promoting the station through personal appearances at dances and theaters.

CONTINUITY OR SCRIPT DIVISION. Many do not realize that most of the words heard on the air have been written. Few performers extemporize completely what they say; they rely upon a script. In radio they read their script. In television several methods are used: (1) read from the script even though the audience is able to see the performer; (2) read from script when "off camera" and memorize material for "on camera" appearances; (3) rely upon "cue cards," large pieces of cardboard containing a word for word script or an outline, which are held at the side of the camera and thus within the performer's line of sight; and (4) refer to "TelePrompter" or similar devices mounted on cameras or placed around the studio which reveal in large type several lines of the script in synchronization with the speed of delivery. The continuity or written material used to introduce programs, performers and musical numbers may be prepared by the announcer in a small station; or by a special continuity department, ranging from one to three writers in a more active program department. These continuity writers prepare copy to suit the MC's style and program format.

Incidental script writing may also be handled by members of a continuity division. Interviews with civic or government officials such as one with the County Health Commissioner about a local epidemic, quiz questions, and stunts for audience participation programs, "voice-over-film" (VOF) narration for film clips used in an "outdoor" series, chatter prepared for "ad-lib" disc-jockey programs, and dialogue for "Husband and Wife" teams are examples of customary assignments. In large stations, specialists may be added to the staff for some of these assignments which require particular craftsmanship, professional competency, and flair. In medium and small stations, the members of the continuity division are expected to be versatile craftsmen.

In co-operation with the commercial departments, the continuity division may be called upon to prepare commercials. In small markets the local merchants may not have advertising agencies handling their accounts. The salesmen who service these accounts relay to the staff writer suggestions from the sponsor for the commercials. Often the continuity writers personally visit the merchants for consultation and ideas. It is not unusual in some small stations to find one of the announcers doubling as a continuity writer and assuming responsibility for preparing commercials. In large stations the continuity division has no responsibilities for writing commercial copy. Advertising agencies send the scripts, slides, and the transcribed and filmed commercials directly to the commercial department.

PRODUCTION DIVISION. Many programs need to be rehearsed and closely supervised by specialists in directorial and production areas while being put on film or presented live. In radio this is especially true for live music, variety, and dramatic programs. In radio stations which depend upon transcribed and recorded music and simple program formats, little or no prebroadcast rehearsal is deemed necessary except perhaps for a "voice-level" check. Whenever studio direction is required, it is handled by an announcer, engineer, writer, or the program director himself. In larger radio stations, an announcer may be assigned part-time studio production duties or a full-time staff producer-director may be hired. Television stations generally rely upon full-time personnel as producer-directors or as studio directors. Many administrative details on programs may be delegated by management to producer-directors. Program talent may be selected and fees arranged, program ideas conceived, staging properties and film budget allocations determined, scripts edited, and script writers supervised. A producer-director also is in direct charge of rehearsal and air presentation. Studio directors in television have no primary budget or administrative responsibilities but supervise the various details encountered in putting a program together, the staging, graphics, music, costumes, properties, editing script or film, blocking action, conducting camera rehearsals, and finally "calling" the camera shots on the air.

An additional group of personnel involved in the presentation of a television program in the production division are the floor managers, also referred to as stage managers. They are the representatives of the director on the studio floor. They relay signals to the performers, and are in charge of the studio crew, the program assistants handling properties and title cards, stage hands moving sets, and other technicians changing lights and producing sound effects.

The directors may have other persons assisting them in the rehearsal and presentation. Assistant or associate directors time the program, make notes about performance and technical details that must be attended to before the broadcast, and render general assistance during the telecast such as reminders about camera movement, lighting effects, and upcoming signals. Some stations call these people "script" or "production" secretaries. Some stations consider that the TV cameramen are a part of the production division. On simple programs such as a local women's program the camera man may double as floor manager. In small stations announcers often act as floor manager, cameramen or direct programs during their schedule. In the larger stations the cameramen are generally considered part of the technical department.

Few radio or TV stations are active enough to require a full-time person in sound effects. When the sounds of newspaper presses, jet planes, or thundering herds of cattle are needed, records with these sound effects are played by the same person who is handling the recorded music. If the special effects are to be done in the studio, such as the closing of a door or a pistol shot, colleagues in the program department are pressed into service.

A card file, with photographs, audition reports, and other information about available talent is maintained in the production division for ready reference when actors, vocalists, dancers, talented youngsters, animal acts, baton twirlers, hog callers, bagpipe players, one-man-band acts, etc., are needed. One or two versatile performers may be put on staff. Generally such persons are employed as specific programs require their services for definite periods of time, ranging from a single appearance to a twenty-six week or a year's contract.

FILM DIVISION. Television stations rely heavily on film of all types: full-length, ninety-minute features; half-hour dramas; cartoons; travel shorts; documentaries; brief, filmed inserts; commercials; delayed, network programs on kinescope (film recordings); and educational or public-service films and kinescopes. One to four persons are employed to keep close track of this film as it comes in and is returned, to screen the film for technical quality and standards of good taste, to schedule it for broadcasting and to do what editing is necessary for insertion of commercials and correct timing. The persons who thread up the film projection equipment and supervise the actual telecast details are generally a part of the engineering department. The photographers and film cameramen who shoot film and stills for station use may be a part of the film division or attached to another division such as news, or be employed on a free-lance or "assignment" basis.

ART DIVISION. In television programs there is a great variety of prepared "visual aids": weather maps, charts to show farm prices, charts to indicate baseball standings, title cards at the opening and closing of programs which carry the cast and production credits, station identification slides, simple animated devices, cartoon-type drawings, commercial slogans on the rear wall of the set, and even humorous or "cute" slides to tell the audience about the difficulties when the station loses its sound or network transmission gives a poor picture. These "visuals" are prepared in the art division. If a station prepares slides for local sponsors or is at all active in studio programming at least two staff artists are needed. Stations may call upon the art department to design and paint or draw murals, background perspectives for street or country scenery, display settings for commercial products, and special promotional material for leaflets and advertisements.

STAGING AND FACILITIES DIVISION. Many of the individual programs had their own distinctive settings—ranging from realistic kitchens to abstract arrangements of light patterns on the floor and draped backgrounds. The responsibility for designing and building the sets, securing large and small properties such as furniture, tables, vases, getting the studio ready for use by putting up the scenery and placing the properties, and changing sets while on the air is given to the staging division. Lighting the sets may also be handled by staging although the general industry pattern is to look upon lighting as a function of engineering.

SPECIALTIES IN THE PROGRAM DEPARTMENT. 1. Public-Service Division. An important division of the program department is the public-service division which deals with education, religious programming, political campaigns, public issues and safety, health, and bond-drive campaigns, Community Chest, Red Cross, and similar appeals. Announcements and interviews are scheduled, special interviews and documentaries prepared and presented, and transcribed or filmed programs from the organization's national headquarters presented. Some of this material is included in sponsored programs and some is donated by the station and presented on a sustaining basis. Everybody at the station may be involved in public-service programs as an addition to their regular duties. One person, however, may be designated the co-ordinator or director of public service for convenient approach by outside organizations. In small stations this person is often the general manager; in somewhat larger stations the program director has charge of this division; and in a few of the very large stations, a specialist is hired. If a political campaign is in progress, the purchase of time by the various political party radio and television chairmen will be handled as any other commercial broadcasts, but the programs are supervised by a key person familiar with the FCC regulations on political broadcasting. Stations differ greatly in the amount of public-service programming and in the choice of person to run the division.

2. Sports. Here again we find a great difference among stations. Some very small stations specialize in sports, with one or two people doing nothing but that. In metropolitan areas, an independent station may secure a consistently high rating whenever it carries play-by-play reports of sporting events, studio recaps, taped and filmed interviews with visiting sports celebrities, or sports news periods. If the station does not have a separate division for sports, one or two of the announcers will usually be chosen to handle the programs.

3. Farm Programs. Many programs are especially designed to assist the farmer with complete weather and market reports, agricultural news, and information about new farming methods and refinements of old methods, by presenting authoritative talks, demonstrations, and interviews featuring government officials, state agricultural college professors, experiment station workers, and successful farmers. Except for a few stations in urban areas, practically every station includes some agriculture programs in its schedule and some make the farm audience their prime consideration. It is a very common practice to have attached to the program department a farm director who is an expert in agricultural matters. The press and film releases of the U. S. Department of Agriculture, State Agricultural Boards, and Agricultural Colleges are available to the station for programming purposes, but an effective series conducted by a farm director will include far more than these releases. The usefulness of a portable tape recorder and film cameras is never more evident than in farm broadcasts. News-reel film and on-the-spot interviews with successful farmers, exhibitors at county and state fairs, and groups conducting various demonstrations are easy to obtain, providing the station's budget permits the farm director and technical personnel to attend these functions. Often the farm director operates the tape recorder or film camera by himself.

4. Women's and children's features. Women's programs are commonly featured on most stations but there are various ways in which these programs are prepared and presented. Medium and large stations may hire a woman to handle the women's features. She may edit and present a woman's program with interviews and homemaking hints. On small stations, a staff member regularly employed as a secretary or clerk may handle whatever women's programs the station offers. Another method is to employ someone

outside the station as special talent. In many newspaper-owned stations, the paper's women's editor will double as a station women's specialist. Some stations develop a trade name for the women's editor so that in the event of change in personnel, the program may continue without having to be adjusted to a new name.

Children's programs fall into several general types. One emphasizes a children's talent revue. Children are auditioned and chosen to appear on the daily or weekly broadcast conducted by a broadcast "uncle," "aunt," or "cousin." Popular or semiclassical songs constitute the bulk of the program and are interspersed with ballet or tap dances, accordion, piano or other instrumental solos or recitations. Some stations also rehearse and train vocal groups from duos to huge choruses and develop children's orchestras. Another general type emphasizes narrations of favorite stories, reading of the comics, or dramatizations with puppets or imaginary characters of familiar fairy and folk tales.

Another favorite juvenile program is the quiz or stunt program, handled by a staff announcer or special-events man. A recent addition to a number of station's schedules is the teen-age MC handling a record show especially aimed toward the junior and senior high school audience.

Engineering Department. Although the members of the home audience are often unaware of the engineering department, a moment's consideration makes it apparent that this department is a vital link in station operation. It is headed by the chief engineer and is usually divided into studio and transmitter divisions.

RADIO. If a station has the transmitter and studio together at one location a smaller compact staff is possible. Normally the two are separated, sometimes by as much as fifteen miles. The studios may be located in the center of town and the transmitter outside the city limits. In a small station the studio engineer may be stationed in master control, while announcers take care of announce-booth equipment and recording turntables. The process may be further simplified by having combination announcer-engineers in a control room overlooking two other studios. In some large stations, engineers may play transcriptions and records, but there is considerable variance in this practice. Many station managers feel that since transcriptions and records are a part of the program department, they should be played by someone in that department, usually the announcer.

Studio engineers are also responsible for making instantaneous recordings on disc recorders, splicing tapes, and servicing tape-recording equipment. Whenever a "nemo" or remote (a program away from the studio) is broadcast, an engineer or combination announcer-engineer is in attendance with the remote amplifying equipment and microphones. Since the FCC prescribes definite rules and regulations for maintenance of technical standards, it is the responsibility of the engineering department to follow these rules and regulations, to anticipate the replacement of obsolete transmitter, monitor, and studio equipment, and to maintain the required broadcast logs. Engineering staffs vary in number from four in small stations to over twenty in some of the large ones.

TELEVISION. Many more engineers are required in television station operation. The WWJ table of organization which appears at the conclusion of this chapter shows that whereas 11 technicians are employed in the radio studios, 38 are needed for the TV studio operation. All of the duties required of radio engineers are present also in television. Added to these are responsibilities for camera operation in the studio, camera switching in the control room, making kinescopes, and regulation of the video controls in the control room, master control, and remote truck. The film projectionists and lighting supervisors may also be engineers. Keeping all of the complex electronic equipment in excellent working order requires considerable time and personnel who have extremely high levels of technical knowledge.

• COMPARISON OF RADIO AND TELEVISION PROGRAM PRODUCTION •

Without dipping too deeply into the techniques of television production for the moment, let us observe the same program in both radio and television studios in order to make a comparison.

Radio: here is a woman's afternoon-shopper's guide program, an everyday affair. In the studio at a table, ready for the radio broadcast, are the commentator, her guest for the day (a celebrated chef), and the announcer. The commercial announcements on the program are in the script together with the notes for the interview. In the control room is a studio engineer. Such production-direction as is needed is taken care of by the announcer who gives simple three-, two-, and one-minute warnings before the show ends. Two production or program people therefore are sufficient to handle the broadcast.

Television: in the studio we find the commentator, her guest and the announcer, but added to the group are 2 cameramen, one for each of the two cameras, who move the cameras into position and change lenses as instructions come from the control room over the telephonic communication system; one floor manager, to relay signals from the control room to the talent and to co-ordinate on-the-air activity; one studio assistant who handles the lights required to illuminate merchandise displays, talent, and the settings (which consist of a comfortable living room set for part of the program, and a kitchen set for the interview); and one studio assistant, in charge of properties, who manipulates the title cards at the opening and closing of the program, places the proper piece of merchandise in its place for an effective camera shot during a commercial, and assists behind the scenes during the salad-tossing demonstration by the chef. In the control room we find the same engineer handling the audio equipment, turning on the microphones and supervising the voice levels throughout the broadcast, but he has been joined by a video engineer who handles control units for both cameras and controls picture quality; a second video engineer or technical director (abbreviated TD) who communicates with the cameramen in the studio on camera placement and lens selection for long shots, medium shots, medium or big close-ups as instructed by the director and who does the actual switching from camera to camera; and the director, who is responsible for co-ordinating the entire operation in the most effective manner. In another room is still another technician (a film projectionist) who, on cue from the technical director in the program control booth, runs the commercial films used by some of the co-operating sponsors on this shopper's guide.

In the case of the radio broadcast, 2 people were sufficient in the immediate area to put the woman commentator's program on the air. In the telecast of the same program 11 were used. The production of the television program could be more elaborate with an additional camera and cameraman, and special engineers to maneuver the dolly camera and boom microphone, more studio assistants for special effects and sets, and an assistant director. When one tries to televise a simple production like this with a bare minimum of personnel, it may be possible to cut down on studio people from 6 to 5 or even to 3 (announcer and 2 cameramen) and to reduce the control room personnel by letting the director do his own switching, but you will still have a minimum of 6 or 7 contrasted to radio's 2.

The same general increase in staff requirements is true for remote television broadcasts, in contrast to radio pick-ups of the same event. Whereas an announcer and an engineer, with an occasional production director to supervise the unit, are quite satisfactory in radio, the remote crew for television, on a minimum basis, will generally consist of:

Two cameramen, one for each of two cameras, stationed to overlook the event being telecast.

One audio engineer, whose duties are much the same as those of the radio engineer mentioned above.

One video engineer, to control picture quality on the two cameras.

One announcer, whose general duties are similar to those in the radio counterpart although he uses different techniques.

One director, who co-ordinates the production, monitors the camera not on the air and calls the shots to be telecast.

One TD, or "switcher" who supervises the technical aspects of the video pick-up and the microwave relay transmitter and does the actual switching from camera to camera.

Commercial Department. The commercial department is the revenue-producing department. Station-break announcements and program commercials are the result of a representative of the commercial department having obtained a contract covering the presentation of a sponsor's message over the station's facilities. The two major sources of advertising contracts available to independent stations are local advertising and national spot-advertising; network-affiliated stations have an additional source of revenue: network advertising. The commercial manager with the assistance of one salesman may handle all sales negotiations for a small station. Medium-sized and large stations keep a full-time sales force of three to six salesmen.

The salesmen and commercial manager work closely with the program department in building programs and writing copy. In small stations the salesman may also be a part-time announcer. To have information available on time-periods open for sponsorship, and to schedule the announcements and programs correctly according to the terms of the contracts, stations rely on a traffic division, generally a branch of the commercial department although in some organizations it comes under the program department.

The traffic manager and his assistants are responsible for preparing the final program log which itemizes exactly what is to be broadcast for which client, at what time, in which studio, by which announcer, and indicates what facilities are to be available, necessary switching cues, and which directors are to supervise. Each member of the station's staff concerned with operations, as well as the executives, receives the program log for ready reference throughout the broadcast day.

Before the compilation of the final log, the program director supplies information to the traffic department listing sustaining programs to be logged, indicating whether originations are local (live or film) or network, and necessary production coverage for sustaining or commercial periods. The commercial manager supplies bookings for commercial announcements and programs according to contractual agreements. Specific transcriptions, slides or film are noted on the log. Either before or after the final typing or duplication of the log, the chief announcer names the announcers to handle the specific announcements and programs. The chief engineer assigns personnel to cover the programs according to technical needs. A master book of a loose-leaf notebook style containing all copy to be read on the air, is assembled in chronological order corresponding to the program log. Transcriptions, film, and slides are placed in an active file. After the broadcast, the announcer signs the announcing copy in the master book and the final "as-broadcast" program log. The traffic department uses these records to bill clients and advertising agencies. Another function of the traffic department is to work out analyses of program types when required by the FCC. The commercial department also includes the bookkeeping or accounting division which enters accounts, renders statements, makes out the station payroll, and pays bills.

Not many people, in normal listening and viewing situations, do exploratory tuning. It is, therefore, to the advantage of a station seeking to increase its audience to make more people aware of its programs on the theory that if you can get people to tune in once, they may tune in again and again. Responsibility for informing people of what is to be on the air is assigned to the promotion and publicity division, which, in many instances, reports to the commercial manager or directly to the general manager. Promotional announcements on the air, billboard, transportation and newspaper advertisements, direct mail, window displays, booklets, blotters, book matches, bread wrappers, collars on milk bottles, movie trailers, listings in the newspapers and magazines, public-relations work with organizations, publicity campaigns in the press, and talent appearances before local clubs, are standard methods for advertising program schedules.

Projects and Exercises

1. Tune in the radio and television stations which are received well in your immediate area. On the basis of this observation, estimate the staff organization each station needs. Each student should take a different period in order to survey varied hours of station programming.
2. Visit one or more stations for "behind-the-scenes" tours. Ask a representative of the station to discuss the actual organization. Discuss later how nearly correct your estimate of the organization staff was.
3. If a class tour is not possible, invite a representative of the station to come to the school and speak.

STATION PERSONNEL CHART, WWJ (AM, FM, TV)

The Detroit News, Detroit, Michigan

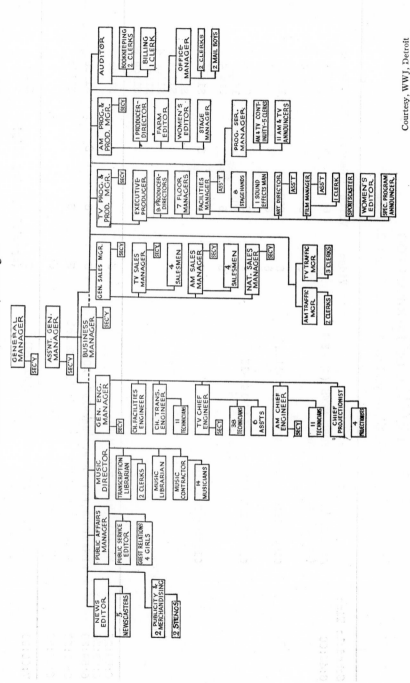

Courtesy, WWJ, Detroit

EXAMPLE OF PROGRAM LOG

Station KRCA-TV, Los Angeles, August 2, 1955 *

Schedule Time	Program	Video	Voice	Record	Film Anncr
6:45:00	JACK LATHAM & THE FORD NEWS (C) 5-F	5	6	5	Slide
	(Ford) Breslow-Runge				Slide
		5	6		Cam 4
	COMMERCIAL (C) #15478 "Invitation"	5	SOF		16mm
		5	6		Cam 4
	COMMERCIAL (C) Copy #LAT-148-15	5	6		Cam 4
	Film #15454	5	SOF		16mm
		5	6		Cam 4
	Closing Credits	5	6	5	Slide 1
					Slide 2
					Slide 3
					Slide 4
					Slide 5
					Slide 6
6:59:25	NI (L) (Mike Roy, M-F)	5			Slide
6:59:26	Chimes				
6:59:30	EXAMINER (C) "Amer. Weekly" 20"	5	6	5	Slide
6:59:50	HAWAIIAN PUNCH (C) Live/Slide & lcl	5	6		Slide
6:59:59	Video fade to black	5			
7:00:00	STEVE DONOVAN WESTERN MARSHALL (C)	5	SOF		35mm
	(Langendorf)	(Special Opening Clip)			
	COMM'L HITCHIKE #LTV-DC-LA-555	5	SOF		16mm
	"Western Marshall"	5	SOF		35mm

Time	Description				
	COMM'L (C) #LWF-155-1R	5	SOF		16mm
	"Western Marshall" Cont.	5	SOF		35mm
	COMM'L (C) #LSD-255-F3	5	SOF		35mm
	"Western Marshall" Cont.	5	SOF		35mm
	"Western Marshall" Concluded	5	SOF		35mm
	(CUTTING ROOM BE SURE TO FADE TO BLACK BEFORE HITCHIKE)				
	COMM'L HITCHIKE (C) #LTV-DC-LA-555	5	SOF		16mm
	SPECIAL CLOSING CLIP	5	SOF		35mm
	CLOSING FILM CREDITS	5	SOF		35mm
	Next Week Plug (If Necessary)	5	6	5	Slide(Wst'nMshl)
7:29:25	NI (L) (Cleve Hermann-11:15PM)	5	5		Slide
7:29:26	Chimes				
7:29:30	COLGATE DENTAL (C) #CDC-61	5	SOF		16mm
7:29:50	ALKA SELTZER (C) #AS-H-2 & 1cl	5	SOF-6		35mm
7:29:59	Video fade to black	5			
7:30:00	Vaughn Monroe	7	7		
7:44:25	NI (N)	7			
7:44:30	FORD (C) "Deal"	5	SOF		16mm
7:44:50	Today Show & 1cl	5	6		Slide
7:44:59	Video fade to black	5			
7:45:00	CAMEL NEWS CARAVAN (C)	7	7		
	(R. J. Reynolds)				

* Courtesy of KRCA-TV, Los Angeles.

❊ 16 ❊

Technical Aspects
of Radio

RADIO COMMUNICATION involves the transmission of sound through space to a point of reception not connected by wires to the point of origin. To accomplish this, microphones are used to convert sound waves into patterns of electrical energy. This energy is amplified and modulated by transmitting apparatus and broadcast on radio frequencies into the ether. At the point of reception, the electrical patterns are converted back to sound waves which emerge from the loudspeaker.

For an elementary understanding of the technical aspects of radio, it is helpful to examine each stage of this process and to describe the equipment which makes radio communication possible.

• MICROPHONES •

The Nature of Sound. Sound consists of waves of air particles in motion. When one speaks, the air expelled by the lungs passes through the vocal folds, which set up vibrations of the air particles. These are amplified by resonators in the head and throat and the resultant product emerging from the mouth and nose is called voice. Musical sound is produced in a violin by vibrating a string with a bow, using the box of the violin as the resonator. Thus sound is a physical product, brought into being by physical energy, and limited in its radius of transmission by the physical strength of the sound and the existence of intervening barriers. Sound produced by a violin or the human voice is usually periodic, or regular in pattern, and thus pleasing to the ear; often, especially among younger violinists or persons with vocal defects, aperiodic sounds are heard; these are irregular and unpleasant, and to them are ascribed such qualities as rasping, noisy, and scraping. Sound is perceived through the ear; the physical movement of air particles caused by the sound vibrates the membrane in the ear which then

244

FREQUENCY RANGE OF MUSICAL INSTRUMENTS
AND HUMAN VOICE

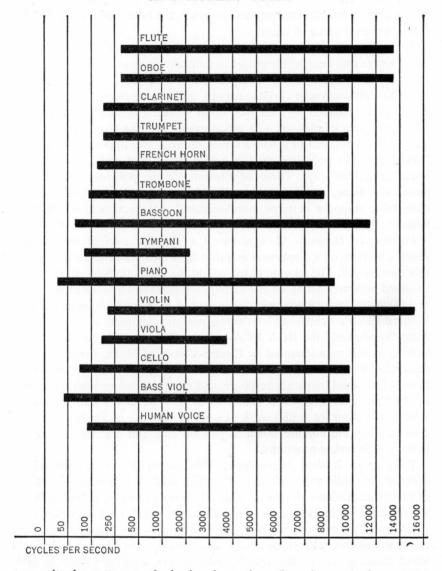

transmits the pattern to the brain where, through various complex nervous processes, meaning is given to the perception of sound.

The sound itself has a frequency, which we perceive as pitch, determined by the number of its vibrations—the greater the number per second, the higher the pitch; a regularity or irregularity of vibrations—with simple to complex patterns—which we perceive as quality; amplitude of vibrations which we perceive as intensity or loudness; and has an existence in time which we perceive as duration.

The more sensitive the reproduction of the full sound, in all its range of frequencies, quality, intensity and duration, the fuller and more satisfying will be the experience of hearing.

Microphone Fundamentals. The purpose of the microphone is to convert sound waves into electrical impulses as faithfully as possible. There are four general types of microphones: (1) pressure or dynamic, (2) velocity or ribbon, (3) combination or variable pattern, and (4) condenser. Microphones may also be classified by their pick-up of sound: (1) nondirectional or a 360-degree area of pick-up, (2) unidirectional or a pick-up on one "live" side, (3) bidirectional or a figure 8 pick-up area, two opposing sides being "alive," and (4) polydirectional, in which the area of pick-up can be adjusted in various ways. These adjustments for the polydirectional microphone give three, or six, or twelve variable patterns based upon the first three basic response patterns, nondirectional, unidirectional, and bidirectional.

Pressure or Dynamic Microphone. The dynamic microphone receives sound vibrations on a diaphragm and translates them into electrical impulses in a moving coil. The moving of the coil in the magnetic field, proportional to sound pressures acting on the diaphragm, generates a small electric current. Dynamic or pressure microphones used in many stations include the Western Electric "eight-ball" (which is not manufactured at present), the Altec "saltshaker," the RCA 88 A and the BK 1A "Commentator," and various models manufactured by Electro-Voice and Shure. Common characteristics of these microphones are ruggedness of construction, small size, light weight, good frequency response, and relative freedom from the effects of wind and moisture which makes them very useful for remotes. Many stations use them for studio work as well, particularly as announce microphones. They are nondirectional in pick-up area and are used for round tables and interview programs.

Velocity or Ribbon Microphone. This microphone has been widely adopted for studio work because of its high fidelity. It consists essentially of a thin duraluminum ribbon suspended between two magnetic poles. When the ribbon is set in motion by sound vibrations, small electric currents are developed. This microphone is equally sensitive on the two opposite sides facing the ribbon but comparatively "dead" on the two edges. The bidirectional characteristic of the velocity microphone, combined with its high fidelity, makes it very useful. The opportunities for subtle shadings of sound perspective due to relative position of the performer directly "on beam" or at the edge of the beam, and the insensitivity on the two "dead" sides are especially important in radio dramatics. The high fidelity (50 to 15,000 cycles) gives lifelike reproduction of music. RCA's 44 BX is the velocity microphone most widely used.

Combination or Variable Pattern. These microphones represent a more recent application of microphone research. By use of the same microphone but with different switch positions, a great variety of pick-up area sensitivity may be achieved. Altec manufactures the 639 A cardioid microphone, which consists of a special ribbon and magnet structure in combination with a dynamic unit. When the cardioid, or heart, pattern is desired, the ribbon and dynamic element are used together for a unidirectional pick-up. It may also be used for nondirectional pick-up patterns with the dynamic unit used alone, and for bidirectional pick-ups with the ribbon alone. The RCA 77 D, a polydirectional microphone, consists of a single ribbon element and a variable acoustic network or labyrinth which permit three broad general adjustments for unidirectional, nondirectional, and bidirectional pick-ups, with additional variations and voice- or music-selector switches. Stations using these microphones profit by their flexibility. Some stations do not use them because there are more opportunities for mistakes when time does not permit careful checking of the switches prior to a broadcast. Frequent manipulation of the switches also results in more wear and tear on the microphones. Two RCA combination type microphones developed primarily for television but which may be used in radio are the small omnidirectional BK 4B designed for "on-camera" use and the unidirectional BK 5A for overhead boom pick-ups.

Condenser Microphone. The condenser microphone was used widely in the early 30's, but its lack of ruggedness imposed certain limitations. Recent improvements have eliminated the source of difficulty. It is nondirectional, does not distort under sudden blasts of sound waves, and has excellent frequency response. The Altec and Telefunken (German manufacture) are the two condenser types generally found in stations.

Public-Address (PA) and Tape-Recorder Microphones. Broadcast microphones are generally not used with inexpensive public-address and portable tape recorders. "Crystal" and low-cost dynamic microphones are commonly substituted. These microphones are "high impedance" in character, matching the PA and tape-recorder amplifiers. However, the high-impedance microphones are not only subject to hum, but they also lose high frequencies when long microphone cables are used. Therefore, when a high fidelity (and expensive) public-address system is installed, transformers may be included so as to permit use of comparable high fidelity broadcast (low-impedance) microphone pick-ups. Some models of tape recorders are designed to allow either a high-impedance or a broadcast microphone to be used. A transformer is attached to the microphone cable in the latter instance.

· STUDIOS ·

Programs may be produced and broadcast from any location ranging from an atomic-powered submarine to a blimp. One musical program featuring Perry Como as soloist, with a vocal group and orchestra, together with announcer, agency director, NBC production representative, and an NBC engineer was broadcast to a coast-to-coast network from an airliner cruising far above the skyscrapers of New York City. The most common point of origination, however, is the station or network studio. A small station may have a combination announce-control room with one adjoining studio and find it highly satisfactory. Regional and clear-channel stations with more complex programming add studios to an average of three or four including one audience studio. Networks, with a greater variety and volume of program origination may have two to four audience studios and six to eight small and medium-sized studios for nonaudience programs.

Studios require acoustical treatment according to the primary use that is made of the studio. In the early days, heavy drapes and thick carpets were used to absorb sound, reduce echo, eliminate extraneous noises, and keep studios from sounding "boomy." Low and high frequencies were dampened out by this method. The speaking voice did not suffer too much as improved microphones, amplifying systems, transmitters, and receivers were introduced, but music and songs did. They sounded lifeless, lacked brilliance and tone color in comparison to concert hall reception due to the reduction in frequency range and the elimination of musical overtones. Some degree of reflected sound or reverberation for brilliance is normal for our hearing. If there is a high degree of reflection, however, it may create an echo or "boomy" effect, and even distort sound to the point where it is "noise."

As studio design improved, "reverberation without echo or distortion" began to be considered, together with the need for isolating the studio from extraneous outside noises. Modern studios are "floating studios." The studio is literally a room within a room, not directly connected by any rigid means to the building that houses it. Special acoustical felt or springs enclosed in absorbent material are used to keep the studio floor, walls, and ceiling isolated from the regular frame of the building. This prevents the transmission of sound and shock vibrations from trains, traffic, street repair, office noises, etc.

In order to prevent corridor noises or sounds coming into the studio from the hall, a sound lock or indirect entrance is usually constructed. A sound lock means that a small foyer or entrance hall is between the studio door and the corridor door. The doors are of extra heavy construction and fit tightly. Any observation windows or control booth windows in the studio have two or three panes of plate glass, and are constructed so as to prevent solid connections between the jambs. With no outside ventilation, relatively noise-less air-conditioning is essential.

In the acoustical treatment of the studio there are two general approaches. One is the "live-end, dead-end" type with a neutral zone between. The live-end section consists of a back wall constructed of seasoned wood or sound reflecting materials, and an approximate third of the adjoining side walls with the same material, but with "saw-tooth" or shallow "V" construction to prevent parallel reverberation surfaces. Opposite the live-end is the dead-end section with special acoustical material designed to absorb the sound without reflection. In this type of studio a greater amount of reverberation may be obtained for singers and instrumentalists by placing them at the live-end, or a lesser degree of reverberation may be obtained by moving the group to the dead end. The degree of reverberation and change of quality are dependent, not only upon (1) the acoustical treatment of the studio, but also upon (2) the directional characteristics of the microphone being used, (3) the placement of the microphone in relation to the location of the performing group, (4) the distance between the microphone and the performing group, (5) individual differences in the musicians and vocalists, and (6) the size of the performing group. It is apparent that the set-up to be used for a particular broadcast can only be determined as the result of experimentation.

The second general type of studio construction is more common among stations which require a more flexible use of their studios. One objection to the definite live-end, dead-end type of studio is that it is restrictive, more useful for single microphone orchestral pick-ups than heavy duty utility work so necessary for a studio in constant use. Further, complications may arise when a large number of microphones have to be used, as on a variety or dramatic program. Acoustical theories and reverberation times figured in the laboratory sometimes do not work out in actual studio operations. A general-purpose type of studio is looked upon with more favor by some stations. It consists of uniformly distributed acoustic treatment. Many have saw tooth or "V" construction on walls and ceiling, used with or without additional half spheres or "bumps" on the walls, or half columns with the rounded portion towards the studio and flat portion toward the wall. The purpose of this type of construction is to prevent "slap" or "bounce" from flat parallel surfaces. Drapes or curtains may be drawn across certain sections to vary the acoustical characteristics. The same general principles of experimentation, before arriving at a set-up, hold true here as with the live-end, dead-end studio, and the same factors of microphone type, distance from performers, and individual performer difference must be taken into account. Examples of various ways to set up programs will be given in subsequent chapters.

• CONTROL ROOM •

The next step in tracing the broadcast circuit is the studio control room. The microphone in the studio turns the sound into minute electric waves (audio current) which travel over special microphone cable into the control room. The first stop is at the studio control console. Here a preamplifier strengthens the weak audio current and it passes through a gain control known as a "fader," "pot," or "mixer" which regulates the volume of the audio current. Referring to clock numerals as many engineers and directors do, at a point at bottom left, about where "7" would be, the fader would be closed and no audio current from that microphone would pass. By turning the fader in a clockwise fashion to the right, audio current is passed according to the distance the fader is turned. *Fading up* the microphone means that the control console fader connected to that microphone "channel" is turned to the right or on. *Fading down* or *off* is the reverse. The console contains a number of these faders, located in parallel series near the bottom, convenient for easy manipulation by the engineer as he is seated at the console overlooking the studio. Each microphone in the studio has its corresponding fader, and the engineer has the responsibility of turning on the number of microphones required, with appropriate level or volume for each according to the needs of the particular program. This is called "riding gain." These faders may be connected with transcription turntables, one fader for each turntable located at either side of the console desk. The number of faders varies according to the elaborateness of the console equipment needed to handle a station's program requirements. Six "channel" mixers are sufficient for normal use, four faders for microphones and two for turntables.

In addition to the individual faders the usual console has a master fader, shortened to "master," which has over-all control of the other faders. With the master, the engineer can fade up or down all the component parts of the program at the same time.

From the microphone faders, the audio signal goes through additional amplification to strengthen the signal enough to boost it along the wire to the master control room or directly to the transmitter. There must be enough amplification for proper transmission, but not so much that the equipment will be overloaded and the sound distorted. A volume indicator, on the face of the console, translates visually the amount of signal being sent. This is a meter containing a fluctuating electric pointer or "needle," a scale arranged to indicate the voltage percentage in black figures from 0 to 100 as the principal scale above the arc, and volume unit or "VU" levels, in decibels from minus 20 to plus 3 in red figures below the arc. *The more gain or volume being sent, the more to the right the "needle" moves across the meter scale in direct proportion to the variations in strength of the signal.* This instrument is referred to by a variety of terms: volume indicator or "VI" is very common due to a carry-over in terminology from an earlier meter; the use of VU, after the newer meter, is more authentic and generally trade-accepted. If the incoming level is too low for proper amplification and transmission, so that the listener at home will not be able to understand it easily, the engineer "riding gain" will turn the fader up; if the VU needle "peaks" over 100 to plus 1, 2 or 3 consistently, the level is too high and the fader has to be turned down. Otherwise, distortion will result as automatic compressors in the transmission equipment go into action to prevent overloading.

The person at the control console regulates the volume during the entire broadcast so that the quality of transmission will not vary and the listener at home will not be distracted by inaudibility or distortion. In addition to the supervision of volume output, he may have the responsibility of (1) having the faders open and closed when they should be, (2) fading the microphones in or out smoothly as needed for certain effects, and (3) balancing and blending the microphones by ear. An example of this is a program, where one microphone picking up a vocalist, is balanced against a second microphone with a selective pick-up of a soft-muted violin section of the orchestra. A third microphone is regulating an eight-voice choir, a fourth microphone is suspended directly over the piano for a rippling piano run, and a fifth microphone is used for an over-all orchestral pick-up.

This operation requires not only manual and mental dexterity, but considerable artistry on the part of the technician. A high degree of co-operation between the engineer, the director supervising the production, and the performing talent is desirable. The example quoted was not selected because of unique difficulties. It would not be out of the ordinary for a station which produces much in the way of live programs. A counterpart in dramatic presentation is a scene where one microphone is covering live organ introductory chords; the second microphone is used for dialogue between characters in the scene; the third controls an isolation booth telephone filter pick-up; the fourth is available for the sound effect of a telephone ring preliminary to a conversation; and a fifth is used both by the announcer for the commercial credits and the narrator for the play.

Above each microphone fader is a key switch for auditioning or listening to another studio, or to a record during the actual broadcast of a program. Additional amplifiers in the console or in a relay rack in the booth permit the engineer or announcer to monitor the program being broadcast or listen to the program source being auditioned. There are various switches on the console providing channels to feed a program to a remote line for cue purposes, and to feed remote lines or the network line to the transmitter or master control. Other controls permit the operator to make announcements from the control room, regulate the volume of the speaker in the booth, and to talk to the people in the studio over the talk-back system. In many small stations a single studio console serves as a master control system, since it is possible to control microphone channels from two studios as well a running the turntables and making announcements directly from the control booth.

An essential piece of equipment for smooth control room operation is an excellent loud speaker with high fidelity. The VU meter can register only the volume; the engineer and director, through the mixing of the microphones, effect the balance and quality of broadcast by "ear" judgment, not by meter readings. The rehearsal period is used to check these items. A control-room loud speaker with faulty response in the higher frequencies may induce a director or engineer to change a set-up to make it sound more pleasing when actually the broadcast would be harmed. There is a reverse caution needed, however. Extremely sensitive control-room loud speakers can lull the production director into thinking that certain tones and certain effects are going to be heard on home receivers when, as a matter of fact, the average set is incapable of reproducing them. A specific example is the sound effect of jingling of coins, which consists primarily of high frequency sounds and is extremely low in volume. A high-fidelity microphone picks up this sound effect authentically as heard over a good control-room speaker. On an average radio, it will be lost completely or be reproduced as the clinking of heavy washers.

Another cause of errors in program production is carrying the control-room loud speaker at too high a level. This may emphasize minute sounds and delicate nuances of tone which seem to be suitable for transmission, but are lost on the average home receiver. To guard against these production errors, many directors and engineers drop the level of the speaker to correspond to home reception during portions of the rehearsal, and some utilize another speaker with less fidelity and a 6- to 8-inch speaker-cone similar to those in the average home set.

Supplementary equipment found in the control room are the jack panels with their associated patch cords. These are used to extend the flexibility of the console in some control rooms by terminating the inputs and outputs of all amplifiers on the jack panels. This allows rapid rerouting of the signal in case of trouble, variation in distribution of the various channels or the use of filter or echo devices to change the quality of the signal.

• MASTER CONTROL ROOM •

If the individual station contains more studios than can be handled with ease by the single control room which feeds the transmitter directly, a master control room is used as the co-ordinating center. Here the various studio outputs, or program feeds, are received and amplified. The master control room may range from a simple extension of the control room to an extremely complex arrangement with relay racks lining the walls. These racks contain power supplies, program and monitor amplifiers feeding several speakers, and jack panels for routing any channel in a countless variety of ways. They also have equipment for receiving and equalizing network and remote channels and sending them into the appropriate studio at the right time, and to the transmitter; and elaborate systems of preset switches, push buttons, signal lights, and countless other pieces of equipment known only to the technicians who expertly and calmly make the necessary adjustments for smooth operation.

• TELEPHONE NETWORK •

The reference to network channels coming into the MC or master control room should be supplemented by a brief description of how network programs get from origination centers to stations affiliated with them. It could be more descriptively termed a "telephone network" because of the thousands of miles of specially leased telephone lines which are used in network broadcasting. Programs go from the network master control room by special telephone circuits to the "long lines" division of the American Telephone and Telegraph Company where they are routed north, east, south, and west. Booster amplifying equipment is located along the lines and at switching centers to keep the volume at proper level. Upon receiving the signal in its master control, each radio station relays the program to its respective transmitter by similar high-fidelity telephone lines. The telephone network can reverse the circuits to receive program feeds from affiliated stations along the network and redistribute the programs in regular fashion.

• TRANSCRIPTIONS AND RECORDINGS •

In addition to programs using live performers, programs may be presented by transcriptions, which are especially prepared for broadcast by the station, or are secured from transcription library services; or by the use of regular commercial phonograph records on sale in record shops.

Many broadcasts are presented by a station on a "delayed" basis, at a period other than the original time on the network because of local commitments. Some programs are repeated after the initial live presentation due to the different time zones across the country. Special auditions also may be prepared for presentation to clients at their convenience. Reference copies of programs may be desired for "as broadcast" checks at a later date. To take care of such demands, stations and networks employ two general methods to make program recordings: instantaneous or disc method, and magnetic tape.

Instantaneous Recording. In this method large 16-inch discs which have an aluminum base covered by acetate and are somewhat thinner than regular records, are placed on a revolving turntable of special design and construction. A continuous spiraling groove (moving in from the edge or out from the center) is cut into the acetate coating by a special diamond or sapphire stylus, leaving an impression on the sides of the grooves. Fifteen minutes of a program can be included on one side. This type of transcription is trade-named after its revolutions per minute (rpm), 33⅓, shortened to "33's." With the newer "microgroove" system, one side can accommodate forty minutes.

These instantaneous recordings or transcriptions (either term is used) develop scratch, and the response, which may have been very good (50 to

10,000 cycles) drops in fidelity with successive play-backs or as copies ("dubbings") are made. When copies are needed in great numbers, master records and pressings, using more durable material, are made. Broadcast transcription companies and library services use the latter method.

ISOMETRIC VIEW OF A STUDIO ARRANGEMENT

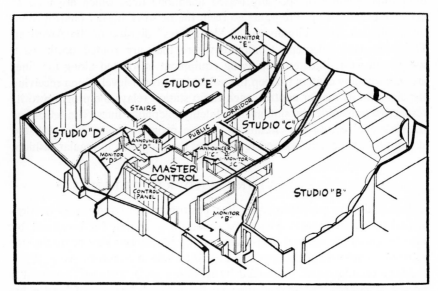

Courtesy of KGW, Portland, Oregon

This is a good example of studio planning for an individual station. The master control room overlooks three studios, yet each studio has its own monitor control room.

Magnetic Tape-Recording Method. In this method a plastic base tape is run from one large reel to another, much the same as in home-movie projection systems, past a magnetic recording mechanism. The tape is run through at speeds of 7½ or 15 inches per second. The frequency range is excellent in machines designed for broadcasting, from 30 or 40 cycles up to 15,000 cycles. The mechanism is small enough to be portable.

This system is very useful because each tape can be used over and over again. The mechanism is so arranged that succeeding recordings wipe off previous ones. In addition, the tape can be spliced quite easily so that changes can be made in the program before it is played on the air, without loss of fidelity. This opportunity to "edit" a program, eliminating faults in production, the portability of the equipment, and the convenience of making tape recordings ahead of scheduled broadcast times have induced many stars and program producers to "tape" their programs. Less expensive versions of instantaneous and tape-recording methods are available to schools and universities. Wire recorders, while less expensive, have not been adopted as widely as tape recorders due to lower fidelity and difficulties in splicing.

Each recording method has its advantages. Although relatively expensive to purchase and operate because precision machinery is required and discs cannot be reused, disc recordings provide permanence of storage. Any portion of the disc may be singled out conveniently. Tape recording equipment gives excellent fidelity at lower cost, permits editing and re-use of the same tape; it is also portable.

Turntables. Transcriptions at 33⅓ rpm and commercial recordings at 33⅓, 45, and 78 rpm are played on turntables similar in function to phonographs. However, since a variety of commercial and instantaneous recordings are used on the air, turntables must be carefully designed and constructed with special filter controls and extremely light pick-up arms. At least two tables are needed to enable the operator to "cue" one record while the other is on the air. Turntables may be placed in studios or control rooms depending on station policy.

• REMOTE PICK-UPS •

When programs originate away from the studios, a special telephone circuit is ordered from the telephone company. This circuit goes from the point of pick-up to the master control of the station. An engineer uses portable remote amplifiers similar in design and function to the control-room console. Suitable microphones are placed for the best pick-up of the program, the engineer mixes and balances the microphones and sends the program along the special telephone circuit to master control. A second circuit may be ordered for communication between the control room and the engineer at the point of pick-up. After a period of test transmission, time signals are given up to the time the program is due to go on the air. The control room at the station may give a "take-it-away" cue, the remote may start on a time basis or immediately following a prearranged word cue included on the program.

For special remote pick-ups, such as golf matches, telephone service is not available and a short-wave transmitter is used instead. The announcer follows the action, using a portable "walkie talkie" to broadcast to a mobile truck which sends the signal by special short-wave transmission to master control.

• TRANSMISSION •

The equipment at the transmitter sends out radio waves according to the licensed power and frequency of a station. The methods of transmission are Amplitude Modulation (AM) and Frequency Modulation (FM).

The Broadcast Spectrum. Let us compare radio and sound waves. Radio waves are caused by electrical vibration or "oscillation" whereas sound waves are air particles set in motion by physical action. Radio waves travel, as do sound waves, in all directions, similar to the familiar illustration of water waves activated by a stone, but they go faster than sound, with a speed of light or 186,000 miles per second instead of the sound velocity rate of 1,090 feet per second, and, of course, travel much farther than sound, to the moon and back, for instance. Whereas sound to our human ear varies in frequency from approximately 16 cycles to 20,000 cycles, radio waves considered useful at present vary from 10 kilocycles (10,000 cycles) to 3,000,000 kilocycles.

With a receiving set possessing no frequency discrimination, a listener would receive a jumble of signals due to the great use of these radio waves for communication: control tower to airplane, ship to shore, amateur to amateur, and commercial and governmental messages for example. As stated before, different frequency bands are assigned to various kinds of communication services by the Federal Communications Commission. The standard or AM broadcast band uses from 540 to 1,600 kilocycles. The United States, following international allocation agreements, has available a total of 106 channels in this band.

Below the standard band are various communication services. The very low frequencies, from 10 to 100 kilocycles, are useful for long-distance communication; those from 100 to 500 kilocycles are used for distances up to a thosuand miles. Above the standard band are other communication services, international short wave, FM and television, and radar and experimental research bands. The VHF television band, numbered for convenience, ranges from an assigned frequency of 54 to 60 megacycles (one megacycle equals one thousand kilocycles) to 210 to 216 megacycles. The FM bands, ranging from 88 to 108 megacycles, are in between the television channels. The UHF band ranges from 470 to 890 megacycles.

Transmitter and Antenna. Modern transmitters are almost self-operated. Engineering science and manufacturing skill provide instruments to insure accuracy and sustained transmission. Except for some small stations, transmitters and antennas are usually located in outlying areas. This is due to intense radiation of energy from the antenna, which tends to "blank out" listener reception in the immediate area, and the need for extensive ground systems consisting of thousands of feet of copper wire buried from six to twelve inches deep. Another important consideration is the electrical interference when the transmitter is located in a thickly populated district.

Transmitters have two functions:

1. Generation of a powerful radio wave initiated by a vacuum tube oscillator and amplified until it reaches the assigned power of the station. This wave is termed the carrier wave because it carries with it on its path through the ether the audio signal produced in the studio.

2. Modulation or superimposure of the audio signal upon the carrier wave. A homely illustration is that this process is like putting coal into a

Broadcast microphones: Clockwise from left: Electro-Voice dynamic 666; RCA 77 D; Altec cardioid 639 B; RCA velocity 44 BX.

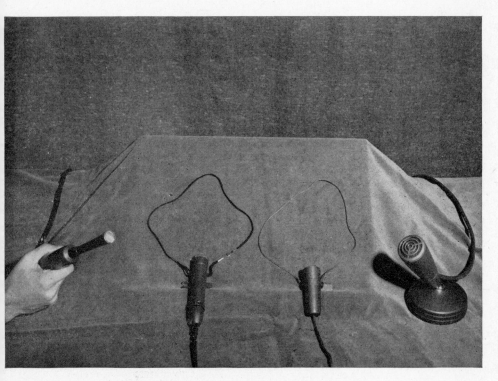

Broadcast microphones. From left: RCA ribbon-pressure "Starmaker" BK 4B; Electro-Voice dynamic 646; RCA miniature dynamic BK 6A; RCA "Commentator" BK 1A.

RCA image orthicon camera with lens turret

Close-up of rear of RCA image orthicon camera

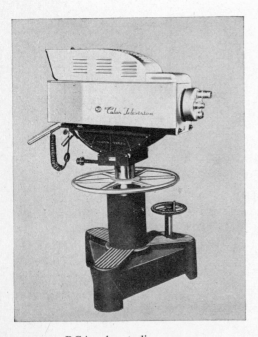

RCA color studio camera

RCA film camera with two TV projectors and multiplexer

A "studio on wheels," Color Television Mobile Unit

Portable video and audio control equipment, rear of RCA Mobile Unit. Top: microwave relay transmitter control unit. Left to right: remote audio amplifier and mixer; TV master monitor; switching system; and two camera controls. Microphone is RCA pressure 88A.

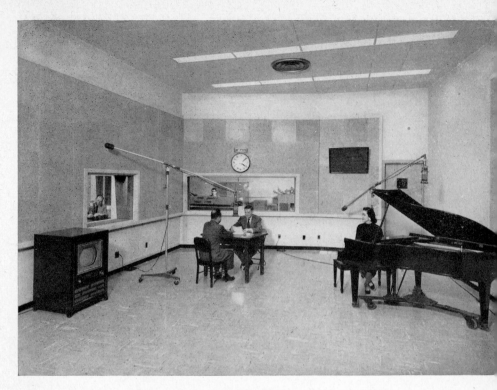

Main radio studio, WHIO, Dayton. Smaller AM studio at left and AM control room through window at rear.

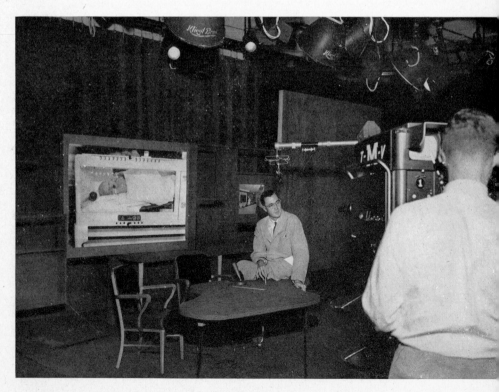

Studio scene, University of Michigan. Note informal posture of Dr. Richard Judge as he talks directly to camera. Photographic blow-up used as set dressing for medical program.

THE BROADCAST SPECTRUM

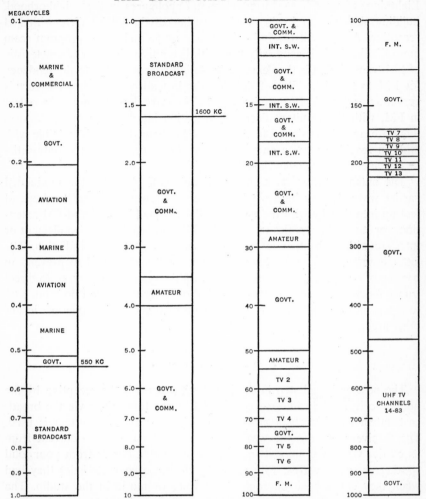

truck and having the truck carry it to your home. The two methods used for this process are:

(*a*) Amplitude modulation or AM. The power or amplitude of the carrier wave is varied. The frequency is the same.

(*b*) Frequency modulation or FM. The frequency of the carrier wave is varied. The amplitude remains the same.

Unless one possesses a great deal of engineering knowledge, a discussion of AM-FM methods of transmission is confusing. A preferable method for nontechnical people is to consider the effect of the two types of transmission. Reception of a wider range of frequencies is possible in the FM system. Lightning, summer heat storms, electrical appliances in the neighborhood, building elevators, and other such disturbances do not interfere with FM reception. As a result the fuller frequency range makes the program seem more lifelike. This is especially true with live music. Another characteristic of FM transmission is the decrease in station coverage, due to the tendency for FM to travel in "line-of-sight" paths instead of following the earth's curvature as does AM transmission. The sky wave does not normally reflect in FM, with the resultant decrease in station interference; more stations, therefore, may be assigned to the same FM channels than is possible with AM. In reaching remote and rural areas, however, AM is the only satisfactory method as yet developed.

The antenna tower serves as the jumping-off place for the modulated carrier wave. It may be a single symmetrical tower reaching hundreds of feet up into the sky with the upper portions containing TV and FM extentions; or it may be a series of vertical spires so placed as to complement or interfere with each other in order to change the pattern of radiation. The latter is referred to as a "directional antenna," and is used to prevent an overlap of coverage with another station on the same frequency, or to direct transmission away from a section of land or water the station does not care to reach, in order to intensify the strength of the station's coverage in another area.

· RECEPTION ·

The next and final step in the broadcast process is the reception by the home receiver. The radio waves sent out by the transmitter via the broadcast antenna are received at home on whatever antenna system is used. The receiver amplifies the weak signal, separates the audio current from its carrier wave, amplifies it some more and out it comes from your loud speaker as sound waves, with relatively the same characteristics they had when they entered the microphone as voice or music in the studio. The "coal truck" has delivered the coal! All of this happens at the speed of light so that the people at home a few feet away from the loud speaker actually hear what happened on microphone before the people in the studio audience!

Projects and Exercises

1. Classify the microphones in your studio according to their respective areas of pick-up—nondirectional, bidirectional, unidirectional. Conduct experiments to determine the operational characteristics of your microphones which give the best results. Use different speakers and musical instruments. Vary the distance from the microphone and location on or off the beam. Decide the most effective locations and distances for different effects which may be desired.

2. Classify your studio set-up as to acoustical construction and treatment. Test isolation characteristics by turning off all microphones and having one person talk in one studio while another listens in an adjoining one. Walk around the studio clapping your hands sharply together and listening to the sound as it comes back to you. Classify the "live" and "dead" areas. Conduct experiments in increasing the "liveness" by removal of rugs and drapes—in increasing the "deadness" by bringing in additional rugs and drapes. Consider the advisability of construction of movable flats hinged together which contain highly absorbent material on one side and reflective surfaces on the other for changing the acoustical conditions of the studios according to need.

3. Practice "riding gain" on a single voice. Then practice on two voices and move into riding gain on two or three microphones. Open and close faders on cue or script markings. Follow hand movements by instructor in fading up or down to acquire dexterity in manipulation of the faders. Play a professional recording and observe the VU meter readings.

4. Practice "patching up" the various combinations possible in your control room. Clear the board after each try for the person who follows.

5. Play a recording and listen to it critically for fidelity and balance as it is patched first through a highly sensitive loud speaker and second through a small "home-type" speaker. Compare the results and draw conclusions about the differences in quality and perception which influence control-room operation. Compare for example, the difference in level for a sound effect of night noises needed to assure clear-cut recognition over the small speaker as contrasted to the level needed when heard over the more sensitive speaker.

6. Observe and practice recording technique using the equipment available at your studio.

7. Observe and practice turntable operation. Chapter 27 contains some specific recommendations for this.

8. Make a field trip to several station transmitters.

9. Report in class on reception differences between AM and FM in your area. Listen in the evening to distant AM stations for confirmation of the "skywave" fading of programs.

❋ 17 ❋

Technical Aspects
of Television

TELEVISION INVOLVES two simultaneous operations: the transmission of sight and sound. The audio (sound) which accompanies video (sight) has been traced in the preceding chapter. The same path is followed by audio in television utilizing the upper one-half megacycle in the assigned frequency band (channel). Turning to video, let us first explain the television process from camera to home and then analyze elements in the "program chain."

• GENERAL EXPLANATION •

You may recall sitting in the movies when a "follow-the-white-dot" singing short was presented. The audience was shown one line of the song at a time with a little white dot moving across that line from left to right indicating which words the audience was to sing, and how long the word was to be held. When it reached the final word at the right, the dot jumped back quickly to the left side of the screen to start again with a new line of lyrics now in view. This is a very rough illustration of the first step in the telecast journey: the action of the electronic camera which scans, moving as the white dot from left to right but at a constant speed, the object or scene to be televised.

The scene in front of the camera is focused by means of a lens on a sensitive photoelectric screen and changed into electrical energy which falls on a glass target plate near the front of the image orthicon tube. This means that instead of an optical image there is an electronic pattern on the plate. Where the light is brighter in the studio scene the electrical charge is stronger; where there are shadows, the electrical charge is weaker. Simultaneously an electron gun is sending a scanning beam, sweeping across in horizontal lines (from left to right), over the back of the target plate at the amazing speed of 525 lines from top to bottom every one-thirtieth of a second (a frame). This beam returns the video signal, electrical patterns of "light" and "dark," to the electronic-multiplier section of the tube where it is boosted in strength and sent along over coaxial cable to control rooms and transmitter for further amplification in order to modulate the carrier wave and be sent out into space. The image orthicon tube which starts the signal on its way is only 17 inches long, has an estimated life of around 500 hours, and costs $1,200.

RCA IMAGE ORTHICON TUBE

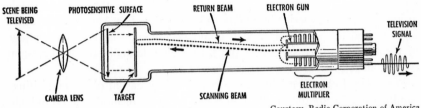

Courtesy, Radio Corporation of America

The television receiving system consists of a special antenna, a combination of tuning and amplifying circuits in the set to select and strengthen the signal, and a kinescope, a picture tube, on the face of which the original scene is recreated by a reverse process of the original action by the camera in the studio. Here an electronic beam scans the inner surface of the picture tube at the synchronized rate of 525 lines every one-thirtieth of a second. The image is thus reassembled in the home receiver for direct view or projection on a screen.

As was noted earlier, the very high and ultra high frequencies used for television-FM transmission do not normally permit much more coverage than "line-of-sight." The station antennas therefore are as high as possible, utilizing skyscrapers in metropolitan centers or nearby heights of land, in order to reach as much area as possible.

The telephone lines used for network radio broadcasting cannot carry the television signal. Special coaxial cable, capable of doing so, has been developed. In conjunction with such cables automatic microwave relay stations are used extensively to provide television network service throughout the country. The original signal is picked up by one relay, amplified and directed in a straight air line to the next point, and so on until the destination is reached. These relays generally are no farther apart than about twenty-five miles.

Another method of presenting one television program to more than one station is that of "kinescope" films. By this method, 35 mm. or 16 mm. films of television programs are made directly off the viewing tube, processed, and distributed for projection over other stations.

Kinescope or television-recording equipment capable of reproducing the program on film within minutes or even in fifty seconds has been developed.

One use for such "hot" processing techniques is in the coverage of special events during the day when regular programs occupy the schedule. Also, live network evening programs are kinescoped at the time of presentation in New York for rebroadcast three hours later on the West Coast.

Magnetic tape recordings of either black and white or color television signals is the newest system to emerge from the laboratory. The elimination of the intermediate step of film processing through the use of an all-electronic process will reduce costs and open up greater opportunities for program re-use and distribution. In 1956, the Ampex Company introduced a magnetic tape recorder, using a two-inch width tape, that produced television recordings superior in quality to kinescopes. The Ampex tape recording required no processing and it could be reused. The many advantages of the tape recorder suggested the future abandonment of the kinescope process in television.

"Organized chaos" might be the reaction of a casual observer visiting a studio scene during the progress of a live program of moderate complexity. He would see a great variety of types of lighting combined to create a blaze of light; massive movable platforms or "dollies," which support boom microphones, moving left or right and extending forward or drawing back as the operators follow the action; additional cameras with pedestal bases being moved around by the cameramen, tilted up and down or swinging right or left; a huge "boom dolly" camera electrically raised up and out in space like a steam shovel ready to take another mouthful of dirt; stage settings, special device mechanisms, and props; milling performers and production personnel; camera, light, and mike cables, and intercommunication wires covering the nonplaying area like a mass of snakes. However, when this casual observer becomes more familiar with the details of program production, he realizes that there are definite reasons for the patterns of activity and the various elements and soon becomes aware of the highly skilled team play which is in operation.

The same congestion appears on the sound stage during the making of a movie and back stage in a theater, but an essential difference exists in television. Here we have "continuality." From the director's call, "dissolve to one" to the end title there is a continuous picture presentation; there is no stopping, as in movies, to reset lights, tear down walls for new camera angles, freshen make-up, or repair cameras; no dropping of curtain to make costume changes and to reset the stage. The television program must continue with a fluid and uninterrupted production.

What are the primary technical facilities which are required for television? They are:

1.	Studios	5.	Control room
2.	Microphones	6.	Film and slide projection
3.	Cameras	7.	Master control
4.	Staging	8.	Transmitter and antenna

An introductory discussion of these facilities follows, excluding staging which is treated in a separate chapter.

· STUDIOS ·

Many early television studios consisted of reconverted radio studios. Many of these were in downtown office buildings high above the ground floor. As program schedules expanded, the required equipment, cameras, microphone booms, sets, lights and numbers of people involved demanded more and more space. Makeshift expansions into halls and adjoining offices became the rule. Numerous difficulties and excessive expenses were encountered in transporting large props and sets up narrow stairs or small service elevators. Although these conditions still prevail, stations generally have recognized the need for specialized design of television studio buildings.

One key principle developed is that of *horizontal* (ground floor) rather than *vertical* planning in order to permit easier and more economical movement in and out of raw stock, finished sets, equipment, and properties. A display of automobiles in the studio is simple when cars may be driven through doors directly into the studio. Station WBAP-TV in Fort Worth has a novel "video-lane" feature which permits movement of autos, trucks, elephants, and even "herds of cattle" across its large studio right before the cameras. Two huge doors (15 x 12 feet), one on each side of the studio facing each other, open directly to the outside of the building. The Budweiser commercial which utilized an 80-foot-long wagon and team of horses was presented live in this studio.

Another principle which is highly important is *traffic flow* or *circulation*. "Such close scheduling of TV broadcasts is necessary, in order to make maximum use of the costly space and equipment, that circulation assumes paramount importance," writes J. P. Allison in the *Architectural Record*. "People and things must flow through the building; control is essential." Functional design is essential to keep the various kinds of groups from interfering with each other as they move in and around the studios. The diagram below lists the types of people and things to be considered. Effective design for plant utilization should not only provide for separation of these groups, but also plan for the shortest possible interior traffic paths. Engineering workshops close to the technical areas, news machines near studios used for news programs, directors' offices near control rooms, and set construction space adjacent to studios are examples of this type of design.

The third key principle in studio design is a provision for *expansion*. It is a commonplace experience for many stations that additional space is needed before the building is finished. Many architects and building consultants recommend an advance over-all, step-by-step development which permits flexible growth in stages as the station increases its program production.

Such a master plan may avoid haphazard space additions as temporary expedients which impose serious limitations on future program production requirements.

Studio buildings are generally constructed on the outskirts of cities in order to secure adequate ground space at less expense and to provide ample parking facilities for station personnel and guests. When existing structures are secured for remodeling, the search for needed space has led officials to

CIRCULATION PROBLEM IN A TV STUDIO

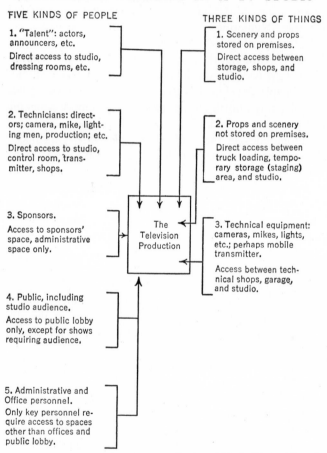

FIVE KINDS OF PEOPLE

1. "Talent": actors, announcers, etc.
Direct access to studio, dressing rooms, etc.

2. Technicians: directors; camera, mike, lighting men, production; etc.
Direct access to studio, control room, transmitter, shops.

3. Sponsors.
Access to sponsors' space, administrative space only.

4. Public, including studio audience.
Access to public lobby only, except for shows requiring audience.

5. Administrative and Office personnel.
Only key personnel require access to spaces other than offices and public lobby.

THREE KINDS OF THINGS

1. Scenery and props stored on premises.
Direct access between storage, shops, and studio.

2. Props and scenery not stored on premises.
Direct access between truck loading, temporary storage (staging) area, and studio.

3. Technical equipment: cameras, mikes, lights, etc.; perhaps mobile transmitter.
Access between technical shops, garage, and studio.

The Television Production

Courtesy of the *Architectural Record*

take over such buildings as riding academies, dance halls, creameries, garages, motion picture sound stages, theaters, armories, and, as the University of Michigan did, a mortuary.

The size and number of the studios depend in large measure upon program activity. A station relying basically upon network schedules may have only one small studio approximately 15 x 30 feet with a 12-to-14-foot ceiling which permits some local live programming and advertising display. The controls may be placed in the master control room to conserve on the number of staff men required. The next step may be for a separate control room, then substitution or addition of a larger studio. A combination of one good-sized studio 50 x 80 feet and a smaller studio 25 x 35, with 14- to 18-foot ceilings, seems to be adequate for a station planning a fair amount of local live productions which include some programs with studio audiences. It is implicit that such a two-studio arrangement must also have allied storage, workshop, dressing-room, and rehearsal areas.

The acoustical requirements of television studios differ from those for radio. Size and shape and wall and ceiling treatment are important factors in radio studio acoustics. In television, however, these factors are reduced in importance due to the many different sets which occupy portions of the studio. Unlike radio, in television there is a necessity for a great deal of physical movement of personnel, properties, and equipment as sets are struck and erected and cameras and microphone booms are changed in position during the actual airing of the program. This activity causes incidental noise. Since microphones are usually kept out of camera range, they are farther from talent and may pick up such undesirable noises. As a consequence, television studios should be "deadened" through use of draperies and considerable sound absorption material on walls and ceilings. Brightness and reverberation when required are frequently obtained through the use of "echo" chambers or electronic devices.

The avoidance of noises from the outside is needed in television as in radio. Similar sound locks and floating-type construction of studios may be employed. Location of studios in surburban areas decreases the traffic noise, but unfortunately sometimes increases the airplane noise potential.

Considerable ingenuity has been exercised by many stations in meeting the demands for studio space. Not every station possesses studio space mentioned earlier as desirable. A striking example of resourcefulness under difficult conditions which attracted considerable trade interest has been described by Ben Greer, Program Director and Production Manager of the UHF station WGVL in Greenville, South Carolina. This station was constructed on a modest budget. Original plans were for only slide and film operation in conjunction with network service the first year, but just prior to going on the air some live programming became desirable. Most of the equipment had been installed; no space was available except for a room adjoining the control room; size, 100 x 120 *inches*. From this oversized closet which wouldn't even accommodate a TV camera, WGVL eventually aired *twenty-two* hours of live programs each week, including some back-to-back scheduling. Not only news, sports, and farm shows, but women's features, interviews, church programs, and even a six-piece band! They did it with bed sheets, steel rollers, a midget piano, a suspended RCA 77-D microphone, thirty-five flood-40 light globes and a mirror 2 x 3 feet. The

UNIVERSITY OF MICHIGAN
TELEVISION STUDIO

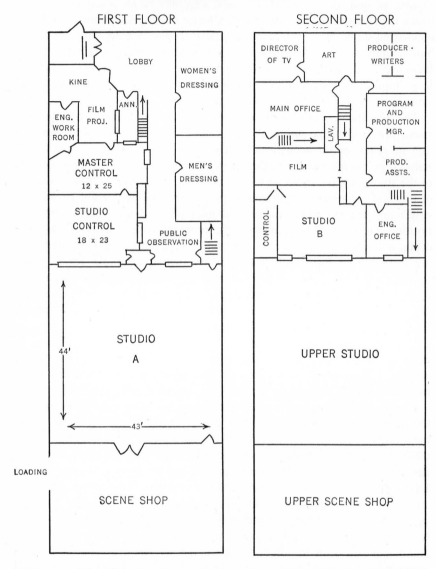

camera was placed in the control room, shooting through a glass window. Since the only space for a window was at one side of the control room, a portion of the closet "studio" was out of camera range. This difficulty was solved by going into slide, film, or opaque for transition and shifting to another camera lens which when focused on the mirror brought the far end of the studio into view. The question of scenery was answered by installing heavy-duty, metal window-shade-type rollers, 8 feet long, with ordinary bed sheets for back drops. A rack was used which would hold eight of these rollers at one time. An alternate system was the use of display paper placed on the wall upon which could be sketched the scenic background required (and saved for subsequent use). Drapes on a track 16 inches away from the wall were also available for use as set dressings. Remember the dimensions of this WGVL closet "studio," 100 x 120 *inches.* And an advantage for the director, for in Mr. Greer's words: "One of the things I liked about this little studio was that nobody could get off the set. There just wasn't any place to go!"

WHIO Studio and Office Building, Dayton, Ohio. Radio and television studios and general offices are contained in a single building occupied by WHIO since March, 1955. It was planned that each operation could be run independently and that certain common facilities would be available to more than one unit. "Traffic segregation" to promote station efficiency has been followed. The circulation legend describes the normal traffic patterns by different groups. Television operations are concentrated in the entire right half of the building. AM operations are located at the left rear, while business offices occupy the left front portion of the building. The television technical area is a two-story section located between the two TV studios. Studio 1 is 30 x 50 feet, studio 2 is 50 x 63 feet. Ceiling clearance is 20 feet. The building, which is situated on the Wilmington Pike, about five miles from downtown Dayton, was originally constructed in 1948 to house a single television studio. The design and construction of the expanded facilities was carried out by The Austin Company, who built the original building. A floor plan of the facilities appears on page 268.

· MICROPHONES ·

In radio the performers move, the microphones are stationary; in television the usual pattern is for the microphones to follow the talent. The two microphones used most generally for this suspended and flexible boom operation are the RCA 77 D and the Altec (WE) Cardioid. The unidirectional pattern is preferred in order to eliminate as much of the incidental studio noise as possible. RCA introduced its Uniaxial BK 5A in 1955 as a type primarily designed for television. This microphone is similar to the 77 D but has better directional properties, less sensitivity to wind noises, and improved shock mount for boom operation. The standard microphone boom permits continuous variations in the length of the boom. It may be extended forward 17 feet into the set and retracted 10 feet; it may be swung in an arc from side to side to follow action; and it has a special attachment

[1] Courtesy of Miami Valley Broadcasting Corporation and The Austin Company. An article in RCA's *Broadcast News,* August, 1955 describes the building and facilities in considerable detail.

WHIO STUDIO AND OFFICE BUILDING

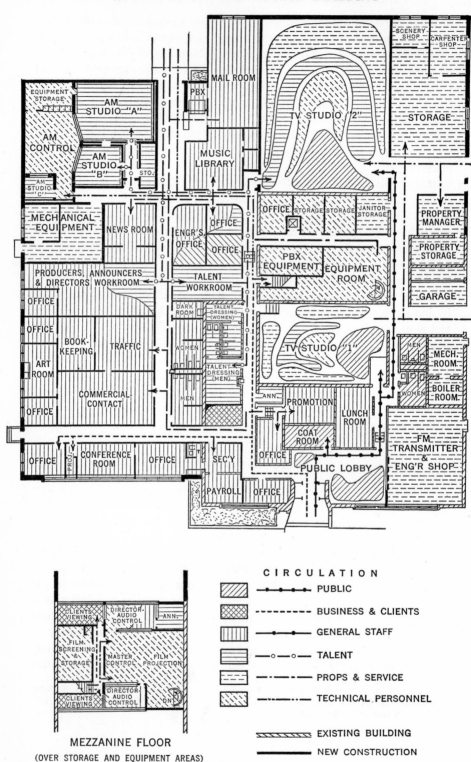

MEZZANINE FLOOR
(OVER STORAGE AND EQUIPMENT AREAS)

CIRCULATION

- ─•─•─•─ PUBLIC
- ─ ─ ─ ─ BUSINESS & CLIENTS
- ─•──•── GENERAL STAFF
- ─○──○── TALENT
- ─•─ ─•─ PROPS & SERVICE
- ─••─ ─••─ TECHNICAL PERSONNEL

EXISTING BUILDING

NEW CONSTRUCTION

which enables the boom operator to rotate the microphone itself in any direction. This latter feature is useful when two persons who are separated in the set are talking to each other. The operator directs the boom to the proper person. If both are speaking, the distance between is split and the boom is adjusted so that the beam covers both. Counterbalancing permits easy movement of the microphone down to the floor and up above the heads of the performers. The boom is usually mounted on a large boom dolly which is movable, has a platform for the operator, and a device for raising the boom pivot position vertically from a height of 6½ feet to 9½ feet. A lighter-weight combined boom-and-tripod base, which is less flexible but which may be moved physically around and in and out of the set, is used in many smaller studios and for supplemental microphone pick-ups in larger studios.

The same types of microphones as in radio are available for off-camera musical accompaniment, announcing, and narration. When television was younger it was assumed that microphones must always be out of sight. With maturity and more critical attention to improvement of the audio portions, it became fashionable to show microphones in discussions or forums where a number of microphones were needed, on news programs and interviews, for MCs, and for occasional vocal selections. Smaller and less conspicuous microphones have found favor with producers. Some of those frequently selected are the RCA BK 1A and 6A pressure types, the RCA ribbon-pressure Starmaker, the Electro-Voice dynamics and the Altec condenser.

Concealed microphones placed in hollowed-out books, flower bouquets, false telephone bases, hidden behind stage properties or tucked away in costumes, may also be used. In addition to the small microphones noted above, tiny crystal microphones, such as the Turner, similar to those used in home tape recorders or public-address systems but with higher fidelity may be preferred for concealed pick-ups.

• CAMERAS •

All makes of studio cameras generally in use employ the image orthicon or "orth" tube which was described at the beginning of this chapter. This camera was developed and refined in the mid-40's. The earlier iconoscope or "ike" cameras which made possible an electronic system and fast scanning when invented by Dr. Zworykin in 1923 are only used now for some types of film cameras. The orth, operating with far less light, has much greater sensitivity than its predecessor. Its smaller size has encouraged the design of cameras which are far lighter, smaller, and less cumbersome, and permits the mounting of a rotating turret with different lenses on the front of the cameras. By simply revolving the turret and adjusting focus, the camera can bring any one of four different focal-length lenses into operation, permitting "big close-ups" to "long shots" from one location without moving the camera.

RCA, General Electric (GE), DuMont, and General Precision Labs (GPL), the four major camera systems, operate basically in the same general way. They all use the image orthicon tube, may be dollied on the air, have the lens turret with four possible lens positions, electronic viewfinders which permit the cameramen to see the exact picture being sent out, and focus by means of moving the orth away or toward the lens. The method of changing lenses on the GPL is by buttons and an electric motor. The other systems switch lenses manually. Focusing on the RCA and GE is by a crank on the side of the camera. DuMont uses a motorcycle-throttle-type focus handle and GPL has a knob on the side of the camera which focuses electrically.

The lenses most frequently employed for studio use are the 50 mm. (2 inch) the 75 mm. (3 inch), which is meeting with increasing favor, the 90 mm. (4 inch), 135 mm. (6 inch), and either an 8 or 8½ inch. Other specialized lenses used are the extreme wide angle 35 mm., the 10 inch, 13 inch and longer; and the Zoomar, Electra-Zoom, and Watson Vari-focal lenses can go from long shot to close-up very rapidly without losing focus. The position of the camera governs the choice of the lens for the desired pick-up. A "two-shot" of interviewer and guest may be secured by any of the lenses listed as those most frequently used. The camera position would vary 6 feet away from the scene for the 50 mm. to 29 feet away for the 8½ inch. The area of pick-up by different lenses when the camera is in a fixed position also varies markedly.

Additional factors affecting mobility and flexibility of cameras in the studio are (1) smooth floor, usually asphalt tile floor covering over carefully leveled concrete; (2) camera friction head which enables the operator to tilt the camera up and down and swing (pan) in a wide horizontal arc; and (3) camera support units with wheels, tripods, pedestals, and cranes.

The tripod is rather difficult to maneuver smoothly on the air, but it is inexpensive. Many stations have all or a portion of their cameras mounted on tripods. Camera height is fixed. The Houston-Fearless pedestal, called "the workhorse of the studio," was especially designed for television work. Like the tripod, it may be handled by only one person. The camera, however, can be easily steered in any direction while on the air through the synchronous alignment of all wheels. It may be raised and lowered between 37 to 60 inches above the floor by a hand crank (earlier model) or by pressure on the steering ring. Networks and larger stations also use crane dollies which were adapted from the movie prototypes. The one most frequently encountered is the Houston-Fearless Panoram which has a small camera boom or "tongue" extending out from a turntable on the base of the dolly and which may be swung in a complete circle. The cameraman may ride the boom or pull the tongue to the side and stand on the platform or studio floor. The services of a dolly pusher who wheels the unit in the desired direction are required. The crane range in height is from 23 to 74 inches. Other more elaborate cranes are made, with the largest one utilizing electric-driven motors to move the unit and large enough to permit the cameraman to be seated with a camera on a special platform extending out from the end of the crane. Two or three dolly assistants are needed to maneuver the "monster." Only the largest studios can accommodate this crane, but when ceiling height and floor space are ample it is very flexible, camera lens height ranging from 2 to 10 feet, and 360 degree rotation of the crane boom is possible.

Another type of television camera, the vidicon, although not used in normal studio operation, should be noted because of its wide use in industrial and military work and for closed-circuit laboratory instruction. A number of schools and colleges have turned to these smaller and less expensive versions of studio cameras for aid in teaching television techniques. A few stations have tried them for studio or "remotes" with varying reports on their applicability. Special electronic synchronizing equipment is required for such broadcast use. Special Vidicon film cameras however have been developed for air use and will be discussed in the section on film projection.

• CONTROL ROOM •

The control room is often referred to as the nerve center in television program production. The persons gathered here have responsibility for unification of the many separate elements into a smoothly blended program "whole."

The selection of the particular camera shots for actual airing is determined by the director of the program. He monitors each camera that is in use by looking at monitor screens, one of which is assigned to each camera. The director, therefore, is able to see what is to be telecast before the picture is sent out. Final "preview" adjustments in focusing and framing the picture, and changes in the shading and quality may be made, together with any re-checking of the lens for the proper shot and shifting of angle of pick-up. The major work, for such directorial duties, should have been accomplished during the camera rehearsal with only refinements remaining to be made during the actual telecast. This does not apply, of course, to situations when the director and technicians are ad libbing or "winging" the program, that is, doing a production without previous rehearsal, or in emergencies when one camera blanks out or develops "bugs" and has to be put out of commission, leaving one less camera available.

The director calls for the camera he wants by using such expressions as "take one," "super slide over three," or "dissolve to two." The technical director (TD) manipulates the controls at the video switching console to accomplish the desired effect. Bright tally lights placed on studio cameras

DESIGN OF A TV CONTROL ROOM

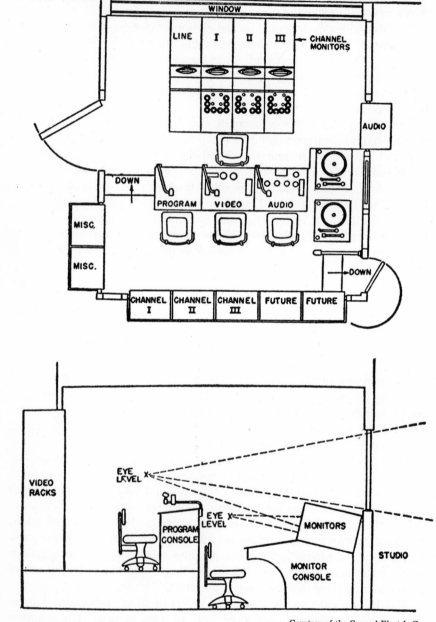

Courtesy of the General Electric Co.

Stations using this design often provide separate monitors mounted above window for the director.

and on control-camera monitors indicate which camera is "hot." A final check of the program is possible by reference to another screen, the line monitor, on which appears the picture actually being telecast. Occasionally an "off-the-air" monitor also is available for inspection. The process of camera-shot selection is similar to motion-picture editing in principle, but quite different in execution because of the continuality factor mentioned earlier.

The camera controls, with viewing picture tubes and oscillograph tubes which reproduce the picture in signal-wave form, are operated by the video engineer; and the audio controls, console, and turntables are handled by an audio engineer. An assistant or associate director (AD) may also be in the control room following the script closely, giving warnings of up-coming shots and pre-arranged switches. He relieves the director of the necessity of looking out for every detail in the script.

Constant communication is necessary between the control room and the technicians in the studio as well as with film projection, announcer's booth, and master control room during the telecast. Such commands by director or TD as "roll film," "stand by to dolly back when guest enters from right," "cue announcer," "flip card," "show him camera three," "boom in the shot" must be made to appropriate technicians. Special wired telephone (PL) circuits with clamp-on head sets and mouthpieces or walkie-talkie radios are used to reach the studio floor, and various types of public-address inter-communication or private telephone lines (PAX) are utilized for reaching film projection, announcer's booth, and master control. A talk-back speaker arrangement which is used in rehearsals for general studio directions has a cut-off switch to prevent use during the broadcast.

The control room is situated so that it looks into the studio. Size, location, and design differ from station to station with no definite and generally accepted pattern as yet. Some have placed the control room far above the studio floor. This trend seems to have lessened because many believe that the necessary traffic between control room and studio becomes rather exhausting under this arrangement. Many people favor the separation of audio from the rest of the personnel and equipment units. These people believe that by this design the engineer may maintain a more critical evaluation of the audio portion. Some stations which operate with small staffs eliminate the TD, permitting the director to do his own switching, and consolidate the video and audio engineering positions. The use of master control as a studio control room was described earlier as a system which allows for a minimum technical staff. Some stations have only audio, monitors, and switching facilities in the control room with the video controls in MCR. A two level-design with director, TD, and audio engineer on a raised level overlooking the video controls is perhaps the most common approach. However, if a separate bank of monitors for the director is not provided, he must be shifting position constantly and craning his neck to view the monitors. More space in the TV control room is required than for radio. It is obvious that far more primary operating personnel are required as well as a much greater amount of equipment. Additional program personnel such as script secretaries, lighting directors, costume and make-up supervisors, choreographer, graphics supervisor, together with writers, producers, agency representatives and observers are frequently present.

A brief discussion of basic shots and continuality editing techniques available to the director is appropriate at this time. It is in the control room that the series of visual images intended for the home viewer are selected, constantly changed and modified.

1. *Distance Between Viewer and Scene May Be Varied.* Three general types of camera shots may be classified in this category; "long shot," "medium shot," and "close-up." An over-all perspective of the setting for the viewer is supplied by the long shot. It is sometimes referred to as an orientation or establishing shot. It aids in indicating "the lay of the land," and the relationship of the various elements. It informs in general terms how many people are on the panel and whether we are in a Western frontier bar or a modern office in New York City. When the audience is comfortable, knowing where it is and who are involved, it is ready to draw closer and join the group. The long shot cannot give much detail, being restricted by the size of the screen on a home receiver. The close-up shots are used to single out details, focus the attention, clearly inform and heighten dramatic emphasis. A combination of a close-up and long shot is often seen. A vocalist, in close-up, might occupy a portion of the screen with a dance group in the background. A new character might enter the side of the frame close to the lens while the camera is on a long shot. The new character can dominate the scene because of his larger size in comparison to the rest of the group. Interesting composition effects may result from such combination arrangements. The medium shots ranging between the two extremes have many gradations. They are utilized heavily in following the action of the main characters and permit arrangements of people and things in good pictorial composition to enhance the mood. It has been estimated that in dramatic programs, medium shots are used about 70 per cent of the time.

Directors, in actual practice, use descriptive functional requests for desired camera pick-up areas such as a "three shot," which will frame as much of the setting needed to include the three performers on the set, "cover shot" to include all of the specific set or action, or "one shot" for a pick-up of a single person. When a shorter distance between viewer and character is wanted terms such as "waist shot," "bust shot," or "shoulder shot" indicate where the bottom edge of the picture frame is to be. "Head shot" or "close-up of hand on the dagger" are examples of pinpointed directions to bring segments of the scene into "big close-up."

2. *Position of Viewer May Be Modified by Camera Movement.* We are standing in an exhibit hall dedicated to American Business and Industry.

On the floor is sketched an outline of the United States with symbols indicating outstanding contributions by the various cities and states: an auto in Michigan, oil derricks in the South and Southwest, motion-picture studios in California, grapefruit in Florida, salmon and lumber in the Northwest, etc. Directly ahead lining the wall are tables containing working models of new machines. At the left are salon photographic prints of industrial scenes. On the ceiling is a huge mural depicting famous inventions. Our physical actions in walking directly forward to one of the models is, in terms of camera movement, a "dolly in"; if we stop and look down to the outline on the floor the head action corresponds to a "tilt down"; looking up to see the mural would be a "tilt up"; as we turn slowly keeping the same physical position looking at the working models and then the photographs it is a "pan left"; or if we walk along the tables of the working models looking at each in turn as we walk it is a "truck shot." The mobility of the television camera permitting a duplication of the freedom of movement by a spectator is one of the medium's unique characteristics. The director is able to guide the viewer's field of view for desired interpretation and emphasis. The sweep of movement also gives to the viewer an emphatic sense of "belonging," of being an active participant and intimately involved in the proceedings.

3. *Position of Viewer May Be Modified by Camera Angle.* The direction from which the viewer observes the scene may be changed by placement of cameras. The discussion of the various camera-support units described the extent of vertical movement by pedestals and cranes. Variations from the normal eye-level, horizontal plane to "low angle" and "high angle" shots may be called for by the director. The use of two or more cameras also permits the easy shifting of direction of view in a horizontal plane. Angle shots from left or right of the subject may be chosen for variety and psychological effect. When two cameras are shooting the scene at approximately 180 degrees, as is frequently done in dialogue scenes between two characters, it is referred to as "reverse-angle" or "over-the-shoulder" shots.

4. *Camera Switching Methods May Be Varied.* In addition to the almost infinite number of different camera shots available through various patterns of distance, movement, and angle, the selection of different transitional techniques or switching methods may also affect visual impressions, tempo, and mood. The "cut" is most frequently employed during dialogue within a scene in drama and for sports, interviews, news, and forums. The change from one camera to another is instantaneous. Care must be taken to keep the audience from becoming aware of the transition from picture to picture. An unusual difference in distance or angle between the shots, a mismatch in focus, or different light intensity may jar the viewer. Cutting in the middle of a sentence or vocal phrase calls attention to the shift.

The classic example of an unwanted, disorientation shock effect through poor cutting occurred during a network coverage of a horse race in the early days of television. One camera was located in the grandstand, the other on the track infield directly opposite. As the horses came down the homestretch, the director called for cutting from one camera to the other. The horses apparently reversed direction, running first one way then the other, with each cut. An amazing effect, but one which unfortunately was extremely distracting, A "dissolve," the fading of one picture out as the other fades in, is a common technique in variety and music programs during the performance of a vocal or dance selection, in commercial demonstrations, and in dramatic programs, to indicate a shift in locale or the lapse of time. Such dissolves may be extremely fast, approximating a cut, or take a number of seconds to execute. The latter type is sometimes called a "lap dissolve." The rhythm of the dissolve is easier, slower, and smoother than the cut. Sometimes a "matched dissolve," going from one object to similar object such as going from an alarm clock to a factory time-machine clock, is used to bind two scenes tightly together. The "fade out" and "fade in" are generally used to indicate a definite break in the progression of the program. It has been compared to the use of a curtain in the theater to end an act or to indicate a lapse in time. In variety programs this switching method is a standard transition between program segments and commercials.

5. *Special Electronic Effects Are Possible*. The director may have many effects at his disposal through specialized equipment in the control room. The "superimposure" is used most frequently. A "super" is achieved by making two cameras "hot" at the same time. One signal is superimposed over another. Many opening and closing titles and credits are supered over the setting or action. Commercial announcements use supers to emphasize the price or particular qualities of the product. Trick dramatic and novelty effects are feasible through utilization of this technique in dream sequences, appearances of ghosts and "magic people," transformation of a vocal trio into a sextet, close up of a tap dancer's feet simultaneously with his entire body, rain and fog, an apparent reduction in a person's size to only 2 or 3 inches in height when compared to other people or objects in the scene.

"Split screen" describes the effect achieved when separate camera images are not supered, but actually occupy adjacent portions of the same screen. An example of dramatic usage of the split screen is where two people in a telephone conversation may be shown. Dialogue between a newscaster or MC in one location and other people in another city is an example of non-dramatic usage. In picking up four correspondents from different parts of the country, for an election coverage, NBC used a four-way split screen. When one picture replaces the other in a horizontal, diagonal or vertical direction this action is called a "wipe." Corner or specially shaped "inserts" allow one picture to replace a portion of the screen.

· FILM AND SLIDE PROJECTION ·

The area where a majority of films, slides, and opaques start on their transmission path is referred to as the "telecine" or film-projection room. A discussion of the various equipment items which are found most generally in the telecine area follows:

16 mm. TV Film Projector. The 35 mm. width film has been standard for use in theaters for many years. Although the networks and a few stations have 35 mm. TV projectors, the television industry has established the 16 mm. width as its standard. Many large film-production companies shoot with 35 mm. and reduce the width to 16 mm. for prints distributed to stations. Lower cost of equipment, raw stock and processing, combined with the existence and availability of many documentary, educational, and industrial films in the 16mm. width were important factors in establishing the 16 mm. standard. The many local fire laws calling for the maintenance of special film vaults when 35 mm. film is used, based upon the inflammable nitrate base formerly used in 35 mm. stock, were also influential in settling upon the smaller size film which has always been the "safety" type. Specialized film-projection equipment has been designed to improve the picture and sound quality for 16 mm. television transmission. Film which is to be projected has been exposed at 24 frames per second. This simply means that the camera shooting the scene has a mechanism which causes the film to pause as it goes past the lens 24 times a second for a series of individual exposures. A shutter keeps the light from the film during the move to the next frame. When the strip of 24 still pictures or frames per second is presented at home or in the theater, it is projected a frame at a time via a "pull down" mechanism. However, it has been noted earlier that television transmission in this country operates at 30 frames per second. This rate is due to the need to synchronize with the standard 60-cycle AC electrical power supply. Normal film projection at 24 frames—television transmission 30 frames! The conversion of 24 frames into the TV 30-frame system is accomplished by the special TV film projector which scans each frame in multiples of 2 and 3 in sequence in order to arrive at the first common denominator of 24 and 30, 120. Thus the first film frame is scanned two times, the next frame three times, the next twice, etc.

TV Film Camera. The camera used most frequently by stations for black-and-white transmission employs the iconoscope tube. The film picture is focused directly on the face of the tube by the lens of the projection machine. No separate camera lenses are required. The operation of this tube is similar in principle to the image orthicon. The iconoscope was the forerunner of the image orthicon, being used for studio work in early days of television. It is cheaper and has longer life than the image orthicon. Its requirement for high light intensity which make it outmoded for studio work is not a handicap in a film camera. Its chief disadvantages are inadaptability for color television, tendency for transmission of unwanted flare at the edge of the picture and the required presence of a skilled shading technician at all times.

The regular studio camera with its image orthicon tube may be used also as a film camera. A special film projector is placed in the studio. The film is projected through a boxed enclosure (a shadow box) on a small translucent screen. The camera transmits this picture. Some stations favor this method and feel that it provides efficient use of expensive camera equipment.

The newer film camera systems which started to move from the laboratories to stations in 1955 are the "vidicon" camera and "flying-spot scanner." The vidicon tube camera is used in the same way as the earlier iconoscope in that the projected picture is focused on the face of the tube. This camera may transmit color film by using three vidicon tubes, one for each of the primary colors. This approach is similar in method to the three-image orthicon tube system used for direct studio pick-up of color telecasts. Other advantages attributed to it are small size, low cost of the vidicon tube, excellence of halftone reproduction, absence of flare and freedom from the necessity of constant shading by a technician. The flying-spot scanner is different from the projector-camera arrangement found in all of the systems described above. The camera tube pick-up of the picture approach is not used. The projector is a continuous-motion projector; the film is not stopped momentarily every time a frame is projected. Photo electric cells replace the camera pick-up tube. The flying-spot scanner is the most complicated in design of any system to date. Its proponents believe, however, that it will become standard equipment for film transmission because of its advantages, smoothness, coolness of operation, adaptability to color by using three photo-electric cells, stability of adjustment which reduces the necessity for constant attention, excellence of halftone reproduction, and lack of flare.

Slide Projector. Many slides are used in the day's operation. A varied assortment of models are available for purchase by stations from the inexpensive 2 x 2-inch projector as used in classrooms to elaborate automatic devices permitting remote operation, dissolves from slide to slide, and accommodations for 3¼ x 4-inch lantern slides as well.

Opaque Projector. This equipment is often referred to as the "telop." Small opaque cards containing lettering, art work, or credit "crawls" are projected on the air from the telop instead of using the live studio cameras. Stations also employ the telop to show the face of an actual clock in operation during time signal commercials, as well as to project polaroid news pictures, book illustrations, map sections, news ticker-tape, and small objects. Stations may construct homemade opaque projectors or order models specially designed for TV work. The use of mirrors permits horizontal placement of cards and objects in the telop.

· MASTER CONTROL, TRANSMITTER, AND ANTENNA ·

As in radio, the master control room is needed when more than one studio and announcing booth are used. MCR takes care of rerouting of the output from various studios and film-projection rooms, amplifies the signals, and makes additional checks on the quality of the pictures. It was noted earlier that occasionally the video controls, instead of being in the studio control room are located in MCR. The transmitter and antenna perform the same function as in radio: transmission of the video and audio signals into the ether. In an effort to obtain as much height as possible, thus increasing the coverage area, transmitting towers ranging from 300 to 400 feet upwards to 1,500 feet have been constructed to support the antenna. In some instances several stations may share the same location or tower, each with its separate transmitter and antenna. Equipment for receiving microwave signals from remote pick-ups may be located on the tower.

· COLOR TELEVISION ·

In 1953, compatible color television was authorized for commercial telecasting. Compatible color means that the color programs can be received in black-and-white on standard black-and-white television sets without special adapters or modifications.

RCA cameras used in color television productions have not one but three image orthicon tubes, one for each primary color: red, green, and blue. They are larger than standard cameras. The light from the original scene reaching the camera lens is separated into the three primary colors with the aid of reflective mirrors and color filters and directed to the corresponding color-sensitive, image orthicon tube. The action of scanning and amplification in each tube is similar to the process described earlier. The video signals from the tubes have separate electronic controls available on the corresponding camera monitor in the control room. Technicians adjust and regulate the separate signals before they are merged by the encoder (colorplexer) into a composite color signal for actual transmission over the air and reception on home receivers in black-and-white or in color.

Relatively very little extra equipment and adjustments are required for stations to convert MCR, transmitter, and antenna for color broadcasts of network programs. The cost of such conversion has been estimated at $20,000 to $25,000. By 1956, 253 stations across the country were able to carry network programs in color. In order to originate live local programs in color, stations will not need any changes in audio or revision in patterns of basic camera shots and continuality editing techniques. The studios will not need any additional space or remodeling, but adequate air-conditioning will be required to take care of the heat generated from extra lighting.

COMPATIBLE COLOR: TRANSMISSION

SCENE BEING TELEVISED

LEGEND
BLUE
GREEN
RED

REFLECTIVE LENS FILTERS CAMERA TUBES
LENS SYSTEM
DICHROIC MIRRORS
STANDARD LENS TURRET
REFLECTIVE MIRROR
COLOR TELEVISION CAMERA
HIGH DEFINITION PRIMARY COLOR SIGNALS
ENCODER FOR COLOR INFORMATION
ADDER FOR BRIGHTNESS INFORMATION
COLOR VIDEO SIGNALS
STANDARD TELEVISION TRANSMITTER
COLOR TELEVISION BROADCAST SIGNALS

COMPATIBLE COLOR: RECEPTION
Drawings from RCA

HIGH DEFINITION PRIMARY COLOR SIGNALS
BRIGHTNESS INFORMATION
TRI-COLOR KINESCOPE
PICTURE TUBE
DECODER FOR COLOR INFORMATION
COLOR VIDEO SIGNALS
SEPARATOR
COLOR TV RECEIVER

COLOR
BLACK AND WHITE
STANDARD TELEVISION RECEIVERS
COLOR TELEVISION BROADCAST SIGNALS
STANDARD BLACK & WHITE KINESCOPE

PICTURE TUBE

UNMODIFIED STANDARD BLACK & WHITE TV RECEIVER

Courtesy, Radio Corporation of America

Cameras and allied equipment are from two to four times as expensive as standard camera chains. This factor may restrict live local programming in color to the larger and more prosperous stations for a number of years. In 1956, WNBQ, the NBC station in Chicago, was equipped to transmit all its local programs in color.

Projects and Exercises

1. Visit a television station for a behind-the-scenes tour.
2. Clip and post on a bulletin board television-programming pictures from magazines and newspapers. Compare studio, microphones, camera types and placement, and control-room design.
3. Arrange for committees or class-viewing periods at television studios for reports to the class. Discuss and comment on camera shots, editing techniques employed, and use of slides, telop cards and film.

Elements of Television Production

AS A VISUAL MEDIUM, television calls on a whole range of theatrical services that, in many instances, are wholly foreign to radio. Program production in television can be a complex operation, as in a major network musical Spectacular, involving as many as 400 people for one show, or a relatively simple operation, as in a local station's interview program involving perhaps 8 or 10 people. Whether the program is large or small, however, certain basic functions are essential to television production. In this chapter we shall attempt to explain these functions in an introductory way so that the discussion of specific production problems covered in later chapters will be understood more clearly.

• "ABOVE-THE-LINE" ELEMENTS •

There has developed in television a convenient division of program production services into "above-the-line" and "below-the-line" elements. This division, suggestive of a bookkeeping arrangement, serves to distinguish production elements for budgetary and cost purposes and for matters of artistic control. Above-the-line elements in television production refer primarily to writing, performing, and producing talents. Included in above-the-line elements are usually the following:

Star performers
Supporting cast, including actors, singers, dancers, and specialty acts
Executive producer
Producer
Associate Producer
Production Assistant
Script Girl

Director
Writers
Script Editor
Choreographer
Choral director
Musicians
Conductor
Music composing, arranging, and copying
Script mimeographing
Announcer
Art Director (in special cases)
Set Designer (in special cases)
Costume Designer (in special cases)
Rehearsal halls and office space
Mail answering service

From this list it can be seen that the above-the-line elements include the main creative talents that make one television show different from another. With the exception of such persons as the choreographer, the art director, and the set and costume designers, the above-the-line elements in television are fundamentally similar to the creative elements required in radio program production. The major distinction between television and radio program production is found below-the-line.

• "BELOW-THE-LINE" ELEMENTS •

"Below-the-line" elements refer to the physical elements necessary to mount a television production and to get it on the air. In this area, the difference between television and radio is almost complete, with television adopting many of the practices used in other visual entertainment media, such as the legitimate theater and the motion picture.

Production Facilities. Production facilities refer to the following, among others:

1. STUDIO USAGE. A television show requires the use of a television studio not simply for air time, but for several hours, and in some instances for days, of "dry" rehearsal and camera rehearsal. Local television shows sometimes manage with only thirty minutes of rehearsal, but network variety and dramatic shows usually rehearse in the studio for at least a full day. This makes it possible to have one dry rehearsal without cameras, a session of camera blocking, a camera run-through of the show, and finally a full dress rehearsal. Television studios are usually rented on an hourly basis; a basic camera complement of three or four cameras is normally included in the studio rental.

2. SPECIAL TECHNICAL EQUIPMENT. Additional cameras, microphones, special camera cranes, mike booms, split screen and "flexitron" devices,

additional studio monitors, and unusual camera lenses, such as the "Electra-zoom," are included in this.

3. FILM STUDIO. If a show uses any film, slides, or similar visual projection materials, a film studio is required in addition to the live studio.

4. MOBILE UNITS. If a show calls for a remote live pick-up from outside the studio building, a mobile unit housed in a truck will be required. The mobile unit has two to four cameras, with its own camera crews and directors.

5. RADIO STUDIOS. Television dramatic shows using live music often require a separate radio studio to house the orchestra. The conductor watches the program on a monitor and over headphones hears the music, integrated with the voices of the actors.

Engineering Personnel. The number of engineers required in a television production varies with the type of show and the number of cameras used. Included in the engineering personnel are the technical director (TD), the lighting director engineer (LDE), the audio and video control men, the cameramen, microphone boom operators, boom pushers, camera dolly pushers, cable men, and utility engineers. When the show has a studio audience, a video PA (Public-Address) man is often required to operate the large television screen on which the audience sees the show.

Staging Services. Staging services include all the activities involved in designing and preparing the physical elements of a show, other than engineering elements, transporting them to the studio, setting them in place, and then, after the show, striking the sets, repacking the materials, and removing them from the studio. Among the main elements included in staging services are the following:

1. SET DESIGN. The services of a scenic designer are required to design the physical layout of the show, just as in the legitimate theater and in motion picture production. The scenic designer is a creative artist who works closely with the writer, director, and producer. He conceives the settings for the production and prepares floor plans and elevations to indicate how the sets should be installed. He also supervises all activities involved in preparing the sets and he orders the furniture, draperies, and set dressings required for the show.

2. CONSTRUCTION OF SCENERY. On the basis of the instructions received from the scenic designer, carpenters construct scenery. Whenever possible, scenery already in stock is adapted to the designer's orders. As in theatrical production, "flats" or "wings" are the basic elements of most sets. Flats are sectional framed units, covered with muslin or canvas duck, with a standard width of 5 feet, 9 inches. For dramatic, comedy, and musical shows, sets are usually quite elaborate and considerable special construction is involved.

3. PAINTING OF SCENERY. Scenic painting is used to suggest perspective and to simulate natural or man-made textures as part of a decorative or

definitive background.[1] The work of the scenic painter ranges from flat "lay-in," a priming coat of paint which dries without any special texture, to various devices such as stippling, glazing, and stencilling. For black-and-white television, painting is done on the basis of gray values, although the actual paint may be in shades of green or brown as well as gray.

4. DRAPERIES, DROPS, AND CYCLORAMAS. For staging purposes, scenic designers also make extensive use of draperies, drops, and cycloramas. Draperies may be used to decorate a set or, in the form of a painted drop, may serve as the background for a scene. "Scrims," drops made from gauze, are useful because, with properly adjusted lighting, they can be made transparent or opaque. Studio cycloramas are curved drops suspended from pipes or a curved track. They can be used to suggest the sky or simply as a neutral background, depending upon their color and the way they are lighted.

5. PROPERTIES AND SET DRESSINGS. Whether it is a simple kitchen set with decorative trivets on the wall or an elaborate imaginative setting for "Your Hit Parade," furniture and set dressings of some sort are required. Even a simple television discussion program requires a table and several chairs. Most properties and set dressings are rented from commercial warehouses or are taken from stock at the station or network. Hand props, such as special-type telephones, firearms, dummy packages or letters, and innumerable other small items required by the script are rented, purchased, borrowed, or constructed in the prop shop. Large network shows often have a unit property man to obtain the necessary props for each week's show.

6. TRUCKING. Sets, draperies, furniture, set dressings, and properties often represent considerable bulk volume that must be transported from warehouses and scenic construction shops to the studio and then returned for final disposition. Because of the heavy trucking expenses involved in these movements, stations and networks prefer whenever possible to have their construction shops in the same buildings that house their studios. At present it is common at network headquarters in New York, where it has not been possible to consolidate operations, to see trucks lined up outside studio buildings ready to unload the sets for the next day's show and to take back the sets from the current day's show.

7. STAGEHAND LABOR. Of key importance in any television show are the stagehands in the studio. Three groups of craftsmen comprise stagehand labor: carpenters, property men, and electricians. The carpenters and property men set up the show under the direction of the scenic designer; the electricians arrange the lighting for the show according to the instructions of the lighting direction engineer. While the show is on the air, the property men hand the props to performers off camera as instructed by the stage manager.

8. GRAPHIC ARTS. Graphic artists are employed to prepare special art

[1] See Robert J. Wade, *Staging TV Programs and Commercials* (New York, 1954), pp. 90-143, for an excellent discussion of television design and scenic painting.

work or lettering required for a show. On most shows this includes, at the minimum, the art work for the title of the show and for the closing credits. This may appear on special "flip" or art cards usually 11 x 14 inches in size, on small "telops" (or "balops") 4 x 5 inches, on 2 x 2-inch slides, on long vertical or horizontal "pan" cards, and on "crawls," long vertical sheets of black paper. The flip cards are placed on flip stands (easels with loose-leaf type binders at the top) and the art cards are placed on easels. In both instances two flip stands and two easels are usually used so that with two cameras it becomes possible to cut or fade directly from one card to the next. Telops are handled by opaque projectors ("balopticons") in a film studio. If a show has already arranged to obtain a film studio for another purpose, using telops instead of flip cards frees the studio cameras from having to cover the opening titles and the closing credits. With pan cards, the studio camera simply pans horizontally or vertically to reveal the credits. A crawl is fastened to a drum and is slowly revolved, either manually or electrically, in front of a studio camera. Stagehands operate the crawl and handle flip cards.

Graphic artists are also used to prepare special visual materials, such as identifying telops that can be used to establish a locale (e.g., a doctor's name plate set against a representation of brickwork sets the scene for a doctor's office), name plates that can be used to identify members of a panel, and special demonstration materials.

9. COSTUME DESIGN. Big network dramatic and variety shows usually require the services of an expert costume designer to design special gowns and period costumes for star performers. Most shows, however, cannot afford special costume design and manage instead with a fashion consultant who arranges to borrow gowns without charge from leading retail outlets in return for a credit on the show.

10. WARDROBE HANDLERS. To help performers in and out of costumes, especially where quick changes are involved, male and female wardrobe handlers are employed. The handlers also are responsible for packing and unpacking costumes used by the show. On nondramatic shows and on dramatic shows not requiring period costumes, actors wear their own clothing whenever the clothing is appropriate to the part; in those instances wardrobe handlers are unnecessary.

11. MAKE-UP DEVELOPMENT. Special make-up is occasionally required on dramatic shows, such as the make-up used on the various characters in Maurice Evans' production of "Alice in Wonderland." Where elaborate make-up creations are involved, this calls for the services of a make-up development artist.

12. MAKE-UP ARTISTS AND HAIR STYLISTS. More common than the preparation of special make-up is the application to performers of standard and character make-up. This is handled by make-up artists. Hair stylists are employed when unusual hairdos are involved.

13. ASSISTANT DIRECTORS AND STAGE MANAGERS. As mentioned in Chapter 17, during rehearsal the assistant director works closely with the director of a show, assumes responsibility for timing the show, lays out positions for actors on the rehearsal floor, and performs similar related duties. While the show is on the air, the assistant director sits next to the director, advises him of cues coming up, checks the timing of the show, and stands ready to take over direction of the show should the director be suddenly indisposed. The stage manager, on the studio floor, receives direct communications from the director over a special battery-operated short-wave radio receiver or over wired telephoned circuits (PL). The stage manager cues the performers and directs the stagehands.

14. SOUND EFFECTS. Television production requires sound effects in the same way that radio production does. As needed, a sound-effects man with a sound-effects truck works in an out-of-the-way spot in the studio, with a special on-the-air monitor to show him the action he must support with sound.

15. PROMPTING DEVICES. On most programs except dramatic shows, prompting devices are used. These may be no more than "cue cards," large white cardboard cards on which the script is printed in large letters. A more efficient device is the electrically operated "TelePrompter" system described earlier. TelePrompters are mounted on each camera and are remotely controlled by a special operator. The script, which appears in large type on TelePrompter, is advanced according to the rate at which the performer reads the lines.

16. SPECIAL EFFECTS AND DEVICES. Special effects refer to such matters as producing rain, snow, and fog, or simulating a burning fire in a fireplace. The NBC Special Effects Department publishes a whole catalog of special effects equipment devised for television. There are other devices, such as the "H-R Cellomatic" which produces effects of semianimation through the use of transparencies. Rear-projection (RP) is another device commonly used in television production. With slides or moving pictures projected on the rear of a latex or lucite screen, it becomes possible to establish a locale or to suggest motion without constructing expensive sets or actually moving on stage. Most scenes set in a moving automobile are actually shot in a stationary car with an RP screen, seen through the rear window, showing traffic in action. With appropriate sound and lighting effects, the impression conveyed to the audience is that of a moving automobile.

All of the below-the-line services described here do not, of course, figure in every television production. Simple television shows require a minimum of production elements; large musical shows require a vast number of services. At NBC the unit manager of a show orders the necessary production facilities and personnel and maintains budgetary control. Working closely with the show producer, the unit manager represents network management. Most of the below-the-line personnel are union craftsmen: the stagehands, make-up artists, and wardrobe handlers are members of the International Association of Theatrical and Stage Employees (IATSE); engineers are usually members of NABET, IBEW, or IATSE. A strict union shop applies to television production in New York, Hollywood, Chicago, and other important television centers.

Projects and Exercises

1. Observe closely a television panel-quiz program and a television musical variety program. Compare the production elements utilized in each, in terms of facilities and personnel.
2. Observe a succession of dramatic programs on television and note the variety in production devices used to establish locale. See if you can detect the use of an RP screen, a photomural, or a scrim.
3. Observe in a succession of television programs the various ways in which closing credits are handled. Which ways seem most effective?

Master control room, WHIO-TV, Dayton, contains not only master switching equipment but also all camera controls and film projection equipment. Studio 2 camera controls are at the left of the main console; studio 1 camera controls at right; film camera controls, preview and line monitors are in the center.

WHIO-TV Studio 2 is 50 feet wide by 63 feet deep. Control room is elevated.

Control room monitors indicate area of pick-up by different lenses from studio cameras each 17 feet from scene: 50 mm., 90 mm., and 8½ inch.

Control room operation for "Wide, Wide World," NBC-TV

Studio scene: "The Great Waltz," a color television "Spectacular" in the "Max Liebman Presents" series on NBC-TV.

Studio scene, network television drama. Eva Le Gallienne and John Kerr in Maurice Evans' production of "The Corn Is Green" on NBC-TV. Carpet pattern is painted on the studio floor to permit camera mobility.

Production scene: "Medic" series on NBC-TV, using one film camera

RCA color vidicon film camera and projectors with multiplexer

❋ 19 ❋

Talking on the Air

"LADIES AND GENTLEMEN, at this time station WDDT is pleased to present a *talk* by . . ."

Click! Off goes the set in the listener's home, the action coming almost like an automatic reflex. Stimulus—the word *talk*. Response—turn off set! "A radio talk is the surest way to get a high rating—*for the competition!*" is a generalization to which practically every station manager would subscribe. And yet, every day *talk* hits the air lanes, sometimes in the disguised cloak of an interview. Sometimes people *do* listen to talks . . . and learn . . . or are entertained . . . or stimulated . . . or convinced.

You are to talk on the air. You realize how easy it is to lose your listeners; you also know how powerful the broadcast word can be when it is effectively prepared and delivered. How, then, should you proceed?

• PREPARATION OF THE RADIO TALK •

1. *Purpose and Attitude.* This is a period of critical evaluation. What do you hope to accomplish by the talk? What is your purpose?

IS IT TO ENTERTAIN? Very few talks on the air have this as the main purpose. Many top entertainers aided and abetted by big name bands and popular vocalists, are available to the listener. It is hard to compete on their level. No $1,000-a-week budget for gag writers is at your disposal.

IS IT TO INFORM? Most broadcast talks have this purpose. The service programs, farm, and homemaking, bring many speakers before the microphone. Experts in government, science, and the arts are frequent studio visitors. The power of radio to bring to so many the words of so few, usually eliminates the "middle man" who digests the opinions of others and rephrases them. Instead, the ideas of the expert himself are broadcast directly to the home.

IS IT TO STIMULATE? Talks may be written for special "one-time" broadcasts, for limited series on patriotic themes, or to encourage a good turnout at the polls. Devotional and inspirational subjects also come within this purpose.

Is it to persuade? Are you after action? Regular commercial advertising with indirect appeals for action is recognized as having this purpose. The radio medium is utilized to solicit funds during community fund drives and appeals from national charitable organizations, in campaigns to increase the purchase of government bonds, and to get votes. Two-to-five-minute talks may be presented during regular programs, or speeches of ten or fifteen minutes may have their own time periods. Longer speeches are usually reserved for national political campaigns or important public addresses by public officials.

This is also the time for determining your attitude. "Get inside the house" is a guiding principle for door-to-door salesmen. The seller of brushes gives away one in order to be allowed to display the complete line inside the house. In radio you enter and are right in the living room as an invited guest. There was no need for "putting the foot" in the door while engaged in rapid high-pressure appeals for entrance. The listener can revoke this invitation, however, by a twist of the wrist. Accordingly, the attitude you must adopt as you start to write the speech, is that of a guest: be friendly and courteous; use a conversational style befitting such a guest; be easy and informal rather than stiff and pedantic. The language and organization should permit instantaneous comprehension and be interesting at all times. Remember, if at any time you become boring, long-winded, complex, confused, superior, stuffy, or insincere, you can be dismissed with a "click." This attitude must be kept in the foreground of consciousness when you prepare a script. You should write an informal one-sided conversation as a friend in the home.

2. *Use of Time-Tested Methods.* Effective communication by the spoken word is not a new development unique to radio. The fundamental principles of oral communication were set forth by Aristotle in his *Rhetoric* and have been amplified by numerous writers. Public speaking, whether from a platform or a radio studio, should adhere to the essential elements of clear organization of evidence and argument, the need for variety to gain and hold attention, and the use of vigorous and vivid language.

3. *Adaptation to the Medium.* Some of the time-tested methods take on new importance when it comes to the use of radio.

(*a*) Gain attention immediately. One adventure broadcast started with the provocative: "Have you ever met a dinosaur? Probably not. Most *certainly* not, as a matter of fact, because there haven't been any dinosaurs perambulating about the earth for millions of years." The opening of a radio speech is crucial. The decision to stay with you or dial elsewhere is often made in a few seconds. You may have only the time taken by a person in getting up from a chair and walking over to the set to capture his interest. Brigance suggests seven devices for gaining and holding attention:

(1) suspense, (2) activity, (3) conflict, (4) humor, (5) the familiar, (6) self-interest, (7) derived interest.[1] Put these devices to work in your speech.

(*b*) ROCOCO IN LANGUAGE SHOULD GO. Avoid ornate and literary words, and overworked clichés. Use and explain only necessary scientific and technical terms and stay away from professional or trade "jargon." Remember that the audience cannot refer to a dictionary. However, strange words and phrases may add spice if capitalized on and skilfully incorporated into the speech. *Caution:* Any chef realizes the value of spices, but he realizes, too, the dangers of "too much pepper."

(*c*) USE SIMPLICITY IN LANGUAGE STYLE. A radio audience is usually unable to follow a long and involved sentence. Short concise sentences that come to the point without qualifying clauses are desirable. Twenty-five words may be a good writing limit on sentences, longer sentences are effective when they are in a loose speech style. Simplicity is essential. Variation in sentence length gives change of pace. The use of contractions, active verbs, and questions are also advisable. The ease of understanding in a "blind" reception situation is the important factor. "Think like a wise man," wrote Aristotle, "but communicate in the language of the people."

(*d*) REPEAT! REPEAT! REPEAT! The radio speaker has no opportunity to clarify the points of his speech as does the platform speaker, who can see the fluctuations in attention in the audience before him. Consider for a moment a speaker who is delivering a speech in an auditorium: over at the left a man and woman come down to the fourth row, sit down and chat for five minutes with the people there, then depart, permitting the occupants of the fourth row to listen to the speech again; at the rear, a baby starts to cry; during the last five minutes of the speech twenty people slip into the rear left section arriving early to hear a violin recital scheduled to be held in the same auditorium at the conclusion of the speech. The speaker would be wholly inadequate if he did not recognize the disturbing effect of such activities on his audience and go over points that might otherwise be missed in the confusion.

Comparable distractions occur in the home, and the speaker must subordinate the unimportant to the important by reducing the number of main ideas he wants to get across. Frequent restatements and summaries for clarification assist in overcoming these home distractions. All of these considerations must enter into the prepared script.

(*e*) BUILD MENTAL PICTURES THROUGH WORDS AND STORIES. A liberal use of pictures has proved valuable in increasing the circulation of tabloid newspapers and picture magazines. Pictorial advertising increases effectiveness. New elementary and high school texts search for illustrative "gimmicks" to increase "comprehensibility" and pupil interest as contrasted to an earlier trust in the dogma: "Learnin' can't be fun!" The use of metaphors,

[1] W. N. Brigance, *Speech Composition* (New York, 1947), pp. 114-120.

illustrations, and anecdotes is standard practice in platform speaking. It is even more important in radio speaking. Build mental pictures through vivid and descriptive words which evoke specific images. Build pictures, human-interest stories, and specific incidents within the experience of the radio audience you will reach.

(*f*) TALK IT OUT. This point is often forgotten. A fluent platform speaker who is accustomed to speaking from an outline or notes writes out his speech for radio's exact time requirements and often uses a stiff and literary style. Talk as you compose, testing the talk by speaking it aloud as you write. Seek an informal and conversational style. Difficult word combinations, tongue twisters which may make you "fluff," should be avoided. What if you had to deliver this: "A statistical statistician is one who surveys statistics statistically." Talk the speech as you write it.

(*g*) "STICK TO YOUR OWN LAST." You are preparing the speech for yourself to deliver. Keep to a style befitting *your* background, *your* personality. If you attempt to change your speech style in an extreme fashion, "what you are" will break through and the audience will become suspicious of your sincerity. No one expects a school superintendent to speak like the manager of the local ball club, or someone from a rural area to pretend he's "above" that and use a style of speech that may be the norm elsewhere. Personality changes come about over a long period of time. If you consider a radio talk as an opportunity of "putting on airs" or "getting down to their level" you fool only yourself. The microphone is sensitive, the audience is close to you and can detect insincerity, lack of naturalness, pretense, "phony" diction, and "parrot-like" statements.

4. *Rehearse, Edit, and Time.* This is the step which puts final polish on your script and enables you to enter the studio with the confidence of knowing you have just the right amount of material for the allotted time. The actual "talk" time may be different than program time. If you have been asked to give a talk on a 6:15 to 6:30 broadcast it means that you probably have only thirteen-and-a-half minutes for your speech. The station break takes thirty seconds, the announcer's introduction another thirty seconds, and the closing announcement thirty seconds. If you are to speak for a certain period during a "round-up" or as a portion of a longer program, the allotted time of two, three, or five minutes probably means that you do have exactly that length of time. Be sure and check with the station before the broadcast to determine exactly how much time you have; don't wait until just before the program.

(*a*) HOW DO YOU TIME A TALK AT HOME? Timing seems to be a "bugaboo" with some professionals and most amateurs. Many directors for example, never get past the "stop-watch" stage and the accolade they treasure most is, "You got the show off on the nose." Timing should be one of the least of a speaker's worries. It actually is very easy and simple. Rehearse at home until you feel you have the right speed for you and your material.

Light frothy material may be read with considerable speed, but important key points and serious material require slower rates for comprehension. Actual rates range from about 115 to 180 words per minute, with 140 to 155 the average for most speakers. Professional radio speakers count by lines instead of by words. Fourteen to sixteen lines per minute is average for typewritten copy running across 8½ x 11 paper with one-inch side margins. Determine your rate by reading aloud a five-minute section of your speech. Use a clock with definite minute markings. Make adjustments in your rate if you seem too high or low in the number of lines you cover in a minute. Go over it at the adjusted pace until you feel comfortable at that speed for the type of material you are using. Don't force a lot of speed on yourself or slow way down. If you do, you will "revert to type" when on the air and ruin the timing. Avoid the tendency to go through the material at a "reading pace" instead of a "speaking pace." Make certain that you pause where you plan to pause, and give full value to emphatic words. Do this with the five-minute section until you have computed your line rate. Then count the lines in the entire script and mark minutes in the left hand margin. You know now how much you need to cut for time. Do not cheat. Don't fool yourself into thinking you can save a carefully polished phrase for which there is no time by reading it faster. Devote the rest of your rehearsal time to improving your delivery, and rechecking the manuscript to insure clarity at all points. Don't waste valuable rehearsal time by laboriously timing the entire speech. If you have access to a stop watch, you may use it but it is not essential.

You now have the exact number of lines of script. Look for several two- or three-line tentative cuts, somewhere about the middle, three-quarters through, and just before the final summary paragraph. Bracket them! This is the expendable material which can go if you slow up on the air. The next step is to mark program clock times on the script. Programs start with the minute hand straight up at the hour, quarter-hour and so on, station breaks come at 14:30, 29:30, 44:30, and 59:30. Let us schedule you for the 6:15-6:30 spot. You know that your program will start right at 6:15:00. The announcer will make his introduction and you will begin at 6:15:30. The first time-mark on your script should be 6:20. Why not 6:18 or 6:19? Because there is no need to start worrying about time too early in the broadcast. You are concerned with the primary job of gaining attention and holding on to the audience. To determine where you should be in the script by 6:20, multiply fourteen (your line rate as determined by rehearsal) by four and one-half (time between end of introduction, 6:15:30, and 6:20). This produces a total of sixty-three lines. Count sixty-three full lines, combining any half lines in your counting, and mark down in the margin to the right "6:20" or in a shortened form "20." This "20" marked in large figures, indicates where you should be by the studio clock.

The next time-mark on your script should be "25," five minutes or seventy lines later; then "27," two minutes later and two minutes before you should be through; "28" one minute to go; and "29," the end of the talk. While you are broadcasting, adjustments in pace may be made, by eliminating one or more of the tentative cuts you have marked and proceeding without interruption.

This is a departure from the usual advice to speakers which recommends marking times at the bottom of each page. The change is suggested as the result of studio experience. This method also permits the announcer or director to give you the professional signals of "two" and "one" minute to go. These signals mean the time remaining for you to complete your remarks.

(*b*) How do you mark your script for interpretation? This question assumes that you will use the rehearsal period and mark the script for interpretation so that you do not have to depend entirely on recall or "doing it by rote" during the broadcast. Each speaker has his own technique for marking scripts. Some underline words once, twice, or three times, according to stress; some use inflection arrows, pronunciation marks, or written directions such as "Hit it here" or "Slow." Parentheses may be used to indicate subordinate phrases. Pauses may be indicated by ". . ." or "/". "//" indicates longer pauses. Experiment with these different methods and use the system you find works best for you.

(*c*) What is the form of the script? The usual practice is to double or triple space the script with ample margins. Use large pica type if possible. Avoid paper that rustles and crackles. Yellow typing paper is quite soft and therefore excellent. The station may desire a copy for its files. This may be used by the announcer or director in following your speech, correcting any changes which may be made during the program by the speaker and to assist in timing. Some stations request copies ahead of time, for press releases or station policy checks.

· DURING THE BROADCAST ·

Now you are in the studio, with your prepared and rehearsed script. The director or announcer greets you and seats you at a table with plenty of knee room. A microphone may be mounted on a desk stand or suspended over the table. You place your script at the right or left side of the microphone if it is on a stand, or under and just behind it if it is suspended. You may then receive some general information about the silent signals required, together with some friendly counsel on what to do for the most effective performance. Following are some items of information a director might give in such a situation:

Studio Signals to Expect. There are a number of standardized signals or cues which are useful when on the air, for control room to studio communication, or for intrastudio work.

MEANING	CUE OR SIGNAL USED
1. Get ready—or stand by for signal to come.	One or two hands raised—palm toward studio.
2. Start your portion, go ahead *now*.	Index finger pointed at respective performer using whole arm motion; or, a head nod towards performer. This latter signal used frequently by announcer or engineer in simple productions.
3. You're speeding. Slow down. Stretch it out. (*Not abruptly but gradually.*)	Drawing hands apart as if pulling taffy or rubber band.
4. You're too slow. Pick it up. Increase rate. (*Gradually.*)	Circular motion of hand with index finger extended. Action goes to right similar to dialing a phone, except it's a larger circle.
5. More energy. More volume. (*Do it gradually.*)	Moving hands up, palms up. One or two hands.
6. Less energy. Less volume. (*Gradually.*)	Moving hands down, palms down. One or two hands.
7. Move closer to microphone. Get in *on-mike.*	Hold hands up, a few inches apart, palms toward each other. Move hands toward each other, repeating gesture—or—bring hand toward face, palm in.
8. Move farther from microphone. Get *off-mike.*	Push hand away from body or face, palm out.
9. Watch director for cue to come.	Tap forehead next to eye.
10. Time going as planned. Don't worry. Relax.	Touch nose.
11. Stop or cut. Using a natural ending such as close of sentence if not prearranged. Also means microphone is dead.	Slash throat with index finger or edge of hand.
12. Good going. Everything is all right. Thanks for what you did.	Circle with thumb and forefinger together, other fingers extended.

Let the Microphone Work for You, Not Against You.

1. DISTANCE AND POSITION: Work directly facing the microphone in a position referred to as "on the beam." Many professionals prefer to work relatively close to the microphone. Six to twelve inches away for velocity, combination type (cardioid or RCA 77 D) and condenser mikes; 4 to 8 inches away for pressure mikes. Working "close" tends to favor the lower frequencies and makes the voice more pleasing for "at-home" listening. It also adds "intimacy" and gives desirable "presence" to the voice.

Many engineers recommend working farther back from mike than the distances given above. It is true that under laboratory conditions, a more faithful reproduction of the entire frequency range is secured when working farther back from the microphone. Any room noise or reverberation is also increased that way. Psychologically, however, the radio audience seems to prefer less reverberation and less room noise, but more intimacy in straight voice transmission. There is no reason to rebel against this listener preference. It is true, however, that less attention needs to be paid to riding gain when the performer is farther from the microphone because of reduced danger of overloading the equipment. This fact gives rise to the customary admonition to newcomers in microphone work to stay back 12 to 18 inches. If you do work close, remember that such a microphone position requires closer supervision by the technician at the controls and more attention to style of delivery by you. When possible and practical, working close is recommended.

2. PROJECTION TECHNIQUE. As noted above, work sitting down. "Elbows on the table" is strongly recommended. There is a sound psychological reason why one should be seated for a studio talk. This helps to break platform habits of vocal projection. A person in a seated position shows a greater tendency toward a conversational style of delivery.

Visualize two of your friends on the other side of the microphone about 5 feet away, and talk to them, not to the microphone. In this way you permit past experience to assist you in adjusting your projection. Forget the microphone and talk to those two people in front of you. You won't blast the microphone because you don't shout at friends that distance away. Normal conversational type gestures may contribute to naturalness and vitality.

Adopt a "First-time" Approach in Interpretation. When you work from script, there is a great tendency to read and not talk it. Keep in mind the chief characteristics of a "first-time" approach. Remember that one is not glib in saying something the first time. There is the "thinking as you go" manner: the slight hesitations before certain words, to ascertain if that word will be the correct one; the repetition of some words; changing a word or phrase after it has been said and substituting another one in its place; using transition words, phrases and vocalized inflections; changes in rate, pitch, and volume during a sentence and presenting the thoughts in word groupings, not word-by-word. To illustrate this point briefly: Instead of a word-by-word style such as *"I-am-here-today."* Use groupings such as *"I'm* heretoday"; or, "I'm *here* today"; or "I'mhere *today."*

Mechanical Details. Count the pages of your script for a final check to see that they are in order. Read a portion aloud on mike. This enables the control operator to obtain a voice level or "balance" and enables the director to check your line rate to help you in timing. Be certain that you read at the rate and the volume you are going to use during the broadcast. Remove staples and paper clips from the script to avoid rattling as you finish each page and turn to the next one. Put the finished page over at the side of the table, sliding or turning it over silently. Don't weave around. Keep your head up and elbows on the table. Acknowledge cues given to you by studio personnel with a slight nod of the head. Don't touch the mike with script or hands. Make certain the mike is off before asking, "How did I do?"

Advice That Is Better Not Given in the Studio. In the above four sections we have summarized information and counsel a director might give in the studio. Nervousness or "mike fright" which should not be mentioned in the studio might well be discussed here. It is natural to have a certain amount of apprehension and tenseness as you get ready to speak. Almost every performer has a touch of it just before "hitting the air." The wise director or announcer does not mention mike fright. It does no good to repeat over and over, "Now don't be nervous." Ignore the subject; instead, chat about other things right up to broadcast time. Focus the speaker's attention on the desirability of "talking to a couple of people just the other side of the microphone," and "thinking of the meaning." Two unobtrusive directorial techniques useful in relieving tension if it persists are: (1) sitting across the microphone opposite the speaker and following the speech with interest, reacting to the material as a sympathetic listener, with appropriate smiles, head and eye gestures; and (2) standing at the side of the speaker and placing your hand gently on the shoulder. These are simple yet effective devices.

· PRODUCTION ASSISTS ·

Not always does the speaker himself have an opportunity to keep the listener from tuning elsewhere. Notice carefully the announcer's introduction presented at the beginning of this chapter, "Ladies and Gentlemen, at this time station WDDT is pleased to present a talk by . . ." The click may come before the audience knows the name of the speaker or his topic. Certain production aids are helpful in the program "format."

1. *Apply Music.* Play a program theme in keeping with the subject and speaker. A bright march or melodic concert orchestra may be useful for many talks of general nature. The use of the speaker's college song may be appropriate. Trite or "corny" themes should be avoided. A "Child Care" series does not need "Oh, What a Beautiful Baby" played by Guy Lombardo.

2. *Provocative Title.* After music is established, fade it down for the title and then bring it up again briefly. The title serves as a newspaper headline. It attracts attention.

3. *Start Abruptly with a Teaser.* The announcer or speaker can give a brief quotation from the speech itself, such as an interesting sentence which attracts attention quickly. The announcer follows the quotation with some such comment as "That represents the view of John Blank who is here. . . ."

4. *Topical References.* A speech by an economist might be prefaced by a capsule report of world or national news on business conditions with the general topic of the speech related to these events before any mention of the word "talk." This technique may be applied to other situations.

5. *Use Sound Effects.* The wail of a siren might aid in establishing a mood for a traffic-safety talk and provide a good beginning tie-in for introductory continuity. Sounds of airplanes, automobiles, and steamboats blending into each other might serve for a travel series. These only suggest the uses to which sound effects may be put to gain attention.

6. *Multiple Voice.* If the station has more than one announcer available at the time, use the second one in the introduction. Alternate the voices in a series of questions appropriate to the material to be covered in the talk. The use of the speaker himself as noted in point 3 is applicable here also.

The purpose of these devices is to persuade the listener not to dismiss the speaker before he gets an opportunity to start. After that it will be up to the speaker. A note of caution is necessary. Some subjects and certain speakers need no such implementations. Indeed, it would be distracting, cheap, and presumptuous. Rely upon good taste in applying the recommendations given above. Subtlety and discrimination are "musts." When used carefully they can be respectable, showmanlike, and helpful in keeping the audience from performing the semiautomatic click response.

· TELEVISION APPLICATIONS ·

Television stations program fewer straight talks than do radio stations. However, TV does schedule remotes from public events such as political conventions, dedication of buildings, presentation of awards, and other ceremonial proceedings. Political parties rely heavily on television during campaign periods. Special studio talks are arranged to supplement the remote telecasts of appearances of candidates at rallies and banquets. Sermons and religious addresses are presented on a regular or one-time basis. The lecture demonstration utilizing visual aids is a modification of the straight talk. Educational institutions and public-service organizations turn to this particular form of presentation for instructional or informational purposes. The advertiser also employs a modification of the television talk in many of the commercial announcements he has prepared in an attempt to motivate the consumer to purchase his product. This specialized area will be discussed at length in another chapter.

· PREPARATION OF THE TELEVISION TALK ·

Much of the discussion about preparing the radio talk applies to the preparation of a speech for television. One must consider the purpose of the talk, strive for a conversational style and utilize time tested methods of effective public speaking. Although speeches may need to be completely written out and presented word for word, it is recommended that whenever possible the television speaker should use an outline. This outline may be kept on a speaker's lectern or desk, held in the lap if seated, or be on large cue cards out of camera range. Intimacy approaching face-to-face contact is achieved when the outline method is adopted. The viewer prefers to have the television performer speak directly to him instead of watching the speaker continually cast his eyes downward to the manuscript. When President Eisenhower gave a TV report to the nation in April, 1954, he surprised the viewers and critics alike. As described by *Life:*

> Instead of entrenching himself behind his desk and reading uneasily, the President lounged against the desk, folded and unfolded his arms casually, smiled easily and often. He used a few simple, telling gestures and from time to time moved about. Speaking without a set speech but cued by notes printed on big cards, the President urged the country not to give in to unreasoning fears over the H-bomb. It was his most professional TV performance to date.[2]

The use of an outline not only gives greater directness and intimacy, but also makes television speaking easier for "nonprofessionals." Radio scripts demand a high degree of reading skill on the part of the performer. Most people, however, are more at ease "just talking" than reading a speech they have written, and therefore are more effective in informal television appearances. The pauses and hesitations which are natural in unrehearsed public appearances or conversation are not as disturbing in television as on radio. The viewer can see the speaker as he gropes for the exact word, as he repeats a phrase or pauses, just as he can when the speaker is physically present in the same room. *Caution:* Attention must be paid to personal mannerisms— raising the eyebrows at the ends of sentences, pressing lips together, fingering a coat lapel—which are passed over lightly when viewed from a distance in a public platform appearance but which are very noticeable in TV. The camera moves everyone up onto the platform immediately in front of the speaker. When a speaker is to make a telecast, a very good friend should preview the action for frank evaluation of "camera-close-up appearance." Visual aids should be considered carefully during the preparation stages. All too often speakers fail to capitalize upon the opportunities which TV affords for securing attention, maintenance of interest, amplification, and clarification through the adroit use of visual aids. Models, rough drawings on a blackboard (or sketch pad on an easel), photographs, slides, maps, cartoons, film clips, magnetic or flannel board for cutouts, animated pull charts and actual objects are some of the devices which may be utilized. Costs of obtaining or preparing the aids, their adaptability to the medium, and studio facilities for using them are important factors in selecting visual aids.

EXAMPLES OF TALK SEQUENCES ON TELEVISION PROGRAMS

(Please note the various script formats that appear throughout Part II of this book. Different stations, networks, agencies, and program packagers

[2] *Life,* April 19, 1954, p. 28.

use their own script formats. Each example reproduced in this book adheres to the format used by the station, network, agency, or program packager which produced the script.)

1. "March of Medicine" [3]

This script illustrates a simple straightforward talk which utilizes a visual design on the studio floor to aid in establishing the points to be made by the speaker regarding radioactive fall-out in the event of an H-bomb explosion. The sequence was presented during the "March of Medicine" broadcast March 29, 1955, over NBC-TV. The script was written by Lou Hazam. The narrator was Ben Grauer. The series was produced by Smith, Kline & French Medical Television Unit.

NARR:

MS NARR. ON STAGE.

So do our scientists in the laboratory
Seek to come to grips
With such radiation problems as would
immediately spring into existence
Should an H-Bomb explode
Here, for example, where I am standing--
Over Los Angeles!
Riding the prevailing wind
In such a direction as this,
We know, from what our government has
    told us,
That radioactive fall-out...
Deadly particles of the bomb,
And dust, debris and water swept up
    in the explosion.....
Might rain down a contaminating plague,
Decreasing in strength as it spreads--
In a cigar-shaped ellipse--
As far as 190 miles away
To (NAME OF CITY).
What special challenges
Does this forbidding aspect
Of the new monster weapon
Pose to our doctors.....
Our first line of medical defense--
Let us ask
A doctor who led the first official
    U.S. Government party
Into bomb-blasted Hiroshima and
    Nagasaki--
The Dean of the Medical School
Of the University of California
    at Los Angeles,
Dr. Stafford Warren...

(1:10)

SWITCH TO CAMERA
ABOVE NARR. REVEALING
FLOOR DESIGN AND HIS
POSITION AT L.A.
THEN SWITCH TO NEW
CAMERA POSITION,
PICKING UP NARR. AS
HE STARTS WALKING
OVER FLOOR DESIGN
TOWARD CAMERA TO 2ND
CITY AT END OF DESIGN

NARR. STOPS AT 2ND
CITY, FACING CAMERA..
DOCTORS IN BG OR TO
ONE SIDE.

PAN TO DR. WARREN
WHO HAS BEEN STANDING
CLOSE BY OR STEPPED
IN. NARR. REMAINS
OUT OF PICTURE.

[3] Courtesy of Smith, Kline & French Laboratories.

DR. WARREN:

Thank you sir.

It is easy to take fright and despair upon the apparently never-ending succession of dramatic announcements about the H-bomb.

To begin, it is good for all of us to remember that however big the blast, there is always an edge where people stop dying and start living. It isn't one edge but many. And at each such point, the doctor--with undiminished equipment and to his fullest power--can go to work to preserve the injured.

WALKS TO EDGE OF DESIGN, AND ABOUT IT.

Now as to the situation within this area of the fall-out. Do not believe that this entire area will be a no-man's land. Although life will not proceed as usual, it will not cease. Medicine will be operating within this area... operating under a new set of ground rules, true, but it will carry on.

MOVES INTO FALL-OUT AREA....

In here, doctors will have to adjust to working in an atmosphere of radiological hazard, and need to take unusual precautions. Radiological monitors may be assigned to each hospital, and staffs trained in the techniques involved in preventing the spread of contamination. For example, there must be prompt removal of contaminated clothing from patients coming in for treatment.

WALKING OUT OF FALL-OUT AREA TOWARD CAMERA. STOPS DIRECTLY BEFORE CAMERA.

Let us have confidence in this: Through special training which many doctors have received...through the use of medical stockpiles which have been, or are, being moved to even more distant outlying areas...with the help of mobile hospitals, land and airborne... You can be sure that the major part of our medical profession is as well prepared--perhaps even better--as a good many of our civil services, to come to the aid of our fellow man.

(2:15)

DOWN TO BLACK.

2. "Tomorrow" [4]

This Johns Hopkins University series, presented over the ABC television network from WAAM, Baltimore, deals with different careers open to young people. Notice the use of film, close-ups of people working with real objects, photographs, advertisements, a plane model, and cartoons to aid the speaker.

[4] Courtesy of Johns Hopkins University.

VIDEO	AUDIO

7:00:00 P.M.--------------MUSIC UP

ROLL STANDARD FILM OPENING------NO NARRATION....Music builds up
to crescendo
As kids reach top of hill

TITLE POPS ON-------------MUSIC UNDER
(Cue narrator)

TITLE STILL ON.........NARRATOR: TOMORROW is presented by the
Johns Hopkins University and WAAM in
Baltimore in cooperation with the ABC
Television Network.

HOLD

CAMPUS SCENE....   NARRATOR: TOMORROW is dedicated to you
Long shot of Gilman   the youth of America...and to the parents
Hall, men across   and teachers anxious to help you select
scene   a career full of worthwhile contributions
and personal satisfactions.

STUDENTS UP STEPS   You who will be the leaders of tomorrow
are now studying on the campuses of
schools and universities like this one
at Johns Hopkins University.

STUDENTS WALK IN   Your future is our security. At this
DOOR   moment you may be wondering what tomorrow has in store for you. You may be
trying to decide what career you should
select.

STUDENTS IN LIBRARY   As you study and work we hope to show
you the highlights of many interesting
careers .... we hope this parade of
career possibilities will help you select
your life's work.
This week we look at the work of

TITLE   "THE HUMAN ENGINEER" .... with
LYNN POOLE -
and his guests for this week -
Dr. Alphonse Chapanis
Dr. Jack Dunlap

7:01:30   PROLOGUE--1 min--30 seconds

CU on hands working   NARRATOR: Nine years ago the psychol-
knobs and buttons   ogists and engineers at Johns Hopkins
University, and other schools throughout
the country, were cutting out knobs and
buttons of different shapes and sizes.

Dolly back to see   These scientists were blindfolding
person blindfolded   people, then asking them to recognize
feeling the knobs   the sizes and shapes of these knobs.
The research people wanted to know which
shapes were most easily recognized.
Which sizes were most easily and quickly
recognized and operated? The studies

were both psychological and mechanical.
This was human engineering.

CU on dashboard of
automobile

Why was this being done? For many
reasons. One of them was this. This is
the dashboard of an automobile. Look at
the knobs which are all the same size and
shape. Is this good? Answer yourself.
How many times have you fumbled in the
dark ... reached for the headlight button
... pulled ... and heard the irritating
swish and spatter of the windshield
wiper? Why not have knobs of different
shapes and sizes so you recognize them
by touch. Of course, your dashboard
construction may be of minor importance.

CU PIC OF
Airplane cockpit

FILM CLIP
airplane flying

But, look at this. This maze, this mass
of knobs and buttons are to be found in
the cockpit of any airplane. Pulling
the right button, turning the right knob
here may mean life or death to fifty-
or-more people!
This is not of minor importance. This
too is a part of human engineering ...
a new profession bursting with
20th-century possibilities for you as an
important, exciting and challenging
career.

Fade to model
of plane in Poole's
hand.

7:03:00
Dolly back from model
plane to Poole

POOLE: Greetings. My name is Lynn
Poole, member of the staff of JHU. For
the past ten years I have had the pleasure of knowing personally and watching
the work of a number of people involved
in human engineering. For ten years
I've been fascinated with their work and
have watched research and experimentation
grow and develop.
A moment ago you saw the dashboard of an
automobile. You saw and heard why it
would be better to have the buttons on
the dashboard be different sizes and
different shapes. This is a problem in
human engineering which affects you and
me .... but the profession of human
engineering may be one of which you have
never heard.
BUT .... right now business and industry
is desperately seeking trained human
engineers.

CU
ADVERTISEMENT

Dolly in to ECU

Look at this advertisement for example
.... here this company is advertising for
many different types of professional
people ... and one of those they seek is

a human engineer. This man is sought
after .... is paid very well .... has
great influence on the economics of the
United States .... has vital effect on
our daily lives.
Who is he? What does he do? How does
he become a human engineer? Our first
guest is a human engineer. A trained
psychologist. He is skilled in mechanics and engineering. He is well
versed in mathematics and anthropology.
All these things and more he must know
to be a human engineer. As a research
director and a professor at Johns Hopkins he is one of the leaders in this
new profession of human engineering ..
and well qualified to tell us exactly what
human engineering is. Our first guest
of the evening is Dr. Alphonse Chapanis.

CHAPANIS BEGINS	six and one-half minute segment--answering
7:04:30	question: What is Human Engineering?
LIVE	CHAPANIS: Mr. Poole, let me begin by saying that the term human engineering sounds as though we spend our time en-gineering humans. Actually, we mean exactly the opposite of this. Human en-gineering means designing and building machines so that instruments can be used more effectively and jobs done most effi-ciently by human operators.
PIC #1 CARTOON	Using our sense of the ridiculous and fantasy, let's approach this definition negatively. Here in the lower central portion you see a human being bending over to twist a giant wheel, while at the same time pulling down an upper-level lever. Here a man turns a cog-wheel and pulls a lever. In the middle, here, you see another human being reaching way back to spin a disk while trying to operate controls on a huge machine. This is all very much like rubbing your tummy with one hand and patting your head with the other.
LIVE	Try it! (Pause and do it) This is a ridiculous drawing. But, let me show you a machine which was designed for actual use, a machine as ridiculous as the drawing.
PIC #2 MAN AT DIAL MACHINE	Here you see a short man, who has to operate controls while he looks way up over his head to read the dials which tell him how his controls are working.

This is a magnificent piece of equipment,
engineering-wise--but, the designer
didn't give enough thought to the human
being who has to operate the machine.

LIVE

This suggests that we need somebody
special to design machines so that they
can be operated by human beings with
efficiency, accuracy, safety, and ease.
Human engineers design apparatus which
take advantage of man's great capacities
--AND his well-known limitations.

LIVE

Another part of the human engineer's job
is to study the physiological and psychological reactions and capabilities of
the human being.

For example ... how much can a man take
before he breaks down?

PIC #5
Man at machine

Here you see a man working at top speed
at a machine that is so badly designed
that it will soon give him a near-nervous
breakdown. The psychologist adds to
human engineering knowledge in this area.

LIVE

There is another human factor involved
in many mechanical operations; factors
which demand a knowledge of psychology.
That is the factor of man's ability to
see, to hear, to assimilate what he sees
and hears--THEN, transmit this information to someone else, as part of a team
of men and machines.

PIC #6
CARTOON

Here is an illustration of this problem.
In the upper right hand corner is an
enemy airplane. Here you see it has been
picked up by radar. The radar-scope
information is read by a human being,
passed on to other human beings who plot
the course and location of the enemy
plane. A human being then radios or
phones this information through a mechanical system to a direction chief. This
human being receives this information
through his earphones ... and with his
vocal cords he then radios the information to interception planes which are
now in the air.

LIVE

Human engineering is mechanical and it is
psychological at the same time. Human
engineering is becoming more and more
important in industry ... in the home ...
and, in fact in almost every part of our
complex every day life--and our lives are
complex!

PIC #3
Old fashioned kitchen

Take this kitchen for example. It is
like one your grandmothers used. It

had a simple wood stove, irons, some
kettles, pots and maybe a pump.

M-S on studio
kitchen, gal busy
in it.

But today's kitchen is literally crammed
with automatic machinery of all sorts.
When you stop to think of it you sometimes feel you need a professor of engineering to operate all the many gadgets.

PIC #4
Man at simple plow

Take a look at the farm. A hundred years
ago the farmer was primarily concerned
with the management of a team of horses
and a few simple instruments--a plow, a
harrow and a wagon.

FILM
Complex harvester,
    etc., etc.

But today's farmer operates a great
variety of machines, each of which is
enormously complex. He has a tractor
to pull these machines. He may even own
an airplane in which he flies from one
part of a farm or ranch to the other.

LIVE

In the face of this increasing mechani-
zation of home, farm and factory, it be-
hooves us to pay attention to the problem
of designing these machines so that we
can use them most efficiently, safely
and with a minimum of training.

LIVE

FILM....
Airplane flying

This is all a part of human engineering
... but, it is only a part. The trouble
with our modern machinery is that it is
becoming so dog-gone complicated. In a
matter of seconds the modern airplane
can whisk a man up to altitudes where the
air is so thin that a match won't even
burn. The pilot and co-pilot of this
airplane are responsible for the lives of
nearly 70 people.
What a terrific responsibility! Let's
look inside an airplane.

FADE OUT TO
PIC #7 Cockpit

Compare this cockpit with the dashboard
of the automobile which Mr. Poole showed
you a few minutes ago. This cockpit is
frightening in its complexity. Think of
what the pilot and his co-pilot must
know, imagine the precision with which
they must operate these knobs, buttons
and switches--think of the dials they
must read instantaneously!!

FILM....
Airplane flying

While you fly in safety and comfort ...
your life depends on the pilot and his
crew, who take you from continent to continent or around the world. Percentage-
wise the airplane is a safe mode of
travel.

FADE out to
PIC #8, crash

But sometimes there are accidents ....
and we know from actual studies that the
largest single cause of aircraft acci-

DIS to PIC #7
again

LIVE

7:11:00

dents is human error ... NOT mechanical
failure .... and when we see the maze of
instruments we can understand why. This
is one job for human engineering---to
make this complex machinery operate
efficiently and safely.

In brief, this is the answer to the question: what is human engineering? It is
the combination of the science of man
and engineering---two fields which co-
ordinate to design machines which work
faster, better, more efficiently, more
safely, with less strain on the operator.
The human engineer is a new specialist
on a design team--a specialist whose
business is people.

• DURING THE BROADCAST •

Studio Signals. Most of the signals are the same as those used in radio.
The floor (or stage) manager relays them to you. He will try to be in position to permit you to see the signals without turning your head. If you are
on camera, do not acknowledge the signal by a head nod as is customary in
radio. You may request the director to have the floor manager give you the
time signals you desire such as "three minutes to go," "two minutes," etc.
The signal for coming to a close (approximately fifteen seconds) varies
from studio to studio. A clenched fist waved back and forth is frequently
employed. Other "wrap-up" signals are revolving of both arms in front of
the body similar to the action in the old "pattycake" nursery rhyme and the
circular motion of one arm similar to the speed-up signal in radio. Due to
possible confusion by the performer, this latter signal has been discarded by
a number of stations. The use of cards with the time signals and rate directions printed in large letters is almost standard practice whenever studio
conditions permit. Cards with such signals usually are easier to comprehend
and help prevent possible errors brought about by the performer missing the
hand signals. You probably will be expected to look at the camera which is
on the air. In this way the viewer at home receives the impression that you
are speaking directly to him. The red tally lights on each camera tell you which
camera is "hot." In case you do not see the tally lights the floor manager may
point to the camera which is hot. Movement of the head and eyes in changing position in order to talk to the proper camera should not be jerky and
abrupt. The movement should be natural and smooth. A glance down to the
floor or to an object you may be holding may be used as a transition device.
In order to achieve a naturalness of style, some directors may prefer that
you not look directly at the camera or recommend that you do not follow
the hot cameras. This may be settled during the rehearsal.

Microphone Techniques. The microphones will be brought to you. If a
boom microphone is used it will be above you and forward. Use slightly

more projection than in radio. If you are walking around the studio, remember that the boom operator must follow you. Don't suddenly rise, sit down or turn your head to the back of the set expecting that the microphone will be in position to pick up your words. A sudden decrease or increase in volume may result in loss of comprehension by the viewer through inaudibility or distortion. When you have a stationary microphone placed before you, try and stay "on beam." You may have to "cheat" in position as you turn to refer to a visual aid in order to keep a satisfactory audio level.

Appearance. The improvement in lighting has done away with the necessity for heavy make-up used several years ago. Men should shave closely before appearances. Some powder is usually applied on the face and on the high forehead when the guest has bald areas. Some types of complexion may require a pancake base applied before the powder. Because of certain image orthicon-tube characteristics, women should avoid cheek rouge. A pancake base with lighter or darker shades according to individual skin pigmentation, lip rouge, and brown pencil for eyebrows are customarily all that is needed. Clothing should be appropriate to the occasion but caution should be exercised in the choice of colors. It is wise to avoid pure black or white on women's dresses. Such use may result in undesirable video effects. Grey or light blue shirts are preferred for men but if a man must wear a white shirt, it should not be starched. The softer oxford material is preferred. Extremely "busy" patterns may be distracting. Jewelry that reflects much light may "bloom" and cause difficulty in effective transmission. Men should avoid highly figured ties and bold chalk stripe or checked suit patterns. Loose-fitting suits make men look heavier on the TV screen than they really are. Women may find that a short jacket or full skirt may not be too becoming as a result of slight horizontal distortion characteristics of the 35 and 50 mm. lenses. Simple and classic styles are generally preferred.

Movement. The speaker may have occasion to handle properties, refer to maps and other graphics and draw or write while on camera. It is highly important to remember the exact movement patterns worked out in rehearsal. Otherwise the close-up of an object, the location on a map, or a picture may be missed. Time must be allowed for the camera man to change to the correct lens and to focus. Rapid movement of hands or properties when close-ups are being used may result in missed shots and confusion as the cameraman tries to follow the action. Allow time for the viewer to see the object or area being described. Most studios have monitor screens referred to as "jeep monitors" available on the studio floor for viewing by the speaker. With a little experience the speaker may become proficient in checking this jeep to see if the viewer at home is seeing what he is describing. If not, he may then make corrections in his description or action to reorient the viewer.

Projects and Exercises

1. Tune in stations in your area and report on radio and television talks broadcast over local stations and networks. Evaluate relative effectiveness, based upon some of the recommendations presented in this chapter.
2. Record your own voice for play-back. Analyze and evaluate the voice and delivery in general terms.
3. Present an informal talk about yourself while on camera. Practice shifting gaze from camera to camera as each camera is hot. Observe yourself in the monitor. Assign class members to report on specific mannerisms which might distract.
4. Determine your line rate for various types of material. Compare your at-home timing with stop-watch timing in the studio.
5. Prepare and present talks for class listening and criticism. Consider the factors noted in the chapter for before-broadcast activities. The instructor may assign special projects. The following activities may also be used:
   - (a) Prepare a two-minute talk for use by you on an early morning disc-jockey program. Subject: Community-wide used clothing drive to be conducted by the schools.
   - (b) Same subject—same length—for use by you on a woman's program over the local television station.
   - (c) Same subject—same length—for use by the local radio sportscaster during the half-time break in his play-by-play account of a game.
   - (d) Prepare a three-minute talk for a series entitled "Men of Action" dealing with leading figures in contemporary business life in your own state. What alternate title can you think up for the series?
   - (e) Prepare a similar series entitled "A Woman's Hand" dealing with famous women in history who influenced the course of governments or social living by their actions—directly or indirectly. What alternate title can you think up for the series?
6. Prepare an outline script and present a two-minute television lecture-demonstration. Utilize several visual aids in your presentation. Sample topics:
   - (a) Interesting facts about a specific hobby.
   - (b) How the fine points of a specific sport may be understood better.
   - (c) Traffic safety.
   - (d) Elementary science experiments.
   - (e) The geography of a nation in the news.
   - (f) Weather forecast.
7. Divide up in pairs. Assign one student as director. Practice any of the talks with the director making suggestions for improvement and then handling the actual presentation.
8. Practice variations in delivery in accordance with signals from the control room or floor manager. Speed up, use more force, move around, etc., as signaled without fluffing or disturbing the effectiveness of the delivery.
9. Prepare "hold-that-audience" formats for different program series. Refer to the Production Assists section in this chapter. Think up appropriate titles and prepare only the opening section leading into the talk.
10. Plan a one-camera pick-up for any of the television talks. What changes are needed in movement and location of the visual aids?

20

The Announcer

THE ANNOUNCER of a station plays many parts. To many people he is the station's spokesman. Behind the scenes at the studio he has other duties and responsibilities. He is, of course, a performer, doing straight announcing, presenting commercials and demonstrating products, newscasting, acting as MC or as straight man to a comic, handling sports, interviews, discussions, quizzes and narration. In addition, in evening hours he may be studio manager; he is frequently a writer, preparing his own material except for commercials; and he may put to effective use supplemental skills such as cartooning or puppet manipulation. The announcer in radio stations is often the person in charge of program production and, in conjunction with announcing assignments, often he is a technician, handling the controls, placing microphones, joining and breaking away from the network, and playing records and transcriptions. The announcer in small local television stations may also assist the director by serving as floor manager, operating a camera, or handling the boom microphone when he is not actively performing on the air. In this chapter, however, we shall concentrate primarily on the announcer as a performer. In this area there is much in common between the work of the announcer in radio and the announcer in television.

The station announcer may join the staff through a "front or side entrance." The procedure at most stations is to audition prospective announcers with varied copy of music continuity, commercial announcements, news, descriptive material, and extemporaneous or ad-lib assignments. Versatility, salesmanship, ability to respond quickly, and basic vocal equipment are judged in this way. Aptitude for on-camera effectiveness may be evaluated in the initial interview or by observation during the microphone audition. Try-outs before the cameras are usually reserved for those applicants who have satisfied all other requirements.

A "side entrance" may be used when a member of a station staff regularly employed as a salesman, engineer, clerk, elevator boy, or writer, to mention but a few, becomes interested in performance and demonstrates that he has an aptitude for announcing. For example, Dave Garroway began his broadcast career as an NBC page. An occasional brief appearance on commercials, woman's hour, or variety program may lead to regular assignments. Persons who are originally hired for positions which involve techniques akin to announcing, such as acting or singing, may also enter announcing through a side entrance. These people may decide to change their professional capacity because of new interests or recognition by program officials of their particular talents. It is true that women have found more opportunities in television than in radio but their appearances as announcers are usually restricted to program MC roles or specialized commercial presentations. Women generally do not serve as station staff announcers.

• AN ANNOUNCER'S KIT OF WORKING TOOLS •

Voice. The basic equipment needed by an announcer is a good voice. A clear resonant and relaxed speaking voice is desirable. A low pitch range, which automatically excluded many candidates from consideration as announcers, is no longer the chief consideration. The intimacy of the broadcasting medium does favor relatively low, rather than high, pitches in the over-all range of an announcer's voice, but clarity and resonance are more important than pitch alone. Unpleasant qualities such as hollowness, harshness, or marked nasality limit opportunities for announcing work. Training and exercise may enable one to increase vocal range and gradually lower average pitch. If extensive work is required for these changes, it should be supervised by a competent voice teacher.

Attitude. The keynote of an announcer's personal attitude should be confidence. He must be poised and confident on the air. Audiences quickly detect nervousness or uncertainty. When attention is focused on the way one speaks instead of on what one is saying, effective communication ceases. Leadership in the announcer-listener relationship must be assumed by the announcer. He must be a dominant, not a retiring, personality. Everything about his delivery must give the listener or viewer the feeling that the announcer is confident of the product's ability to live up to the claims for it, and of the talent's ability to be as good as the announcer claims. Broadcasting has no place for the timid, "Why am *I* here today?" announcing approach. What the announcer does and says from "The following was transcribed earlier for broadcast at this time." To "Shop at Blanks and Save!" must be spoken with assurance and dominance. *A note of caution:* When this confident and self-assured manner becomes exaggerated and merges into a bullying, shouting, and superior style, with an undercurrent thread of "See how good I am" running through it, then one has become afflicted with "announceritis," a swelled head. Controlled confidence is the desired goal.

Style. This may be referred to as the announcer's "air personality." One announcer may have sincere warmth and vitality and seem like an interested friend; another may capitalize on a homey approach, talking as one neighbor to another over the back fence; another may rely on a quiet authoritative assurance, apparently unruffled by anything or anybody; another has worked out a bouncy, breezy manner. Other approaches are those of the soft, professional sympathizer; the circus barker or pitchman; the staccato, human machine gun; and the naive "It's-simply-wonderful" style. This list could be extended and modified, but it illustrates the impressions listeners receive. Each announcer has to determine for himself the particular style best suited to him. An added responsibility of a station-staff announcer is to develop a multiplicity of styles or approaches according to the various programs he handles. It is in flexibility and adaptability that many young announcers fail. To be familiar and jocular on a popular music show, then serious and sincere on a hymn period, then informal and kidding in an audience-participation period, and then dignified and authoritative on a classical music program requires skill and concentration. Conversely, the demand for general adaptability, a program "chameleon," may be dangerous to an announcer concerned with a long-term professional outlook. The better-paid network and free-lance positions call for specialists with distinctive "air" personalities. If individuality, or show-business "color," is lacking, audiences may accept the message without remembering the person. *Again a note of caution:* The style should not become so important that communication suffers.

Understanding. It is possible for an announcer to present his material without actually understanding its meaning. If he does deliver his script as a mechanical mouthpiece, however, he may get by only in less critical situations. An announcer should strive to understand the significance of the material he is reading. He should not become absorbed with the mechanics of the vocal process, listening to his own voice and speaking with a pride in how he is saying it, but should "think the thought" instead.

Pronunciation. Many are the discussions on "correct" pronunciation among network personalities and in stations throughout the country. So much attention is given the subject because these people know they are considered authorities by listeners. Broadcasting is effective, along with the movies, in furthering a trend toward standardization of American pronunciation. Even station personnel in regional areas tend to follow the lead of their contemporaries on the networks, and to eliminate their regional speech habits. The type of pronunciation labeled "General American" appears to be the standard radio and television speech, with individual differences according to the regional background of announcers. It is an accepted custom among many announcers to check the latest complete dictionary recommendations, keeping in mind that the dictionaries record the prevailing usage deemed best by social standards; to compare these recommendations with actual pronunciations by personalities in the public eye who might be considered "authorities"; and to double-check by their own reactions the appropriateness of the pronunciation for them as individuals, and for the program.

Foreign place names and proper names create special problems. The press services and the networks compile word lists as the names appear in the news. The general practice is toward Anglicizing foreign names. Two reference volumes, other than recognized dictionaries, which are of special value, are *NBC Handbook of Pronunciation* and CBS's *World Words*. These volumes are consulted by many announcers.

The question of which of several pronunciations is "right" cannot always be decided with any finality. The pronunciation "preferred" by the reference works, by public figures, and by co-workers should guide an announcer. When you choose a pronunciation, use it with assurance and confidence. *Caution:* Overly precise, pedantic pronunciation will cause the audience to react negatively to the announcer and to his message.

Articulation. Articulation is concerned with the utterance of vowels, consonants, and diphthongs. Good articulation aids in effective communication. Articulation must be distinct and pleasing without calling attention to itself. Consider again the position of the listener or viewer in relation to the person on mike. The microphone is only a few inches away from the speaker. The person at home is really just as close to the speaker, due to the electrical increase in speaker volume. Very few people, except relatives and intimate friends, ever get as close to a person as a microphone does. The microphone reveals much about speech and personality that is hidden by distance. As a microscope brings out minute flaws and rough spots in material which to the eye is apparently flawless, the microphone highlights what might be disregarded in other situations. The amplifying system serves to bring the voice to us in magnified detail for "microscopic" *sound* examination. The listener does not expect a high degree of careful articulation from the casual performer, but he is quick to detect slovenliness and indistinctness in indifferent or untrained announcers.

Good articulation demands: (1) an ample supply of air, (2) a relaxed throat, (3) the use of head, throat, and chest resonators in correct proportion, and (4) the strong and agile movement of lips, tongue, and jaw. You may be familiar with the announcer who uses *dubya* for *double u* or *git* for *get, probly* for *probably, godder* for *got to, kuz* for *because, jest* for *just, gonna* for *going to, l'll* for *little,* and *in'* in *ing* endings. You may be familiar too with the overarticulation of "stage-trained" or "platform-minded" announcers who carry over speech habits from their activities in fields where it is necessary to project to the rear of a theatre without electrical amplification.

Both sloppy and exaggerated articulation adversely affect judgments of an announcer's personality. When one is as frequent a caller in the home as is an announcer, minor faults of articulation may grow into major irritations.

The following appears frequently in announcer's audition copy. Try it as a challenge:

```
SHE: (TO PLUMBER) Are you copper plating those pipes?
HE:  No Mum!  I'm aluminuming 'em, Mum!
```

Or, for a change of pace, five stand-bys:

```
1. "Is this the sixth sister's zither?"
2. The seething sea ceaseth, and it sufficeth us.
3. He thrusts his fists against the posts and still insists he
   sees the ghosts.
4. The green glow grew, a glowing gleam, growing greener.
5. Geese cackle, cattle low, crows caw, cocks crow.
```

And an announcement which completely threw an announcer when he read it at sight:

```
Rome wasn't built in a day... and you can't serve a good cocktail
or good punch in a minute...that is, not unless you serve Pic-
cadilly Cocktail or Piccadilly Punch, the bottled cocktail and
punch that the famous house of Old Nobility has made available to
smart hosts everywhere.  Old Nobility Piccadilly Cocktail and Old
Nobility Piccadilly Punch come bottled...ready-prepared for you
to chill and serve in a jiffy.  Your neighborhood dealer has Old
Nobility Piccadilly Cocktail and Old Nobility Piccadilly Punch
at only $1.45 a large bottle.
```

Emphasis. The announcer uses emphasis to point out for the audience the important and unimportant ideas in the spoken material. A platform speaker, of course, uses gestures to give emphasis and clarity to ideas, but radio listeners cannot see an index finger pointed at them on the sentence, *"This* is important news for *you,"* or *"Shop* at *Blanks . . .* and *save!"* accompanied by a nod of the head and a smile of satisfaction on *save!* Television, of course, permits the viewer to see the gestures. However, a radio announcer may profit by using gestures, even though they are not part of the audible code. Speaking with gestures is very common in good conversation; incipient radio announcers who avoid gestures break their conversational speaking patterns and risk a dull and lifeless presentation of their material.

One method of emphasis is vocally to underscore key words:

```
Your tea is easier to make, more delightful to taste, more
flavorful and satisfying.
```

Another method is to separate key words or phrases with appropriate pauses:

```
The orchestra plays a favorite of yesterday...Lady Be Good.
Remember the address...Main and Second.
```

Climactic emphasis may be achieved by increasing or decreasing force.

```
It's priced to save you money.  Don't delay--buy today!
It's mild...mild...mild.
```

A note of caution to the announcer: An emphatic and enthusiastic treatment is acceptable if it is in keeping with the product and the program, but if the announcer resorts to "shouting" or "barking" for emphasis, he may make the audience weary of him.

Word Color. Word color is closely related to emphasis. Emphasis is concerned primarily with volume, and word color with quality of tone and emotional undercurrents. Not only the generally accepted denotations, but associated impressions, attitudes, and mood are communicated.

Consider this narrative setting for Hawthorne's "Ethan Brand": "Within the furnace were to be seen the curling and riotous flames, and the burning marble, almost molten with the intensity of the heat . . . while outside, the reflection of the fire quivered on the darkness of the surrounding forest." This selection requires care and skill in setting a mood through word color.

In musical continuity, word color is the announcer's stock in trade:

```
Hold on to your hats, here's Jimmy Lunceford's treatment of "Run-
nin' Wild."
An Irish medley...first a lively jig..."The Irish Washerwoman"
...then, the tenderly nostalgic "Danny Boy"...and finally "Come
Back to Erin."
Majestic, resplendent with regal beauty and appeal, the orches-
tra's interpretation of "Pomp and Circumstance."
Music Sweet...Music Hot...the Rhythm Parade!
```

In announcing commercials, consider the implicit meanings brought out in word color by:

```
The lowest-priced...The car of the year...Blank pipe tobacco
smokes sweet and fragrant...It's smart to wear a Blank hat.
```

Rate. There are two factors involved in rate. One is the over-all pace, the line rate or number of words per minute; the second is the speed with which individual words are spoken. Announcing requires variety in pacing, because of the many different types of material broadcast. Mood and pace are closely related. Consider the following:

```
Jones leads with a right to the jaw.  Brown brushes it off be-
fore it reaches him...Jones gives him a left hook...there's
another left hook...and now Jones is following Brown...a short
jab by Jones a right to the jaw...Brown blocked it...There's a
clinch...they're apart...Now Jones gives a left to the stomach
...another left...a straight right lead...and a powerful...but
powerful left hook.
```

With variations in pacing, an impression can be given of a slow, extremely tense, or a fast bout.

The choice of pace can influence the degree of comprehension. Consider this narrative description of ways of detecting counterfeit money:

NARR 1:   The best way to recognize illegal money is to know what genuine bills look like. Open your purse--that's right --now take out a dollar bill. Go ahead--there--hold up the side with Washington's portrait...now look at the numerals in the upper corners.

WOMAN: Why they're set against a pattern of fine lines--it's almost like a lace doily. And--the lines are traced along the entire border.

NARR 1:   The tracing is much more complicated than most of us realize from a quick glance. Made by a skilled crafts- man using a geometric lathe.

NARR 2:   This type of geometric lathe is a special engraving machine capable of cutting precise lines into a steel die--the designs it makes are so involved they can never be reproduced. These machines were developed solely to defeat counterfeiters.

NARR 1:   Now look at the portrait of Washington. This part was done by hand. Those fine lines--even the ones around the eyes and mouth--were cut into hard steel by the skilled hand of an expert engraver. A counterfeiter cannot produce work of such high quality. If he could he would demand a legitimate job at very high pay.

NARR 2:   Actually there are only about twenty-five men in the world who could be called competent in this work. These engravers must have the delicate touch of an artist and the sense of precision of an engineer.

NARR 1:   If you ever see a bill where the portrait is dark--or the eyes dull--or the hair lines blurred--that bill is a counterfeit.[1]

If this selection is read at a fast clip, it will communicate nothing. The auditor must feel close to the narrators, as though they were right at his shoulder, examining the same bill with him, in the same intimate manner a golf professional might give instructions on how to grip a club. Knowing when to slow down, how to capitalize upon contrast in rhythm, how to use pauses, are refinements and subtleties which give announcing professional flavor.

EXAMPLE OF A TELEVISION COMMERCIAL

The television commercial which follows calls for careful attention to emphasis, word color, and rate. The sponsor has indicated, by underlining, the words and phrases which require special consideration for effective presentation.[2]

[1] Courtesy of the author, Rollin Quimby, and University of Michigan Department of Speech.
[2] Courtesy of Kraft Food Company.

VIDEO	AUDIO
DISSOLVE TO SLIDE READING KRAFT TELEVISION THEATRE.	ANNCR: We'll be back in a moment with the third act of..... .....featuring..........and brought to you on the Kraft Television Theatre by the Kraft Foods Company whose good cooks tonight bring you...
DISSOLVE TO SANDWICHES AND JUICE GLASSES.	ANNCR:...some wonderful, little cheese appetizers that you can serve before dinner with a glass of tart juice. Or, you could use them for dainty sandwiches at a tea. First thing we do is...
DISSOLVE TO BREADBOARD ON WHICH HANDS ARE CUTTING BREAD SLICE WITH FLOWER-SHAPED CUTTER. COOKIE SHEET WITH SOME FLOWERS ALREADY CUT IS AT SIDE. ABOUT ON CUE "HANDY KRAFT CHEESE SPREADS" START SPREADING FLOWERS CU FROM OPEN OLIVE PIMENTO JAR.	ANNCR:...cut thinly sliced white bread with a flower-shaped cutter. (Or use any cookie cutter that will give you a similar form.) To cover our appetizers, we're going to use several of the handy Kraft Cheese Spreads, which we have let soften awhile at room temperature. We'll spread the "flower" part of some with Kraft Olive Pimento Cheese Spread that looks so festive and tastes so good. By the way, for picnics, Kraft Cheese Spreads are grand to take along because they not only make quick, tasty sandwiches but are so easy to pack. And there's an
ON CUE "FOR THE STEMS" START SPREADING STEM OF ONE WITH OLD ENGLISH.	assortment of eight varieties to choose from. Now then, for the stems of these, we're going to use Old English Cheese Spread. Of course, you can make other combinations such as...
DISSOLVE TO COOKIE SHEET WITH SOME PIMENTO - PHILADELPHIA VARIETY ALREADY SPREAD. HANDS ARE GARNISHING ACCORDING TO RECIPE DIRECTIONS, AS CLOSE TO CUES AS POSSIBLE.	ANNCR:...these, which we have already spread with Kraft Pimento Cheese Spread and Philadelphia Brand Cream Cheese. (Soften the Philadelphia Brand with a bit of milk.) For the garnishes we use slices of

stuffed olives on some of the "blossoms" and tiny squares of green pepper on the others. These garnishes look fancy, but as you see, they're really very simple. We'll decorate all the "leaves" and "stems" with slivers of green pepper and then...

DISSOLVE TO CU OF ATTRACTIVE TRAY. HANDS TAKE ONE OR TWO OFF, AS IF TO EAT.

ANNCR:...arange them on a big tray so folks can just serve themselves. You can easily make these grand party sandwiches if you...

DISSOLVE TO REVOLVING TURNTABLE IN FRONT OF PLAIN BACKGROUND. ON CUE "JUST LOOK AT" HAND BRINGS ONE GLASS ECU, TURNS IT TO DISPLAY PATTERN, SETS IT ASIDE. ON CUE "START YOUR SET" START REVOLVING TURNTABLE TO DISPLAY EACH LABEL ON CUE.

ANNCR:...always have a supply of Kraft Cheese Spreads on hand. And just look at this colorful brand new "Bachelor Button" design on all the glasses. You'll use these handy glasses again and again ...so...start your set tomorrow by getting Old English Brand...or Kraft Pimento...or Kraft Olive Pimento. We also have Kraft Bacon...Kraft Garlic ...Kraft Relish...Kraft Pineapple...and Kraft Roka Blue. Get them tomorrow...the handy Kraft Cheese Spreads in new bright Bachelor Button design glasses.

EXAMPLE OF TELEVISION NARRATION

"Ten Years After Hiroshima" [3]

The opening narrative passages from the "March of Medicine" television program over NBC-TV March 29, 1955, were prepared to be read over special film footage taken in Hiroshima, Japan. This material calls for the utmost in professional skill for effective presentation. The script was written by Lou Hazam. The series was produced by the Smith, Kline & French Medical Television Unit.

AUDIO	VIDEO
MUSIC:	
SNEAK IN DOLEFUL SAMISEN, ESTABLISH, THEN HOLD UNDER FAINTLY IN BG.	UP ON STOCK FOOTAGE, VIEWS OF DESTROYED CITY HOLD FOR ABOUT 8 SEC. WITHOUT NARRATION

[3] Courtesy of Smith. Kline & French Laboratories.

NARR: (QUIETLY, ON CUE)

This was Hiroshima
In the recollection of a Dr.
    Hachiya
Who lived through its most remem-
    bered day:

DR. HACHIYA:

BEGINS DESCRIPTION OF MEDICAL
SITUATION IN JAPANESE, THEN DOWN
TO COVER WITH NARRATOR'S TRANS-
LATION...

NARR:

90% of the doctors were casual-
ties...(JAPANESE UP AND DOWN)...
Only 30 were able to carry on
their duties...Almost all our
nurses were injured and died...
Medical facilities were non-exist-
ent...Medical supplies were destroyed & the treatment of the
severely wounded had to be improvised. The dead--more than half
of Hiroshima's 300,000 population
--were slow to be recovered...

MUSIC: DISSOLVE TO REBUILT CITY,

SEGUE TO MORE SPRIGHTLY THEME AND   AND PAN...DISTANT SHOT...
DOWN UNDER   (15")

NARR:

This is Hiroshima....
The new Hiroshima that was built
Over the ashes of the old...
Ashes that it was once erroneously
    believed
Would not again support human
    habitation
For 75 years....
This railroad station   3000 METER VIEW   (15")
Is roughly 2 miles from point   RAILROAD STATION
    zero,
Where the A-Bomb burst.
From here on out damage was not
    great,
Radiation delivered insignifi-
    cant...
(PAUSE)
Moving in
From about a mile and a quarter   2000 METER VIEW   (15")
    from point zero,   ROLLING SHOT, STREET
Of the 100,000 survivors   SCENES
More than a third
Were within this 2000 meter radius
And many showed definite signs
Of radiation effects.
(PAUSE)
At 750 yards   ROLLING SHOT, FUKUYA DEPT.

The Fukuya Department Store,	STORE (22")
Once gutted,	
Is today restored and in opera-	
tion...	
(PAUSE)	

MUSIC OUT

You are now at point zero.	POINT ZERO...HYPOCENTER,
(PAUSE)	FULL SHOT...PAN UP (13")
This is the hypocenter	
Which--once standing proudly	
As a hall of science and indus-	
try--	
Is the bomb's last significant	
material vestige.	
And this is the cloudless sky	CLOUDLESS SKY (15")
In which--at 8:15 A.M. on August	
6, 1945--	
A single "miniature sun"	
Exploded some 650 yards above the	
ground,	
The ghost of a building that	PAN DOWN TO SOUVENIR STAND
remains	...TOURIST PURCHASING CARD
Is preserved as a memorial	(17")
Of that moment, that day, that	
event,	
And to the souvenir stand at its	
foot	
Come Japanese tourists daily,	
To purchase tokens of their visit.	
There are still other vestiges	MS WOMAN'S HAND REACHING
Of the atom	...CU OF ARM, SLEEVE FALL-
Not often observed anymore...	ING DOWN, REVEALING SCAR.
Burns from the bomb	MS AS SHE PAYS MONEY AND
Barely visible on this woman's	MOVES OFF INTO CROWD (15")
hand,	
Have long since been healed	
And been noted in the Medical	
Notebooks	
But in this unique population of	THE CROWD MILLING. PAN UP
Hiroshima	TO SEE ABCC IN DISTANCE.
Might there be unseen effects	(10")
Delayed effects	
Destined to turn up in these	
people?	
Those are the questions	MS ABCC FROM TOWN CLOSER
Being asked upon the hill	OVERALL SHOT ABCC...
Overlooking the town,	PEOPLE, ARRIVING FOR WORK
Where--since 1946--	FRONT YARD AND ENTRANCE
The U.S. Atomic Bomb Casualty	(25")
Commission	
Has gathered together a select	
staff	
Of American doctors	
And Japanese doctors and techni-	
cians--	
A monument to cooperation between	
East & West--	

```
To study the effects of radiation
On the A-Bomb survivors.
The scope and purpose of this--
One of the world's most absorbing
      scientific investigations--
Is described (for the March of
      Medicine)
By the director of the ABCC.
Dr. Robert H. Holmes...
```

Inflection. The English language has its own characteristic melody patterns. An incident widely quoted in the broadcasting industry illustrates this. On a dramatic broadcast from Hollywod, the usual practice is to have a star reappear after the play, to give an "oral trailer" about the program to come. This continuity sometimes does not get rehearsed due to exigencies of time, or late confirmation of broadcast details. A prominent star began the following trailer in good form. It read:

```
Next week this program will feature in the starring role the very
talented and brilliant young actor, John Blank!
```

Just as he was about to give the name of the person he was lauding, the star saw it for the first time. His amazement and horror at such praise for this particular actor of little standing or prestige in the profession was perfectly reproduced by the melody pattern, a questioning snort, with which he uttered the words: "John ... Blank?" He had never spoken a more expressive phrase in his entire acting career.

Students of speech should be familiar with the drills in variation of meaning and emotion; saying "Oh" or "Yes" in many different ways. The physical "nearness" of the auditor to the broadcaster permits extensive use of inflection to signify minute shades of thought and feeling. The attitude of the announcer towards the product he is talking about, towards the talent, musical selections, and the personalities mentioned in the news broadcasts are revealed in the melody patterns of his speech. His state of health, his poise or confidence in his ability, and clues to his personality are suggested by his vocal inflections. It might be well to mention three very common melody patterns which are particularly distracting: (1) a mechanical, transitional vocal hold, (2) sing-song, and (3) recurrent up-or-down patterns.

1. MECHANICAL, TRANSITIONAL VOCAL HOLD. This is the result of the working conditions in many radio studios. The announcer, in addition to reading copy, may be cueing in records while one turntable is on the air, filling out a program and announcement log, editing news for the next program, checking out-going program levels, auditioning microphone placement for a studio program, pulling records from the transcription library, and answering the phone. In television studios some of the same duties are his, together with signals for film projection and watching the monitor as he reads the copy. With all of this responsibility and activity the announcer

may not have sufficient time to rehearse his continuity and commercial announcements. He may be obliged to read from sight. Therefore, to insure himself enough time to glance ahead quickly and get some general sense of the copy, an announcer may fall into the habit of mechanically lifting his voice at ends of phrases and holding the final note. While holding this note he may look aside to check a title or the console controls. After a time the habit is firmly established. Consider the following:

```
You know, Mothers, every child going to school needs lots of
energy to do good work.  If your child comes home after school
feeling tired and worn out maybe it's because he's not getting
the right kind of food at lunch.  Now bread is a very important
part of any lunch...and it's important that the bread you use...
be full of all the food energy that children need so much.
```

This is a straightforward commercial announcement. It needs a direct and friendly approach. An announcer who has fallen into the mechanical, transitional vocal hold habit may read it very unevenly. The underlined words below indicate the trouble spots for such announcers.

```
You know, Mothers, every child going to school needs lots of
energy to do good work.  If your child comes home after school
feeling tired and worn out maybe it's because he's not getting
the right kind of food at lunch...and it's important that the
bread you use...be full of all the food energy that children
need so much.
```

The habit of separating phrases and sentences by three and five dots used indiscriminately by some copy writers, tends to encourage this faulty reading style. The announcer is never certain where the end of the thought comes unless he studies the script carefully.

2. SING-SONG. This is sometimes referred to as "ministerial" pattern. Translating the announcement into sing-song style, indicating pitch levels and relative stress, we might get something that looks like this:

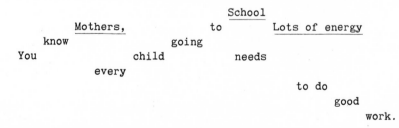

3. RECURRENT UP-OR-DOWN PATTERNS. Another melody trap is present when the performer gets past the word-by-word style of delivery and into the word-combinations phase. With a close correlation to breathing rhythm, usually short half-breaths, the inflections always go up, or always go down,

at ends of phrases and sentences. The melody curve can be plotted if one
follows it with a pencil in hand. The same announcement is read:

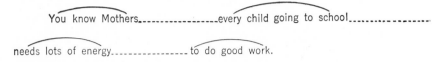

Or, the curve may be just reversed and will go up instead of down. This
style leads to monotony.

Resourcefulness. Adroit ad-libbing by the announcer may be needed
when unforeseen contingencies arise in radio or television. A notable
example of such occurred during the initial appearance of a woman announcer substituting for a vacationing colleague on a top network TV
dramatic program. One of the characteristics of the new-model refrigerator
being advertised was the ease with which it opened when the homemaker
was laden down with packages. One of those horrible and frustrating night-
mare situations resulted. The woman described its "finger-tip" opening
action and confidently pressed the door plate. Nothing happened. The
woman tried again and again, but the refrigerator door refused to swing
open. The remainder of the announcement dealt with the features inside the
refrigerator. Without apparent discomfiture the woman announcer ad-libbed
a vague reference to the fact that the refrigerator power outlet had been
disconnected after the show rehearsal, and went on to point out desirable
features of specific areas behind the closed door which the viewers *would*
have seen. Moving slightly away from the stubborn machine she continued
to talk smoothly about the refrigerator while the camera moved in on a
close-up. At the conclusion of the announcement, upon signal from the
floor manager that the refrigerator was tractable again (without permitting
the audience to see that she had received such a signal), she moved back to
the refrigerator door, gave it only the slight pressure she had mentioned as
required, and, with the viewers, watched the door swing ajar. Never once
did she lose her poise.

• STRICTLY TELEVISION •

Appearance. This factor has no bearing on effectiveness in radio or in
those phases of TV announcing where no one is seen on camera. Much live
TV and film work by station staff announcers never demands personal
appearances. However, as soon as the announcer moves into specialized
and feature assignments on camera, appearance is extremely important. In
the early days of network telecasts one prominent announcer who was
completely bald except for side fringes worked a transformation in his
appearance by the purchase of a series of toupées, each with a gradual increase in the amount of hair until he attained the "well-groomed" look.

It was first assumed that announcers would need to have the "Hollywood" gloss, and program producers attempted to hire announcers on appearance alone. Agencies handling photographer's models were approached. The casting files of agencies handling actors for motion pictures were examined. Men who looked handsome and distinguished, women who were striking and glamorous, were in demand.

Soon, however, the absence of the many other factors which make for effectiveness became apparent when these persons were entrusted with responsibilities for persuasive broadcast salesmanship. A trade-association study points out that

> most TV station managers have found that the great majority of their radio announcers are sufficient on this count [appearance] to handle a TV job. Most TV station managers feel that an honest sincere pleasant face will stand up best over the long haul. . . . However those with physical defects which show up before the camera, also those who are extreme physical types—for example, very tall, very short, very fat or very thin—are not acceptable for television. It is important to keep in mind here that these are characteristics of general applicability. Exceptions may and do exist.[4]

Related to appearance are good grooming, naturalness of posture, facial expression, gesture, and movement. Announcers must not possess irritating facial or gesture mannerisms distracting to the viewer, and they must sit and move gracefully. Since much of the camera shooting will be in close-ups, extreme gestures, where hands and arms are extended towards the camera, may lead to considerable distortion as well as to distraction. Crossing one's legs towards the camera may exaggerate their length and size. The appearance of the announcer is, of course, also related to his age. Many radio announcers are quite young. Their vocal qualities alone may give an impression of maturity. When these announcers appear on the screen, however, the viewing audience takes its primary cue from what it sees. As a result, many advertisers and program producers prefer announcers who "look" as well as "sound" mature. Announcers may compensate somewhat for their "youth" by paying careful attention to their choice of clothing and of hair cut in order to avoid a "collegiate" appearance.

A minor yet specialized aspect of appearance is in the "freeze" of the facial expression following the conclusion of the announcement. The director frequently will hold a closing shot of the announcer for a few seconds before taking the next shot or ordering a slow dissolve. The announcer must not move or take on a "sickly" self-conscious or "blank" look during this period. A break in mood might completely ruin the effect of the message just concluded. This subtle yet professional skill takes practice.

Memorization. Many commercial announcements and much program continuity must be committed to memory. The pressures of the schedule

---

[4] National Association of Radio and Television Broadcasters, *Station Management Takes a Look at Television Jobs* (Washington, 1952), p. 7.

seldom permit the announcer to have time to learn the copy over a period of days. "Quick studies" are the rule. Any mental struggle to remember specific words must be concealed from the audience. Since pictures and words must be synchronized, a process that requires careful camera work, the announcer must present the commercial on the air in the exact sequence as rehearsed. The announcer may have access to automatic prompting devices or cue cards which display the copy to be presented. To use such aids without detection by the viewers requires considerable practice. It is preferable that the announcer have the content partially memorized by broadcast time.

Synchronization. We have said that the radio announcer must imagine that the listener is close beside him when he reads descriptive narration. In television, in contrast to radio, the viewer is guided primarily by the picture on the screen. It is as though the announcer is beside the viewer: both are examining a photo album or a sales leaflet as the anouncer comments on each. The announcer must know what is actually being shown in order to direct the attention of the viewer and, through nuances in his delivery, to emphasize certain points. Thus, it is clear that the television announcer has much less freedom than the radio announcer in determining his rate of speech. If he reads the credits at the close of the drama faster than the names are displayed on the scroll, if he is enthusiastic about the excellent taste of the salad before the actress has tried it, if he refers to action or details not being captured by the camera and seen on the home screen, the mismatch of words and pictures results in confusion that may be comic or otherwise. Effective communication of mood or message has been lost. Constant reference to a monitor in the studio or announce booth must be made during this type of announcing assignment.

EXAMPLES OF RADIO CONTINUITY

1. "Your Concert Hall" and 2. "Meet the Artist" [5]

Excerpts from continuity service available to stations from Broadcast Music Inc. (BMI)

| YOUR CONCERT HALL | TIME: 59:30 |

ANNCR: (STATION/SPONSOR).................presents...YOUR CONCERT HALL.

MUSIC: ESTABLISH THEME: ANDANTE FROM SYMPHONY NO. 5 IN C MINOR (Opus 67) FADE AT 0:40 (Beethoven/PD)

ANNCR: This is a program of concert music for your listening pleasure...recorded melodies to enjoy, brought to you by (STATION/SPONSOR)....................

MUSIC: THEME UP - OUT AT 1:00

[5] Courtesy of Broadcast Music Inc. Material copyright, 1954.

ANNCR: Perspective on an artist's development is often gained by
reviewing his earliest efforts. Beethoven's (BAY-toh-
ven) FIRST SYMPHONY admirably fore-tells the growth in
creative powers that was imminent.

For cogency of idea and intensity of expression this work
is unique. Now on YOUR CONCERT HALL we hear Beethoven's
SYMPHONY NO. 1 IN C MAJOR.

MUSIC: SYMPHONY NO. 1 IN C MAJOR, OP. 21 (Beethoven/PD)

VICTOR LCT 1023

ANNCR: Opening YOUR CONCERT HALL Arturo Toscanini (ar-TOO-roh
tos-cah-NEE-nee) has conducted the BBC Orchestra in
Beethoven's FIRST SYMPHONY. To continue our concert we
hear a FLUTE CONCERTO by Mozart (MOH-tsart).

During his second trip to Paris in search of work and a
secure position, Mozart wrote several compositions for
the flute, on commission from "a gentleman of means and a
lover of all the sciences."

In the CONCERTO NO. 1 IN G MAJOR FOR FLUTE, we hear John
Wummer (WUM-mer) as soloist - with Pablo Casals (PAH-blow
cah-SAHLS) conducting the Festival Orchestra.

MUSIC: CONCERTO NO. 1 IN G MAJOR FOR FLUTE, K. 313 (Mozart/PD)

COLUMBIA ML 4567

ANNCR: On YOUR CONCERT HALL John Wummer has played Mozart's
FIRST FLUTE CONCERTO IN G MAJOR.

Regarding his own work, a prominent contemporary composer
has said: "After studying many pages of a certain composer, I sense his musical personality and, like a detective, reconstruct his musical experience."

In hearing our next selection, which is called SCENES DE
BALLET (SENN duh b-LAY), we discover that our prominent
tune-detective is none other than the great Igor Stravinsky (EE-gor strah-VIN-skee).

MUSIC: SCENES DE BALLET (Stravinsky/Schott-AMP)

COLUMBIA ML 4047

ANNCR: The New York Philharmonic has performed Stravinsky's
SCENES DE BALLET - with the composer conducting.

MUSIC: FADE IN THEME - PLAY IN B.G.

ANNCR: ...And so we come to the end of another of YOUR CONCERT
HALL programs. (STATION/SPONSOR).......................
invites you to tune in again.........at..........for
another program of recorded concert music dedicated to
your listening pleasure. Your commentator has been
....

MUSIC: THEME UP FOR TIME

59:30

MEET THE ARTIST   TIME. 14:30

ANNCR: (STATION/SPONSOR)...................invites you backstage
to MEET THE ARTIST!

THEME: "DANSERO" - HAYMAN-MERCURY 70166 - B&F MUSIC ESTABLISH -
FADE AT :15 FOR:

ANNCR: Would you like to know more about your favorite recording
artists? Well...MEET THE ARTIST puts the spotlight on the
stars...America's most popular music-makers. Come with
us now as we take you backstage into the lives of those
YOU have made famous. Today, let's get acquainted with
one of America's most popular singers and Academy Award
winning actor...FRANK SINATRA.

THEME: "DANSERO"
UP AND OUT.

MUSIC: "THIS LOVE OF MINE" - SINATRA - VICTOR/EMBASSY
ESTABLISH - CUT AT SUITABLE BREAK FOR:

ANNCR: Yes, that's the million dollar voice, and we'll hear
more of it after this message.

(INSERT COMMERCIAL HERE)

ANNCR: And now to officially meet Sinatra. You know, in this
business, we play a lot of records and hear a lot of
success stories.

But I don't think there's been anything to equal Frank
Sinatra's fabulous rise to fame. In 1943, he hit the
headlines like a comet and has been shooting upwards ever
since. From a fifteen dollar a week singing waiter to a
twenty five thousand dollar a week national idol. That's
what can happen in show business! So let's listen to one
of Frank Sinatra's own compositions. "This Love of Mine,"
originally recorded with Tommy Dorsey, and which has since
become his theme song.

MUSIC: "THIS LOVE OF MINE."

ANNCR: If there ever was such a thing as an average American boy,
it was probably Frank Sinatra! Born December 12th,1917
in Hoboken, New Jersey, he did all the things expected of
a normally active youngster...including getting his head
caught in the roof of a carousel! Needless to say, Frankie
lost most of his hair and the carousel had to be torn
apart to get him out!

A few years later, while in High School, he was burning a
path as a track star. He was a great swimmer, and a
member of a championship basketball team. Sure, Frankie
sang too! At the Demarest High School, he was with both
the school band and the Glee Club. After school he worked
on a delivery truck of the Hudson Observer, which gave
him ambitions to be a newspaperman.

That was Frank Sinatra - a nice average kid. But more
about that episode in a moment. Right now, a song for
lovers, young and old. Frank Sinatra suggests "VIOLETS
FOR YOUR FURS."

MUSIC: "VIOLETS FOR YOUR FURS." - SINATRA - CAPITOL/EMBASSY

ANNCR: Can you believe that a man who sings like that was once a
newspaper copy boy and sports editor? Well, that's exactly
what Frank Sinatra was upon leaving High School. But it
didn't last long. One day he went to a local movie and
saw a Bing Crosby show. Overnight, Frankie decided to be
a professional singer. He did it too...as a fifteen dollar a week singing waiter at a roadhouse near Hoboken!

The next break came in 1938 when he was signed with Harry James at seventy five dollars a week, then with Tommy Dorsey at one hundred and fifty a week! Teen-agers began to swoon and the Sinatra legend swept the nation! The rest of Frank Sinatra's story is sweet music whichever way you look at it. He was booked at New York's Paramount Theatre at a thousand a week and broke all records. For his return engagement he got over seven thousand dollars. Yet, for all this, Sinatra is a nice guy...unassuming, friendly and a hard worker. And, as he most recently proved in the movie, "From Here to Eternity,"...he can act too! Frank has big things lined up for 1954. For instance, this early hit..."YOUNG AT HEART."

MUSIC: "YOUNG AT HEART." - SINATRA - CAPITOL/SUNBEAM

> (INSERT SECOND COMMERCIAL HERE)

THEME: "DANSERO"
ESTABLISH - FADE FOR:

ANNCR: Today, MEET THE ARTIST featured FRANK SINATRA.

THEME: "DANSERO"
UP APPROXIMATELY :15 - FADE FOR:

ANNCR: Listen again....................at........when (STATION/ SPONSOR).....................invites you along to MEET THE ARTIST, a special radio feature which brings you the interesting and unusual stories about today's most popular recording artists. Next....................at........we have a date to meet lovely ROSEMARY CLOONEY.

THEME: "DANSERO"
UP TO TIME.

14:30

3. Excerpts from RCA Recorded Program Service supplied to subscribers to its library service.[6]

917-A THEME: FROM A TO Z IN NOVELTY (MR)
(HOLD 30 SECONDS, THEN FADE UNDER AND OUT)

ANNCR: It's A to Z in Novelty! Yes, friends, it's time for another rhythm party. This time we hear music by the Sammy Herman Trio and the spirituals of the Golden Gate Quartet. So for swing and rhythm, it's plain to see... it's novelty from A to Z!
(THEME UP TO CLOSE   :58)

First, a bright Spanish dance...styled by the Sammy Herman Trio. LA SORRELLA!

983-K LA SORRELLA (PD)   (HERMAN TRIO) 2:00

Next...the Golden Gate Quartet comes calling for a first song--and from long ago, and in beautiful harmony, the boys sing--PREPARE ME LORD.

1122-J PREPARE ME LORD (MR)   (GOLDEN GATE) 2:25

975-H THEME: CHURCH IN THE WILDWOOD (PD)
(HOLD 35 SECONDS: THEN FADE UNDER)

[6] Courtesy of RCA Recorded Program Service.

ANNCR: The time has come again to share inspiration and song
with neighbors and friends, while John Seagle sings your
favorite hymns from the CHURCH IN THE WILDWOOD.
(THEME: UP AND OUT FAST AT 1:05)

Our hymn service begins with a unique hymn. The music is
by Haydn and the words by John Newton, a soldier of fortune who became a preacher. John Seagle sings--GLORIOUS
THINGS OF THEE ARE SPOKEN.

832-B GLORIOUS THINGS, ETC. (PD)   (SEAGLE)   2:10

Next--I'M A PILGRIM, from an old Italian air.

937-B I'M A PILGRIM (BMI)   (SEAGLE)   2:25

With music by William Doane and words by Fanny Crosby,
John Seagle presents the sacred song--SAVIOUR, MORE THAN
LIFE. (START MUSIC) "Behold I am laying in Zion a stone
that will make men stumble, a rock that will make them
fall; and he who believes in Him will not be put to
shame."

964-D SAVIOUR, ETC. (PD)   (SEAGLE)   2:45

1228-A OPENING THEME: SONGS THAT MY MOTHER SANG TO ME (BMI)
(HOLD 37 SECONDS: THEN FADE UNDER AND OUT)

ANNCR: Greetings, neighbor. SLIM BRYANT AND HIS WILDCATS are
set to entertain you with ballads and dance tunes
gathered from the hills and plains all over the country.
By way of getting things off to a good start, here are
Slim and the boys with...THE AIRLINE POLKA.

1317-L AIRLINE POLKA (BMI)   (BRYANT)   1:33

ANNCR: Our favorite hillbilly vocalist, Ken Newton, provides us
with one of his best hillbilly vocals--ALL MY LIFE.

1373-C ALL MY LIFE (BMI)   (BRYANT & NEWTON)   3:00

ANNCR: Here's a fast bit of melody put together by Jerry Wallace,
the Wildcats' guitarist. Jerry calls it--WALKIN' THE
PUP.

1494-D WALKIN' THE PUP (BMI)   (BRYANT)   1:22

EXAMPLE OF TELEVISION OPENING ANNOUNCEMENT

"The Growing World," [7] Sunday, July 24, 1955.

AUDIO	VIDEO
THEME: "LA VIE EN ROSE"	Flower Opening film

ANNCR: How would you like - absolutely
free - as a souvenir, a Maori "Tiki",
a good luck charm? Listen later in
the program for details.
Yes, today the fabulous land from
"down under" -- New Zealand -- is our

[8] Courtesy of Station KRCA-TV, Los Angeles, California.

plantsmen's locale as we bring you another edition of the NBC show, "The
Growing World"....
Yes, Southern California is indebted
to New Zealand for hundreds of fine
ornamentals.
...Your host is Norvell Gillespie,
world traveler, author, and garden
editor of the Pictorial Living Magazine of the Los Angeles Examiner.

Slides: Growing World
         Gillespie
         Pictorial Living

...Our special guest is Arthur Feslier, Deputy Travel Commissioner for
the U. S. and Canada for the New
Zealand Government Tourist Bureau.
...You'll see the famed Kiwi bird....
nocturnal, meat-eating bird which does
not fly -- yet lays huge eggs......

CU OF FESLIER, with
poster in background,
turning pages of book

CU of Kiwi Bird

ANNCR: You'll see the Kaka beak -- the
brilliant blood colored native vine
with a flower like a parrot's beak --
and many other oddities.
....Stan Hayes, world famed spraying
authority is here to give some summer
pest control hints.
...And, Jack Savarese, West Coast Director for Teleflora is here to demonstrate new ways to arrange tuberous
begonias properly.
...Right now, here's your garden gad-
about, without a New Zealand accent, I
might add, Norv Gillespie.

Kaka beak, C.U.

CU of Hayes studying
insects

Savarese with bowl of
begonias

Norv at desk

EXAMPLE OF LOCAL STATION
LIVE TELEVISION COMMERCIAL

Security–First National Bank, Mary McAdoo Subjects, July 3, 1955.[8]

1. CLOSE SHOT - MONTHLY CALENDAR (July, 1955)

   The whole month of July has been circled with a bold black
   line. Printed inside circle is the word: VACATION!

                    MARY'S VOICE
         Friends, this is the time of year when
         vacations are uppermost in everybody's
         mind.

   CAMERA PULLS BACK and PANS to include Mary, who stands beside
   a large world globe.

                       MARY
                 (indicating globe)
         And in these days of super-rapid
         transportation the whole world is yours
         to choose from

8 Courtesy of Station KRCA-TV, Los Angeles, California.

> (she starts the globe
> spinning with her hand)
> Hawaii...Alaska...Mexico...Cuba...
> Italy...Switzerland...France...England --
> any place that suits your fancy.

Mary slows the spinning globe with her hand and CAMERA MOVES
IN as she rotates the globe so the North American Continent
can be seen in a BIG CLOSEUP.

> MARY'S VOICE
> But for most Americans, vacation-time
> means "Seeing America First."

2. MED. CLOSE - MARY AND GLOBE

Mary turns from the globe and speaks into CAMERA:

> MARY
> And to help people enjoy their vacations
> more, SECURITY-FIRST NATIONAL BANK has a
> simply wonderful plan -- about which I'll
> tell you later.
> > (she gestures off)
> But, first, I want you to meet a typical
> American family -- the Dillworthys, who
> are dreaming about a typical vacation
> place -- let's just call it "Paradise Point."

CAMERA PANS down to --

3. CLOSEUP OF FRAMED PHOTOGRAPH - MR. DILLWORTHY

An average husband-father type, with a pleasant personality
and smile.

> MARY'S VOICE
> This is Mr. Dillworthy -- Class of '31
> Devoted husband...father...and family
> breadwinner.

4. MED. CLOSE SHOT - MRS. DILLWORTHY - AT KITCHEN DOOR

An attractive type, she is sitting on a kitchen-type stool,
staring dreamy-eyed into space -- oblivious of the fact that
she is paring the potato away into nothingness. (Alternate
gag: perhaps she tosses potato out of scene, and puts peeling
into bowl.)

> MARY'S VOICE
> And this is Mrs. Dillworthy, day-dreaming
> about the wonderful vacation the whole
> family could have at Paradise Point --
> if only they could afford it.

Mrs. Dillworthy starts dreamily peeling another potato -- or
slicing one not yet peeled.

> MARY'S VOICE
> She's imagining how heavenly it would be
> with no meals to cook...no dishes to wash...
> no lunch boxes to fix...no floors to wax...

no beds to make...no clothes to wash...
no sox to darn. Oh, that <u>would</u> be Paradise!

Mrs. Dillworthy, still in a dreamy-eyed fog, continues to
whittle a potato into nothingness. CAMERA PANS AWAY TO --

5. INT. LIVING ROOM - JUDY DILLWORTHY

She is a girl of 10 or 11, and should be wearing pedal-
pushers. She is vacuuming the floor -- but is <u>riding astride</u>
the vacuum cleaner tube, prancing about as though it were a
<u>horse.</u> She glances behind her to see where she is vacuuming.

                    MARY'S VOICE
        This is Judy Dillworthy -- who simply <u>loves</u>
        horses, and dreams of riding horseback at
        Paradise Point.

CAMERA PANS AWAY from Judy to her brother, who enters scene,
wearing swim-trunks and a skin-diver's mask. He is about 12
and carries a pronged fishing spear -- and starts stalking to
<u>goldfish</u> in a bowl set atop a pedestal.

                    MARY'S VOICE
        And <u>this</u> is Junior -- whose passion is
        <u>spear-fishing.</u> He knows the family can't
        afford a vacation at Paradise Point this
        year -- but he's "practising" nevertheless.

Mr. Dillworthy now enters scene, dressed in business suit and
hat (to convey he just came home from work.) Slung over one
shoulder is a new fishing creel, and in his hand he carries a
brand new fishing rod. He is in a gay, exuberant mood. Immediately Mrs. Dillworthy and the two children gather about
him -- expectantly.

                    MARY'S VOICE
                  (over the above)
        And here comes Mr. Dillworthy, with
        momentous news.

Mr. Dillworthy produces from his pocket a SECURITY-FIRST
NATIONAL BANK "Vacation Club" <u>check</u> -- and exhibits it pride-
fully.

                    MARY'S VOICE
        <u>This year</u>, the whole family <u>is</u> going to
        <u>Paradise Point!</u> -- for two glorious
        weeks!

Mrs. Dillworthy and the children are overjoyed by this stun-
ning revelation. They embrace him joyfully, and he beams.

                    MARY'S VOICE
        Yes, because Mr. Dillworthy had the foresight,
        <u>a year ago</u>, to join SECURITY BANK'S "Vacation
        Club" -- and the check he so proudly exhibits
        will make their vacation dreams come <u>true.</u>

6. MED. CLOSE MARY -

                    MARY
        Friends, <u>you</u> can make your vacation dreams

come true, too. Join SECURITY-FIRST NATIONAL
BANK'S "Vacation Club"...Now!
> (exhibits Coupon Book)

You get this handy Coupon Book...make 25
twice-monthly deposits...and <u>then</u> you receive
your Vacation Club Check -- <u>including interest!</u>
> (pauses)

So, go to your nearest branch of SECURITY-FIRST
NATIONAL BANK...and open a "Vacation Club"
account...You can start <u>any time.</u>
> (smiles)

And, be sure to tell the folks at SECURITY
That Mary McAdoo sent you...

EXAMPLE OF NETWORK LIVE TELEVISION COMMERCIAL

First commercial of the "Ford Star Jubilee," Sept. 24, 1955, on CBS.[9]

VIDEO	AUDIO
1. MEDIUM CLOSEUP M.C.	EMCEE: To all of you who remember the early days of show business, the old Palace Theatre in New York has a special meaning. Willie and Eugene Howard, Gallagher and Shean, Sophie Tucker, Eddie Cantor, Al Jolson ...those are names that bring to mind the good old days of two-a-day at the Palace. But
JUDY JOINS HIM. (JUDY GARLAND)	two-a-day was never enough to satisfy the crowds that lined up outside the Palace when our gal Judy played there a couple of years ago. You really warmed a lot of hearts, Judy.
	JUDY: And I have a special place in <u>my</u> heart for the Palace. Everyone was so nice to me, I just can't describe the feeling I got sitting there on the edge of the Palace stage, looking out and singing all the old songs.
2. DISSOLVE TO SILHOUETTE OF NEW YORK SKYLINE.	EMCEE: Well, Judy, since your next number will re-create some of those memorable songs from your days at the Palace, we've got something to put you in the

[9] Courtesy of Ford Division of Ford Motor Company and J. Walter Thompson Company.

mood. Recognize that silhouette?

JUDY:
Who wouldn't? New York, New
York -- it's a wonderful town.

**3. DISSOLVE TO SUNLINER
SILHOUETTE.**

ANNOUNCER:
And here's another famous
American silhouette that I'm
sure you'll also recognize,
Judy.

JUDY:
Do I! That's the car right
from over the rainbow -- the
Ford Thunderbird!

**4. BRING UP LIGHTS ON RED AND
WHITE SUNLINER AGAINST ABSTRACT
BEACH BACKGROUND.**

ANNOUNCER:
Thunderbird styling, Judy.
Actually, you are getting your
first look at the 1956 Ford!

MUSIC UP
But you didn't mistake that
long, low silhouette or those
clean, crisp lines. That's
styling that only the Thunderbird could inspire.

**5. DISSOLVE TO FRONT 3/4 VIEW
OF VICTORIA. AGAINST ABSTRACT
BACKGROUND OF WALDORF ASTORIA
OR OTHER FASHIONABLE HOTEL SET-
TING. (FASHIONABLE SETTING MAY
BE SUGGESTED BY CANOPY AND ONE
POST AND RED CARPET). DOORMAN
COMES OUT AND HOLDS DOOR FOR
MODEL. DOLLY INTO MEDIUM
CLOSEUP OF GRILLE AND FRONT
END.**

PAN UP TO HEADLIGHT.

And for 1956, Ford carries the
Thunderbird look into a whole
new line of fine cars. Ford's
new Fairlane Victoria, for example, shows its Thunderbird
heritage in every detail.
Notice the graceful simplicity
of the grille...how it wraps
around the front end in one
fluid motion...

...and just look at the forward
sweep of the headlights. This
car looks as though it hates to
stand still!

**6. CUT TO 3/4 REAR VIEW OF
VICTORIA. PAN TO SHOW CHROME
ON SIDE.**

Even the taillights have that
Thunderbird flair -- and the
new Chrome trim accents its
low, road-hugging look.

**7. INSERT SLIDE OF ROOF LINE
PHOTO WITH ANIMATED DOTTED LINE
RUNNING TWO INCHES ABOVE VIC-
TORIA'S ROOF LINE. LINE IS
LABELED "1955".**

And as you can see here, it
actually is lower. The roof
line of the Victoria is almost
two inches lower than it was in
'55. And without sacrificing
head room inside.

**8. CUT TO PROFILE SHOT OF
VICTORIA.**

Everything about this car says
"Take me anywhere - everywhere
- I belong."

9. DISSOLVE TO CU REAR OF
COUNTRY SEDAN. MAN AND BOY
TAKE SKIFF OUT OF REAR. BACK-
GROUND IS ABSTRACT DESIGN OF
MOUNTAINS. BOY CLOSES REAR
DECK. DOLLY BACK TO REVEAL
ENTIRE CAR.

And that's true of Ford's new
Station Wagons, too. Wherever
you go - you'll always have
plenty of room in this four-
door eight-passenger Country
Sedan. And it's only one of
six station wagons Ford is
offering for '56.

10. DISSOLVE TO 3/4 FRONT OF
PARKLANE IN FRONT OF HOME (IN
ABSTRACT DESIGN). SOCIETY MAN
AND WOMAN.

Here's another -- the all-new
Parklane. This fashionable addition to Ford's Station Wagon
line is the most luxurious of
all the two-door six-passenger
wagons.

11. DISSOLVE TO CUSTOMLINE
TUDOR IN FRONT OF ABSTRACT
SHOPPING CENTER. TWO MOTHERS,
WITH CHILDREN, TALKING ALONG-
SIDE.

Or, if you prefer a two-door
sedan, then take a good look at
Ford's new Customline Tudor.
Notice the entirely new long,
low look that reflects the
Thunderbird silhouette. This
practical beauty is sure to be
a big family favorite.

12. CAMERA MOVES TO FAIRLANE
FORDOR IN FRONT OF SAME BACK-
GROUND.

Unless, of course, the new '56
Fairlane Fordor steals your
heart away. Most distinguished
four-door sedan in its field,
the Fairlane Fordor offers you
a choice of 25 interior and
exterior color combinations.

13. DISSOLVE TO PROFILE OF
SUNLINER.

You've seen just a few of
Ford's 19 models for '56 --
just a sampling from Ford's
rainbow of 58 different color
schemes. Make your selection
at your Ford Dealer's.

14. FADE LIGHTS ON SUNLINER TO
REVEAL SILHOUETTE ON SCRIM.

But Thunderbird styling is only
one reason the '56 Ford is
America's fine car at half the
fine car price. We'll have
even bigger news for you later
in the evening.

Projects and Exercises

1. Assign announcer's copy found in the chapter and in scripts elsewhere in the
   text. Study these announcements before presentation in class. Class criticism,
   evaluation and drill.
2. Tune in stations in your area and report on the work of the announcers.
   Compare radio and television styles.
3. Prepare brief pronunciation check lists on the basis of such observation.
   Each student should bring in ten words heard on the air with their pronunciation as given. Discuss "correctness" of presentation.

4. Prepare a practical announcer's audition for another student. Include:

   (*a*) An ad-lib assignment to reveal ease of delivery without script and appearance on camera.

   (*b*) News copy to reveal general ability in reading from script and style together with the auditionee's command of pronunciation of foreign and domestic place names.

   (*c*) Musical continuity to reveal familiarity with composers and selections. Do not select the very obscure composers or too technical terminology.

   (*d*) Voice-over narration to check on ability to synchronize delivery with film. Still pictures may be used instead of film.

   (*e*) Commercial copy.
   Alternate presentations of audition material. Criticize delivery and material.

❋ 21 ❋

Announcements

THE ANNOUNCEMENT in radio and television has a spotlight on it. While it is being presented, it is "center-stage." There is no competition for the attention of the listener by other program features. Edward R. Murrow stops his presentation to permit the audience to attend to his sponsor's announcement. A star comic is not in the middle of a routine while the commercial message is presented. The spokesman for United States Steel talks without the Theatre Guild's production of a play continuing in the background. This is not so with newspaper advertising, magazine advertising, or billboards.

This is a decided advantage for the copy writer and producer who try to attract attention, arouse interest, stimulate desire, and impel action. If commercials which come between entertainment portions of programming are ingenious and interesting, are sincerely and honestly related to the audience's personal interests and problems, and are presented in vivid and meaningful fashion, they will usually be accepted and widely acted upon.

The spotlight on commercials is detrimental, however, if the commercials are displeasing. Rude or annoying announcements are offensive because they are practically inescapable interludes when broadcast between program units.

· TYPES OF ANNOUNCEMENTS ·

Station Breaks. These come between programs during the pauses used for station identification.

SERVICE ANNOUNCEMENTS. These are short five- or ten-second commercials accompanying time signals or weather reports:

```
It is now 10:00 o'clock Central Standard time, ...courtesy Blank
Watch Company.  Choose a "Blank" Watch for your gift to her!
```

Many national advertisers, such as Bulova and Benrus, use service announcements—using slogans, headlines, and simple phrases—on a saturation basis as "reminder" copy.

"ID" OR TEN-SECOND STATION-IDENTIFICATION ANNOUNCEMENTS. These are common in television. Segments of the slide which displays the call letters and channel may be utilized simultaneously for a brief eight-second commercial. Film with such station identification data super-imposed or spliced in at the close is also used. The two-second audio station identification follows the commercial message.

CHAIN BREAKS. When stations are affiliated with one of the networks the period between sponsored programs is a valuable source of revenue for the station. It is desired by advertisers because of the opportunity it offers to reach the audience attracted by the network program. A twenty-second spot, the time between the network and the local station identification, is available to a client. Both local market and national advertisers use these periods. Since only a brief time is available for the commercial message, unity and concreteness of expression are essential. Most radio stations designate fifty or sixty words as the maximum for chain breaks.

Program breaks between the station's own adjacent commercials or popular sustaining features may also be selected by advertisers. The timing of these announcements runs the same as for chain breaks. Television, with its heavy reliance upon film, has standardized the timing of such filmed commercials for either chain or program breaks at twenty seconds.

ONE-MINUTE SPOTS. Many independent stations schedule their noncommercial programs on a fourteen- or twenty-nine-minute basis to permit the use of one-minute announcements during station breaks. If the program is commercial, the program which follows is held up for an additional thirty seconds. Network affiliates may schedule one-minute announcements between sustaining feeds from the network, fading out the network program at a logical place and signing it off locally; or, they may take the preceding program to its conclusion and join the network late, following the station's one-minute announcement.

Participating Announcements. These are similar to one-minute station-break announcements. Many transcribed or filmed one-minute commercials can be used interchangeably as station breaks or as participating announcements, worked into the body of a program. There are only a limited number of chain and station breaks available in a single broadcast day. Consequently, some periods of programming are designated as participation periods in order to carry commercial announcements. No one sponsor purchases the entire program. Disc jockeys, women's features, musical clock, breakfast chatter, household hints, and straight music on radio stations are frequently presented in the form of participating commercial programs. Television programs with similar formats may follow the same procedure. In addition, a highly important source of revenue for many stations is in the showing of feature length films which are interrupted every fifteen or twenty minutes for different participating anouncements. The high cost of network television program sponsorship has stimulated the use of participating announcements. "Home" and "Today" on NBC are examples of network participating programs. An outstanding "air" personality who also delivers commercials helps to hold the elements of the program together. Participating commercial programs are very flexible. One person may devote a great proportion of the program to information or entertainment and deliver the commercial announcements one after the other. Other broadcasters arrange the program so that the entertainment or information portions run for a few minutes, then a live, filmed, or transcribed commercial, followed by entertainment or information. Commercial announcements that last two or three minutes may occasionally be included on programs of this type.

"Cowcatchers," "Trailers," and "Hitch-Hikes." Sometimes a company that sells several different products, such as Procter & Gamble (Ivory Soap, Crisco, Spic and Span, Prell, Cheer, Joy, Tide, Gleem, Duz, Camay, etc.), may use program time for brief announcements advertising products other than the one usually identified with the program. If the announcements come at the beginning of the program they are termed "cowcatchers"; if they come at the end of the program, they are termed "trailers" or "hitch-hikes." In order to avoid a string of commercial announcements around station-break time the networks require that such announcements be included within the program frame.

Co-op Announcements. These are sold on network shows to different sponsors in local markets and vary in length and position according to the program format. In a daytime drama there may be an opening announcement, no middle, and a closing announcement. In an evening half-hour entertainment program the local co-op announcements may be divided into three one-minute periods at opening, middle, and close, and incorporated within the program frame.

Program Announcements. These are the commercial credits which are used when a sponsor purchases a segment or an entire program on a weekly, alternating or "one-shot" basis. Here he has an opportunity to select programs which serve to attract the audience most likely to purchase his product: daytime programs for women, late afternoon programs or Saturday morning for children, early evening sports round-ups for men, and programs with widespread appeal, comedy, variety, drama in the evening. The commercials will vary in style, emotional appeal, and form according to the individual program. The maximum time available to commercials is regulated by the codes of the National Association of Radio and Television Broadcasters.[1]

---

[1] See Chapter 10 for the NARTB television code.

EXAMPLES OF DIFFERENT TYPES OF COMMERCIALS

1. Station-break Announcements

Radio commercials with the same theme used for twenty-second and one-minute versions.[2]

ANNCR: Now <u>Kraft</u> brings you a wonderful timesaver! It's <u>Cheez
        Whiz</u> -- a delicious pasteurized process cheese spread that
        starts to <u>melt</u> the minute it touches <u>hot food</u>. <u>Spoon</u>
        Cheez Whiz into hot macaroni. Or <u>heat it</u> for a smooth
        cheese sauce. Or <u>spread it</u> for snacks and sandwiches.
        It's delicious! Get a jar of <u>Kraft's Cheez Whiz</u>!

ANNCR: Have <u>you</u> tried <u>Cheez Whiz</u> -- Kraft's exciting, <u>new</u> pas-
        teurized process cheese food? Here's a remarkable <u>time-
        saver</u> for all kinds of hot cheese dishes. Cheez Whiz
        actually starts to <u>melt</u> the instant it touches hot food.
        You can <u>spoon it</u> right from the jar into macaroni or any
        hot dish. Or you can <u>heat it</u> for a perfect, golden cheese
        sauce. Or you can <u>spread it</u> on crackers or bread for
        quick snacks and sandwiches. Cheez Whiz is creamy-thick
        and smooth just as it comes from the jar. And it has a
        marvelous <u>rich</u> cheese flavor. Cheez Whiz is <u>completely</u>
        <u>different</u> from any other pasteurized process cheese
        spread you've ever had before. Try it. You'll discover
        dozens of ways to use it for fast cheese treats. Stop at
        <u>your</u> grocer's today, and take home a jar of Kraft's won-
        derful <u>Cheez Whiz</u>.

2. Participating Announcements

Television commercial on "Home" which is presented by the star, as well as by the program announcer.[3]

<u>(NATURAL SOUND: TINKLE OF NEWS
BELLS)</u>

HUGH DOWNS:
(OFF CAMERA: READING OVER
SOUND OF BELLS)

It's coffee time...with WEAR-
EVER ALUMINUM COFFEE MAKERS!

Ah...that's always good news,
Hugh...because it means that
it's time to talk about the
best way to make delicious
coffee.

CLOSE SHOT: NEWS HEADLINER:
"IT'S COFFEE TIME...WITH
WEAR-EVER ALUMINUM COFFEE
MAKERS":

CLOSE SHOT OF ARLENE
FRANCIS UPSTAGE OF COOKING
AREA: ARLENE FRANCIS POURS
CUP OF COFFEE FROM ONE OF THE
COFFEE MAKERS: SHOULD BE <u>PERK</u>:

---

[2] Courtesy of Kraft Foods Company.
[3] Courtesy of The Aluminum Cooking Utensil Co., Inc.

Just be sure you use a WEAR-
EVER ALUMINUM COFFEE MAKER....

PULL BACK TO INCLUDE COFFEE
MAKERS IN SHOT WITH ARLENE
FRANCIS HANGING FROM END OF
COUNTER (UPSTAGE) IS A BANNER
THAT READS: "WEAR-EVER
ALUMINUM COFFEE MAKERS" AND
TWO BLOW-UPS. ONE A PERK AND
ONE A DRIP:

a PERK...or a DRIP.

ARLENE FRANCIS INDICATES EACH
OF THE COFFEE MAKERS ON CUE:

You can't go wrong...because
leading university scientists
designed the construction
that's used in WEAR-EVER'S
COFFEE MAKERS.

ARLENE FRANCIS POINTS TO OTHER
COFFEE MAKERS ON RANGE.
COUNTER AREA: PICKS UP A PERK
BEGINS TO TAKE OUT BASKET.

You see, the coffee basket has
just the right number of holes
...the right size...and in just
the right location--only across
the bottom. That means ALL the
water goes through ALL the
coffee...and at just the right
speed.

CLOSE SHOT OF COFFEE BASKET
AS ARLENE FRANCIS DEMONSTRATES
ON CUE:

That's why you get rich-
flavored coffee every time...
and that's why you use less
coffee and save money with
WEAR-EVER COFFEE MAKERS.

SHOT OF ARLENE FRANCIS STANDING
BY IDENTIFYING SIGN WITH THE
WEAR-EVER COFFEE MAKERS ON THE
RANGE BESIDE HER:

HUGH DOWNS:
You sure do, Arlene...and you
can get WEAR-EVER COFFEE MAKERS
in any size you want: from 2
to 16 cups.

CUT TO HUGH DOWNS STANDING AT
WEAR-EVER DISPLAY: HE HOLDS A
CUP OF COFFEE: CAMERA PANS
DISPLAY SLOWLY, INCLUDING SMALL
CARD THAT READS: "WEAR-EVER
ALUMINUM COFFEE MAKERS"!

Just make sure you say WEAR-
EVER ALUMINUM COFFEE MAKERS...
it's the name that's been
famous in America's kitchens
for over 50 years.

EXTREME CLOSE SHOT OF CARD,
SCENE 8, THAT READS: "WEAR-
EVER ALUMINUM COFFEE MAKERS":

3. Program Announcements

Television commercial on film for "Medic" [4]

VIDEO	AUDIO
SPOTLIGHTED HAND IN CORNER OF SCREEN. TURNING OFF ALARM.	From the moment that alarm goes off, you're off to the most frantic ninety minutes of your
FADE OUT HAND, FADE IN SECOND HAND IN SECOND CORNER OF SCREEN	day -- cooking breakfast... getting the children dressed

[4] Courtesy of the Dow Chemical Company.

HOLDING FRYING PAN. FADE OUT
SECOND HAND, FADE IN THIRD HAND
BUTTONING COAT. FADE OUT
THIRD, FADE IN FOURTH HAND IN
FOURTH CORNER OF SCREEN FIXING
LUNCH BOX. MONTAGE SHOT OF ALL
FOUR HANDS DOING VARIOUS JOBS.

DISSOLVE FROM ABOVE MONTAGE TO
MORE RELAXED SHOT OF HANDS
WORKING AT TABLE FIXING LUNCH
BOX.

DOLLY BACK TO SHOW SARAN WRAP
BOX ON THE TABLE NEXT TO
LUNCHBOX.

HANDS PULL OUT PIECE OF SARAN
WRAP FROM BOX AND WRAP CHICKEN
LEG. VCU OF WRAPPING JOB TO
SHOW CLINGING.

HANDS WRAP SLICED TOMATOES AND
HANDS PUT TOMATOES INTO
LUNCHBOX.

HANDS WRAP GREEN ONIONS AND PUT
THEM IN LUNCHBOX NEXT TO
WRAPPED PIECE OF CAKE.

DISSOLVE TO LUNCHBOX ON WORK-
BENCH OR SCHOOLTABLE WITH HAND
REACHING IN TO TAKE OUT AND
UNWRAP PIECE OF CAKE VCU OF
INSIDE OF BOX TO SHOW VISIBIL-
ITY OF ITEMS.

PAN TO SHOW BOX OF SARAN WRAP
ON TABLE. HAND PICKS UP BOX
AND BRINGS IT UP TO FULL
SCREEN.

for school...fixing lunch boxes
for the whole family. If you
only had three pairs of hands,
your job would be so easy.
Actually there's a way to cut
out the most time-consuming of
all those jobs -- preparing
lunches. It's Saran Wrap --
the crystalclear plastic wrap
that keeps more foods fresh
longer. Saran Wrap lets you
fix all your lunch box foods
the night before....and you
know they'll be fresh and
delicious when they're eaten
the next day. That's because
Saran Wrap is a moisture-proof
plastic that clings by itself.
Once it clings around food,
Saran Wrap becomes a tight
moisture barrier that just
won't let food freshness
escape. What's more, there's
just no end to the wonderful
variety of foods you can pack
with Saran Wrap. Take sliced
tomatoes, for instance...
neither their flavor nor their
juices can escape. Saran Wrap
is perfect for strong foods
like green onions and cheeses,
too...and you'll never have to
worry about a light, fluffy
piece of cake picking up the
flavor of the onions. If
you're looking for a way to put
new appetite appeal into the
lunch box -- or if you'd just
like a way to make life in the
kitchen easier, try a roll of
Saran Wrap tomorrow. It's sold
in food stores throughout the
United States and Canada.

(ALTERNATE CLOSING FOR SAME COMMERCIAL TO TIE IN
WITH SPRING LUNCHBOX PROMOTION)

DISSOLVE TO LIMBO SHOT OF
DISPLAY PIECE.

PAN TO VCU OF MENU SUGGESTION
CARD. HAND COMES IN AND TEARS
OFF COPY OF SUGGESTIONS FROM
CARD. HAND STILL HOLDING CARD
MOVES DOWN TO BIN CONTAINING
BOXES OF SARAN WRAP AND TAKES
OUT BOX. THEN BOX UP TO FULL
SCREEN.

Next time you're in your
favorite food store, look for
this display and especially for
this card of lunchbox menu
suggestions. Be sure to take
your copy of these menu suggestions home with you along with
a box or two of Saran Wrap.
Saran Wrap is sold in stores
throughout the United States
and Canada.

• FORMS OF RADIO COMMERCIALS •

No matter which type of commercial is being used, form must be considered. The time available governs the choice of form, but it does not rule out any of the following. Combinations of the different forms may be used:

1. Straight selling or description.   5. Dialogue.
2. Testimonial.   6. Humorous.
3. Educational.   7. Musical.
4. Multivoice.

Straight Selling or Description. This is the most common and most widely used. Principal advantages are directness and unified development of a single appeal. It depends on the announcer and "copy for the ear." A question often raised is "Should the announcer give the commercial as *his* personal recommendations?" The practice on most stations is for the announcer not to do so in regular staff work, but he may be permitted to do so on "personality shows." Statements such as, "Come to *our* store" and *"We* have been doing business in the same location" tend to confuse the station and sponsor relationship. The usual practice is to avoid them unless they are phrased as quotations from the sponsor.

Testimonial. This may be a personal recommendation by the program star, announcer, or guest, or a quotation from a celebrity or "satisfied user." Testimonials can impart additional impact, due to the feeling of gratitude many listeners have. They may try a product recommended by a radio "friend," the announcer or the star. If this appeal is not tactfully presented it may induce a negative reaction. The indirect method is used by many comedians. The Gillette Razor Company and R. J. Reynolds Company (Camel cigarettes) often use testimonial copy.

Educational. This form may be used when the writer is using "long-circuit" or "reason-why" appeals. "They provide information for the consumer who does deliberate before he makes a purchase, comparing values and weighing pros and cons . . . They are most used in the advertising of products which are rather high in price . . . and consumed only over a relatively long period of time." [5] The Sunbeam Corporation and The DuPont Company use this type of commercial extensively.

Multivoice. This may consist of a series of alternate voices in climactic arrangement; a question-and-answer frame which permits an abrupt beginning; a device for pinpointing attention on a slogan or phrase; or reinforcement through repetition.

Dialogue. These commercials may be simple in form or little productions complete with sound effects and music. An announcer may engage in conversational banter with the performer. Daytime serials have utilized a fic-

[5] Albert W. Frey, *Advertising* (New York, 1947), p. 168.

tional character such as "Granny" or "Cousin Mary" who, in conversation with the announcer, speaks with authority about household duties. Some sponsors use the playlet idea by incorporating the "Boy-meets-girl, boy-loses-girl, boy-wins-girl!" formula into the commercial. Dialogue commercials win attention and interest, but listeners resent commercials that are too far-fetched or too glowing in the claims made for the product. The humorous form is an outgrowth of dialogue technique.

Humorous. Humorous commercials are frequently used on comedy programs, and also by disc jockeys and personality "salesmen" such as Arthur Godfrey. The Jack Benny radio series used the Sportsmen Quartet with especially prepared lyrics to popular songs. This same technique has been transferred to Jack Benny's television series. The sound track from humorous cartoon-type television commercials may also be employed for transcribed radio spots.

Musical Commercials. Musical commercials are widely used. Some of them have original melodies; others are based on popular songs or themes from the classics. "Chiquita Banana" became so intriguing in 1944-1945 that it was published as a popular song. Singing commercials are usually transcribed or filmed. Vocal stars such as Rosemary Clooney and Vaughn Monroe may be featured. As noted above, additional use for the sound track of filmed television musical commercials may be obtained via transcribed radio announcements.

EXAMPLES OF DIFFERENT FORMS
OF RADIO COMMERCIALS

1. Westinghouse Refrigerator [6]

This announcement is primarily straight selling, but it utilizes the multivoice technique for attention at the opening. The first portions are transcribed. The closing paragraph is presented live in order to permit identification of local Westinghouse dealers.

```
ANNCR I:      (LOW, LOW BASS VOICE)  Low...low...low
ANNCR II:     Yes, right now for the lowest price ever...you can
              get a brand-new WESTINGHOUSE Frost-Free Refriger-
              ator.  It's the kind of refrigerator you've always
              wanted.  It's Frost-Free!  No defrosting in the
              Refrigerator and no defrosting in the Freezer.  No
              mess...no bother.  And it's a big family-size
              WESTINGHOUSE Food-File Refrigerator...with a full-
              width Freezer...roll-out shelves...special places
              for fresh vegetables...eggs...butter...and fruit.
              And remember -- you can get this brand-new WESTING-
```

[6] Courtesy of Westinghouse Electric Corporation and McCann-Erickson, Inc.

HOUSE Frost-Free Refrigerator now at the lowest
price in history!

LOCAL ANNCR: Trade-in now and save! Yes, (DEALER'S NAME) is
offering such a liberal trade-in allowance on your
old refrigerator...you just can't afford not to get
a brand-new WESTINGHOUSE Frost-Free. Pay as little
as $_____ a week. See (DEALER'S NAME AND ADDRESS)
today!

2. A & P Food Stores [7]

This commercial from "The Margaret Arlen Program" combines dialogue and personal endorsement by the featured woman's commentator.
Harry Marble is the program announcer. He also participates in the interviews with guests as well as in discussions on topics of the day with Miss
Arlen.

ARLEN: This may sound like double talk Harry...but do you know
a half a ham isn't a half of ham?

MARBLE: Margaret, I don't see how a half of ham can ever be
anything but just that.

ARLEN: Well, at A & P they don't consider a half a ham the real
thing unless it's a full half a ham...that is a ham from
which the choice center slices have not been removed.

MARBLE: Oh - then you can buy half hams without the center
slices, in other stores?

ARLEN: Yes - but of course it isn't fair to have to pay the
same price for a half ham without the center slices as
for a half ham with the center slices.

MARBLE: And you don't - at A & P.

ARLEN: No. At A & P you can buy your ham six different ways.
For 65¢ a pound you can buy a whole ham...a full shank
half...or a full butt half. For 99¢ a pound...you can
buy the center slices.:.for 57¢ a pound, the butt
portion...and for 49¢ a pound, the shank portion.

MARBLE: I see - at A & P when you buy a half ham you get all the
choice center slices with it - your full money's worth.

ARLEN: You bet you do. And speaking of money it strikes me
that A & P can save you a tidy sum when you shop there.

MARBLE: Remember...A & P's hams are not only priced to give you
the most for your money...but they're all top-quality,
famous brands, specially selected. So, if you're planning to have a ham for the Fourth...better select it at
A & P.

ARLEN: And if you want some other ideas on how to get more good
food for your money...read A & P's ads. Then Shop at
A & P...and see for yourself how much further your money
goes.

[7] Courtesy of The Great Atlantic and Pacific Tea Company and WCBS, New York
City.

3. Vitalis [8]

This announcement illustrates a multivoice form.

ANNCR: Men, in case you didn't happen to know...and you probably didn't...today is a very special day. We're calling it "Advice-for-Men-Who-Don't-Know Day."

MAN: Men who don't know what, Fred?

ANNCR: How to make their best girls greet them with...

GIRL: Hello handsome!

MAN: Say...I could use that advice myself.

ANNCR: Well, remember, good looks begin at the top. Good looks begin with good looking hair.

MAN: But I've got dry hair that never stays put. What's the answer?

ANNCR: Vitalis is the answer! For Vitalis contains natural vegetable oils that keep your hair under control...and with that natural, masculine look. No mineral oil...no slick, greasy shine. In addition, Vitalis and the famous sixty-second workout brings you an extra advantage so many hair preparations cannot provide.

MAN: Something special?

ANNCR: Yes, it's that distinctive "Vitalis feel"...that wonderfully refreshing, scalp stimulation. So...if you want her to say...

GIRL: Hello handsome!

ANNCR: Get Vitalis...available now at drug counters and barbershops everywhere.

4. Ford Cars [9]

This announcement illustrates a musical one-minute commercial which features "name" personalities. These transcribed commercials were prepared for Ford dealers to use on local radio stations prior to the first public showings of the new models of Ford cars.

(Tune: "Where Will the Dimple Be?")

ANNOUNCER: Now Rosemary Clooney and Mitch Miller have news about the '56 Ford.

BASS: When will it be?

CLOONEY: Oh the kissin' cousin of the Thunderbird
Arrives September twenty-third.
That's when the big new Ford bows in.
In power and style its Thunderbird kin.
New Lifeguard design in this Ford you'll see
Friday's when it will be.

[8] Courtesy of Bristol-Myers Company.
[9] Courtesy of Ford Division of Ford Motor Company and J. Walter Thompson Co.

BASS: <u>When will it oe?</u>

CLOONEY: On September twenty-third,
           Oh the very latest word
           In new cars at your Ford Dealer's you will find.
           Ford's a fine car--and what's nice
           It's at half the fine-car price.
           And Ford's safer 'cause Ford's got Lifeguard design.

CLOONEY: Oh th' kissin' cousin of the Thunderbird
           Arrives September twenty-third.
           That's when the big new Ford bows in.
           Power and style, it's Thunderbird kin.
           Lifeguard design in this Ford you'll see
           Friday's when it will be.

5. Western Union [10]

This commercial, which was presented on NBC's "Monitor," combines multivoice, music, and straight selling.

JINGLE #2 (RECORD)	Song:	It's wise to wire --
	Voice:	(ON FILTER) Western Union --
	MOM & DAD:	Happy birthday, dear son, (OR: Greetings to you, dear son) (OR: Best wishes, dear son)
	VOICE:	Western Union --
	MAN:	Close deal by wire -- each minute counts!
	VOICE:	Western Union --
	GIRL:	I'll arrive tomorrow on the 8:01! (OR: I'll arrive tomorrow on the 8:03!)
	VOICE:	Western Union --
	MAN:	It's a boy! Seven pounds one ounce! (OR: It's a boy! And he looks like me!)
	SONG:	Good news travels faster by Western Union, It's wise to wire!
	ANNCR: (LIVE)	Going away next weekend? Suppose the resort you're going to is filled when you get there? Don't take chances... check on your reservation right now... by Telegram. And ask for a confirmation by wire. It takes only a few minutes and you'll be <u>sure</u> of getting just the space you want. And remember, you now get 15 words to start with in every fast wire...that's right 15. Just call Western Union and --

[10] Courtesy of Western Union Telegraph Company and Albert Frank-Guenther Law, Inc.

```
JINGLE #1                    Send it -- Western Union, Western
(RECORD)                     Union, Western Union, Western Union!
                             It's wise to wire!
```

NOTE: MUSICAL JINGLE RECORDINGS <u>IMMEDIATELY PRECEDE AND IMMEDI-</u>
<u>ATELY FOLLOW</u> LIVE COPY. <u>THERE SHOULD BE NO PAUSE.</u>

· WRITING COMMERCIAL COPY ·

In writing radio announcements, the seven points discussed in Chapter 19 should be kept in mind: (1) Gain attention quickly, (2) rococo in language should go, (3) use simplicity in sentence style, (4) repeat with skillful rephrasing and restatement, (5) build word pictures, (6) talk it out, and (7) "stick to your own last." In writing commercial copy you may be writing announcements to be read by someone other than yourself. If so, familiarize yourself with that person's air personality.

The basic appeal to be used for motivating acceptance and purchase of a commercial product is the first thing to be decided by the writer. One or more appeals may be chosen from our basic and impelling motives: the desire for good food and drink, comfortable surroundings, escape from pain and danger, sexual satisfaction, social prestige, and pride.

After choosing your basic appeals, consider the make-up of the audience that will hear the announcement. Note the time and day of the broadcast, and the age and buying habits of potential listeners. Examine the station's programming profile and select the appeal for individuals who may be attracted by such offerings. Study any marketing surveys that have been made for the station. People have local habits, likes and dislikes: in some areas, brown eggs are preferred, whereas white eggs are preferred in others. Your community may rank high in home ownership, another in apartment rentals. There may be differences in shopping habits. "In Washington, D. C. . . . Friday is more than twice as important a shopping day as Wednesday, whereas Friday in Cincinnati is only one-fourth as important as Wednesday. In Houston, Texas, Monday is the most important shopping day, about one-and-one eighth as important as Saturday." [11] Different areas and different groups respond to different motive appeals. Whereas "style for social prestige" may be the best appeal for a college set, "long wear and economy" may be the best for low-income or rural areas. The specific individual in a special environment must be considered in selecting the appeal.

The particular product must also enter into the selection of appeals. A copywriter may have to prepare copy for a shoe store that wants to stress a certain line of men's shoes. "Style" and "price" appeals are usually used in such copy, but in an area where there are poor transportation facilities and walking long distances is common, "feel" and "fit" appeals stressing comfort may be more effective. Questions like the following should be

[11] H. W. Hepner, *Effective Advertising* (New York, 1949), p. 47.

asked: "Is this product a new and unfamiliar one?" "Is it a luxury or necessity?" "Is it an inexpensive product bought on impulse or one purchased
after considerable thought and planning?" "Is it seasonal or all year round?"
"Who purchases it, men or teen-age boys?"

An example of the type of consumer analysis helpful to a copywriter is
the classification of women into sales-approach types published by the
Printz-Biederman Company of Cleveland, a women's clothing manufacturer.
The analysis is included here to indicate how a station-staff writer may get
away from stock appeals in preparing spot announcements.

1. *The young unmarried woman:* She is very sensitive about the opinion
   of others. She is susceptible to offense where the fatness of her own or her
   family's pocketbook is in question. If the girl is in business, she can be
   talked to on the topic of durability, but beware of allowing her to feel
   that you have the least idea that her life outside her business hours is not
   as frivolous and full of pleasure as that of her idle sisters.
2. *The young married woman, without children:* She wants becomingness
   and style. She wants to look more attractive than anyone else to her
   husband and wants the other young matrons with whom she spends her
   time to see that her husband can and does give her as beautiful, if not
   more beautiful, things than any of them have.
3. *The young married woman, with children:* She is less concerned about
   becomingness and style and more concerned about price and durability.
   She still has her youth and her little vanities, but she is beginning to plan
   for a family as well as to be a charming young lady. This makes her
   wiser, more practical, and more careful in her purchases.
4. *The middle-aged unmarried woman:* She is interested in dressing in such
   a way as to appear still young. She is usually interested in quality and fit.
   If she is of the slender- or heavy-figure type, she wishes to minimize her
   bad points and make the most of her good ones.
5. *The middle-aged married woman, without children:* Appeal to her is very
   much the same as to the unmarried woman of her age group, but with
   less emphasis on price and rather more on style, fit, and becomingness as
   factors which tend to increase her own self-esteem and her husband's
   pride in her.
6. *The middle-aged woman, with children:* The main consideration is price.
   She must make those dollars go as far as she possibly can and still not
   be a disappointment to her children and their friends.
7. *The elderly unmarried woman:* She is appealed to by becomingness,
   workmanship, and in some cases by style. Quality appeals more and more
   strongly to her as she grows older, especially if she has grown older
   gracefully and dresses with dignity and real beauty.
8. *The elderly married woman, without children:* Women of this age group
   are apt to have unusual figures. These customers must never be made
   to feel that they are ugly and impossible to fit. Garments should be sold
   to them which minimize stooped shoulders or other ungraceful features.
   If the customer is in an income group below the average, more stress
   must be laid on the price factor. And where the individual is socially
   prominent, more emphasis is put on style.
9. *The elderly married woman, with children:* She is keenly interested
   in the way she appears to her children. For this reason more money is

often spent and more care taken in the choice of the garment than is the case where only she and her husband need be pleased.

10. *The unmarried professional or business woman:* She has a healthy curiosity about the workmanship and about processes of manufacture.

11. *The married professional or business woman:* In addition to the interests of the unmarried professional woman she is also interested in becomingness for the sake of the husband. She has greater confidence in the article if she is taken behind the scenes a little and is shown the why's and wherefore's.

· WRITING TELEVISION COMMERCIALS ·

In the preceding section we stressed the importance of the copywriter's selecting the proper appeals for the theme of the radio commercial in order to relate the announcement to the needs and wants of the consumer. The proper choice of effect is equally important in writing television commercials. Information from marketing studies to determine *who* the potential customers are, *where* they live, and *when* they buy, are also needed in preparing television copy. In planning and writing the actual commercial, one must avoid the error of thinking that the pictures on the screen merely illustrate and reinforce the spoken copy. The commercial must be approached with primary consideration for what can be shown on the screen. Words should not be used to describe what can be easily demonstrated visually.

When sight was added to sound in broadcasting, it brought with it the variety and flexibility provided by action, staging, costumes, cards, still photographs, special graphic devices, slides and moving pictures. Many new and different ways of presenting announcements resulted. As one advertising agency executive expressed it, "Think of what the copywriter has to work with! For his television commercial he can draw on radio, movies, the legitimate theater, musical comedy, magazines, billboards, animation—yes, even skywriting. The only thing he's limited by is his imagination. And his client's budget." [12]

The contrast between various advertising media has been described by another agency executive as follows:

Advertising in magazines and newspapers always has presented the limitations of space. You can't have a dramatic picture of a boy eating a piece of pie, *and* a huge mouth-watering photograph of the rest of the pie from which the boy's piece was cut, *and* a recipe for making the pie, *and* a striking illustration of your product that makes the pie look and taste so good, *and* the several convincing reasons why—*all* the way you want them in any affordable space unit that I know.[13]

[12] Joseph A. Moran, "Commercials: How They Got That Way," *Broadcasting-Telecasting,* September 28, 1953, p. 123.

[13] Fairfax M. Cone, "10 TV Commercials I Wish We Had Made," *Broadcasting-Telecasting,* December 7, 1953, p. 90.

He points out that in print it may be possible either to picture the boy's satisfaction or the pie and that in radio you may only talk about the picture or product. However, in the television commercial *all* elements may be included.

The Television Story Board. The story board is a series of drawings, or "roughs" which show the sequence of picture action, optical effects, settings and camera or shooting angles, with caption notations indicating what words, sound effects, and music are to be heard as the sequence is presented. The story board resembles the layouts used extensively in agencies preparing advertisements for print. This technique has had its widest use in television filmed commercials, but it is becoming increasingly important for live studio commercial presentations as well. Since the commercial is presented on a visual medium, the use of the story-board technique is helpful for the copywriter because from the beginning it requires him to think in terms of the pictures. In addition, those who have to approve the commercial—agency executives and the sponsor—have an opportunity to appraise the visualization of the copy. Without the story board, different people reading a script may have markedly different impressions of what will actually be seen on the air.

The cost of studio rehearsal and film does not allow much leeway for experimentation and basic changes during the final stages of production. It is better, therefore, to check and recheck any questionable details in the commercial during the story-board stage. In order to anticipate any possible studio shooting problems, the director for the commercial usually is given an opportunity to review the story board. In this way, he can eliminate unpractical or impossible action and staging. Besides acting as a check against possible errors, the story-board technique makes it possible for creative artists connected with the production to suggest to the writer small changes or touches that will increase the impact of the commercial. Various agencies and production firms utilize different formats for their story boards. An example appears on pages 352-354.

• FORMS OF TELEVISION COMMERCIALS •

The forms of television commercials roughly approximate the forms of radio commercials discussed earlier; straight selling, testimonial, dialogue, etc. Because the method of presentation is so varied and flexible, however, it seems wise to classify the forms of television commercials with the elements of variety and flexibility in mind.

Live—with Talent in View. An announcer, or specialized talent, is usually seen during the commercial. The amount of time on camera varies considerably. He may be on the screen for practically the entire period, standing by the product if it is large, such as a car, or displaying the package if it is small, such as holding a box of cereal. He may show charts or cut-away

EXAMPLE OF STORY-BOARD FORMAT
JELL-O INSTANT PUDDING

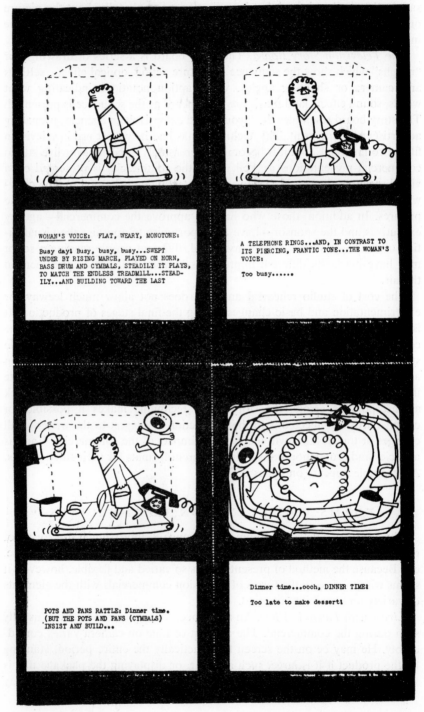

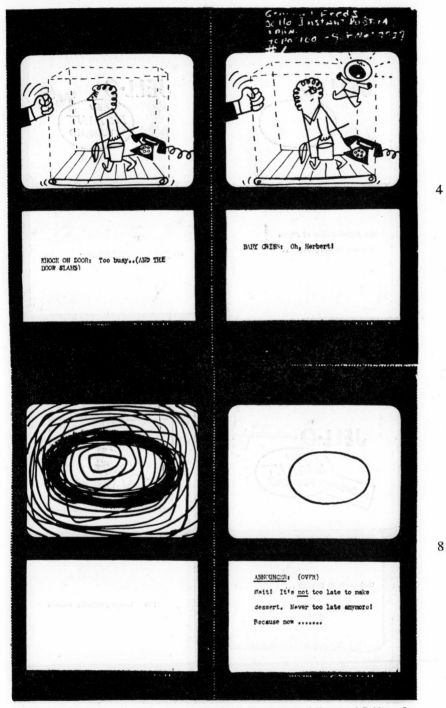

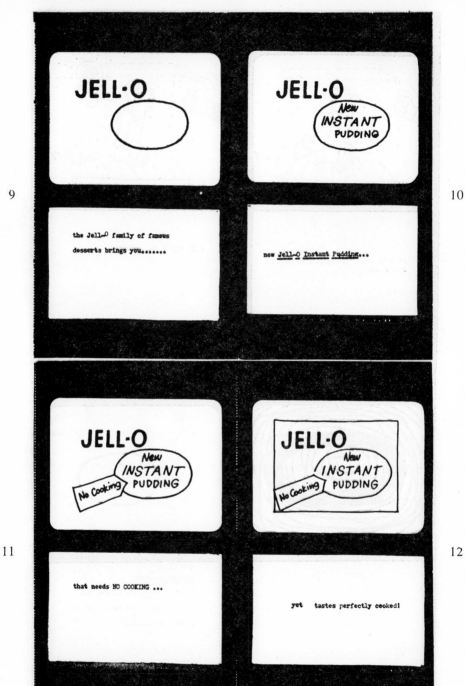

sections, he may demonstrate its action and point out main features. Key words, specific prices, and slogans may be superimposed or shot full-screen. The announcer usually handles the display of the product or the demonstration. His personality is supposed to add to his persuasive appeal. His presentation carries with it his personal endorsement, implicitly or explicitly conveyed. Consequently, this form of commercial is often employed on programs in which the star can also act as salesman. This method is not too expensive and allows for considerable variation. It is considered to be well suited for daily programs broadcast over local stations.

Live—Voice Over. This method of presentation focuses attention on the visual aspects of the product display and the demonstration. Several subdivisions may be noted:

1. Talent may be seen as they display the product or demonstrate, but the audio comes from off camera.

2. Slides, photographs, or cards may be shown on the screen. This is a common method used for local station-break commercials and sustaining promotional announcements.

3. Silent film footage may be projected. Many product displays and demonstrations cannot be produced live in the studio. Film is used instead. This method may be used to aid local accounts by stations that have facilities for shooting film. A cover shot and a slow pan, showing many used cars may serve, together with appropriate audio commentary, as an effective commercial for a used-car dealer. Stock footage such as shots of scenic views in the West may be used for a lead into a local travel-agency spot.

Film—Realistic Action. Essentially the same approaches are used as those described for the live commercials. Film insures that the commercial will be presented in an approved form without the danger of slips of tongue or errors in production. When talent forgets lines, stumbles over the name of the product or gives the competitive product's name, or when demonstrations fail to work, all of which instances have happened on the air in live commercials, the take is discarded.[14]

---

[14] The following off-the-air transcription illustrates what may happen in a live commercial. The scene is in a shop following the completion of a dramatic scene.

Clerk: Well, the police say they got the man who led it. That's something anyway.

Customer: I hope they got the right one.

Clerk: Well, I'm not 100% sure about that myself (fluffed 100%)

Customer: Well, cheer up. Here's something you were 100% right about—(Blank) cigarettes—the most unusual cigarettes I've ever tasted.

Clerk: That's what I told you,—the nicotine is reduced but not your enjoyment.

Customer: Oh, I believe you about the nicotine. After all (pause and cough) you showed me uh writing here on the uh.

Clerk: Yeah, guaranteed less than 1% less nicotine. And as I pointed out the guarantee refers only to the tobacco in (Blank) cigarettes.

Customer: I understand that too, yessir. Absolutely less tobacco in the nicotine. Absolutely less tobacco in the cigarette itself.

Only the "right" takes are used. Film increases flexibility and permits effects which cannot be attained in live presentation. An example of this is the contrast between "before" and "after" in a shampoo commercial.

Film—Nonrealistic Action. Many different production techniques are available to those who create commercials: dancing, electronic effects, cartoons, puppets, animation, and stop-motion photography. These commercials usually have music, vocals, signature melodies or music to reinforce the mood and backing for words and action. Many humorous announcements use this form. Detailed explanations of a technical nature may be presented in an entertaining and informative manner. New ways may be explored to express commercial messages visually. John Baxter of the Earle Ludgin Advertising Agency, says that

> A writer of a television commercial should be as concerned about his pictures as he is about his words. When we planned this series for Manor House, [included in this chapter] practically all the TV commercials for instant coffees presented their case to the public in pretty much the same manner. They had a picture showing how easy this product was to use. Invariably, the announcer put a spoonful into a cup, added hot water, and stirred. This was usually followed by a lip smacking picture to indicate how good the product tasted.
>
> This posed quite a problem for us.
>
> To avoid the usual pictorial clichés, we sought for new ways to bring our message to the public visually. It was this kind of thinking that led us into the present series which employs abstract patterns to illustrate words rather than the usual literal picture.

Combination. Commercials, live or film, often employ more than one of the different types of presentation. Many different combinations may be observed on the air. For example, the announcer may be seen live for a few seconds, followed by film. Realistic action may be framed with a filmed cartoon opening and closing. Some of the commercials, especially film commercials, are designed to permit the extraction of a twenty-second station-break announcement from the matrix of the one-minute version. Some advertisers require that the announcements be planned so that the audio may be put on transcription and be used on radio.

Clerk: Well uh there's actually less than $\frac{1}{10}$ of 1% nicotine in a (Blank) smoke, by scientific measurement. Now that's less nicotine than in any leading cigarette.

Customer: I know, with less nicotine, well (Blank) cigarettes are the best cigarettes I have ever tasted.

Clerk: Well, that wonderful (Blank) taste clinches it for you.

Customer: That's right (long pause). You give me a carton of (Blank) cigarettes.

Clerk: Right you are, and say, will you do me a favor?

Customer: Yep.

Clerk: Will you please tell your friends the minute they start smoking (Blank) cigarettes they can stop worrying about nicotine (jerkily). There's your change. Thank you very much.

Customer: Thank you.

Check List for Increasing Effectiveness of TV Commercials. NBC has released the findings of a special Schwerin Research Corporation study dealing with television commercial effectiveness. The results are applicable in a discussion of television announcements. A brief summary of the key points follows: [15]

1. Correlate audio and video. Failure to observe this simple rule was often found to have been overlooked. A commercial for a baking mix which stressed quality of ingredients was discovered to have greater impact when the video showed the items which went into the mix, milk, eggs, etc., at the same time each item was mentioned, as contrasted to the identical audio message delivered while the video showed a housewife merely using the mix. The double sensory impression fixed the sales point more firmly.

2. Demonstrate. . . . Demonstrate. . . . Demonstrate. People are more likely to remember advertiser's claims when they see them proved by demonstrations. A sales idea in a cleanser announcement was that the product makes it easy to clean greasy pans. One approach, which showed the housewife holding a cleanser in one hand and the cleaned frying pan in the other, was not as effective as an alternate approach, in which the TV audience followed the process as the housewife started with a greasy pan and used the cleanser to demonstrate its speed, ease, and efficiency of operation. The research study emphasis is that far-fetched demonstrations or those which smack somewhat of the sleight-of-hand are less successful than realistic demonstrations.

3. Keep it simple. The number of elements and the way in which they are to be presented should be kept as simple as possible. When cause-and-effect sequences were utilized, it was found that when the effect was described first followed by the cause, it was usually more effective. A clear recapitulation of the sales points aids the impact. Tricky camera effects may be effective, but often a complicated approach may weaken the results. When the effects strengthen the sales point, however, they may reinforce the sales point. An illustration of this was found in the reaction to one commercial in which the announcer held a product while he explained what it was not. Results were poor. However, an alternate approach utilizing stop-motion photography was very effective. The camera focused on a row of products clearly identifiable as a soap, a cream, a lotion, and finally the advertised product. When the announcer said the product wasn't soap, the bar of soap disappeared; when he explained it wasn't a lotion, the bottle of lotion was eliminated. When he finally said that the product was absolutely unique, there was nothing on the screen but the product itself.

4. Use the right personality. The person who is chosen to represent the product and present the idea should be compatible with the product or idea and his identity and function should be clearly conveyed. Voice over audio appeared to be less effective than when the presenter talked directly to the viewers or identified himself and introduced the commercial message prior to the voice over. The Schwerin findings indicated that, when appropriate, the use of an "authority" increases impact. The person selected by the advertiser as the authority, however, may not be regarded by viewers as the person best qualified to present claims for the product. Thus, in several deodorant commercials the use of a white-coated druggist as the

[15] Courtesy National Broadcasting Company, abstracted from "How to Increase Effectiveness of Television Commercials."

authority was not nearly as effective as the testimony of a typical woman. The misuse of authority may weaken the sales point. The sales theme for commercials of a prepared baking mix was that the mix makes it simple to achieve perfect baking results. In one commercial the authority was a chef in a test kitchen who was shown pulling some pastry out of an oven and explaining how simple it was to insure consistent baking success by using this mix. It was not as effective as a second commercial in which the same sales point was made by a little girl, who was exceedingly proud of the pastry she had just made with the product.

Certainly the professional chef outranked the child as a culinary authority. But in this instance he was too expert for the advertiser's purpose. What was simple for him might not be easy for the average housewife. He was therefore, not nearly as desirable a spokesman for the advertiser's sales point as the little girl. If she could use this product and get good results with it, obviously any housewife would be able to obtain the same results.

Distractions of any kind reduce the sales effectiveness of a commercial. A scantily clad model diverted attention away from a sales message. The advantages from the use of the star of a program were not clear cut—the results depended on how he or she was used. The mere presence of the star holding the advertised package did not automatically insure greater impact. The star had seriously to assume the role of a commercial spokesman.

5. Keep the setting authentic. Every element in the setting should contribute to the impression the advertiser wishes to make. Commercial personalities who were out of place in the setting such as a program MC attempting to demonstrate a baking mix were less effective than a beaming mother bringing muffins (made with the advertised mix) to the family group at the table. Additional sensory impressions should be used when possible to increase impact. In a commercial for a pancake flour, a steaming plate of hot-cakes was shown being brought to the table. The dialogue was full of praise for the color, lightness, and taste of the hot-cakes. The setting was right. However, an extra setting, a camera shot of the pancake just about done on the griddle was inserted ahead of the sequence noted above and increased the impact through another favorable sensory impression—hot-cakes on the griddle.

EXAMPLES OF DIFFERENT FORMS OF TELEVISION COMMERCIALS

1. "Kraft Television Theater" Commercial [16]

This dramatic series has long featured the preparation of recipes. The announcer is not visible. The commercial is presented live. Different stages in the preparation of the recipes are illustrated.

VIDEO	AUDIO
DISSOLVE TO SLIDE READING "KRAFT TELEVISION THEATRE."	ANNCR: (VOICE OVER): We'll be back in a moment with some news about next week's show. But first...the Kraft Foods Company

[16] Courtesy of Kraft Food Company.

DISSOLVE TO MCU OF SERVING
BOWL FROM WHICH HANDS ARE
SPOONING SALAD MIXTURE INTO
INDIVIDUAL DISHES.

has this tasty salad idea borrowed from Italy to show you.
Italians call it "Insalata
Mista"...Kraft's good cooks
call it "Vegetable Medley"...
but whatever you call it...it's
delicious because you make it

DISSOLVE TO WORK SURFACE ON
WHICH IS AN OPEN HYDRATOR
FILLED WITH DEWY-FRESH VEGE-
TABLES. BESIDE THIS, IN FORE-
GROUND, IS A BOTTLE OF ITALIAN
DRESSING, AND, NOT SO PROMI-
NENTLY, A JAR OF STUFFED
OLIVES. ON CUE, HAND SHOWS
DRESSING BOTTLE TO CAMERA, SETS
IT DOWN, THEN SHOWS VEGETABLES
FROM HYDRATOR, AND THE BOTTLE
OF OLIVES.

with wonderful new Kraft
Italian Dressing...along with
these other good things...red,
ripe tomatoes...crisp cucumber
...and onion...crunchy celery
...and pimento stuffed olives.

DISSOLVE TO HANDS ADDING
CHOPPED CUCUMBER TO CHOPPED
TOMATOES IN SERVING BOWL.
HANDS ADD CHOPPED ONION.

Here's the easy way we do it:
We're adding one cup of
chopped, peeled cucumber to
three cups of chopped, peeled
tomatoes. Next we'll put in
half a cup of chopped onion...
cut a little finer than the tomatoes and cucumber.

HANDS ADD SLICED CELERY AND
STUFFED OLIVES.

Here we're adding one cup of
thinly sliced celery...and half
a cup of sliced, stuffed
olives. So....

HANDS PICK UP BOTTLE OF ITALIAN
DRESSING AND START TO SHAKE IT
VIGOROUSLY, TURNING IT COM-
PLETELY UPSIDE DOWN TO RE-BLEND
INGREDIENTS.

now we're ready for the Kraft
Italian Dressing...it's really
terrific! A light...clear...
oil-and-vinegar base...seasoned
with rare herbs and spices...
and a little onion and garlic.
We're shaking the bottle thoroughly...to re-blend the perfectly proportioned ingredients

HANDS OPEN BOTTLE AND POUR
DRESSING ON VEGETABLES, STIR
WITH SPOON TILL VEGETABLES ARE
WELL COATED.

before we pour the Kraft
Italian over the vegetables.
Use enough to cover them...and
then stir gently till every
morsel is glistening...

DOLLY IN TO SHOW CU OF GLISTEN-
ING, DRESSING-COATED VEGETABLES
AS HAND SPOONS UP SALAD.

and coated with that fabulous
new flavor. Kraft Italian
clings to the salad makings...
doesn't slide off"...because of
a special pre-blending process.

DISSOLVE TO SHELF DISPLAY OF
KRAFT ITALIAN DRESSING. SHOP-
PER'S HAND GUIDES MARKET CART

Tomorrow...when you're shopping
...look for Kraft Italian
Dressing at your grocer's. This

ANIMATED COMMERCIAL

He rose to the occasion, went flying
through the air —

'till we put a stick of dynamite under-
neath his chair —

My brother was so lazy he wouldn't
move no-where —

INTO LOWER PORTION OF FRAME, REACHES UP AND SELECTS BOTTLE OF KRAFT ITALIAN AND SHOWS IT TO CAMERA FOR CU.	is the bottle to look for... with the
DISSOLVE TO CU OF LABEL.	shiny red and green and white label that says...Kraft Italian Dressing.

2. Smyth Van and Storage Company Animated Commercial [17]

This is a film commercial viewed on the Pacific Coast. A catchy "clap hands" rhythm which has a simple lilting melody is used. Different attention-getting verses are used. The story board on pages 360-361 illustrates one. Following the opening fourteen-second verse, changed from announcement to announcement, the same close is presented. It was produced by the Telepix Corporation of Hollywood and George Glavin and Grant Merrill, now of the Pacific National Advertising Agency, Seattle, Washington.

VIDEO	AUDIO
FURNITURE WITH FACES MARCHING DOWN THE STREET.	"Move me with Smyth the Smoother Mover, Smyth, not Smith, the Smoother Mover;
FURNITURE IN RHYTHM, MARCHES UP RAMP INTO PADDED VAN.	Put me in a padded van - and I'll be a happy man, Always a winner not a loser.
SMYTH VAN MOVES DOWN THE STREET.	Move me with Smyth the Smoother Mover, Smyth, not Smith, the Smoother Mover, No matter where he moves me - he'll handle me so smoothly,
PIX OF VAN WITH LETTER "Y" CHANGING TO "I" AND BACK TO "Y", VAN MOVES ON.	Smyth - not Smith, Smyth, not Smith, Smyth, the Smoother Mover. (CHEERS).

3. McLaughlin's Instant Manor House Coffee Announcement [18]

The story board on pages 363-365 illustrates a nonrealistic animated film commercial. It was prepared for W. C. McLaughlin & Company by Earle Ludgin & Company, Advertising.

• SUSTAINING ANNOUNCEMENTS •

Staff writers are responsible for preparing all noncommercial announcements. These usually consist of "public-service" announcements which may be of any type and form listed in the discussion of the commercial announce-

[17] Courtesy of George Glavin, Pacific National Advertising Agency.
[18] Courtesy of John H. Baxter, Earle Ludgin & Company.

A NONREALISTIC ANIMATED COMMERCIAL

1. Do you have a closed mind?

2. Lots of people bar themselves...
(BARS COME DOWN)

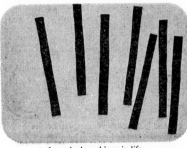

3. from the best things in life.

4. They stay off in a corner...

5. all by themselves.
(BARS FORM DOOR)

6. But may we ask you to open
your mind for a moment?

7. We'd like to tell you about a
brand new instant coffee.
(DOOR OPENS)

8. No, don't close your mind!
(DOOR SLAMS)

Courtesy, John H. Baxter, Earle Ludgin & Company

9. This is McLaughlin's Instant
Manor House Coffee!
(DOOR OPENS)

10. Everybody's talking about it!

11. Delightful! . . . What flavor! . . .
So easy to make! . . . Real coffee taste!
(QUOTES FORM)

12. And it all adds up because Real coffee
gives it that real coffee flavor!
(EACH QUOTE BECOMES A WORD)

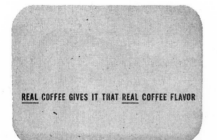

13. And that's not just talk!

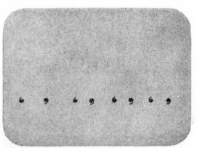

14. Yes, real coffee gives it that
real coffee flavor!
(WORDS CHANGE INTO QUOTES)

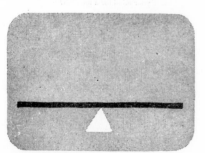

15. Actually, it's so concentrated, it
takes pounds of real coffee . . .
(QUOTES BECOME BAR)

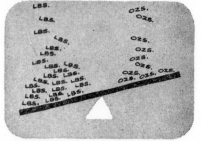

16. to make just ounces of McLaughlin's
Instant Manor House Coffee.

17. So in your house . . .

18. serve McLaughlin's . . .

19. Instant Manor House Coffee.

20. You'll like it instantly!
(DOOR CLOSES)

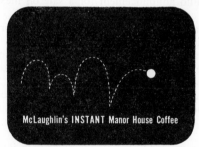

21. (DOORKNOB BECOMES BALL WHICH
BOUNCES OFF IN TIME WITH MANOR
HOUSE MUSICAL THEME.)

ments. They are broadcast during local and national drives for funds. Many of the same techniques and appeals are used. Reminders to vote, tolerance notes, traffic safety suggestions, information on special community events and what to do to meet disaster emergencies or epidemics come under this classification.

Stations also face the problem of keeping old and attracting new listeners. Promotional "on-the-air" announcements are prepared to acquaint the audience with the start of a new series, or to "billboard" coming program features. Variety in approach is necessary. One method frequently utilized is to assign a definite period for these announcements and work them into a program format. Interviews with personalities heard on the station is one device for entertainment "bait."

Projects and Exercises

1. Visit an advertising agency for a "behind-the-scenes" tour. Request one of the account executives to discuss a current advertising campaign.
2. Tune in a station for an assigned period. Report on the general motives appealed to, and specific forms used in the radio and television commercials.
3. Discuss the relative effectiveness of the above commercials.
4. Using the Printz-Biederman classification prepare commercials for women's clothing suitable for a local department store:
    (a) Straight radio announcement for a sale on inexpensive cloth winter coats.
    (b) Educational 150-word television commercial for live presentation on an expensive fur coat.
    (c) Commercial for a woman's participation program for introduction of a new line of smartly tailored classic suits. Alternate radio and television presentations.
    (d) Twenty-second jingle for station-break announcement which may be used on both radio and television. Suggest visual treatment for the television commercial. The subject should be inexpensive evening gowns.
5. Follow a specific program to become familiar with it. Then prepare appropriate radio or television commercials in harmony with the program and its current advertising campaign.
6. Prepare seasonal sixty-word radio station-break announcements, using actual companies and products in your area, as follows:
    (a) A toy store in the first week of December.
    (b) A florist in the week before St. Valentine's Day.
    (c) A sale of snow shovels by a local hardware store in November.
    (d) A dry cleaners company two weeks before Easter.
    (e) A garden supply store in the Spring.
    (f) A soft drink in the middle of Summer.
    (g) A used-car dealer's sale in September.
7. Prepare television commercials for the same companies. Presentations should be live or voice over. Discuss how film might be used.
8. Prepare musical commercials based upon public domain songs or current popular melodies.
9. Outline or sketch out in rough form a commercial story board.

☀ 22 ☀

Interviews, Quizzes, and Audience-Participation Shows

DIRECTORS of programs have found that, except in unusual circumstances, it is generally easier to hold an audience with an interview than with a straight talk. Quizzes and audience-participation shows are applications of the interview technique. An interviewer or MC on such programs must think not only of himself and his presentation, but he must always consider the answers and actions of those in the studio with him. Something may happen that makes the next question inappropriate; a contestant may become frightened or blurt out censorable material; a telephone call may not go through as planned; the correct identification of a mystery voice may occur before it is expected; a long-winded answer may upset the timing; all of these "surprise" factors must be anticipated in some degree and handled with apparent smoothness and assurance.

· INTERVIEWS ·

Interviews may be classified in three general types: (1) opinion, (2) information, and (3) personality. These may be presented entirely ad lib, from an outline, from a complete script, or by using a combination of these methods.

Opinion Interviews. The opinion interview is used throughout radio as a basic program frame. The "Man-on-the-Street" format is adapted to an individual station's requirements. An informal presentation is very common; an announcer stations himself on a busy corner and stops the passersby for a chat on the "topic of the day" which may range from "What would you do if someone gave you a million dollars?" to "Who will be the next President and why do you think so?" This cross-section of public opinion is interesting to the audience. They like to know what others are thinking. The newspapers used similar techniques long before broadcasting.

Adaptations of this approach may be observed in various programs. Members of the audience may be invited to write to the station about their pet peeves and the writers of the best letters asked to come to the station for an interview. A program may originate each week in a different location, inside a factory, in a private home, or at a railway terminal. A concealed microphone may pick up the reactions of persons unaware until afterwards that their words have been recorded for play-back on the air.

These programs are largely ad lib. The vernacular speech adds flavor. A prepared script would destroy the spontaneous conversational manner. The interviewer may have an outline, as a guide. He should prepare for the program whenever possible by reading about the subject. An audience may forgive the ignorance of the man in the street, but it expects an announcer to have more than a casual acquaintanceship with his subject. The interviewer must make sure that the "interviewee" is heard on the air with satisfactory volume. A few personal questions provide an opening wedge and let the interviewee forget about "mike fright." Instead of saying, "Now don't be shy" or "You're not scared of talking into a microphone are you?" which may cause the person to be nervous, he is asked something about himself or about the preceding guest's answers. The person begins to think about the topic. The microphone is held casually between the two of them. The less stress given to the "broadcast" angle, the more naturalness results. The questions should be phrased in such a way that the person will not answer "Yes" or "No," but if he does, more details should be requested. Abrupt transitions from one question to another should be avoided. The interviewer should lead into the next question by referring back to the preceding thought. Summaries and restatements for the listeners are desirable.

Information Interviews. This type of interview is used with great frequency in public-service programs. A doctor may give information on child care, a physicist on the Geiger counter, a social worker on the service of a Red Feather agency, a person from overseas on differences in habits of living. Many of these are completely scripted; if not, they are at least outlined and discussed in advance. Most persons have difficulty in reading from scripts. The writer must capture the individual's natural method of talking and not force formalized language and sentences upon him. Writers should talk to the person who is to be interviewed before preparing the script. Notes can be made listing specific phrases and expressions that come up in this preliminary conversation. These notes should be referred to, along with the writer's memory of the individual's style of speech, while preparing the script.

Enough time should be allowed for several complete microphone rehearsals ahead of the broadcast. The director handling the program should encourage the interviewee to make his own changes in the script to conform to his own conversational style. He should watch for words which seem to give difficulty and phrases which sound awkward when the person read's them aloud. Most interviews of this type sound artificial unless great care is taken both in writing the script and in rehearsing it. A good method is to have an outline of questions and ad-lib replies. The type of information interview where the announcer feeds the speaker a leading question and then retires into the background during a long reply is not desirable, however. This frame is nothing more than a thinly disguised talk and turns the interviewer into a stooge.

Whether a script is used or not, the audience should receive the impression that there is none. Repetition of words and phrases, conversational pauses and interruptions in the presentation may help in creating a general "first-time" naturalness.

A great responsibility rests upon the interviewer for preparation ahead of time. A young announcer may well take a lesson from Ben Grauer, who is recognized as a top man in his field. Grauer works hard before an interview, getting facts on the particular subject and reading extensively. He is not content to go into one without this preparation, even though he can handle almost any interview completely "cold," due to his long and varied experience.

Personality Interviews. In personality interviews the person interviewed is important primarily because of what has happened to him, what he has done, or because of the position he holds in the public eye. It may be a feature-story interview presented when the occasion arises, or built as a regular series. It may be a celebrity interview.

Feature-story interviews range from novelties and stunts to eyewitness accounts of disasters. Great flexibility and sensitivity must be possessed by the interviewers. Language and delivery must match the mood of the occasion. This seems obvious and yet announcers have been guilty of bad taste in pursuit of a feature interview after a disaster, capitalizing upon personal grief or using a type of delivery more suited to a sports account. When novelty or stunt interviews are conducted, an announcer must be careful not to seem superior or to be making fun of the "interviewee." An objective attitude may be hard to maintain when one encounters eccentrics who come into public attention through their activities. The audience may decide to ridicule the person on the basis of the interview, but the announcer should not slant it in that direction. Avoid correcting grammatical errors made by the interviewee or commenting on gaps in his knowledge. The audience does not like a smart-aleck interviewer, it prefers an interviewer who is genuinely interested in the subject of the interview.

One of the more successful celebrity interview series in the Midwest is the "Show World" series of Dick Osgood, broadcast over WXYZ, Detroit. Due to the high calibre of his interviewing, Osgood has the respect of the

stars who play the city. Osgood offers seven very practical rules for interviewing celebrities.

1. Know as much as possible about your subject.
2. Avoid obvious or trite questions.
3. Keep a file of background material.
4. Do not put the celebrity "on the spot" by asking questions that will
   embarrass him.
5. If you want information on a touchy subject, take an oblique or indirect
   approach before you get on the air.
6. Don't wait to talk with the celebrity until you are both on the air.
7. Give every personality the plush treatment.

• RADIO QUIZZES AND
AUDIENCE-PARTICIPATION SHOWS •

"I have a lady in the balcony, Doctor!"; "The $64,000 question"; "Aren't
we devils?"; "Think carefully, can you tell me . . ." These phrases represent
key expressions of quiz and audience-participation shows which have
brought pleasure to many, and condemnation by many. The personality of
the MC is one determining factor in effectiveness, and the program format
is the other.

The early quiz shows were simple in idea and production, such as a
spelling bee, a team of men pitted against women, or questions drawn out
of a basket. Variations on the standard formats were developed in the early
40's. By the end of the decade, quizzes and audience-participation programs
were so widespread that they were considered an economic threat to actors
and vocalists.

Quizzes may be classified in two general types:

1. A panel receives questions submitted by listeners. The contest element for the audience, necessary for interest, is in observing how well these
experts answer the questions, together with a race to guess the answers
ahead of the panel. A small prize is given for the use of the questions and
a larger amount is distributed in the event the experts fail to answer them
correctly.

2. Individuals are selected to answer the questions. These individuals
may be selected from the studio audience by a casual or chance selection;
by elimination contests during the warm-up period; or from those who
send in letters and are invited to come to the studio to participate. The
contestants may be selected from the radio audience, the names being
selected at random from telephone directories and the individuals called by
phone, or by a "best-written-letter" method. "Give-aways" have relied on
telephone selection in order to secure many listeners, each waiting for the
telephone to ring in his home. Some give-aways have permitted the studio
audience to compete when the telephone contestant failed to supply the
correct answer.

The audience-participation programs rely on stunts performed by participants for the entertainment of the audience. These stunts may range in complexity from a pie hurled in the face to elaborate and fantastic situations. "People Are Funny" describes its stunts as "basically psychological." The producers explain:

> Art Linkletter along with his partner and producer, John Guedel, and the gag men, employ basic human weaknesses and foibles as the fundamental beginnings of all stunts. Jealousy, greed, love, pride, fear, ambition and the innate hamminess of ordinary people are played upon and enlarged to major sized proportions for their stunts.
>
> Take the case of Mrs. Virginia Taylor of Pasadena, California. Mrs. Taylor had never attended any radio show until one Tuesday night when some friends took Mr. and Mrs. Taylor to the NBC studios to see "People Are Funny." During the warm-up Linkletter called for married couples without children. Mr. and Mrs. Taylor responded along with several other couples, won out over the others and found themselves in a typical "People Are Funny" predicament.
>
> Linkletter offered Mrs. Taylor one thousand dollars cash if she could keep quiet for one solid week. Mrs. Taylor said she could do it easily, probably thinking in her own mind that no one would be around to check on her. But she didn't count on the wacky Linkletter. Art sent a cute little movie starlet to their home to live with them, the stipulation being that if Mrs. Taylor spoke *one word,* for any reason, the starlet would get the thousand bucks. She not only didn't speak for one week, but refused to speak one word on the following Tuesday's show until Linkletter placed the one thousand dollars in her hands.[1]

Many more questions and stunts than one anticipates using should be available for emergencies. An audience-participation program with its elaborate stunts is more difficult to time than a quiz program. Extra stunts are prepared and held in readiness. These vary from very short "quickie" gags to longer ones.

"People Are Funny" refers to these quickies as "cuckoos." Here is an example: [2]

WHAT HUSBAND DOESN'T LIKE ABOUT YOU

Raleigh Cigarettes will give you 50 dollars if you can tell me what your husband doesn't like about you for the next 30 seconds without pausing.

If I can count to <u>five</u> during your pauses, you get no money.

Okay...Go!

(PRODUCER YELLS TIME)

IF LOSES: Here's a carton of Raleigh 903's and we'll send you a table radio.

The personality of the MC must be such as to inspire the confidence of participants. He must be extremely facile in identifying co-operative and stubborn contestants. He must be intelligent enough to know when a reply

[1] Courtesy of John Guedel Radio Productions.
[2] Courtesy of John Guedel Radio Productions.

other than the one marked on his script answers the question satisfactorily. He must keep the radio audience informed of the activities in the studio in order to keep them from feeling cheated. He must have contagious enthusiasm without artificiality. He must be able to take anything in his stride, from an off-color remark to microphone fright, and deal with it diplomatically. He must not appear to ridicule the contestants by reference to their nationality, race, or personal characteristics. He must be extremely fair and courteous to those on his program.

· DIRECTION ·

The informality and ad-lib factors in many interviews, quizzes, and audience-participation broadcasts do not permit much rehearsal before air time. This precludes advance timing. Adjustments must be made during the performance. When interviewees or contestants are going on the air for the first time, an entire course on microphone technique would serve to confuse rather than to put them at ease. A few simple instructions about distance from the microphone and how loud to talk are enough. A quick microphone-level check may help before the broadcast. If the person moves off mike during the broadcast, a signal to the announcer or MC can be given. A nonchalant "Would you come in a bit closer to the microphone," spoken aloud to the person does not sound out of place. Another technique is to place a hand on the shoulder and gently move the person towards the microphone. This may be done by the director if he is working in the studio, or by an announcer.

Timing an interview program depends in large measure on the interviewer. He follows a studio clock or a stop watch and concludes at the time agreed upon prior to the broadcast. "Stretch" material should be available for use during the closing period. This material may be a recapitulation of the setting of the interview, or the background of the guest. If a director is assigned to the program, he may signal three minutes to go, two minutes to go, and a final one minute to go. A quick glance at the studio clock when this final signal is received indicates to the interviewer the exact position of the second hand. He does not have to figure in his head the time it signifies, just the position. Then he knows that he has until the second hand goes once around the clock to that position again to complete the interview. An alternative plan is to give the interviewer a stop watch, started from zero, at the one-minute warning time. The interviewer has only to watch the second hand going around to the top of the dial as he brings the interview to a close "on the nose." The interviewer should not be required to add minutes and seconds in order to compute when the interview portion should be completed, because he should be able to concern himself almost entirely with the content of the interview.

A quiz or audience-participation broadcast is prepared in blocks or units.

A timing sheet is worked out prior to the broadcast, indicating in studio-clock times the completion times of each unit. Such timings are "ideal" timings and never work out exactly as marked. However, they provide guideposts. If the first round goes quickly, a stretch signal to the MC can indicate that he can engage in more chatter with those in the second round. The MC's script is also marked with the clock timings for the completion of each unit of a quiz show to check the timing quickly. Similar contraction or stretch of the various units continues during the broadcast. With audience-participation broadcasts a similar timing sheet is prepared with approximations of time for individual stunts. These times may be completely off in some instances, so that stand-by stunts are necessary. Timing deadlines in early portions should not be considered as absolute deadlines. If a particular contestant is exceptionally entertaining, it would be bad showmanship to cut him down. It is well to cut short the dull participant as diplomatically as possible.

• TELEVISION APPLICATIONS •

Many of the same basic radio formats for interviews, quizzes, and audience-participation programs have been transferred to television. Most of the discussion of techniques is applicable to the newer medium. It is important that consideration be given, however, to the opportunities for visual implementation and re-enforcement. As with talks, utilization of charts, models, objects, drawings, photographs, slides, film, costume and staging may increase the effectiveness of the broadcast. The information interview in particular is aided by the ability of the medium to show and to permit demonstrations.

EXAMPLE OF A TELEVISION INTERVIEW

The following excerpt from a "March of Medicine" script presented over NBC-TV October 31, 1954, illustrates this. The first sequence has an interviewer and guest seated in a moving automobile. This introductory material, filmed prior to the broadcast, leads directly into the second sequence, a live remote pick-up. The script was written by Lou Hazam. The series was produced by the Smith, Kline & French Medical Television Unit.[3]

AUDIO	VIDEO
	SMITH, KLINE AND FRENCH LABORATORIES AND THE AMERICAN MEDICAL ASSOCIATION PRESENT THE MARCH OF MEDICINE Search for Sanity
(CAR SEQUENCE)	

[3] Courtesy of Smith, Kline & French Laboratories.

MUELLER: (S.O.F.)

This is Merrill Mueller entering the
grounds of the Hudson River State
Hospital for the mentally ill, in
Poughkeepsie, New York ... With me
is Dr. O. Arnold Kilpatrick, Director of the Hospital, who -- with Dr.
Newton Bigelow, State Commissioner
of Mental Hygiene -- has willingly
agreed to permit television cameras
inside, for the first time, to help
bring your attention to the most
compelling medical problem that con-
fronts the nation -- mental illness ... How many mentally sick
Americans are in hospitals today?

CU MUELLER IN CAR WITH
KILPATRICK...DETAIL TO BE
WORKED OUT...BUT SUGGEST
WE GO DIRECTLY TO CLOSEUP,
THEN TO EXTERIOR SHOT AS
WE SEE SIGN "HUDSON RIVER
STATE HOSPITAL", THEN BACK
TO INTERIOR OF CAR.

DR. KILPATRICK:

Six hundred and fifty thousand of
them -- believe it or not, half of
all the patients in all the hospitals in the country. And every
three minutes of every day somewhere
hospital doors open to admit still
another mental patient.

MUELLER:

Well, we've come here to New York
State for our report because we've
heard that New York spends more in
caring for its mentally sick than
any other state in the country.

DR. KILPATRICK:

That's true. And Hudson River is
one of our State's model set-ups.
You see, we feel that the surroundings in which the patient lives are
almost as important as the treatment we apply. Here we've tried to
create a peaceful, pleasant atmosphere... That golf course, for example, is used by some of our
patients...

CUT IN SHOT (FROM SIDE
WINDOW OF CAR) OF GOLF
COURSE, AS CAR DRIVES BY
... THEN GROUP OF PATIENTS
GATHERED OUTSIDE....

MUELLER:

Certainly a far cry from the picture
most people have of mental hospitals... Are those patients I see
over on this side?

DR. KILPATRICK:

Yes, when we have nice weather like
this, patients are always taken out
in groups to get the benefit of the
sun and air ... That's our recreational building there where the

RECREATIONAL BUILDING

patients hold their dances and have
get-togethers. You see, we've
changed the emphasis in recreational
therapy from just exercise and
amusement toward socialization and
companionship ...

    MUELLER:

I see... What are <u>those</u> buildings?   PORCH BUILDINGS

    DR. KILPATRICK:

Those buildings house some patients
who require longer term treatment...
And that's our <u>farm</u>, there ...   FARM SHOT: PERHAPS PLUS
helps supply our food. Patients   FARM COTTAGE
work the farm and are housed in a
cottage close by....

    MUELLER:

I can see what you mean by the
proper physical setting to help
create just the right emotional
climate ...

    DR. KILPATRICK:

We're proudest, of course, of this   CHENEY THROUGH WINDSHIELD
- Cheney - which houses all our   AS CAR PULLS UP TO IT...
acute treatment facilities. And
it is our hope that newly admitted
patients may be treated here and go
from here directly home. It's the
last word in mental care facilities.

    MUELLER:

Yes, Doctor .... and our cameras
are standing by on the sixth floor
of Cheney to take our audience
inside....   (SWITCH TO CHENEY BLDG.)
        (3:00)

It is true that opinion and personality interviews rely heavily on a straightforward question-and-answer approach. No special attention is paid to
visuals. Sometimes this technique has been casually dismissed with the
phrasing "It's not really television but visual radio!" One must remember,
however, that the audience is able to be present during the interview, to see
for itself first-hand the facial expressions, to observe details of dress,
and to make personality judgments from the way the guest moves, talks,
and reacts. The viewer in a real sense is sharing experiences, sensing the
emotional tone or mood of the interview. When sight as well as sound is
possible, a new dimension has been added.

EXAMPLE OF TV PERSONALITY INTERVIEW

In the "March of Medicine" broadcast quoted below the closing interview may be cited as an example of the personality interview. The director used a close-up of the girl's face as she answered Ben Grauer's questions sincerely and honestly and spoke her fervent plea for better understanding of the mentally ill. The impact upon the viewer was powerful and moving, an inspirational message of hope for the future.[4]

AUDIO	VIDEO

GRAUER: (ON CAMERA)
As we close our report, now,
Here in the Lobby of Cheney
      Memorial,
We would like you to meet --
As an example of what can be
done for our mentally ill, with
top facilities and care --
An ex-patient of this hospital
Who has the courage
To come here today
And reveal herself to you on
      television.
	CAMERA ON GRAUER IN LOBBY
	OF CHENEY MEMORIAL.

	CAMERA PULLS BACK TO REVEAL AUDREY COLE WITH GRAUER.
GRAUER: Audrey ... when were you a patient here?	
MISS COLE: From March, 1952 for about a year, Mr. Grauer.	
GRAUER: How do you feel now?	
MISS COLE: Never better!	
GRAUER: Wonderful! -- Any plans for the future?	
MISS COLE: It's great to be able to make plans again. I'm looking forward to going back to college.	
GRAUER: Audrey, as one who has been mentally sick and recovered, what do you have to say to us about your experience?	

[4] Courtesy of Smith, Kline & French Laboratories.

MISS COLE:
What I want most to do is to tell
people not to _fear_ mental disease
... to get help when they need it.
And to please change their attitude
about mental illness.

GRAUER:
What do you mean by that?

MISS COLE:
I've known patients who were afraid
to go home because of what people
would say about them. If we would
only regard mental disease as "respectable" as any other disease --
that's _so_ important.

GRAUER:
Have you been troubled by the wrong
attitude since your return?

MISS COLE:
No, I've been lucky. My family and
friends have been kind and understanding, and I'll always be grateful. It's the _others_ I'm thinking
about.

GRAUER:
Well, bless you Audrey Cole for
having the courage to speak for
them. And -- good luck!

MISS COLE:
Thank you, Mr. Grauer.

(FINAL CLOSING)

GRAUER: As Audrey Cole, Full of new hopes and plans Departs again The place to which she once came Lost to the world of reality, Let us not forget those she leaves behind	CAMERA FOLLOWS MISS COLE AS SHE TURNS AND WALKS DOWN THE MAIN HALL OF CHENEY AND OUT OF THE DOOR.

(SWITCH TO SOF)
It is Sunday afternoon, here at
      Hudson River State hospital,
And the patients are gathered in
      Union Chapel,
Not far from where we stand,
Giving testament, in prayer and
      hymn,
To their faith in God ...
Asking him to accept them --
Even as _we_ must learn to,
If we are truly to help them --
Accept them
"Just as they are ...."
      (45")
	SWITCH TO SOF, PATIENTS AT
	CHAPEL SINGING HYMN
	"JUST AS I AM"
	
	HYMN UP FULL TO END.

The panel quiz has been more widely accepted in television than its alternate type wherein questions are directed to individual members of the audience. A pioneer in this program area which has become a prototype is "What's My Line?" The format is simple: a panel tries to guess the occupation of the contestant. Spice and glamour are added by the appearance of a mystery guest, a national celebrity in sports, politics, or the entertainment world. The excitement and fun come from by-play between panel members as well as the "chase" as the panel tracks down the right occupation. The panel members have definite video personalities and are chosen so as to complement each other. Many "switches" or modifications of this general format have been developed. One example is "Masquerade Party" where the panel members guess the identity of assorted celebrities who appear dressed in elaborate costume and make-up. Another example is found in a series where panel members race against the clock to identify a news event in which the guest was involved. Panel members and MC should possess a facile wit, be able to ad lib adroitly, and be refreshingly natural.

Audience-participation programs continue to emphasize stunts performed by the participants. "Beat the Clock" with Bud Collyer employs a race against time for its contestants. Series such as "People Are Funny" and "Truth or Consequences" select stunts with high visual interest. One stunt which was presented on the latter program in 1955 capitalized upon the nation's revived interest in huge "give-aways" stimulated by the success of "The $64,000 Question." The television audience watched a young lady placed under hypnosis. Then a total of $100,000 in currency was stacked up on a table before her. The money was to be hers if she could break the spell and reach the money. She did not!

• DIRECTION •

Before the Broadcast. Since many interview and quiz programs have little actual camera rehearsal but are directed ad lib, preplanning is highly important. The director cannot stop the broadcast to change the background set from a busy one to a plain drape because of the elaborate frock worn by a participant, to change the microphone from the boom to the desk for the guest who has a weak delivery, or to order a 10-inch lens on a camera for a close-up of a rare postage stamp. His opportunity to make such changes has been lost. The staging requirements must be kept simple when ad-lib programs are presented. If only one camera is to be used it should be obvious that rapid shifts in the size of the picture to be transmitted should be avoided. Without a studio zoom lens, even the most professional cameraman cannot dolly in from a three-shot to a tight close-up of a piece of jewelry on a coffee table during the space of these short sentences by the guest: "See this bracelet. Notice the intricate carving!" With a zoom lens such a spurt of movement back and forth would tend to upset the viewer. The director needs to talk with the guests about the objects to be displayed ahead of time in order to preplan his camera direction. Considerable practice is required in order to hold objects in the air for tight camera close-ups. Slight variations in position may move the object out of camera range. The director can save himself trouble if he shows the guest ahead of the broadcast how to place the objects on a table or platform at the same location each time. In this way the director may be ready to cut to a close-up of the object at the appropriate time. Few details of this sort should be left to chance. A beginning director who carefully examined various color slides on an ordinary slide projector was horrified to realize when his show was on the air that the iconoscope in the film chain was "color blind" and many of the slides were unintelligible.

Off-camera rehearsals should be held whenever possible. Stand-ins for contestants on an audience-participation program may be helpful while working out stunts. Rehearsals should be on the same set which is to be used on the air. Home work by the director on movements and shots is just as essential as for a dramatic broadcast. Timing procedures are worked out ahead of the broadcast as in radio. Instead of a stop watch being given to the interviewer, the floor manager relays the information through cards or hand signals. Run-down or timing sheets are also prepared. In addition to the usual "stretch" material which is included in the script outline and rehearsed, television utilizes the timing of the closing credits as a "cushion." The title drum, flip cards, or telops may be speeded up or slowed down as desired.

Camera Direction. The shots that are basic for most interview programs include the two-shot, a close-up of the interviewer and of the guest. Changing camera pick-up angles and distance, such as starting with a close-up of the MC and pulling back to reveal the guest, add visual variety. The placement of the interviewer and guest side-by-side on a couch is frowned upon by most directors. This grouping makes it difficult to secure full-face shots. If the person speaking turns away from his companion and looks straight ahead in order to provide a full-face shot, the conversational flavor of close communication between the two participants is broken. People usually look at each other when they converse. Restricting this impulse in order to play to the camera results in artificiality. If naturalism wins out the television audience can see only "half a face." Instead of this horizontal grouping many directors favor putting chairs at an angle or placing the people at adjoining sides of a table. As the two persons talk, cameras may be moved to left and right to catch full-face close-ups as they look at each other.

A general principle to follow is: "Never force lay people to assume the role of professional talent." Instead, the director should plan to place them so that the cameras can shoot them effectively without making them aware of the technique employed. Often the tally lights on cameras are disconnected to keep from revealing to guests which camera is on the air. Some directors feel that static grouping of some interviews may be lessened by taking a close-up of the interviewer, and then following him as he moves into another area of the set where the guest is waiting. Visuals, charts, pictures, objects, etc., may be handled by the interview participants and shown to the camera, or be beside the group for direct reference through word or by a pointer, or shot "wild." Shooting wild means that the visual is placed in another set or in another area of the same set, but away from the group. This technique is often used to control the lighting and to insure effective close-ups. Errors which may be avoided by this technique include photographs shown by the guest to the wrong camera, or tilted in such a manner as to reflect the light from a studio spotlight, thereby causing undesirable glare. Sometimes duplicate material is used. A guest may show a small card to the audience. Instead of moving one of the cameras forward and trusting that the guest will not spoil the shot, a duplicate card is held by a stagehand elsewhere in the studio in the correct position for the close-up. Some directors keep cameras on two shots for overly long periods of time. This often causes attention to be shifted away from the guest's answers and be directed instead to the random movements by the interviewer, such as glancing toward the floor manager for time signals or looking at notes or cue cards. The interviewer should be careful not to engage in distracting movements, but to look at and listen to the guest. The director can help direct the viewers' attention by use of close-ups of the guest alone. Other directors go to the opposite extreme and call for many cuts back and forth from interviewer to guest, as questions and answers proceed. Cut to interviewer for the question; cut to the guest for answer; cut back to interviewer for the next question; cut to guest for the next answer, etc., with never a two-shot to vary the pace. This staccato cutting technique of camera direction is extremely annoying to the viewer during ordinary conversational interplay. And all too often the camera may be on the wrong person as the director attempts to out-guess the participants.

Directors of quiz programs where panels are employed seldom use long shots showing both the panel and MC. The more general camera shots employed are close-ups of MC and an alternating cover shot of the panel, with close-ups of individual panel members who speak. Occasionally the person seated next to the panel member who is answering is included to show his facial reactions. A pan to other members of the panel is easily made from such a two-shot. Since the format of audience participation shows differ greatly, the method of camera direction also varies. One general principle is usually followed. Since contestants and MC may move quickly without warning during the ad-lib portions, the director attempts to keep one camera available with a wider angle or cover shot during close-ups on another camera.

EXAMPLE OF A TELEVISION CELEBRITY INTERVIEW, PARTIALLY REHEARSED

"Person to Person," CBS Television Network, January 22, 1954.[5]

This "as broadcast" transcript illustrates the informality and conversational quality achieved in the television series, "Person to Person." Edward R. Murrow is seated in the studio separated from his guests by anywhere from a few blocks to 3,000 miles. Special technical systems have been evolved which permit both parties to see and hear each other as Mr. Murrow talks with his guests, as though he and the viewing audience were actually in the same room with the guests.

MURROW: Now, we propose to visit Mrs. Eleanor Roosevelt of whom you may have heard. Mrs. Roosevelt lives in this red brick house on East 62nd Street here in New York, not far from the home the Roosevelts once maintained for some 34 years while business took them to Albany and Washington. Mrs. Roosevelt has a five room duplex apartment, with a small garden in the back. For five months now this has been home. It is just a few yards away from the 3rd Avenue El. I remember once reading an out of town newspaper that said to say that Mrs. Roosevelt stayed at the hotel is probably wholly inaccurate because she never stays anywhere, but tonight I believe and hope that she is at home for you.

Good evening, Mrs. Roosevelt.

MRS. ROOSEVELT: Good evening, Mr. Murrow.

MURROW: Tell me, Mrs. Roosevelt, do you still find people are amused at the amount of travelling you do and the way you get about?

MRS. ROOSEVELT: Oh yes, they are always amused at many things when they are not angry.

MURROW: I gather you are in your office now, aren't you?

MRS. ROOSEVELT: Yes, I am in the office, in the house here.

MURROW: Is this where you write your column generally?

MRS. ROOSEVELT: Yes, this is where I write the column. This is where I do all the work that comes my way.

MURROW: How long does it take you to write the column, Mrs. Roosevelt?

MRS. ROOSEVELT: I dictate directly to the typewriter -- to my secretary on the typewriter, and then I correct it and I think it takes about a half hour. But then, of course, I do think about it during the daytime and I am all ready when I sit down.

MURROW: Do you have to handle very much mail?

MRS. ROOSEVELT: Yes, a considerable amount, a good deal is always on my desk every night when my secretary goes home.

MURROW: About how much?

MRS. ROOSEVELT: Well, between Hyde Park and New York I suppose we get about 100 letters a day. Of course it goes up, if there is anything exciting going on and it goes down at other times.

MURROW: What is the general nature of it, Mrs. Roosevelt?

MRS. ROOSEVELT: Oh, everything, everything in the world - questions from children, a great many children like me to write their themes for them. And then people who want me - who think I can still do what I could once, when in the White House, and people who want all kinds of help and a great many invitations to speak here and there and everywhere.

MURROW: Is most of this mail friendly or is most of it still abusive?

MRS. ROOSEVELT: Oh, I guess a certain amount. I have certain people who don't like me or my husband or my children or anything I do. Some of them are anonymous; some of them signed, but any signed letter I try to answer as clearly as I can. But after a certain amount of exchanges you reach a point where you feel it would be better to let it drop.

MURROW: Does this critical mail bother you?

MRS. ROOSEVELT: No sir, no. You have to do the best you can in this world and if you have done that, that is all you can do.

MURROW: Well, I know you have hundreds of photographs around your apartment there. Could you show us a few.

MRS. ROOSEVELT: Yes.

MURROW: Could you identify them for us? That one you don't need to identify.

MRS. ROOSEVELT: Well, that is an old one of my husband. I think it appeared in the Times and under him is Mr. Churchill and the date on that I think is 1942, when he came over. That was taken in the White House garden, I think.

MURROW: He is wearing his siren suit, isn't he?

MRS. ROOSEVELT: Yes, he is wearing his siren suit; and below that is a photograph that was taken on the porch of Hyde Park on one of the evenings when they came down to congratulate my husband after the election returns came in. I think it was '36 but I am not certain.

MURROW: I am sure it was '36. I was there.

MRS. ROOSEVELT: Were you?

MURROW: Yes. Mrs. Roosevelt, is it true you once said that Mr. Churchill had not changed his mind about anything in 60 years?

MRS. ROOSEVELT: I perhaps didn't say it quite that way, but I think I meant that he looked at life much the way he had 60 years ago.

MURROW: Mrs. Roosevelt, how do you keep in touch with your large family now?

MRS. ROOSEVELT: I write very regularly and they write to me and when anything really must be told we hear very quickly. There is a telephone you know.

MURROW: Who is the star correspondent among your family?

MRS. ROOSEVELT: My daughter. My daughter writes more regularly than the boys do, of course.

MURROW: Mrs. Roosevelt,I want to ask you another question. This is about the animal family that you have in your apartment. Don't you have Fala's grandson there?

MRS. ROOSEVELT: Yes, this is Fala's grandson Tamis and this is Duff, who was given me by two children in Toledo who read in the paper that Fala had died and they had a new puppy. At first I thought I couldn't possibly bring up a new pup but Tamis was so sad that I accepted gratefully. He chewed up almost everything.

MURROW: Are they fairly obedient dogs?

MRS. ROOSEVELT: Yes, at times. At times they are quite

obedient but you know Scotties have minds of their own. They
like to be independent.

MURROW: You don't mind independent people around the house?

MRS. ROOSEVELT: No, I have lived with rebels a good deal.

MURROW: Mrs. Roosevelt, I wonder if we could go down stairs?

MRS. ROOSEVELT: Surely, with great pleasure.

MURROW: We are on the second floor now in your office, aren't
we?

MRS. ROOSEVELT: Yes, we are.

MURROW: I was wondering if you ever got homesick for the
White House?

MRS. ROOSEVELT: One couldn't get homesick for the White
House. One might miss the beauty of the White House because, of
course, it has wonderful proportions and is a lovely house. But
one couldn't be homesick for the White House.

MURROW: How many rooms in the White House? Can you remember,
compared to the house you now have?

MRS. ROOSEVELT: No, this house has only five rooms, but I
don't know quite how many there are now in the White House.
They made a good many more when they changed the White House.

MURROW: I wonder if you would take us down and let us get a
glimpse of the kitchen?

MRS. ROOSEVELT: Yes, indeed, I will be glad to do that.

MURROW: Do you do much cooking, Mrs. Roosevelt?

MRS. ROOSEVELT: No, I do very little cooking. I have never
done much more than scramble eggs on Sunday night.

MURROW: I remember you did that on Pearl Harbor Day, on
Sunday night in the White House.

MRS. ROOSEVELT: I did. I did it in the White House.

MURROW: You don't require as much help in this kitchen as you
did in the White House?

MRS. ROOSEVELT: No, this is better suited to the number of
people that now are apt to be in this apartment.

MURROW: During all the traveling you do, the lectures you
give, living in different hotels, is food a problem for you?

MRS. ROOSEVELT: No, I'm afraid that I don't really know when
food is good or not. I like, well, I eat when it is before me
but I don't think I am ever really very hungry and if it isn't
there I don't mind.

MURROW: Your living room is just, so to speak, off the
kitchen, isn't it?

MRS. ROOSEVELT: Yes, there is a little bit of a passage way
but we are practically just across the hall.

MURROW: Isn't that a Japanese print just beside you?

MRS. ROOSEVELT: Yes, these are two Japanese prints that I
brought home from Japan this summer and I think they are
decorative. I had some my father brought home 90-odd years ago
and I just thought it was interesting to have the two together.

MURROW: Mrs. Roosevelt, you are just recently back from a
trip around the world and I wanted to ask you if you would tell
us who was the most interesting individual you met in the course
of that trip?

MRS. ROOSEVELT: Oh, I think on the whole the most interesting
person was President Tito.

MURROW: Where was that?

MRS. ROOSEVELT: In Jugoslavia on the way home.

MURROW: Why did you feel he was the most interesting?

MRS. ROOSEVELT: I felt that he was a leader and you could

feel that he was a leader and then he expresses himself pic-
turesquely and clearly.

MURROW: In this long career that you have had what would you
regard as your greatest or most satisfying achievement?

MRS. ROOSEVELT: Well, I had never thought about achievements.
I don't know that I would call anything an achievement. I have
just done whatever came along to do but the thing that I remember
giving me the greatest pleasure was at the end of the first
session in London of the United Nations. I had gone in fear and
trembling and I had felt that I had to walk very carefully because I was the first woman on the delegation and a woman must do
well or it hurts all women. At the end of a session in which we
had had a disagreement about the return of people against their
will to the countries of their origin both Mr. Dulles and Senator
Vandenburg were kind enough to follow me up and say in saying
good-by that they were glad that I had been on the delegation;
and while they had opposed me and begged the President not to
appoint me they had found it good to work with me. I think that
pleased me more than anything that could have happened.

MURROW: That must have been very gratifying. Mrs. Roosevelt,
this is a question I have wanted to ask you a long time. I don't
know how to put it, so I will put it bluntly. Why do you work so
hard?

MRS. ROOSEVELT: What else would I do? I live alone. My
children are all busy and all have lives of their own. I
wouldn't want them to be worrying about Mother having to do so
I might as well work as long as I am well enough.

MURROW: It occurs to me that a lot of people don't know what
your average day is like. Could you tell us about your day?

MRS. ROOSEVELT: Oh, I write a good deal about my day. Well,
I get up every morning around a quarter to eight, sometimes a
little earlier and go to work at the office when I am in New
York. And then I do other things, like making a speech or two,
perhaps for a lunch or an afternoon thing, and I write a column
and I attend to the mail. I usually finish the mail at night
after I come home from wherever I may have been dining. And
then that is the end of the day.

MURROW: Let's just ramble a bit, shall we? Who was the most
difficult guest you ever entertained at the White House?

MRS. ROOSEVELT: I don't think any guest in the White House
was ever really difficult because you had all the service that
was necessary to look after them. You didn't have to do it yourself. You just had to think a little bit and tell other people,
so it was easy. But I think perhaps for the people in the White
House, Harry Hopkins might have been fairly difficult because he
always had to have a diet. Alexander Woollcott wanted coffee all
hours of the day and night and also guests at all times.

MURROW: I seem to remember Alex was rather fond of having
guests at the White House.

MRS. ROOSEVELT: He wanted guests for breakfast any hour of
the morning and he would wander around the house at times. I
always remember that once when I left him in the White House -
he was acting in a play at that time and living in the White
House -- I came in from New York and he met me on the door
steps, the front of the White House, and he said, "come right in,
Mrs. Roosevelt; I am delighted to see you."

MURROW: Mrs. Roosevelt, have you read any good books lately?

MRS. ROOSEVELT: I think Chester Bowles book on India is per-

haps the most interesting I have read just lately. I hope everybody reads it. It is called AN AMBASSADOR'S REPORT and it is
certainly a remarkable book on India.

    MURROW: Are you going to write another book?

    MRS. ROOSEVELT: I hope not, not at the moment anyway. I am
much too busy traveling around making speeches.

    MURROW: Mostly on behalf of the United Nations?

    MRS. ROOSEVELT: Yes, most of them are on the United Nations.

    MURROW: Mrs. Roosevelt, permit me to say our thanks for per-
mitting us to come and visit you this evening. We are most
grateful and thank you very much indeed.

    MRS. ROOSEVELT. Thank you.

Projects and Exercises

1. Present for class evaluation the various interviews included in this chapter
   and elsewhere in the text.
2. Tune in locally produced radio and television interviews in your area and
   classify them as to type. Do the same for any locally produced quizzes and
   audience-participation programs. Time with a stop watch and note format
   breakdown.
3. Record several class ad-lib interviews and prepare a written transcript. Assign
   another pair to read these transcripts and compare the results.
4. Study the above transcripts and draw conclusions about characteristics of
   informal speech style. Then write an interview on a similar subject. Keep the
   flavor of the ad-lib style, but do not attempt to incorporate all the repetitions,
   interruptions, and hesitations, nor write in the exact same loose style. Rehearse
   delivery and present for class as an ad-lib interview. See if the class can detect
   that it is from script.
5. Prepare and present television interviews with only a few visuals. Select the
   visuals carefully in order to assure that the interview could not be presented
   as effectively on radio.
6. Use sound effects (street background—industrial sounds—railroad station
   or airport—harbor noises—baseball game crowd—theatre lobby—etc.) to
   simulate a background for a series of "Traveling Mike" or "TV Close-ups"
   interviews. Adhere to the type of questions appropriate to such a program
   series.
7. Present a series of informational radio or television interviews entitled "The
   Hobby Clinic." Keep to an exact three-minute timing excepting a few seconds
   leeway *under* but not over the time. The interviewer may prepare opening
   and closing material (reading from script for radio and from cue cards for
   television), but the remainder of the interview should be ad lib. Conferences
   with the persons to be interviewed may be held. Brief outline material may
   be used.
8. Prepare and present a series of four-and-one-half or nine-and-one-half
   minute quiz or audience-participation programs. A suggested method of
   procedure: Divide the class into groups by counting off one through four.
   Assign duties. Number ones are directors; number twos are announcers;
   number threes are writers; and fours are MCs. Four rounds of this project
   permit alternation of duties. Each group is permitted to present its choice
   of program type and format, including specific title, sponsor, radio or television, and station or network. A group other than the performance group
   assists in technical areas, another group is used for the participants, other
   groups serve as the audience. Class criticism follows each presentation.

❋ 23 ❋

Discussion Programs

IT IS axiomatic that there is an impelling need in a democracy for public discussion as a means by which issues may be clarified, the public informed and enlightened, and majorities and minorities brought into the active intercourse out of which will emerge the compromises that characterize the democratic way. The methods of discussion and debate are uniquely the tools of democracy because they invite and require direct confrontation of advocates and an open clash of views. It is the element of confrontation that gives substance to the process of opinion-making in a democracy— confrontation around a cracker barrel, in a courtroom, on the floor of Congress, before a radio microphone, or in front of television cameras.

Television and radio contribute to this democratic process through discussion programs. These programs have proved themselves to be one of broadcasting's most effective ways of handling controversial issues because they present various points of view to biased listeners and viewers who otherwise might tune in to their favorite speakers only.

"Broadcast discussions are useful for clarifying issues that have become confused in the public mind," says Lyman Bryson. "They are good for exposing the arguments on both sides of issues that are at the same time being discussed in homes and meeting places and in the press all over the country. Discussion programs, when they are doing their best work can help people to think." [1]

The objective of a television or radio forum or round table is to present to listeners an organized, balanced, and interesting discussion of an important subject in a way that reveals the real questions or problems at issue. A forum that fails to be interesting defeats its own purpose because it will lose its audience; a forum that capitalizes on personality clashes at the price of elucidation of issues serves mainly to confuse neutral listeners and to impassion partisans. "Those taking part in forums," says Francis Williams, "should have both knowledge and a degree of open-mindedness: the discus-

---

[1] Lyman Bryson, *Time for Reason About Radio* (New York, 1948), p. 126.

sion should be an inquiry beginning from different points of view, and not a platform on which spokesmen . . . demonstrate the inflexibility of their loyalty to a party point of view and their fervid inaccessibility to argument." [2] Audience surveys indicate that, in comparison with good entertainment programs, round tables and forums do not have very large audiences, but those audiences consist of people who tend to be more influential in their own social circles. Even a very low Nielsen rating may still mean that perhaps 250,000 to a million people are listening to a network television or radio forum, and that figure is considerably greater than the audiences attracted to one-sided discussions in the press or on the lecture platform.

Round-table discussions can be used to explore both controversial and noncontroversial topics. "Invitation to Learning," a CBS radio discussion program of many years standing, offers panel discussions on literary subjects. In such discussions, there may be no strong differences of viewpoint at all, but merely a many-sided expository presentation of an interesting topic. The round table thus becomes a device for the conversational presentation of material to which an audience might not tune in if it were a straight talk. In fact, a successful radio discussion series entitled "Conversation" was broadcast for some time over NBC radio.

Some discussion program series select controversial topics and invite two or three exponents of different views to state their cases informally in a group discussion. Still others devote themselves almost entirely to informal debates on controversial issues and generally offer two speakers and an active moderator who regulates, guides, and interprets the interplay of ideas.

Various stations have developed debate formats using two, and occasionally four, speakers. In such programs, the issue is explicitly stated in the debate question. Each speaker makes an opening statement of his case, following which are heard rebuttals, cross-examinations, and summaries. The best-known radio network debate-forum of this type for many years has been ABC's "America's Town Meeting," which uses two or more speakers and a moderator. After opening statements the speakers interrogate each other. The remainder of the program is thrown open to the audience in the studio and questions are directed to individual speakers. Shortly before the end of the program, the speakers summarize their cases. "Junior Town Meetings," following roughly the same format but using junior high school and high school students as participants, have also been fairly successful.

In the first few years of television, there were a considerable number of discussion programs, but the number has since declined. Programs such as "Youth Wants to Know" and "The American Forum," broadcast on both radio and television, really approach the press-conference type of news program that is discussed in Chapter 24. "Facts Forum Panel," a syndicated television program, attempts to follow a general debate format in covering controversial issues.

[2] *BBC Year Book, 1949,* p. 14.

In the final analysis, regardless of twists and "gimmicks" in format, the success of any debate or discussion program in radio or in television depends foremost on the ability of the speakers, the care with which they are chosen to represent different points of view, and the skill of the moderator.

• PLANNING THE DISCUSSION PROGRAM •

The primary responsibility for any series of discussion programs rests with the individuals who plan and moderate them. The public-service director of a large station, the program or news director of a small station, or a representative from an educational institution may assume this task. Planning a series of round tables involves choosing good topics every week and engaging capable representatives from the fields of law, labor, business, journalism, government, education, etc. Successful series have also been developed using school children or college students as the speakers. Topics must be timely and of general interest and should concern matters of policy, judgment, or interpretation. Simple questions of fact are not appropriate for discussion programs. Such broad questions of interpretation as "What is Democracy?" "What is Communism?" "What is a liberal education?" often lend themselves to good discussions. Controversial questions should be stated neutrally, in such form as "What should be our policy toward the Soviet Union?" "How can we strengthen the United Nations?" or "What should be our policy toward UNESCO?" Since round tables are usually broadcast on sustaining time, talent fees are generally not available, although some stations make it a practice to give small honoraria to guests. It is important, therefore, that the person responsible for a discussion series have excellent contacts with community leaders, since he will be obliged to ask them to participate purely as a public service.

When topics and speakers have been decided upon, the moderator should indicate to the participants the exact format of the program, and what he expects each of them to do. If scripts are used, speakers should be informed of the deadline for clearing the scripts at the station. The amount of actual planning and rehearsing of a round table or forum varies from one series to another. All programs seek the quality of spontaneity that good extemporaneous discussion or debate can provide, but many moderators have learned that, without some previous planning in consultation with the speakers, the program may achieve spontaneity at the expense of good coverage of the question. One speaker may find that he has devoted half of his speech to a point which his opponent has been willing to concede all along. Or the speakers may tangle during the broadcast on which aspect of the question they should discuss. The result is that the program is disorganized and valuable air time is wasted.

Planning and rehearsing the program should be limited to setting the format of the program, deciding what issues will be discussed, and in what order, and making a rough allotment of time for each major issue. Conceded matter can then be merely stated and need not be debated, and the crucial questions at issue can be explored more thoroughly. The moderator may prepare an outline which indicates the order of topics, and give copies of it to the speakers. All of these matters can be handled through correspondence, or at a luncheon meeting where the moderator and his guests can review in a friendly fashion what they will later discuss on the air.

Some discussion programs follow a practice of very thorough planning and preparation for broadcast. Participants may actually make one or two "dry runs" of a program before it goes on the air. This method assures that most irrelevancies will be eliminated before broadcast, and clear lines of difference are set forth. But such detailed preparation often results in dull broadcast discussions. The speakers lose their spontaneity and anticipate their opponent's statements. The controversy has been practically "talked out" of the program in advance of broadcast. Indeed, in one instance a participant discovered that the arguments he had used in prebroadcast sessions were being refuted by his opponent before he had a chance to state them on the air. The producers of such round tables must ask themselves whether, in sacrificing spontaneity for orderly discussion, they have organized their program to death.

Planning the broadcast is considerably simpler if the format calls for prepared statements by the individual speakers. Several procedures can be followed. The moderator may work the program "cold." Neither the moderator nor the opponent examines the speech before it is delivered over the air. At the conclusion of the talks, a question period ensues. In such an arrangement, the moderator must be confident that his speakers will not commit libel and that they are sufficiently quick-witted to work up questions as they hear their opponents speak. In another procedure, the moderator may ask to see the scripts in advance of broadcast and see how the lines of conflict have developed. Observing a scrupulous fairness at all times, he may advise both speakers that their scripts reveal that they are not clashing on the issues and, accordingly, he may suggest some revisions. It is also possible to go a step further and, after binding the speakers to their original speeches, the moderator may submit copies of all the scripts to them shortly before the broadcast to give them additional time to prepare questions. The moderator, himself, would be wise to draw up lists of questions so that there is no fear of a break in the continuity should one speaker be unable to respond quickly.

· PRODUCING THE RADIO DISCUSSION PROGRAM ·

The production of a radio round table or forum is relatively simple if there is no studio audience. It is somewhat more complex when a studio audience is invited to participate in the question period.

In a round table discussion without a visible audience, it is generally wise to seat the speakers opposite each other across a bidirectional ribbon microphone. A nondirectional microphone may also be used. In both cases, it is essential to check voice levels prior to the broadcast so that the speakers may adjust their physical positions to achieve a vocal balance on the air. It is very difficult for the control-room engineer to ride gain on a microphone being used by two people who are improperly balanced. Whenever possible, the moderator should have a microphone of his own so that he may break into the discussion at once should he feel an interruption desirable. The moderator should face the control room so that he can receive production signals from the engineer or director and observe the studio clock.

The moderator should work out a rough timing on his outline, so that the entire broadcast will not be limited to only a few of the questions that were planned for discussion. Getting the program off the air on time can be managed by back-timing the final announcement in rehearsal, and having the director give three-, two-, and one-minute signals to the moderator as the program approaches its close. The last two minutes of a discussion can profitably be devoted to a summary made either by the moderator or by the participants themselves.

During the discussion, the moderator carries the dual responsibility of maintaining order and of listening carefully to the talks and comments to judge whether further clarification of any points is necessary. The moderator should identify each speaker until he is fairly certain that the radio audience can associate the speaker's voice with his name. He should also try to prevent any one speaker from "hogging" the mike. The moderator should be quick to note digressions and bring the discussion back to the issue under discussion. In a "People's Platform" discussion on the role of the U. S. Navy, moderator Dwight Cooke brought the digressing speakers back to the subject with a quick, "Gentlemen, I'm afraid we're sailing full steam away from our subject." The moderator must exert a firm control over the discussion when it becomes disorderly or seems to be going astray, but he must not stifle the freedom of the speakers to express themselves vigorously on the questions at issue. Maturity, intelligence, and great tact are required of the moderator to accomplish these seemingly contradictory objectives. The obsequious moderator, who remains quiet while the discussion turns into a verbal brawl will be criticized by the radio audience as much as the moderator who appears to be imposing his own views or interrupting speakers when they are making legitimate points. Either type of moderator will find it difficult to get good speakers to reappear on his program.

The speakers themselves should try to make their points concisely and simply. It is most important to retain emotional poise throughout the discussion regardless of provocation, and to have a fluent command of language to express one's ideas forcefully and clearly. In preparing for a brief opening talk on a forum program, the advice given in Chapter 19 should prove helpful. In preparing for the question-and-answer period, the best advice for a speaker is to make a thorough study of his subject, outline his position, and work up a number of basic questions he would like to put to his opponent. A few main headings from the outline will serve as the basis for a summary at the end of the program.

In audience-participation forum programs, the production is somewhat more involved because additional production personnel and equipment are necessary to handle questions from the audience. "America's Town Meeting" uses several announcers or production assistants with roving microphones connected by long cables to the control room for this purpose. Members of the audience may indicate they have questions by raising their hands, rising to their feet, or handing written questions to the assistants. The moderator indicates to his assistants which person will be called upon for the next question, and the microphone is swiftly moved into position.

Some moderators find it helpful to conduct a warm-up session with the audience before the program goes on the air. On "America's Town Meeting," the moderator conducts a free-for-all discussion before the program actually begins. This period tends to make the audience more responsive to the speakers during the broadcast, and also provides an emotional outlet for some people who feel strongly about the issues under discussion. A keen moderator can spot people with good questions during this period, and also note people to be avoided during the broadcast because of their inability to express themselves clearly or rationally. In such audience-participation forums, it is usually wise to provide a lectern and a single microphone for the speakers. Each speaker delivers his talk from the same microphone in a standing position and remains in his seat on the platform during the parts of the program when he is not in action. If questions come repeatedly to one or two speakers, the moderator may suggest that they remain on their feet in order not to waste time.

It is also important in the production of these shows to avoid situations where the members of the studio audience are all on one side. This is unfair to one or more of the speakers and will also upset radio listeners who hold contrary points of view. In distributing tickets of admission to such programs, care should be taken to obtain a balanced representation. One way to do this in very controversial discussions is to make equal batches of tickets available for distribution to the members of organizations publicly committed to various sides of the question, and the rest of the tickets available to the general public through schools, community groups, or mail requests.

The interest of the studio audience may be heightened if a prize is offered for the best question put to the speakers. Such productions become more elaborate, however, and require several judges to rule on the questions, since it is desirable to announce the winner before the end of the program.

· PRODUCING THE TELEVISION DISCUSSION PROGRAM ·

The production of a television discussion program is basically similar to that of a radio discussion program, with certain adaptations to the needs of the television screen. All speakers should be seated so that direct views of them can be obtained by the television cameras. Sometimes it is desirable to seat the moderator at a separate table, covered by a special camera, but this tends to make it difficult for the moderator to work closely in developing the discussion among the participants. An Electra-zoom lens on one pedestal camera, with two other cameras using standard lenses, are usually adequate for good visual coverage of the discussion. Name plates of each participant, printed white on light gray and set in front of each speaker, provide simple identification throughout the program. Separate microphones set in front of each speaker provide the best audio control. One or two water pitchers and several drinking glasses are usually advisable. Placed in front of a simple three-fold set or gray velour drapes, the discussion program can be conducted very simply. With an announcer, appropriate opening and closing title and credit cards, and possibly some recorded music to go over the closing credits, the basic production elements necessary for the program are present. The camera director must be alert to the way the discussion is moving so that the cameras will pick up not only the speaker, but the reactions of those listening. These reactions not only will indicate who the next speaker probably will be, but may also provide an interesting picture to put on the air. The moderator of the program takes opening and closing cues from the stage manager.

Projects and Exercises

1. Listen to several network and local station round-table and forum broadcasts and compare the work of the moderators.
2. Make an intensive listening analysis of one discussion program to detect whether an outline is being followed and when the discussion digressed from the main issues.
3. Study transcripts of "America's Town Meeting of the Air" and "The American Forum" and criticize the speakers and moderators in terms of the criteria set forth in this chapter.
4. Plan and present round table discussions on the following questions:
    (a) What kind of plays should a college theater produce?
    (b) How can we eliminate group prejudice?
    (c) What should we do to combat juvenile delinquency?
    (d) What is the best public policy for television broadcasting?

5. Plan and present half-hour audience-participation forum programs debating the following questions:
   (*a*) Is the two-party system a failure?
   (*b*) Should we adopt a national program of compulsory health insurance?
   (*c*) Should broadcast stations be permitted to editorialize in their own name?
   (*d*) Should atheists be given time on the air?

❖ 24 ❖

News Programs

"AT NO PERIOD in our history has the function of news and public affairs broadcasting been so critical and important to our national life," said William S. Paley, Chairman of the Board of CBS, in a recent address to professional broadcasters.

> The movement of world events on both the national and international scenes takes on increasing significance each day in terms of the welfare and security of each citizen. These conditions and circumstances provide the broadcaster with an unprecedented opportunity to move ahead in this field of news and public affairs. We have today within our grasp the opportunity to provide an extraordinary public service in a troubled world and, at the same time, to increase our stature and strength as broadcasters.

The broadcasting of news and, to a more limited extent, commentary and "news-in-depth" is an activity in which practically every radio and television station engages. News operations range from large-scale undertakings involving staffs of news editors and reporters to small-scale operations run by staff announcers. Because of the great audience for news broadcasts and the public faith in the reliability of broadcast news, it is essential that news broadcasters have a high sense of responsibility and the intellectual equipment required for professional journalism. A staff announcer who is required to prepare and present news summaries should at least have a clear knowledge of what constitutes news and of the processes by which news is gathered and edited, a keen sense of news values, and skill in the construction and delivery of newscasts.

• WHAT IS NEWS? •

"News exists in the minds of men," writes Wilbur Schramm. "It is not an event; it is something perceived *after* the event. It is not identical with the event; it is an attempt to reconstruct the essential framework of the event—*essential* being defined against a frame of reference which is calculated to make the event meaningful to the reader [or listener]." [1]

Millions of events occur daily: your awakening in the morning is an event, just as your failure to awaken on schedule, or your death is an event. Which of these events is worthy of a news report? Your rising according to schedule may be a matter of such regularity that even you do not consider it of any significance; should you oversleep some morning, however, you would consider the event of some significance if it made you late for school or forced you to miss an appointment, and you might make a first-hand report of the event to the person you kept waiting. Should you fail to get up in the morning because you had died in your sleep, the event would unquestionably be reported as news to a circle of your social and business acquaintances and might even be reported to the community at large by local newspapers or radio and television stations. Should you fail to rise because you are a victim of a rare sleeping sickness which keeps you in a coma for days, weeks, or months on end, this unusual event might be reported by the press throughout the country. If you happened to be a high government official, the news of your illness or death might be transmitted around the world.

News is related to events which in some way *interest* people. People are interested in reports of events which directly or indirectly affect their own lives, and in reports of any irregularities in the course of human affairs which arouse intellectual or emotional curiosity. News of natural disasters, such as floods, hurricanes, and fires interest many people. Departures from moral and legal codes of behavior interest more people than strict observance of these codes. The commission of a crime, the apprehension of the suspected criminal, and his trial, conviction, or acquittal are events usually reported as news. Important governmental actions, such as the enactment of a law, the issuance of an executive order, or a court decision, are reported as news when they affect our lives in some way. Speeches and interviews by important public officials are newsworthy because they provide clues to future governmental action.

We may see, then, that the occurrence of an event of common interest is the basis for any news story, and that speeches, interviews, and public statements become newsworthy as they are related to past and future events. It is true, of course, that there are several figures in the world whose every public statement serves as material for news reports. The President of the United States is one of those figures because his remarks may indicate what our government will do next. George Bernard Shaw was another such figure because he established a tremendous personal reputation for pungency of language. Greta Garbo illustrates the type of public figure who makes a fetish of silence and whose rare public comments are therefore always re-

[1] Wilbur Schramm, "The Nature of News," *Journalism Quarterly,* Vol. XVI (September, 1949), p. 259.

ported as news. The radio and television newsman must maintain at all times a clear understanding of the nature of news so that he will be able to distinguish between news accounts that are worthy of broadcast and stories which are nothing more than advertising or inconsequential statements of opinion.

· GATHERING AND DISSEMINATING NEWS ·

A knowledge of the process by which news is gathered, compiled, and disseminated enables the television and radio newsman to evaluate the reliability of various news items. News may be gathered by on-the-scene reporters who describe an event as they see it. If reporters arrive after an event has occurred, they may interview people who were present at the time, and then write second-hand accounts. Reporters seldom witness airplane crashes, but they are often able to interview surviving passengers, people who saw the crash, or people who arrived on the scene shortly after the crash occurred. From this information, the reporter reconstructs the event as best he can. In this news-gathering process, possibilities for error exist in the original observation, in the narration of it, and in the semantic difficulties involved in the use of language for descriptive purposes. Readers and listeners do not always interpret words in the sense intended by the reporter.

Some events, however, cannot be *seen,* in the sense that they take place behind closed doors and all that a reporter sees is a sheet of paper stating that something has occurred. A doctor releases a note stating that his patient has passed away, the Presidential press secretary releases an announcement of a Presidential appointment, or a clerk of the Supreme Court hands out a paper saying that the court will honor an appeal in a very important case. In such instances, reporters have to summarize the history leading up to the event to indicate its current news value.

Some events are purposely staged to provide material for news stories. Public rallies are scheduled to create newsworthy events in order to publicize certain ideas. Specialists in publicity know how to dramatize occurrences in order to attract public attention. An American soldier in Germany who wanted to protest our occupation policy found that he could get no newspaper space for his views until he dramatically created an event by resigning his American citizenship; then his story was carried by all the news-gathering agencies. Several years ago, John L. Lewis, a master of dramatizing events in labor affairs, had to notify William Green, then head of the American Federation of Labor, that the United Mine Workers were seceding from the Federation. Instead of following the prosaic course of sending a formal letter, Lewis, in the presence of reporters, scrawled on a scrap of paper, "GREEN WE DISAFFILIATE LEWIS," and dispatched the note by messenger. The very manner in which Lewis broke from the A. F. of L. contributed to the interest in the event.

When a reporter has prepared a written report of an event, he submits it to the newspaper or broadcast station for which he works. There the report may be edited to make it fit space and style requirements. If the story has more than local interest, it will be further edited and then transmitted to the regional or national headquarters of the wire-service agency to which the newspaper or station may subscribe. There are three main wire service agencies which engage in the business of news-gathering and dissemination: Associated Press, United Press, and International News Service. In addition, there are several news feature agencies, such as the North American Newspaper Alliance, King Features, Overseas News Agency, and Gannett News Service.

The Associated Press is a membership corporation which provides vast news coverage through a unique arrangement with its affiliated newspapers. Newspapers that join AP agree to send to AP headquarters news of any local events which have regional or national interest. This means that AP can depend upon the reporters of all its member papers to provide it with news coverage. AP supplements these sources with its own reporters located in many news centers, and large staffs of newsmen in key cities like Washington, New York, and foreign capitals. Into AP's New York headquarters flow the news reports from regional offices which channel the reports received from individual papers. From overseas come the cable reports of foreign correspondents. AP editors in New York process and rewrite these reports for transmission to all member newspapers which then use the material to make up their papers. In this way, a story that breaks in some remote community where an AP correspondent or a reporter of an AP newspaper is present, can be communicated to the entire AP membership within a matter of minutes.

For television and radio, the Associated Press rewrites the newspaper material and transmits its copy over its own teletype system of communication to subscribing stations. To provide for regional and state coverage, AP stops its national transmissions several times a day for "splits" which are transmitted from regional headquarters to stations within a limited geographical area. Teletype machines are electrically operated typewriters which automatically reproduce copy received over wires at the rate of sixty words a minute. These machines are usually operated 24 hours a day because AP transmits material round-the-clock, although the quantity of material sent out in the hours after midnight is much smaller than during daytime transmissions. As many as two hundred or more numbered items may be sent out in a single day, or far more than any one station can possibly use in its newscasts. These items include individual news and feature stories, headline summaries, five- and fifteen-minute summaries, and feature commentaries. Very important news stories are labeled "bulletins" and urgent dispatches are called "flashes." Most of the summaries are rewrites of earlier stories, but they include new information and late stories. For television, AP Photofax and Wirephoto services provide spot picture coverage.

The United Press is a wire-service agency affiliated with the Scripps-Howard newspaper chain and run differently than AP, since it is not a membership corporation. UP depends for its news material on its own correspondents here and abroad. UP rewrites news stories for broadcast presentation and transmits its copy over its own teletype system. For radio, UP provides news; news features on sports, women's interests, general human interest, farming, business, and science; and commentary and reviews of outstanding news events and national and international affairs. For television, UP supplies motion-picture news film, spot news pictures by Telephoto and facsimile, teletyped scripts for motion-picture news films, round-the-clock news, sports, and weather shows, and week-end sports reviews. United Press Movietone Television News also provides motion-picture news coverage, comprising sound and silent film, with teletyped scripts. This is produced jointly by United Press and 20th Century-Fox Movietone News. United Press Newspictures provides news photos and telops to television stations by mail, messenger, and Telephoto service. UP Newspictures also supplies 35 mm. transparencies with timed scripts; sports shows; a baseball scoreboard, including cartoons; and weather maps, slides, and film, with appropriate scripts.

The International News Service is a Hearst news agency organized primarily to exchange news material among Hearst newspapers and to supplement this with the reports of INS domestic and foreign reporters. In association with Hearst Metronome News, INS supplies stations with world-wide news and news feature coverage by a round-the-clock teletype printer. INS maintains a special facsimile circuit for television stations carrying spot news and sports photos, and supplies them with on-the-spot audio recordings, maps, and other visual aids. INS turns out a daily television news film, a weekly television newsreel, and a weekly television sports reel.

· THE RADIO NEWSROOM ·

A radio station that schedules news programs must subscribe to one or more of the wire-service agencies to get its basic news material. Some small stations manage with only one service, and the announcers read the material taken from the news ticker, making practically no changes in it. This type of newscast suffers from the lack of editorial adaptation to local needs and interests, and from inaccuracies or inadvertent bias in the wire service material. Editors in New York work with great care to avoid such departures from high quality news reporting, but all local news editors should double-check material for accuracy and fairness. Another drawback in reading the wire-service material without modification is that, when more than one station in the same area engages in this practice, listeners hear identically-worded programs over different stations, and competition suffers.

A small radio newsroom may be nothing more than a closet housing a news ticker, and a small office with a desk, some reference books and maps for the use of one or more news editors. The editors check the ticker copy, rewrite some stories completely to give a local angle or to improve the manner of presentation, retouch other stories by cutting their length, and then piece the stories together to make new and more effective arrangements. Large radio newsrooms employ several editors and subscribe to a number of wire-service agencies out of whose combined reports the editors write their own newscasts.

A survey of thirty-four radio stations in Iowa made several years ago by Robert E. Widmark provides a basis for generalizing about common newsroom practices. Widmark found that the larger the stations, the more specialized were their news personnel. Staffs ranged from an average of four-and-one-third newsmen at stations of 5000 watts and over, to three-and-one-quarter newsmen at 1000-watt stations, and three-and-one-third at 250-500-watt stations. Three-fourths of the stations said that the persons who read newscasts on the air also help in their preparation. A majority reported they had full-time news directors, with many of the directors supervising special events, farm programs, and sport shows as well. Sixty-five per cent of the stations subscribed to only one news wire. Over three-fourths made an effort to check local news sources either by using their own reporters or by telephone. A few stations had one fulltime reporter, with newspaper-owned stations depending on affiliated papers for local news. About a third had special arrangements other than the wire services to get news from the state capital or Washington. Low-powered stations used local news sources more extensively than high-powered stations. Five- and fifteen-minute newscasts were most common, and 38 per cent had at least one regular newscast devoted exclusively to local news.[2]

· CONSTRUCTING THE RADIO NEWSCAST ·

The main problems in constructing a radio newscast are deciding what items to include, in what order, and how to present each. The first two problems involve exercises in news judgment and the third involves skill in radio writing. It is well to remember that radio does not have headline type to highlight important stories, nor can a story be buried in the back pages to be caught by only a few. Indications of a story's importance must be made by placing it at the beginning of the newscast, by allowing more time for its presentation or by directly stating its importance in the report itself. But stories of lesser importance, though they are broadcast later in the program, will still be the center of attention for the thirty or so seconds it may take to read them.

[2] Robert E. Widmark, unpublished master's thesis, State University of Iowa, summarized in *Broadcasting-Telecasting,* August 8, 1949, p. 68.

A fifteen-minute sponsored newscast, which actually runs about twelve minutes, allowing time for commercial announcements, can comfortably handle as many as twenty or thirty different items. Seldom should one story run over two minutes in length, unless it has very unusual interest for the local audience. The items should be arranged within geographical or topical compartments as far as possible, and transitional phrases, such as "On the labor front today," or "Turning now to news from Washington," should be used to hold the units together. It is usually wise to take up national news, foreign news, labor news, and local news as separate units. Failure to maintain some organization in the news presentation tends to confuse many listeners.

The choice of stories to be included should be influenced by the audience to be reached at the time the program is broadcast: midmorning and afternoon newscasts reach women listeners mainly and items should be selected with them in mind. The time of day also influences the kind of news material available for broadcast. While certain news events, such as disasters, may be reported at any hour, news of public events is generally reported on a fairly well-established schedule. Early morning newscasts usually review the previous evening's news, and mention events scheduled to take place that day. Noon news programs may report on Presidential press conferences, Congressional committee hearings, and European developments. Dinner-hour newscasts usually have an abundance of news material covering the entire day's events, while late evening newscasts can do little more than restate earlier newscasts or discuss events scheduled for the next day unless an unscheduled event, such as a natural disaster, breaks during the evening. Sundays are generally very dull news days because there is little official activity to make news. If you listen carefully to Sunday newscasts, you will probably discover much greater use of feature stories and summaries of earlier events than you commonly hear on weekday newscasts.

Tape-recorded, on-the-scene interviews and descriptions may supplement the material from AP, UP, or INS in constructing a newscast. Widmark's survey showed that 41 per cent of the Iowa stations made some use of tape recordings in their news programs.

In writing radio news, an editor must avoid carrying over the "inverted pyramid" style of writing used on many newspapers. Newspapers usually try to cram all the essential facts about a story into the opening sentence or paragraph. A radio newscast, on the other hand, uses a narrative technique to relate the facts in a more colloquial fashion that will be instantly intelligible to the listener who, unlike the newspaper reader, cannot dwell on any one sentence or go back to check a confusing word.

Consider the following news story which appeared in a New York newspaper a few years ago:

Assistant District Attorney Milton Altschuler, of the Bronx, said yesterday that a seventy-five-year-old woman was fatally injured

at 4:20 p.m. Wednesday afternoon when she was knocked down by a
seventeen-year-old Bronx youth who was playing street football,
and that the youth and another boy will be subpoenaed today for
appearance in his office on Dec. 1.

The woman, Mrs. Esther Beck, of 27 West 181st Street, the
Bronx, was knocked down as she crossed 181st Street at Grand
Avenue, and died at 8:40 p.m. at Morrisania Hospital. Mr. Alt-
schuler said that Irwin Chazin, of 44 Buchanan Place, admitted he
had run into the woman while catching a football thrown by
Charles Gregg, sixteen, of 2181 Davidson Avenue, the Bronx.
Other participants in the game are being sought, Mr. Altschuler
said.

The story contains the names of four different people, three ages, four
hours and days, five addresses, and nine related events—all in 133 words
divided into four sentences. Read the story aloud. Note that while it may
be satisfactory as newspaper copy, it is awkward for the reader and confusing to the listener. Compare it with the following account, which is a
rewrite of the story for radio:

A game of street football played by Bronx teen-age youths resulted in tragedy yesterday afternoon. Seventeen-year-old Irwin
Chazin, of Buchanan Place, was trying to catch a football when
he knocked down a seventy-five-year-old woman who was crossing
the street at the time. The woman, Mrs. Esther Beck, of West
181st street in the Bronx, was taken to Morrisania Hospital
where she died several hours later. The district attorney's
office is investigating the accident and will issue subpoenas for
both Chazin and sixteen-year-old Charles Gregg who threw the
football. Other participants in the game are also being sought
for questioning.

The rewritten story relates the essential facts in 26 fewer words than
the newspaper story in a way that is both easier for the announcer to read
and for the listener to understand.

In writing a newscast, complex sentence structures and difficult words
should be avoided. Verbs should be used in active rather than passive
voice whenever possible. Whereas newspapers usually employ the simple
past tense to describe events that have occurred the previous day, newscasts are often able to use the present or past perfect tense to describe
events that have occurred a few hours or minutes before broadcast time.

Governor Williams has signed the modified version of the Bonine
Tripp Law...but he says he doesn't like it,

is an example of radio's way of narrating recent events. Tongue twisters
and phrasings that might be misinterpreted by listeners should be eliminated
from all news copy. When a fairly long story tells about one individual,
some variety can be obtained by referring to the person in different ways.

Editorializing on the news through the use of emotionally-loaded adjectives or by quoting only one side in a controversy should be scrupulously
avoided. Although the practice of describing some individuals involved in

political controversy as "handsome and slim" and others as "short, gruff, or pudgy" is quite common in many news magazines and papers, it does not contribute to a fair evaluation of the controversy by listeners. Such descriptive adjectives "personalize" the news to arouse more listener interest, but they often serve to load a news story emotionally in favor of one side or another. This is not to say that descriptive adjectives should be avoided altogether; they should, however, be used with great care in reporting political news. In covering controversial news, efforts should be made to balance the news report by quoting comment from both sides and indicating the sources of all opinions. One national wire-service agency recently reported a Supreme Court decision by devoting one paragraph to the minority opinion and another to the opinion of the lower court that had been overruled. In failing to explain the majority opinion which had become the law of the land, the wire service was guilty of what, in effect, was poor and biased reporting. In this instance, a station news editor registered a complaint with the service, and New York headquarters forthwith repaired the error by adding a paragraph from the majority opinion.

Crime news should be handled with extreme care. "Morbid, sensational or alarming details not essential to the factual report, especially in connection with stories of crime or sex, should be avoided," according to the code of the National Association of Radio and Television Broadcasters.

· DELIVERING RADIO NEWSCASTS ·

The most efficient rate for delivering newscasts appears to be somewhere between 175 and 200 words per minute.[3] This rate is somewhat faster than normal radio speaking. Actually, the rate of speech in newscasts should vary according to the content and style of each story. If a newscast is constructed out of stories of widely different topics and events, a responsive reader will derive vocal variety from the changes in meaning and moods of the stories.

The reading should be clear, direct, and confident. A hesitant delivery indicates a lack of assurance, and the radio audience seems to prefer speakers who give the impression that they know what they are talking about. Newscasts should be rehearsed aloud, if time permits, to check the smoothness of sentences and to ferret out any tongue twisters. Pronunciations of place and personal names should be checked in dictionaries or in the pronunciation guides that the wire services provide daily. Many newscasters find it helpful to underline or overscore key words or names in the script and to indicate major pauses or transitions with pencilled notations so that they will have additional cues to aid their interpretation on the air.

Timing the newscast is handled much the same as timing an ordinary radio talk. Determine the average number of lines of teletype copy you

---

[3] Harold E. Nelson, "The Effect of Variations of Rate on the Recall by Radio Listeners of 'Straight' Newscasts," *Speech Monographs*, XV (1948), No. 2.

read in a minute, and compute from that the total number of lines you can handle in the broadcast period. Back-time the closing announcement and your final story. Several brief additional items should be taken into the studio as a precautionary measure to cover unexpected situations such as a miscalculation in timing. Few things can be more embarrassing to an announcer than to run short on his newscast and have to fill with announcements or music.

In reading news, an announcer should remember to avoid saying anything in any way that might conceivably alarm his listeners, for panic is epidemic, and great damage can be caused by the broadcast of frightening reports. The decision to interrupt a program on the air to broadcast important news bulletins or flashes should be made by the news director. Such interruptions should be reserved for bulletins of transcendent importance. With less important news bulletins, the news director must decide whether it is wiser to wait until a station break when the bulletin may be substituted for the scheduled announcement. Decisions like these are exercises in judgment that require a keen sense of news values and cannot be based on rules laid down in advance.

· COMMENTARY PROGRAMS ·

The main difference between programs of news and programs of commentary is found in their purpose. A newscast aims to provide news without editorial comment, while a news commentary has as its main purpose the presentation of background information and opinion to enable the listener to interpret the significance of the news. News commentaries have become a highly personal affair in American broadcasting, and there is little consistency in the manner of presentation of leading network commentators.

Six different elements can be detected in many news commentaries, however:

1. *Narration of Straight News Reports.* The available facts are stated, but inferences are not drawn. Editorial judgment determines the selection of reports for the narration of news events which provides a springboard for interpretative comment.

2. *Analyses of Personalities and Historical Forces Which Indicate the Meaning of Events.* Here the commentator tries to throw light on news developments by providing a frame of reference in which the known facts that preceded or immediately followed an event are assembled to supply interpretative perspective. The commentator points out all the relevant and significant evidence, but he makes no effort to intrude his own conclusions upon the listener.

3. *Statements of Personal Opinion.* Here the commentator expresses his own beliefs and judgments on the significance of events. These personal opinions may be expressed outright, but some commentators use the ques-

tionable technique of disguising their purely personal belief as expert or majority opinion.

4. *Prophecies of Future Events.* The desire to know what is going to happen in advance of its occurrence is a wholly normal desire. Attempts to peer into the future in social and political affairs, however, are extremely hazardous in view of all the uncontrolled variables in human and social behavior and the many limitations on available information. Prophecy, nevertheless, has become a staple of much commentary and, depending on whether it is based on verifiable evidence, "inside information," or simple hunches, it takes forms ranging from outright forecasts to meaningless ambiguities.

5. *Advocacy, or the Direct Pleading for a Cause.* This turns the commentary into little more than a political talk, with the commentator making use of his privileged position on the air to advance projects close to his personal interest and to attack others. This element of commentary has probably given rise to more controversy than any other.

6. *Drama.* Here the commentator uses narrative and dramatic techniques to create an atmosphere of excitement and the aura of importance and prestige. Sound effects of racing news tickers, "date lines," impressive introductions, and a breathless manner do much to achieve this purpose. A commentator often builds up his own prestige by referring to his associations with men in power or to his broad travels; he may refer to himself in the third person, a technique used by Walter Winchell and Fulton Lewis, Jr.; or he may set up a conflict between himself and individuals or groups with whom he differs. Great amounts of dramatic excitement have been created by some much-criticized commentators who make seemingly libelous attacks on the character or motives of persons in public life.

Occasionally a commentator creates a news event himself by revealing previously undisclosed information in the form of an interview with a public figure or the summation of his personal research. For this purpose, some commentators maintain a staff of research assistants and part-time reporters who do the leg work in developing a story.

Commentaries also differ from ordinary newscasts in that a commentator may make no effort to cover all the leading news events, but may mention less than 10 items and give extended comment to perhaps two or three stories. The personality of the commentator is usually reflected in his style of commentary. No one should undertake to broadcast commentary until he has sufficient education and experience to make his comments on political and economic events worth listening to. No one, of course, is qualified to speak on every subject that may arise in the news. A responsible commentator refrains from commenting on subjects about which he knows very little. All commentators should continually broaden their own backgrounds, but they should be aware of their present limitations and not go beyond them in their broadcasts.

Following are ten rules which have been suggested as guides of conduct for commentators:

1. Separate facts from opinions, and clearly identify the source of each.

2. If you are advancing an argument, state the premises on which you base your reasoning.

3. In your choice of topics, don't ride a hobby horse by harping on the same subject day in and day out.

4. Check and recheck all statements of fact to verify their accuracy.

5. Avoid exaggerations.

6. Do not attempt to make yourself appear infallible. Not an overweening self-assurance, but a humility derived from knowing the limitations of your evidence and the pitfalls of prediction should characterize your work.

7. Do not induce panic or extreme insecurity in listeners through excessive emotionalism.

8. Do not prejudice listeners through innuendo, distortions of fact, or suppression of vital information.

9. Do not employ your ability to dramatize an opinion on one side of an issue only.

10. Be prepared to make a sincere and equal retraction if necessary and to provide reply time to those you may attack unfairly in a broadcast.

· TELEVISION NEWSCASTS ·

Televised news programs resemble their radio equivalents quite closely, the primary difference being the addition of still and moving pictures of various news stories. Where pictures of important stories are not available, the newscaster, himself, must report about the events, making use of the material supplied by correspondents and the wire-service agencies. One technique for televising a newscast is to have the announcer sit behind a desk in front of a simple set featuring an enlarged map. At his side may be put a dummy teletype machine to suggest a newsroom, and on his desk may be placed a dummy telephone to conceal a microphone. When he reads his stories without visual aids, the camera is focused on the announcer who must develop considerable skill in memorization and manuscript delivery so that he can look at the camera instead of his script. When newsreel material or slides are used to illustrate or dramatize an event, they can be inserted into the newscast at the appropriate point, and the announcer, speaking off camera, supplies a background explanation. Sound effects of teletype machines may be used to introduce and close the show.

TV news programs have not shown any great superiority over radio news programs, except in special cases. Good news film is difficult to obtain because most of the important events of the day do not take place in front of a newsreel camera. If a photographer is lucky enough to be in the right place at the exact moment an event occurs, such as happened in the magnificent coverage of the 1955 floods in New England, excellent news shots may result. But most newsreel pictures, like most photographs that appear in newspapers, have to be posed. Cameras can be set up to take pictures of scheduled news events, but they are not always of the most interesting type. The television audience gets tired of seeing foreign ambassadors landing at the National Airport from four-motored planes day after day.

Newsreels and still pictures, moreover, do not explain the significance of events. Television cameras may picture the signing of a treaty, but they cannot summarize what the treaty says except in a very crude way, and they certainly cannot weigh its significance. Where a newscast or commentary aims to stimulate the thought processes of the viewers, it finds no significant advantage in TV over radio, except through the use of visual demonstration materials. In scheduled news events such as a Presidential inauguration or a parade, where thought stimulation is not the primary object, television has no peer, but these constitute only a small percentage of the daily fare of news.

Newscasts which try to incorporate visual material at the price of news value of the stories themselves soon take on the character of weekly movie newsreels. Instead of providing the comprehensive news coverage to which radio has accustomed the listener, these TV newscasts feature bathing-beauty contests, ski slides, and pictures of the President pinning decorations on outstanding citizens. It is not yet certain whether listeners will prefer newscasts which feature such visual materials or whether they will stick to the radio type newscast. It is true, of course, that a TV newscast can merely picture the newscaster reading his script in the fashion of a radio news program. The only criticism that has been voiced against presentations of this type has been the feeling that television audiences do not respond as favorably to the sight of a man reading his material as they do to hearing him without seeing him.

It is significant to note that on the national television networks only one regular evening newscast is scheduled per network, in contrast to the numerous news shows that are regularly carried in the evening by the radio networks. The cost of producing television news programs is many times greater than the cost of radio newscasts because of the expense involved in shooting or buying news film. The greatly increased cost, combined with the reduced number of programs against which these costs can be written off, poses a very real problem for the future of network television news.

Local television newscasts can be produced on a relatively modest scale, if incorporated with the material supplied by one of the wire-service agencies. Even so, the costs are considerably higher than most stations are accustomed to spend on radio newscasts. Station WHAS-TV, in Louisville has developed a successful locally-produced news show with a staff of only 3 full-time men—a film cameraman, a director-writer-editor, and a newscaster-supervisor. The cameraman shoots the local news film in Louisville, using an automobile to get around; the second man edits the film, writes the narration, backstops as a second film cameraman when two stories are breaking at the same time, and directs the news program; the third man is the general supervisor and does the on-camera newscasting, as well as reading of film narration. Out of this operation the station obtains each day about five minutes of edited film.[4] With the use of still photographs of people and situations in the news, mounted on art cards and set on an easel, it is possible to give visual variety to even the simplest television newscast. Just as photographs serve to add interest to newspaper reading, so even a still photo of a person or a scene renders a news report more interesting and meaningful to the viewer.

Following is a script and film-spot sheet for a typical news item on a television newscast. From this script it can be seen how carefully narration must be written and spoken in connection with news film. The news writer plans the copy to cover the picture on the screen; the newscaster must deliver the copy with an eye on the television monitor to maintain the exact speed required to remain abreast of the on-the-air film.

EXAMPLE OF SCRIPT AND FILM-SPOT SHEET
FOR A TELEVISION NEWSCAST

Title: Denver, Col. - Midget Races   Length: 43 ft. (16 mm)
                                             Time   :   71 seconds

Scene No.	Total Feet	Total Time	P I X	SOUND
A.	2	3	(TITLE)	
1.	9	15	MIDGETS LINED UP INTO SEATS	At Denver, Colorado, the smallest midget racers yet take to
2.	10	16	CROWD	the track... Piloting the pee-
3.	14	22	RACES START	wee racers are four kids - from 6 to 9 years old. The cars were built by their fathers--- like regular racing cars, they have no clutches...it takes a man-sized push to get the kid-sized racers off.....
4.	15	24	FLAG	They're under the flag for a
5.	17	28	PAST CAMERA	perfect start...Lawnmower
6.	20	33	AROUND TURN	motors furnish the power. The
7.	22	37	LS RACE	cars are half-size models of
8.	26	42	INTO STRETCH	standard midget racers. The dirt track is one-twentieth of a mile, and the kids average about 15 miles an hour...
9.	32	53	AROUND TURN	The kids slam around the turns
10.	32	54	CROWD	like pros...jockeying for posi-tion like experts...

[4] *Broadcasting-Telecasting,* June 29, 1953, p. 95.

11.	35	58	CAR SPINS-STALLS	One bantam flyer goes into a skid and stalls...he's out of the running in this race...
12.	41	68	CARE IN FINAL STRETCH	Only two cars go into the home stretch, and there's a real battle as they go under the wire...
13.	43	71	WINNER PAST FLAG	The winner ... and champion of the half-pint league!

• NEWS-IN-DEPTH PROGRAMS •

Programs that go beyond the surface of the news and penetrate into the meaning and significance of news events are often referred to as "news-in-depth" programs. The most outstanding program of this type in television has been "See It Now," produced on CBS by Edward R. Murrow and Fred W. Friendly. "See It Now" developed from Murrow and Friendly's radio news-in-depth show, "Hear It Now," which used tape-recorded voices of people involved in the news, edited into a meaningful presentation of a major news event. In "See It Now," Murrow and Friendly use specially-shot news film to tell a visual story. In a succession of highly effective programs, including special reports on the American soldier in the Korean war, the controversy over Senator McCarthy, and the security discharge, subsequently rescinded, of an Army major, "See It Now" established itself as a major influence in American public opinion. Other television programs have attempted treatments of news-in-depth; the most successful have been special one-shot shows on particular subjects of current importance.

• PRESS CONFERENCE PROGRAMS •

One major development in television news programming has been the broadcast press conference. While this type of program was broadcast over radio prior to television, it never succeeded in getting the kind of public and press attention that it has obtained in television. Programs such as "Meet the Press," "Face the Nation," and "College Press Conference" are actually a form of press conference in which a group of news reporters question a person in the news. Many public figures have used these programs to make the first public announcement of important news statements. "Meet the Press" has been especially successful in choosing timely subjects for the conference and has created many news breaks. As a result, these programs are covered regularly by the wire services for possible news. Instead of simply covering an aspect of the news, these programs thus create news themselves. The telecasts of the Presidential press conferences in Washington are, of course, news-making programs.

On a smaller scale, the press-conference type of program can be used on local stations or on educational stations. A local community leader, public official, or educator who has been involved in the news can serve as the basis for an interesting program produced in simple fashion along the lines of the discussion-type program described in Chapter 23.

Projects and Exercises

1. Have every member of the class read aloud the newscast printed on the following pages to determine his most effective rate of news reading and to demonstrate his interpretative skills.
2. Rewrite a leading news story from a local newspaper for radio broadcast.
3. Rewrite a short news account from the inside pages of a newspaper for radio broadcast.
4. Prepare a five-minute world news summary for radio broadcast, drawing on a newspaper for your material.
5. Visit your local radio station and discuss news problems with the news director. Observe the operations of the teletype machine.
6. Prepare a two-minute local news report that might be included in a national news round-up.
7. Prepare a five-minute news summary of local news for broadcast over your local station. Draw upon local and college newspapers and interviews for your material.
8. Using news photographs taken from a newspaper, prepare a short television newscast.

EXAMPLE OF A WIRE RELEASE, GENERAL NEWS

Associated Press Fifteen-Minute Summary, October 27, 1955 [5]

```
AP124
        THIRD 15-MINUTE SUMMARY
    HERE IS THE LATEST NEWS FROM THE ASSOCIATED PRESS:

    (INTRO)
    PRINCESS MARGARET HAS PAID A SURPRISE VISIT TO THE ARCHBISHOP
OF CANTERBURY, WHO IS KNOWN TO OPPOSE ANY PLAN FOR HER TO MARRY
PETER TOWNSEND...

    PRESIDENT EISENHOWER HAS CONFERRED WITH AIDES ON HIS STATE-OF-
THE-UNION MESSAGE TO CONGRESS, DUE NEXT JANUARY...

    THE BIG 4 FOREIGN MINISTERS HAVE BEGUN THEIR GENEVA CONFER-
ENCES AMID PESSIMISTIC EXPECTATIONS ON GERMAN UNIFICATION...

    AND THIS YEAR'S NOBEL PRIZE FOR LITERATURE HAS GONE TO THE
ICELANDIC NOVELIST, HALLDOR LAXNESS (HAHL'-DOR LOCKS'-NESS).

    NOW--THE LATEST DETAILS:

    (MARGARET)
    LONDON HAS BEEN SURPRISED BY A VISIT TODAY BY THE PRINCESS
MARGARET TO THE ARCHBISHOP OF CANTERBURY.
    SHE WAS IN THE ARCHBISHOP'S RESIDENCE, LAMBETH PALACE, FOR
```

[5] Courtesy of The Associated Press.

ALMOST ONE HOUR. THE ASSUMPTION IS THAT THE PRINCESS WENT TO SEE
THE CHURCH OF ENGLAND'S RANKING PRELATE ABOUT HER ROMANCE WITH
PETER TOWNSEND. A BARRIER TO THEIR MARRIAGE IS THAT THE 40-YEAR-
OLD R-A-F HERO IS DIVORCED. THE CHURCH OF ENGLAND FROWNS ON THE
RE-MARRIAGE OF DIVORCED PERSONS WHILE THEIR FORMER MATES STILL
ARE ALIVE--AS IS THE FIRST MRS. TOWNSEND.

(JOKE)
THE USUALLY STAID BRITISH BROADCASTING CORPORATION HAS, FOR
THE FIRST TIME, PERMITTED A COMEDIAN TO CRACK A JOKE ON ONE OF
ITS SHOWS ABOUT THE ROMANCE BETWEEN PRINCESS AND COMMONER. THE
GAG WAS:
"BRITAIN IS FACING ANOTHER CRISIS--THEY HAD TEA TOGETHER AGAIN
TODAY."

(GENEVA)
THE BIG 4 FOREIGN MINISTERS CONVENED IN GENEVA TODAY--IN THE
COUNCIL ROOM OF THE PALACE OF NATIONS--FOR THE CONFERENCE WHICH
GREW OUT OF LAST SUMMER'S MEETING AT THE SUMMIT.
THE FIRST DISPATCHES ARE NOT OPTIMISTIC. THEY SAY THERE AP-
PEARS TO BE NO PROSPECT OF A COMPROMISE AT THE GENEVA MEETING
BETWEEN THE WESTERN AND RUSSIAN APPROACHES TO THE MAIN PROBLEMS:
UNIFYING GERMANY AND OBTAINING A PERMANENT PEACE FOR EUROPE.
SITTING ALONGSIDE SECRETARY OF STATE DULLES IN THE AMERICAN
DELEGATION TODAY WAS DEFENSE SECRETARY WILSON.

(POSITIONS)
THE U-S, BRITAIN, AND FRANCE ARE PREPARED TO OFFER A GUARANTEE
TO RUSSIA AGAINST ANY FUTURE GERMAN AGGRESSION, IF THE SOVIET
UNION WILL AGREE TO A FREE ELECTION THROUGHOUT GERMANY AS PART OF
GERMAN UNIFICATION. UNLESS THERE IS A REMARKABLE REVERSAL OF
RUSSIAN POLICY, SOVIET FOREIGN MINISTER MOLOTOV IS EXPECTED TO
INSIST THAT FIRST THE NORTH ATLANTIC ALLIANCE BE ABOLISHED, AND
THAT A NEW EUROPEAN-WIDE SECURITY SYSTEM BE DEVISED, BEFORE EAST
AND WEST GERMANY ARE COMBINED.

(MIDEAST)
IT HAS BEEN ANOTHER DAY OF SHOOTING BETWEEN ARABS AND JEWS IN
THE MIDDLE EAST, WHICH WASHINGTON OFFICIALS CALL THE MOST CRITI-
CAL THEATER OF THE INTERNATIONAL COLD WAR.
ACCORDING TO THE ISRAELIS, TROOPS OF THE NEW ARAB MILITARY
ALLIES--EGYPT AND SYRIA--ATTACKED INSIDE ISRAEL'S TERRITORY IN
2 DIFFERENT DE-MILITARIZED ZONES. FOR THE 2ND DAY IN A ROW, THE
EGYPTIANS ARE SAID TO HAVE PENETRATED INTO THE AL AUJA (EL
OW-JAH) ZONE IN THE SOUTH, SETTING UP A 2ND ENTRENCHMENT. AND IN
NORTHERN ISRAEL, A SYRIAN FORCE IS SAID BY ISRAEL TO HAVE CLASHED
WITH AN ISRAELI FRONTIER PATROL IN NORTHEASTERN GALILEE, BUT TO
HAVE RETREATED CARRYING THE BODY OF ONE OF THEIR MEN.
IN CAIRO, OFFICIALS OF EGYPT AND SAUDI ARABIA TODAY SIGNED A
MILITARY ALLIANCE SAID TO BE PATTERNED AFTER THE ONE BETWEEN
EGYPT AND SYRIA.
AND LEBANON'S PRIME MINISTER HAS ARRIVED IN THE SYRIAN CAPITAL
FOR TALKS ON A MILITARY ALLIANCE BETWEEN THOSE 2 ARAB COUNTRIES.
ALTHOUGH WASHINGTON IS DESCRIBED AS INCREASINGLY ALARMED OVER
WHAT IS GOING ON IN THE MIDDLE EAST, THE STATE DEPARTMENT IS SAID
TO FEEL THAT ALL IT SHOULD DO FOR THE PRESENT IS URGE EVERYBODY
CONCERNED TO REMAIN CALM.

(SHARETT)
FOLLOWING HIS PARIS CONFERENCES YESTERDAY WITH SECRETARY OF
STATE DULLES AND THE BRITISH FOREIGN SECRETARY, ISRAEL'S PREMIER

SHARETT FOLLOWED THEM TO GENEVA TODAY FOR ADDITIONAL TALKS.

HE ALSO EXPECTS TO CONFER WITH FOREIGN MINISTER MOLOTOV OF
RUSSIA. SHARETT CHARGES MOSCOW IS RESPONSIBLE FOR WHAT HE CALLS
THE VERY SERIOUS DANGER CONFRONTING ISRAEL: THE ACQUISITION BY
EGYPT OF LARGE QUANTITIES OF WEAPONS FROM COMMUNIST CZECHO-
SLOVAKIA. A NEWSMAN ASKED WHETHER ISRAEL MIGHT START A PRE-
VENTIVE WAR AGAINST EGYPT. THE PRIME MINISTER REPLIED:

"I HOPE TO GOD THAT ISRAEL WILL NOT BE DRIVEN TO THIS--TO
WHAT MIGHT APPEAR TO BE A SHORT CUT TO THE SOLUTION OF OUR GRAVE
PROBLEMS."

THEN HE ADDED: "IT'S NOT THE CASE OF A PREVENTIVE WAR. IT'S
THE CASE OF MEETING AGGRESSION."

(CHINA)
ONE FLOOR BELOW THE GENEVA PALACE OF NATIONS CHAMBER WHERE THE
BIG 4 MEET, ANOTHER CONFERENCE OF INTERNATIONAL IMPORT WAS HELD
TODAY.

THIS WAS BETWEEN THE U-S AND CHINESE COMMUNIST ENVOYS WHO HAVE
BEEN PARLEYING THE PAST 12 WEEKS. ALTHOUGH TODAY'S DISCUSSION,
THE 23RD AND LONGEST SO FAR IN THE SERIES, LASTED NEARLY 3 HOURS,
THERE WAS NO ANNOUNCEMENT AS TO WHAT IT CONCERNED.

(AMERICANS)
TWO MORE AMERICAN CIVILIANS IMPRISONED IN RED CHINA ARE EX-
PECTED TO BE FREED TOMORROW, AND A 3RD IS SAID TO HAVE BEEN GIVEN
AN EXIT PERMIT.

THE 2 EXPECTED IN HONG KONG SHORTLY ARE A JESUIT PRIEST, THE
REVEREND ARMAND PROULX OF LOWELL, MASSACHUSETTS, AND MISS HARRIET
MILLS OF NEW YORK. A COMMUNIST BROADCAST SAYS A FORMER BROUGH-
TON, PENNSYLVANIA, WOMAN, MISS LAURA AUGENSTEIN, IS EXPECTED TO
LEAVE CHINA AT ANY MOMENT. SHE IS A MISSIONARY.

(NOBEL)
THIS YEAR'S NOBEL PRIZE FOR LITERATURE HAS GONE TO A WRITER
OF NOVELS ABOUT ICELAND--HALLDOR LAXNESS (HAHL'-DOR LOCKS'-NESS),
WHO IS WELL KNOWN TO AMERICAN READERS AND TO HOLLYWOOD.

IT MEANS A CASH AWARD OF ALMOST $37,000 FOR THE 53-YEAR-OLD
ONETIME SHEPHERD BOY WHO--SINCE HE WAS 17--HAS BEEN A WANDERER
ALL OVER EUROPE AND THE U-S. LAXNESS, WHO IS DESCRIBED AS A
LEFTIST, IS THE AUTHOR OF SUCH GOOD SELLERS AS "INDEPENDENT
PEOPLE," "SALKA WALKA," AND THE "THE ATOMIC STATION."

(SMOG)
FOR THE 2ND SUCCESSIVE DAY, TRAFFIC IN THE NEW ORLEANS AREA
WAS HARASSED THIS MORNING BY A HEAVY SMOG WHICH IS HELD RE-
SPONSIBLE FOR AN OUTBREAK OF ASTHMA.

TWO ASTHMA DEATHS YESTERDAY WERE BLAMED ON THE SMOG AND 350
OTHER PERSONS WERE TREATED IN NEW ORLEANS HOSPITALS. BEFORE THE
SMOG BEGAN TO LIFT TODAY, HUNDREDS OF CARS WERE MAROONED INCLUD-
ING SEVERAL ARMORED TRUCKS REPORTEDLY CARRYING 16 (M) MILLION
DOLLARS IN FEDERAL RESERVE FUNDS.

(BENSON)
A SPLIT WITHIN THE PRESIDENT'S CABINET OVER AN ATTEMPT TO GET
RID OF AGRICULTURE SECRETARY BENSON IS REPORTED BY THE MONTHLY
MAGAZINE "FARM JOURNAL."

THE MAGAZINE SAYS THAT SHORTLY AFTER PRESIDENT EISENHOWER'S
HEART ATTACK, ATTORNEY GENERAL BROWNELL, POSTMASTER GENERAL
SUMMERFIELD, AND DISARMAMENT ADVISER HAROLD STASSEN GOT BEHIND A
MOVE TO OUST BENSON AS PART OF A PLAN TO REGAIN FARM SUPPORT.
BUT, ACCORDING TO THE FARM JOURNAL, THE REST OF THE CABINET

BACKED THE AGRICULTURE SECRETARY AND NOW, IT ADDS: "VICE-PRESI-
DENT NIXON IS HAVING BENSON IN FOR CHUMMY LUNCHEONS."

(POLITICS)
THE 1956 PRESIDENTIAL CAMPAIGN WARMUP BRINGS THESE DEVELOP-
MENTS:
COMMERCE SECRETARY WEEKS SAYS PRESIDENT EISENHOWER IS HIS
CANDIDATE UNTIL HE SAYS HE IS NOT, AND AS WEEKS ADDS: "OUR PRESI-
DENT IS ON THE SIDELINES, BUT HE HASN'T GONE TO THE SHOWERS.
HE WILL BE BACK SOON."
DEMOCRATIC SENATOR ESTES KEFAUVER PREDICTS THAT ADLAI STEVEN-
SON WILL ANNOUNCE HIS CANDIDACY FOR THE DEMOCRATIC NOMINATION IN
A SPEECH IN DULUTH, MINNESOTA THIS SATURDAY NIGHT. FORMER PRESI-
DENT TRUMAN'S ONETIME NEWS SECRETARY, ROGER TUBBY, IS TAKING A
SIMILAR JOB WITH STEVENSON NEXT WEEK.

(TAX)
WHAT ARE CALLED THE MORE CONTROVERSIAL CASES AMONG MORE THAN
32,000 ORGANIZATIONS WHICH ESCAPE FEDERAL TAXES ARE BEING CHECKED
BY INCOME TAX AUTHORITIES IN WASHINGTON.
TREASURY OFFICIALS ARE MUM, BUT IT IS LEARNED THAT THEY ARE
GIVING GREATER ATTENTION TO WHAT IS CALLED A RAPIDLY GROWING
PROBLEM: HOW TO SEPARATE POLITICAL ACTION GROUPS WHICH AVOID
FEDERAL TAXES AS FOUNDATIONS OR TRUSTS, FROM GROUPS REGARDED AS
NOT TRYING ACTIVELY TO INFLUENCE LEGISLATION.

(RULING)
THE U-S COURT OF APPEALS IN WASHINGTON HAS RULED THAT A LABOR
UNION MAY ENGAGE IN HARASSING TACTICS DURING NEGOTIATIONS WITH AN
EMPLOYER WITHOUT BEING GUILTY OF FAILING TO BARGAIN IN GOOD
FAITH.
THE COURT VOTED, 2 TO 1, THAT THE HARASSMENTS COULD INCLUDE
SLOW-DOWNS. AND IT THEREBY OVERRULED A NATIONAL LABOR RELATIONS
BOARD DECISION THAT BY SUCH ACTIONS THE C-I-O TEXTILE UNION DID
NOT BARGAIN IN GOOD FAITH WITH THE PERSONAL PRODUCTS CORPORATION
OF NEW JERSEY. THE 2 U-S COURT OF APPEAL JUDGES IN THE MAJORITY
DECISION SAID THE LABOR LAW DOES NOT FORBID THE USE OF ECONOMIC
PRESSURE IN SUPPORT OF LAWFUL DEMANDS.

(WESTINGHOUSE)
ADDITIONAL NEW CONTRACT NEGOTIATIONS ARE ON TAP--- But
LITTLE HOPE OF A QUICK SETTLEMENT IS SEEN---IN THE C-I-O AND
INDEPENDENT ELECTRICAL UNION STRIKES WHICH HAVE CRIPPLED THE
WESTINGHOUSE ELECTRIC CORPORATION. WESTINGHOUSE ATTRIBUTES
PREVIOUS WALKOUTS AND A DROP IN DEFENSE ORDERS FOR A REDUCTION IN
PROFITS DURING JULY, AUGUST, AND SEPTEMBER. ITS NET INCOME FOR
THOSE 3 MONTHS TOTALED ALMOST 14 AND ONE HALF (M) MILLION
DOLLARS.

ALSO IN THE DAY'S NEWS:
IN NEW YORK-- MARILYN MONROE, WHOSE DIVORCE FROM BASEBALL
GREAT JOE DIMAGGIO BECAME FINAL TODAY, SAYS MARRIAGE IS THE
FARTHEST THING FROM HER MIND...

IN ROME-- POLICE EXPLAIN THAT MISS FINLAND OF 1955, 20-YEAR
OLD MERVA ARVONEN, HAS BEEN REFUSED PERMISSION TO ENTER ITALY ON
THE COMPLAINT OF THE WIFE OF SOMEONE CALLED A SECRETARY OF EXILED
FORMER KING FAROUK OF EGYPT. THE POLICE SAID NO BLAME IS
ATTACHED TO MISS FINLAND...IT'S JUST THAT THE EGYPTIAN WOMAN
WARNED THERE MIGHT BE TROUBLE BECAUSE OF HER HUSBAND'S INTEREST
IN THE GIRL. ONE ROME NEWSPAPER TODAY CALLED THE SITUATION
"ABSURD."

IN HOLLYWOOD-- GLORIA VANDERBILT IS RETURNING TO THE MOVIES; TO PLAY IN A WESTERN OPPOSITE FRANK SINATRA.

IN NORWALK, CALIFORIA---CHARGED WITH SMASHING A BIG WINDOW IN THE SHERIFF'S OFFICE, 39-YEAR-OLD WILLIAM PIVAR IS QUOTED AS SAYING: "I JUST HAD AN URGE TO BREAK A WINDOW. I FEEL BETTER NOW."

IN MEXICO-- WALTER WINCHELL'S DAUGHTER AND HER HUSBAND ARE ON A 2ND HONEYMOON AFTER CANCELLING DIVORCE PLANS.

(BRIEFS)
IN BURBANK, CALIFORNIA--THE LOCKHEED AIRCRAFT CORPORATION REPORTS THE AIR FORCE HAS ORDERED AN ADDITIONAL 25 (M) MILLION DOLLARS WORTH OF JET TRAINING PLANES.

IN KAPLAN, LOUISIANA-- JUST AS OIL DRILLERS FELT THEY WERE WITHIN A FEW HOURS OF BRINGING IN A BIG GUSHER, THE WELL BLEW OUT AND CAUGHT FIRE.

(FEATURE)
OUT OF WORK AND WITH THINGS, AS SHE SAYS, NOT EXACTLY PROS-PEROUS, YOU CAN IMAGINE THE EXPRESSION ON MISS STELLA KOTEWICZ'S FACE AT WHAT HAPPENED WHEN SHE BEGAN UNWRAPPING THE PACKAGES SHE JUST BROUGHT HOME FROM THE GROCERY IN PITTSBURGH, PENNSYLVANIA.
MONEY BEGAN FALLING ON THE FLOOR. MORE MONEY, SHE SAYS, THAN SHE HAD EVER SEEN.
THERE WAS $2,146 IN THE PACKAGE WHICH, IT TURNED OUT, HAD BEEN LEFT BEHIND ON THE GROCERY COUNTER BY A MAN. AND THIS PACKAGE WITH THE MONEY GOT MIXED UP WITH MISS KOTEWICZ'S BUNDLE. SHE HURRIED RIGHT BACK WITH THE MONEY, AND THE OWNER GAVE HER A $50 REWARD. MISS KOTEWICZ SAYS SHE HOPES THIS WILL CARRY HER OVER THE ROUGH SPOTS UNTIL SHE FINDS ANOTHER JOB.

MT&B225PED 27

❊ 25 ❊

Women's, Children's, and Feature Programs

MANY SPECIALIZED programs are relatively simple in structure and utilize a minimum of personnel in the performance. Examples of such programs are: (1) those featuring a commentator who presents, through individual talk and demonstration, interview, or dialogue with announcer, advice and news in the general areas of homemaking, child rearing practices, health and beauty, and news of interest to women; (2) stories for children which utilize single-voice narrations with sound and music in radio and with pictures or drawings to illustrate the narratives in television; (3) nonspot news feature programs highlighting unusual or human-interest stories, hobbies, and social or scientific advances. The latter are similar to magazine digest articles or Sunday newspaper features. The problems and techniques involved in these specialized programs are considered in this chapter.

• WOMEN'S FEATURES •

This program type has acquired a good following in radio and has received excellent response from television viewers. Women are featured as program hostesses, narrators, and interviewers. They present sales talk as homemaking consultants, or as beauty and fashion experts. The over-all personality of the woman broadcaster is extremely important, and goes beyond matters of appearance or voice quality alone. Most successful women commentators are not beauty queens or film stars, many have thin and even high-pitched voices. A pleasant, well-groomed appearance (implied in radio, evident in TV), sincerity, knowledge of subject matter, a warm, friendly, and conversational style of delivery, vital interest in people and things, and a sense of close contact with the audience, are key elements in achieving effectiveness. Those who give an impression of superiority or "talking down" to the audience, who treasure the manner of speaking over naturalness and meaningful communication, who gush or enthuse, or who are overly formal in attire and manners, do not survive in the broadcasting world. A station executive summarized these ideas as follows: "The personality should fit right into your living room. The super-sophisticate or the squealing life-of-the-party type might be all right on occasion, but a daily association with this girl is apt to get a little tiresome." [1]

If a station has any live programming at all, it usually discovers that women's features are important sources of revenue, and aid in fulfilling the station's public-service requirements. It is both good business practice and professional showmanship to "accentuate the local" in program planning. The women's commentator should analyze the interests and needs of her potential audience, participate in local affairs, become adept at public relations, develop contacts for information on upcoming events, organize campaigns for civic and social improvement, initiate rather than passively report on happenings in the station area. The need to personalize material instead of relying on "canned" releases sent to the station, and to adapt this material to the interests of her audience are vital. It should be remembered also that not all programming activity need be confined to the studio or to guests who come to the station. The tape recorder, and the still- or sound-film camera, can add authenticity to first-hand reports of visits to "Garden Day," "Juvenile Court," "Centennial Celebration," "Bake Sale," or "Girl Scout's Juliette Low Birthday Observance."

Several years ago women's programs were restricted to the broadcast of recipes and information on such topics as fashions and interior decorating. Today women's programs include social and political topics of local and international significance. Many programs attempt to combat juvenile delinquency; introduce women to labor-saving techniques; improve child care; expand the horizon of the audience with book reviews and interviews on cultural activities; and increase the knowledge and understanding of scientific advancements and world organizations. Of course, the lighter side of the news and human interest features are not neglected.

EXAMPLE OF A NETWORK WOMAN'S PROGRAM
"Home," NBC-TV, October 25, 1954 [2]

The "Home" show with Arlene Francis as MC was introduced on NBC as a part of its "Magazine" approach to television programming. It has been well received. In 1955, the results of a survey were released which showed that "Home" led all specifically named publications except one, plus all newspapers, radio, and other TV programs, as "a main source of home-making information and ideas in the urban United States." [3]

---

[1] Franklin Sisson, of WOOD-TV, in *Thirty Two Television Talks* (New York, 1955), p. 144.
[2] Courtesy of National Broadcasting Company.
[3] *Variety,* August 17, 1955, p. 31.

Three segments of the hour broadcast are reproduced. Hugh Downs is the announcer. The term "logo" refers to the program's identifying symbol.

OPENING

CU: <u>HANDY AID BOOKS</u>

HUGH: (VO)
Do you know what this is? It's just
one of the many things you'll see
today on HOME.

WIDE SHOT OF STUDIO

SUPER LOGO

HUGH: (VO)
NBC presents the 169th daily edtion
of HOME, starring Arlene Francis-----

ARLENE:
Good Morning.

(LIFTS OPEN COPY OF "ALICE IN WONDER-
LAND" FROM DESK)
Here's a bit of verse familiar to
most everybody. Six lines from Lewis
Carroll's nonsense poem, "The Walrus
and the Carpenter"...
(READS)
"The time has come," the Walrus said,
"To talk of many things:
Of shoes--and ships--and sealing wax
Of cabbages--and kings--
And why the sea is boiling hot--
And whether pigs have wings."

(CLOSES BOOK) Well, we all know that
pigs don't have wings and now a
recent news item tells us that
<u>giraffes</u> can't fly either....It seems
that recently one Mr. Alton V.
Freeman arrived at the United States
Animal Quarantine Station in Clifton,
New Jersey, planning to ship a
giraffe by airplane to the Dade
County Zoo in Miami....The giraffe
was a mere slip of a girl, weighing a
thousand pounds and only nine feet
high in her stocking feet...but this
was a shade too high for air travel.
It was evident that our gangling girl
would have to stick her neck and head
out all the way south and this just
wouldn't work.....You know, rarefied
air bad for the nostrils, whistling
wind might blow off her eyelashes,
flatten her horns and all that sort
of thing....The upshot was Mr.
Freeman had to settle on truck travel
for his nine foot hitch-hiker and

ARLENE WITH LARGE OPENED
COPY OF "ALICE IN
WONDERLAND"

even <u>that</u> method promises trouble....
underpasses, low bridges and so
forth. It was decided that at such
moments our girl would just have to
duck, that's all....Luckily giraffes
have no voices or this one might be
crooning-----

(SINGS, TUNE OF "LOW BRIDGE")
"Low bridge, everybody down, I'm a
traveling giraffe, and I'm going to
town!"

(SMILES) That's all. Folksinger
Francis now signing off......Now, in
a more serious vein, let's consider
singing, consider the joy and the
great release that a song can bring
to us.....

GOD'S WONDERFUL WORLD   GOD'S WONDERFUL WORLD

ARLENE:
A song.....a song of inspired words
and music, is an expression of deep
feeling. There are love songs and
comic songs. Songs that make us
laugh and cry. There are convivial
and patriotic songs.

And...There are songs about God....   DISSOLVE ARLENE IN FRONT
                                        OF AREA A: FADE IN KIDS
                                        SINGING IN AREA F

CUE: CHORAL GROUP

(FIRST SONG: "JESUS LOVES ME")

                                        DISSOLVE KIDS: FADE
ARLENE: IN ARLENE
Thank you children. That was fine.
In just a minute we'll hear from you
again. But first I would like to
tell our viewers something about you
and your inspired leaders, Mrs. Agnes
Mason and Mrs. Phyllis Ohanian.

Mrs. Mason and Mrs. Ohanian are the
authors of a unique and joyous song-
book for children that has just been
published. It is called "God's
Wonderful World."

(ARLENE HOLDS UP POCKET AND STANDARD   CU OF BOOKS
BOOKS)

It contains more than one-hundred-
and-fifty songs and hymns. Stories
from the bible; stories of wonders
that surround a child; and stories
about people. The two authors of the
book are also mothers and teach at
the Saugatuck Congregational Sunday
school in Westport, Conn. Through

their interest in music and love of
children this book came to be.

(ARLENE MOVES TO AREA G, NEAR PIANO)   PAN ARLENE INTO PIANO

ARLENE:
Good morning........
Are these members of your Sunday
school classes?

Tell us, Mrs. Mason, when was it that
you decided to compile these songs
for children?

MASON:
Several years ago, I felt the need
for more songs about God and His
World, which were suitable and under-
standable to young children.
(AD LIB SEARCH AND DIFFICULTY IN
FINDING SUITABLE SONGS OF THIS TYVE
FOR CHILDREN)

ARLENE:
And the songs in the book, are they
both original and old favorites?

OHANIAN:
(AD LIB 100 ORIGINAL AND 59 FOLK AND
CHURCH SONGS)

ARLENE:
Did one of you compose the music and
the other the words?

MASON:
(AD LIB ANSWER)

ARLENE:
Why do you feel that children need
their own songs? Didn't you feel
there already existed enough hymns
and religious songs?

OHANIAN AND MASON:
(AD LIB: FIRST, LACK OF MUSICAL
SIMPLICITY IN MOST SONGS: SECOND,
CONFUSION DUE TO SYMBOLISM IN TEXT OF
EXISTING SONGS)

ARLENE:
Your choristers look all ready to
sing again. (TO KIDS) Would you
like to sing for us again?

OHANIAN:
How about something seasonal, Arlene?
From one of the sections in the book,
called the seasons "Goodbye Dear
Robin."   GOOD BYE DEAR ROBIN, KIDS

CUE: CHILDREN SING

ARLENE:
(SITTING DOWN WITH CHILDREN)
Fine, etc... and what other kind of
songs is there in the book?

OHANIAN:
They know a song about Elephants,
from the section of animal songs.

CUE: "ELEPHANTS"   KIDS SING "ELEPHANTS"

ARLENE:
Fine, etc...(GOES TO PIANO) I see
there's a section of songs about
HOME...how about one from there?

CUE KIDS: KIDS SING "HERE'S A BALL
                                         FOR BABY"
(IF TIME, ARLENE ASKS ABOUT CO-OPER-
ATION BEHIND THIS WORK AND ENCOURAGE-
MENT FROM MINISTERS, TEACHERS ETC.
WHILE BOOK WAS BEING WRITTEN)

ARLENE:
It's only Monday but after all,
Monday is close to Sunday. Do the
children know a song about going to
church?

MASON:
(AD LIB FINAL SELECTION INTRO: STATE
IMPORTANCE OF GESTURES)

CUE: KIDS SING "OUR MINISTER"   KIDS SING: "OUR MINISTER"

ARLENE:
(CLOSE)
Thank you for being with us on HOME   USE ARLENE'S CLOSE AS
today....etc....and...I know that it   WARN CUT-AWAY CUE FOR OUT
must be a rewarding experience for   OF TOWN STATIONS
both of you to realize that these
songs...many of them your songs...
will be sung by children many times,
for many, many years to come. Truly,
you have accomplished something fine,
in explaining God's Wonderful World
to children.....in verse and music.   CUT-AWAY

....

                                         ECU FREEZE-DRIED
                                         (DEHYDRATED) STEAK IN
                                         ARLENE'S HAND.

ARLENE: (VO)
Well, well! What won't they think of   PULL BACK MS ARLENE &
next? Just look at this.....   STEAK

HUGH: (VO)
What is it? A tired old sponge?

ARLENE:
You're not even warm, Hugh, but I
will admit it'll look better after
it's soaked in water.

HUGH:
(ENTERS SHOT, TAKES A LOOK AT STEAK)   TWO SHOT AS HUGH ENTERS
It's a steak! (FEELS IT GINGERLY)
Or is it?

ARLENE:
Good boy! Yes, it's a dehydrated--or
Freeze-Dried T-Bone Steak. It came
from the Agricultural Experiment
Station of the College of Agriculture
of the University of California.

HUGH:
(PATS HER SHOULDER) Good girl! That
was quite a mouthful.

ARLENE:
And so will this be after it's soaked
for fifteen minutes.

HUGH:
Arlene, I don't want to be a doubting
Thomas, -- but I doubt it.

ARLENE:
No, this is for real. The Department
of Food Technology out there sent it
to us, knowing our viewers would be
interested in the latest developments
in food preservation. While it looks
pretty anemic at the moment, this
steak can be rehydrated by submerging
it in room temperature water for 15
minutes.

HUGH:
(TURNS STEAK OVER, INSPECTS IT)
Doesn't look very red-blooded to me.

ARLENE:
Not now, but they say that once it's
cooked it will look and taste just
like any other steak.

HUGH:
This isn't for sale in grocery and
meat stores, yet, is it?

ARLENE:
No. Freeze-dried meat products are
still in the research stage....Hugh,
let's do a little research right here
at HOME. I'll ask Chef Phillip to
soak this and cook it for us later
this week and we'll show it to our
viewers and tell them what it tastes
like.

HUGH:
(DUBIOUSLY) Er....Who's going to
taste it?

ARLENE:
(GRINS) We'll toss a coin.

HUGH:
I have a feeling I'm not going to get
the break.

ARLENE:
At this point, <u>everybody</u> gets a break
---a station break and then we'll be
back with some brand new party games.
LOGO
MUSIC

BREAK

• CHILDREN'S PROGRAMS •

Narrative programs directed toward young children are economical to produce and attract loyal audiences. Phonograph record companies have discovered this market and have become quite active in production of albums. It is a field in which the smallest radio or television station can be active. Even the station which has no live studio cameras can still produce such series by using voice over narration during visual transmission of drawings on its opaque projectors.

The many volumes of children's literature are excellent program sources if the station does not have a writer for original scripts and an artist to illustrate them. Publishers may authorize use of their stories, and even illustrations, providing a small fee is paid. It may be feasible to work out co-operative arrangements with local book stores to reduce or eliminate the fee. When such a series is produced as a sustainer without a commercial sponsor, either by the station directly, or in co-operation with a local public-service organization, the library or public school system, etc., the publisher may permit the use of his story without charge. Many classical and folk stories are in the public domain and may be used at will. These stories generally require some editing and simplifying for children's broadcasts.

In building a series of children's programs, it is important to consider the general interests of children according to age groups. A story well suited for a six-year-old will be too simple for a ten-year-old. Children are less discriminating toward dramatic programs, however. A ten-year-old will listen to dramatic versions of stories, which he will neither listen to in narrative form nor read himself. Generalizations about the interests of children are difficult to make because of individual differences, but a rough classification may be helpful for those planning series of children's programs. Regional differences, of course, influence these classifications.

Age 4-5

The Mother Goose stories, repetitive jingles and stories dealing with very familiar things around the home or farm. Sample titles: *The Three Bears, Red Hen, Chicken Little, The Pig with a Straight Tail, Noisy Books, Big Dog Little Dog.*

Age 6-7

Stories with a little plot. Familiar transportation methods and animals and some simple fairy stories. Sample titles: *Jack and the Beanstalk, The Tinderbox, Cry Fairy, How the Camel Got its Hump, Golden Touch, The Little*

Engine That Could, Hop O My Thumb, Honk the Moose, Choo Choo the Little Switch Engine.

Age 8-9

The fairy story is well liked. Beginning of folk tales and stories from other lands. Continued interest in animal stories. Sample titles: Grimm and Hans Christian Andersen stories, Oz stories, *Winnie the Pooh, The Wind in the Willows, Mother West Wind* series, *Li Lun Lad of Courage.*

Age 10-12

More attention to the outside world and reality instead of fairy stories. Beginning of sharp divisions of interest between boys and girls. Biography and animal stories have appeal to both. Adventure, invention, and sports have great interest for the boys. Romantic fiction and stories of home and school hold more interest for the girls. Some classic titles: *Treasure Island, Heidi, Swiss Family Robinson, Robin Hood, Hans Brinker, Black Beauty, Tom Sawyer.*

The writer of children's narratives should approach the subjects from the child's point of view, not from the adult's. The child has the thrill of the new world unfolding before him and is highly imaginative. He accepts the fantasy of toads and trees talking. The concentrated attention which the child gives to the program makes it possible to have several characters and a simple plot. He will follow and remember correctly many specific details and characters, if they are properly identified. This does not mean that the writer can take advantage of this habit of attention and introduce long descriptive passages. Interest must be maintained through the action of the story. Direct conversational style is imperative. Classic fairy stories should not be presented as they appear in print, but edited to make the speech smooth and fluent. Horror passages usually can be changed to retain the excitement of the story without inducing fright. A narrative which casually tells about a witch cutting off sixty-seven heads may be accepted, whereas a dramatization of the same event would be too gruesome for broadcast.

EXAMPLE OF ADAPTATION TECHNIQUES (RADIO)

"The Snow Queen," A classic story, rewritten by Ethel Joyce Atchinson.[4]

Parallel columns indicate the changes in style between the original version and adaptation.

1. THE FRIENDLY BEGINNING

"Now we are about to begin and you must attend; and when we get to the end of the story, you will know more than you do now about a very wicked hobgoblin."

Hello there! This is the story about a wicked old hobgoblin, who was so very, very wicked that--well, just listen to this story about all the terrible things that he did.

[4] Courtesy of the author and University of Michigan Department of Speech.

2. DESCRIPTION

"The most beautiful landscapes reflected in it looked like boiled spinach and the best people became hideous or else they were upside down and had no bodies. Their faces were distorted beyond recognition and if they even had one freckle it appeared to spread all over the nose and mouth. The demon thought this immensely amusing."

In the mirror the trees looked all brown and wilted, the grass and flowers lost all their color. And the people! In the mirror, people were all upside down. Their noses looked a foot long and the corners of their mouths always turned down. How the demon laughed when he saw how ugly the mirror made people look.

3. MODERNIZING AND UNIVERSALITY

"The roses were in splendid bloom that summer; the little girl had learnt a hymn and there was something in it about roses and that made her think of her own. She sang it to the little boy and then he sang it with her —'where the roses deck the flowery vale, there, Infant Jesus, we thee hail.' The children took each other by the hands, kissed the roses and rejoiced in God's bright sunshine and spoke to it as if the Child Jesus were there."

The roses in the tiny garden were so beautiful that summer. The little girl and boy would make up songs about the roses and dance and sing in the bright sun. The sun, the roses and happiness...what a wonderful summer!

4. CREATING SUSPENSE

"Kay and Gerda were looking at a picture book of birds and animals one day—it had just struck five by the church clock—when Kay said, 'Oh, something struck my heart, and I have got something in my eye.' The little girl put her arms around his neck, he blinked his eye, there was nothing to be seen."

One day when Gerda and Kay were playing in the garden a terrible thing happened. Just as the clock in the village struck five, Kay screamed! Gerda ran to him! What was the matter, what could it be! Why had Kay screamed so? "Ohhh!" was all that Kay could say. "Oh, Kay," said Gerda, "what has happened?" "I don't know," said Kay, "All of a sudden I had a funny feeling in my heart." "In your heart?" "Yes, and then it got in my eye," said Kay. Gerda didn't know what to think. Was something wrong with her friend?

5. DRAWING IMAGINATIVE PICTURES

"The snow-flakes grew bigger and bigger till at last they looked like big white chickens. All at once they sprang on one side, the big sledge stopped and the person who drove got up, coat and cap smothered in snow. It was a tall and upright lady all shining white, the Snow Queen herself."

The snow flakes grew bigger and bigger and bigger until they looked almost like soft white feathery clouds. Suddenly the big sleigh stopped and the driver of the sleigh turned to look at Kay. And do you know who the driver was? Standing right there before Kay was a beautiful lady all dressed in the purest of white fur. Tiny sparkling diamonds were scattered all over her huge muff and hat. The lady was the most beautiful that Kay had ever seen as she stood there before him all white and sparkling, just like ice and snow when the sun shines on it. Why it was the Snow Queen herself!

Men or women may be featured in presentation of children's stories. In most stations this duty is assigned to the woman's editor. In television, when men are used, frequently a character role is developed, such as a Western cowboy, "old timer," clown, "uncle or cousin," or, as at WHA-TV in Madison, Wisconsin, "The Friendly Giant." Gushiness, mock enthusiasm, and artificial manners are taboo in the narration of these tales; the delivery must reveal genuine interest in the story. Exaggerated characterizations, playing with nonsense words and rhythms, and reacting to the action in the story with an illusion that the performer is also hearing or seeing it for the "first time" help in achieving a professional presentation. Direct visual contact is gained in television by talking directly to the lens. Spontaneous and facile facial expressions and gestures are effective when they are motivated by the material. Children are suspicious of "overplaying." The rate of delivery should be somewhat slower in children's narratives than in other types of narratives. The child has to imagine the scene in radio or to absorb the visual in television. Too rapid a pace, as is likely to happen when beginners are involved, may confuse him.

Radio. Sound and live or recorded music should be used when appropriate. Several music bridges are recommended. These permit breaks in attention. Many children have not learned to take advantage of relatively static passages to shift attention as adults do. The music bridges almost force them to relax their attention for a while. Sound effects are also effective production devices. Here you have an interesting contrast. Sound effects in scenes which are close to the experience of the children—cars, telephone, running, planes, trains, horses—should be authentic and realistic. Children are quick to spot the difference between the real sound and the sound effect. It would be better to let them use their imagination about sounds, or use vocalizations in exaggerated manner if realistic sound is not possible in these instances. In fantasies and fairy stories, however, children will accept sounds of a highly imaginative nature. A slide whistle can be a magic carpet to transport Aladdin's palace to the Far East, it can be the rapid growth of Jack's magic beanstalk into the sky, it can be the shrinking of a child into a tiny elf.

Television. Not only is the child able to see the story teller in television, but the writer and director have, in addition to sound and music, visuals of various kinds, puppets, and marionettes, actors, action, and camera and electronic tricks to interest and tell the story. Some children's program series such as "Disneyland," "Howdy Doody," "Mickey Mouse Club," "Ding Dong School," "Lassie," "Rin Tin Tin," "Kukla Fran and Ollie," "Roy Rogers," "My Friend Flicka," and many Westerns have achieved great popularity. It is true that children would not have been termed "TV's most avid fans" if they watched only the children's programs. As all surveys point out, they begin at an early age to tune in the adult situation comedies, quizzes, mysteries, detective stories, variety shows, half-hour dramas, serials, and any movie. However, we are concerned here in those programs with relatively simple formats, especially designed for children. These programs might be produced by a station staff or by organizations or institutions such as schools, universities, libraries, Junior Leagues, who build programs for broadcast.

• SIMPLE FORMATS FOR CHILDREN'S TV PROGRAMS •

1. *Narrator with Stills*—drawings in the studio or on opaque projector, RP or regular slides, photographs. Camera shots vary from full- to shoulder-shots of story teller as he talks directly to the audience. Cut to stills in harmony with story progression. Proportion of camera time allotted to stills and talent depends upon personality of the performer and number of available visuals. Variety and heightened interest may result from camera movement during the showing of a visual. A single drawing may be designed to serve for several shots. For example, a neutral still of the lead character may be shot with head shot, extreme close-up of eyes, waist-shot, or as a one-shot at different times in the story while he is supposed to be talking or thinking. Dollies in and back may give additional variety. Another example might be a street-scene shot in a sequence of different framed shots as the camera tilts up following the character in the story walk along the street. Then the camera pulls back for a cover shot and fades to black as a magic carpet wafts him away from the city. And a final example is a pan back and forth, or dissolves between two cameras, from the face of a mother

bird talking to a fledgling during dialogue between them about problems of learning to fly. Writer, director, and artist should each bear in mind the many uses of visuals as they approach the story. The set for this type as well as those to follow may be only a draped background, a standard set simulating a "circus tent," "magic story room," "garden nook," "old timer's ranch," "giant's castle" etc., or varied from program to program with display paper sketched background, realistic or stylized set or rear screen projection background.

2. *Narrator with Children in the Studio.* One, two, or a group of children may gather to listen to the story and engage in dialogue with the narrator. Camera shots which transmit their reactions, usually intriguing and natural, may be employed during the presentation. The children may be requested to re-enact segments, participate in rhymes or physical action, or answer questions about the story.

3. *Story Teller Who Draws the Illustrations While the Narrative Is Told.* This action may be very effective in keeping interest. Pausing while the sketching is in progress may be desirable at times. Finishing a cartoon with a flourish may reinforce a "punch" line. This approach may be varied by having some of the sketches predrawn, partially drawn ahead of air time, or by having another person, an artist partner (either on or off camera) draw while the story is in progress.

4. *Narration with Stills and Off-Camera Voices for Dialogue Sections.* The voice over segments may be best used when the camera is on the visuals. Properly used, this technique may approximate a dramatic presentation, but without the need for rehearsing action and memorizing lines. The actors read their speeches "off camera."

5. *Narration with Pantomime.* Child actors or staff members may act out the story in pantomime while it is being told. The characters may or may not be in costume, with or without props and set, in full view or in silhouette.

6. *Narration with Film.* Standard film from library sources or special film. One director secured footage of a German circus which had been photographed by a visitor overseas. He brought in a group of children into the studio who watched the film with the narrator and then drew, on camera, their impressions of the individual scenes or characters which interested them most. Film of a local zoo, fire or police station, farm, dairy, bakery, quarry, etc., may be incorporated into the stories or used as "teasers."

7. *Performer with Other Types of Visuals*—the cardboard cut-out type, standing free or pinned up on boards, felt figures placed on felt board, pipe-cleaner figures, or toy houses, dolls, animals, cars, railroads, farm yards, trees, etc. Movement may be accomplished through animation, pulls, camera "superimps," magnet boards, operating and manipulating toys by wires, or by moving cameras. "The Friendly Giant" series opens with a camera pan along a miniature outdoor set, using toy objects and figures, which the viewing audience accepts as life size. Then suddenly huge boots

are seen as the camera continues to pan, dwarfing the landscape. A slow tilt up and up to the giant's face reinforces the impression of hugeness.

8. *Performer, Dialogue, Singing, with Hand Puppets or Marionettes.* This technique has been adopted widely and dates back to the phenomenal success of the "Kukla, Fran, and Ollie" program which began in 1947. Many variations may be found across the country. Complete stories or sequences may be performed or acted out with pantomime and dialogue. Actors off camera read the lines. Bil and Cora Baird and their puppets also illustrate this type of presentation. A human being may appear on camera working with and talking to the puppets or marionettes. "The Strange Adventures of Maggie Muggins," which is included in this chapter, illustrates an approach where a little girl is featured with the animal characters. A complex network version where several adults participate is NBC's "Howdy Doody." It has vaudeville or variety show units incorporated in a thin story line.

9. *Preschool or Kindergarten Home-Participation.* The performer talks directly to the young fry, telling stories, singing songs, demonstrating how-to-do-it projects suitable for their age. Emphasis is upon stimulation of activity by the child. The performer teaches them games and songs, shows them how to construct a cut-out puzzle from a magazine advertisement, a tambourine from paper plates, or a tom-tom from a cereal container, interspersed with "exercise sessions." Miss Frances Horwich's "Ding Dong School" on NBC established a pattern which has had considerable influence. Performers must have an intimate and thorough knowledge of the interests and capabilities of the preschool child, speaking and moving in harmony with the rhythm and frame of reference of the child's world. Excitable, fast chatter and a rapid style are ineffective. The director must remember also that too much camera movement and too many camera cuts may confuse and distract the child viewer.

10. *Variety Show Format.* (*a*) Performers work in regular street clothes or in costume and make-up for a character role. Examples of the latter may be a circus clown, a magician, a Western ranch hand, a magic story lady. Children's talent shows are frequently broadcast. An MC may introduce film shorts and cartoons, speciality vaudeville or circus acts, phonograph-record pantomime units, or broad slapstick comedy sequences. A story line may run through one program or a series.

(*b*) Basically the same as above but with a ventriloquist and dummy partner. Real persons and puppets may be included, as in the "Paul Winchell-Jerry Mahoney Show." WJAR-TV, Providence, Rhode Island, has programmed a one-camera daily show using little more space than the width of a puppet theater. The "Children's Theater" series features Ted Knight, who is a ventriloquist, his dummy, and various other puppets including a St. Bernard dog puppet that has become a favorite. Considerable dialogue is used. Included in the program are two to three six-minute cartoon films. Mr. Knight frequently conducts campaigns which call for participation by the home audience, snapshots for comments by characters, contests to name new characters, rhymes, or drawings.

Producers and talent alike should bear in mind the advice on children's programs developed by the NBC Children's Program Review Committee and discussed in Chapter 10. The following summary of the essential qualities in a TV children's program set down several years ago by Burr Tillstrom, creator of "Kukla, Fran, and Ollie," will also prove very helpful.

> First among the qualities to be sought after is simple sincerity. The wise showman won't try to do any faking before a young audience: neither will he attempt subtleties. The first they are likely to see through, the second they are not likely to understand.
>
> This is particularly true in television, where characters and situations are much more real and infinitely closer than they ever could be in any other medium. The camera takes you right into the living room, and there is no place to hide; everything you do is seen, and the television camera is almost unbearably honest.
>
> Therefore, the fewer complications involved in a children's program, the better. The simplest props and the least complicated plots have the most appeal. Even adults tire of the too-elaborate.
>
> Secondly, a children's program should be certain of its facts. When anyone on a children's show trips up on pronunciation or on the historical, geographical or arithmetical details, you can be sure the program hears from children and from all ages. As long as the program-planners make sure that the children never see or hear anything unkind, however, the correspondents are correspondingly gentle. Then the corrections are as lovable as a compliment.
>
> A third quality to be aimed at is that of imagination. For while children are intensely practical, they're also highly imaginative. Much of their play is make-believe, and, universally, they love fairy tales, the Oz books and similar fantasies. They find a show that makes that sort of stories real to them a delight.
>
> Informality or intimacy is the fourth point to be stressed for young audiences (although I think it can apply to older audiences as well). Children love to feel that they are a part of the show; and if your audiences are part of you, you are pretty certain of their loyalty.[5]

EXAMPLE OF CHILDREN'S PROGRAM WITH PUPPETS AND REAL PERSON

"The Strange Adventures of Maggie Muggins," Part 13, by Mary E. Grannan.[6]

This series has an established record of audience popularity in Canada. Miss Grannan is a staff writer for the CBC. The series was originally adapted from the "Maggie Muggins" series of books published by the Thomas Allen Publishing Company. Miss Joanne Hughes is the producer.

[5] *New York Times,* April 24, 1949. Courtesy of *New York Times* and Burr Tillstrom.

[6] Courtesy of the author and the Canadian Broadcasting Corporation.

The series was supervised by the Television Children's Department of the CBC at CBLT, Toronto, Canada, Fred B. Rainsberry, Supervising Producer.

The basic puppet house set has an "L" shape. The little girl works in the area where two stages are joined so that she is framed by the stage from various angled camera shots. An opening scene in a standard garden set with Maggie's friend, Mr. McGarrity, also a real person, reveals that Maggie is going to the circus to watch her animal friend, Fitzgerald, who is a field mouse, enter a contest at a circus. The script concerns itself with what happens at the circus, including a fall for the mouse who bragged too much —a fall which was broken by a haystack.

DISSOLVE TO MOUSE HOUSE. FITZGERALD'S PANTS ARE SEQUINED. THERE IS ONE SEQUIN ON EACH EAR. HE IS DOING PUSH-UPS.

FROG: (ON ROCKING CHAIR) Fitzgerald, I don't know as I am too happy about this venture of yours...

FITZ: That's too bad, Grandmother Frog, just too bad. (GETS UP ...GOES TO HER) But you'll be both proud and happy when you see my silver cup on the piano.

FROG: Your life is worth more than a silver cup and I feel it in my bones that this is going to come to no good end.

FITZ: Do you know what you feel in your bones? That same rheumatism you're always groaning about, and it has nothing to do with my sway pole exhibition...(BACK TO EXERCISE) Got to limber up a little...One...two...three...four...one...two...three... four...

MAGGIE (OFF) Yooo hoo...anybody home...? (ENTER)

FITZ: TO FEET...BOW...LEFT...RIGHT...CENTRE...

MAGGIE: Oh Fitzgerald, you look sweet...just like a real circus mouse.

FITZ: Pretty Snazi, eh? I'm all spangled up for the big show...

FROG: I don't feel too good about the whole thing, Maggie. I wish he'd forget about this contest.

FITZ: Well I won't. Adventure is in my blood. Today I am about to become the most famous sway pole artist in the world...(ARM UP EXPANSIVE) My name will be emblazoned in lights...I'll be the toast of the town.

MAGGIE: It doesn't matter what you say, Fitzgerald. I'm like Grandmother Frog...I'm worried too...What if you lost your balance.

DISSOLVE TO CIRCUS TENT SCENE...BG IS LIKE SIDES OF CIRCUS BIGTOP ...IN DISTANCE BLEACHERS SHOWS DOTS OF PEOPLE ON OTHER SIDE OF RING...WE NEED A PLATFORM FOR LION...LION WORKS ON FOUR FEET... MUST BE ABOUT 18 INCHES WIDE...MAGGIE ENTER WITH FROG ON SHOULDER FIND PLACE TO SIT...RAIL IN FRONT OF THEM...FROG LEAPS TO RAIL... MUSIC...CIRCUS MARCH BG...FROG WALKS RAIL NERVOUSLY

MAGGIE: Sit down, Grandmother Frog... sit down and enjoy yourself.

FROG: I can't, Maggie...I'm worried...I have a feeling of approaching doom.

MAGGIE: Don't be silly...I don't feel a bit doomy.

VOICE: (OFF) Ladies and Gentlemen...Your attention please. (MUSIC OUT) We bring you today, for the first time, that charming...that enchanting personality..."Rumble, the Gentle Lion"...He will sing for you...Ladies and Gentlemen...He will dance for you...He will win your hearts...Ladies and Gentlemen ...And now, here he is..."Rumble, the Gentle Lion"...

LION ENTER...BOW COYLY...
SOUND APPLAUSE

LION: (SING...YANKEE DOODLE)
I am a very gentle lion
And my name is Rumble
And I came from South Africa
My home is in the jungle.
I dance and dance, and dance and sing
I jump about and tumble
I am a very gentle lion
Although my name is Rumble.

SOUND APPLAUSE

MAGGIE: Isn't he sweet, Grandmother Frog?

FROG: I don't know.   I can't think of anything but Fitzgerald on that pole.

MUSIC UP
CLOSE-UP OF LION DANCING   (OUT ON CUE)
MUSIC OUT
SOUND APPLAUSE
LION BOW OUT EXIT

• FEATURES •

Other programs which attract good audiences, though perhaps not the highest ratings, may be constructed in straight narrative or multivoice fashion. These programs present information which is unusual or little-known, material of specialized interest, human-interest stories, and background and interpretative material for better understanding of the world. Feature programs may provide an attractive package program for sale by a local station or a feature segment may be included within the framework of another station or network program. Tape recordings with on-the-spot inserts give added impact and realism to radio features. Silent film with voice over narrative or sound film do the same for television. Staging, interviews, and demonstrations may be added, of course, as productions become more complex.

If the program is a solo presentation, it is essential that the narrator possess a definite air personality. The reputation of the individual as a world traveler, historian, sportsman, agricultural specialist, newspaper columnist, publisher or drama critic may attract the people at the start of a series, but the audience will not continue to tune in regularly if the individual is not intrinsically interesting. An announcer's style of delivery is not necessary— some persons may be very informal in manner and others more formal; but all should be direct, vital, and stimulating. John Nesbitt and his "Passing Parade," Cedric Adams in the Midwest, Bill Leonard in New York, and Paul Coates in Los Angeles are examples of personalities who established themselves in feature programming. Earl Selby, a well-known personality in Philadelphia, may serve as a representative example of a successful local-feature series. Selby has a 5-minute telecast at 6:25 on WCAU-TV each week day. He combines his television assignment with other duties as a reporter and columnist on the *Philadelphia Bulletin*. He explains, "It's kind of like leaning on the back fence chatting. The problems may not be earth-shakers but they hit the neighbor where he lives." The series is entitled, "Mr. Fixit." In addition to personal discussions on civic improvement issues he helps people by: discovering a store that carries young ladies' size 5-AAAA shoes in fashionable styles; instructing a Scottish bride-to-be how to season steak before broiling; locating at a thrift shop a $3 prom dress for a girl who could not afford regular prices; and transmitting expert advice on how a man could get rid of bats in his window shutters.[7]

The interest of a segment of the audience may be keen enough in a specialized subject that they will tune in to programs dealing with it, even though a recognized authority is not handling the presentation. Traffic reports by a police official assigned to the safety detail, case histories of confidence games, swindles and other rackets, weather reports from local U. S. Weather Bureau stations, as well as series on wild life and the outdoors, stamp collections, humane society activities and "how-to-do-it," are a few of the types of programs which fall into this category. When special talent is not practical, a staff member of a station who is able to "speak the language" may do a satisfactory job. Many sources of material are available to writers of these narrative features: government reports and surveys, standard reference books, private business booklets, and research organizations, college and university bulletins, and first-hand personal investigation. Articles in magazines and newspapers may provide a springboard to develop a topic with local tie-ins and applications.

On page 588 is an example of a TV film feature, "Theodore Roosevelt's House," which employs single-voice narration.

EXAMPLE OF A RADIO FEATURE NARRATIVE
Excerpt from "Michigan Journal of the Air" [8]

The straight radio narrative is changed in this example to use two announcers and one woman's voice. Many beginning narrators have a tendency to use a delivery that is too hurried and overly dramatic.

[7] *Time,* August 29, 1955, pp. 37-38.
[8] Courtesy of the University of Michigan Department of Speech.

ANNCR:　Page one of the Journal. Invitation to Burglary!

WOMAN:　We'll be gone for a few days. Won't you drop in and help yourself?

NARR I:　This sort of invitation is lying around for a burglar to accept. Skilled housebreakers work throughout every sizeable community in the country regardless of all measures taken to stop them.

WOMAN:　But things like that never happen here.

NARR II:　Your own community is no exception. According to Ann Arbor Police Chief Casper Enkemann, there were 169 robberies from buildings and 61 breaking and entering cases reported in Ann Arbor during the past year.

WOMAN:　Well, what can I do to keep my home safe while I'm away?

NARR I:　Take a few precautions next time you leave home. The "invitation" is usually some telltale sign that you leave behind telling the burglar that you have gone away.

WOMAN:　Sign? What sort of sign tells him no one is home?

NARR II:　Some of the burglar's methods have been described by Mr. P. D. Keating in a recent issue of Better Homes and Gardens. This Week has summarized the recommendations of police officials.

NARR I:　Remember these points. Sometimes your burglar friend will learn you are not home by phoning you. If someone answers the phone, he fakes a wrong number. If there's no answer, he'll phone again in half an hour to be doubly sure that you're out.

NARR II:　Another thing to keep in mind is the newspaper. You might not be the only one who likes to see your name in print. Our same burglar likes to read that "Mr. and Mrs. D. A. Smith are spending two weeks at Island Lake."

NARR I:　Newspapers can show that you are gone in another way. A stack of papers on your front porch along with full milk bottles and a mailbox full of letters is a clear sign that you are away. It's better to stop the milk and newspaper and have the postoffice hold your mail. Leave the shades up...make it look like some one is around at all times.

WOMAN:　But what can I do when I'm gone for just an evening?

NARR II:　Lights mean a great deal to a burglar. A porch light on with the rest of the house dark is a sure sign that you are gone. A light shining dimly from the living room or hall won't fool him either. Police advise plenty of lights. They even suggest leaving the radio on. They have also found that a lighted bathroom usually convinces a burglar that someone is home.

NARR I:　Just a few small precautions before you leave home for any length of time may keep your home safe from a prowler. So, don't leave an invitation to burglary for anyone that might want to "drop in."

MUSIC:　BRIDGE.

• AGRICULTURAL FEATURES •

Station managers have learned through experience that by being of service to agriculture they can secure loyal audiences. Many programs are presented especially for farmers. Weather and market reports are included in news programs. There are specialized agricultural feature programs broadcast daily. The use of portable tape recording and film equipment has given impetus to broadcasts of this type. The success of a farmer in an upstate county in increasing egg production through his methods of culling the flock and feeding a balanced ration, as reported by on-the-spot recording or film, carries more weight and attracts more attention than a straight reading from a state agricultural bulletin. In addition to "how-to-do-it," technical farm reports and general farm news broadcasts, some stations such as WNAX, Yankton, South Dakota, also prepare programs dealing with economic subjects which affect farmers and rural community businessmen. A portion of one of these programs follows.

EXAMPLE OF AGRICULTURAL ECONOMICS RADIO PROGRAM

"Farm Chats," featuring Chet Randolph, Farm Service Director, WNAX, Yankton, South Dakota, 6:15 P.M. May 14, 1955 [9]

A few months ago, I reported that the hams imported from other countries was only a drop in the bucket...only 1%. It's different now...it's serious. About one-third of all canned hams sold in America are from other countries. That should mean to the pork industry what an alarm clock means to the sleeper...It's time to wake up.

The first thought of many is to rush to Washington and try to force a law to keep those hams out...to fight it. But let's profit by the experience of the dairy industry. A moment's reflection recalls all those years and millions of dollars dairymen spent fighting oleo. In fact, you know a few years ago, I wouldn't have dared say that sentence. Everytime the dairyman mentioned the word, oleo, he sold another pound. Homemakers in Chicago weren't one bit interested in how early the dairyman had to get up to take that milk away from the cow nor did she take the trouble to search out some of nature's best food. Still the butter industry continued to fight. Fortunately progressive leadership took over and after things were bad enough, farmers began to accept what industry had built on...You must have first a quality product and then you must get out and sell it...promote it. When dairy leaders stopped "fighting against" and started "positive selling" they really moved ahead.

I've already heard some farmer groups beginning to fight against these imported hams and it takes me back to the butter fight and how butter sales went down and down as the fight got hotter and hotter. No, the answer lies not in stopping imports, but in producing hams of equal quality because it's all a matter

[9] Courtesy of Chet Randolph, WNAX, Yankton, South Dakota.

of fat. It should come as no surprise...we had warnings years
ago that homemakers were simply going to rebel against all that
fat. This only brings it out in the open. Imported hams have
increased 28% the past year. The canned hams coming in from
Denmark, the Netherlands, Germany and Poland equal the production
of nearly 5½ million hogs. I repeat...over 1/3rd of all canned
hams are from other countries.

In New York most delicatessens are carrying only imported hams
...not because they are cheaper...oh no...but because they are
leaner. Not because they are "agin" the farmer but because they
buy and sell what the customer wants. It's so simple that many
will not accept it. People like the imported hams better and
they'll pay a premium for them. Every ham is well shaped, lean
with every inch a beautiful slice of meat. One packer salesman
hunted for two days here in America and couldn't find a single
ham that matched in quality a random sample imported ham according to Successful Farming.

People are not buying as much pork as formerly, but they are
buying as much beef...simply because people don't like fat pork.
All of this serves notice on the farmer and the packer. Both
have a stake in this. The two must get together because until
the packer starts paying for quality, then there's no reason
for the farmer to go to quality...he can't be that altruistic.

Denmark faced that same situation 50 years ago..fat hogs and
no market. They were forced to a quality trade to get the
business in England. I've had an opportunity to see the Danish
breeding program first hand. These quality hams of theirs are
not something they just inherited. It's a result of years and
years of hard work..selection and organized effort toward Number
1 hams. And they are really strict. The result is a ham famous
the world over...consistently tops. When it's Danish Number 1
you can bet your bottom dollars it's tops and homemakers the
world over recognize that. That's why I urge our hogmen not to
start fighting these imported hams but profit by the experience
of the dairy industry and take this as the fact that tripped the
alarm clock. Then wake up and get a product that will equal what
farmers in other countries can do. Take a cue from the beef boys
and get out and sell pork. That's the positive approach that
will pay off. We have many breeders who can show us quality hams
...we have a few packers who pay for quality... as the industry
follows these leaders restaurants and homemakers will go back to
buying American hams...because they're better.

The dairy industry is truly showing agriculture the way.
Their sponsorship of Disneyland was one of the wisest moves in
years the way it looks from here. Now in Disney's fabulous park
they'll have a big exhibit featuring dairy foods...put up in a
way that appeals to the city consumer instead of the dairyman who
already drinks milk. Then the ADA is undertaking a major study
to find out what the American homemaker thinks of our dairy
products. A real step forward..instead of telling her what we
want to sell her we'll ask her what she wants. That sums up the
complete switch made in the last 5 years.

Canned hams are not a threat...they are a signal.

Projects and Exercises

1. Tune in stations in your area and prepare reports on different types of women's, children's, and feature programs currently broadcast. Compare and evaluate relative effectiveness.
2. Prepare and present a three-minute woman's program. Use magazines and newspapers for material. Alternate radio presentations intended for:
   (*a*) Station serving a small metropolitan area.
   (*b*) Station serving a large rural audience.
   (*c*) Station in New York, Chicago, or Los Angeles.
3. Discuss what changes and modifications would be needed if these programs were to be presented on television. Present them again, this time for television.
4. Prepare and present five-minute children's programs. These may be original or adaptations. Alternate radio and television presentations. Test for effectiveness by inviting a group of children to the studio. Note carefully the actions of the children during the presentation. Check the places where attention drifted or special interest was shown. Discuss story details with the group following the presentation to check on comprehension.
5. Prepare and present feature radio narratives, some single-voice, others incorporating sound and multivoice narrations. Discuss how radio features might be adapted for television.
6. Prepare a shooting script for a two-minute television feature. Do not confine the script to silent or sound film. Suggestions for using stills may be given. Typical topics for such features are:
   (*a*) A salute to your institution for use on a regional or national network between the halves of a football game telecast.
   (*b*) A "behind-the-scenes" tour of a local business firm, factory, or farm.
   (*c*) A simple "how-to-do-it" sequence for use on a hobby series.
   (*d*) A human-interest feature on "A Day in the Park" or "School Recess Time."
   (*e*) A "Trip by Film" to local scenic or historical points of interest.

❋ 26 ❋

_____

Sports and Special Events

THE LARGEST audiences in radio and television are reached usually when sports and special events are presented. Local stations find these programs useful in competing successfully with large stations. The larger stations and networks compete in obtaining exclusive rights to sporting events and "dreaming up" new twists for coverage of the spectacular. A classic example of the latter was the NBC radio broadcast in 1937 which entailed a 7,000-mile journey by announcer George Hicks, his technical crew, and four tons of radio equipment to tiny Canton Island in the South Pacific for an eyewitness account of a total eclipse of the sun, which lasted three minutes and thirty-three seconds.

In television, the initial NBC "Wide, Wide World" telecast in 1955 startled blasé viewers by a 32,000-mile panorama of live pick-ups in a ninety-minute journey back and forth between New York City and Washington, D.C., Iowa, Denver, Salt Lake City, and the Rockies, traveling down to southern California and then up to Canada for a Shakespeare festival, to Mt. Hood, Oregon, for skiing, and to Tiajuana, Mexico, for a fiesta. The climax came as the view of the darkness of Manhattan Island with its skyscrapers silhouetted by sparkling lights was shifted in a split second to a glimpse of the bright sun behind the San Francisco skyline.

• SPORTS •

Sports announcers are daily visitors in millions of homes. Their voices are recognized at once and their pet personal expressions find their way into the vocabulary of sports enthusiasts. Many of the points on general announcing hold true for announcing sports and conducting sports programs. However, the techniques and problems of presenting a running account of a game are highly specialized. The opinions of some top-flight sports broadcasters will be incorporated in our discussion.

General Considerations. Many early sportscasters entered this field be-

436

cause they had a flair for talking easily and well without script. Even though their descriptions were colorful and exciting, those who knew sports thoroughly found in the broadcasts numerous factual errors, unwarranted excitement, and too much "color" at the expense of describing what was actually taking place. These criticisms are still made of some sportscasters. Most present top-ranking sportscasters know sports extremely well and make their announcing vital and exciting, but they do not artificially inject excitement into their broadcasts.

Marty Glickman, of WMGM and CBS-TV, a Paramount news sportscaster and *Variety*'s sports columnist, says:

> In reporting a ball game, my idea is to take the listener from his seat and bring him into the broadcast booth with me. I want to have him see what I see and react the way I react. The net result should be that the listener can later discuss the game with as much facility as a friend of his who was actually present at the contest. The *broadcaster* should not have been exciting. The *game* should have been exciting, and the broadcaster can do no more than mirror the action.

Walter "Red" Barber, one of the leading figures in broadcasting of sports for many years, feels that

> the single most important thing is a person's industry coupled with honesty in reporting a game. The sportscaster must seek to eliminate all the feelings of a fan. The caring for who wins and who loses is beyond the province of the play-by-play man. His job is merely that of a reporter. It's up to this reporter to have a reportorial or almost a judicial frame of mind. From this judicial frame of mind it's important to study as much of the literature and rules of the game as he can get his hands on. Personal acquaintanceship with the people in the sport, players, coaches, managers, umpires, is important. In other words one has to make a business of the sport. With these ideas as a foundation, the rest is a matter of experience, detail and individual personality.

Mel Allen, who is the voice of the New York Yankees and is known nationally through his World Series and Rose Bowl broadcasts, subordinates color to the factual reporting of a contest. He feels that the average fan tunes in to an event primarily to find out what is going on insofar as the action of the game is concerned. He does not feel that there is anything wrong with color *per se,* but it should be used sparingly and judiciously, when the action has slowed down sufficiently to permit it. Allen's personal goal has been to "sacrifice the terminology of color for the sake of accuracy." He continues:

> I like to bring in color as much as anybody, but primarily I'm interested in getting across who's got the ball, for example, where he went, how far, who tackled him and so forth. The more you can concentrate on *individual movements* before the snapping of the ball (in football), or the pitching of it (in baseball), the more vivid is the picture of what is developing.

By this Allen means the little things that lend themselves to drama: runners' actions, movements of the coaches, and idiosyncrasies of players

before the pitcher releases the ball in a baseball game. Allen strongly objects
to the announcer who tries consciously to be a star in his own right, or as
Allen puts it,

> making himself more important than the event. Where some announcers might
> become very popular very quickly through little pre-conceived tricks and
> acted-out enthusiasms, making themselves more important than the event, yet
> over the long run, the fellow who concentrates on making the play the thing,
> and who strives for *accuracy* above everything else, will grow slowly perhaps,
> but surely. You must realize that the audience today knows more about sports
> than ever before. The current pulse of the public is that they dislike anything
> too gaudy, too dressed up. Psychologists can possibly explain this better than
> I, but the fans want everything stripped down to the barest essentials. Give
> them that first, and then if you have time, you can sugar-coat a little with
> your "color."

Effect of Television. With the advent of television, many persons believed
that completely new techniques would be required for sportscasting. It was
reasoned that since the audience was able to view the action there was little
need for the announcer to talk. However, when this was tried, unexpected
results ensued. Many viewers simply tuned in the picture on the TV set, but
kept the audio off, and used a radio set for the play-by-play description.
If one now listens for a brief period to a sportscaster's voice only, while he
is broadcasting some sports, it is difficult to determine whether he is presenting a radio or a television account. Sometimes he is actually doing both.
Stations and sponsors have found it economical in manpower to rely upon
"simulcasts." This is true particularly where a number of games are regularly scheduled over both media. Jimmy Powers, who has announced boxing
from New York for many years, feels, however, that in boxing one should
not talk while the fighters are hard at it.

> I talk only in the low spots of the bout when the action is dull ... The ideal
> show is when the viewer is listening but doesn't know it. I try to give him
> enough information pointing out different things so he thinks he saw it
> himself without my telling him. I keep my voice at the same level all the time,
> putting in a little tenseness if I want to make it dramatic.[1]

Most sportscasters attempt to keep an eye on a monitor when play permits
to be informed about what the viewer at home is seeing. They then weave
into their commentary references to the specific scene shown on the screen.
In sports with fast action, such as hockey and basketball, this may not be
possible during sustained periods of continuous play. Mel Allen summarizes
some generally accepted points of view concerning television techniques:

> Now that the fan sees the plays as they occur we've got to help him under-
> stand the more complicated ones and "color" the routine plays with relevant
> facts. In video the sportscaster ... has to supply the commentary with a
> certain amount of anecdotal material, background, and the like that adds to

[1] *New York Times,* June 8, 1952.

the viewer's enjoyment. . . . He's got to revert to radio techniques once in a while because it can't be forgotten that not everyone watching the game is a complete scholar of the game.[2]

Television places a premium upon accuracy and knowledge of the game. In radio presentations some sportscasters of national reputation were guilty of calling plays wrong, losing track of a down, or giving incorrect balls and strikes counts. In order to pull themselves out of a hole they resorted to description of mythical action on the field. Such errors by announcers are detected easily by ardent fans on TV. An announcer who attempts to brazen out an error or oversight by inventing a play which is "off camera" is in for serious trouble. It is imperative that accurate records be kept during the game.

EXAMPLES OF A SPORTSCAST PLAY-BY-PLAY DESCRIPTION

Radio and television coverage are compared in the following exact and unedited transcripts secured from off-the-air tape recordings.

1. *Baseball*

All-Star game July 12, 1955. The radio account was by Bob Neal on Mutual; the television by Al Helfer on NBC-TV.[3]

RADIO	TELEVISION
This is Bob Neal with Earl Golespy in the Milwaukee County Stadium, the All Star game of 1955. Robin Roberts on the mound, he's making his fifth start here in the All Star classics, he started in 1950, worked three innings and gave up three hits, one run, one error, one strike out, and one base on balls. In 1951 worked two innings, gave up four hits, one run. In 1953 gave up only one hit, struck out two, walked one, and in 1954 was touched for five hits, four runs, five strike outs, two bases on balls. So Robin Roberts, 6'1½", 190 pounder, a bonus baby, signed back in 19 -- let's see, back about 7 or 8 years ago, born September 30, 1926. The infield for the National League has Eddie Mathews at third base, Banks at	.....The National League is taking the field and the first man to come up here for the American League will be Harvey Kuenn, the youthful shortstop of the Detroit Tigers. So we'll set the distances here for you because we expect a lot of them to be poked out of this park here this afternoon. Down the right field line, a distance of 315 feet, falling away to 355 feet in right field, in right center field 394 feet, to straight away center field to the six foot fence, it's 402 feet, it falls away to 394 in left center, 355 in dead left and 320 down the left field line. Now here is Harvey Kuenn, the first batter to come up here for the American League in this the twenty-second playing of the All Star game. Harvey Kuenn is 0 for 1

[2] *Variety,* July 28, 1954.
[3] Courtesy of Ford Frick, Commissioner of Baseball.

RADIO

short, Schoendienst is at sec-
ond, Kluszewski at first, Robin
Roberts pitching to Harvey
Kuenn.

The first pitch of the ball
game is a fast ball on the outside corner, strike one. The
outfield playing straight away.
Eddie Mathews, the third baseman about two steps back at
third and about five steps inside the line. Red Schoendienst is deep in second, the
outfield straight away, Duke
Snider looking on.

There's a ground ball hit to
the left side, by Mathews out
into left field, the first hit
of the ball game, Harvey Kuenn
is a great place hitter and he
picked out the spot there. "He
puts them where they ain't," as
the saying goes. The first hit
of the ball game by Harvey
Kuenn. And Robin Roberts now
will stretch and look over at
first, Kluszewski, is holding
Kuenn.

The first pitch to Nellie Fox,
high inside, ball one. Charg-
ing in was Eddie Mathews, the
third baseman, with Nellie Fox,
the little left hand batter,
Fox, of course, is now batting
currently in the American
League 326. He's got five home
runs. He stands deep in the
box, he chokes that bat.

The next pitch, he swings and
he fouls one in the lower deck
out of play. So the count is
one ball, one strike to Nellie
Fox. The American League has a
runner at first base in Harvey
Kuenn... Nobody out, Roberts
looks into Dell Crandall who's
catching for the National
League, Fox waiting--

TELEVISION

in All Star play, he got in the
ball game last year. He is
batting 320 for the season so
let's lean back and see what
happens in this one.......
Robin Roberts on the mound, in
All Star play has pitched 11
innings.

Strike one on Kuenn. Kuenn
will be followed by Fox and
then by Williams....

Ball hit through, past Mathews,
into left field for a base hit
and Harvey Kuenn is on, so we
have the first base hit given
up by Roberts. That will be
the fourteenth hit in this type
of play. The boy placed that
ball pretty well through the
infield. He's a great place
hitter this Harvey Kuenn, puts
them just where they don't
happen to be.

Nellie Fox, and the pitch to
him, ball 1. Nelson Fox on a
regular season batting 326,
making his fourth appearance in
the All Star game....

One ball, 1 strike... "Little
Pepper Pot" from St. Thomas,
Pennsylvania....

#####

RADIO

Here's the 1-1 delivered from Roberts and it's on the inside corner for a strike. One ball, two strikes as Nellie Fox took a curve ball on the inside corner about belt high. Deep in right field, Don Mueller for the National League, Duke Snider is straight away in center field. Ennis playing shallow in left.

\#\#\#\#\#

TELEVISION

Strike 2..... Harvey Kuenn who opened this ball game here as you saw with a single hit sharply into left field is the only native Milwaukeean in the starting line-up. He was born and raised and still lives here......

\#\#\#\#\#

2. *Football*

Game between Ohio State University and the University of Michigan, November 20, 1954. The radio broadcast over station WWJ, Detroit, was by Bill Fleming. The television description over the ABC network was by Jack Drees.[4] The transcripts appear on pages 442-443.

Preparation for a Play-By-Play Report. Each sport has its own vocabulary, pace, traditions, rules, and customs. The sportscaster must learn these traits over a period of years as a player or fan, or in a shorter period of time by concentrating on the literature of the sport and by talking shop with writers and players. In preparing for an individual contest, it is necessary to become familiar with the plays and players. This problem is simplified somewhat if you handle all the home games of a college or professional club. Only the visiting squad and its particular plays must be learned. Marty Glickman, who handles over one hundred basketball games a season, involving teams from all sections of the country, says that ideally the broadcaster should attend at least two or three practice sessions of both teams. Since many of these are "secret," the broadcaster has an ethical responsibility to respect the confidence imposed on him. At these sessions, one can learn how to identify the individual players by physical aspects. One player may be extremely tall, another short; one stocky, another lean, and so on. Characteristic movements are also helpful in distinguishing players. If there is no opportunity for such advance preparation, close observation is essential during warm-up periods.

Mel Allen says that the week before a game is

like boning for an exam, learning to associate a player's name with his number until it's almost automatic. Also in advance of the game I'll secure offensive diagrams from the various coaches in order to tell where men are likely to play in certain situations. This is not to dismiss defensive play entirely, but the announcer, in a sense, is always on the offensive. This is natural because to the listener, advancing is the big thing. People are not too concerned with who

[4] Radio account courtesy of Bill Fleming and WWJ, Detroit; television account courtesy of Jack Drees and ABC.

RADIO	Words (Radio)	Time Elapsed	Words (TV)	TELEVISION
All set to go. Here is Dugger, moving back. He's on the 31 yard line. He moves forward on the ball and here's the boot. Coming over to the right, taken by Baldacci at the 18, back to the 20, to the 25, runs into his own man, staggers for a moment, still stays on his feet, and is thrown out at the 32 yard line by Francis Lachinski. ...So he's brought down at the 32 in his own territory, 18 yards in from the far side of the field. It will be first and 10 for the Wolverines.	112	:30	99	Now we are ready. Kline and Shannon to receive the kickoff. Kline on the far side of the field, Shannon nearest us, Dugger gets under the ball. Loops one up in the air. It is going to come down short and it drops down into the hands of Baldacci across the 20. He's up to the 25 now and still scrambles along there to go to the 30 yard line to cross it where Francis Lachinski brought him down for Ohio State so the Wolverines took the ball. Michigan's ball, first and 10 on their own 32 yard line.
Wolverines go into a huddle back on the 23 yard line.... Out over the ball comes Jean Snyder, sophomore center from Hamtramck.... Unbalanced line to the right, the wing-back is flanked out. ...The ball comes directly to the left halfback, Danny Kline, he finds the hole, drives across the 35 to the 37, gets in the open to the 45 to the 50, and is finally pulled down on the 42 yard line... ...A beautiful run by Danny Kline who found daylight as he started off the right tackle spot and kept staggering... and stuttering as he went down to the 45 of Ohio State and finally he was pulled down by Bob Thornton, and it looked	199	1:00	203	Michigan,....blue jerseys...and the maize numerals and pants. Single wing is over to the right. ...Shannon in the wingback, Dane Kline in the tailback, taking the pass from center, gets good blocking as they ride the ends out. The secondary is up in a hurry, but he twists out of their grasps. He's across the 45, still on his feet, he's at the 50. That boy is running in and out of the arms of tacklers faster than we can keep up with him. And he takes it down through the Ohio State 41 yard line before Bob Thornton finally put him down... to stay.

like he might get loose, but he was pulled out on the 41 yard line of the Buckeyes.

...Ohio has a man injured on the play. That was the first play from scrimmage and a total of 32 yards.

...So the Wolverines opening a gigantic hole through the right side of their own line, the left defensive side of the Ohio State Buckeyes, reeling off 32 yards on the first play from scrimmage, and now they are taking a look at the Ohio State player who is flat on his back at the 45 yard line. Michigan is seated on the far side, the Ohio State bench is down in front of us on this Western side line and we can't identify, I don't believe yet

I think it's Watkins....It's Bob Watkins...the ace right halfback of the Ohio State Buckeyes who is now on his feet. Bobby is a boy from New Bedford, Massachusetts. He's starting his third game against Michigan today, one of the finest halfbacks in the Western conference, both as an offensive threat and a defensive player. He is a big boy, 5'9" and 196... pounds and he packs a lot of steam behind those quick openers. He's going to stay in the ball game.

#####

Correction on that first play, a 27 yard pick-up, not 32 as I originally said, 27 yards on that first play for Michigan.

#####

322   1:30

265

420   2:00

355

2:15

One of the Buckeyes was shaken up in the play as Dan Kline, the left half-back for the University of Michigan went storming up the field...was hit ...on at least three different occasions by more than one Ohio State tackler only to twist free and keep on going....

Dave Hill is coming in at...

Bobby Watkins it is who... is injured for Ohio State. There is quite a story on Dan Kline, Number 44. As a matter of fact, that's the title of the story in the current issue of Sports Illustrated and ...what it clearly illustrates is you never know what your ..possible results may be when you do a favor for a youngster. Tommy Harmon here at my elbow,...when he was...achieving All-American greatness at the University of Michigan through an aunt of Tommy's who knew Dan Kline, sent him an auto-graphed picture and said... on the picture..."To Dan Kline, class of '51, University of Michigan squad, "Best Regards, Tom Harmon." And get-ting that autographed picture with the prophesy that he would go to Michigan, as the story brings out, actually got him to the University of Michigan. It was the school that from that moment on, he wanted to attend and Bennie Oosterbaan is mighty happy to have him as a member of the backfield.

#####

makes the tackle until after the play is run. They are concerned with who's got the ball, where he's going, how far he went and who blocks for him.

Different sports require more memory work than others. Baseball, with its more leisurely pace and relatively static positions of the teams on the field, allows more time to identify the players. In football, however, entirely new teams may come onto the field at one time. The huddle or calling of signals gives a little time for identifying players, but a good memory is most helpful in such situations. The speed of hockey, according to Geoff Davis, sports director of WROW, Albany, New York, who has also covered hockey for the Canadian Broadcasting Corporation, requires one to memorize identifications of players before the game, either by number or physical characteristics. He notes that, added to the speed of the game, the complications created by substitutions of whole lines "on the run" make accurate identification very difficult. A description of a horse race, with numerous entries and rapid changes of position during the race demands instant recognition of horses and jockeys.

Other aids in preparing for a particular contest may be found in the press releases given out by the teams before the contest. These include information sheets, statistics, form charts, and human-interest stories on players. This is termed "filler" or "background" material. Many sportscasters pin these sheets up in the announcing booth or put them together on clip boards for use during lulls in the game and time-out breaks.

Mechanical Devices and Identification Charts. Mechanical or spotting devices make possible more accurate coverage of events. These devices vary from one sportscaster to another. Ted Husing's electrical board system for football has been adopted in modified form by many others. Husing's board was a complicated affair worked by assistants or spotters who pressed buttons that lighted up an individual player's name.

Mel Allen uses a relatively simple football chart. A large pasteboard is prepared for each team with individual squares for each player. In the center of the board are seven blocks, one for each line-man. Beneath these are four blocks, one for each back. The eleven blocks constitute the starting, first string, or offensive team. On top of the seven blocks are two rows of seven blocks for the substitutes. Below the backs, the same arrangement applies. In order to tell who is playing at any particular moment, Allen has only to look at the board which will have eleven tacks stuck in the appropriate squares. A spotter for each team takes care of this.

Baseball reporters may also use a cardboard with separate name cards tacked on it according to position. Some use the tack-up method in basketball and hockey. Others rely on memory because they have to keep their eyes on the ball or puck.

"Recaps" and Audience Orientation. The sportscaster has to look at the playing area most of the time in order to keep the audience informed on the progress of the game. Fans also like to know the facts about what happened

earlier in the game because much of their listening is intermittent. Few people tune in at the beginning of a game and stay before the set all the way through. And even those people do not keep a score card. Many sports announcers have assistants to compile statistics. Sometimes this task will be combined with the work of a spotter. When there are interruptions in the game Mel Allen prefers to use "recaps" instead of "filler" material. The

FOOTBALL CHART FOR BROADCASTING

	LE	LT	LG	C	RG	RT	RE
SUB							
SUB							
1st STRING OR STARTERS							

	LH	QB	FB	RH
STARTERS				
SUB				
SUB				

TYPICAL SQUARE

HT.	WT.	AGE	CLASS	HOME TOWN
6-1	190	23	JR	Detroit Mich.

57   BILL
         JONES

Courtesy of Mel Allen

recaps will please those who tune in late. Someone tuning in during the sixth inning is pleased to hear a quick summary, such as: "The Yankees got their three runs in the third" and a rapid and clear review of the details on a big inning. Budd Lynch of Detroit who broadcasts the hockey games has an unusual situation. Because of network conflicts three different television stations carry parts of the play-by-play account of the games. He emphasizes recaps after successive channel shifts. Marty Glickman makes it a rule in basketball to give the score as of the moment and time of play remaining, every time a basket is scored.

The TV camera can transmit part of the atmosphere of the scene by shots of the time clocks and scoreboard devices used for the audience attending the event in person. Special visual aids may also be prepared for the TV summaries. Plays may be explained and interpreted.

Football, unlike baseball, does not have a set, of scoring symbols. Mel Allen uses his own system to keep track of events in order to permit recaps. On an ordinary tablet he rules off several sheets in three vertical columns. To the left of each of these columns he notes the series of "downs" and records every play. For example, in a Columbia-Army game he might note 1-10-30-C. That would be Columbia's ball, first down, ten to go, on the thirty yard line. If the play gained two yards the next entry would read 2-8-32-C, and so forth. In this manner all plays leading up to the scoring play are available at all times. The numbers on the jerseys of the players involved on key plays are also set down. In his recap, the sportscaster can take as few or as many of the lead-up plays to the touchdown as he needs. This procedure also adds to the accuracy of the account. The announcer knows at all times what the down is and where the ball is.

A recommended procedure in baseball is to "set" the teams offensively and defensively during the game in order to give those who tuned in late a better understanding of what is happening. One may name the players at their various posts and, if it is a TV broadcast, show them by a cover shot or by a succession of area-shots, right half of the infield, then left half, etc. Batting averages as of that moment, not the night before, may be given, comments on where the infield or outfield is playing for a particular hitter, whether a bunt is expected in this situation and any number of such interpretative analyses may be offered. The name of each batter may be superimposed on the bottom of the screen to reinforce the identification.

Keeping the listener oriented toward the location of the ball in radio is simplified in those sports which have a definite geography. "Silver River is ahead by a length coming into the stretch," "It's Notre Dame's ball first down and 10 to go on the 15-yard line," or "There are runners on first and third with one out."

Marty Glickman reminds us that in basketball

there is no specific geography so we've created a great deal of it. We follow the ball "to the right corner"—"to the elbow"—"just outside the keyhole" and so on. We have educated our listeners to these terms through the years until a listener is now oriented almost as well as he would be on a football broadcast.

Hockey broadcasters, according to Geoff Davis, also need to work out a series of expressions pleasing to the audience and descriptive enough to cover the very rapid action peculiar to hockey. Examples of this would include the terms to cover the breakaway play, full-length rushes down the ice, player jam ups near the goal crease, etc.

The viewer's orientation must always be kept in mind in placing cameras and selecting camera shots. Programs that are relatively static (in terms of location) during events such as wrestling or boxing are not as difficult to televise as events where the action takes place over a wider area—baseball, football, horse racing, basketball, and hockey. With these sports, eye-straining pans or a multiplicity of fast cuts in an attempt to keep up with rapid action on the field may be very disturbing to the viewer. Sudden shifts of the basic angle of sight occasioned by cameras located on opposite sides of the playing field may create confusion. An example of the latter is a tele-cast of a race where one camera is located on top of the grandstand and another inside the track. Switching from grandstand camera to track camera gives the effect of the horses (or racing cars or runners) suddenly reversing the direction in which they are running. The excessive use of the split screen or the upper-corner insert of different players also may be irritating. Speeding up the action of the Zoomar lens with its ability to move from a cover-shot to a close-up can also result in making the viewer feel uncomfortable.

Spotters or assistants may work with the sportscaster in keeping track of the play, of incoming substitutions and in compiling statistics for use in recaps or during breaks in the game. Some relieve the regular sportscaster on microphone to handle the color and statistics. The featured play-by-play reporter will be held responsible by the audience, however, for the accuracy of the descriptions of the game in progress. Here is a word of advice from "Red" Barber: "Most mistakes come from carelessness, a momentary break in concentration. The first essential is *complete concentration* on your play-by-play-assignment."

Daily Sportscast. The peak audiences come with the presentation of the actual sporting event. But large and loyal audiences also follow the many daily sportscasts scheduled at the dinner hour or late evening. Some of these broadcasts are merely summaries of results and the press services provide material for them. Other sportscasts combine press material rewrit-ten for the individual sportscaster, still pictures, both silent- and sound-film clips and interviews. Geoff Davis gives his view of how to proceed:

> The preparation of a daily sportscast differs slightly depending upon the point of view of its origination. For example, in New York, a man beaming to a local audience would have so much action going on in any single day that results alone would take a considerable amount of time. The most efficient means of setting up this type of show is to start with the top sport in season and gradually progress through the less important items. In summer, base-ball scores of the major leagues come first followed by "off the diamond news" of this sport, injuries, sales and trades and other executive business of im-portance. Next come boxing, horseracing and seasonal events of a purely local nature. For a network show out of New York, also lead off with baseball but you must necessarily look across the country and mention national events, big time fights, Davis cup tennis, international swimming, college sports of importance, etc. The main thing to remember in network presentation is that the program must not be too confined to the local scene.
>
> Interviews have become an important part of every sports reporter's presen-

tation to his public. The thing to remember about interviews is not to overdo them, either in number or in length because prepare them as you will, like fashions, they come back eventually over the same cycle.

Daily sports broadcasts derive their interest from clear, concise presentation in good taste. Actual delivery is usually somewhat faster than normal, but again it is wise to remember not to overdo the speed because increased rate sometimes gets in the way of clarity.

Directing Procedures. In radio, a local station rarely assigns a director to sports pick-ups. When a director is present he assists in timing, lining up guests for interviews, and listening carefully to the description in order to detect any errors. However, a director is required in television coverage. He usually is stationed in the "remote" truck or mobile unit which contains the field equipment—camera controls, amplifiers, power supply units, sync generators, switching panels, off-the-air and off-the-line monitors, audio console, and telephone connections with cameramen, sportscaster, and studio master control.

The television director follows the same general procedures as in studio work. He, or the TD, instructs the cameramen about upcoming shots and calls for appropriate switching from camera to camera as the action of the game and announcers' comments prescribe. He is also responsible for timing and inserting live or filmed commercials at the proper moments.

Usually three cameras as a minimum are used for most sports other than boxing or wrestling. The fast action required of all program and technical personnel demands close teamwork. Ideally, the director, cameramen, and TD should be thoroughly acquainted with the fine points of the sport they are covering. There is little time for deliberation before camera movement or switching to other cameras to follow the play and to obtain proper close-ups. Pre-established patterns and areas of coverage are often assigned to cameramen ahead of the action. The switching must be done fast, often a quick hand signal to the TD is used instead of a vocal command. A brief outline follows which indicates respective camera placements in a few of the major sports with which the director works.

BASEBALL. The physical design of the individual ball park and the direction of sunlight may require special locations. The main camera is generally placed behind home plate. It is equipped with a Zoomar lens in order to follow the ball to any part of the field for close-ups. The location of the other cameras varies considerably—some directors prefer the other cameras grouped together on either side of the main camera, others separate them with one along the first-base line and the other between home and third. Jack Murphy, of WPIX, New York, recommends that the second camera be placed by the side of the main camera as a spare and to supplement the wide-angle cover shots through cuts and close-ups without a Zoomar action. The third camera would be placed along first-base line for coverage of infield plays, close-ups of right-handed batters and tight coverage of plays at any base, including home plate, from a different perspective. World Series coverage employs additional cameras in the two locker rooms or on the field for pre- and postgame interviews and color. Commercials may be presented before one of the three basic cameras or they may require one or more cameras for exclusive use.

FOOTBALL. It is easy to make mistakes in trying to follow the ball in play in football. In covering football, sportscasters should have an intimate knowledge of the fundamentals of the game and should learn the styles of play of various teams. Different teams are usually covered each week. Observation of practice sessions and briefing by opposing coaches are extremely important. Many fans are agreeably surprised to see how expertly complex plays are followed on TV without confusion or hesitation. Two cameras are usually placed close together at the fifty-yard line in the press box or on top of the grandstand. One camera, sometimes both, has a Zoomar lens. The third may be stationed alongside of the announcer for commercials and summaries and supplemental color coverage. Additional cameras may be located to good advantage on the field itself or at an exit ramp just slightly above field level. Pick-ups of band maneuvers and festivities at half-time are aided when a camera is available for different perspectives and eye-level close-ups.

BOXING AND WRESTLING. Usually two cameras are sufficient for boxing and wrestling because of the limited area of action. One camera can supply a cover shot of the ring and the other camera tight two-shots or close-ups. A special platform is often erected above the spectators but not too far back from the ring. When shots are taken from the rear of the arena the characteristics of the long lenses make the fighters appear short and squat. If the announcer is at ringside he should be stationed on the same side of the ring as the cameras in order not to confuse the viewers in references to "right" or "left." Close-ups of the sportscasters during commercials or interviews are also facilitated. If an additional camera is available, a location which permits "low-angle" shots close to the ringside is desirable and will add considerable dramatic impact to the visual presentation.

• SCHEDULED EVENTS •

Scheduled special events provide an opportunity for advance preparation. Examples of scheduled special events are: election-night returns, political conventions, dedication ceremonies, banquets, parades, arrival of dignitaries, opening ceremonies of fairs and conventions, fashion shows, and publicity stunts. The station may have an opportunity to adjust the time schedule of some of these events in order to secure a better audience. The atmospheric color achieved by the transmission of "on-location" sights and sounds are important factors in the high degree of interest audiences have in such programs.

The advance preparations for technical pick-up facilities affects the polish and smoothness of special-events programs. In arranging radio coverage, special audio "loops" and "cueing circuits" are ordered from the local telephone company. If origination points are outside the immediate community then the Long Lines Division of A.T.&T. is called upon to obtain such facilities. Facilities for television remotes are handled either through orders to the telephone company or by the station's own microwave equipment. When the station has sole responsibility, it utilizes a small portable transmitter placed adjacent to the mobile unit on a high point which has a direct line-of-sight approach to the receiving "dish" located on the tower at the station's transmitter. When buildings or hilly terrain interfere with such a line-of-sight connection, another microwave relay link must be used to send the signal to the transmitter in two "hops." The microwave equipment may be used also for color television transmission; it is also capable of transmitting the audio portions.

An outstanding example of complex microwave relays arranged for a one-time broadcast by an individual station was the first live television pick-up of an atomic bomb test from Yucca Flats, Nevada.[5] Klaus Landsberg of KTLA, Los Angeles, supervised a dramatic race against time and the elements of nature to install facilities which sent the signal picked up by the cameras at News Nob, 7 miles from the scene of the blast, to the station transmitter about 300 miles away. A series of four hops from mountain peak to mountain peak including one 140-mile relay over the California desert was required. Things looked dark indeed at one crucial point. An 8,000-foot mountain peak was needed as a relay station, but there was no way to travel up the steep trail except by foot or burro. The U. S. Marines literally came to the rescue. Twenty-four flights of Marine helicopters transported 12,000 pounds of electronic gear, food, gasoline supplies, and four engineers to the peak. The 8-foot receiving dish was tied on by rope. Both a heavy sandstorm and a blizzard knocked out the relay system during test periods. Undaunted, the men worked on; and Landsberg and his staff succeeded in sending to the station, and thence to the nation, the first live television broadcast of an atomic blast. The entire project, including transportation of equipment, location, and installation of the relay links, and arduous checking and testing, took sixteen days.

Script material for use during the broadcast can be prepared ahead of the scheduled event for the opening and closing announcements, continuity for emergencies, for delays in the progress of the event, and for providing background comments on the occasion, speakers, or other participants. A thorough announcer or writer collects newspaper clippings, maps, press releases,

---

[5] Address by Charter Heslep of the U.S. Atomic Energy Commission, *The Story of the First Live Television of an Atomic Detonation,* before Georgia Radio and Television Institute, Henry W. Grady School of Journalism, University of Georgia, May 9, 1952.

and articles, and writes copy for almost every contingency. Interviews with various personalities can be arranged. The skill with which prepared material and interviews are woven into the ad-lib description of the actual event as it takes place marks the difference between a professional job and an amateurish one. It should be noted that present-day broadcasting does not place a premium on the ability to talk on and on when there is no need to stay at the scene. A switch-back to the control point for films, music, or narrative comments by others in the studio is the customary practice. In the early days of broadcasting, technical facilities were such that repeated returns to the studio were not feasible. As a result, radio's program history contains such epic stretches of ad-lib prowess as Norman Brokenshire's two-hour solo at the microphone when rain held up the Presidential inauguration ceremonies in 1929. Monitors should be available for use by announcers in remote televised pick-ups. Otherwise the announcer may be describing a completely different scene from the picture selected for transmission by the director. It is difficult to generalize on how much television commentary is necessary and desirable at a special event. In evaluating the coverage of the Republican Presidential convention in 1952, Walter Cronkite, of CBS-TV, concluded that he had not talked enough, whereas Bill Henry of NBC-TV felt that he had talked too much. The latter commentator said bluntly: "If the television people directing the show in the studio would let me alone, I'd never talk except during a lull. . . . But the television people want you to talk. It's a terrible hangover from radio." [6] Walter Cronkite, on the other hand, states: "I would have liked to explain a little more . . . the big problem is that you don't know your audience. Is it intelligent or is it made up of people who know nothing about political procedure? I received several telegrams from viewers asking 'What is a caucus?' I explained it on the air but the people who already knew must have wondered why I didn't shut up." [7]

• UNSCHEDULED EVENTS •

The other broad area of special events deals with the unexpected. These events may occur during a regular program pick-up, such as the explosion of the Hindenburg at Lakehurst, New Jersey, which took place before the eyes of Herbert Morrison, of WLS, who was there to record a routine description of the landing of the giant dirigible. The need to cover unexpected special events may arise at any moment when disaster strikes. Radio stations have covered many such events through the years, and television stations, through film and mobile units, have begun to establish a similar reputation for public service—to inform people what to do, where to go, and what is coming next in such crises as hurricanes, tornadoes, floods, and tidal waves. Such broadcasts demand great sincerity and naturalness in presentation.

[6] *New York Times,* July 20, 1952.
[7] *Ibid.*

No showmanship tricks, no pretentiousness, no capitalizing on the sufferings of those involved should be tolerated.

• USE OF TAPE RECORDINGS AND FILM •

The portability of tape recording equipment and the flexibility in editing the tape before broadcast make it possible for any station to cover special events. It takes only the time to get to the scene, the time for the interview or description, and the trip back, to cover special events. The tape recorder permits coverage of events far from the studio, where regular pick-ups would be impractical due to the great cost of telephone lines. The announcer must remember that the tape may have to be cut and spliced to eliminate certain portions. Provisions for pauses between parts of the description and interviews should be made during the recording. Each unit should be complete in itself, and not contain a reference to other portions of the description. Background sounds can be recorded separately on other portions of the tape, for blending during the broadcast.

Film coverage recreates the event for the television audience when live facilities are not available. The description in the chapter on Film deals with this aspect at more length.

• AD LIBBING •

Whether the event is scheduled or unexpected, live, filmed, or taped, the announcer must be proficient in extemporaneous speaking. Vivid expressive language, keen observation and accurate description are essential. A brief summary of the scene to orient the audience is a good way to begin the broadcast. A conversational progression from that point should follow. Brief summaries of past activities may also be used if they are necessary for understanding. Avoid long and elaborate summaries. Many announcers work their summaries in along the way rather than at the opening. The rate of speech and emotional overtones should, of course, be appropriate to the event and its significance. Emotional reactions need not be suppressed; if the event is truly exciting or solemn, it should be reflected in the voice and delivery. Excesses in emotion, however, should be avoided. Stock phrases and repetitive transitional phrases should be avoided. A straightforward progression of ideas and human-interest material should be the pattern.

Projects and Exercises

1. Each class member should read aloud and define twenty-five words or phrases for a particular sport which have special significance and meaning. Select the words and phrases which are distinctive and descriptive of the sport—a vocabulary which would be used by a sports announcer in a broad-

cast of that sport. "Single wing back" in football and "Texas Leaguer" in baseball are examples.

2. Make an off-the-air recording of a sports event description, radio or television, and have it transcribed in written script form for class analysis and evaluation. Compare it with newspaper accounts. If any sports event is covered by two stations, attempt to have the two announcers recorded as they describe the same thing. Discuss and evaluate the two styles.

3. Monitor television coverage of different sports. Have one class member watch the screen (with the sound off) and describe the game on a tape recorder. Have another class member record the professional description on another tape recorder over a different set. Play back the two recordings for comparison and criticism.

4. Obtain film footage which shows a game in progress. Class members should take turns in describing the game, first as for radio and then as for television during the projection of the film. Class evaluation of different styles should follow.

5. Prepare background material and work out scoring and identification systems. Then take a tape recorder to different practice sessions or actual games for use by class members alternating as sportscasters and spotters. Play back these tapes for class criticism.

6. Cover special events on campus and community via tape recording, or film. Prepare advance copy and arrange for interviews to fill in as needed.

* 27 *

Music and Variety Programming

AS TELEVISION has assumed the dominant role in broadcasting, radio stations have turned more and more to the programming of music, which is not dependent upon visual interest. Stations stress disc-jockey personalities who are concerned primarily with popular tunes, and schedule programs featuring Western, folk, and standard melodies, as well as light concert and serious music. Television employs recorded or transcribed music extensively for background use, but has relatively few music programs except for those featuring an individual vocalist singing current tunes. Variety programs which include music and dance as well as specialty acts and comedy routines are among the most popular programs. In this chapter, we shall examine the sources of music available to stations, the problems of planning musical programs, preparation of continuity, and music production techniques. A discussion of some of the specialized aspects of variety programming for television is included.

· SOURCES OF MUSIC ·

Recorded or Transcribed. In the very early days of broadcasting, recorded music was supplied by a hand-wound phonograph which turned out tinny melodies through its funnel-type speaker horn to be picked up by crude carbon microphones. Today, with high-fidelity recording processes, it is almost impossible to detect any differences between live and recorded music. As a result, most stations rely on recordings and transcriptions for the bulk of their music programs. (Transcriptions are special pressings used by broadcasting stations and not distributed for home use.)

Stations may subscribe to various transcription library services. The charges for these library services vary according to the size of the station, and the number of selections in the library. The transcriptions remain the property of the company and are distributed complete with special filing cabinets, catalog and index material which gives detailed information about type of selection, performing artists, playing time and background data for use in continuity; and preplanned programs with script and selections timed and ready for broadcasting. Some companies emphasize "all-round" libraries; others specialize in popular music; and still others concentrate on Western, folk, old-time, and sacred selections. If they make much use of music, stations may subscribe to one or as many as four or five transcription library services to have available a wider range of choice. Stations receive releases of new popular tunes and additional "standards" or classical numbers from the transcription services at periodic intervals, usually each month. Generally each transcription contains several different selections by the same performance group.

Television stations also subscribe to film library services. Short musical numbers of varied types, from concert to popular melodies, and highlighting different performers and groups, are filmed. Stations receive these in the same manner as transcriptions. The musical shorts are catalogued and filed and may be incorporated into programs.

Commercial recordings are secured through regular channels, usually the manufacturer's distributor. Popular releases are distributed to stations without charge, in the hope that such promotion methods may sell more copies of recordings. That this assumption is correct has been proved many times by phenomenal sales of old recordings as well as new releases, due to the publicity given them by established disc jockeys. RCA Victor, Columbia, Decca, and Capitol are the major recording companies. They issue releases in either 45 or 33⅓ rpm. Many foreign and older American releases have a speed of 78 rpm.

Live Music. The amount of live music broadcast on stations varies greatly. Some stations do well with a single staff musician or small performance group, or, in some instances, get along with none at all. Stations with small staffs may capitalize instead on amateur and school organizations in their area. Promotion of local talent can be mutually profitable: the station secures good music programs and favorable word-of-mouth publicity; and the talent gains experience, public recognition, opportunity for learning broadcasting techniques, and a possible foothold on a professional career. Talented children, church choirs, and soloists, high school and college bands and glee clubs, local hillbilly and popular dance bands, folk singers, amateur vocal organizations, and advanced music students can be called upon for live music. Contracts and agreements with locals of the American Federation of Musicians (AFM) may determine the number of musicians on staff and the degree to which nonpaid talent is used. J. Leonard Reinsch, a station manager of long experience, recommends: "Pay *all* talent something." [1] Vocalists in some areas are affiliated with the American Federation of

[1] J. Leonard Reinsch, *Radio Station Management* (New York, 1948), p. 26.

Television and Radio Artists (AFTRA) and a contract with the union will determine their wage rates.

Live musical programs may originate from a station's studios or as remotes from local dance halls, auditoriums, schools, and armories. TV stations schedule fewer such remotes than radio stations. Modern tape-recording equipment, which is very portable, now permits radio stations to go far afield for music features.

A desire on the part of both the station and local talent to have live music should not, however, be the decisive factor in scheduling such broadcasts. Good quality of performance should be required. Auditions under broadcast conditions, supervised by the musical director of the station, an orchestra conductor, or the program director, should be the rule. Local talent programs may be included in order to provide an outlet for the airing of home-town aspirants. The customary format for handling this type of program is the contest. The audience, by applause in the studio or by a mail vote, selects the winners.

Judgment of instrumental or vocal talent is a highly individual matter. Very poor talent can usually be recognized quite quickly by a trained ear. The performance by a singer may be evaluated by such items as:

1. TONE PRODUCTION, whether the quality is harsh, nasal, and whether it has sufficient volume and power.

2. SENSE OF PITCH, whether the singer has ability to stay on key and has no excessive vibrato.

3. DICTION, whether one can hear the words clearly, whether they are enunciated slovenly or too precisely.

4. RANGE, whether the voice's range is narrow and limited or extensive, whether it washes out in upper or lower registers.

5. FLEXIBILITY, the ability to perform more than one general type so as to avoid the dulling effect of uniform approach and mood; quick adaptation to changing circumstances, to make adjustments in treatment, to speed or to slow down without being flustered as required by program circumstances and studio conditions.

6. INTERPRETATION, "to think the lyrics" with expression instead of mechanical recitations.

7. STYLE, whether the singer has an individuality of presentation which marks him as a creative artist, or has a commonplace and unexciting personality.

8. STAGE PRESENCE (for TV), appraisal of the impression the audience will receive when talent is on camera. Is the appearance in harmony with the type of music? Does the singer have good grooming and pleasant features? Does the singer have good co-ordination, effective gestures, and graceful movement on stage?

Staff accompanists must be resourceful and familiar with the whole field of musical literature from be-bop and rock-and-roll to Bach. In evaluating small vocal and large choral groups, blending, precision, clarity, and quality of arrangements are particular points to check.

The electric Hammond organ with its economy and flexibility came as a welcome source of live music to many stations. When played by an expert musician who knows the possibilities of the instrument, it can be of great assistance in solo and accompaniment work as well as for themes and music bridges in plays and narrations. If the staff organist doubles as a pianist, additional variety may be obtained.

• PLANNING MUSIC PROGRAMS •

Copyright Regulations. The first factor in planning music programs is to know which numbers can be played without danger of copyright violations. Musical selections, like written works, come under the copyright laws. Copyrighted works of any type are protected from unauthorized performances for a period of twenty-eight years after first publication and may be renewed for an additional twenty-eight years at the expiration of the first period. If not renewed at the expiration of the first period, or after a total of fifty-six years, the work is considered to be in the public domain and may be performed by anyone at any time. An important point to remember is that arrangements of public-domain numbers may be protected by copyright. A station, therefore, must be certain that the music it broadcasts is either an original public domain (PD) version, or one it is permitted to use under a license agreement with representatives of holders of the copyright.

The oldest and largest licensing organization is ASCAP (American Society of Composers, Authors and Publishers), founded in 1914 by Victor Herbert, Gene Buck, and others to protect themselves from widespread violations of copyright. The organization serves all affiliated authors, composers, and publishers and allocates payment to them from the license fees it collects. It has agreements with similar foreign licensing groups in order to permit performances in this country. Stations may take out two general types of license with ASCAP: a blanket agreement which permits unlimited performance of numbers, or a per-program agreement based on actual performance of certain selections. Payment is on a percentage basis according to the size and revenue classification of a station. Reduced rates are allowed for sustaining programs and for noncommercial stations. BMI (Broadcast Music Inc.), a competitor of ASCAP, was organized in 1939 by the radio industry as a protest against an increase in licensing fees by ASCAP. BMI also publishes music in addition to representing composers, publishers, and foreign licensing organizations, particularly Latin-American companies. Blanket or per-program licenses may be secured from BMI.

The third major company is SESAC (Society of European Stage Authors and Composers), which has extended its representation to include many American composers and publishers, especially in the field of Western, hillbilly, and religious numbers, and also has expanded into the field of transcription library service. It offers only blanket licenses. BMI and SESAC permit both sustaining and commercial use under a single agreement.

Program Formats. The next step is to decide on the program idea and work out the format. This is where imagination, showmanship, and knowledge of audience tastes enter into the picture. The specific period of time and day of the broadcast, the MC, the availability of talent, live, recorded or filmed, the sponsor if the program is commercial, the balance in the schedule, and the competition must all be considered.

Here are several questions which should be raised in planning a series of musical programs:

1. WHERE IS THE SPOTLIGHT? Is the audience to pay particular attention to the MC, the program idea, or the talent? For whom is the program a showcase? What ingredients will attract the listeners? What gets top billing? Names attract listeners; the disc jockey, band leader, and symphony conductor, may be featured. The impact of an imaginative and clever program idea or the pull of an accustomed and familiar idea may also be utilized.

2. DOES THE SERIES HAVE UNITY? Audiences live by the clock—they are used to tuning in for a specific program type. A program which presents a swing number for the first selection, a symphony movement for the second selection, a vocal quintet for the third, and concludes with a soft waltz, does not attract a loyal audience. Grab-bag routining is ineffective.

3. DOES THE PROGRAM HAVE VARIETY? A program without this ingredient makes for dull listening. Extreme variations are not necessary, but changes in mood and style of arrangements, staging (for TV), instrumentation, featured vocalists and vocal groups, rhythm, and tempo, are desirable for live programming. A change of talent is also possible with transcriptions, film shorts, and records.

4. DOES THE SERIES NEED A NEW TWIST OR "GIMMICK"? Two dress designers have the same basic ingredients to work with, but one prepares a "creation" while the other has an acceptable but ordinary costume. We term the process of reassembling existing items in a new pattern, invention. Effective program building requires invention. It may be just a slight flourish, as a salad may be distinctive because of the carrot curls framing it, and nothing more. The addition of sound effects of a crowd applauding soloists after vocal choruses and at the completion of numbers, has given a new twist to many radio record shows; singing along with the artist on transcription put another disc jockey out in front. "Your Hit Parade" reflected a change from presenting popular favorites of the day in the usual way to a manner which capitalized on the sales of sheet music and records and public performances. The staging for TV, with different visual treatment each week of the same number, received high praise from professional colleagues and excellent audience response.

New "gimmicks" are not easy to devise. Invention is not simple and it may account for the fact that in the need to program so many hours of the day, every day, every week, stations tend to copy and repeat formulas which are developed elsewhere. To copy an existing program and yet give it a new angle is a regular assignment for many program directors. This process may actually result in the new program's possessing individuality of its own. This does not mean that every music program must be "hypoed" by tricks. Some sustaining programs may be just pleasant listening interludes.

5. WHAT HAPPENS ON THE TWENTY-SEVENTH PROGRAM? Many excellent programs are developed which run for the first thirteen-weeks' cycle and even manage to get through the next thirteen. The real test for a program is what happens the twenty-seventh week. Almost without exception, the first program series planned by a newcomer will be a "Musical Journey" format. "How easy it is, you have 'Music of England' the first week, then 'Music of Spain' the second, and so on. A fine series!" With this "chestnut" idea the program builder has limited himself to only as many programs as there are countries with indigenous music. The format must be elastic and not too restrictive in application.

6. WHAT WILL THE TV AUDIENCE WATCH? If you are programming a disc-jockey TV series and plan to play popular records, what will be on the screen during the two-and-one-half to three minutes it takes for each record? Pantomime a story told by the number? Have cast members or guests "lip sync" the lyrics? Show film clips? Pan across the audience as they dance to the music? Study reactions of a panel of "experts" who are to rate the numbers as to expected popularity? Watch an artist sketch? Turn the camera on fish tanks and animal cages? If the series features live music, what about long instrumental introductions to vocals or complete instrumental selections? Will various sections of the orchestra be shot as they play specific passages interspersed by close-ups of individual players and fingering techniques? Do you have a dancer or dance teams who may perform? Is a choreographer on staff to plan the dances? Is there a scenic designer to supervise special sets for staging of the dance numbers? These questions are typical of those that must be answered by the TV producer in addition to those mentioned earlier.

• PREPARATION OF CONTINUITY •

Musical selections and programs are introduced and described by an announcer, MC, or a special narrator who may be one of the performers. The written material dealing with the program and performer identification, and the transition material which comes between the various selections, are referred to as continuity. Whenever practicable, the continuity is written in advance. Stations with small staffs and limited rehearsal time often permit ad-libbed continuity. Many personality or disc-jockey shows capitalize on the casualness and informality of the proceedings. Apparently informal ad libs, however, may have been carefully prepared in advance. Some comedy-gag writers, for example, may write in malapropisms or slips of the tongue followed by the appropriate "ad-lib" recovery. Dependence upon actual ad-lib continuity usually deteriorates into a succession of stock phrases used over and over again. Every guest is "outstanding," selections are "terrific," each unit is "something you'll really like," or each dance is "amazing." A pet adjective is soon applied to everything, such as "distinctive treatment," "distinctive version," "distinctive styling," "distinctive presentation."

Classical Music Continuity. It is desirable for writers of classical music continuity to possess a thorough knowledge of music. Max Wylie sounds a note of caution, however: ". . . knowledge of music does not mean opus numbers. The pedantry of the opus number has no more to do with the delights of music than the patent number of the Bessemer process has to do with the romance of steel." [2] The early practice of giving extensive program notes on detailed analyses of the degree of "contrapuntal ingenuity" exercised by the composer as he sat at his clavicitherium [3] in a dimly-lighted attic in old Vienna has given way to a "less-talk-and-more-music" approach. Such talk is devoted to human interest material and nontechnical explanations necessary for increased enjoyment of the music. The comments must be accurate, however, for many listeners to classical music programs are very familiar with composers, performers, and selections. Reference guides, clippings, personal conversation with performing artists may fill in the writer's gaps of knowledge. Music continuity for these programs should be conversational in style and should avoid criticism. Enjoyment of music is personal and highly individualized. Capsule generalizations such as "This rondo is the *finest example* of such compositions" may be violently objected to by members of the audience, especially if such a Jovian pronouncement comes from a young staff announcer.

Semiclassical. The emphasis in semiclassical music is less on the composer and composition and more on the mood of the music and the memories of other lands and other times the music evokes. The program idea is more in evidence and the continuity may be much briefer. The performing artists may be highlighted somewhat more.

Popular and Specialized Music. In popular and specialized music the resourcefulness of the writer must be called into play to find a method of introducing the same number, the latest hit or standard favorites, time after time. The program idea, the performers, and miscellaneous techniques, such as "word play" on the title, and patter between MC and performers are utilized for continuity. Familiarity with correct terminology is needed. Each special music type attracts its own faithful listeners. Continuity appropriate to the type of music is therefore essential. Reference to "Chicago jazz," "tail-gate rhythm," "barrel house," "gut bucket," "sending out of the head"

[2] Max Wylie, *Radio Writing* (New York, 1939), p. 388.
[3] Obsolete type of harpsichord.

without appreciating the meaning that type of music has for devotees, leads to contempt for the speaker by the affected segment of the audience. Just a title may serve to introduce a number, as on a Sunday morning program: "Give me your tired . . . your poor." Read by the announcer with appropriate feeling of reverence, it was an example of effective continuity. This same program utilized simple continuity and fine interpretation with "And here's just *one* way to say . . . 'I Love You.' " But how banal and coy it might have sounded! The writer must consider the delivery of the person who will present the continuity. The "gag" style of continuity may contribute to the general pleasurable effect of music and talk, but when humor which requires subtlety and finesse in timing is delivered flat or with timing that is off, it is embarrassing for all concerned.

A SUMMARY OF TABOOS FOR CONTINUITY

1. Avoid overusing stereotyped phrases, such as: "Raises his baton," "mounts the podium," "the orchestra renders."
2. Avoid overusing repetitive transitional phrases, such as: "And now," . . . "And now" . . . "And now." "Next we have" . . . "Next" . . . "Next."
3. Avoid overusing flowery superlatives, such as: "ever popular," "thrilling," "distinctive," "unusual," "incomparable."
4. Avoid overusing "cute" talk, such as this "as broadcast" example: "A tune dedicated to one of America's greatest hobbies and most pleasant pastimes . . . Pettin' in the Park."
5. Avoid overusing technical "gobbledegook" or affectation, such as in this "as broadcast" example: "The spirit of adaptability and conformity to the occasion and mood, expressed in piano rhythms and harmonies. 'Improvisations' with Forbus Drapus at the keyboard of the grand. We have heard variations on themes and melodies—impromptu meanderings through the scales and keys—striking contrasts and blendings—'Improvisations' with Forbus Drapus!"
6. Avoid overusing title lead-ins or tie-ins as in these examples:
    "What are you going to sing, Ginny Drapus?"
    "My Hero."
    "Thanks, honey, I go for you too, but what are you going to sing?"
    "My Hero."

    "I'd better let Ginny Drapus ask the questions from now on. What is the question, Ginny?"
    "How Deep Is the Ocean?"

The warnings against overuse should not be interpreted as forbidding *any use*. The program and the performers make the difference. One person can give an announcement using "cute" talk and make it entertaining. The simplicity of "And now" may serve perfectly for another introduction, such as "And now, 'The Rosary,' sung by Stuart Churchill." An arrangement actually may be "unusual." Use showmanship and be aware of the appropriateness of an announcement.

EXAMPLE OF LIVE MUSIC CONTINUITY

A Quarter-Hour of Organ Music, Written by Larry Frommer, Production Director, WOL, Washington, D. C.[4]

```
ORGAN: (SHORT RUN)
ANNCR: It's KEATON on the Keys.
THEME: (UP...AND FADE ON CUE)

ANNCR: Those ten talented fingers, tripping with skill over the
       keys of the organ, belong to Charles Keaton, who presides
       at the console every Saturday at this time from the Mutual
       studios in our nation's capital.  For the next quarter
       hour, it's KEATON ON THE KEYS.
MUSIC: FIVE FOOT TWO...UP TO END...SEGUE INTO

MUSIC: I'LL STRING ALONG WITH YOU...UP...AND FADE ON CUE

ANNCR: You may not be an angel...cause angels are so few;
       But until the day that one comes along, I'll string along
       with you...
       Let's string along with KEATON ON THE KEYS.
MUSIC: I'LL STRING ALONG WITH YOU.

ANNCR: You are listening to KEATON ON THE KEYS, with capers on
       the keyboard, provided by Charles Keaton.
MUSIC: SPEAK LOW...UP...AND FADE FOR

ANNCR: A bit of melodic caution proffered by Keaton on the Keys.
       When you speak LOVE...speak LOW.
MUSIC: SPEAK LOW...SEGUE INTO

MUSIC: STARDUST...UP...AND FADE FOR

MUSIC: Seated at an old, beaten piano on the campus of Indiana
       University just twenty years ago, a young man by name of
       Hoagy Carmichael composed what might be considered the
       most popular song ever written.  And seated at the con-
       sole...twenty years later, a young man named Keaton,
       combines piano, organ and celeste to do ample justice to
       the other young man's STARDUST.
MUSIC: STARDUST

ANNCR: You've been keeping company with KEATON ON THE KEYS, hold-
       ing forth from Mutual's studios in our nation's capital.
       One week from today Charles Keaton and console will greet
       you again.  Hope you'll be listening for KEATON ON THE
       KEYS.
THEME: (UP FOR TIME)

ANNCR: _____speaking.  THIS is the Mutual Broadcasting System.
```

[4] Courtesy of Larry Frommer.

EXAMPLE OF TRANSCRIBED MUSIC CONTINUITY

Portions of Programs, KHQ, Spokane [5]

ANNCR: BY TRANSCRIPTION Here is a DESIGN FOR LISTENING!

THEME: YOU KEEP COMING BACK LIKE A SONG...

ANNCR: KHQ is happy to bring you again this evening the voices of
Margel Ayers and Byron Swanson in duet. With songs long
remembered--and bright new notes--they fashion two-tone
harmonies--the songs you love to hear in a DESIGN FOR
LISTENING.

THEME: OUT

ANNCR: Tonight Mangel and Byron feature songs long remembered
from the days of old Vienna, choosing first a melody older
than Lehar or Strauss--This lovely air is truly in the
public domain for it belongs to everyone--THE OLD REFRAIN.

MUSIC: THE OLD REFRAIN

ANNCR: "To waltz is to dream," they say, and surely there is no
more graceful and effortless rhythm than the easy measures
of three-quarter time. Gay Vienna took the waltz as her
own, and the music of old Vienna is as happy and lilting
as Margel's next song--A WALTZ DREAM.

THEME: SOMETHING TO REMEMBER YOU BY...EST. AND UNDER:

ANNCR: We bring you--REMINISCENT RHYTHM--a flashback in music to
what was going on just a tune or two ago! Say not "Time
marches on"...it dances to the songs we remember when
headlines are forgotten.

THEME: SOMETHING TO REMEMBER YOU BY...TO BREAK AND OUT

ANNCR: Do you remember when this number flashed across the country?--THE CONTINENTAL!

MUSIC: CONTINENTAL...CAP B 57 1 2:24

ANNCR: Every year brings out its song titles that are variations
on the theme "I Love You." The titles are distinguished
only by the few words added--as Peggy Lee and the Four of
a Kind Do it--it's I CAN'T BELIEVE THAT YOU'RE IN LOVE
WITH ME.

MUSIC: I CAN'T BELIEVE...CAP B 189 2 1:42

[5] Courtesy of KHQ, Spokane.

EXAMPLE OF TV CONTINUITY FOR STATION PROGRAM

"The Dick Contino Show," Station KRCA-TV, Los Angeles [6]

	FADE UP ON:
DICK CONTINO SILHOUETTED AGAINST SPLASH OF LIGHT. HE PLAYS OPENING PHRASE OF "LADY OF SPAIN"	
	CUT TO: SLIDE: CONTINO BILLBOARD
ANNCR The Dick Contino Show!	
	DISS: TO: COMMCL OPENING FILM
ANNCR Riviera, the department store of sofa beds...the original house of convertibles with fourteen beautiful showrooms in Southern California presents a half hour of fun, music and surprises... featuring the song stylings of pretty Gloria Grey....And the star of our show, Dick Contino! (APPLAUSE)	
	CUT TO:
DICK, NOW SPOTLIGHTED. HE PLAYS "HINDUSTAN"	

(APPLAUSE)

        DICK

Hi again, everybody. And a great big
old fashioned welcome from our sponsor,
the folks who make those fine Riviera
sofa beds.

DICK CROSSES DOWN TO CENTER OF ROOM TO
TABLE OF BOILING FLAGONS, RETORTS, ETC.

Tonight there's magic in the air. Our
guest is a famous magician. Gloria
Grey's voice is enchanted.
And my accordion is completely bewitched.

THERE IS A PUFF OF SMOKE AND WE

                                       DISSOLVE TO:

EXTERIOR: MAGIC LANDSCAPE AS DICK EXITS
FROM CASTLE AND PLAYS "BEWITCHED."

GLORIA, INTERIOR CASTLE, SINGS "IT'S MAGIC."

DICK, EXTERIOR, FINISHES "BEWITCHED."

(APPLAUSE)

DICK TURNS TO GLORIA, AS SHE ENTERS.

        DICK
Hi Gloria. Do you know any magic songs?

[6] Courtesy of KRCA-TV, Los Angeles.

GLORIA
Magic songs? Sure, I do. Hundreds and
hundreds.

DICK (DOUBTFULLY)
That's an awful lot of songs about
magic.

GLORIA
Well, not really. The way I look at it,
love is a pretty mysterious and magic
thing. And any song that's about
love.......

DICK (SMILING)
I get it. (LOOKS OFF TOWARD ORK) All
right, maestro. Play us some magic
music.

DUET: "I GET A KICK OUT OF YOU."

(APPLAUSE)

ON APPLAUSE, DICK CROSSES TO INTERIOR OF
CASTLE AND MOVES TO A SPOT JUST BEHIND
TABLE. HE PICKS UP A SQUARE, ORNATE BOX.

DICK
We call this our "Riviera Box," 'cause
we keep all our commercials locked up
inside. Come on, take a look.

PUSH IN TO BOX UNTIL WE FILL FRAME WITH
BLACKNESS INSIDE BOX. DISSOLVE TO
COMMERCIAL.

MUSIC: SHORT TAG
        (APPLAUSE)

                                    FADE TO BLACK

DICK SPOTLIGHTED AGAINST BLACKNESS. LONG
SHOT. ORCH INTRO BEGINS UNDER.

ANNCR (OFF)

                                    FADE UP ON:

Ladies and gentlemen, Dick Contino plays
the very exciting and dramatic,
"Two Guitars!"

DICK PLAYS "TWO GUITARS"

(APPLAUSE)

· PRESENTATION OF MUSICAL PROGRAMS ·

Use of Turntables. Transcribed and recorded musical selections are
played on turntables especially constructed for broadcasting. Two turntables
are used, so that one may be cued while the other is on the air. Announcers
in small stations often operate their own turntables; in such cases, the
tables are placed on both sides of the console.

Cueing a transcription may be handled as follows:

1. With the turntable fader closed and the motor off, place the transcription on the table and gently lower the pick-up arm on the smooth

area between the separate cuts on the transcription. Examine the label to determine whether the transcription plays from the outside-in or inside-out. The separate cuts are numbered or lettered accordingly: cut number two or "B," for example, would be the second from the outside if it is an outside-in transcription. Then move the arm across the smooth area into the beginning of a particular cut.

2. Leaving the pick-up needle in the beginning groove, use your index finger to rotate the transcription at a brisk rate until you hear some sound. Rotate the transcription back and forth slightly to establish the exact point at which the music begins. Head phones may be used to determine the start of the music. They are plugged into the cueing circuit which is operative with the fader moved past the "off" position to "cue."

3. "Back-track" (rotate the pressing backwards) a quarter of a turn for 33s and three-quarters of a turn for 45s and 78s. One must be exceedingly careful with microgroove commercial records. The pick-up arm may jump across several grooves if this motion is sharp or jerky.

4. Just before the number is to be played, the motor switch is turned on. A slight pressure of the fingers prevents the transcription from spinning.

5. As the introductory comments are concluded, release the transcription and turn up the volume fader. If you cue the transcription too close, a "scoop" or "wow" may be the result. These are distortions in the music due to the failure of the transcription to attain full speed before the start of the music. Make a practice of releasing the transcription before turning up the fader.

Repeated cueing of a selection may cut into the walls or bottom of the grooves at the place where the selection starts. As a result an objectionable "pop" or surface noise may be transmitted. With instantaneous acetate transcriptions, which use softer material, back-tracking only a few times may give this pop. One may cue such discs by a "count of the turns." Count the exact number of turns until you hear the music, using the headphones, and mark the number on the script or label. When it is time to play the selection, place the pick-up arm in the first groove at the same starting spot used in counting the turns and run the record one-half turn less than the number of turns you counted. This eliminates the necessity for spinning the record back and forth.

Other controls on the turntable to which attention must be paid are the speed regulators (the high-pitched squeals and chatter which occur when 33s are played at 78 are distracting when not intentionally used for comedy); and the filter switch, with appropriate response characteristics befitting commercial transcriptions, commercial recordings, or instantaneous transcriptions.

Cross-fading ("segue") from one turntable to another, superimposing one upon the other, and holding music down to background (BG) level behind announcements are special production devices for variation and special effects. It may be desirable to "spot" a record somewhere during the selection, to play only the final vocal chorus, for example. A simple technique is to mark the record with a white or yellow china-marking pencil (a dot or circular band) at the approximate place. For exact cueing, monitoring the number by head phone or speaker is preferable, if time permits. Some announcers and engineers become expert at reading the patterns made by the cutting stylus in the walls of the grooves, and use this method for cueing.

Studio Production. When programs originate live, questions concerning the best placement of microphones in the studio or for the remote pick-up, the microphone types, the program personnel, and the arrangements of compositions must be answered. In some television programs, the microphones may be shown; in others they must be concealed or kept out of camera range. Each program or selection has its own individual requirements. Here a soloist has a soft voice and the pianist a forceful attack; here a small combination features the pianist as vocalist while he continues to play; here is a remote dance band pick-up with the bandstand down close to the milling crowd; and here is a vocal quartet, swing quintet, and full eighteen-piece orchestra. A strenuous song and dance routine may need to have the audio prerecorded, a technique often employed in the movies. The performer makes a recording of the selection before the actual performance on camera. Lip sync movement is used as the lyrics are heard. Directors usually refrain from too many close-ups on such numbers, shooting the dance in medium or long shots.

It is important that the sound be "balanced" in the control room and not in the studio. Certain rules of thumb may be worked out from experience, however, for approximate placements, or for actual broadcast use when time is pressing. These rules are based on the principle of placing weaker instruments close to microphone and on beam, stronger instruments some distance away or even off beam. The purpose of this balancing is to permit every instrument of an orchestra or unit to be heard in its proper proportion as it might be heard by a listener in a theater or concert hall.

There is one reason why this goal cannot be attained completely under present broadcasting conditions. When a sound comes from the right, the right ear receives the impression with greater strength than does the left, and so we interpret it as "coming from the right." At a concert or dance hall, notice how people turn from right to left to single out the soloist or the particular section of the orchestra being featured. A person in the fifth row center can turn his head and focus attention on a harp run at audience left, practically blotting out the tympani roll at audience right. Binaural listening and focus of attention highlight sounds for the listener.

What is the situation in broadcasting? The audience member at home hears all the sound coming from the one place: the loud speaker. The audio channel in the studio acts as a single ear, and the reception through a loud speaker cannot be separated for binaural perception. The focus of attention

MICROPHONE PLACEMENT FOR PIANO RECITAL
PIANO LID RAISED

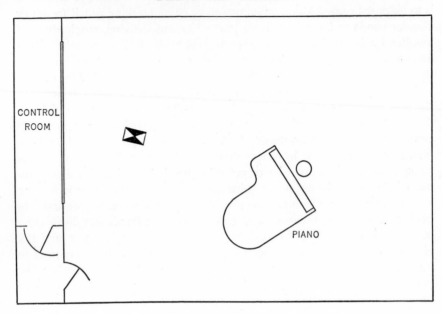

MICROPHONE PLACEMENT FOR STRING QUARTET

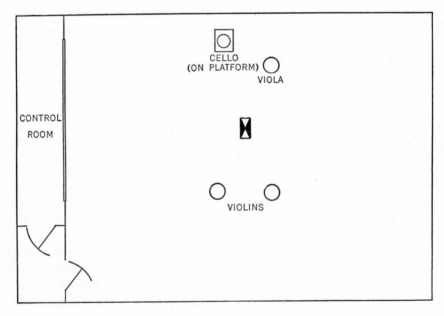

is taken care of by the audio engineer who regulates the volume of sound picked up by the different microphones, and thus does *for* the listener what he would be doing for himself if he were in the studio. Even though a TV camera may be shooting a close up of a vocalist or solo instrument, the viewer cannot compensate by sight the errors in sound balance by an audio engineer.

MICROPHONE PLACEMENT FOR TEN-PIECE POPULAR DANCE ORCHESTRA

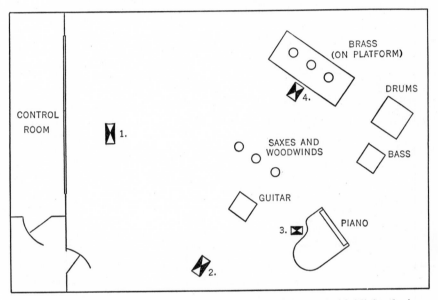

Mike 1, solo vocalist; 2, for over-all orchestra pick-up; 3, highlighted piano passages; 4, soft brass passages.

The particular arrangements used by the orchestra must be worked out with microphone placement and technique in mind. Such features as a soft-muted trumpet figure or a celeste ripple would not be possible without electrical amplification. This is why more than one microphone is used for modern arrangements of semiclassical show tunes and popular numbers, and as many as six or seven microphones for large musical organizations. Concert and symphonic arrangements adhere to a more traditional style where the balancing is accomplished within the orchestra by composer and conductor; as a result, a one mike pick-up is standard for programs of that type.

When it comes to visual presentation of vocals, the director should select camera shots to emphasize the performer. Tricky camera angles and super-impositions may overshadow the talent. Alan Handley, who has produced

FLOOR PLAN AND MICROPHONE PLACEMENT FOR
FRED WARING'S PENNSYLVANIANS

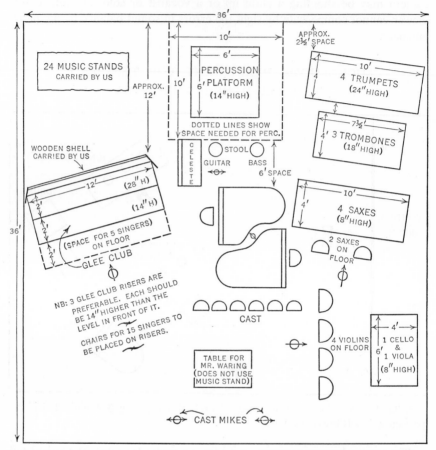

Courtesy of Fred Waring's Pennsylvanians

This is the floor plan sent ahead to stops on the organization's tours. The shell indicated behind the Glee Club is a large folding wooden screen. Four more violins are used at present. They are placed in a row ahead of the four indicated. All platform heights are approximate, except Glee Club which are exact. Other dimensions are minimum and do not include space for audience, nor space for control booth on remote broadcasts.

and directed the "Dinah Shore" and "Eddie Fisher" shows, says that the director should resist excessive cutting in ballads. He says, "A good ballad is a story being told to you as a viewer. You have may noticed yourself when you met an expert raconteur that your tendency is to be drawn to the story teller. You resent the raconteur turning away from you during the story if it is interesting. I consequently resent camera cutting on a ballad." When rhythm tunes are presented, however, Handley points out that "camera cuts sometimes help to punctuate the brightness of the music."

Directors should refrain from complicating the staging and production of quarter-hour popular music series. A proclivity to reach for extremes of lighting effects or the cute and "gimmicky" in story line or action during the presentation, at the sacrifice of the music, has all too often embarrassed talent and marred their personal charm and individualistic style. It is well for directors to recall the highlight of the first Spectacular variety program, the Ford Motor Company two network anniversary telecast in 1953. Ethel Merman and Mary Martin sat on two stools on a bare stage and sang song after song with which they had been personally identified. Jack Gould, television critic of *The New York Times,* mirrored the reaction of viewers when he gave high praise to the "imaginative simplicity brought to the staging of this duet."

Instrumental music, not only popular but chamber and symphonic music, represents an area which is relatively neglected in television. The basic problem is simple. TV is primarily a visual medium, instrumental music appeals primarily to the ear. What is seen is not the important element. But what techniques should be used in production of such programs? Should the camera faithfully show in close-ups the mechanics of presentation and performance techniques of the various musicians and sections of the orchestra? Should a cover shot of the entire performance unit be held for long periods of time, even though the small size of the home television screen may reduce the players to tiny blurs? Should interpretative dance sequences be employed? Should abstract or descriptive art forms or light patterns be prepared to "visualize" the music? Should superimpositions and clear shots of the conductor be utilized? Should film clips of nature in varying moods, drifting clouds, ominous clouds, lightning flashes, high waterfall, tumbling tumbleweeds, stormy sea, calm placid pool, rippling stream, etc., be projected to reinforce or interpret the mood of the music? Opinions differ widely on these questions. The most generally accepted procedures appear to be: (1) use of dance for popular music, with camera cuts to talent, trick camera effects, special angle shots, and close-ups. "The Hit Parade" is the outstanding example of a series which does this. (2) Succession of cover shots, slow dollies in and back, crane up and down, slow truck shots along sections, shots of entire sections, and close-ups of performers, scores, musicians, and conductor.

EXAMPLES OF STAGING SUGGESTIONS FOR TV

BMI issues regularly a *Television Sketchbook* which is designed to assist stations who use its music, either live or via recordings. Alternate sketches are given for both the current popular tunes and "standards." This material may be used by the licensee as presented or regarded as a basis for elaboration.[7]

"Sh-Boom"

(Life Could Be a Dream)

SET: Chicken wire fence fronting leafy background. To all intents and purposes this is fenced-in tennis court of summer resort.

CAST: Male vocalist in shorts, tee shirt, sneaks, carrying handball gloves.
Female actress in blouse, shorts, carrying tennis racket.

BIZ: A summer vacation romance turns into the real thing.

DIR: Open on boy behind fence moving head from right to left and back to right in timed relation to whack of tennis ball being hit and heard on audio. Game ends and girl's squeal of delight is heard as boy is seen grinning broadly. Girl appears, out of breath, tennis racket in hand, and greets boy, asking him how he did in handball. He says he didn't do as well as she just did in tennis, and then, becoming serious, he asks her when she's leaving. She answers right after lunch. He tells her he wishes she could stay on but she says her vacation is over and she must return to work. He reiterates he wishes she could stay on and she asks why. Music intros and he goes into song. They try, during rendition, to intertwine fingers through wire fencing but are able to touch finger tips only. At conclusion, she nods affirmatively, he disappears off camera and comes about to her side. Fade on their embrace.

Rehearsal and Timing. With transcriptions, records, or TV film shorts as the basis of program talent, a session of arithmetic is about all the rehearsal and timing needed for a music broadcast, except checking the quality of the recorded or filmed selections. The total time of the numbers, plus commercial and continuity reading time, and usual theme timings can be compared with the scheduled period. If the total estimated time is short by thirty seconds or so, stretching the theme at opening and close as well as a few announcements will easily do the job. If there is more time to fill, a substitute number of greater length or the addition of a short number are possibilities. If the program is long according to estimated times, shortening the theme or speeding up announcements is not recommended; omitting one chorus or one entire number is preferable.

Back-timing the theme is a technique that makes it possible for the theme to come to its close instead of having to be faded out in the middle. This means that the exact playing time of the theme is marked on the label, say 2:23. By subtracting this figure from the clock time at which you want to conclude the theme, say 14:25, you get 12:02. No matter what is happening

[7] Courtesy of BMI Inc.

on the air, at 12:02 the theme is started "from the edge" (the beginning of the theme), *but with the fader closed.* You are then able to fade the theme in under the closing announcement, hold it BG, and bring it up following the closing announcement to its natural finale right at 14:25, the station identification cue following in the clear. It is a clean way of ending a program.

With live music, the director times each number during the rehearsal. Usually no complete dress rehearsal of a radio music program is held except in the case of some network commercial shows. The numbers may be rehearsed in any order, but not necessarily in the order in which they will be broadcast. The timing of each number is noted on a timing sheet, which contains the routine, opposite the particular selection title. This procedure continues until the director has rehearsal timings for each musical selection. He marks down theme timings, reading times for any commercials used on the program and introductions to the numbers, and he totals the timings. The total should be very close to the program length, but not more than thirty seconds over or under. If the program timing runs over more than thirty seconds, the conductor may make cuts in the selections by eliminating a few bars or half a chorus; if the program runs under by more than thirty seconds, a chorus may be repeated or another number added. Since some numbers occasionally do not work out well in rehearsal, it is a usual practice to clear copyright on more selections than are actually needed for broadcast, and to have several of these in the individual musician's folders. Whatever rehearsal time remains after completing the timing computations may be used by the conductor to polish the performances while the director enters estimated running times on the timing sheet. This sheet can be followed during broadcast, the director giving appropriate signals to conductor and the announcer about the progress of the program. Slight speeding or stretching of announcements, or selections, or of both, provide opportunities for the necessary adjustments to bring the program out "on the nose." The theme may have several versions—short to long—and the conductor can use the appropriate one upon signal from the director. Other devices such as sneaking in the musical introduction under the announcer or segues between numbers, the announcer's introduction being given over the musical selection, are used to pick up time or to give a different pacing to the program.

Music programs in television follow the same general procedure as in radio for the "dry run" and audio rehearsals and timing of selections held prior to putting the program on camera. In order to avoid costly camera time, many stations may use only a brief period immediately ahead of broadcast to check lighting, establish camera positions for key shots, and to go over the talent's transitional action. Stations often rely on a standard set for regular series in order to save time in lighting and staging. The director may shoot the program completely ad lib. When budgets permit, both camera and dress rehearsals are scheduled. "The Dick Contino Show" which has its script reproduced on page 464 uses the following schedule:

```
12:30 - 2:45    Lighting
 1:30 - 3:00    Music Rehearsal
 2:45 - 3.45    Eat
 3:45 - 4:00    Dry Walk-through
 4:00 - 5:30    Camera Rehearsal
 5:30 - 6:00    Trim Lights
 6:00 - 6:30    Dress Rehearsal
 6:30 - 7:00    Audience and Trim Production
 7:00 - 7:30    AIR
```

SAMPLE TIMING SHEET

This same form may be used for radio or TV, straight music or variety format.

Program Routine	Individual Timings	Running Time Rehearsal	Running Time Broadcast	
Opening- Theme and Anncr.	:20	:20	:20	
MC	:10	:30	:30	
Commercial	:15	:45	:45	
MC	:25	1:10	1:10	
First number	1:50	3:00	2:50	(—10)
MC	:15	3:15	3:05	
Commercial	1:00	4:15	4:05	
MC	:20	4:35	4:30	(+5)
Second number	2:10	6:45	6:40	
MC and Guest dialogue	:30	7:15	7:25	(+15)
Guest spot Medley	3:10	10:25	10:45	(+10)
MC	:20	10:45	11:05	
Final number	1:40	12:25	12:45	
MC	:10	12:35	12:55	
Commercial MC Teaser for next show	1:00	13:35	13:55	
(Cushion)	:20	13:55	-----	(—20)
Closing theme Credits Anncr.	:30	14:25	14:25	
Station Identification	:05	14:30	14:30	

The first number ran ten seconds less than estimated time, the MC stretched his introduction to the second number, the interview with the guest, and the guest medley ran over so that twenty seconds had to be cut during the latter portion of the program. The teaser for the next program, which serves as a "cushion" and may be stretched or cut as needed, was eliminated and the program ended on time.

• VARIETY PROGRAMS •

Television has utilized the variety format to a great degree. When it became possible for the audience to see as well as hear broadcast programs, many more types of entertainment became available to program producers, including "sight" gags, pantomime, and slapstick routines in comedy; circus and vaudeville specialties, such as jugglers, acrobats, magicians, bell ringers, trained animals, etc.; scenes from operas with costumes and staging; semi-dramatized or production vocal numbers; singing and dancing choruses; and dancers, dancers, dancers.

Several versions of the variety format have been developed. One of the most successful is the revue—the succession of different acts. Instead of the signs posted at either side of the vaudeville house listing the name of the act to appear on stage, an MC introduces each act. The role of the MC has assumed great importance with some series, such as "Toast of the Town" which became the "Ed Sullivan Show" after several years. He emerged as a personality in his own right. The MC, in addition to introducing the various acts, may also be starred in performance portions of the program. He may be a comic, such as Milton Berle, or a singer or dancer. When this format is employed, fewer separate and distinct acts are programmed. Comedy, songs and dances are stressed. Many individual stations still retain some form of the straightforward variety format.

Variety shows use other forms, however, than the revue:

1. A theme is chosen as a "peg" on which to hang the frame. Composers such as Irving Berlin or Rogers and Hammerstein may be "saluted"; a general locale, country or city such as New Orleans, Mexico, etc., may serve as a springboard; a cavalcade of tunes and dances associated with a colorful period of history, the showboat days, for example; a reenactment of the rise to fame by a star may be the unifying device, e.g., "The Gertrude Lawrence Story," or the background in making a movie may be presented.

2. A story line similar to the "book" of Broadway musical comedy is utilized to highlight a comedy star or comic team. This approach stresses the "plot" and eliminates many of the individual specialty acts. Comedy, music, and dancing are woven into the continuity. If the story line takes the star to a Central American fiesta, for example, the dancers may be dressed in appropriate costumes; if the star visits a night club, the usual show girl parade and dancing chorus appear; or if the star plays himself in simulated attendance at a rehearsal of his own program, the dances and music may be presented with the company dressed in informal practice clothes and with backstage properties and sets. Instead of "stand-up" comedy monologues, the laughs come from lines that are delivered in character and arise out of situations.

Programs which start out as variety programs may move over into close approximation of situation comedy. The "Jackie Gleason Show" on the

DuMont network in the early 1950's was a straight variety program. When it was transferred to the CBS network, fewer acts were featured and the comedy routines featuring Gleason in several comic character roles became longer. One characterization, the husband in "The Honeymooners" sketch, gradually was expanded and expanded, and in the fall of 1955 the one-hour format was abandoned in favor of a half-hour situation comedy.

3. Combination sketches and variety acts. Some programs combine one or two longer sketches which have a story line with music numbers and dances or guest spots. The Sid Caesar show is an example of this type. A husband and wife "Commuters" sketch may take half an hour, vocals, dance specialties, motion-picture satire, and a pantomime or monologue spot by Caesar may fill the remainder of the hour. The importance of the partners and supporting players becomes very evident in program formats described under (2) and (3).

The effectiveness of variety programs depends upon (a) the ability of the acts and stars; (b) the balance of the over-all production with placement or routining; (c) creativity and imaginative writing and staging. Program producers turn to night clubs, Broadway musicals, and movies, or tour other countries in search of talent. In variety programs heavy reliance is placed upon music. The traditional routining of vaudeville acts, with the acrobats or an animal act in the opening spot and the star "next to closing" is rarely followed now. Competition with the programming on opposition stations has increased the demand for getting off to a good start with a top act. Producers generally attempt to give audiences a contrast between successive specialties. Two short acts, one after another are usually avoided. A fast and bouncy act may well be followed by a "smooth" romantic ballad or flowing dance act. The practicalities of staging may prescribe that a routine such as an elaborate song and dance which takes up the full stage should be followed by a solo number front-of-the-curtain.

It is very difficult for writers to prepare a fresh comedy script week after week, coming up with new twists to old themes. They must be skilled in preparing the script for the particular comedian. It is essential that they become very familiar with the types of routines the star does best and write material in keeping with the characterization or personality the audience associates with him. The same general comments on continuity given earlier also hold true for the introductions to the guests and numbers. Considerable banter and straight dialogue may have to be written for the talent. Naturalness and conversational sparkle sound effortless when delivered by professionals, but may represent considerable time and effort by the writer as well as the possession of a keen ear for the language, sentence construction and rhythms of speech.

The dance numbers must be staged with the limitations of the medium in mind. Cover shots of large groups spread out over huge areas of the studio make the dancers appear mere specks when seen on the average home receiver. Complicated movements by dancers who swirl back and forth and in and around each other may result in a blur when the director attempts any close-ups. TV choreographers tend to emphasize these principles: careful blocking to confine movements to small areas; hold to relatively small groups, six usually being the maximum for an ensemble; plan movement diagonally or in straight lines to and away from the camera to reduce the need for broad sweeping pans to follow extreme horizontal movement; and stress an interpretative or story-line theme.

Rehearsals of variety programs are conducted in much the same way as music, usually spread out over three or four days for an hour show. Music, of course, is an important part of most variety shows. Not only are vocals spotlighted but dance routines, specialty acts, and a number of comedy routines have the support of music backgrounds. Orchestral introductions and payoffs also frame the units. A piano is used for preliminary workouts of vocals and dance numbers; the orchestra is not called in until the program rehearsals are well under way. Comedy sequences are rehearsed with walk-throughs and preliminary on-camera work without the orchestra. The separate elements are not put together until the time of the first camera run-through. A timing sheet has been used during this period of individual unit rehearsals.

Programs with comedy sequences must rely on estimates of "spread" to compute timing. Most programs of this type are broadcast before a live audience. Laughter and applause are expected as the show is seen in person. Program directors must allow for the time consumed by audience reactions. Another unknown factor is the rate of delivery of stars. Most comedians read their lines faster in rehearsal when no audience is present than in performance on the air. Action and business play faster in rehearsal. The directors must evaluate by past experience how much slower the lines will be delivered, how much laughter, how much the performers will "milk" the comedy bits when the show "hits the air." A common practice is to add an arbitrary percentage of rehearsal time to a sequence for spread. This figure may range from 20 per cent to 100 per cent. A five-minute sequence by rehearsal timing, therefore, is marked down on the timing sheet as six minutes if the lower percentage is taken, as ten minutes if the higher, or somewhere in between.

Knowing how a comic works, whether or not he tends to ad lib and expand a routine, or whether the sequence is likely to induce slight chuckles or hilarious "show-stopping" gales of laughter are all taken into account in determining the percentage for spread. Since the best guesses are not always correct, a cushion sequence is inserted which may be included or cut according to time. This cushion may be an introduction to the final number in short and long versions, a section of the final comedy sequence which may be omitted, a final dance "theme" sequence, an extra song by one of the stars, additional choruses of a scheduled song, or a talk by the MC or star about "coming attractions." Sometimes the timing may be off and a stretch in the final moments is needed. The MC or star may bring back the guests of the program for an interview about future plans and another exchange of pleasantries with expressions of thanks. He may bring the entire cast on stage for a curtain call. The director may pan across the audience applauding the program, or run the credits through as slowly as possible.

EXAMPLE OF TELEVISION MUSIC PROGRAM

"Omnibus III," Vol. 5, November 14, 1954.[8]
Beethoven-Bernstein Feature

One of the highlights of the "Omnibus" 1954-55 schedule was the sequence dealing with Beethoven's Fifth Symphony. Two excerpts from "Omnibus" produced by the TV-Radio Workshop of The Ford Foundation over the facilities of the CBS Television Network follow. The script was written by Arnold Sundgaard.

```
INTRO TO BERNSTEIN AND BEETHOVEN

        COOKE

Probably the most famous notes in music are the ones that Ludwig
Van Beethoven, going blind and gone deaf, used for the opening
theme of his Fifth Symphony.  This afternoon, a distinguished
American composer and conductor, Mr. Leonard Bernstein, will
show what these notes meant to Beethoven:  how he scored them;
for what instruments; how he changed his mind here and there -
because he had the sort of mind that could throw away a merely
brilliant phrase for the one his genius told him was exactly
right.

Leonard Bernstein will analyze the music, and it will then be
played by Toscanini's NBC Symphony Orchestra, which has re-
organized itself as the Symphony of the Air.

        (DISSOLVE TO BEETHOVEN SCORE)

        (VOICE OVER)

The evolution of a masterpiece - Beethoven's Symphony number 5
in C Minor

FADE UP ON COVER OF B & H EDITION OF BEETHOVEN'S FIFTH:

MUSIC:  ORCHESTRA PLAYS FIRST FOUR NOTES

DISSOLVE OUT THE MAT OF

        B E E T H O V E N

        Symphony #5

            C Minor

            Op. 67

        S C O R E

REVEALING HIGH, WIDE SHOT OF BERNSTEIN STANDING ON THE SCORE.
MUSIC:  ORCHESTRA PLAYS SECOND GROUP OF FOUR NOTES.  AS WE HEAR
```

[8] Courtesy of TV-Radio Workshop of The Ford Foundation.

THE MUSIC DISSOLVE OUT THE DECORATIVE FRAME OF THE B & H COVER,
CAMERA SWOOPS IN TO BERNSTEIN.

            BERNSTEIN

That's the perfect beginning for a symphony. It's simple, strong
and right. And so economical -- why, almost every bar of this
first movement is a direct development of these opening four
notes.

HE INDICATES NOTES WITH HIS FOOT.

Here they are.

HUMS THE NOTES.

And what are these notes that they should be so pregnant and
meaningful. Three G's and an E-flat. Nothing more. Anyone
might have thought of them -- maybe.

CAMERA LOWERS AND TIGHTENS IN A CU OF BERNSTEIN WHO WALKS TOWARD
CAMERA. CAMERA PULLS EQUI-DISTANT TO HIM.

            BERNSTEIN (Cont)

People have wondered for years what it is that endows this
musical figure with such potency. All kinds of music appreciation theories have been advanced that it is based on the song of
a bird Beethoven heard in the Vienna woods; that it is the announcement of Judgment Day: that it is the letter V in Morse
Code -- three shorts and a long -- and thus during the last war
it became the musical symbol of "V for Victory." These, and
more. It has been played slowly, quickly, wildly, pompously,
percussively. Every conductor has another idea of how to bring
out its real meaning. But none of these interpretations begin
to tell us of its real musical meaning. The truth is that the
real meaning lies in the notes that follow it - all the notes
of all the 500 measures that follow it. And Beethoven, more
than any other composer before or after him, I think, had the
ability to find these exactly right notes -- notes that grow as
naturally as fingernails out of his thematic material.

. . . .

(TWELVE MUSICIANS WITH THEIR INSTRUMENTS ARE LIGHTED UP STANDING
ON THEIR OWN STAFF LINES BETWEEN INSTRUMENT NAME AND CLEFF SIGN)

These are the 12 instruments Beethoven chose to use in his opening movement. A full orchestra is made up of these 12 instruments multiplied from 2 to 18 times. Starting at the top of the
page they are:
Flute

    Then the Oboe

        The Clarinet

            The Bassoon

                Horn

                    Trumpet

You see that break across the page? It divides the higher
register instruments from the lower register instruments.
After that, the First Violin
    And the Second Violin

    The Viola

     'cello

      Double Bass

They must be kept in the symphony composer's mind at all times.

THE MUSICIANS SLOWLY WALK ACROSS THE PAGE OF MUSIC.

BERNSTEIN AD LIBS REMARKS ABOUT THE COMPLEXITY OF THE VOICES --
HOW THEY CAN BE USED, CHORDALLY, CONTRAPUNTALLY OR NOT AT ALL.

BERNSTEIN AD LIB SINGS STRAUSS WALTZ, EXPLAINS SIMPLICITY OF
COMPOSING THAT AS CONTRASTED WITH SYMPHONY.

THIS SHOULD START WITH CAMERA STILL ON MUSICIANS. COME BACK TO
BERNSTEIN DURING SPEECH ABOUT STRAUSS WALTZ.

DURING THIS TIME, OFF CAMERA, MUSICIANS RETURN TO STARTING
POSITION.

BERNSTEIN AD LIBS selecting of instruments by Beethoven to make
his opening statement. He points to 12 musicians and says Ludwig
Van Beethoven selected these.

7 MUSICIANS: FLUTE, CLARINET, 1st and 2nd VIOLINS, VIOLA, CELLO
AND DOUBLE BASS STEP ONTO SCORE.

BERNSTEIN HOLDS MS.

          BERNSTEIN

Here is the manuscript as he started it. But here is something
crossed out, the music given to the flute. So we know that
Beethoven,for one wild second, was going to include the flute.
Why did he cross it out? Let us hear how it would have sounded
with the flute left in:

BERNSTEIN AND ORCHESTRA, FAVORING ORCHESTRA

ORCHESTRA: EX. 1

          BERNSTEIN

The high, piping notes of the flute don't seem to fit into the
generally rude and brusque atmosphere of the opening bars.
Beethoven clearly wanted these notes to be a strong, masculine
utterance; and he therefore orchestrated entirely with instruments that play normally in the register of the male singing-
voice.

The flute, being the instrumental equivalent of a soprano, would
be intruding here like a delicate lady at a club smoker. So out
came the flute.

FLUTE PLAYER STEPS OFF SCORE.

and now let's hear how masculine it sounds without him.

PLAY MUSIC: EX. 2

You see a lot of us assume when we hear the Symphony today it
must have spilled out of Beethoven in one steady gush--clear
and right from the beginning. It is as though he had a direct
telephone wire to heaven, where the symphony was already made
and waiting; and all he had to do was to listen and put it down
on paper. But not at all. Beethoven left pages and pages of
discarded material, similar to this, enough to fill a whole book.
The man listened, rejected, rewrote, scratched out, tore up, and

sometimes altered as many as twenty times. We can see some of it here in this facsimile of the original orchestral manuscript score.

Projects and Exercises

1. Tune in the stations in your area and determine station policy regarding musical program planning: How elaborate are the productions? What program formats are used? How are unity and variety achieved? Any evidence of effective twists or "gimmicks"? What are the respective merits and demerits of the continuity? What staging is attempted for the television programs?

2. Do the same for any variety program originated by the local stations. Report on the routing of the acts on any revue type productions.

3. Visit the stations and discuss with representatives of the engineering or programming departments the types of microphones used for live music pick-ups and microphone placement.

4. Write substitute continuity for scripts included in this chapter. Refer to current issues of *Variety* and *Billboard* for authoritative surveys of best-selling records, sheet music and broadcast performances. Refer to standard musical encyclopedias for information on classical and semiclassical compositions and composers.

5. Attempt pantomime lip sync to current records. Practice this assignment out of class before presentation before classmates.

6. Divide the class into groups—four in each group. One runs the turntables, the second directs, the third writes the continuity, and the fourth announces recorded or transcribed five- or ten-minute programs. Use the facilities at hand and alternate duties on each round. Present both radio and television programs. Each group has free choice of program type, format, station, time of performance, and sponsor. Play only portions of numbers but cue them in so that the cuts are not obvious. Class criticism and evaluation after each presentation.

7. Audition class members and friends for a live-talent variety program, either radio or television. Rehearse and present before the class. Criticize and evaluate.

8. Prepare and present for class performance a television version of scenes from a musical comedy or operetta. Secure the co-operation of the music department in a simulated televised broadcast.

9. Experiment with the placement of different types of microphones in your own studio. Enlist the services of amateur or professional vocalists or instrumentalists from the class or school. Move them around in different positions and use different microphones. Try changing the reverberation characteristics of the studio by movable screens. Attempt concealed microphones for television pick-ups.

❖ 28 ❖

Television and Radio Drama

"WHEREVER AND WHENEVER humans have progressed beyond the mere struggle for physical existence, to gods and recreation and self-expression, there has been theatre in some sense; an inevitable place for acting, dancing, dialogue, drama, in the ordered scheme of life." [1]

Production of drama through the ages has been influenced not only by the cultural environment of the people, but also by the physical dimensions of the setting where the drama is presented and the technical devices available to the dramatist and director. Modern day audiences that watch or listen for hours have their predecessors in ancient Greece when theatrical attendance was an all-day family affair. Thousands gathered in large amphitheaters cut into the hillside. Since the faces of actors could not be distinguished by the audiences seated far from the stage, huge masks were used to identify the different characters. In Shakespeare's time, dialogue references instead of realistic settings informed those in pit and balcony where the scene was to be—a battlefield, a castle, or an island. In later years the theater developed the "picture-window" stage, with an emphasis upon more or less realistic scenery viewed by the audience through a fixed proscenium arch. The development of motion pictures introduced a new set of techniques that were available to the dramatist and the director. Similarly, the radio and television media have developed dramatic forms of their own.

It is appropriate in this chapter to discuss the nature and characteristics of radio and television drama; then to compare them with the legitimate theater and motion pictures to analyze and appraise their similarities and differences.

Radio. The absence of sight makes possible a radio theater of the imagination. The listeners, each in his own way, are co-operating playwrights.

[1] Sheldon Cheney, *The Theatre* (New York, 1929), p. 1.

482

Each listener provides the setting for the play in his mind; with mental imagery he gives visual characterization to the participants in the play. Radio drama draws its aesthetic form from the following: (1) the intimacy of the medium, which makes the audience feel it is on stage with the performers, (2) the absence of sight which means that setting, characterizations, and plot must be conveyed through dialogue, narration, sound effects or music, and (3) the complete freedom of locale, time, and characterizations made possible by the absence of sight and limited only by the extent to which our imagination is stimulated.

In radio drama the setting may be transferred to any place, at any time, in a matter of seconds. It takes only

```
ANNCR:   The time: Twenty thousand years from tomorrow.
MUSIC:   LAUGHING MOTIF, FADING OUT BEHIND
THE MAN: (FADE IN LAUGHING VIGOROUSLY, TRYING VAINLY TO CONTROL
         HIS LAUGHTER). Excuse me please! I--I'm laughing--I
         know it isn't polite! I--I can't help it! [2]
```

And we are with "The Laughing Man" in a civilization twenty thousand years ahead in time when society doesn't believe that there could have been an era of air bombings.

```
MUSIC:   WILLIAM TELL OVERTURE THEME
ANNCR:   Now he was the masked mystery rider once again.  He
         leaped astride the great horse, Silver, and shouted...
RANGER:  Hi, yo, Silver!  Away-y-y
SOUND:   HOOFS
MUSIC:   WILLIAM TELL OVERTURE THEME [3]
```

And now we are in that great West of yesterday, riding with the Lone Ranger to the rescue of his faithful Indian companion, Tonto.

```
TUPAC:   I come to you out of the dry and folded years of the past.
         I speak to you from beyond the grave.  I am Tupac Amaru...
         last of the Incas. [4]
```

And further back in time to another era of yesterday when the Incas were the proud rulers of Peru, to be annihilated later by the Spanish conquerors.

```
STUDIO ANNCR: (OROTUND AND PROFESSIONAL)
              Ladies and gentlemen:
              This broadcast comes to you from the city. [5]
```

And now we are in a huge city, existing somewhere in space and time overlooking a "great square," the populace awaiting "the master."

[2] Arch Oboler, *Fourteen Radio Plays* (New York, 1940), p. 3.

[3] "The Lone Ranger" written by Fran Stryker, in Max Wylie, *Best Broadcasts of 1939-40* (New York, 1940), p. 289.

[4] Morton Wishengrad, "The Last Inca," published in Joseph Liss (ed.), *Radio's Best Plays* (New York, 1947), p. 222.

[5] Archibald MacLeish, "The Fall of the City," in *ibid.*, p. 8.

RUNYON: (Timidly). Is this the department of lost dogs?
CLERK: Yes.
RUNYON: I'm looking for my dog.
CLERK: (Perfunctorily) Your name?
RUNYON: Runyon Jones.[6]

This time we are in the hereafter, a particularly whimsical hereafter, where in Purgatory we meet Father Time, Mother Nature, a talking Harp, and a Board of Directors as they are encountered by our companion, Runyon Jones.

And for our final example we go inside the brain of a man—at "Central" where messages are phoned in from the various parts of a "Mr. Jones"—Optical, Nerves, Old Age, Dental, Framework, Skin, Bloodstream, Building and Repair, and Energy—each stating his food requirements.

NARR: Stand by, America. For now HOME IS WHAT YOU MAKE IT
         takes you--INSIDE Mr. Jones!
SOUND: (OSCILLATOR, CARRYING US IN AN AMUSING-SOUNDING "SPIRAL,"
         INSIDE MR. JONES)
(MUSIC: USE, IF DESIRED, IN ACCOMPANIMENT WITH OSCILLATOR...)
SOUND: (DEEP INSIDE MR. JONES--AS IF IN AN INDUSTRIAL PLANT--
         NOISE OF MACHINERY, THE WHIRRING OF MOTORS, THE CLANGING
         OF BELLS, BURPING AND BUBBLING, OFF...ANYTHING TO SUG-
         GEST THE HEART THROBBING, THE BLOOD FLOWING, THE WHOLE
         HUMAN ORGANISM NOISILY AT WORK...HOLD UNTIL ESTABLISHED,
         THEN UNDER AS B.G. FOR:)
NARR: (IN THE MANNER OF A SPECIAL-EVENTS ANNOUNCER...SLIGHTLY
         MUFFLED AT FIRST) Hello, America! We are greeting you
         from the interior of Mr. Jones. Lots of interesting
         things are going on here, which we'll want to describe
         to you in a moment, but first perhaps we ought to tell
         you where we are. As near as I can make out, we're in a
         sort of nerve center in Mr. Jones' mind. Here, ap-
         parently, is where messages are received from all parts
         of the body that are ultimately relayed to Mr. Jones'
         consciousness.
                (START MELTING INTO THE EFFECTS OF A HUGE
                  TELEPHONE SWITCHBOARD, HOLD AS B.G.)
         "Hectic", is the word for it. I don't believe there's
         a livelier spot to be found in all of Mr. Jones' five
         feet, seven-and-a-half inches. Fortunately, I've man-
         aged to find some one here who seems to know what it's
         all about. And here he is!--How do you do, sir.
CHIEF: (HARRIED: RAPID-SPEAKING: EDWARD-EVERETT-HORTON TYPE)
         How'd do. I'm sorry, I can only spare a minute. This
         is the busiest day we've had in Jones' last ten years.
         I don't know when there have ever been so many com-
         plaints! I do wish Mr. Jones would take better care of
         himself.
         (IMPATIENTLY) Now, what is it...What is it?

---

[6] Norman Corwin, "The Odyssey of Runyon Jones," in *Thirteen by Corwin* (New York, 1942), p. 3.

```
NARR:    First, what do you call this place, sir?
CHIEF:   "Central."  Jones--Central.  I'm in charge.
NARR:    What do you do?
CHIEF:   What do you do, he asks!--We handle messages from the
         various anatomic parts of Mr. Jones--muscles, blood
         stream, morphological structure, heart--
NARR:    All kinds of messages?
CHIEF:   (HORRIFIED)  All kinds?!  What do you think we are,
         here, young man?  No indeed!  Food messages only.  The
         human body, sir, is a highly complicated organism.
         We've enough to do specializing on food alone.  Even at
         that, at the end of an ordinary day with Mr. Jones, I'm
         just plain worn out!
NARR:    But what sort of complaints do you get?
CHIEF:   You hang around and listen in.  There's simply no end to
         them!  Anyone would think that Jones' health was our
         fault, the way the various Department Heads fuss at us!
         But all we at Central can do is pass on their warnings,
         and if Jones chooses to ignore them, our hands are tied.
         And what makes it especially difficult is--they always
         complain at once...
SOUND:   (A BATTERY OF TELEPHONES, WITH DIFFERENT BELL SOUNDS,
         SOUNDING OFF AT THE SAME TIME.)
CHIEF:   (OVER SOUND.  AT WIT'S END)  See what I mean?  (FADE)
         It never fails!
(MUSIC:  IN TO COVER TELEPHONES, THEN UP WILDLY TO:) 7
```

Television. Television drama has developed an aesthetic form that is quite distinct from the drama of radio, the theater, and motion pictures at the same time that it uses techniques characteristic of the other aesthetic media. Television drama has the same intimacy as radio drama and it makes much use of sound effects and music, but in other respects it shows a greater kinship for the theater and motion pictures. It lacks the flexibility of time and space found in radio and the movies, but it has greater freedom of movement than the theater. It has all the added values of sight to convey character, mood, action, and plot. The television camera becomes a moving proscenium arch that extends the audience's horizontal range of vision to all possible angles within 360°; it offers an adjustable vertical range, and practically unlimited variations in depth, from extreme close-ups to long shots limited only by the visual requirements of relatively small television viewing screens. Albert McCleery's "cameo" style of television directing concentrates almost exclusively on close-ups and medium shots and avoids long shots almost entirely. This style has won considerable critical recognition as a distinct aesthetic form of television drama.

Consider for a moment how the varying degrees of depth of affection or intensity of hate are more easily comprehended when we can see as well as hear. The ability to direct the viewers' attention to specific

7 Lou Hazam, "Daily Problem of Food." Courtesy of the National Broadcasting Company.

detail by appropriate camera movement and selection of camera shots has great significance in television drama. The writer and director may place emphasis where they see fit. A camera close-up of a gun on a table during a bitter quarrel between a thug and young heroine is intended to increase the dramatic force of the action when the girl suddenly seizes the revolver. The opening camera shot of "Marcia Akers" in the script found on page 556 illustrates how attention can be directed to specific detail. In David Shaw's script, "Native Dancer," written for the Goodyear Television Playhouse, camera action anticipates dialogue revealing certain ambitions held by a leading character. After an opening establishing shot of Broadway, the camera dollies in to a drug store exterior and then dissolves into the busy scene inside. A waitress is shouting orders across the counter to a short order clerk (Shirley) who is racing to fill the orders. During the rapid-fire exchange of dialogue the camera tilts down to Shirley's feet and reveals that she is wearing ballet slippers and is practising some classic positions while she works. The camera then tilts up again as the scene continues:

```
    FRANCES
Is my toasted American working?

    SHIRLEY
No harder than I am.

    FRANCES
Well, it'd be a lot easier on you if you
did your ballet lessons on your own time.

    SHIRLEY
My teacher says every minute counts if you
want to be a great dancer.

    FRANCES
Sure, what does he care?  He doesn't have to
eat here.  Shirley, the customers are beginning
to complain about the service.

    SHIRLEY
Tell them I'm on my toes.   (AND SHE IS).8
```

Television and Radio Compared to Theater and Film. LOCALE OR PLAY-ING AREA. Theatrical drama is influenced by the physical stage or playing area, and the physical location of the audience. Most modern theaters have a proscenium arch. Some plays such as "Our Town," and "Death of a Salesman" use different areas and levels together with special lighting and staging devices in attempts to achieve a degree of freedom from the "picture-frame" stage. Most stage plays, however, adhere to a conventional stage setting with an open "fourth wall" through which the audience can see the play. Radio drama, of course, is not limited by physical stage settings. Live television drama does not have the same freedom as radio drama, but it does make use of "detail sets," "limbos," rear-screen projection (RP), electronic

8 Irving Settel (ed.), *Top TV Shows of the Year* (New York, 1955), p. 142.

matt inserts, photo murals, film inserts, and unit or multiple sets to increase its range of movement. Film has less flexibility in selection of locale than radio, more than television, and, of course, much more than theater. Outdoor or on-location scenes, chase sequences, and spectacles, such as huge crowds, battle scenes, and picturesque exteriors, are possible, limited only by time and budget.

AUDIENCE ORIENTATION. In the theater each member of the audience watches the performance from the same fixed position. The listener in radio may accompany the actor right by his side as he is on the move, or the listener may stay while the actor leaves. The listener may share the innermost thoughts of a character or be only a distant observer. Narrative and dialogue, distances from the microphone, and variations in voice levels create these differences in perspective. Film and television also have great flexibility in changing audience orientation. The cameras move in and around—we look into back corners of the locale—we can see how the characters appear to each other from their respective locations. We can become very close to the characters when we move from a cover view, as though we were in the fourteenth row, right up to the players "on stage." This change of audience orientation may account for the greater emphasis in film and television upon *reaction* rather than on *action,* as in theater and radio. Observe as you watch film or television, how many times the camera directs your attention to a character other than the one speaking in order to show you the effects of the words or action.

The ability of the camera to move around, taking the viewer with it and changing the view as it moves, and the ability to cut from camera to camera so that a viewer can be far away, a little distance away, or very close, in front or behind, below or above, are distinctive elements of film and television drama. Intensification of emotion may be accomplished by the moving camera, the angle of camera shots, self-identification (empathy) with a character, and cuts from one camera to another. Alfred Hitchcock, in his classic film, *The Thirty-nine Steps,* moved a camera into an extreme close-up of the mouth of a hotel maid as she started to scream when she discovered the corpse of a beautiful woman on a bed in a cheap hotel. The blow-up of a portion of the face increased the impact of shock and horror. In some television dramatic scenes, a camera may stand in for a character. The camera simulates the eyes of the person as he looks around the scene and moves towards and away from other actors. The way the world of the grownups appears to a youngster has been suggested by shooting from the youngster's eye level up towards the adults. How a scene appears to one who is losing consciousness is often portrayed by having the camera gradually lose focus or by rotating the lens, or other camera tricks. This "subjective-camera" technique, however, should be used sparingly. It is mentioned here because it illustrates vividly the contrast between audience orientation in the theater and what may be accomplished in television and film.

DIALOGUE. Radio drama depends primarily upon words to convey character and plot. The audience has to understand instantly. When a number of persons are involved in a scene, failure to identify characters through spoken names or family relationships (Dad, Sis, Mom, Uncle Joe) results in audience confusion. Since the audience cannot see the setting of any scene, meaningful references through dialogue, narration, and sound effects must be incorporated in the script.

```
JOE:     Don't forget...two AM...at the hotel side entrance.
         Be there.
MUSIC:   BRIDGE

JANE:    Oh, it's so quiet and scary here, George.  Are you sure
         this is where we are to meet him?  On this deserted
         street?

GEORGE:  Right here at the hotel's side entrance -- that's where
         Joe said.  He should be here any minute.  Don't be
         nervous, Jane.
```

From the dialogue in scenes before this, the audience is able to tell whether this scene involves the payment of ransom, or is just an arrangement for an elopement. We know the setting, however. The listener's imagination will fill in the background details. Writers must be cautious not to be too blunt or to use opening speeches to pile on exposition. Here is an exaggerated example to illustrate what should *not* be done.

```
JANE:    Here we are, at the side entrance on West 57th street,
         all ready to meet Joe with money I saved from six months'
         clerking at Macy's and train tickets I purchased at Grand
         Central at 4:15, but Joe isn't here.  It's quiet and
         scary, and I'm nervous, George.
```

Stage plays also depend primarily upon dialogue. It is true, of course, that action, setting, lighting, costumes, and physical appearance of the actors are very important, but because of the physical limitations of the playing area and the fixed location of the audience the playwright usually turns to dialogue to set forth the problem, to develop the conflict, to proceed to a climax, and to state the resolution.

The editing of camera shots plays an important role in live television and filmed dramas. The tempo of different sequences in a drama is established by the length of time each shot is held and the speed of switching from shot to shot, whether by fast cuts, slow dissolves, or fast dissolves. An identical scene shot in one tempo and then shot in another will differ strikingly in mood. Consider how a series of fast cuts would dissipate the suspense of the slow tortured crawl of a badly wounded man across the floor towards a time bomb set to go off momentarily.

The pattern of different camera shots also influences the dramatic meaning conveyed. A classic example from motion picture film is the final sequence in *All Quiet on the Western Front*. Paul, a German soldier, is the leading character. He is in a front-line trench in World War I during the final moments before the Armistice goes into effect. He sees a butterfly, is attracted by its beauty, studies it as it rests on a twig, and finally reaches out his hand for it. As he does so, we see a close-up of his hand going limp. The various camera shots of Paul are interspersed by camera shots of a French sniper. The sniper loads his rifle and aims it; a close-up of his fingers reveals that the trigger is being pressed; a close-up of the rifle shows it being fired. The cuts back and forth between the camera shots of Paul and the sniper heightens the emotional effect upon the audience which can anticipate the outcome; it also emphasizes the irony of Paul's absorption with the butterfly under the shadow of death. And additional meaning may be found in the implied comparison between Paul and the insect. The individual soldier has no more control over his fate in modern warfare than a trapped butterfly. This juxtaposition of different series of camera shots "enables the film director to endow his shots with a meaning beyond the scope of their apparent ideological content." [9]

In a contrary vein, Gilbert Seldes describes how a director can use television techniques in an imaginary production of *Hamlet* to

> destroy all the poetry and philosophy of the original, reducing it to a roaring melodrama of murder and revenge. . . . He will prevent the audience from concentrating on Hamlet by placing him in the background of long shots, never giving him a close shot; he will disconcert the audience further by giving close-ups to Claudius, to the gravedigger, to Osric. He will cut rapidly and he will cut against the tempo of speeches; the more thoughtful and poetic the speech the jumpier will be the cut from one shot to another, he will cut half a dozen times in the first three lines of any soliloquy. He will avoid the slow fade, doing the entire play in a single tempo, and that a fast one, so that in the end he will have a melodrama. The line of action will be clear; the line of thought and feeling that underlies the action will vanish . . .[10]

NARRATOR. The narrator is "the most useful dramatic personage since the Greek chorus . . . an integral part of radio technique." [11] The use of the program narrator permits the radio writer to speak directly to the audience. This technique permits him to tell where the scene is, to set the mood, to establish the relationship of the characters, to recapitulate the action in previous episodes or scenes and to comment on the attitude the audience should have toward the play, *before* the play actually begins. During the play the narrator can summarize, change the scene, comment on the action, talk to the characters in the play. At the conclusion he can draw loose ends together, state the moral, and comment on it or its application. The charac-

---

[9] Joseph and Harry Feldman, *Dynamics of the Film* (New York, 1952), p. 55. A more detailed description of this shot sequence may be found in this volume.

[10] Gilbert Seldes, *Writing for Television* (New York, 1952), p. 64.

[11] Archibald MacLeish, quoted in Joseph Liss (ed.), *Radio's Best Plays* (New York, 1947), p. 7.

ter narrator, a member of the cast of the play, may talk directly to the audience, or he may tell his story to an imaginary third person as the audience listens in.

Arch Oboler, one of the outstanding radio playwrights of the late 30's and early 40's, began a radio play, "This Lonely Heart," dealing with a love affair of the composer, Tschaikowsky, as follows:

VOICE: I'm weary of these everlasting alarms of war. I'm tired of cruelty and the bitterness between men. Come -- let us have a play of love -- a strange love...

MUSIC: "NONE BUT THE LONELY HEART," DOWN AND CONTINUING FAR BEHIND.

VOICE 2: In a darkened room sits a woman...an old woman...She sits very quietly, white hands motionless...[12]

As the play progresses Oboler uses the "stream-of-consciousness" technique to give voice to the thoughts in mind of the old woman, Nadejda:

NADEJDA: Piotr...Piotr...why are you in my mind? Why do I think of you now? Why is your song with me here in the darkness? Why today Piotr....[13]

As she thinks of the past, voices are heard as she recalls how the people spoke to her. This dialogue is presented by other actors:

NADEJDA: I told myself I would always help you, Piotr... When I got home that night, the children...

VLADIMIR: (FADE IN FAST) Mother, where did you go? The carriage waited -- you didn't come out!

JULIA: Mother, where have you been?...(FADE) You walked home. Why did you walk? Why?

NADEJDA: I did not answer them...[14]

In the use of the narrator, radio drama has been compared to the short story and novel. In stage plays, the narrator has been used occasionally for introductions, transitions and exposition, dating back to the chorus in Greek plays, but the device of a main character, the novelist's "I," as a narrator who addresses the audience directly, is seldom used. However, Thornton Wilder's *Our Town,* Tennessee Williams' *The Glass Menagerie,* and John Van Druten's *I Remember Mama* are modern plays which do utilize such narrators.

Feature films for theatrical release generally do not use narration except to identify dates or locale or to give the audience some background information. In *The Blackboard Jungle,* a film on juvenile delinquency in a high school, a foreword was shown in written form to justify the picture and to

---

[12] Arch Oboler, *Fourteen Radio Plays* (New York, 1940), p. 9.
[13] *Ibid.,* p. 10.
[14] *Ibid.,* p. 17.

disclaim any implication that the situations portrayed were typical of normal school conditions. Some pictures are produced with a character narrator. *Sunset Boulevard* used a character narrator who, at the end of the picture, is revealed to have been dead. Half-hour dramatic films for television tend to use narration in order to pack as much story as possible into the brief time period. Live television dramas frequently employ program narration— through title cards or words to be read by the viewer or by an announcer speaking over camera shots of the opening scene. The use of character narration has increased as television dramatic writers have moved away from the more rigid techniques copied from stage plays in the first days of television and have reached for greater freedom of form. It should be stressed, however, that in drama for any medium an excessive reliance upon narration instead of on dramatic action and dialogue usually weakens a play.

TIME. Radio and television dramas are ruled by time. The program lengths for presentation are restricted in time to a half hour, hour, and in-frequently ninety minutes—*including commercials.* A so-called half-hour drama is actually only twenty six-and-a-half minutes long; an hour drama fifty-three-and-a-half minutes, including opening and closing titles and credits as well as commercial billboards. Rehearsal periods prior to pro-duction are established and fairly inflexible. The element of continuous performance in live television precludes elaborate costume changes or transformations by actors from one age to another age when they are involved in successive scenes. "Cover" material must be planned to advance the plot and keep action going while principal characters leave one set and move into new positions in the scene to follow. The play must start at a specific time, gain the immediate interest of the audience who might other-wise "do the dishes" or tune to another station, stop at specified times for commercials, and complete the play on time.

Theater and film do not have the same degree of time tyranny regulating them. The length of the play is not arbitrarily restricted, although plays running more than two hours are rare. Rehearsal schedules have more lee-way. Intermissions in the theater and the system in film of shooting scenes separately, permit necessary costume and make-up changes to be made without pressure. The audience has gathered together in a theater away from the competing environmental activities in the home following the pur-chase of tickets. It seldom leaves—even if the play does not attract interest in the opening minutes. And "a word from the sponsor" never intrudes upon the progression of the story.

Half-hour radio and television dramas generally eliminate subplots from adaptations and rarely include them in original works; the audience's atten-tion is directed towards only a few principal participants. One playwright comments: "I have only one rule that I consider absolute and arbitrary, and that is: a drama can have only one story. It can have only one leading character. All other stories and all other characters are used in the script only as they facilitate the main story." [15] Although radio dramas permit considerable physical action, television plays minimize pageantry and spectacle and, excluding mysteries and situation comedies, tend to be dramas of character development rather than complicated plot and action. "Television drama . . . must expand in depth. In the last year or so, television writers have learned that they can write intimate dramas—'intimate' meaning minutely detailed studies of small moments of life. . . . Now, the word for television drama is depth, the digging under the surface of life for the more profound truths of human relationships." [16]

Creative dramatic writers and directors who are inclined to become disturbed by the various restrictions radio and television imposes upon them may be stimulated and reassured by Goethe's observation that the master hand reveals itself when it works within the limitations of the medium.

EXAMPLES OF TELEVISION DRAMA

1. "Marty," by Paddy Chayefsky [17]

John Crosby, *New York Herald Tribune* syndicated radio and television critic, has referred to Paddy Chayefsky as "one of TV's most honest and distinctive writers." Following the presentation of "Marty" on NBC-TV, a movie was produced which won many of the top critical awards, including a sweep of four 1956 Academy "Oscars" for best screen play, direction, actor, and picture. In his discussion of this script, contained in the published edition of six of his plays, the author indicates that the play represents "the sort of material that does best on television. . . . [It deals] with the world of the mundane, the ordinary, and the untheatrical. The main characters are typical, rather than exceptional; the situations are easily identifiable by the audience; and the relationships are as common as people." He feels that the essence of the show lies in its "literal reality." "I tried to write the dialogue as if it had been wire-tapped. I tried to envision the scenes as if a camera had been focused upon the unsuspecting characters and had caught them in an untouched moment of life." In addition to illustrating the style of Chayefsky's writing, the excerpt which follows also indicates time compression and economy of staging found in television drama. The motion-picture treatment added two scenes immediately ahead of the excerpt included here. One scene was located at the bottom of the stairway going up to the dance hall. The young man (who later approaches Marty) and his companion talk briefly while engaged in obtaining a package of cigarettes

---

[15] Paddy Chayefsky, *Television Plays* (New York, 1955), p. 81. This collection of plays by one of television's most gifted writers contains excellent essays on various aspects of television drama.

[16] *Ibid.,* p. 132.

[17] From Chayefsky, *Television Plays.* Courtesy of the author. Copyright 1954 as an unpublished dramatic composition by Paddy Chayefsky. Copyright 1955 by Paddy Chayefsky.

from a vending machine. The audience learns of his disgust with his blind date. The second scene is in the lobby where the young man encounters an old flame and decides to "ditch" his blind date. In the original television version a photograph of a building exterior was used to establish the locale. The camera dollied in on the entrance of the dance hall and then panned up to the second floor. A dissolve from the photograph revealed a live shot of a portion of the dance hall.[18]

DISSOLVE TO: Live shot - a row of stags along a wall. Camera is looking lengthwise down the row. Camera dollies slowly past each face, each staring out at the dance floor, watching in his own manner of hungry eagerness. Short, fat, tall, thin stags. Some pretend diffidence. Some exhibit patent hunger.

Near the end of the line, we find Marty and Angie, freshly shaved and groomed. They are leaning against the wall, smoking, watching their more fortunate brethren out on the floor.

ANGIE: Not a bad crowd tonight, you know?

MARTY: There was one nice-looking one there in a black dress and beads, but she was a little tall for me.

ANGIE: (Looking down past Marty along the wall right into the camera) There's a nice-looking little short one for you right now.

MARTY: (Following his gaze) Where?

ANGIE: Down there. That little one there.

The camera cuts about eight faces down, to where the girls are now standing. Two are against the wall. One is facing them, with her back to the dance floor. This last is the one Angie has in mind. She is a cute little kid, about twenty, and she has a bright smile on - as if the other two girls are just amusing her to death.

MARTY: Yeah, she looks all right from here.

ANGIE: Well, go on over and ask her. You don't hurry up, somebody else'll grab her.

Marty scowls, shrugs.

MARTY: Okay, let's go.

They slouch along past the eight stags, a picture of nonchalant unconcern. The three girls, aware of their approach, stiffen, and their chatter comes to a halt. Angie advances to one of the girls along the wall.

ANGIE: Waddaya say, you wanna dance?

The girl looks surprised - as if this were an extraordinary invitation to receive in this place - looks confounded at her two friends, shrugs, detaches herself from the group, moves to the outer fringe of the pack of dancers, raises her hand languidly to dancing position, and awaits Angie with ineffable boredom. Marty, smiling shyly, addresses the short girl.

MARTY: Excuse me, would you care for this dance?

The short girl gives Marty a quick glance of appraisal, then looks quickly at her remaining friend.

[18] Chayefsky, *op. cit.,* pp. 149-153, 173.

SHORT GIRL: (Not unpleasantly) Sorry. I just don't feel like dancing just yet.

MARTY: Sure.

He turns and moves back past the eight stags, all of whom have covertly watched his attempt. He finds his old niche by the wall, leans there. A moment later he looks guardedly down to where the short girl and her friend are. A young, dapper boy is approaching the short girl. He asks her to dance. The short girl smiles, excuses herself to her friend and follows the boy out onto the floor. Marty turns back to watching the dancers bleakly. A moment later he is aware that someone on his right is talking to him....He turns his head. It is a young man of about twenty-eight.

MARTY: You say something to me?

YOUNG MAN: Yeah, I was just asking you if you was here stag or with a girl.

MARTY: I'm stag.

YOUNG MAN: Well, I'll tell you. I got stuck onna blind date with a dog, and I just picked up a nice chick, and I was wondering how I'm gonna get ridda the dog. Somebody to take her home, you know what I mean? I be glad to pay you five bucks if you take the dog home for me.

MARTY: (A little confused) What?

YOUNG MAN: I'll take you over, and I'll introduce you as an old army buddy of mine, and then I'll cut out. Because I got this chick waiting for me out by the hatcheck, and I'll pay you five bucks.

MARTY: (Stares at the young man) Are you kidding?

YOUNG MAN: No, I'm not kidding.

MARTY: You can't just walk off onna girl like that.

The young man grimaces impatiently and moves down the line of stags...Marty watches him, still a little shocked at the proposition. About two stags down, the young man broaches his plan to another stag. This stag, frowning and pursuing his lips, seems more receptive to the idea....The young man takes out a wallet and gives the stag a five-dollar bill. The stag detaches himself from the wall and, a little ill at ease, follows the young man back past Marty and into the lounge. Marty pauses a moment and then, concerned, walks to the archway that separates the lounge from the ballroom and looks in.

The lounge is a narrow room with a bar and booths. In contrast to the ballroom, it is brightly lighted - causing Marty to squint.

In the second booth from the archway sits a girl, about twenty-eight. Despite the careful grooming that she has put into her cosmetics, she is blatantly plain. The young man and the stag are standing, talking to her. She is looking up at the young man, her hands nervously gripping her Coca-Cola glass. We cannot hear what the young man is saying, but it is apparent that he is introducing his new-found army buddy and is going through some cock-and-bull story about being called away on an emergency. The stag is presented as her escortto-be, who will see to it that she gets home safely. The girl apparently is not taken in at all by this, though she is trying hard not to seem affected.

She politely rejects the stag's company and will get home by herself, thanks for asking anyway. The young man makes a few mild protestations, and then he and the stag leave the booth and come back to the archway from where Marty has been watching the scene. As they pass Marty, we overhear a snatch of dialogue.

YOUNG MAN: ...In that case, as long as she's going home alone, give me the five bucks back...

STAG: ...Look, Mac, you paid me five bucks. I was willing. It's my five bucks...

They pass on. Marty returns his attention to the girl. She is still sitting as she was, gripping and ungripping the glass of Coca-Cola in front of her. Her eyes are closed. Then, with a little nervous shake of her head, she gets out of the booth and stands - momentarily at a loss for what to do next. The open fire doors leading out onto the large fire escape catch her eye. She crosses to the fire escape, nervous, frowning, and disappears outside.

Marty stares after her, then slowly shuffles to the open fire-escape doorway. It is a large fire escape, almost the size of a small balcony. The girl is standing by the railing, her back to the doorway, her head slunk down on her bosom. For a moment Marty is unaware that she is crying. Then he notices the shivering tremors running through her body and the quivering shoulders. He moves a step onto the fire escape. He tries to think of something to say.

MARTY: Excuse me, Miss. Would you care to dance?

The girl slowly turns to him, her face streaked with tears, her lips trembling. Then, in one of those peculiar moments of simultaneous impulse, she lurches to Marty with a sob, and Marty takes her to him. For a moment, they stand in an awkward embrace, Marty a little embarrassed, looking out through the doors to the lounge, wondering if anybody is seeing them. Reaching back with one hand, he closes the fire doors, and then, replacing the hand around her shoulder, he stands stiffly, allowing her to cry on his chest.

2. "Rosie," by Milton Gelman [19]

Fantasy has not been presented very often on television. "Rosie" by Milton Gelman, broadcast on NBC-TV's "Robert Montgomery Presents," was one of the rare instances when a fantasy-melodrama was presented effectively. The author exploits the potentials for technical effects which are possible in live television but which are neglected by many writers who do not yet understand the medium. The excerpt which follows came at the opening of the play. The characters we encounter are described by the author as:

ROSIE ZELDA . . . Blonde, pale, dumpy, either a young 40 or an old 36. She is the symbol of the commonplace.

[19] Courtesy of the author.

She wears her hair parted in the middle,
combed straight back, held tightly in place in
the rear by a comb.

HENNIG DORK . . . Rosie's sadistic supervisor of the ledger dept.
Crafty, sneaky, given to making examples of his
staff who are nothing but cogs in his well-
oiled office machine. I hate him. You'll
loathe him.

OPEN IN BLACK

A CIRCULAR POOL OF LIGHT SLOWLY BEGINS TO ILLUMINATE A TIME CLOCK
AND TIME CARD RACK HANGING IN LIMBO.

(SOUND: AS THE LIGHT BRIGHTENS, WE HEAR THE STEADY, MEASURED
CLOCK TICKS. BRING UP FULL AND KEEP UNDER THE FOLLOWING ACTION.)

THE TIME CLOCK HAS A SLOT AT THE BASE FOR THE TIME CARD AND A
METAL LEVER TO THE RIGHT OF THE SLOT WHICH, WHEN BANGED, PUNCHES
THE TIME AND RINGS A BELL.

THE HANDS OF THE CLOCK ARE ALMOST, BUT NOT QUITE ON 9:30.

THE TIME CARD RACK IS IN TWO SECTIONS. ONE IS MARKED "OUT",
THE OTHER "IN".

ALL THE CARDS EXCEPT TWO ARE IN THE "IN" SECTION. EACH OF THE
TWO CARDS STILL IN THE "IN" RACK ARE UNDER SEPARATE COLUMNS.

UNDER THE COLUMN MARKED "CLERKS", IS ONE MARKED "ZELDA, ROSE".

UNDER THE COLUMN MARKED "SUPERVISOR", IS THE OTHER MARKED "DORK,
HENNIG".

WE NOW SEE ROSIE ZELDA WALK TO THE TIME CLOCK QUICKLY, NERVOUSLY.
SHE PULLS OUT HER CARD, HASTILY PUNCHES IT AS THE BELL RINGS.
NOW SHE SEES THAT DORK'S CARD IS STILL NOT PUNCHED. SHE SIGHS
WITH RELIEF AND RELAXES A LITTLE. SHE NOW WALKS OUT OF THIS
LIGHT POOL, INTO THE BLACKNESS AND OUT INTO ANOTHER POOL OF LIGHT
WHICH BRIGHTENS SHOWING THE FOLLOWING IN LIMBO:

A WATER COOLER, WITH CUP DISPENSER AND WASTEBASKET. ABOUT IT,
HANGING IN LIMBO, AS IF ON A WALL, IS THE FOLLOWING SIGN:

NECESSITY is the
MOTHER of INVENTION

ROSIE TAKES A QUICK DRINK, STARING AT THE SIGN. SHE CRUMPLES
THE CUP AND WALKS OUT OF LIGHT THROUGH DARKNESS TO A THIRD POOL
OF LIGHT WHICH NOW BRIGHTENS IN LIMBO.

HERE THERE IS A RACK OF LARGE LEDGERS. ABOVE THE RACK, AS IF
HANGING ON A WALL, IS THE FOLLOWING SIGN:

INDUSTRY is the
FATHER of SUCCESS

ROSIE SELECTS A LARGE, HEAVY LEDGER MARKED "H" ON THE SPINE,
LOOKS UP AT THE SIGN AND, WEIGHTED DOWN, WALKS OUT OF THIS POOL
OF LIGHT THROUGH DARKNESS TO THE NEXT BRIGHTENING LIGHT POOL IN
LIMBO CONTAINING:

THE INEVITABLE SIGN, HANGING IN LIMBO AS IF FROM A WALL READING:

SUCCESSFUL INVENTION is the
CHILD of
NECESSARY INDUSTRY

BELOW THE SIGN IS ROSIE'S DESK. IT IS VERY PLAIN WITH A DRAWER.
IT IS PLACARDED "DESK 8".

ROSIE FLOPS THE LEDGER ON HER DESK, AND WITH A SIGH, SITS ON HER
STOOL. SHE FLOPS OPEN THE LEDGER, GETS HER PEN READY, POISED
ABOVE THE LEDGER. NOW SHE LOOKS UP AND ACROSS AS, BEYOND HER,
THE POOL OF LIGHT CONTAINING THE TIME CLOCK SETUP BRIGHTENS.

WE SEE HENNIG DORK MARCH IN. HE'S NARROW EYED, WEASELY, GRIM.
HE GRIMLY LOOKS ACROSS AT ROSIE AND SEES TO HIS SATISFACTION THAT
SHE IS READY FOR WORK, HER HAND POISED, FROZEN. SATISFIED, HE
LOOKS AT THE HANDS OF THE CLOCK. THEY ARE SQUARELY ON 9:30.
HE REACHES OVER, TAKES HIS TIME CARD, PUTS IT IN THE SLOT AND
BANGS HIS FIST DOWN ON THE LEVER.

SOUND: THE TIME CLOCK BELL BANGS LOUDLY LIKE THE RING BELL AT A
FIGHT. SIMULTANEOUSLY, AS IF TO THE BELL'S GO SIGNAL, WE HEAR
THE CLATTERING OF OFFICE MACHINES AND THE RHYTHMIC SCRATCHING
OF PENS AS:

WITH THE BELL ROSIE DROPS HER HAND AND STARTS WORKING.

ROSIE IS INDUSTRIOUSLY DOING JUST ONE THING: SHE IS MARKING THE
NUMBER 4 ON EACH PAGE OF THE LEDGER--4, TURN THE PAGE, 4, TURN
THE PAGE, ETC.

(PAN DOWN: TO SHOW ROSIE'S WORK, THEN:

                    END OF TEASER

OUT OF COMMERCIAL

(SOUND: BRING UP THE SOUND OF OFFICE MACHINES BANGING AWAY, THE
SCRATCHING OF PENS, ETC. BRING UP FULL, THEN KEEP UNDER THE
FOLLOWING:)

FADE ON:

THE THREE POOLS OF LIGHT: DORK TAKING A DRINK AT THE WATER
COOLER, THE LEDGER RACK POOL, AND ROSIE'S DESK.

DORK, WHO HAS JUST FINISHED HIS DRINK, CRUMPLES THE CUP AND
THROWS IT IN THE WASTEBASKET. HE NOW TURNS AND NARROWLY EX-
AMINES ROSIE, WHO IS INDUSTRIOUSLY WORKING AWAY AT THE LEDGER.
DORK'S EYES TRAVEL SLOWLY FROM LEFT TO RIGHT AS:
                    DORK'S VOICE   (RECORDED)
Desk 6, ledger F, good work. Desk 7, ledger G, all right.

(HIS EYES GO BACK TO ROSIE AND NARROW.)
Desk 8, ledger H...hm-m...
                    ROSIE'S VOICE   (RECORDED)
Four turn the page, Four turn the page...
                    DORK'S VOICE   (RECORDED)
Bears watching, that girl. Watch her, Dork!
                    ROSIE'S VOICE   (RECORDED)
Four, turn the page...
                    DORK'S VOICE   (RECORDED)
Too modest, too unassuming, wonder who she thinks she is...

(ROSIE SIGHS. SHE LOOKS UP FOR A MINUTE, SUDDENLY SEES DORK
WATCHING, DUCKS HER HEAD AND GOES BACK TO WORK.

             ROSIE'S VOICE   (RECORDED)
Four, turn the page...
             DORK'S VOICE   (RECORDED)
Aha! Almost got her that time! Too quiet, that one. Too
unassuming. Too careful about getting into trouble. Still
waters run deep!
             ROSIE'S VOICE   (RECORDED)
Four, turn the page...
             DORK'S VOICE   (RECORDED)
Set a trap, that's it.

(HE LOOKS AROUND KEENLY, SEES THE LEDGER SPOT. HIS LOOK CHANGES
TO ONE OF BOREDOM. HE DELIBERATELY SAUNTERS OUT OF HIS SPOT AND
DISAPPEARS INTO THE LIMBO BLACKNESS.)

(SUDDENLY, HIS HEAD POPS UP BEHIND THE LEDGERS. HE LOOKS LIKE A
CAT ABOUT TO POUNCE ON A MOUSE AS HE STUDIES ROSIE.)
             DORK'S VOICE   (RECORDED)
Who does she think she is, one of those Plain Janes, sneaky,
never yet gave me the chance to deliver my inspirational speech
about getting on the ball, the office, solemn responsibility and
all that. Watch that girl, Dork! Watch her!

(ROSIE SIGHS AND LOOKS UP AGAIN. SHE SEES THAT DORK IS NO LONGER
AT THE COOLER.)
             ROSIE'S VOICE   (RECORDED)
That Mr. Dork. Who does he think I am?

(DORK, WATCHING HER GOOF FROM BEHIND THE LEDGERS, RUBS HIS HANDS
IN GLEE AND ANTICIPATION.)

For that matter---just exactly who am I? Who am I to Mr. Dork?
(HER VOICE IMITATES DORK'S AND HER FACIAL EXPRESSION CHANGES TO
AN IMITATION OF HIS AS:)

"Desk 8, Ledger H. Make those fours neat!" Or the waitress at
the cafeteria downstairs.

(HER FACE CHANGES TO THAT OF A BORED, GUM-CHEWING WAITRESS AND
HER VOICE CHANGES TO A BRONX-TYPE ACCENT)

"toastedcheeseonwhitecawfeeonelump..."
Or that man at the payroll window...

(HER VOICE AND FACE CHANGE AGAIN AS:)

"Zelda, Rose, forty nine fifty per week, one deduction, next
please, move along..." Or my landlady--

(NOW HER VOICE AND FACE CHANGE AS SHE IMITATES A SNIDE, SUSPI-
CIOUS, SLATTERNLY LANDLADY)

"tenant in room six, sober, quiet, single, very regular in her
hours and rent payments"

(ROSIE BECOMES HERSELF AGAIN. SHE DOESN'T SEE DORK, DELIGHTED,
SNEAK AWAY FROM THE LEDGERS, DISAPPEAR IN LIMBO AND POP UP BEHIND
HER, READY TO POUNCE.)

Does anybody really know who I am? Do I?

(SHE LOOKS DOWN AT HER DESK DRAWER. SHE SLIDES IT OPEN AND
SLOWLY EXTRACTS A PACKET HELD TOGETHER BY RUBBER BANDS. IT IS
A BUNCH OF WILDCAT URANIUM STOCK. AS SHE BRINGS IT UP TO HER

DESK, WE SEE THE COVER IS ORNATE, SCROLLED, CLEARLY PRINTED IS
THE LEGEND:
>   SECRET HOPE
>   URANIUM MINE
>   ONE SHARE

Is this my dream, my future? Who am I...
(SHE IS SUDDENLY JERKED BACK TO REALITY AS DORK POUNCES:)

                    DORK
Miss Zelda!

(ROSIE JUMPS) Just exactly who do you think you are?

(SOUND: DEAD OUT)

STARTLED, ROSIE TWISTS AROUND AND LOOKS UP AT DORK. HER HAND,
NEXT TO THE STOCKS ON HER DESK, SLOWLY REACHES OVER TO COVER
THEM UP. ROSIE'S LOOK OF SHOCK TURNS TO ONE OF CURIOSITY AS SHE
LOOKS UP AT DORK.)

                    ROSIE
You know, Mr. Dork, that's a good question.

(DORK'S JAW DROPS IN SURPRISE. THE MOUSE IS NOT IN FLIGHT.)

Just exactly who do you think I am?

                    DORK
(BITTERLY) I'm just beginning to find out, Miss Zelda.

                    ROSIE
Really?

                    DORK
You are a thief, Miss Zelda!

(ROSIE LOOKS HORRIFIED.)

And I've caught you in the act!

(OFF, WE HEAR A FEW TITTERS. ROSIE, RATTLED, LOOKS TO BOTH SIDES
AS IF SHE IS TRAPPED BY THE SCORN OF HER FELLOW EMPLOYEES. DORK
RELISHES THIS. WE CAN SEE HE IS PLAYING TO THE HELP.)

Stealing, Miss Zelda, stealing the most precious thing in our
little world. Stealing company time!

                    ROSIE
But Mr. Dork--

                    DORK
And insubordination!

(OFF, WE HEAR A MUTTER OF VOICES. ROSIE LOOKS TRAPPED.)

I'm sorry, Miss Zelda, but I must make an example of you.

(DORK NOW SEES ROSIE'S HAND COVERING THE STOCK ISSUES. HE POINTS
A QUIVERING FINGER AT IT.)

                    DORK
What's that? What are you hiding?

(ROSIE TRIES TO PICK THE STOCK UP BUT SHE'S TOO LATE. DORK
SWOOPS DOWN AND GRABS IT FROM HER. SHE JUMPS UP FROM HER CHAIR
AND FACES HIM AS HE STUDIES IT.)

Uranium stock! Well! a gambler in our midst! Wildcat uranium
stock!

                         ROSIE
My dream.

(DORK LAUGHS SCORNFULLY. OFF, THE VOICES PARROT HIM AND LAUGH
SCORNFULLY. ROSIE TAKES THE STOCK FROM HIM AND CLUTCHES IT TO
HER BREAST.)

                         DORK
Your dream! Who do you think you are?

(ROSIE TAKES A DEEP BREATH AND SUMMONS RABBIT COURAGE.)

                         ROSIE
I don't know. I want to find out.

                         DORK
Well, Miss Zelda. This office is built on reliability,
stability--

                         ROSIE
I can be anything I want to be if this mine comes in!

                         DORK
The office is just not big enough for someone who gambles so
cavalierly with their money.

                         ROSIE
I don't want to be me, just a four, turn the page four, I want
to be somebody else--

                         DORK
Who knows, Miss Zelda--with your mind on your wildcat investments, your pen might slip, a two might be entered instead of a
four in your ledger and then where are we?

(OFF, WE HEAR THE VOICES GASP IN HORROR. ROSIE IS COVERED WITH
BLUSHING SHAME. DORK IS TRIUMPHANT. HE ADVANCES ON HER. SHE
RETREATS, CLUTCHING THE STOCK TO HER BOSOM.)

                         ROSIE
Just a four, turn the page, four...

                         DORK
I'm sorry, but you now are no longer even that.

(ROSIE DISAPPEARS INTO THE BLACKNESS AROUND THE SPOT AS:)

You're a ZERO!

(ROSIE REAPPEARS AT THE WATERCOOLER SPOT, STILL BACKING AWAY.
DORK ADVANCES ON HER INTO THE SPOT.)

You're through, Miss Zelda. Through! Punch out!

(ROSIE RETREATS OUT OF THE SPOT AS THE TITTERING, JEERING
LAUGHTER WELLS. SHE REAPPEARS IN THE TIME CLOCK SPOT, FOLLOWED
BY DORK.)

(DORK POINTS TO HER CARD IN THE "IN" FILE. ROSIE, CRUSHED,
SLOWLY TAKES IT OUT AND PUTS IT INTO THE SLOT BENEATH THE CLOCK.)

(OFF, THE TITTERING VOICES GASP IN ANTICIPATION.)

(ROSIE BACKS OFF TO THE EDGE OF THE POOL OF LIGHT AS DORK
GRANDIOSELY SURVEYS HIS DOMAIN, WATCHING TO MAKE SURE EVERYBODY
IS WATCHING HIS EXAMPLE-MAKING.)

(ROSIE TAKES A STEP FORWARD, REACHES A HAND OUT ENTREATINGLY.
DORK GRIMLY SHAKES HIS HEAD, THEN RAISES HIS FIST OVER THE TIME
CLOCK LEVER.)

(ROSIE DROPS HER HEAD IN SHAME AND BACKS OUT OF THE SPOT AS DORK BANGS HIS FIST DOWN ON THE LEVER.)

(SOUND: THE BELL BANGS, AND SIMULTANEOUSLY, AS IF IT'S THE "GO" SIGNAL, THE CLATTER OF OFFICE MACHINES AND SCRATCHING OF PENS ABRUPTLY STARTS, BUILDING TO A CRESCENDO AS WE MOVE IN CLOSE FOR A SHOT OF DORK GLOATING, NARROW-EYED, WATCHING HIS BEAUTIFUL OFFICE MACHINE RACKET AWAY.)

COMPARISON OF NOVEL AND TELEVISION DRAMA

It is informative and revealing to compare an original text as written for the reading public with a television version of the same scene. The interrupted wedding scene in *Jane Eyre* is reproduced first as found in the novel, then as adapted for television.

NOVEL

Chapter 26 from *Jane Eyre,* by Charlotte Brontë.

Sophie came at seven to dress me; she was very long indeed in accomplishing her task; so long that Mr. Rochester, grown, I suppose, impatient of my delay, sent up to ask why I did not come. She was just fastening my veil (the plain square of blond after all) to my hair with a brooch; I hurried from under her hands as soon as I could.

"Stop!" she cried in French. "Look at yourself in the mirror: you have not taken one peep."

So I turned at the door: I saw a robed and veiled figure, so unlike my usual self that it seemed almost the image of a stranger. "Jane!" called a voice, and I hastened down. I was received at the foot of the stairs by Mr. Rochester.

"Lingerer," he said, "my brain is on fire with impatience; and you tarry so long!"

He took me into the dining-room, surveyed me keenly all over, pronounced me "fair as a lily, and not only the pride of his life, but the desire of his eyes," and then telling me he would give me but ten minutes to eat some breakfast, he rang the bell. One of his lately hired servants, a footman, answered it.

"Is John getting the carriage ready?"

"Yes, sir."

"Is the luggage brought down?"

"They are bringing it down, sir."

"Go you to the church: see if Mr. Wood (the clergyman) and the clerk are there: return and tell me."

The church, as the reader knows, was but just beyond the gates: the footman soon returned.

"Mr. Wood is in the vestry, sir, putting on his surplice."

"And the carriage?"

"The horses are harnessing."

"We shall not want it to go to church; but it must be ready the moment we return: all the boxes and luggage arranged and strapped on, and the coachman in his seat."

"Yes, sir."

"Jane, are you ready?"

I rose. There were no groomsmen, no bridesmaids, no relatives to wait for or marshal: none but Mr. Rochester and I. Mrs. Fairfax stood in the hall as we passed. I would fain have spoken to her, but my hand was held by a grasp of iron: I was hurried along by a stride I could hardly follow; and to look at Mr. Rochester's face was to feel that not a second of delay would be tolerated for any purpose. I wonder what other bridegroom ever looked as he did—so bent up to a purpose, so grimly resolute: or who, under such steadfast brows, ever revealed such flaming and flashing eyes.

I know not whether the day was fair or foul; in descending the drive, I gazed neither on sky nor earth: my heart was with my eyes; and both seemed migrated into Mr. Rochester's frame. I wanted to see the invisible thing on which, as we went along, he appeared to fasten a glance fierce and fell. I wanted to feel the thoughts whose force he seemed breasting and resisting.

At the churchyard wicket he stopped: he discovered I was quite out of breath. "Am I cruel in my love?" he said. "Delay an instant: lean on me, Jane."

And now I can recall the picture of the grey old house of God rising calm before me, of a rook wheeling round the steeple, of a ruddy morning sky beyond. I remember something, too, of the green grave-mounds; and I have not forgotten, either, two figures of strangers, straying amongst the low hillocks, and reading the mementoes graven on the few mossy head-stones. I noticed them, because, as they saw us, they passed round to the back of the church; and I doubted not they were going to enter by the side aisle door, and witness the ceremony. By Mr. Rochester they were not observed; he was earnestly looking at my face, from which the blood had, I daresay, momentarily fled: for I felt my forehead dewy, and my cheeks and lips cold. When I rallied, which I soon did, he walked gently with me up the path to the porch.

We entered the quiet and humble temple; the priest waited in his white surplice at the lowly altar, the clerk beside him. All was still: two shadows only moved in a remote corner. My conjecture had been correct: the strangers had slipped in before us, and they now stood by the vault of the Rochesters, their backs towards us, viewing through the rails the old time-stained marble tomb, where a kneeling angel guarded the remains of Damer de Rochester, slain at Marston Moor in the time of the civil wars; and of Elizabeth, his wife.

Our place was taken at the communion rails. Hearing a cautious step behind me, I glanced over my shoulder: one of the strangers—a gentleman, evidently —was advancing up the chancel. The service began. The explanation of the intent of matrimony was gone through; and then the clergyman came a step further forward, and, bending slightly towards Mr. Rochester, went on.

"I require and charge you both (as ye will answer at the dreadful day of judgment, when the secrets of all hearts shall be disclosed) that if either of you know any impediment why ye may not lawfully be joined together in matrimony, ye do now confess it; for be ye well assured that so many as are coupled together otherwise than God's word doth allow, are not joined together by God, neither is their matrimony lawful."

He paused, as the custom is. When is the pause after that sentence ever broken by reply? Not, perhaps, once in a hundred years. And the clergyman, who had not lifted his eyes from his book, and had held his breath but for a moment, was proceeding: his hand was already stretched towards Mr. Rochester, as his lips unclosed to ask, "Wilt thou have this woman for thy wedded wife?"— when a distinct and near voice said:—

"The marriage cannot go on: I declare the existence of an impediment."

The clergyman looked up at the speaker, and stood mute; the clerk did the same; Mr. Rochester moved slightly, as if an earthquake had rolled under his feet: taking a firmer footing, and not turning his head or eyes, he said, "Proceed."

Profound silence fell when he had uttered that word, with deep but low intonation. Presently Mr. Wood said:—

"I cannot proceed without some investigation into what has been asserted, and evidence of its truth or falsehood."

"The ceremony is quite broken off," subjoined the voice behind us. "I am in a condition to prove my allegation: an insuperable impediment to this marriage exists."

Mr. Rochester heard, but heeded not: he stood stubborn and rigid: making no movement, but to possess himself of my hand. What a hot and strong grasp he had!—and how like quarried marble was his pale, firm, massive front at this moment! How his eye shone, still, watchful, and yet wild beneath!

Mr. Wood seemed at a loss. "What is the nature of the impediment?" he asked. "Perhaps it may be got over—explained away?"

"Hardly," was the answer: "I have called it insuperable, and I speak advisedly."

The speaker came forwards, and leaned on the rails. He continued, uttering each word distinctly, calmly, steadily, but not loudly.

"It simply consists in the existence of a previous marriage. Mr. Rochester has a wife now living."

My nerves vibrated to those low-spoken words as they had never vibrated to thunder—my blood felt their subtle violence as it had never felt frost or fire: but I was collected, and in no danger of swooning. I looked at Mr. Rochester: I made him look at me. His whole face was colourless rock: his eye was both spark and flint. He disavowed nothing; he seemed as if he would defy all things. Without speaking; without smiling; without seeming to recognise in me a human being, he only twined my waist with his arm, and riveted me to his side.

"Who are you?" he asked of the intruder.

"My name is Briggs—a solicitor of —Street, London."

"And you would thrust on me a wife?"

"I would remind you of your lady's existence, sir; which the law recognises, if you do not."

"Favour me with an account of her—with her name, her parentage, her place of abode."

"Certainly." Mr. Briggs calmly took a paper from his pocket, and read out in a sort of official, nasal voice:—

" 'I affirm and can prove that on the 20th of October, A.D.,—(a date of fifteen years back) Edward Fairfax Rochester, of Thornfield Hall, in the county of—, and of Ferndean Manor, in —shire, England, was married to my sister, Bertha Antoinetta Mason, daughter of Jonas Mason, merchant, and of Antoinetta his wife, a Creole—at—church, Spanish Town, Jamaica. The record of the marriage will be found in the register of that church—a copy of it is now in my possession. Signed, Richard Mason.' "

"That—if a genuine document—may prove I have been married, but it does not prove that the woman mentioned therein as my wife is still living."

"She was still living three months ago," returned the lawyer.

"How do you know?"

"I have a witness to the fact; whose testimony even you, sir, will scarcely controvert."

"Produce him—or go to hell."

"I will produce him first—he is on the spot: Mr. Mason, have the goodness to step forward."

Mr. Rochester, on hearing the name, set his teeth; he experienced, too, a sort of strong convulsive quiver; near to him as I was, I felt the spasmodic movement of fury or despair run through his frame. The second stranger, who had hitherto lingered in the background, now drew near; a pale face looked over the solicitor's shoulder—yes, it was Mason himself. Mr. Rochester turned and glared at him. His eye, as I have often said, was a black eye: it had now a tawny, nay a bloody light in its gloom; and his face flushed—olive cheek, and hueless forehead received a glow, as from spreading, ascending heart-fire: and he stirred, lifted his strong arm—he could have struck Mason—dashed him on the church-floor —shocked by ruthless blow the breath from his body—but Mason shrank away, and cried faintly, "Good God!" Contempt fell cool on Mr. Rochester—his passion died as if a blight had shrivelled it up: he only asked, "What have *you* to say?"

An inaudible reply escaped Mason's white lips.

"The devil is in it if you cannot answer distinctly. I again demand, what have *you* to say?"

"Sir—sir"—interrupted the clergyman, "do not forget you are in a sacred place." Then addressing Mason, he inquired gently, "Are you aware, sir, whether or not this gentleman's wife is still living?"

"Courage," urged the lawyer,—"speak out."

"She is now living at Thornfield Hall," said Mason, in more articulate tones: "I saw her there last April. I am her brother."

"At Thornfield Hall!" ejaculated the clergyman. "Impossible! I am an old resident in this neighbourhood, sir, and I never heard of a Mrs. Rochester at Thornfield Hall."

I saw a grim smile contort Mr. Rochester's lip, and he muttered:—"No—by God! I took care that none should hear of it—or of her under that name." He mused—for ten minutes he held counsel with himself: he formed his resolve, and announced it:—

"Enough—all shall bolt out at once, like the bullet from the barrel.—Wood, close your book, and take off your surplice; John Green (to the clerk), leave the church: there will be no wedding to-day." The man obeyed.

TELEVISION

4. "Studio One," "Jane Eyre"
Excerpt from "Jane Eyre," as adapted by Sumner Locke Elliott.[20]

(FADE IN ON LARGE WEDDING POSY OF FLOWERS. PULL BACK TO SHOW ADELE IN PARTY DRESS AND MANY RIBBONS SEATED IN THE LIBRARY. SHE IS BORED AND PLAYING WITH THE FLOWERS. MRS. FAIRFAX IN HER BEST GOWN COMES HASTILY INTO THE LIBRARY.)

MRS. FAIRFAX
Adele? What are you doing here?

ADELE
Waiting.

MRS. FAIRFAX

Get up, child, it is time for you to be ready to attend Miss Eyre
...for she is dressed.

ADELE

Oh, Mamoiselle looks so beautiful, Leah allowed me to peep
through the door.

MRS. FAIRFAX

(SIGHS) Yes, doubtless, love has lent beauty to the plain Miss
Eyre, I have heard it said that great love can make beauty.
Now come, for it is almost time.
(SHE TAKES ADELE BY THE HAND AND WE FOLLOW THEM AS THEY PASS THE
FRENCH WINDOWS. WE SEE ROCHESTER IN LS. IN GARDEN WITH THE
MINISTER. WE SEE HIM TAKE OUT HIS WATCH AND LOOK AT IT IM-
PATIENTLY.)
Tut, Tut, I have never seen a man so impatient. There, he is
looking at his watch again.
(WE FOLLOW ADELE AND MRS. FAIRFAX OUT THE SLIDING DOORS TO THE
HALLWAY AND TO THE STAIRS. AS THEY GO UP THE STAIRS.)

ADELE

Are they going away, Mrs. Fairfax?

MRS. FAIRFAX

Yes, they are leaving immediately after the wedding.
(THEY DISAPPEAR UPSTAIRS AS WE HEAR THE FRONT DOOR BELL RING
AND LEAH HASTENS ACROSS THE HALL AND OPENS THE DOOR. MASON
ENTERS, A TALL, DARK MAN, FOLLOWED BY BRIGGS, A NERVOUS MIDDLE-
AGED SOLICITOR.)

RICHARD MASON

We wish to see Mrs. Poole immediately.

LEAH

Mrs. Poole? Well...

RICHARD MASON

Tell Mrs. Poole, Mr. Mason is returned from the West Indies and
desires to see her.

LEAH

Yes sir.   (LEAH GOES UPSTAIRS.)
(MASON AND BRIGGS STAND LOOKING AROUND AS JOHN THE SERVANT ENTERS
FROM BACK STAIRS CARRYING A WEDDING CAKE TOWARDS THE DINING ROOM.
HE GOES OUT. WE SEE MASON GLANCE AT BRIGGS.)

RICHARD MASON

Then what we have heard is correct, it seems.
(GRACE POOLE COMES DOWNSTAIRS. ON SEEING MASON SHE IS OBVIOUSLY
AGITATED...SHE GLANCES AROUND FURTIVELY.)
Mrs. Poole!

GRACE

Mr. Mason, this is most unexpected. We did not know that you
were in England.

RICHARD MASON

On urgent business.

GRACE

Have you seen Mr. Rochester?

RICHARD MASON

No, we have only just arrived in Thornfield.

                    GRACE
You have come at a most inconvenient time, sir.

                    RICHARD MASON
That is obvious, Mrs. Poole. But it should also be obvious that
I have not come to see Mr. Rochester. How is she?

                    GRACE
Tolerably well, Mr. Mason. (SHE GLANCES AT THE STAIRS.)   At
times better than others.

                    RICHARD MASON
You seem most agitated, Mrs. Poole.

                    GRACE
I do not wish to be caught here talking to you without the consent of Mr. Rochester.

                    RICHARD MASON
Then let us go upstairs to your rooms.

                    GRACE
If you will excuse me, I shall take you up the backstairs. We
are less likely to run into any...of the members of the house-
hold.
(SHE LEADS THE WAY TOWARD THE BACK OF THE HALL. MASON AND
BRIGGS FOLLOW. WE PAN FROM THEM TO THE STAIRS AND SEE ADELE
LEADING THE WAY WITH JANE FOLLOWING IN HER WEDDING DRESS AND
VEIL, THEN MRS. FAIRFAX. WE FOLLOW THE PROCESSION THROUGH THE
LIBRARY AND TO THE FRENCH WINDOWS TO THE GARDEN. WE SEE
ROCHESTER TURN TO FACE JANE. HE SMILES. WE PAN TO ROCHESTER
WHO TURNS AS JANE COMES TO HIS SIDE THEN TO MINISTER, THE
REV. MR. WOOD.)

                    REVEREND WOOD
Will you join hands?
(JANE AND ROCHESTER TAKE HANDS. AS WE TRUCK BACK WE HEAR WOOD'S
VOICE FADING QUICKLY...)
Dearly beloved, we are gathered together today in the sight of
God, and his Holy Tabernacle to join this man and woman...
(MUSIC CHANGES TO OMINOUS MOTIF AS WE PAN TO C.U. THE WINDOW
OF THE HOUSE. WE SEE THE MADWOMAN STARING FROM THE WINDOW, HER
FACE ABLAZE WITH HATE AND FURY. ANOTHER SLOW PAN DOWN TO FRENCH
WINDOWS AND WE SEE MASON WITH BRIGGS COMING TO HIS SIDE.)
(WE SHOOT OVER MASON'S SHOULDER TO LS. THE GARDEN AS THEY WATCH
THE CEREMONY.)
(CUT TO MINISTER READING.)

                    REVEREND WOOD
.....and if either of you know of any impediment why we should
not lawfully be joined together in matrimony, ye do now confess
it for...
(WE SEE BRIGGS STEP OUT FROM THE FRENCH WINDOWS.)

                    MR. BRIGGS
Stop!
(ROCHESTER DRAWS BACK WITH A CRY. THE WEDDING RING SLIPS FROM
HIS HAND ONTO THE STONES.)

                    MR. BRIGGS
Stop! I declare an impediment. I declare this marriage is
illegal.
(C.U. JANE'S FACE STRICKEN. GAZING AT ROCHESTER.)

REVEREND WOOD
(CALMLY) What is the nature of this impediment? Perhaps we
can...

ROCHESTER
Get Adele inside quickly.
(MRS. FAIRFAX TAKES ADELE BY THE HAND AND LEADS HER AWAY.)

ADELE
(GOING) What is happening, Mrs. Fairfax?

REVEREND WOOD
What is the nature of this impediment?

MR. BRIGGS
A previous marriage. Mr. Rochester has a wife living.
(C.U. JANE. HER HAND GOES TO HER MOUTH STIFLING A CRY.)

ROCHESTER
Who are you?

MR. BRIGGS
My name is Briggs, a solicitor of Chesney Lane, London.

ROCHESTER
What proof have you of this?

MR. BRIGGS
(TAKES PAPER FROM SATCHEL.) I have here an affidavit signed by
a client of mine which reads as follows: (READS QUICKLY) "I
affirm and prove that on the 20th of October, 1842, Edward
Fairfax Rochester was married to my sister Bertha Mason at
Spanish Town, Jamaica. The record of marriage will be found in
the register at that church."
(HE HANDS PAPER TO ROCHESTER. JANE WATCHES.)

ROCHESTER
Then, if this be a genuine document, it may prove marriage, but
it does not prove that my first wife is still living.

MR. BRIGGS
She is living in this house at the moment.
(JANE LETS OUT A CRY.)
I have a witness to the fact.
(MASON STEPS OUT OF THE HOUSE. ROCHESTER SEES HIM. HE GIVES A
TERRIBLE CRY. RUSHES TO MASON TO STRIKE HIM. BRIGGS AND REV.
WOOD BOTH RESTRAIN HIM. JANE SINKS ONTO THE SEAT DROPPING HER
FLOWERS, NEARLY FAINTING.)

REVEREND WOOD
Mr. Rochester!

RICHARD MASON
His wife is my sister, and she is living here at Thornfield Hall.
In fact, I have just seen her.

REVEREND WOOD
Impossible! I have known Mr. Rochester these fifteen years.

RICHARD MASON
I have just returned from the Indies, and heard by accident of
this impending ceremony in London.
(A CRY BREAKS FROM ROCHESTER. WE PAN UP TO HIM. HE LIFTS HIS
FACE TO THE SKY.)

ROCHESTER

Now God punish me! As though I had not been punished enough.
There will be no wedding today.
(WE COME UP TO BIG CU. HIS FACE. TEARS IN HIS EYES.)
(FADE OUT.)

Projects and Exercises

1. Listen to radio plays or read script collections and report on specific techniques employed to identify setting, time and character relationships.
2. Tune in television plays or read script collections and report on techniques employed to identify locale, change of audience orientation, and "cover material" during transitions.
3. Compare radio, television, and film techniques used in opening sequences for a specific type of program such as romantic comedy, melodrama, or murder mystery.
4. Analyze pattern and pacing of camera shots in different type television dramas.
5. Report on a current motion picture regarding pattern and editing of camera shots for intensification of emotion and dramatic meaning. For example, *To Catch a Thief,* a 1955 movie produced and directed by Alfred Hitchcock, uses the same technique of an extreme close-up of a woman's face as she screams that was described on page 487. In the opening scenes of the movie, Hitchcock intersperses several sequences of shots of a black cat first walking across a tiled slanted roof toward the camera and then away from the camera between close-ups of the gloved hand of a jewel thief opening jewel boxes and removing jewels from under pillows. The audience later learns, through a display of newspaper headlines, that a burglar who has committed daring nighttime thefts, is referred to as "The Cat."
6. Write transitions for radio or television dramas for:
    (*a*) From a death cell in Sing Sing to a scene in an amusement park twenty years later.
    (*b*) From the living room of an apartment to an office.
    (*c*) From a hitchhiker at the roadside to a hospital bed after a wreck.
    (*d*) From Idlewild Airport in New York City to a uranium claim in Canada.
Use dialogue only for radio; detail sets only for television. Discuss the scripts. Present them on microphone or camera. Evaluate effectiveness.
7. Write for class presentation a series of radio scripts (two-and-one-half minutes each) entitled "Murder to Order," with the following conditions:
    (*a*) Three characters only. Two men and one woman or two women and one man.
    (*b*) A murder is committed on microphone as a result of a triangle; love, revenge, greed are motives. No actual sound effects are heard in the presentation, but they are indicated and suggested by dialogue. Shooting is too common, so eliminate it as a method—any other is acceptable. No narrator—no announcer—no music.
    (*c*) The dialogue alone must reveal the characters—names and relationship to each other; the setting—on a train, New York town house, motor boat, penthouse apartment, jungle, etc.; movement of characters including one entrance of a character and one exit of one or two characters; and motivation for the murder.

This exercise is designed to focus attention directly upon the function and importance of dialogue in radio writing. Each script is to be presented on microphone (with or without rehearsal) and is to follow the script exactly without editing by actors. Discussion immediately following the presentation should consist of questions such as: Who were the people? Where were they? How was the murder committed? etc. The author should listen and learn at first-hand how many of his classmates completely miss or misinterpret matters he thought perfectly clear. Unnatural dialogue; too obvious identification of people, movement, setting, objects; awkward monologues; and poorly drawn characterizations will stand out in bold relief.

8. Write adaptations to television of the original "Murder to Order" scripts. Which ones do not adapt well? Why?
9. Report on a comparison of television writing with novel writing after study of *Jane Eyre*.
10. Discuss how you might suggest to a writer how he might adapt to television the following:
    (*a*) Lord Dunsany's *A Night at the Inn*—a one-act play.
    (*b*) Ernest Hemingway's "The Killers"—a classic short story.
    (*c*) *Aesop: Fables for Today*—a radio documentary. See pp. 533-549.
    (*d*) Other assigned plays, stories, or radio broadcasts familiar to the class.

Sound Effects and Music

SOUND EFFECTS were referred to as "the stuff of radio" by an early British writer-producer in broadcasting.[1] Sound effects are used less in television than in radio, but they still assist materially in drama, documentaries, and comedy programs. The usefulness of music in radio drama and in film has been well established. Television has incorporated music in accordance with practices developed in radio. The dramatic writer, director, or producer should be thoroughly acquainted with the possible uses of sound effects and music and should seek to discover new ways to weave imaginative spells with sound and music. The desire to experiment with and exploit these tools should not, however, overshadow the more important objective of telling a story clearly and sincerely.

· SOUND EFFECTS ·

The first classification of sound effects is according to their function in the dramatic script. Why are they there? What can they do?

Sound Effects Can Establish the Locale or Setting. An examination of the sound effects record catalogues reveals at once the types of locale that can be suggested imaginatively through the use of sound effects. Here are some illustrative catalogue descriptions: [2]

Bugle Calls (Standard 402)
402A　1.　Retreat, Army & Navy, 29"; 2. Fire call, Army & Navy, 15"; 3.　To arms, Army; Torpedo, defense quarters, Navy, 16"; 4. To horse, Cavalry, 07"; 5. Boy Scout call, 05".

[1] Lance Sieveking, *The Stuff of Radio* (London, 1934).
[2] Catalogue descriptions from:
Standard Transcription Services, Inc., 360 North Michigan Ave., Chicago 1, Illinois.
EMI (British) Distributed in the United States by Charles Michelson Inc., 23 West 47th Street, New York 19, New York.

402B   1. Call to post, race track, 05"; 2. First sergeant's call, Army, 05"; 3. Officer's call, Army, 05"; 4. Church call, Army, 30"; 5. Recall, Army, 07"; 6. To the colors, Army & Navy, 30".   ·

Crickets (Standard 153)
153A   Crickets and Frogs. (Continuous) Recorded specifically for background to any nighttime scene where it might be appropriate. Should be played only at low level, otherwise ground noise becomes apparent. 2'40"
153B   Crickets (continuous) This effect is one of the most realistic scenes. Recommended as background for evening country scenes. 2'40"

Crowd (Standard 270)
270A   Restaurant Background 1. Clatter of dishes in kitchen (with voices). 1'25"; 2. Same as above with dishwasher, 1'25"
270B   Restaurant Background Crowd noise with clatter of dishes. Two spirals for cueing cash register. 3'07"

Farmyard (EMI CM-1028)
1028A   Farmyard Animals: Cows:
            (a) Cows, Calves and Heifers, 3:00; (b) Milking Time, :30
1028B   Cock Crows, Hens, Guinea Fowl, Bantams, 3:10

Marine (Standard 350)
350A   Ship Engine Room (Continuous) Large steamship. Heavy throb of pistons is accompanied by slap of cam-rods, and escaping steam is heard at intervals. Bell signals and whistles purposely left out as these are best added as needed in the studio, 2'40".
350B   Boat Whistles 1. Liner, 3 long blasts, 35"; 2. Two tugs, signalling, 1'00"; 3. Liner, 4 short, 1 long, 22"; 4. Liner, 2 short, 05".

Railway (EMI CMX-2015)
2015A   Terminus (English): Terminus 1
            (a) Express Departure (Steam), 1:40; (b) Express Arrival (Steam) and Station Announcer, 1:21
2015B   Train Interior, Continuous running, 4:00   (2)

It is apparent that with such sound effects, the listener may be transported to an Army post, to outdoors in the country, to a restaurant, to a farm yard, to an ocean liner, or to a British railway station. The list may be extended at length. In the studio, actors may be reading scripts on microphone and a sound effects technician may be playing a record on a sound effects turntable truck; but in the listener's imagination two heroic adventurers are in the frozen Arctic or up the Amazon.

On the television set the actors may appear to be on the seashore because of a rear-screen projection or a few rocks and palm trees in the scene. Appropriate sound effects of surf and wind give the picture a true-to-life setting.

VOLUME LEVEL OF SOUND: A BASIC SELECTIVITY PRINCIPLE. In the use of sound for backgrounds and settings, we must distinguish between realistic representation and imaginative suggestion. The multiplicity of sounds in any one locality as well as the normal volume of these sounds should not be reproduced faithfully. The program personnel must do for the listener what he would do for himself: select some sounds for conscious perception, and blot out unwanted or meaningless sounds. To illustrate: Stop for a minute to attend to everything around you. You may now be acutely conscious of many sounds. There is the ticking of a clock, the hum of the refrigerator, traffic noises from passing cars, conversation in another room, and even the radio or television set. You shift attention to first one sound and then the other, bringing some into conscious focus and ignoring others. If a microphone replaced you where you are, it would not be able to differentiate to shifts in attention. Each sound would register according to its relative strength and characteristics. The writer, the sound technician in charge of sound production, the engineer at the controls, and the director as coordinator and final supervisor of what is sent out, must do the selecting for the listener.

AN APPLICATION TO A SCENE. A man enters a restaurant at noon to meet his girl friend. The place is jammed with people. The cash register is in constant use, the bell ringing and the drawer opening and closing. Silverware and tableware are being distributed. Bus boys are piling empty dishes on huge trays and taking them out. Waitresses are rushing around, taking orders, and relaying orders to the kitchen. As the man enters, this wave of sound sweeps towards him. He is conscious of a jumble of sound pressing against his ears and around him, as he walks down to his table and sits down across from his girl friend. Does that sound continue to press against his ears with the same volume as he talks to her? Certainly not. His attention to her may completely blot out all sound. When we transfer this scene to radio or TV, we may give a fair amount of level to the restaurant background effects, not to every sound, but to some characteristic sounds, such as the murmur of voices and light silverware. A creative sound technician may add the cash register as an additional bit of atmospheric color, and then fade the sounds down gradually with the start of the dialogue, and continue to fade the sound down to a very low background or completely out, as the man and the girl talk. If for some reason the setting should be brought to attention again, a gradual fade-in of some of the sound takes care of it adequately.

It is interesting to note in this scene how an immediate change in setting in a radio drama is effected by adding or substituting some sounds. Play the scene as indicated and you have the setting as a typical medium-priced, busy restaurant. Add to it a record of a tinny upright piano and you get a low dive. Or add a record of a string quartet playing a Strauss waltz, and you get an upper-class or expensive hotel dining room. Use the same sounds as described above, but spotlight the sound of a cork being pulled out of a bottle and a clink of bottle to empty glass and you get a bar. Use the same sound, but use a hand-operated cash register, add steady steps on wood, and an upright piano in the background playing "Oh, Susanna" and you are back in the Old West (especially if you have a horse whinny as the man enters from the outside).

IDENTIFICATION OF SOUNDS: A BASIC PRINCIPLE. Don't depend on sound to identify itself. Few sounds are absolutely self-identifying. In radio assist the listener either directly by specific identification by the program announcer or in dialogue, or indirectly, by suggestive "trade terms" in dialogue. The roar of Niagara Falls is easily confused with a heavy truck motor. Identify a sound before or concurrently with its appearance in the script. The listener is jolted if he has visualized a couple riding along in a heavy truck, only to awaken suddenly to realize that the couple is looking at "The Horseshoe Falls." A valuable instructional practice in writing and production classes is to play unidentified records, letting members of the class identify the sounds. The variation in response to such a frequently used sound as an automobile motor may come as a surprise. The misinterpretation of less frequently used sounds such as tractors, buses, or motorcycles, will serve as a forceful reminder of the necessity for clear identification of sounds.

In television, when sound effects are matched with action, such as in a scene where the sound of an auto motor running at high speed is played behind a scene of two policemen in a cut-away car prop, identification is much easier. However, sound in television drama which occurs off-camera requires care in identification through a camera shot of a small prop such as a sign marked "Bus Stop" or appropriate dialogue. In the Kraft Television Theater's "Elisha and the Long Knives," written by Dale Wasserman and Jack Balch, which had its setting in the mountains along the Santa Fé trail in 1840, a bird call was identified as follows: [3]

(A BIRD'S WHISTLE SOUNDS CLEAR AND CHEERFUL ON THE MORNING AIR.
BOONE LIFTS HIS HEAD ALERTLY)

BOONE
What kind of bird is that?

MACE
That's plain ol' curlew.

BOONE (INTRIGUED)
Can I learn to do that?

MACE
Nothin' to it, ol' hoss. Jeb kin do it better than me. Show
him, Jeb.

JEB (PLEASED BUT EMBARRASSED)
Aw, I ain't so good. Brack, now - he's got Injun blood. He
kin do it better than the bird hisself kin.

(THE CURLEW'S WHISTLE SOUNDS AGAIN. JEB LOOKS ABOUT)

In fack - that is Brack.

[3] Irving Settel (ed.), *Top TV Shows of the Year* (New York, 1955), p. 115.

Exaggerated sounds for comedy effect are effectively used in radio comedy as in the following excerpt from a Bob Hope script. Notice how the dialogue identifies the sound.[4]

HOPE: ...Okay, you win, Ed (Edward Robinson)...Here...I've got
         my wallet out now...I'll open it up.

SOUND: VERY LOUD RATCHET..HORRIBLE SQUEAKING OF METAL...RATCHET
         AGAIN, LOUD AND JERKY WITH SQUEAKING.

HOPE: Hm...The zipper needs a little oil!

This comedy "bit" could be presented exactly the same way in television, but without the preliminary identification line. The camera would show Hope struggling with the purse as sound "off-camera" matched the action. This same ratchet sound has been employed frequently for a creak of the neck.

Sound Can Advance the Action.

         CAR

JANE: Be careful John, that looks like a sharp curve ahead.
         There might be...

JOHN: Nonsense Jane...why I know this road like a book...see how
         I can...

JANE: Oh no! John...look...a truck! Ohhh...
         TIRE SKID COMING IN UNDER ABOVE AND CRASH (THE GOOD OLD
         STANDARD RECORD WITH LOTS OF GLASS)

This segment of script is heard almost every day with slight variations; the particular crash record is almost too authentic, but it does advance the action. We get much of the sense of movement in many radio scripts by the use of sound which accompanies the actors. Walks, autos, planes, trains, horses, take our actors from one place to another. They may be shot, hit over the head by a vase, run down by a subway train, sawed in half by a band saw, or knocked down by a sock to the jaw. *Caution:* overuse can clutter up and actually confuse the action. Observe the selectivity principle. Footsteps are not always appropriate sound effects. Don't forget that some rooms do have carpets. *Caution:* timing of the sound effects is very important. If the audience hears the actor say, "Why you—take that!" with an accompanying tenseness in the voice and an emphasis on the last word to signify a good solid punch to the jaw, a comedy effect ensues if the blow comes a count later. One of the more effective comedy sounds utilized on the "Buck Benny Rides Again" series was based on the ridiculousness of the image brought on by incongruous timing. Racing across the plains with great speed, the horse at a full gallop, "Buck Benny" called with a "Lone Ranger" flourish, "Whoa. . . ." The horse took only three steps and quit cold! Handled improperly, the sound of the opening and closing of a door

---

[4] Courtesy of Bob Hope.

can destroy the authenticity of a tense scene. The exact timing of a body fall—not too quick a drop after the blow—is vital in a violent scene. This is a difficult problem for many amateur sound technicians. Authentic synchronization of sound with the action of the act on mike may be obtained by watching the actors, listening to their lines, and matching sound with action.

Since much of the film used for scene transitions in television, planes, trains, steamships, etc., is silent footage, sound effects must be played in synchronization with pictured action.

Sound Can Tell Time. Sound is frequently used to tell time: clocks strike, cocks crow, crickets chirp, birds sing, factory whistles blow, the bell in the steeple rings, and we know the time of day. A cold wind blows, birds chirp, thunder claps, snow crunches underfoot, fire in the fireplace crackles, and we know something of the season. A sad fact that disturbs many writers is that snow makes no sound as it drifts down. A favorite story at one of the networks concerns the action of a technician when this impossible sound was requested by a "genius" director. Operating a good distance across the studio, this technician finally resorted to wiggling his fingers in the air as though snow flakes were falling through his fingers. Immediate approval was expressed through the talk-back by the director—the effect was just right! The listener is not the only one who can bring imagination into play for visualization of action! *Caution:* be careful of the standard scene opening, "Clock strikes midnight." Try this in rehearsal and see the length of time it takes to reach twelve. If one or two o'clock won't do, fade in on the supposed last two or three strokes and have the characters identify it as twelve o'clock.

Sound Can Establish Mood. The chirp of a single cricket can invest a quiet night scene with ominous undercurrents as a frightened girl finds herself isolated in a deserted place. Terror can be added to fright with the slow and methodical crunch of approaching footsteps down a gravel road. In the original radio presentation of "Sorry, Wrong Number" the use of the insistent telephone rings to heighten the suspense and mounting horror prior to the murder was climaxed by the click of the receiver as it was replaced on the phone cradle. Sound effects can also impart gaiety and frivolity, as in a carnival scene; excitement and tension, with heightened speeds of autos and planes; calmness and serenity, with the steady rhythm of the surf at low tide; or cold lonesomeness, with the really "wet" rain recordings. Alfred Hitchcock, in two British film classics, *The Thirty-nine Steps* and *The Lady Vanishes,* used a cross-fade of a woman's scream into a shrill English train whistle, matched to the dissolve from her face to a shot of the train, for powerful shock climaxes to action scenes.

Sound effects used for a "montage" on the air in the following excerpt from the documentary, "Milestones on the Road to Peace," gave an uplifting paean of thanks for America's might in aiding the countries of the world in World War II. Boat whistles were used for sound effects, but the blended pattern of many whistles of every type and the increasing wave of sound sweeping in and up to a thrilling climax created a rare moment. It was artistry in sound composed by Keene Crockett.

JOHN W. VANDERCOOK: All this time many of us went about our business...expecting war to reach our shores at any moment...dreading the time it might come. And finally one day the lethargy was gone and America decided to roll up her sleeves and prepare to cope with the future. The day was October 29th, 1940...and this is a record of the broadcast you heard...coming to you from Washington.

(RECORD 2, BAND 6--20 SECONDS)

FRANKLIN D. ROOSEVELT: --The Secretary of War will now draw the first number...the first number drawn by the Secretary of War is Serial Number 158

...(BACKGROUND, A WOMAN SCREAMS)

VANDERCOOK: The scream of the woman you heard that day was echoed in many homes...as sons and husbands left their loved ones to join the Armed Forces. America was being mobilized for war.

(MUSIC: AGITATO...FADE UNDER AND OUT)

DON HOLLENBECK: The year 1941 was a momentous year...for many reasons. Lend-Lease was one of them.

(BOAT WHISTLE)

VOICE I: (OFF) Cast off.

VOICE II: Aye, aye, sir.

(BOAT WHISTLE)

HOLLENBECK: Convoys laden with lend-lease supplies crept out in the night and spanned the oceans. (BOAT WHISTLE) Lend-lease supplies for Britain in her hour of darkest need...food and guns...bringing life and hope...Strengthening the will to resist... and the means of resisting.

(BOAT WHISTLE)

VOICE I: Cast off.

VOICE II: Aye, aye, sir.

HOLLENBECK: Lend-lease for China...fighting desperately alone, almost forgotten. Meager supplies, not one tenth enough...but supplies.

(BOAT WHISTLES IN AND HOLD)

HOLLENBECK: Lend-lease for the Polish armies in exile...

```
                    (MORE BOAT WHISTLES IN)
                For the fighting French...
                    (MORE BOAT WHISTLES IN WITH EACH
                    PHRASE)
                For the Belgian squadrons...for the fight-
                ing Norwegians...for the Czech soldiers...
                for the Dutch.  Supplies to stem the tide
                of aggression.
                    (BOAT WHISTLES HOLD FOR CLIMAX)
(MUSIC:         STAB TO COVER) 5
```

Another classification of sound effects is in the method of presentation. The two broad divisions are manual and recorded. A miscellaneous division includes several other methods.

Manual Sound Effects. Manual sound effects are produced live by an actor or sound-effects technician. In earlier days, elaborate equipment involving "Rube Goldberg" concoctions, was constructed for much of the sound. Rain machines, for example, stood about six feet high. The sound of rain was produced by a continuous sifting of bird seed down upon a ping-pong ball, then on to other surfaces: starched linen sheets, paper sacks, and finally open tissue paper at the bottom. These manually operated devices have generally been replaced by recordings made from life. The improved fidelity of broadcasting equipment revealed that the simulated sounds were imitations. A budget factor also was important; $2.00 for a sound effects record of automobile sounds was less expensive than the purchase of a car, and the record took up much less space.

It is fun for class broadcasts to experiment with gadgets such as a roller skate for an elevator, an egg beater for a wagon, a basketball bladder with BB shot inside for explosions and surf, a dowel striking a leather cushion for shots. Sometimes such effects are satisfactory for air use.

There are a number of sound effects that are best presented live. A knock on a door, for example. It might be given in a great variety of ways— a light tap by a timid little girl—a vigorous pounding by the police—a knocking in code—one bang or two—on a light door or a heavy door—far off-mike or on-beam. It is obvious that no recording can give such a variety of door knocks. The same is true with walks. There are such characteristics as: duration of the steps, whether they are going up or down stairs, whether they are on concrete or gravel. The following sounds are usually produced manually:

Body blows, falls, struggle
Destruction (crashing in doors—breaking glass)
Door knocks

---

[5] "Milestones on the Road to Peace." V-E Day Documentary, broadcast on NBC May 8, 1945. Script by Ben Kagan, direction by Garnet R. Garrison. Courtesy of the National Broadcasting Company.

Doors (houses and auto)
Fire (broomstraw and cellophane—blended with recordings for large fires)
Footsteps
Gunshots (pistols and rifles)
Horses (blended with recordings)
Motor noises (whine of elevator, etc.)
"Off-beat" comedy and phantasy effects (ratchets, slide whistle, etc.)
Silverware and dishes
Telephone rings and receiver sounds
Water sounds (washing dishes, swimming, rowing, etc.)
Whistles (police, slide, and toy)

It is often difficult to decide the best position in which to place these sound effects around the microphone to secure the most effective pick-up. A succession of manual effects in the script entails careful planning and experimentation in placement according to the microphones used.

In television, the actor may be seen as he knocks on the door, washes dishes, has a fight, etc. He creates the sound realistically with actual properties as a part of his characterization and the microphone that picks up the dialogue also transmits the sound. However, when the sound occurs off-camera, such as a door opening down the hall, a telephone ring, a distant rifle shot, or when sound supplies the aural background for a setting on-camera, such as a scene placed inside an elevator which requires the sound of a motor whining, continuous running and then stopping to give a touch of realism and movement to the scene, then sound-effects technicians perform these effects before a separate microphone in the same manner as in radio. They look at picture monitors to obtain accurate synchronization of sound to action.

Sound-effects technicians may also use vocal effects requiring no properties, such as baby cries and animal imitations. Specialized talent for these vocal effects may be employed.

Recorded Sound Effects. Thousands of individual cuts are available to the sound technician on records taken, in most instances, from life. Far less expensive than process shots used in making films, they may nevertheless be used in the same way. Recorded sound effects are played on (1) sound trucks in the studio, or (2) control-room transcription turntables.

1. "Sound truck" is the term used to designate a specially constructed movable cabinet equipped with three turntables and four to six pick-up arms, connected to a movable speaker cabinet. The records are played on these turntables and the sound comes out of the loud speaker. A microphone is placed before the speaker in such a fashion as to give the best fidelity of pick-up from the speaker and at the same time pick up the various manual sound effects being produced. It is possible to purchase special turntables which permit the operator to speed up or slow down the turntable. Filtering equipment may be connected to the output of the pick-up arms; monitor equipment for cueing can be incorporated; and record spotting devices can

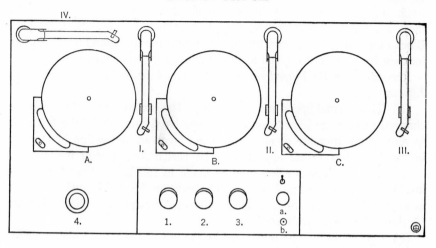

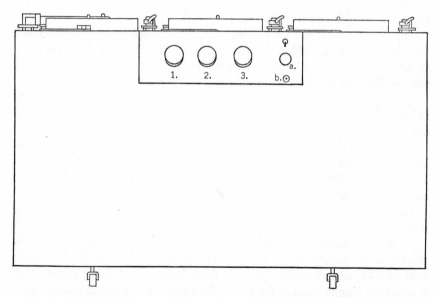

Above, view of sound truck from top. Volume controls 1-4 for pick-up arms I-IV. A, B, C, turntables, a, dynamic noise suppressor. b, phone jack for head set monitoring. *Below,* view of sound truck from front. Volume controls 1-3, panel sloping.

be utilized. If commercial construction costs prove very expensive, a sound truck may quite easily be built by a small station or college. On page 519 there are top and front views of such a cabinet housing the turntables. Block diagrams, a list of construction materials for this sound truck, and an inexpensive version are given at the conclusion of the chapter.

Records May Be Played on a Sound Truck to Produce a Variety of Effects:

(*a*) The normal speed may be varied. The steady auto effect may be changed to give the impression of stopping by slowing down the turntable to zero speed. Increase of turntable speed gives an impression of increase in speed of auto. Other records may be varied for different impressions.

(*b*) One continuous effect may be made to run longer than the record itself by using a second pick-up arm. The arms are located in such a manner as to permit two arms on any one turntable. An airplane in flight may run for the entire sequence if needed.

(*c*) One effect may be reinforced by the use of the second pick-up arm. Two horses can appear to be in motion from the sound effects record of one. One car passing another by manipulation of the volume controls on a single record is another example.

(*d*) Blending of two or three records gives a great variety of impressions. A continuous tire skid may be blended in with the sound of a running car motor for a short corner skid, a wide sweeping skid, or in between. A third record of a crash can write a tragedy ending.

(*e*) Effects other than those listed in the catalogues and on the labels may be secured by playing records at 33 instead of 78. Eerie and strange or comical and fantasy impressions may be obtained this way. A wolf howl, surf, or Big Ben turn into interesting and useful impressions.

(*f*) Cutting out the highs or lows changes the quality of sounds. A simple switch of a continuous train from regular tone to filtered position may, with correct timing, give the impression of walking from one car to another.

(*g*) Any of the above techniques may be modified by a change in volume. Fading-in a sound or the reverse may help indicate movement by the actors. For example, with appropriate dialogue the fading-in of a church bell can create the picture of movement towards the church.

Imagination and experimentation by the sound-effects technician are needed for full realization of the flexibility of recorded effects.

2. Control-room transcription turntables are used by many stations for playing sound records if they do not have a sound truck, when the TV studio is filled with scenery and props, or in those instances when the sound effect is relatively simple, such as the use of news presses as a sound effects theme for a news program. The turntables do not have the sound truck's variations in speed. Blending and special effects are, therefore, not very practical on control-room turntables.

3. Spotting records. The same general procedure described for cueing

transcriptions applies to spotting sound-effects records. *Exceptions:* revolving the records back and forth to find a particular spot is frowned upon because of possible damage to records. Counting turns is a common practice for specific sounds such as thunder. Marking a specific spot may be accomplished also by the use of china-marking pencils or a small piece of scotch tape. If the effect does not have to be spotted at a particular place—the scene opening in a car which is running continuously—cueing is no problem. The needle may be placed anywhere in the record. Mechanical spotting devices permit adjustment by micrometer dial readings ahead of time—the pick-up arm dropping down at the preselected place when the technician presses a push-button release switch. These automatic devices are not only expensive, but require great skill in manipulation for exact spotting. Many technicians prefer to count the turns even if the sound truck has a mechanical spotting device.

• MUSIC •

Modern "mood music" for radio and television drama is a direct heritage from the movies of another generation. The old-time piano players who improvised as they liked during a show would hardly recognize their craft as broadcast media have developed it. Present masters of cue music were thoroughly trained in basic musical education at the finest schools in Europe and America. Network composers such as Morris Mamorsky, Harry Sosnik, Bernard Herrmann, Alexander Semmler, and Vladimir Selinsky, to mention only a few, combine this soundness in musical knowledge with versatility, imagination, and ability to produce fine work in a brief time.

The cue music can ruin a production if the accompaniment is not subordinated to the paramount dramatic idea. "When the audience says, 'The orchestra is playing,' the music director of the program has failed," Bernard Herrmann warns. "Attention is distracted from the drama and the whole aim of the cue music is defeated."

Not every network program and very few local stations can afford the luxury of a specially composed score. Music from the files is pulled according to various published indices of mood music or those developed by the station or network music librarian. The NBC files contain many broad classifications from Agitato to Western, and each major classification has many subdivisions, each with its own pieces of music to suggest the mood. In the "horror" section of the file, for example, one card recommends "In Gloomy Forest" by William Axt to suggest "sinister, gruesome suspense in lonely places." Pianists and organists may refer to such files or use collections which have been published.

Special care must be taken to avoid the very well-known compositions and those older cues which have been used too often. They may call attention to the music or create erroneous pictures due to previously established associations. Burlesque or comedy effects from such familiar music are constantly used. "Hearts and Flowers," "Sailing, Sailing, Over the Bounding Main," "The Bowery," and "Good Night Ladies" are often so used.

Recorded Music for Dramas. Ordinary commercial records are used frequently by radio and television networks, to provide the music for dramas. Symphonies, ballet music, suites, musical comedies, special mood albums by orchestras, and music used in films or stage productions may be auditioned and selected for use. The various transcription library services include selections for use on dramas as part of their service. The sound-effects companies make available some public-domain and specially composed music.

The same advice to avoid music that is too familiar or stylized should be closely observed here. *Caution:* avoid mixing instrumentations—symphony for one bridge, small concert orchestra for another, organ for a third.

A representative list of recorded music is given at the end of the chapter. The albums issued by the recording companies should be regularly auditioned if much use is to be made of music in dramatic productions.

On long-playing (33 rpm) records, which have very little space between grooves, it is extremely difficult to "spot-cue" a specific passage. A general practice is to "dub" the music to be used on to acetate disc recordings or on to tape instead of attempting to use the regular records during the on-the-air performance.

Functions of Music in Drama. THEMES. Themes serve to identify a program series. A situation comedy, however, requires a different theme than a serious drama. Good themes are not easy to compose. They must wear well. If the theme is very repetitive it will not hold up well if a "stretch" is needed at the close. If the theme is too familiar, a steady diet of it may be wearying. If the theme is too heavy and full, the announcer may have to blast to be heard over it. Some original themes, such as those written for "Dragnet" and "Medic," became so popular that they were recorded commercially for general release. To locate a good theme often requires arduous hours of trial-and-error auditioning. Some dramatic series which feature different types of plays from week to week, such as CBS-TV "Studio One," have a standard series theme supplemented by different program themes according to the type of play presented.

LOCALE AND SETTING. These may be indicated directly by a musical selection which the audience knows, or indirectly by music which suggests the locale or setting. The latter is preferred for most dramas except light romances and broad comedy shows. *Caution:* the title of the selection should not be relied upon to provide a clue to the audience as to the locale of the drama. Association of titles and music is very weak at best, and to expect the audience to know that the next scene is in Alabama because of an eight-second bridge based on "Alabamy Bound" is foolhardy.

TRANSITION. This is a common function of music in drama. Music serves to comment on the scene that is ending and to match its mood; and to transfer the audience to the next scene and anticipate its mood. With an effective music bridge in radio or combined with the pictured scenes in television, the audience can move from the tragedy of illness and death to happiness and warm affection. It is particularly useful in fantasy. In the adaptation of Robert Ayre's short story "Mr. Sycamore" on the Columbia Workshop series, Bernard Herrmann effected the transfiguration of John Gwilt, the postman, into a tree, with a harp run segued into a sustained flute meody.[6]

Selection of appropriate recorded transitional music sometimes falls into a hit-or-miss pattern disregarding the subtleties of the mood of the scene that is ending and the one coming up. Hours of auditioning may be necessary to find appropriate music to link two scenes. If the music is to back the narrator or film sequences for any length of time, the selection of music is even more difficult.

ATMOSPHERE AND MOOD. Music is effective for suggesting and creating mood and atmosphere. Somehow, it does not trouble the audience that a tender love scene on a porch in the moonlight is backed by a muted string and a woodwind theme of romance. The presence of the music is accepted without the audience's being consciously aware of it.

Those who use recorded background music must avoid overly elaborate orchestrations. Selections with too clearly defined melodies should also be avoided because the audience may listen to the tune.

SOUND EFFECTS. Music may be used instead of sound effects where some stylization is desired. Example: In the original version of "Skyscraper," a stream-of-consciousness radio play, the climax of the drama includes the fall of a man down the many floors of a skyscraper under construction. The audience heard the thoughts of the falling man. The impact of his body as it hit the ground was conveyed as a sound effect. In a revival of the play, music was substituted with equal dramatic impact, but with less specific visualization of the actual event in the minds of the listeners. This symbolizing of violent death is suggested by music on many programs. Special effects, such as a run by the string section ending in a brass discord for the sound of an arrow in flight, can be obtained. Such music is found frequently in modern compositions available on records.

MONTAGES. Music is constantly relied upon for assistance in "montages," a series of short scenes, or statements, that (1) advance the action at a faster than normal pace; or (2) give a panoramic picture of various aspects of the action in progress. The term is taken from the movies where the technique is widely used. Music serves as a unifying force. In the following excerpt from "Milestones on the Road to Peace," a radio documentary, sound is used to punctuate and reduce the climax in a minor mood in the first montage; in the second montage music is used for a climactic turning of the tide. The rapid segue from one selection to another, as indicated,

[6] The "Mr. Sycamore" script and score is reproduced in Max Wylie, *Radio Writing* (New York, 1939), pp. 341-361.

could not be duplicated with separate records. If records must be used in such a program, a single selection that builds to a climax should be chosen. This recording could then be used for the montage, fading it up between narrative lines. Careful back-timing is needed to make certain that the musical curtain will be there when it is needed.

NARR: Throughout the summer of 1942 the news continued to be dreary and the future dismal.

(EXPLOSION--SUSTAINED LOW RUMBLE WITH OTHERS SUPERIMPOSED)

Submarine warfare was at an all time high.

(EXPLOSION)

Tobruk had fallen.

(EXPLOSION)

The Germans had launched a major offensive in the Caucasus.

(EXPLOSION)

The Japanese had landed in Kiska and Attu in the Aleutians.

(MUSIC: UP TO PEAK AND HOLD)

NARR: And then...in August, the tide suddenly turned.

(MUSIC: "MARINE SONG"...UNDER)

VOICE I: U. S. Marines land on Guadalcanal.

(MUSIC: SEGUE TO PIPES...UNDER)

VOICE II: General Montgomery begins 1500 mile chase of Rommel across North Africa.

(MUSIC: SEGUE TO "SONG OF THE PLAINS" UNDER)

VOICE III: Russia launches sweeping offensive at Stalingrad.

(MUSIC: SEGUE TO "STARS AND STRIPES FOREVER" UNDER:)
(SHOUTING AS BEFORE)

VOICE IV: U. S. and British troops open new front in Africa.

(MUSIC: UP FOR CLIMAX AND FADE UNDER)

HOLLENBECK: Yes, the tide had turned. The United Nations were on the offensive...[7]

[7] "Milestones on the Road to Peace," V-E Day Documentary, NBC, May 8, 1945. Courtesy of National Broadcasting Company.

SOUND-EFFECTS LIST—A SUGGESTED MINIMUM

Manual

Berrybaskets (to crush).

Broom straw for fire and brush (also cellophane).

Car door (mounted in frame).

Door buzzer.

Glass (to break for crashes).

Leather pad and *dowel* (for shots).

Metronome.

Dishes and silverware

Door (half or full size—workable with hardware).

Door bell and *chimes.*

Motor, electric, with rheostat.

Rubber plungers and *half coconut shells* (for horses).

Steps—four steps and landing.

Telephones—French type with dial, receiver on hook.

Telephone phone bell (rings two bells not one).

Tools—hammers and saws.

Walk platform—two by six feet.

Water tank—lined with canvas.

Whistles—all types.

Recorded

Forty records suggested

Airplanes (three records)

Multi-motor.

Single plane, idling, in full flight, landing.

Animals (seven records)

Birds.

Cattle.

Dogs.

Horses—whinny, horse and wagon, single horse trotting and galloping.

Posse.

Automobiles (six records)

Various types, old and modern. Continuous running, start, skid and crash.

Horns.

Squad car with siren.

Traffic, small and large city.

Crowds (four records)

Small and large polite conversation.

Applause, straight and with boos and hisses.

Excited crowds, large.

Restaurant.

Babies crying—also single baby.

Industrial (one record)

Factory noises and machinery.

Marine (three records)

Harbor noises—fog horn.

Ocean liner—whistles.

Outboard motor.

Music (one record)

Calliope.

Train (four records)

Passenger train, steam and Diesel—continuous running, whistles.

Train start in station and stopping with RR station background.

Freight train over trestle.

Warfare (four records)

Pistol shots and pitched battle.

Modern artillery fire and machine guns.

Explosions with shell whine and falling debris.

Western style guns and rifles.

Weather (three records)

Rain and thunder.

Wind, various types.

Surf.

Miscellaneous (four records)

Printing presses and teletype.

Big Ben and clock bells.

Church bells.

Fire—with police and fire apparatus.

BLOCK DIAGRAM FOR SOUND TRUCK
ILLUSTRATED ON PAGE 519

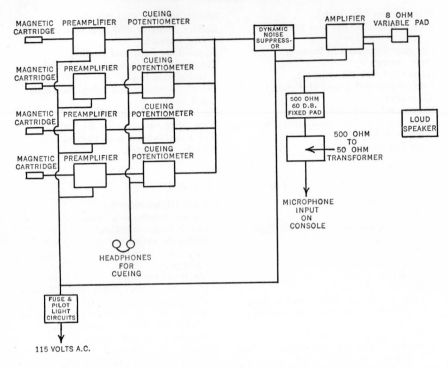

BLOCK DIAGRAM OF INEXPENSIVE SOUND TRUCK

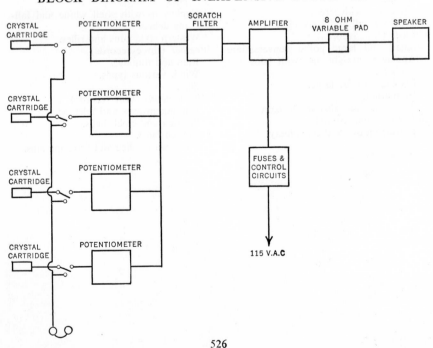

EQUIPMENT LIST FOR SOUND TRUCK
WITH APPROXIMATE PRICES

Regular Broadcast Truck

1 Radio Craftsman RC 400 10 watt amplifier	$ 43.00
2 Rek-o-kut 3 speed turntables @ 120.00	240.00
1 Rek-o-kut variable speed turntable	85.00
4 GE A1-501 Transcription arm @ 35.50	142.00
4 GE Cartridges and pre-amps @ 20.00	80.00
(RPX 050 Cartridge and UPX 003A pre-amp with power supply)	
4 Daven 500,000 ohm potentiometers—3 db steps—Linear—cueing type @ 11.00	44.00
1 UTC LS-30 Transformer	16.00
1 Altec 600 B 12 inch speaker and cabinet	80.00
Miscellaneous parts	25.00
Wood—⅝ plywood, 2 x 4's and 3" casters.	35.00
Total	$790.00

A variable sound effects filter, (RCA BE 21 B) may be added if desired. Cost $275.00. Insert between pre-amplifier and cueing potentiometer for one channel or between noise suppressor and amplifier to affect output of all channels.

Inexpensive Version

1 Radio Craftsman RC 400 10 watt amplifier	$ 43.00
2 General Industries DSS 3 speed turntables @ 15.00	30.00
1 Rek-o-kut variable speed turntable	85.00
3 Astatic Model 400-CAC-D pick-up arms @ 15.00	45.00
3 Anti-capacity key switches DPDT @ 2.50	7.50
Standard type 10 or 12 inch speaker and cabinet	40.00
Miscellaneous parts and volume controls	15.00
Wood—⅜ plywood, 2 x 4's and 3" casters	22.00
Total	$287.50

SUGGESTED RECORDED BRIDGE AND BACKGROUND
MUSIC FOR DRAMAS

Title	Composer	Recording Co.	Performance Unit
American Music for Orchestra	Various	Victor	Eastman Symphony
Concerto in F	Gershwin	Victor	Boston "Pops"
Damnation of Faust	Berlioz	Columbia	London Philharmonic
Death and Transfiguration	Strauss	Victor	New York Symphony
Duel in the Sun Music	Tiomkin	Victor	Boston "Pops"
Escales (Ports of Call)	Ibert	Victor	San Francisco Symphony
Feste Romana (Roman Carnival)	Respighi	Columbia	Philadelphia Orch.
Film Music	Varied	London	London Symphony
Firebird Suite	Stravinsky	Columbia	New York Philharmonic
Five Portraits	Thompson	Columbia	Philadelphia Symphony
Interplay for Piano and Orch.	Gould	Columbia	Robin Hood Dell Orch.

Title	Composer	Recording Co.	Performance Unit
La Mer	Debussy	Victor	Boston Symphony
London Again Suite	Coates	Columbia	Coates Symphony
Mark Twain Suite	Kern	Columbia	Andre Kostelanetz
Music for the Theatre	Copland	Victor	Eastman Symphony
Ozark Set	Siegmeister	Columbia	Minneapolis Symphony
Pictures at an Exhibition	Moussorgsky-Ravel	Columbia	New York Philharmonic
Pines of Rome	Respighi	Columbia	Philadelphia Symphony
Program of Cesar Franck	Franck	Victor	Chicago Symphony
Rite of Spring	Stravinsky	Victor	San Francisco Orch.
Rhythms (Vol. 1-6)	Various	Victor	Varied
Suite Provençale	Milhaud	Victor	St. Louis Symphony
Symphony Fantastique	Berlioz	Victor	Cleveland Orchestra
Till Eulenspiegel	Strauss	Victor	Boston Symphony

Projects and Exercises

1. Hand out two sound-effects records to each member of the class. Each student writes a melodramatic scene (two to two-and-one-half minutes) incorporating at least three of the sounds contained on these records. This exercise is to focus attention on the selectivity of sound principle; how script techniques can identify sound when identification is needed; and how sound effects establish locale, advance action, and create mood. Produce these scenes exactly as written for class criticism.

2. Perform the manual sound noted in the following script in keeping with the mood of the dialogue. The scene should be played in many different ways. A few suggested ways are: a girl seeking refuge after escaping from a gang of crooks at two A.M.; same situation, but with the gang only a floor below her; a young wife with arms full of bundles and unable to reach her keys; a young wife after a quarrel with her husband coming to the apartment of a former flame; same character coming back to her husband after the same quarrel, but this time only after a walk around the park; a sultry siren after a naive young man; and the girl a day late for a meeting of a couple of crooks at an assigned hideout after pulling off a big job.

    KNOCK ON DOOR

GIRL: Come on...let me in. (KNOCK) Let me in. (KNOCK)

MAN: (CALLING OTHER SIDE OF DOOR) Just a minute.

GIRL: Ah--it's about time.

MAN: Well...hello Mary.

3. Perform the manual sound as indicated in following script in a realistic manner. Differentiate between steps on stairs and level floors. Observe how people use heels and soles of shoes going upstairs—walking along—going downstairs—men or women walking.

    STEPS ON PAVEMENT TWO MEN

BILL: Just wait till you meet Marie, Jim. You'll agree she's one in a million.

JIM: Well, why are we just ambling along, then? Hurry up Bill. Don't be such a slow poke.

BILL: O.K. but we're just about there.

BILL: Here's the house. Right up this way.

STEPS ON STAIRS

DOOR OPEN AND CLOSE

Just up to the second floor.
And in we go.

STEPS ON STAIRS

JIM: You never did tell me where you met this girl who's "one in a million," Bill...Break down and tell me.

BILL: Sounds funny but I really fell for her the first time I saw her. I was skating over at Rockefeller Plaza--tried to do a fancy step--and took a tumble--right in front of her.

JIM: Sounds phoney. Didn't you plan it that way?

BILL: Confidentially--I did. (STEPS ON LANDING) Oh--here we are and apartment B 4 is over there.

(STEPS)

(DOOR BUZZER--DOOR OPENS)

GIRL: Yes?

BILL: Why where's Marie?

GIRL: Marie...? Oh you must mean the girl who moved out this morning. She's getting married the super told me.

BILL: Married?

GIRL: That's right.--she's probably being married right now. The ceremony was to be at 3 o'clock.

BILL: Oh...No...(BODY FALL)

4. Select and play appropriate themes, background, mood, montage, and transition music for scripts included in the book as designated by the instructor.
5. Play over and classify possible future uses of the music albums at hand. Prepare a file catalogue listing your recommendations.
6. Enlist the services of a college music major and experiment with original scores for dramas.

❄ 30 ❄

Acting

AN ACTOR has two tasks: to sell and to create. The selling of an actor's ability takes place in the audition where a casting director or producer passes judgment on the quality of his work. The actor usually works alone, in front of a microphone in radio where the director listens in the control room, or off-camera in television, without benefit of scenery or lighting. In radio, the creative aspect comes in a studio where the actor, reading from a script, brings a character to life with a sound-effects technician as his *alter ego,* walking for him, fighting for him, and dying for him, speaking on cue and with movements determined by microphone pick-up patterns. In television, the actor, having memorized his part, performs without benefit of audience and is circumscribed in all he does by the complex equipment which is necessary to transmit the picture.

This chapter considers specialized problems of radio and television acting. Our discussion presupposes basic training in acting. We first treat the audition, then we proceed to a multiscene half-hour radio script and to excerpts from a television play to give the student practice in creating different characterizations.

• AUDITIONS •

General auditions give the actor an opportunity to present capsule versions of his skill in portraying different roles. The actor's own evaluation of his strong points should influence his choice of material. When an actor is being considered for a specific part, special auditions are often held. The casting director may request a number of actors "to read for the part" in order to determine which one is best suited and is most responsive to directorial suggestions. Instead of working alone, the actor may be given a partner. His appearance in costume or on camera may be checked. Short screen tests may be shot when an actor is being appraised for a film role. The calls for special auditions or readings may be awarded to actors on the basis of past credits, personal observation by the director, recommendations by an agent, or results of the general audition.

1. The first step in preparing for auditions is the selection of material. For many, this seemingly simple task takes on the proportions of a tremendous obstacle. Since the audition is to enable the actor to be heard and viewed in the characterizations he feels most capable of performing, he should choose first from the roles he has played elsewhere, provided he did a commendable job. The advantage in this procedure is familiarity with the material. If this material is not available, roles from other sources, such as stage plays or TV and radio scripts may be selected. It is usually desirable to avoid Shakespeare, Greek tragedy and other classical plays, because TV and radio do not have many such programs. They should also be avoided because very few actors can do them well. To be avoided, too, are the excerpts for drill which appear in acting manuals. These have been used so many times by so many candidates that directors are unable dispassionately to hear them again. A tally at a particular studio revealed that out of twenty auditions by ingenues in one week, the drugstore speech in "Our Town" was used seven times, Alexandra's curtain speech in "The Little Foxes" six times, and Katrin's opening narration in "I Remember Mama" and Olive's phone call in "Voice of the Turtle" four times each. Even if any of these roles is close to the heart of the aspirant, a different scene should be selected. For the record, however, it should be noted that an occasional interpretation of these "chestnuts" is so striking that the performer stands out head and shoulders above the crowd and makes a vivid impression.

2. The customary time allowed for an audition is from five to eight minutes. In radio, about five selections, a minute each, should give a fairly accurate picture of the actor's capabilities. In television three selections of two-and-a-half minutes each should be sufficient. The next step is the arrangement of the selections.

Study the station, agency, or production company. If it does nothing but serials, it will avail you little to go far afield from serial roles. If they specialize in "whodunits," choose your material accordingly. Don't attempt roles you cannot handle. If you cannot do crooks well, but can play lawyers (the so-called "professionals"), present characters of that type doing different things and in different moods: an excited lawyer, a lawyer cross-examining a witness, a lawyer delivering an emotional plea for the life of a client, etc. If you cannot do dialects authentically and with assurance, avoid them. Dialects require a keen ear, close observation of physical mannerisms, and memory of rhythm and melody patterns. Even if you played numerous character roles in a college or community theater, remember that in professional television you are facing competition from established character actors with many years of experience who do not need elaborate make-up to look the age of a character.

The following is suggested for general auditions. In radio, let the first of five selections be a straight or neutral character fairly close to your own age. The second, to demonstrate flexibility in age range, can be a more youthful role. The third may demonstrate the older limits of your range. Both second and third should provide a change in pace and emotion. The fourth selection may provide a climax of some sort. It may be an intense scene played with a sharp dynamic attack, but it should be in your own age range. The fifth selection should provide as much contrast as you can handle, such as sincere emotion of great depth. In television, the second and third selections may be eliminated because of the tendency of producers to cast actors who look the age they must portray. If you are a specialist in accents, comedy, character roles, or a combination vocalist-actor, you may wish to vary this arrangement. A brief pantomime piece may also be included.

NBC-TV ACTOR'S FILE CARD	CLASS:
NAME:	AGE RANGE:
HOME PHONE: MESSAGES:	AGENT:
HEIGHT: WEIGHT: HAIR:	EYES:
LANGUAGES.	FILED:
DIALECTS:	AUDITIONED:
BROADWAY:	
STOCK:	
SEASONS:	
OFF BROADWAY:	
REP ETC:	
TV PLAYED:	
WALK-ONS:	
OTHER TALENTS:	INTERVIEWED:

3. The third step is the actual presentation of the audition. Identify the selection briefly by general type: "The first is a straight lead, from 'Mister Roberts.'" This enables the director to check your performance against what you think you are doing, and keeps him from falling into the very human habit of attempting to guess the particular play and the role. In radio, work directly on the beam for most acting, 6 to 12 inches away from the microphone; slightly farther away for a dynamic delivery. Avoid stage projection and overly precise articulation. Voice alone must communicate the character and the meaning. This does not mean that you should refrain from bodily action. Let your body help you in the portrayal of the roles. In television, as in radio, remember that there is an intimate relationship between the actor and the audience. Physical movement and facial expressions will

be seen by an audience which may be thought of as being present on the stage with you.

4. Evaluation of the audition. What are the standards of judgment? What does the director look for? The first reaction may be a general evaluation: "This actor isn't up to desirable standards." And for the purposes of an audition from the director's point of view, that may be the final reaction —a big "No" on your card. However, we may probe a little deeper and examine some of the specific things that are considered in arriving at a judgment.

One of the first items is the positiveness of attack. This is a signpost of professionalism. The characterization may be faulty, the interpretation muddy, but the poise and the assurance with which the actor proceeds, is important. *Caution:* There is no direct correlation, however, between frenetic activity or great volume and positiveness of attack.

Another key item brought into focus by the demands of radio and television is the reality of the presentations: whether the characters seem real or seem artificial or exaggerated. The microphone and camera show quickly where technique overshadows meaning; where the actor is more conscious of how he is "doing a part" than what the scene means in a real flesh-and-blood situation. We must observe the actor thinking, reacting, and feeling, not reciting.

In arriving at a judgment, also considered are a number of other factors, many of which are essential in the art of acting: control of voice and body, portrayal of emotion, meaning of phrases and sentences, timing of physical action and lines, ability to pause and nuances of emphasis.

EXAMPLE OF RADIO ACTING SCRIPT

An "as broadcast" radio script of "Aesop: Fables for Today and Tomorrow" is included here for laboratory study. This script is extremely useful because of its vignette construction. The individual scenes lend themselves to performance by separate groups, and provide opportunities for doubling roles as is often required in actual broadcasting. After the script appears comments on mike technique, suggestions for characterizations, and recommendations for playing the scenes.

"Home Is What You Make It" [1]

Episode #139, Greece, "Aesop: Fables for Today and Tomorrow," by Lou Hazam.

(MUSIC: ACCENTS EACH COUNTRY WITH A STING)

1. NARR: (ECHO)   Canada...China...England...France...(FADE) Greece...Denmark...India...

[1] Courtesy of the National Broadcasting Company.

(MUSIC: SWELLS TO COVER)

2. ANNCR: For a better and more tolerant understanding among
nations and the promotion of enduring peace...

(MUSIC: UP A TONE TO HANG FOR)

3. ANNCR: HOME IS WHAT YOU MAKE IT, brought to you weekly by
the National Broadcasting Company and its affiliated
independent stations, presents the eighth program in
its summer series devoted to the contribution of the
peoples of the world to American culture and home-
life! Today, we acknowledge our debt to--

4. VOICE: Greece!

(MUSIC: SALUTE AND OUT)

5. ANNCR: "Aesop--Fables For Today and Tomorrow!"

(MUSIC: THEME IN AND UNDER)

6. ANNCR: Here is your narrator, Ben Grauer...

7. NARR: To Greece we Americans can bow for many things. For
some of the greatest works of sculpture that have
ever been born of the hands of man. For a style of
architecture by which we have built public buildings
in virtually every city of our nation. For the drama
of Aristophanes...for the wisdom of Aristotle and
Plato. Indeed, for the very way in which we govern
ourselves--for Greece was the first democracy. But
today, we choose to salute a lesser appreciated in-
heritance from ancient Greece--a man whose ideas
have been just as enduring as Greek art and wisdom.
Aesop! (CHANGE NOW TO MORE INFORMAL TONE) Yessir,
Aesop of the famous fables.--We don't know very
much about Aesop, my friends. They say he was a
slave, who--discharged by his master--rose to play
an important part in the political life of his day.
The story goes that somebody finally framed him
and he ended up condemned to be thrown from a high
cliff.--But this much we do know. The fables which
bear his name pack just as much of a wallop today
as they ever did--are just as filled with meaning
to guide our future actions. To prove it...to show
how the fables of Aesop can be readily applied
today to individual matters, family matters and
national affairs-- we've corralled two extremely
versatile actors. Here first is Miss Mitzi Gould.

8. WOMAN: How do you do.

9. NARR: And Joe De Santis.

10. MAN: How do you do.

11. NARR: Well now, here's what these two, Miss Gould and Mr.
De Santis, are going to do. They are going to perform a variety of typical scenes from our present
day life--and then defy me to find an Aesop fable
that applies to each scene. In short--to see if
the scene literally strikes a bell in my mind and
I can make with the appropriate message. So lend

us your ears, my friends, and listen for that bell
--for remember what Aesop said:

(MUSIC: STING)

(ECHO) He who refuses advice may some day vainly
seek it.

(MUSIC: IN AND UNDER)

12. NARR: First we have a typical "family" scene. Hubby is
just coming home from work...

(SCREEN DOOR OPENING AND CLOSING)

13. MAN: (AS HUSBAND; GAY AND CHIPPER) Oh, hello, darling...
and how's my lovey-dovey wife tonight?

14. WOMAN: (ON VERGE OF TEARS) Hello...Jim.

15. MAN: Hey--what's the matter? What's wrong?

16. WOMAN: (BETWEEN SNIFFLES) Junior...

17. MAN: (QUICKLY) What's he done?

18. WOMAN: He wanted to eat early...but he left the table...he
wouldn't eat his spinach.

19. MAN: What! How dare he do a thing like that? Where is
he?

20. WOMAN: He went out. He said he wouldn't touch the...the
darn stuff.

21. MAN: He did, did he? Well, I'll fix him. Who does he
think he is around here?...

(OPENING THE SCREEN DOOR)

(CALLING FORCEFULLY) Junior! (ANGRILY) Junior!
(SORE AND GRUMBLING) Not wanting what's good for
him. How does he expect to grow up into anything,
answer me that! (CALLS) Junior!

22. WOMAN: (ALMOST WEEPING) I don't know what to do with him.

23. MAN: I'll show him who's boss around here. When I say
eat spinach he'll eat it and like it, by gosh!
(CALLS) (DOOR OPENS) Junior! Jun-ior! (DOOR BANGS
SHUT) (TURNING TO WIFE) By the way what's for dinner for us tonight?

24. WOMAN: Steak, potatoes 'n--spinach.

25. MAN: Spinach? Me? Good heavens, Grace, you know I
can't abide spinach! Open a can of peas or some-
thing--(CALLING, AS IF HE SEES HIM NOW) Oh, there
you are, Junior--Junior--come and eat your spinach!
(BELL)

26. NARR: Yessir it rings a bell with me right off. I am reminded of Aesop's fable which goes like this.

(MUSIC: SNEAKS UNDER)

Once a mother crab and her son were taking a walk
on the sand. Said the mother crab--"Child, why do
you walk so ungracefully crooked? Walk straight,
my child, without twisting." "Pray, mother," said

the young crab..."do but show me the way and I will
follow you."--Moral...

(MUSIC: STOP)

(ECHO) Example is the best precept.

(MUSIC: UP AND OUT)

27. NARR: Score one for Ben Grauer. And now an office scene.
                    (INTERCOM BUZZER; SWITCH)

28. MAN: (BOSS, BIG, BLUSTERY TYPE) Yes?

29. WOMAN: (AS SECRETARY, FILTER) I finally got Miss Wilson,
          sir. She's waiting to see you.

30. MAN: Well, it's about time! Send her in.

31. WOMAN: (FILTER) Yessir.

                    (SWITCH)
                    (DOOR OPEN AND CLOSE)

32. WOMAN: (AS STENO; TIMIDLY) Did...Did you want to see me,
          Mr. Merriam?

33. MAN: Of course I wanted to see you or I wouldn't have
          sent for you!--Where have you been?

34. WOMAN: Well, I--

35. MAN: Sit down.

36. WOMAN: Yessir.

37. MAN: Look here, Miss Wilson. I run an office here, not a
          country club. I notice from your time card that
          you've been late twice this week. And three times
          this week your typing has shown errors.

38. WOMAN: Well, I....

39. MAN: Now, Miss Wilson. We pay you what we believe to be
          a fine salary. We naturally expect a proper return
          for that salary.

40. WOMAN: If you'd only let me explain, Mr. Merriam--

41. MAN: I can't understand why you're not cooperating.
          After all I don't treat you unfairly.--Now, what is
          your explanation?

42. WOMAN: I...I'm awfully sorry about it all, Mr. Merriam, but
          you see--my mother's been awfully sick. I've had
          to do a lot of things at home that I wouldn't or-
          dinarily do and that's what made me late.
          As for the typing mistakes, I've been so worried
          about her--well, really, Mr. Merriam, I shouldn't
          be at work at all....I should be home taking care
          of her. I asked to have my vacation moved up, but
          I was told--

43. MAN: You were told it was impossible and it is impos-
          sible. While we sympathize with you, Miss Wilson,
          you can't expect us to run an office to conform to
          home emergencies.--I can't understand you people
          I employ here. I don't seem to be able to get

anything but the most average work out of the whole
lot of you!

(THE STRIKING OF A BELL)

44. NARR: Well that incident reminds me of Aesop's fable of
the Wind and the Sun. Remember?

(MUSIC: SNEAKS UNDER)

Once the Wind and the Sun had an argument about
which one was stronger. "I know we can tell who is
the stronger," said the Sun. "Look down there at
the traveler walking along the road. Let's test our
strength by seeing who can cause him to remove his
cloak.'' The wind tried first. It blew as hard as
it could...

(WIND IMPRESSION)

But the harder it blew, the tighter the traveler
held his cloak about him. At last the Wind gave
up in despair. Then the Sun began to try.

(WIND FADES--BIRDS)

It warmed the air and calmed the breeze. It shone
pleasanter and pleasanter upon the traveler. At
first he loosened his cloak and then finally he
removed it entirely.--Which all goes to show...

(MUSIC: STOP)

(ECHO)

Kindness brings better results than severity.

(MUSIC: UP AND OUT)

45. NARR: So far, so good--we continue. Along a main highway
a nice looking woman stands staring dejectedly at a
flat tire on her car. Along comes a kind motor-
ist....

(CAR PULLING UP TO A STOP)

46. MAN: Can I help you, madam?

47. WOMAN: Oh dear...I would be so obliged! Looks like I've
gone and got a flat tire.

48. MAN: Oh yes...well...Let's see what I can do with it.

(CAR DOOR CLOSES AS HE CLIMBS OUT)

49. WOMAN: So kind of you to stop.

50. MAN: Not at all...not at all, madam.--There was something
about your face that reminded me of my sister.

51. WOMAN: Oh, how nice.

52. MAN: (EXAMINING TIRE) I think I can fix this for you in a
jiffy. Shouldn't be hard at all.

53. WOMAN: Oh, how wonderful...It really is so sweet of you...

54. MAN: Not at all. Not at all...

55. WOMAN: May I hold your coat and vest--so you won't get them
dirty?

56. MAN: Oh,--well, that's real thoughtful of you--

57. WOMAN: Hate to see a man soil his suit--particularly a nice
    one like yours.

58. MAN: (EFFORT) Here 'tis. Thanks. Yes--well, I'll get
    my stuff out of the back of my car and get to work
    on this tire right now. (FADE) Won't take long...

    (MUSIC: BRIDGE)

    (SOME LAST FEW BANGS. PERHAPS THE JACK)

59. MAN: (JOB FINISHED) There you are.--I think that will be
    all right now.

60. WOMAN: Oh, I can't tell you how very grateful I am!

61. MAN: That's all right. Don't mention it.--Here, I'll
    open the door for you.

    (CAR DOOR OPENING)

62. WOMAN: (EFFORT) Thank you again. I really appreciate it a
    whole lot!

63. MAN: You're quite welcome.

64. WOMAN: Here's your coat and vest.

65. MAN: Thank you.--Goodbye.

    (CAR DOOR CLOSES)

66. WOMAN: Goodbye.

    (CAR STARTING UP, AND MOVING OFF)

67. MAN: (TO SELF, AFTER CAR SOUND FADES OFF) Sweet woman.--
    (CHANGE) Well, I've been delayed. Wonder what time
    it is? (PATTING POCKETS) (PAUSE; THEN A STARTLED
    EXCLAMATION) My watch! Gone!--(THEN, AFTER A
    QUICK CHECK, GIVES OUT WITH A SHRIEKING) MY WALLET!

    (BELL...)

68. NARR: Aesop could have warned that man--with his fable of
    "The Wolf in Sheep's Clothing." It goes like
    this...

    (MUSIC: IN AND UNDER AS B.G.)

    There was once a greedy wolf who had trouble catch-
    ing sheep. So one day he decided to disguise
    himself. He found a sheepskin and covered himself
    with it. Then he went in and mingled with the
    flock. One at a time, the young lambs who belonged
    to the sheep whose skin he had taken, followed him
    away...And as soon as they had gone a little apart
    from the flock, he pounced upon them and ate them.
    --Proving--

    (MUSIC: STOP)

    (ECHO)

    Appearances are deceptive.

    (MUSIC: UP AND OUT)

69. NARR: Score three for Grauer.--Onward and upward with Aesop!

(MUSIC: FANFARE)

Our scene now--an office to the back of a night club...Attendez!

70. MAN: O.K., Trixie...What's it about...Why did you want to talk to me?

71. WOMAN: (NITE-CLUB TYPE; ARGUING AND PLEADING) Listen, Mr. Bragato...I don't see why you don't give me a break. After all I been workin' for this run-down honky-tonk for two years now...

72. MAN: But, Trixie--I already give you a break. You're the hit of the floor show. You come out last draped in that white mink sarong with the red spotlight.

73. WOMAN: But I wanna sing!

74. MAN: You're beautiful, Trixie. People who come want to look at you, not hear you. You're the most beautiful showgirl in New York!

75. WOMAN: But I'm tired of being the most beautiful showgirl in New York.--I wanna sing! Listen to me, Mr. Bragato, I can sing...Listen!

76. MAN: No no, please, Trixie, no no...

77. WOMAN: (BURSTS OUT SINGING)
I'll be comin' in a taxi honey,
Better be ready at hap-past eight,
Now sweetie don't be late...

78. MAN: (OVER SINGING) Please, Trixie...please...

79. WOMAN: (CONTINUING UNDETERRED) I wanna get there when the band starts playin'...

(MUSIC: PICKS UP REFRAIN AND CURTAINS)

(BELL)

80. NARR: Believe it or not, I've got an Aesop that hits that one right on the nose!--Stand by, folks, for "The Peacock and Juno..."

(MUSIC: IN AND UNDER AS B.G.)

Once upon a time there was a peacock who, in spite of all his attractions, was not satisfied with his fate. So the peacock went to the goddess Juno and petitioned her that she add to his endowments the voice of a nightingale. Juno refused. But the peacock persisted. He reminded Juno that he was her favorite bird. But Juno wouldn't listen. Finally, when Juno could stand no more, she turned upon the peacock and said:

(MUSIC: STOP)

(ECHO)

Be happy with your lot in life. One cannot be first in everything.

(MUSIC: UP AND OUT)

81. NARR: Next scene, Anytown, U.S.A.

(CAR SPEEDING)

Mrs. Peyton Smith speeds along the highway with
scarcely a glance in her rear view mirror until...

(MOTORCYCLE COP'S SIREN)

82. WOMAN: Oh dear...

83. MAN: (OFFICER: CALLING) Pull over to the curb. Where do
you think you're goin'?

(CAR HALTING)

84. MAN: (COMING ON) You must be mighty late for that bridge
game.

85. WOMAN: But, officer...I didn't do anything. I can't
imagine why you stopped me!

86. MAN: You weren't doin' anythin'--but 50 miles an hour,
madam--in a 25 mile zone!

87. WOMAN: But, officer, that's ridiculous! Your speedometer
must be wrong.

88. MAN: (SIGHING) Sure and that's a new one, that is. Now
I've heard everything. You tell that one to the
judge, mam--he gets tired, he does, of the same
stories all the time--

89. WOMAN: (PROTESTING) But, officer--!

(MUSIC: BRIDGE)

(GAVEL--TWO BANGS)

90. MAN: (JUDGE) Next case--Mrs. Peyton Smith. Charge,
speeding, Main Street off Taylor Avenue.

91. WOMAN: Your Honor...it's all a mistake.

92. MAN: (BORED) Do you plead guilty or not guilty, Mrs.
Smith?

93. WOMAN: Not guilty, of course!

94. MAN: The officer's report says you were going fifty miles
an hour in a twenty...

95. WOMAN: (INTERRUPTING) But I couldn't have been doing that,
Your Honor! I never speed. I must ask you to take
my word as the wife of a leading citizen of this
community. I'm a great believer in respecting
traffic laws. I never go beyond the speed that's
posted. I've driven down Taylor Street a million
times and turned on to Main and never been stopped
before!

96. MAN: Down Taylor Street, Mrs. Smith?

97. WOMAN: That's right--time and time again!

98. MAN: You're fined 10 dollars for speeding...and ten
dollars for wrong-way driving!

99. WOMAN: But, Your Honor!

100. MAN: Taylor Street, Mrs. Smith, which you've driven <u>down</u> a million times, is a one-way street--<u>going up!</u>

(BELL)

101. NARR: Alas, poor Mrs. Peyton Smith. She should have read Aesop's "The Mole and Her Mother," and been fore-warned...

(MUSIC: SNEAK UNDER)

It seems that once a young mole cried out to her mother: "Mother---I can see!" To try her, the mother found an onion and held it before the young mole's face. "What is it, my child?" she asked. "A stone," cried the young one eagerly "...a stone!" "Alas, my poor child," said the mole, "Not only are you blind, but you cannot even smell!" --Remember, then--

(MUSIC: STOPS)

(ECHO)

Brag, and you betray yourself.

(MUSIC: UP AND OUT)

102. NARR: Now we give you two lovers--who are able to keep in touch with each other only through the grace of a certain A. G. Bell...

(TELEPHONE RINGING, RECEIVER PICK-UP)

103. WOMAN: Hello?

104. MAN: (FILTER, THROUGHOUT) Oh hello, honey.

105. WOMAN: (THRILLED, BUT CAUTIOUS) Oh, it's you. (CHANGE, AS SHE'S IN EARSHOT OF HER FATHER) I'm sorry you troubled to call, Mildred, I won't be available this evening.

106. MAN: (DEFIANTLY) Won't be available? Why not?

107. WOMAN: Well, Dad thinks I'd better stay in and hit the hay early.

108. MAN: You mean your father's home and hears what you're saying?

109. WOMAN: Yes.

110. MAN: But I've got to see you, Betty...I haven't seen you for two whole days!

111. WOMAN: Er..aha...I know it is, Mildred. I feel the same way.

112. MAN: Isn't the old bozo going out this evening?

113. WOMAN: Well...Dad is going out in a litle while to the club meeting...but I've promised to stay home tonight and get some badly needed rest.

114. MAN: What time is the meeting?...

115. WOMAN: Yes, I saw the gang at nine o'clock. They're all
     carrying on pretty much the same way--nothing new.

116. MAN: You mean he's driving?

117. WOMAN: Yes.

118. MAN: Well, I'll be parked around the corner, out of
     sight. When I see him go by I'll drive around and
     come on up.

119. WOMAN: So you're going to buy a new dress! Well, I'd be
     real careful if I were you. I always preferred a
     real dark color for evening...

120. MAN: Don't worry...I'll pick out a dark spot where he
     won't see me.

121. WOMAN: Goodbye, Mildred. I'm glad you called. I can't
     wait to see how you look--

122. MAN: And me, to see you, honey. Gosh, it'll be like
     heaven again. See you soon.

     (MUSIC: BRIDGE)

123. MAN: Darling!

124. WOMAN: Oh, Wilbur! You had me so worried. I was sure
     you'd bump into him!

125. MAN: Missed him by a mile. I'm too smart for him!--How
     about a kiss?

126. WOMAN: (GIGGLES) (STOPS)

127. MAN: (PAUSE) Darling. Gosh, I don't see how I can live
     another day without you!

128. WOMAN: Sweetheart!

     (OFF, DOOR OPENING AND SLAMMING)

129. MAN: (QUICKLY) Who's that--

130. WOMAN: I don't know unless--he forgot something and--
     (STOPS THEN, AS IF HE'S JUST COME IN THE ROOM) Dad!

131. MAN: (AN ESCAPING WORRIED SIGH) Oh me!

     (BELL)

132. NARR: No, the fabulous Aesop didn't forget advice for you
     lovelorn, either. He made up a fable especially for
     people in your predicament called--"The Lion in
     Love"...listen--

     (MUSIC: SNEAKS UNDER)

     A lion once fell in love with a woodcutter's daugh-
     ter, and went to the father to ask for his
     daughter's hand in marriage. The woodcutter did not
     care for the match, but he was afraid to decline the
     ferocious King of the Beasts. So he said to the
     lion, "Very well, I give you my consent. But, good
     lion, my daughter would not like your sharp claws
     and big teeth. She'd be frightened of you. Why
     not have your claws and teeth removed and come back
     tomorrow. Then the wedding can take place." So

enamoured of the daughter was the lion that he went
at once to rid himself of his teeth and claws.
When he returned, there was the woodcutter awaiting
him with a club. And since the lion could no longer
defend himself, he was driven away!--Heed this
moral, lovers all--

(MUSIC: STOP)

(ECHO)

Beware lest the eagerness of love bring your undoing!

(MUSIC: UP AND OUT)

133. NARR: That makes six down and I haven't failed yet to
              match an Aesop fable--containing a practical message
              --to every scene!--But let's see what we have next,
              here...

                  (TYPEWRITER UNDER)

134. WOMAN: (BEFUDDLED SECRETARY) Dear Mama: Just thought I'd
              take my typewriter in hand and let you know how I'm
              doing on my new job. Up until yesterday, I liked
              working for Wheeler, Webster and Wiggin. But yes-
              terday--Jeepers--everything seemed to go wrong.
              First it was Mr. Wheeler. He decided that from now
              on I was to type all office memorandum in small
              type. Said it saved paper and paper was scarce.
              But when I sent the first memorandum through that
              way, Mr. Webster--he's the second partner--came
              out fit to be tied! He said what did I think his
              eyes were--magnifying glasses? He said he couldn't
              read the small type. I told him Mr. Wheeler told
              me to use the small type, but he said he didn't care
              what Mr. Wheeler told me, I was to type things so's
              people read them. So I started to use the large
              type again when what should happen but out should
              come Mr. Wiggin--he's the third partner. He said
              that his secretary and I were to switch typewriters.
              Hers was too noisy, he said, and it disturbed him
              and mine was a noiseless. Then Mr. Wiggin gave me
              her typewriter, which--as you can see from this
              letter--has medium type!

              Now if I send office memorandums through on medium
              type, why Mr. Wheeler will say it's too big, Mr.
              Webster will say it's too little, and only heaven
              knows what Mr. Wiggin will say!--Mama, what should
              I do?

                  (BELL)

135. NARR: (WITH A LAUGH) Do? Why open a book of Aesop's
              fables, of course, and read the story of "The Man
              and His Two Wives."--Don't you know it?

              (MUSIC: SNEAKS UNDER)

              Back in olden days, when men had more than one wife,
              there was a middle-aged man who had two. One wife

was old and the other was young. Each of them loved him a great deal, and wanted him to appear as each desired him. His young wife did not like to see his hair turning grey. So every night, as she combed his hair, she plucked out the grey ones. The elder wife was grey herself. So every night she combed his hair she plucked out all the black hairs she could find. This went on and on until the man, who tried to be pleasing to both wives, found himself completely bald!--Which is to say--

(MUSIC: STOPS)

(ECHO)

Try to satisfy everyone and you'll satisfy no one.

(MUSIC: UP AND OUT)

136. NARR: We have time for just a few more.--We let you listen, next, to a telephone conversation...

(PHONE RINGING; RECEIVER PICK-UP)

137. MAN: (PLEASANT, UNCONCERNED TYPE) Hello.

138. WOMAN: (FILTER THROUGHOUT...UPSET AND DETERMINED) Mr. O'Hare?

139. MAN: Yes, this is Mr. O'Hare.

140. WOMAN: I'm Mrs. Lawson...a couple of blocks up the street.

141. MAN: Oh yes, Mrs. Lawson...

142. WOMAN: I'm calling to complain about your son, John.

143. MAN: Oh yes? What's Johnny been doin'?

144. WOMAN: He's been constantly annoying my Albert, that's what he's been doing. This morning he actually whipped my Albert because Albert said his catcher's mitt was better than Johnny's pitcher's glove.

145. MAN: (BELITTLING) Well...

146. WOMAN: Apparently, Mr. O'Hare, your son's idea of solving an argument is to whip anybody who disagrees with him!

147. MAN: Well I'm sure that--

148. WOMAN: And another thing--

149. MAN: Yes.

150. WOMAN: Yesterday, Albert lost his baseball and your Johnny found it and absolutely refused to return it, claiming it was his. Now that's downright stealing, Mr. O'Hare, and I think--

151. MAN: (LAUGHING IT OFF) Oh come, come, now, Mrs. Lawson. You're letting yourself get too excited. Boys will be boys, you know.

152. WOMAN: I think it's a far more important matter than just "boys will be boys", Mr. O'Hare! Bullying and stealing are not my idea of--

153. MAN: (BORED, CUTTING IN) Well, I'll speak to him about it, Mrs. Lawson--

154. WOMAN: I should think that's the <u>least</u> thing you'd do. I should think you'd be interested in seeing that--

155. MAN: (CUTTING HER SHORT) Thank you very much, Mrs. Lawson. Goodbye.

    (CRADLING PHONE)

(SIGHS WEARILY) Women! Cackle, cackle, cackle just like hens! Probably nothing but a chronic complainer...

    (BELL)

156. NARR: So Mr. O'Hare does nothing about Johnny's youthful transgressions. Oh, if he'd only known Aesop's story of "The Thief and His Mother".

(MUSIC: SNEAK UNDER)

There was once a young man who was caught stealing. Upon being condemned to death, he asked if he couldn't see his mother. His wish was granted and they brought his old mother to him. He leaned over his mother, as if to whisper in her ear. Suddenly, instead of whispering, he almost bit her ear off! The court attendants jumped upon him and pulled him away, horrified at such inhuman conduct. "Why do you bite your own mother!" they cried. "So that she may be punished," he said. When I was a child, I began stealing little things and bringing them home. My mother, instead of punishing me as she should, laughed and said it would not be noticed. It is because my mother did not punish me then that I am condemned to die today!--For...

(MUSIC: STOP)

(ECHO)

Evil should be nipped in the bud.

(MUSIC: UP AND OUT)

157. NARR: We might call the next one a summer scene. Engrossed in the travel section of the Sunday paper, Madam wife looks up to Mr. Husband and exclaims--

158. WOMAN: (THRILLED) Bermuda!...The magic Caribbean! Gentle trade winds...velvet seas!--(EAGERLY) Why can't we go to Bermuda on our vacation?

159. MAN: (IRRITABLE TYPE) Are you insane Gladys?

160. WOMAN: Of course I'm not insane! What's so impossible about going to Bermuda?

161. MAN: (BLUNTLY) The expense.

162. WOMAN: Oh, ridiculous. You know we can afford the trip.

163. MAN: I refuse to concede any such thing.

164. WOMAN: Look, dear. <u>Before</u> the war, we were too busy to go

anywhere...<u>during</u> the war it wasn't patriotic. But now there's no reason on earth why we can't--

165. MAN: (FINISHING IT FOR HER) <u>Stay put</u>.--I can't see any point in going traveling half way around the world just to--

166. WOMAN: But it isn't half way around the world to Bermuda! It's just a few hours by plane, or we can make a cruise in--

167. MAN: (FIRMLY) The answer is no!

168. WOMAN: It would be wonderful for the children--educational and everything and--

169. MAN: My dear. I do not intend to spend my life making money only to squander it on vacation trips.

170. WOMAN: But you've done remarkably well this year--it wouldn't cripple our bank account at all!

171. MAN: We'll go to Oxyboxo lake, like we always do...

172. WOMAN: Flies! Mosquitoes!

173. MAN: We can get a cottage there for next to nothing.

174.. WOMAN: Mud instead of sand!

175. MAN: I can commute to work.

176. WOMAN: The same old faces in the same old places!

177. MAN: (CONCLUDING) We'll <u>save money</u>.

          (BELL)

     (MUSIC: SNEAK UNDER)

178. NARR: There was once a miser, says Aesop, who buried a bag of gold under a tree. Each day he would come and look at it. One day a thief saw the miser dig in the earth, take out his bag of gold, fondle it and put it back again. When the miser had gone, the thief dug up the gold and put in its place a bag of stones. The next day the miser returned and when he saw his bag of gold was gone, and in its place was a bag of stones, he raised such an outcry that all his neighbors came running to him. "My gold is stolen," he cried. "Stolen!" "What did you do with the gold when you had it?" asked one. "Why, I came each day and looked at it," replied the miser. "In that case," said the other, "come each day and look at the bag of stones. It will do you just as much good."--In other words--

     (MUSIC: STOP)

     (ECHO)

     <u>Wealth unused may as well never exist.</u>

     (MUSIC: UP AND OUT)

179. NARR: We have time for just one more, my friends. So far Aesop has taught us--

Kindness brings better results than severity...
Example is the best precept...Appearances are deceptive...Be happy with your lot...Brag and you
betray yourself...Beware lest the eagerness of love
bring your undoing...Try to satisfy everyone, and
you'll satisfy no one...Evil should be nipped in
the bud...Wealth unused may as well never exist.
--Yes, each scene from our present day life has
struck a bell in my mind and I haven't failed yet
to match it with an ancient fable! Now let's see
how I make out on the last one...The scene, a large
hall crowded to the rafters--with an arm-waving
speaker holding forth from the stage--

(CROWD SNEAKS IN ABOVE)

180. MAN: (SLIGHT ECHO--POLITICIAN, SHOUTING) And so I say
to you, my friends...far from finding peace and
justice in the United Nations, we can only find
trouble! Let us, then, sever this artificial connection with foreign nations!...Let us turn to the
solution of our own problems in our own individual
way! Let us show the world that we can get along
without the help of other countries, even if they
cannot! I propose that we devote our total energies not to the United Nations--no no!--but to
one nation--our own--the American nation!

(APPLAUSE)

181. NARR: Oh-oh...That one's got me stumped--no bell!
(WORRIED) Let me see now--surely Aesop couldn't
have failed us on the most important principles in
international life!...What did that speaker say,
now...(MUMBLING) Sever connections with other
nations...go on our own way alone...--(SUDDENLY)
Wait a minute, now, it's coming...it's coming!--

(THE CLANG OF THE BELL...CONTINUING EXCITINGLY
FAR EXCEEDING THE PREVIOUS EFFECTS)

Ah, I knew it...I knew it! I knew Aesop wouldn't
let us down.--(HURRIEDLY) Listen to this...

(MUSIC: SNEAK UNDER)

182. NARR: There was once a father who had a family of sons
who were always quarreling. When his exhortations
failed to stop them, he determined to give them a
practical lesson in the evils of disunion. One
day, he instructed his sons to bring him a bundle
of sticks. When they did so he gave each one in
turn the bundle and told them to break all the
sticks at the same time. Each of his sons tried
with all his strength, but was not able to do so.
Next the father separated the sticks, one by one,
and again put them in their hands. This time each
son broke the sticks with ease.--Then said the
father to his sons..."Remember, my sons--

(MUSIC: STOP)

(ECHO)

In unity, there is strength!"

(MUSIC: UP AND CURTAIN BIG)

183. NARR: To Greece, then, my friends...not only for its
sculpture, architecture, drama and philosophy...but
for the enduring fables of its one-time slave, Aesop
--fables which are packed today with as much significance to the individual, the family, the nation
as ever...fables by which we can help shape our
future--to Greece, "thank you."

(MUSIC: THEME IN AND FADE OUT UNDER)

184. ANNCR: You have just heard the 139th program of HOME IS
WHAT YOU MAKE IT, and the eighth in the summer
series, devoted to contributions of other peoples to
American culture and home-life. The program saluted
Greece and was entitled "Aesop--Fables For Today
and Tomorrow!"--speaking of Aesop, did you know
that in his fable "The Clock and The Dial" he makes
this signicant point--

(MUSIC: STING)

185. AESOP: (ECHO) No person can do without help.

186. ANNCR: That's one reason why HOME IS WHAT YOU MAKE IT has
prepared for its listeners, a handbook on the
Family.

187. NARR: Tell us about it, Ray...

188. ANNCR: It's fifty-six pages long, Ben--and packed with all
sorts of information not readily available to homemakers elsewhere.

189. NARR: For instance?

190. ANNCR: Such information as--What Families Are For...Doing
Things Together...Getting and Spending the Family
Income...Families Alive to Religion.--Copies of this
useful handbook can be secured by simply sending 25
cents--the non-profit price--to NBC, Box 30,
Station J., New York 27, New York. The address
again--for the family handbook, send 25 cents to
NBC, Box 30, Station J., New York 27, New York.
Act now, for again remember what Aesop said--

191. MAN: (ECHO) We often forget what is most useful to us.

(MUSIC: THEME IN AND UNDER)

192. ANNCR: HOME IS WHAT YOU MAKE IT is presented as a Uni-
versity of the Air feature by the National Broad-
casting Company and its affiliated independent
stations--in cooperation with the American Home
Economics Association, the General Federation of
Women's Clubs, the National Congress of Parents and
Teachers and the United Council of Churchwomen.
Your narrator was Ben Grauer. Music was by Jack
Ward. Mitzi Gould and Joe DeSantis were featured.

(MUSIC: UP AND DOWN)

HOME IS WHAT YOU MAKE IT is written by Lou Hazam.
The series is directed by Garnet R. Garrison. Be
sure to listen next week when we will present the
ninth dramatization in the new summer series--
A Salute to Poland, entitled, Paderewski--Pianist
and Patriot.

This is Ray Barret, and
THIS IS THE NATIONAL BROADCASTING COMPANY.

It is apparent from reading the script that flexibility is certainly required of a radio actor. Joe DeSantis and Mitzi Gould played ten different roles. They met the challenge extremely well. Neither dialects nor extreme character types were used.

Scene 1: Speeches 13-25. This scene requires a naturalness which strikes a responsive chord for many parents who have had difficulty in getting children to eat certain foods. The husband starts enthusiastically and dominates the scene, keeping the lead throughout. He has a low threshold of irritability and seeks any path to stop a wife's tears. The wife must convey the relief she feels in transferring to her husband the responsibility for the child which brought her to the breaking point. Both are on-mike at the beginning. Movement is achieved by a fade-off of the man on speech 21, representing a walk to the back door, a fade of 2 or 3 feet, directly on beam. The voice is directed slightly off-beam as he calls. He fades back on at the end of the speech. The same impression of pacing to the door and back comes in speech 23 by fading off and on. The contrast between the "Junior!" and the "By the way . . ." line can be sudden. Emotional outbursts directed toward children are turned on and off with ease by many parents. The tag, speech 25, must carry the punch, the explosive personal reaction to "spinach," then the uncompromising order to the child. The phrase in speech 25 where he sees Junior at the door, "Oh, there you are, Junior," was a write-in during rehearsal to help the picture for the radio audience; it represents a transition from the throw-away line "Open a can of peas or something." The pace is fast, about farce tempo, and the asides from the husband in speeches 21, 23, and 25 can almost be mumbled. The solicitude in speech 15 is a troublesome one for many students who give it as a honeymoon husband or "fraught with emotion." He isn't embracing her—the time does not permit—nor is it a serious line.

Scene 2: Speeches 28-43. This employer is an interesting character because he can be played in so many different ways and still be a petty office tyrant and inhuman boss. There is danger in a too literal interpretation of the directions from the writer, "big blustery type" which might permit the character to become a stereotype caricature. An excellent opportunity for clues to the boss's pettiness and absorption in money is found in word coloring of "office" contrasted to "country club," "twice" and "three times" and repetition of "salary." For a change in pace from the first scene, this scene can be given in a lower-keyed delivery. The boss brushes aside the girl's attempts to speak in speeches 33-41. He is not actually emotionally disturbed by his employees in the final speech, and is just thinking aloud as he dismisses the girl. The girl as the secretary can use a straight delivery, reflecting the neutral detachment of secretaries.

The filter changes the characteristics of the voice in several different ways. Some people have trouble talking on filter. A slightly slower pace is recommended without much pitch variation. Work about 2 or 3 inches from the filter and use less projection. The stenographer has a pleasant young manner, with butterflies in the stomach, revealed so well in radio by slightly vocalized nuances and breathiness. When the girl finally gets an opportunity to explain, she is hesitant at first to reveal the personal aspects, but overcomes the reluctance and rushes through the exposition, expecting to be stopped at any moment. A recommended mike position for the girl is in close, in order to permit a breathy pick-up.

Scene 3: Speeches 45-67. The effectiveness of this scene depends upon the credibility of the man. He's not a wolf, but a good hearted "big brother" type. The woman is gracious and normal and avoids any tip-off as to her real character as she proceeds, but has a slight glibness and smoothness that the audience can recall afterwards and say, "I felt there was something fishy about her." The visualization of action here can be aided by the actor's physical movement as the man gets out of the car in speech 48. Indicate some effort of opening the door and changing from a sitting position to a standing position. Speech 52, where he looks at the tire, can be given some perspective by changing the head position, a slight fade combined with moving the head as he talks.

A general rule for all actors to follow is: *Move as you talk*—not between phrases. "Effort" was written in at speech 58 to suggest the man's action of taking off his coat and vest. Most actors find it desirable to do the indicated action in pantomime. Physically jogging up and down in front of the mike, for instance, heels hitting solidly—helps to complete the picture of "man on horse" when the movement is accompanied by sound effects. It is a little incongruous, to have a smooth-flowing delivery in such instances.

The fade in speech 58 before the music bridge may be taken by the engineer in the control room (*a board fade*) or may be taken by the actor (*a physical fade*). Don't leave the end of the speech up in the air. Complete such phrases. It is distracting to hear an actor stop in the middle of the line as sometimes happens. Such cessation of utterance spotlights the mechanics and destroys the illusion of reality. Effort in speech 59 and again in 61 help the picture. The same for the woman in 62 as she gets into the car and hands the man his coat and vest. The monologue in speech 67 must be very intimate, almost stream-of-consciousness, the actor moving in on mike slightly and physically following the action for correct timing of the sound-effects direction, "patting pockets." The final blackout line, "My wallet" should contain, along with the blackout tag, a sudden realization of what an easy mark he had been.

Scene 4: Speeches 70-79. This is strictly for fun. The nightclub show girl can be a tall, languid, "beautiful-but-dumb" type, with a narrow pitch range and husky delivery, possessing a rhythm suggestive in itself of the show girl's glide. Don't worry about articulation, the jaws can be almost immovable throughout the entire scene. An organist can match and cover the actor's melody and pitch, otherwise a board or physical fade is used. In contrast to the singer, the man can be the loud pink-shirt, cigar-in-corner-of-mouth type, with staccato delivery. He is a realist, a dealer in contrived sensuality.

Scene 5: Speeches 82-100. Mrs. Peyton Smith is the overprecise social leader with a contempt for those not in the Social Register. If played too broadly, the role loses its effectiveness. The lady is not a Bob Hope comedy stooge. The policeman may be played with a touch of Irish brogue, but inasmuch as there are so many of this type on the radio, a straight approach is recommended. The authority and assurance of "a policeman on a motor-cycle" can be revealed both in general attitude, and more specifically, on the speech 84 fade-in, and in speech 86 where he suggests by voice the stiff-legged police walk, modeled in swagger after its prototype, the "cow-boy-on-the-range" walk—even to the hoist of the gun belt by the policeman in speech 88. The sound perspective in the opening of the scene, the woman in the car and the policeman coming up alongside, is aided by the call by the policeman, speech 83, which begins far off-mike and comes to full volume by the end of the speech. The judge may be played in a number of ways. He is a small town judge, but not a "hick." Working close to mike should help to create the picture of the judge in the foreground, with Mrs. Smith a few feet away. That distance permits Mrs. Smith to speak up more and it heightens the contrast between the two characters. The judge says his lines in a semi-sing-song, routine traffic-case flavor, except for the slight rising climax at the close.

Scene 6: Speeches 103-131. This phone call is given a setting through the explanatory dialogue. In rehearsal, the picture of the girl pretending to talk to a girl friend while her father was overhearing the conversation, was not quite clear enough until speech 108 was written in, "and hears what you're saying?" This scene provides good exercise in interpretation and the high-lighting of key words and phrases which carry meaning to the young lover, such as "Dad thinks" in speech 107, "nine o'clock" and "nothing new" in speech 115, "real careful" and "dark color" in speech 119.

A special note about phone conversations. In order to distinguish a telephone call on the air, actors copy the habit of many people by using a slightly higher pitch and more projection. It is helpful for the actor to listen to people for similar guides in other situations.

Another common habit is to increase volume while talking to people who are quite old. Without costume and make-up, old age is difficult to suggest by voice alone. Accordingly, if the actor playing opposite slightly increases his volume and enunciates more carefully, the listener will accept the old age characterization more easily.

This side issue of age characterization on the radio is appropriate during a discussion of this scene because of the youth of the characters. The suggestion of adolescence, as portrayed by voice, is intensified by remembering that speech involves the entire body. It is difficult for actors in a slouched position to portray the bodily rhythms of adolescence and youthful enthusiasm and energies. The actor on stage would be assisted by adolescent movements. Without moving away from the microphone, the radio actor may stand on his toes and use spasmodic shallow breathing. An acute sensitivity to different vocal rhythms for different ages is important to the radio actor. This section of the script must be played with extreme changes of pitch. The foibles of adolescence must not be satirized; they must be played with understanding.

Scene 7: Speech 134. This monologue should not be dragged out. The actress should match the typing rhythm at the opening to suggest the scene, but she should not continue this rhythm for more than a few lines. A segue should lead her into the breezy and conversational style of a girl who can really talk one's head off with her problems. If the actress uses hand gestures, the listener can imagine their effusiveness. Minimizing some of the lines—throwing them away—and spotlighting the significant parallel portions is essential for good pacing. Watch out for the tag. It should not be "milked."

Scene 8: Speeches 137-155. This is a tricky one in that the actors must be careful not to slant it too much in favor of Mr. O'Hare at the sacrifice of the message. The scene is a natural one, and we do have a touch of sympathy for the man. However, when the narrator points out the moral, we should be able to look back in memory, and feel a sharp prick of conscience because we didn't realize the justice of the complaint. The woman must be fast-talking without being too nasty. Overlapping of speeches is used from 150 on to build the climax. It is at 153 where he changes from indifference to bored irritation. Overlapping of speeches should not be used too frequently in radio because of the audience's inability to focus attention on one of two simultaneous speeches presented at the same volume. The actor learns in radio to fade the words quickly after the other actor cuts in. It is not an abrupt stop but a fast withdrawal from the radio spotlight.

Scene 9: Speeches 157-177. Stage business with the newspaper would help this scene in the movies, stage, and television. It would be apparent that Gladys is reading the travel ad half to herself and half to her husband. A close pick-up and almost lazy enunciation helps this impression in radio. Without any cues in the script, it might be helpful for an actor to think of the man here as a trifle on the fat side, with an affinity for the easy chair and slippers. We must feel sorry for the wife, who has to live with a man as superior and overbearing as an old lord of the manor. The timing of the lines in which he enumerates the qualities of Oxyboxo lake and brushes aside her interjection without listening to her point of view is very revealing character portrayal. This is the reverse of the usual suggestion for creating naturalness in dialogue by listening to the speech before yours and letting the audience feel that your response is a reaction to what was said. The woman must not appear very strong-willed in this scene. If Gladys works slightly off mike, the dominance-submissiveness relationship is emphasized.

Scene 10: Speech 180. The actor should remember his "favorite" dema-gogue and let go with both barrels. He shouldn't be all sound and fury, but he should have an insidious persuasiveness which would attract followers if it were not for a touch of the charlatan which the actor introduces by over-using word color. The actor can work a good distance away from the micro-phone here. The echo chamber alone won't create the impression of a hall. The actor's projection is also needed.

• TELEVISION ACTING •

A few generalizations should be borne in mind as students begin prac-tice and work in television acting:

1. The television actor should be quick in memorizing his role. The brief time available for rehearsals does not allow the cast much time to learn lines. One director of an hour dramatic series requested that his actors have their lines completely memorized by the second rehearsal, forty-eight hours after the first meeting of the cast. A background in stock company acting is valuable because of the experience one gains in quick study. It is generally advisable to memorize words and action simultaneously.

2. Never look directly at the camera lens unless specifically directed to do so. This is completely opposite to the style used by announcers and speakers.

3. Don't drop out of character at any time during scenes, even when off-camera, or at the tag of a scene, until released by the stage manager. Some-thing may go awry with the cameras, and instead of close-ups or medium shots which exclude you, you may be in the scene. Staying in character also helps other actors playing opposite you by giving them some degree of inter-action and response. A "freeze" at the end of a scene is difficult to do and yet stay in character. However, the director may have difficulty in lining up the next shot and may have to keep the cameras on you. It may seem ages to the actor who is on camera before he is released by the stage manager. He should not break the freeze until he receives a signal.

4. Learn to take cues from the stage manager without looking directly at him. It is distracting to have a scene appear on the air and catch the actor just standing motionless, staring in a fixed direction, then spring into action.

Directors should issue cues for action before the camera takes, but often they cannot. Actors should be in character and whenever possible be engaged in some movement suitable to the character and situation slightly ahead of the camera take.

5. Actors should become proficient in "hitting the mark." Chalk marks on the studio floor are used to guide the actor to where he is to stand for certain effects. The director may want a small light spot beamed up from a floor stand to illuminate the actor's eyes, or a tight over-the-shoulder shot may have been plotted. Just the slightest error in position by the actor may spoil the effect. If marks are not used the actor may be told where to stand in reference to properties or furniture. Freedom of movement is not one of the television actor's prerogatives. It takes considerable practice to learn how to attend to hitting the mark while performing on camera without revealing the techniques to the audience.

6. Television is a close-up medium. Actors should work for mobile facial expressions. The camera is frequently focused on faces of actors who are not speaking, but are listening and reacting. Television, like film, emphasizes the effects of speech and action upon others in the scene. An impassive "dead-pan" look conveys to an audience little of the thoughts and emotions that should be mirrored on the face. *A note of warning:* do not make the error of gross facial movements or "mugging" which irritate and distract when seen in close-up. The intimacy of the medium calls for naturalness in bodily action. What appears as natural to the television viewer, however, may have come about as the result of long arduous practice by actors. Gestures must not be aimless or unrestrained. An arm extended towards the camera may be distorted out of correct proportions if the scene is being shot on a 35 mm. wide-angle lens. A close-up of a handclasp may be blurred if performed in a vigorous up-and-down hand-pumping manner. Shifting of weight from foot to foot can be distracting in a tight waist (from the waist up) shot because the actor may appear to weave from right to left of the screen. Working with other actors while standing or sitting only inches apart is difficult for some to learn. Scenes which are played "nose to nose" in the studio may be strangely uncomfortable to the actors but appear "natural" when viewed on the small television screen.

7. Actors should become proficient at pantomime. Often a narrator describes the setting or action while actors are performing in pantomime. Prerecording thoughts is a technique frequently utilized. The actor is seen without lip action while the recording of his thoughts is being played. A loud speaker in the studio permits the actor to hear the recording. If the camera is on a close-up, resorting to extremes of facial expressions in an attempt to reflect the emotional undercurrents or "inner speech" may distract the viewers. An impassive, "poker face" may be almost as bad.

8. The audio side of television cannot be ignored. It is true that, in contrast to radio, where the actors move to and from the microphone, in

television the microphone follows the actor. However, TV actors also must be aware of microphone pick-up patterns. An actor who moves from one portion of the set to another may have to time his delivery so that he does not speak while he is crossing an area not covered by a boom microphone. In studios where only one boom microphone is available, actors may have to make adjustments. For example, if the microphone is covering a conversation between one actor on the set at camera right and another across the set on the left, each must project more than if the same conversation was taking place with both seated together on a couch. It may be advisable for actors not to speak when turned away from the beam. Sometimes an actor may have to engage in "stage business" to invest a pause with significance and meaning—the pause being necessary to permit the microphone to be swung around into position for the next speech.

9. Actors should be prepared to begin or end a scene alone. Scenes may have to start or conclude with a character supposedly talking to another person in the scene when actually the second character is not physically present. He may be moving to or from another set or making a fast costume change. The audience must not be aware that this is the case. Camera shots exclude the missing actor. It takes considerable poise to talk in convincing manner to some one who isn't there.

10. The actor must act, and act well, even though he may conclude that he is only a piece of machinery at the mercy of technicians. He is pushed here, then there, started and stopped by the wave of a stage manager's hand, huge cameras are pointed at him, lights shine in his eyes, microphones weave in and out and up and down, just above his head, scenery and costumes are changed all around him—and all this without a live audience to listen to him, to give him "feed-back," to respond to his acting! Actress Judith Evelyn made an observation sometime ago which is still applicable. She felt the restrictions upon the player are

> out of all proportion to reason. . . . It is a nerve-wracking ordeal, for example, to be playing a violent love scene with one's brain, voice and body, and at the same time having to keep one eye in constant vigil to see which camera is taking the picture at which particular point.

Advantages may result from the hectic atmosphere, however, if one agrees with the conclusions reached by another actress, Maria Riva:

> The more obstacles you have the more you work to overcome them. Under stress and strain, you get added vitality. Television teaches you to capsule things, to think, to be on your toes. . . . Television is the finest training today that an actor can get.

EXAMPLE OF TV ACTING SCRIPT

"Philco Television Playhouse"—"Marcia Akers" [2]
by William Kendall Clarke

These opening scenes call for intensity of attack in the dialogue by Jake and Patty, cool sophistication by Marcia, and quick establishment of definite attitudes and characterizations by the townspeople in the town clerk's office.

FADE IN:

<u>CLOSE UP</u> OF GIRL'S LEGS, CROSSED, SILK-CLAD, THE EPITOME OF SVELTE ELEGANCE. SHOES ARE FRENCH-HEELED, ULTRA-FASHIONABLE. ONE LEG MOVES INDOLENTLY, BACK AND FORTH. A LAZILY RELAXED MOTION IN SHARP CONTRAST TO ANGER OF VOICES HEARD OFF. HOLD THIS SHOT FOR:

         JAKE (OFF)
So six years ago she lights outta this town like it was poison - today she comes back like it was honey - okay, so she's back - why must she move in here?

         PATTY (OFF)
Because she belongs here!

         JAKE (OFF)
Like ketchup belongs on ice cream, she belongs here. How come she can't go to a hotel? How come?

CAMERA MOVES UNHURRIEDLY UPWARD, PAST VARIOUS DETAILS OF THE WELL-DRESSED YOUNG LADY, TO REACH FACE OF MARCIA AKERS - WHO LISTENS WITH DETACHED AMUSEMENT, SUPERIOR INDIFFERENCE, TO HEAT OF ARGUMENT WHICH CONTINUES DURING CAMERA'S SURVEY.

         PATTY (OFF)
Jake, she's my sister --!

         JAKE (OFF)
I'm your husband. Your husband don't want your sister moving in here, Patty.

         PATTY (OFF)
Oh, really! -- Marcia, darling, don't pay any attention to Jake --

CAMERA HAS NOW REACHED MARCIA'S FACE. HER HEAD TURNS POLITELY AS JAKE ROARS AN ANSWER TO THIS. SHE FOLLOWS THIS VERBAL EX-CHANGE LIKE A SPECTATOR AT A TENNIS MATCH.

         JAKE (OFF)
She better pay attention to Jake! .. Listen - we got one room, one bedroom, here. This is a dump -- you don't want to stay here. They redecorated the hotel three years ago - it's real comfortable ...

         PATTY (OFF)
You might think of me - what I'd like --

[2] Courtesy of the author, William Kendall Clarke.

           JAKE (OFF)
I'm thinking of us! She's no good for you and me, Patty.
Trouble, plus -- that's Marcia ..

           PATTY (OFF)
Oh, golly! - Marcia, I'm so sorry you had to listen to this ...
AS MARCIA SMILES, ENTIRELY UNTOUCHED BY JAKE'S ACRIMONY OR
PATTY'S EMBARRASSMENT,
                          CUT TO:
CLOSE UP OF PATTY, AS SHE TURNS ON JAKE.

           PATTY
... but you'd better understand that my sister stays right here,
if she wants to, as long as we've got one bedroom! - whether you
like it or not, Jake Callahan!

THE VIOLENCE OF HER OWN WORDS DISMAYS HER. SHE BITES HER LIP,
BUT THEY'VE ALREADY BEEN SAID - AND AS HER REACTION REGISTERS,
                          CUT TO:
CLOSE UP OF JAKE. HIS ARM IS RAISED IN A SHOULDER-BRACE-CAST.
HE, TOO, IS DISMAYED BY PATTY'S OUTBURST, BUT HE RECOVERS AND
FACES MARCIA, TIGHT-LIPPED.

           JAKE
There's nothing in this town to interest you. Why'd you come
back?
                     CUT TO:
FULL SHOT CALLAHAN APARTMENT. MARCIA UNCROSSES HER LEGS,
SMOOTHS DRESS, MEETS JAKE'S GLARE WITH BLANDNESS.

           MARCIA
I was born in Newbury - remember, Jake, dear? Marcia's a Newbury
girl. After six years in the big city, I'm tired.

A GLINT OF STEEL SHOWS THROUGH HER POISE

I wanted to come home. It's that simple.

           JAKE
Nothing's that simple, with you.
HE LOOKS HER OVER, DELIBERATELY.
Looks like you did okay for yourself in the big city.

MARCIA SMILES

           MARCIA
We both knew I would, didn't we?

           JAKE
Yes, sir, a real big time success.

           PATTY
You do look just wonderful, Marcia!

           JAKE
How'd a small town girl manage that? -exactly?

           MARCIA
The way anyone manages success -- know what you want and work
hard to get it.

           JAKE
Work hard? - you?

           PATTY
Now stop it. Jake!

THEN, PLEADING, HER HAND GENTLY ON HIS

Please, darling?

HE FROWNS AT HER, NOT WANTING TO BE WON OVER. WITH HER HAND
STILL ON HIS, SHE SPEAKS TO MARCIA.

Jake hasn't worked for three months. He's not getting compensation --

JAKE JERKS AWAY FROM HER

-- he's worried -- on edge --

          JAKE
That's not her business.

PATTY IGNORES HIM

          PATTY
Marcia, what I mean is - is --

          MARCIA
I know, honey. Poor Jake.

HER LOOK AT HIM IS MOCKING
I'll make allowances. Well ---

SHE RISES
-- now that the welcoming speeches are over, where do I lay my
head?

          PATTY
In here.

SHE PICKS UP SUITCASE, STARTS OFF R.
I'll clean out a couple of bureau drawers so you'll have some
place to put things.

SHE EXITS DOWN R. MARCIA AND JAKE EYE EACH OTHER FOR A MOMENT.
THEN:

          MARCIA
Relax! It won't be for long.

          JAKE
How long?

SHE LAUGHS
          MARCIA
Jake H. Callahan! - 'H' for hospitality!

SHE STARTS FOR BEDROOM

          JAKE
The town won't take you back so easy.

SHE BRUSHES PAST HIM WITHOUT ANSWERING. AT BEDROOM DOOR SHE
TURNS BACK.

          MARCIA
The town'll open its arms to little Marcia -- wide!

          JAKE
I want to see that.

          MARCIA
You will, Jake, dear. Make book on it - you will.
SHE GOES INTO BEDROOM AS JAKE STARES AFTER HER, ANGRY, APPRE-
HENSIVE.

DISSOLVE TO:

CLOSE UP OF DOOR, LETTERED "TOWN CLERK." IT OPENS, AND WE SEE
OFFICE AS CAMERA MOVES IN WITH MRS. WYMAN: SHE HEADS FOR COUNTER,
AND WE PASS REVEREND WITHERS, ALREADY DOING BUSINESS WITH A YOUNG
MAN ASSISTANT AT COUNTER. SEEING MRS. WYMAN, A MIDDLE-AGED
WOMAN ASSISTANT LEAVES HER DESK AND COMES UP TO COUNTER - CAMERA
MOVES ON PAST THEM TO END OF COUNTER, L., AND AMOS DRAKE, A
HOUND DOG, AND A YOUNG WOMAN ASSISTANT, WHO IS BEHIND COUNTER.

>   AMOS
Tax on this, tax on that - up and up and up ...

>   YOUNG WOMAN
Dog licenses haven't gone up in price, Mr. Drake.

>   AMOS
They're two dollars.

>   YOUNG WOMAN
That's what I mean. Last year --

>   AMOS
Ten years ago they was one dollar.

>   YOUNG WOMAN
Well, I wouldn't know about --

>   AMOS
Twenty years ago, wasn't no fancy-dancy dog tags in Newbury
County a-tall!

HE GROPES IN POCKET FOR MONEY

Next thing, they'll be taxin' the taxes ...

CAMERA MOVES PAST THEM, PASSING UPON MRS. WYMAN AND WOMAN

>   MRS. WYMAN
I never knew I paid a traffic fine here.

>   WOMAN
When you plead guilty, it saves the fuss of going to court.
SHE BRINGS UP RECEIPT PAD.

>   MRS. WYMAN
Well, I did park beside that fireplug - but I'm not guilty!
Lands! What I did, I told Amy -that's my daughter, Amy ---
CAMERA STARTS TO MOVE PAST THEM
-- I told her I'd pick her up at Gordon's Hardware on Main
Street ..

CAMERA PAUSES UPON REVEREND WITHERS AND YOUNG MAN, WHO IS SEARCH-
ING THROUGH A LARGE DUSTY FILE ON COUNTER.

>   YOUNG MAN
Here we are - 'Deeds and Titles' -- 1870-1880 .. When does the
new chapel go up on this property, Reverend?

>   WITHERS
Next Spring - supposing our Building Fund Drive is successful.
DOOR DOWN R OPENS AND MRS. ADAMS ENTERS.
I'm most optimistic about that, by the way.

>   MRS. ADAMS
Good morning, Reverend.

WITHERS TURNS WITH A SMILE

Or is it a good morning?

> WITHERS
> God's sunshine was never more abundant, Mrs. Adams.

> MRS. ADAMS
> I'm that aggravated, I didn't notice the sunshine.

SHE SETS UP HER PIECE OF NEWS

Marcia Akers has come back!

> WITHERS
> Marcia - - - ? Oh? Has she, indeed.

THEY HAVE ATTENTION OF MRS. WYMAN AND THE WOMAN ASSISTANT.

> MRS. ADAMS
> I passed her on the street -- this close! -- and she was brazen
> enough to smile!

> MRS. WYMAN
> 'Morning Hetty. Did I hear you say Marcia Akers --?

> MRS. ADAMS
> Dolly, she's come back!

> YOUNG MAN
> Well, what d'you know!

HE IS GRINNING. OTHERS FROWN UPON HIS REACTION, AND HE COMPOSES
HIMSELF. THE YOUNG WOMAN, EN ROUTE TO CASH BOX, SPEAKS TO WOMAN
ASSISTANT.
> CUT TO:

CLOSE UP YOUNG WOMAN AND WOMAN.

> YOUNG WOMAN
> That old man's Mr. Drake!

> WOMAN
> It is.

> YOUNG WOMAN
> Imagine! - with all his money! - fussing about a two dollar dog
> license!

> WOMAN
> He's not the Mr. Drake. The one with the money is Alden Drake,
> his son.
> CUT TO:

GROUP AS BEFORE, AS YOUNG WOMAN GOES ON TO CASH-BOX AT ONE OF
DESKS.

> MRS. WYMAN
> Why, Hetty? - why do you suppose she's come back?

> MRS. ADAMS
> I don't know. But I for one want no part of her . . .

> WITHERS
> I never knew Marcia well. I've been curious about the resentment
> there seems to be toward her . .

                MRS. ADAMS
Did you ever see that girl inside your church, Reverend?

HE SHAKES HIS HEAD, STARTING TO SPEAK

                WOMAN
Any church! She never went to church.

                WITHERS
That's unfortunate, of course. But it is hardly sufficient
to - - -

                MRS. WYMAN
I say if this town wasn't good enough for her six years ago, it's
too good for her now!

                WOMAN
I agree.

                MRS. ADAMS
Little Miss High and Mighty! she had a trick, you know? - made
you feel like the clothes you were wearing smelled of moth-
balls . .

                WOMAN
I know just what you mean.

                YOUNG MAN
Don't you suppose that was just - - well, just Marcia's way? - -

                MRS. WYMAN
It's the wrong way to get along in this town!

AT END OF COUNTER, AMOS DRAKE IS BEING GIVEN HIS CHANGE AND
LICENSE

Anyhow, it wasn't just that. Not that anything was ever proved,
mind you - - -

                WOMAN
- - but there was talk . .

                MRS. ADAMS
Talk? Half the men in town, mooning about - - and her too good
for any of them!

                WOMAN
Harry Ellis admitted right out he was crazy about her.

                MRS. WYMAN
And his wife not in her grave two years!

CAMERA PULLS BACK SLOWLY FROM GROUP AS AMOS LEAVES COUNTER,
CROSSING R.

                MRS. ADAMS
Well, I'm not one to gossip. Like Dolly said, nobody ever proved
anything against her . . but - - -

CAMERA NOW FOLLOWS AMOS AND HIS DOG TO DOOR. AS HE OPENS IT
AND GLANCES TOWARD GROUP AT COUNTER,
                              CUT TO:
CLOSE UP OF AMOS AND DOG
                AMOS
They're whettin' up the knives, Mister Buchanan. Makes us favor
Marcia Akers, sight unseen, eh? Ssssh! - - -

```
HE OPENS DOOR
-- dassn't say so, here!  You want to get us skinned alive?
HE GOES OUT, AS WE
                    DISSOLVE
```

Projects and Exercises

1. Prepare and present an acting audition for the following:
   - (*a*) University radio station.
   - (*b*) A television audition for a production agency specializing in daytime serials.
   - (*c*) A combination radio and television audition for an advertising agency holding general auditions.
   - (*d*) A television audition for a situation comedy series being held by the package agency in charge of production.

   Class criticism of material selected by the student and the presentation.
2. Divide into groups to prepare and present the scenes from "Aesop's Fables" script.
3. Divide into groups to prepare and present the scenes from the television excerpts.
4. Bring in brief scenes from script collections which may be rehearsed outside of class by each group.
5. Record actual persons of all ages and dialects speaking naturally. Prepare a written transcript and then record the same material as delivered by a class member. Compare the two.
6. Film the face of a classmate as he reacts to some emotional speech presented by a fellow student. Project the film for the class and see if the class can tell which emotion is portrayed on the screen. Project the same footage for different age groups and secure their reactions. Evaluate results.
7. Listen to radio plays and watch acting on TV for class reports and discussion.

❋ 31 ❋

Directing

THE PERSON who takes the script from the writer and actively guides its progress until it has been brought to life through a radio performance or telecast is the director. Sometimes the writer is also the director. The supervisor of a series, a producer, may direct the program in addition to his executive work. This chapter deals with the directorial responsibilities and techniques.

The director must be able to view radio or TV dramas in enlarged detail, as through a microscope, in order to suggest specific recommendations to members of the program company on aspects of their performances; but the director must also see the play as a whole to make qualitative judgments on general aspects of the production.

The director is obliged to supervise many details in putting together a broadcast or telecast. The necessity to decide which details require attention first and which are of lesser importance led one network to give the following dictum to newly-hired directors: "There are *fifty* specific things you need to do before a broadcast, but the rehearsal time allotted makes it possible to do only *twenty-five* out of the fifty. The choice of which twenty-five you do makes the difference between a good showmanlike production and a poor one which may have polish in unimportant details but misses fire."

Experience proves the soundness of this statement. No one can set down ironclad recommendations as to what any individual director should do. In mathematics the figure four is always four, but not so in directing. What works today with one actor, one engineer, one cameraman, one sound technician, may not work tomorrow. The pattern changes with people, script, studio, and time of day. The director should adjust himself to these changes and vary his techniques accordingly.

· RADIO ·

Following is a list of activities the director of a half-hour radio drama may find helpful.

Before Studio Rehearsal.

1. Read the script through without interruption to get an over-all impression of it. First impressions are important to the director because he knows the audience receives nothing but first impressions.

2. Reread the script carefully, observing its details. Determine the general type of treatment it requires; comedy, fantasy, melodrama, and other types directly affect the music, casting, sound effects, and the way the play will be paced. If the script is one of a regular series, examine it to see whether it harmonizes with the others in the series. Estimate the over-all length, by timing several representative pages. Solid narrative passages take much longer to read than short-sentence dialogue. Determine whether rewriting is needed to improve the story, or whether minor adjustments should be made before the script is sent to the typist.

3. Schedule a script conference with the writer, if a meeting can be arranged. Have the writer give you tentative cuts and approve those you have made. Raise any questions you have on character analysis, and check to see if he agrees with your general approach. The writer's views should be given great weight.

4. Send the revised script to the typist. Include revised directions to sound-effects men and actors on perspective changes, such as "off-mike," that you want incorporated in the script. Directions included in the script save precious rehearsal time later. Don't clutter up the script with directions, however. The actors have to be able to find their lines.

5. Schedule a music conference with the organist, composer, or the person who is to obtain the records. Indicate where music is to "Sneak," "Stab," "Fade Out," the length of bridges, the flavor of desired music, and other such details. Welcome suggestions from your musical adviser, but you must make the final decisions.

6. Cast the actors. Do this on the basis of past experience, audition cards, by consulting other directors, or by special voice tests for the program. Be sure to audition on microphone. A large character man may not sound as virile on microphone as he looks on stage.

Decide on the number and type of characters you need, figuring in the doubles. A chart may be helpful for large casts in order to check "doubling possibilities."

Scene	Pages	
1	1-3	Narrator
		Policeman (bit)
		John (Lead) (32)

Scene	Pages	
2	4-6	John
		Clerk (Female—Comic)
3	6-7	Jane (John's wife—lead)
		Susan (Sister 15, bit)

Character juggling now goes on to find the most economical use of actors without limiting their effectiveness. Actor A may be able to double as an old man and a stockbroker, but the two roles may be too close together in the script, whereas Actor B may do the policeman and stockbroker. Unavailability of one actor may cause a reshuffling in your tentative casting before rehearsal.

In addition to suitability for the part, consider the actor's own personality and the balance of his voice with others in the cast. One actor who likes to direct others, or fool around, or thinks he is above direction may destroy the necessary sense of a co-operative "in group" feeling.

7. Order whatever is necessary in manpower and equipment for the program. Reserve the studio, request the engineer for a particular time, sound effects, and such things as filters, echo chambers, platforms, screens, turntables, etc.

8. Schedule a conference with the sound-effects man if anything unusual is required.

First Read Through—Off-Mike. (One hour of a four-and-one-half-hour rehearsal period).

1. Greet the company. Gather round a table, introduce those who are new. Distribute scripts, assign parts, and allow time for the actors to mark their scripts.

2. Briefly explain the treatment you are going to follow in the script, outlining in general terms, describing the characterizations as you see them at this point. Don't be too specific or long-winded. Such comments as "Play the policeman straight," "The clerk is fussy and a little eccentric, likable but comical," "John is a young lawyer with his eye on the Supreme Court— a driver—who worked his way through college," should be sufficient to set the actors on the right track.

3. Have the actors read aloud through the script from beginning to end. Hold a stop watch on the read-through and mark the minutes in the left margin of the script. Allow time for sound and music bridges and program credits. Cue as you have planned for the broadcast. This gives the actors time to establish a habit of waiting for a cue. This seemingly minor point may be very important because in the strain of a performance an actor may jump a cue because he has taken the cue by himself up to dress rehearsal. Running through without any interruptions gives the actor a feeling of the whole, and enables the director to check how the play fits together.

4. Determine whether the script runs overtime. If so, make the cuts you

tentatively marked. The reading rehearsal usually takes less time than the actual performance so you usually can cut with impunity down to 29:30. It is wasteful to rehearse portions you later cut. Don't fool yourself into believing that you can make up time.

5. Correct any characterizations that are completely "off." Approve those that are on the right track. Now that they have read the script, the actors may have questions about their parts. Discuss their roles with them. Don't let the direction get out of your hands, but if suggestions advanced by actors seem to make sense, change your approach. If certain members of the company need stringent correction, try to do this privately without fanfare.

6. Give the company a rehearsal break: "Take Five."

Production Rehearsal on Mike. (Two-and-one-half hours.)

1. Forget timing during this rehearsal unless you have an assistant. Work in the control room.

2. Start at the beginning and continue scene by scene to the end of the script. Sound effects are included and music, too, if an organist or recorded music is being used. Orchestra rehearsal is usually separate and concentrated for budget reasons. In normal practice, rehearsal of the orchestra would come at the end of the production rehearsal period.

3. Work carefully on each scene before going on to the next. This is the creative period. Sound patterns are introduced and integrated with the dialogue. With the sound-effects technicians, try different levels and microphone positions for manual effects. Experiment with different records. Avoid too much sound, however, and bear the selectivity principle in mind. Above all, do not become a director who rehearses for a quarter-hour on one body fall and neglects the interpretation by the actors. Don't be "cue happy" and throw cues for every sound. Retain control of enough cues for adjustments on the air as you may feel necessary. A longer pause may "feel" right to you on the air. If you have control of the cue you can control the pause.

4. Pacing of the whole scene should not be neglected while concentrating on the details. One scene may furnish the necessary balance between scenes of tension and action. One may be the climactic scene for the first half. Establish the tempo for each scene before moving to the next. If you have an assistant, he can compare scene-by-scene timing with first timing.

5. Characterizations should begin to jell now. Before hammering away on individual interpretation, correct the over-all attack. Vary the approach to each actor. One actor may react best to the short, succinct, "More speed here," or "Don't ham this line." Another actor may resent this as a mechanical approach, and want suggestions of another type: "This man is frustrated here. Remember we had a clue in the first scene where . . . See if you can give me a bit more of an inner resentment against the world

which takes the form of irritation with this poor clerk in the department store." One actor may respond best to gentle chiding, another to bluntness. Use whichever attack is needed to build and set the character and interpretation. The director must be a good practical psychologist.

MICROPHONE PLACEMENT FOR TYPICAL DRAMATIC PROGRAM

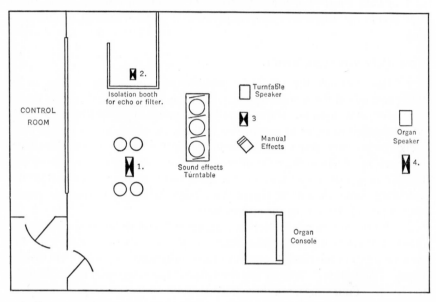

Mike 1, actors; 2, actors on echo or filter; 3, recorded and manual sound effects; 4, organ speaker.

6. Work closely with the engineer during this period. He will be marking his script. Check with him about the levels. Be aware of his problems, don't expect him to be able to use more than two hands in making board fades, bringing in effects, and controlling multiple microphones. The usual number of microphones consists of one cast mike or possibly two, if there are many people on mike at the same time; one sound mike, one filter or echo, and one music mike. Don't have the engineer run the turntables if you are using recorded music, because he won't be able to ride gain well if he does. Be co-operative and respect his advice, but keep the control of the show in your own hands. Weigh seriously the advantages of getting good "presence" out of a close pick-up against working farther away from the mike. The latter does permit less supervision of the VU, but does not carry the impact of the first method. Work with your actors to get intensity without blasting, but don't let them get too far back. A general recommendation has been given for 6 to 12 inches away from velocity mikes for

conversational delivery. In scenes where the actors are shouting or projecting a great deal, move them back. Fades on the beam are recommended
for most scenes. The faster fade-out by going to the dead side of the mike is
disturbing in many sound-perspective sequences. Experiment with relative
placement of actors on-mike. Having both people in a conversation at the
same distance may give a flatness of perspective—move one back a few
inches or to the edge of the beam.

7. "Take Five!" Let it run to 10 or 15 minutes if possible. This break
may divide the rehearsal into two periods. It will be welcomed by everyone.

Dress Rehearsal. (one hour).

1. Run through the complete performance. Place the timings every
thirty seconds in the margin at the right of the script. Some directors prefer
more frequent timings. Unless you have an assistant, thirty seconds is
recommended in order to permit you to listen closely to the program. Individual habits vary, some like to put timing on the exact word in the script,
but markings made to the right of the line are recommended for easy vision.
Use big numerals. Exact time of entrances into bridges and the start of the
following scene should be noted. You may use music bridges as minor
stretch periods for on-the-air adjustments.

2. Jot down reminder notes on performance and production points. Put
these in the left margin. Make them simple and specific enough to jog
your memory in the final discussion before broadcast. Such as: "Hit wrong
word," "Too close," "Watch me for fade," "Tag final speech," "Sound in
too soon," "Four stings, not three."

3. Warn engineer of upcoming fades, sudden sounds, shouts, filter mike,
etc.

4. Listen to the show as a whole with the first-time approach of an
ordinary radio listener.

5. After the run-through, see what time adjustments need to be made.
Many professionals on the actual performance tend to stretch death or
sentimental scenes, so anticipate this and cut enough to compensate. Also
cut enough to give you twenty to thirty seconds to "play with." Many
amateurs tend to pick up speed on the actual broadcast instead of stretching. You won't need to overcut in those instances. Give the cuts to the cast
before any break. Announce the cuts distinctly, and check to see that all—
engineers, musicians, and sound-effect men—in addition to the cast, have
them correctly. Some provisional cuts may be marked for use if needed on
the air.

6. Re-rehearse any difficult scenes, tricky sound synchronization, crowd
backgrounds, etc.

7. Do not change actors' characterizations at this point. You had your
opportunity before.

8. "Take Five!" Relax. Even if you don't feel like it, relax outwardly for the sake of company morale and confidence.

On the Air.

1. Cue clearly as previously rehearsed. Follow the script, looking ahead to warn the engineer and to check that the cast is ready for the next scene.

2. Keep close contact with the members of your cast. Watch them, as well as your script, and encourage and commend them by visible expressions of your interest in their performance. There should be a close bond between cast and director. *Live* the script with the performers, if you can, and react to the presentation. It is not only discourteous, but distracting for a performer on microphone to look into the control room and see a director looking bored or disgruntled, or talking with others in the control room.

3. Be in control of the show. Check the timings as compared to the dress rehearsal. Mark the as-broadcast times on the right margin, crossing out the dress-rehearsal times. Give any necessary signals for stretching or picking up time. Indicate ahead of time, if everything is going along satisfactorily and a provisional cut isn't needed. Or, if required, give signals to the cast to make the provisional cut.

4. Disregard any fluffs made. Don't rebuke a member of the cast from your position of authority in the control room because the entire cast may tense up and more fluffs may occur.

5. Make adjustments in tempo and pacing as you consider necessary. Be sensitive to the empathic responses the home audience may be having. *Listen, feel, and direct the broadcast.*

Following the Program.

1. Thank the cast. Give compliments sincerely when they are deserved. A reassuring smile is in order when the members of the cast have done their best. This is no time for recriminations.

2. Fill out any reports and talent sheets.

3. Leave the show in the studio. Don't brood over the mistakes. Don't direct it again at night before going to sleep. Evaluate your work another day.

• TELEVISION DIRECTING •

The physical location of the director during the rehearsal and actual performance on the air has been described in the chapter on "Technical Aspects of Television." When one is located in the confines of a control room, surrounded by people (engineers, production assistants, associate directors, agency representatives, and observers) and equipment, (camera and film-chain monitors, oscilloscopes, preview monitors, line monitors, switching panel, talk-back microphones, audio panels, loud speakers, amplifiers, power supplies, turntables, etc.) and somewhere "out there" is the studio with more people and more equipment, one realizes the loss in direct personal contact between the director and his company. The director turns to the stage manager to take care of the cueing and signals to cast and production personnel in the studio; he turns to the technical director (TD) to transmit his instructions to the members of the technical team if he isn't permitted by union regulations to do so himself; and turns to his AD for timing cues and reminders of upcoming directorial instructions.

The number of personnel connected with the production increases the responsibility for co-ordination and leadership by the director. Some of t problems that face the motion-picture or stage director are about the same ' television. In the planning of scenery, design of costumes, procurement o properties and furniture, and the like, the routine is similar. The basic and highly important differences, however are (1) the continuality of presentation in live television with its maintenance of a fluid, uninterrupted story, (2) compressed rehearsal period, (3) closeness of contact between cast and home audience, and (4) the 4:3 aspect ratio and small size of the TV screen.

Following is a list of suggested activities for a director of a one-hour drama. It should be stressed that this list is only representative. Budgets and practice differ, resulting in variation in time allotted for rehearsals. Also different directors have evolved alternate sequences and methods.

Before Rehearsal. 1. Study script for theme, content, and first impressions. Keep in mind what is to appear on the screen. Re-read with consideration of the budget and facilities available, size of the studio, number of cameras, number and style of sets, costumes and costume changes, and number and types of actors indicated.

2. Script conference with writer. Discuss possible changes in story line, dialogue, transitions, and tentative cuts. Available facilities at your disposal and live television limitations may necessitate changes. That outdoor scene on a mountain side beside a tiny brook may not be possible. The flashback scene where the mature mother sees herself as a young bride may have to be switched around because of costume and make-up problems for the actress concerned.

3. After editing, send script to typist.

4. Confer with the designer who is to work with you on the staging. You have certain suggestions in mind about the style and number of sets. Perhaps you have sketched out some of your ideas in rough form and indicated how they may be placed in the studio. The designer can approve, modify, and recommend alternate approaches. It is important to arrive at some basic conclusions on the staging as soon as possible. The blocking out of action and planning camera shots cannot be started until you know about the sets. The theme, flavor, and type of play, whether it is a serious story, farce, fantasy, or comedy, affect the staging.

5. Work out with the designer a detailed floor plan and elevations with sets and furniture indicated. This plan may be traced or duplicated and sent to the various departments concerned in the production. Begin to block out action and plan camera shots. Use scale models of furniture and sets or mark down the dimensions on the plan by using a home furnishings template. Plan the shots by using a "shot plotter" (protractor or separate plastic triangle for each lens) which shows the area covered by the various camera lenses according to position and angle of shooting. Do not forget to leave space for microphone dollies and booms. Consider, also, the audio problems when you block out the action.

6. Through the unit manager assigned to the show, order production facilities, engineering and physical needs, such as film clips, rear-screen projection (RP), sound effects, music, and properties. Art work, such as titles, may be ordered. The credits are delayed until the cast is complete. Conferences with specialists may have to be held if the show requirements are out of the ordinary. If the play is to be located on a submarine, which is tossed around by huge waves while going to the rescue of another sub, a considerable number of conferences will have to be held. The music director will have to be consulted early if special music scores are to be composed. On-location film inserts require considerable advance scheduling.

7. Cast the play. Confer with the casting director, if the organization has one. Select a tentative cast, with alternate choices. Conduct audition-reading sessions to decide upon final choices for leads. If you are not familiar with the work of the supporting players you may desire to hear them, too. Issue definite casting calls with an established rehearsal schedule. Selection of the right actor for the right part is not easy. Consider carefully the type of play and the visual requirements. Experience in the medium is important. The compressed rehearsal schedule (20-30 hours in all) and other characteristics of live television mean that when you get into rehearsal and studio production, detail after detail will press in upon you, and you will have little time to work individually with weak actors. Take sufficient time to choose your actors.

8. Now that the cast is selected, confer with the wardrobe department and order costumes. Give the department as much time as you can. Costumes should be in keeping with the period and style of the play. Some costumes are available through regular costume rental firms, others may have to be designed and made, others may have to be refurbished from the stock on hand. Actors may be requested to furnish their own clothing. They then receive a small extra fee.

Off-Camera Rehearsal. 1. FIRST MEETING. Distribute scripts and tell actors which parts they have been assigned. Briefly explain the play and characters. Read through the play, taking a very rough timing, for an estimate of approximate length. It is uneconomical in time and budget to spend much time rehearsing scenes that will have to be cut later. Perhaps a set may not have to be constructed. Obviously this timing should not be considered absolutely accurate. It does provide the director with a guide. Time should be allowed for action which will take place. The rehearsal hall may be marked with masking tape or chalk, simulating entrances, sets, furniture, and large properties. A second reading may take place with the director giving the cast the action which has been blocked out on paper.

2. SECOND MEETING. Lines should be memorized for at least the first of three acts. Rehearse, working on characterization and following the action as blocked. The director has an opportunity to see the results of his planning. A small hand-held optical view-finder, similar in shape to a small flashlight, permits the director to look through it and see a close approximation of the way the TV lens will pick up the scene. The director can move around into different positions comparable to those to be taken by the three or four cameras he may have at his disposal. He is able to view the movement and groupings of the actors and thus evaluate composition. It is appropriate at this point to list a few generalizations about composition which are applicable to television drama direction.

CHECK LIST ON COMPOSITION.

(a) Group the figures into some form or pattern instead of a haphazard arrangement. Stress simplicity of form. The triangle grouping is considered more pleasing than squares, T forms, circles, or rectangles. The triangle may be formed vertically with differences in height and levels, in depth on a horizontal plane at varying distances from the camera, or a combination of both. Attention is usually directed to the apex of the triangle, making that figure dominant.

(b) Avoid formal balance. The key subject should be located above, right or left of center. Objects such as furniture, wall paintings or decorations, or other people may be placed in the other areas of the frame for more pleasing informal balance. Reverse angle- (over-the-shoulder) shots and facial close-ups should be in slight profile. Keep away from camera shots which have a vertical or horizontal line in the background, dividing the picture symmetrically.

(c) Including another person or object in the foreground of a shot tends to give a more interesting perspective, a feeling of depth to the scene. Examples of this technique are shots through a door frame, a window, or stairway rails. A camera may be on a close-up of an object in a room as a scene opens, pulling back to reveal actors in the scene but with the object remaining in the foreground for a period of time. Sometimes a shot is taken of subjects through openings framed by arms or legs of other characters. A full-face view of one actor shooting across the face of another actor is quite common.

(d) Shots which have too much empty space on the margins or between figures are dull. Examples of this are when a wide expanse of floor occupies a considerable portion of the bottom of the frame or when two actors are apart on the edges of the screen with a wide gap of blank wall between them. The director must remember also, that the framing of the picture as seen in the view-finder or control-room monitor is not the same as received at home. There may be considerable loss of the transmitted picture, up to one sixth of width or height as viewed on the home TV set. This comes about by some loss in transmission, but more importantly from errors in centering and the adjustment of picture size. Various controls at the back of the set regulate the framing. Often the owner attempts such adjustments during regular broadcast hours when no test pattern is being transmitted. When directors place key subjects too close to the side margins, not only poor composition may result, but the figures may be completely out of the frame.

(e) The angle of the camera shot affects composition. Looking down tends to weaken the subject, looking up gives the subject more strength and power. Placing people in a shot so that there is difference in height as the camera shoots up slightly to include them, makes the taller people dominant. Sets, properties, or furniture may be handled in the same way. An actor can be reduced to insignificance when placed deep in the set under a high arch as the camera is angled down shooting from a high position. If he is moved closer to the camera so that he appears larger in relationship to the arch which is now behind him, and the camera is moved down so that the angle of shooting is up toward the actor, he will then appear dominant.

(f) Not only the static relationship between people and objects must be considered as in a still photograph or in painting, but also their relationship in motion—the movement of actors within the frame, the movement of cameras (giving the audience the impression of shifting position), or the simultaneous movement of both cameras and actors. Generally speaking, movements across the screen towards or from the camera on straight or diagonal lines are more interesting than horizontal movements across the screen.

(g) Space or mass occupied in the frame affects dominance and audience identification. A long shot of an actor in a scene tends to submerge the individual and to make the audience feel that they are spectators. Closer shots tend to involve the audience into more personal relationship and to highlight the subject of the close-up. When movement is added, such as dollying in from long shots to close-ups, dramatic impact is increased on two counts, the personal involvement of the audience and focus of attention. A dolly back reduces the involvement and diffuses attention. This technique is often applied to "draw the curtain" at the conclusion of a scene. Sudden moves in or out may disturb the orientation of the audience. A shock effect may be produced.

3. THIRD, FOURTH, AND FIFTH MEETINGS. Continue through the script as in the second meeting. Minor script changes may be required now that the

lines are actually being delivered. Writers may be present at these meetings to observe and make the necessary rewrites. Occasionally plot or character flaws are discovered which require major revisions by the writer. It is better to do this than polish the production of a weak script. The story is still the most important single item. By the conclusion of the fifth meeting you should have completed blocking out the entire play. Characterizations should be close to what is desired.

4. SIXTH MEETING. Several complete "dry-runs," going through the play as though on the air, but without equipment. If time and budget permit, request that the stage manager, TD, and lighting director attend. Allowing them to become familiar with the show may save valuable studio rehearsal time. The dry-run permits you to make a more accurate timing check. You may evaluate changes made in blocking and camera shots.

Production Rehearsal in the Studio. The following activities may take place over several days, sometimes in only one—the day of the broadcast.

1. THE DIRECTOR ARRIVES TO INSPECT AND CHECK THE SET. Staging crews, supervised by the scenic designer, have erected the flats, placed large physical properties in position, and distributed small props and wall decorations. The lighting director and his staff are hanging the lights in accordance with the plan previously discussed and approved. Costumes are checked in and placed in the dressing rooms. The engineering personnel begin to assemble and prepare for their part in the rehearsal. The studio is a beehive of activity as the various members of the production team are busy with their specific assignments. The director checks on countless numbers of details, approving changes or modifications in the light of their effect upon planned action and camera shots.

2. A "WALK-THROUGH" REHEARSAL WITH CAST. This is the first time the cast has actually worked with the scenery, furniture, and properties. Some adjustments may be necessary in action or business. The TD, audio engineer, lighting director, and cameramen are present to observe and make any corrections in their planned procedures. The walk-through is a stop-and-start affair. The emphasis is upon the mechanical and technical. The studio floor is marked for actors' positions, location of respective cameras, and microphone boom dollies, and placement of floor lighting units. Chalk of various colors may be used to avoid confusion. Camera shots are numbered in sequence in the script and separate camera run-down sheets are prepared for each cameraman, indicating position and lens for the shots to be taken by that camera. "Kill shot 34" or "Shot 47 is changed from a waist to a shoulder shot" are examples of directions which may be given later to speed up rehearsal and reduce opportunities for error.

3. CAMERA BLOCKING. Different methods are used in conducting the camera rehearsal. Some directors prefer to work a considerable length of time on a small section of a scene, going over it again and again until it is perfected, before moving on. Others work by the "whole" method,

preferring to run through several scenes or an entire act without stopping to make detailed corrections. They would rather "plow through" to give everyone the general feel of the performance. They summarize and correct the errors at the conclusion of each unit. Some of the British directors refer to the first rehearsal periods on camera as the "stagger-through." It is a most descriptive term and has been adopted by some studios. It is in this period that the director displays his creative prowess. He now has an opportunity to appraise the dramatic and artistic quality of the camera shots as he views them on the control-room monitors. He observes the lighting to see if it is adjusted correctly to the composition, harmonizes with the mood, and permits clarity of vision. He evaluates the camera cuts he has planned. He judges the appropriateness of the music played behind scenes and during transitions and the sound effects chosen by the sound technicians. He issues the commands required to lead and co-ordinate the efforts of the entire technical crew and cast to create an "illusion of reality" for the home viewer. He must know when to seek advice from the many specialists gathered together in the studio, since he cannot be an expert in all fields. He must be decisive in his directions in the control room and over the PL (Private Line) without resorting to strident demands or shouting. He must be flexible and alert, sensing when he must vary his methods—remembering constantly that he is working with people and not with machines.

4. CAMERA CHECKS OF MAKE-UP AND COSTUME. Practice costume changes which must take place within seconds. Repositioning of lights as required. Adjustments by staging or technical crews as needed. Comments to the cast on characterizations, meaning, and pace.

5. PREDRESS RUN-THROUGH. Cast in costume, and complete run-through on camera with as few stops as possible. Polish rough spots which have been revealed by the run-through. This step may not be included in some series because of budget restrictions.

6. DRESS REHEARSAL. This is a complete performance without interruptions. Secure an exact timing. Final instructions are now given to cast and crew. Try to avoid making any major changes or adjustments at this point. In giving the necessary cuts for timing, make certain that everyone concerned has them corrected in their scripts and camera run-down sheets. The actors may be requested to "talk through" the cuts. Give at least an hour for relaxation and last minute costume and make-up retouching before the performance.

On the Air. From the opening camera calls to final release of studio channel, the director must watch his script, the camera-control monitors, the preview and line monitors. The allocation of responsibilities for giving on-the-air cues differs from studio to studio. The TD may handle camera directions and instructions to film projection, the lighting director may signal for the light changes, and the audio engineer may warn the boom operators about upcoming moves. The director, however, may assume part or all of these duties in some studios. He alone has the responsibility for cueing action. The director must always be prepared for emergencies, such as a camera "conking out," which might demand wholesale reshuffling in the prepared sequences of shots. And through it all, he must remain calm and poised, never flustered.

Following the Telecast.

1. Thank the control-room team. Circulate in the studio to give compliments sincerely when deserved, or at least a reassuring smile or pat on the back when the members of the company have done their best.

2. Fill out reports.

3. Leave the show in the studio! (The unit manager is responsible for seeing that the settings, properties, furniture, drapes, etc. are all returned to their proper places).

EXAMPLE OF AN "AS-BROADCAST" TELEVISION DRAMA SCRIPT

"The Prize Winner," by Jerome Ross [1]

The excerpt which follows is taken from a television drama by Jerome Ross presented on NBC-TV's "Goodyear Television Playhouse." The director was Jack Smight.

Mattie has won a twelve-day cruise to the West Indies with her entry in a "fill in the last line of the jingle" contest. Kenneth is a shipboard acquaintance who had spurned her the first night on shipboard. It is now the final evening before the end of the cruise and Kenneth has "rediscovered" her. In the excerpt the first few speeches are from a scene (realistically staged) in the ship's Veranda Café. Mattie and Kenneth then move to a section of the top-deck. The staging of this scene illustrates the use of a detail set in live television. Shooting across a short section of a ship's rail as the actors look "out" at the ocean; placing a characteristic shipboard prop, such as a large funnel, in the background; selecting appropriate "moonlight" lighting; playing sound effects records of ocean waves; using a silent electric fan to create a slight breeze and blow their hair; and using a few extras strolling by the railing are techniques employed by the playwright and director to create the illusion of an authentic setting. The final scene in Mattie's cabin was shot most effectively by placing the camera presumably outside of the ship. The director opened the scene with the porthole framed in the center of the shot. The cabin is dark except for a shaft of moonlight across the floor. Then in long shot we observe the cabin door open and Mattie enter. She stands motionless for a moment, still stunned by the intense emotional impact of what has happened. No longer required to keep up appearances now that she is

---

[1] Courtesy of the author, Jerome Ross, and director, Jack Smight.

alone in her cabin, she starts to sob most deeply. Seeking solace from the vastness of nature, the open sea, she half-walks, half-stumbles across the floor to the open porthole (and toward camera) and collapses. Her face, streaked with tears, rests on her hands, which tightly grasp the metal frame of the porthole. She remembers the events and wonders about her future. The camera dollies in to a full close-up of her face as the act ends.

(// is the director's marking to indicate camera "take." The numerals at the right refer to the camera on the air.)

KENNETH: You sure you wouldn't like to dance? //	FADE JAZZ X/S AT MATTIE	2
MATTIE: Well ...		
KENNETH (AWKWARDLY) Look, about that first night, I feel pretty awful --	RISE	
MATTIE: Oh please. Don't say anything. I understood perfectly.	HOLD RISE AND PAN THEM OUT	
KENNETH: Let's dance.		
(THEY LEAVE THE TABLE AND HEAD TO- WARDS THE DANCE MUSIC	MUSIC SNEAKDECK MUSIC - STARLIGHT SOUND	
//	Q EXTRA X OVERS	1
(THE DECK IN THE MOONLIGHT. THE DANCE MUSIC CAN BE HEARD, OFF) EXTRAS IN (PRESENTLY MATTIE AND KENNETH COME TO THE RAIL)	LET MATTIE AND KENNETH IN	
MATTIE: Well, you see, we work in Pur- chasing and that's how I hap- pen to know that your firm's spooling equipment is about the best on the market for our purposes.	HOLD AS TIGHT AS POSSIBLE	
KENNETH: That number seven-eighteen, traverse spooler? We'll sell it to all the textile mills down your way.		
(THEY ARE GAZING OUT NOW, OVER THE WATER) Pretty romantic, isn't it?		
MATTIE: Lovely, just lovely.		

KENNETH:
Did you notice, last night and
the night before, that phos-
phorous goop? The whole ocean
was glowing.

MATTIE:
No, I didn't see it.

Q COUPLE BY
LOOSEN TO SEE EXTRAS
BG - HOLD BIZ - THEN
TIGHTEN.
AFTER KISS   X/S

(A COUPLE PASSES THEM, LOCKED //
IN AMOROUS EMBRACE)

2

MATTIE:
I ... This is the first time
I've been up here at night.

KENNETH:
Really?

MATTIE:
A bunch of us started to come
out once, but it looked sort
of occupied, so we went back
inside. //

X/S AT
SLOW FADE MUSIC

1

KENNETH:
Yeah, the traffic's been pretty
heavy.

SOUND MORE PROMINENT

MATTIE:
That's what Rita told me.
(SHE GAZES OUT AT THE WATER,
SHIVERING A TRIFLE)

START TRUCK AROUND
TO X/S AT KENNETH

KENNETH:
You chilly? You want to go
down?

MATTIE:
No, no. I mean -- well -- just
a wee bit, but I don't mind, I
never get head colds. I'd like
to stay out. It's just so
beautiful ... //

ON KENNETH'S TURN
X/S AT HER

2

(SHE SMILES AT HIM, THEN,
SHYLY --)

I -- I'd like to thank you,
Kenneth.

KENNETH:
What for?

MATTIE:
Well, it was very nice of you,
making my last evening such a
pleasant one. Dancing with me,
and all this. //

X/S
AT KENNETH

1

KENNETH:
Well, I've enjoyed it. We
certainly talked a lot. You're
very easy to talk to, Mattie.//

SAME

2

MATTIE:
I am? //   SAME   1

    KENNETH:
You're remarkably well informed   SNEAK
about textile machinery.   MUSIC
                                        THEME

(KENNETH PUTS HIS ARM AROUND
MATTIE AS SHE STANDS AT THE RAIL.
SHE SEEMS FRIGHTENED, UNCERTAIN)

You want to know something?
You're very nice, Mattie.

(HE KISSES HER LIGHTLY)
(SHE STARES AT HIM, NOT RESPOND-
ING, NOT QUITE BELIEVING WHAT'S
HAPPENED, NOT KNOWING WHAT TO DO)   TITEN ECU

Wasn't I a dope, giving you
the brush-off 'til the last
night on board? We ought to
make up for lost time --

(HE TRIES TO EMBRACE HER, BUT SHE
BREAKS AWAY FROM HIM)

    MATTIE:
Please, Kenneth -- don't --

    KENNETH:
Aw, don't be silly. You know
you're dying for me to kiss
you.

(WHEN HE MAKES ANOTHER ATTEMPT TO   SLAP
DO SO, SHE SLAPS HIM: MUSIC OUT

Well, for crying out loud!

(HE LAUGHS UNCOMFORTABLY)
The prudish type, h'm? //
               (ON TURN)   X/S MATTIE

    MATTIE:
No. No, that isn't it, at all.
You're thinking: somebody
like me ought to be grateful,
and say thank you. You're taking me for granted, just because it's moonlight and you're
a man, and I haven't been able
to attract a man the whole
trip.

    KENNETH:
No wonder, the way you're act-
ing --   PUSH IN CU MATTIE

    MATTIE:
You think I'm like the rest of
them, the whole pathetic boat-
load. Just hoping for a man.
Well, I gave up hoping years
ago. I'm unattractive. I'm a

wet blanket. Maybe that's why
I can be honest. But I still
have too much pride to let you
make love to me just because
it's the thing to do.

(KENNETH LOOKS SHEEPISH. HE CON-
SULTS HIS WRISTWATCH   //   2/S   1

    KENNETH: (VERY SUBDUED)
We probably both got a lot of
packing to do in the morning.
I'll take you down to your
cabin.   LET MATTIE OUT

    MATTIE: MUSIC
Thanks. That's sweet of you,   SNEAK THEME
but don't bother.   LET HER OUT

(SHE EXITS. AFTER A MOMENT HE   DI CU KENNETH
LEAVES)   MUSIC UP ON DISSOLVE
(DISSOLVE TO GIRL'S CABIN - DARK)   Q MATTIE IN
                             (X FADE TO CURTAIN)
                         //   LOOKING THRU PORTHOLE   3
                               SEE MATTIE ENTER ROOM -
(FADE OUT)   X TO PORT HOLE
                               DI CU MATTIE
                               FADE   B

                   END OF ACT TWO

Projects and Exercises

1. Divide the class into groups of three or four. Alternate as director for each round. When each member serves as the director of his group he may select a five-minute portion of a radio or television play in one of the published collections. The script should suit the actors he has at his disposal. Rehearse and present it for class criticism.

2. Work with assigned actors in scenes from the TV excerpts included in the text. Assign different groups to the same scene. Compare the presentations. If cameras are not available, describe the camera shots as the scene is presented.

3. Distribute to each student a copy of the identical half-hour radio script. Assign to different groups specific periods of time which must be cut out of the script: one group to cut the script by five minutes, another group ten minutes, and another fifteen minutes. Compare the various cuttings and discuss reasons for differences in the editing.

4. Distribute to each student a copy of the identical television script. Assign students in pairs. One student should sketch out in rough form the staging which he might recommend. The other plan the action and camera shots. Report to class the decisions which have been reached by each pair. Class discussion of different approaches.

5. Visit a radio or television studio for observation of a play in rehearsal.

6. Watch a television play. Report on composition and shot patterns used by the director.

✣ 32 ✣

Film in Television

PRODUCTION OF FILMS for television is now a business of vast proportions. By 1955, Hollywood was producing at least ten times as much film for television as for theatrical motion-picture exhibition.[1] Thirty to forty per cent of the average television station's programming utilizes film.[2] Hollywood's annual feature film production, which supported the entire motion-picture industry for more than thirty years prior to television, would fill only some two weeks of television film programming for markets as large as New York or Los Angeles.[3]

• SOURCES OF FILM •

Features. Stations may secure films produced originally for release in motion-picture houses. Some pictures are leased on an individual basis for one-time projection only. More generally a "package" or group of films is leased to a specific sponsor or station. The costs may be very high for films made available for first television showings in a large city—$5,000 to $15,000 for each feature is not unusual. Packages of second-, third-, or fourth-run films cost less and some of the very old Westerns, British, and American features may be secured for local markets for as little as $25 each. A station may elect to purchase a feature film library which permits two, three, or four runs for each film in one year or 18 months. Some libraries permit unlimited showings during the rental period. Different clients may sponsor an individual film in turn as it is scheduled during this period. Instead of one sponsor taking the entire feature, individual spot announcements are often inserted. A national survey indicated that the number of breaks for commercials during a feature average between two and five, with more interruptions by stations in the smaller markets.[4] If no sponsors are obtained, the station must absorb the costs itself.

[1] *New York Times,* July 3, 1955, p. 1.
[2] See p. 64.
[3] G. Bennett Larsen, *22 Television Talks* (New York, 1953), p. 1.
[4] *Broadcasting-Telecasting,* April 12, 1954, p. 70.

Except for a period of time in the early development of television, networks did not make use of feature films for network showing until late in 1955 when ABC bought the first television rights to a large number of good quality British films that had previously been shown in American motion-picture houses. NBC was the first network to obtain the television rights to a new feature-length starring film prior to its exhibition in motion-picture houses, NBC followed this up by obtaining for a reported $500,000 first screening rights to Sir Laurence Olivier's three-hour epic film, *Richard III.*

The film department is responsible for carefully screening all the film received by the station to check sound and picture quality. Features which are "bicycled" (sent directly by each film department from station to station) may arrive with defective splices, objectionable scratches, or even missing or reversed reels. Viewers have been startled to see a drawing room romance suddenly shift into a chase across the plains as the U. S. Cavalry rushes to the rescue of a wagon train. Someone in the film department failed to check the order of the reels.

The films also must be screened in order to determine the best places to insert commercials as well as to edit the films to meet program time requirements. When a Western was found to be several minutes short, one ingenious film department clipped out a chase sequence from a different picture and made a continuous film loop out of it. At an appropriate place in the scheduled picture the additional chase sequence was faded in on a second projector and the "bad cowboys" kept running after the "good men" round and round through the brush and hilly terrain for the required minutes needed to meet the time limits. The film department claims that no one suspected anything amiss!

Industrial, Governmental, and Audio-Visual Films. An examination of any catalog of films distributed by a university or school audio-visual center reveals a great variety of short films prepared by business firms. General Electric, for example, released in 1954 a twelve-minute short entitled "The Atom Goes to Sea." This film tells the story of the atom-submarine and attempts to answer questions such as why a submarine was selected to be the first vessel run by atomic energy and how the atom-sub works. American Airlines, the Ford Motor Company, General Motors, and Greyhound Bus prepare many travel shorts. Trade associations, and national organizations, such as the National Association of Manufacturers with its "Industry on Parade," have films available for general distribution. Various governmental agencies, such as the Federal Security Agency, Department of Agriculture, and different branches of the Armed Forces, maintain active film-production units. Sample titles are:

"Europe Looks Ahead." Economic Cooperation Administration. The progress of Western Europe with the help of the Marshall Plan.

"That Men May Fly." U. S. Department of the Air Force. Activities of the Air Surgeon and accomplishments of the School of Aviation Medicine and the Aero Medical Laboratory.

"The Desert People." U. S. Indian Service, Department of the Interior. Story of the Papago Indians who have lived on the desert for centuries.

"A Tree Grows for Christmas." U. S. Department of Agriculture. The Christmas Tree in history and legend and the Christmas Tree industry of today.

Information services of the different states and of foreign countries have many films available. For example, the British Information Services in 1955 released "English Farm" which describes activities of a typical small farmer in southern England. A number of companies such as the Encyclopaedia Britannica Films and Coronet specialize in the distribution of films for general audio-visual use. University audio-visual centers produce and distribute films. The University of Minnesota had a 1955 release entitled "Youth and the United Nations" which reported the highlights of a pilgrimage to the U.N. by a group of high school students. There are numerous other films of this kind.

Many of these films are available to TV stations without charge. Usually they must be presented in their entirety. If rental charges are required the fees are generally quite reasonable. Station program directors often relegate these films to "filler" or fringe-time segments in the day's schedule. The factors which rule against widespread use of audio-visual film material are: (1) the time required for separate negotiations with various companies; (2) poor quality of prints which are used indiscriminately on a variety of nonbroadcast projectors; (3) the informational rather than entertainment nature of the majority of the films; (4) absence of "name" personalities; and (5) lack of continuity between films.

Commercial and Syndicated Series. These are films, usually half-hour in length, which have been prepared especially for television presentation. Several types of series fall under this general classification. When the sponsor's product has national distribution, he may commission a producer to film a program series exclusively for him or contract for first-run privileges of a series controlled by the producer or by a network. Examples of this type are "Lassie," "Medic," "I Love Lucy," "Dragnet," and "Disneyland." The sponsor may also elect to purchase re-run privileges of a popular series from the film producer or owner of the distribution rights. These programs may be carried on a network or placed on individual stations on a spot basis. Television stations may obtain local or regional sponsors for programs secured from film syndicators such as "The Guy Lombardo Show" and "Kit Carson" from the Music Corporation of America; "Mr. District Attorney" and "Cisco Kid" from Ziv, "Liberace" from Guild Films, "Badge 714" ("Dragnet" under a different title) from NBC, or "Amos and Andy" from CBS. "Syndicated film enables the TV station to fill its local program hours with entertainment and information of a kind not available through local origination." [5]

The rise of syndicated film production was spectacular from 1950 to 1955. Many free-lance package producers thought that on the basis of a pilot film they would sell the series to stations across the nation not only for first-run privileges but for re-run after re-run. It was assumed that fabulous profits would result. Although a few did manage to establish successful film companies, many persons lost the money invested in the pilot films. It is now evident that substantial financial and production resources along with a sound knowledge of programming, film techniques, and broadcasting fundamentals are required. Instead of the small free-lance producer with one or two series to offer stations, the general pattern by 1955 found the networks, large corporations with extensive show business experience, and the independent and major Hollywood film studios dominating the film syndication field. The success of Walt Disney in producing film for TV, including "Davy Crockett" which appeared first as a TV film series and then was released as a regular theatrical feature in wide-screen color, was a major factor in removing the final doubts that had delayed the entrance into television of the major Hollywood companies.

Charges for syndicated films vary according to the size of the market served by the station and the anticipated popularity of the series. If the station contracts for other and possibly less popular series distributed by the same syndication company, "package discount" rates may be applicable. One executive has estimated that the average production cost of a syndicated half-hour film in 1954 was $22,500.[6] Additional costs for prints, promotion, advertising, salesmen's salaries, commissions, and merchandising kits run the figure up to $30,000. Thus a series of twenty-six films in a series represents an investment of $780,000. It is obvious that such a sum requires sales in many major markets before a company can recoup its investment. Sample weekly production costs of film series shown on national networks were estimated by *Variety* in 1954 as follows: [7]

Gene Autry	$22,500	Make Room For Daddy	$40,000
Disneyland	65,000	(Danny Thomas)	
(One Hour)		Medic	31,000
Dragnet	30,000	Topper	35,000
I Love Lucy	40,000	You Bet Your Life	35,000
Lassie	25,000	(Groucho Marx)	

Miscellaneous Sources. Stations also need film to incorporate into live programs. A film of waves dashing upon a rocky shore may be effective for rear-screen projection behind a vocalist in a popular music program; a view

[5] Robert W. Sarnoff, President of NBC, in *Variety,* January 6, 1954, p. 93.

[6] Les Harris. "The Thorny Side of Syndicated Film," *Broadcasting-Telecasting,* November 8, 1954, pp. 94-96.

[7] *Variety,* November 10, 1954, pp. 34-38.

of heavy highway traffic may add atmosphere to a documentary on traffic safety; the producer of a sports program may require an opening montage of scenes from different athletic events for a standard introduction; or the writer of a foreign policies series may feel that a succession of one shot after another of the different Premiers who headed the French government from 1950 to 1955 can result in visual reinforcement of his comments and greater dramatic effect.

Stock shot footage from a film library is an answer to such needs. The NBC-TV Film Library is reported to have the largest collection of stock footage especially photographed for use in the television field. Millions of feet of film are cross-indexed and available to stations and film producers. Costs of processing are borne by those requesting such footage, plus $2.50 per 16 mm. foot for one-time use, or $6.25 for use in TV film programs. A partial listing of the subjects under "C" indicates the scope of areas included:

Cabarets	Christmas	cooks
California	circuses	corpses
camps	cliffs	Costa Rica
Canada	clouds	counterfeiters
canneries	coal	cowboys
capital cities	Coast Guard	crops
C.A.R.E.	colleges	cross bows
castles	collisions	crowds
cattle	confetti	cruisers
caverns	Congress of United States	cyclones
children	conventions	Czechoslovakia

Television counterparts of the radio transcription services are sound-film libraries of musical shorts. Popular, semiclassical, and concert selections are filmed and leased to stations for specified periods of time. These filmed musical numbers are used in the same way as radio stations employ transcriptions.

Stations that desire broader coverage of national news than that obtained by use of still photographs may subscribe to national television newsreel services. Regular releases of topical film coverage are rushed by air express to the stations. Script material is supplied when silent footage is sent. The sound on film (SOF) releases generally do not contain any narrative comments but are confined to the speeches and statements by the figures in the news. Some stations have reservations about TV newsreel film. They hold that the filmed news stories are limited in coverage, are a day or two old when they reach the station, and some of the same releases have already been shown on the networks.

Kinescopes of network programs may be arranged for by stations that are not able to receive direct live transmissions. In other instances kine-

FILM FILE CARD [8]

FILE UNDER	NATIONAL BROADCASTING COMPANY, Inc. TELEVISION DEPARTMENT FILM DIVISION LIBRARY CARDS	STOCK SCENES OF SAN FRANCISCO, CALIFORNIA SEE ALSO 930	CAN NO. 929
CALIFORNIA: SAN FRANCISCO: STOCK SHOTS			FT. 786 SOURCE Birch

SYNOPSIS		SUBJECTS		SOURCE
LS- Ferry bldg, at ft. of market St.	12	LS- Alcatraz Island from Telegraph Hill	15	Birch
MS- Tower of Ferry Bldg.	10	LS- Same	13	
LS- Colt Tower on top of Telegraph hill	10	MS- NBC camera car down hill of typical Frisco St.	9	not used
MS- NBC Camera car comes over hill to Frisco St. and past camera	23	MCU- Trolley Powell and Mason Sts.	4	USED
MS- Travel shot thru windshield of car down Frisco St.	39	MLS- To turntable Powell and Market Sts. turned around and pushed onto other track	56	NEG. 35mm orig. Neg. POS.
CU- Sign "Telegraph Hill" Colt Tower	3			
MS- Colt Tower-girl sitting in fg	19			
MS- People walking towards Colt Tower pan up to top of tower	29	MS- Trolley towards cam. stops	8	
LS- San Francisco from top of Telegraph Hill	16	MS- Three scenes trolley manually turned on turntable on Powell St.	22	
LS- Same-pan across city-trees in fg	30	CMS- Trolley towards camera-passes	16	
LS- Same looking toward Knob Hill with man walks thru fg	20	CMS-MCU-Several scenes trolley being turned on turntable and then manually pushed off (Powell and Eddy St.)	76	
LS- Pan of Frisco from Telegraph Hill	39	MLS-Same hi angle sv scenes	84	
LS- Tree framed shot of Knob Hill with Mark Hopkins Hotel from Telegraph Hill	12	MLS-Sv scenes-trolley up	Over	

scopes are used when prior commitments prevent a station from taking a network feed at the scheduled time. A number of educational production centers make available to stations the kinescopes of various series prepared in their studios. In 1955, 17 commercial stations received 45 programs each week which had been kinescoped at the University of Michigan. Non-commercial stations across the nation were linked together with a kinescope or film network starting in 1954. The Educational Television and Radio Center in Ann Arbor inaugurated a program distribution service to its affiliates. Initial weekly distribution consisted of five hours of programming.

The film department also receives regular shipments of TV film commercials from advertising agencies for use on air time purchased by the agency. National organizations such as the Girl Scouts, Red Cross, etc. send public-service spot announcements. Two inch x two inch slides (35 mm. film transparencies mounted in glass or cardboard frames 2 inches square) are sometimes used instead of film for commercials or public-service spots.

It should be apparent from the number of different sources of film that the film department of a station has an extremely complex operation to handle. Detailed records and well established routines are necessary in order to see that the right film is received, screened for quality, accurately timed, commercials inserted, correctly marked and taken to the projection room prior to the scheduled time of broadcast, and then to disassemble the film reels following the broadcast, to package, label, and send out the different prints according to plan.

· INTERNAL SOURCES OF FILM ·

Many stations supplement their external sources of film by establishing their own film production units. Some stations have extremely limited facilities that permit only still photos. Speed Graphic models are standard newspaper type cameras used for this type of photography. The Polaroid camera which produces a 3¼- x 4¼-inch print in one minute after exposure is a recent development which may be used to good advantage. On the spot Polaroid shots may be taken by amateurs for inclusion on news and sports programs. Stations with these cameras report getting photos on the air within minutes after disasters or special events in their area. An example of this was the experience of WTTV, Bloomington, Indiana, in covering a $100,000 warehouse fire: "The fire broke out at 11 A.M. and we arrived with two Polaroids fifteen minutes later. We were able to show twelve Polaroid pictures on the noon news with ad-lib commentary by the reporter who took the pictures." [9] Stations may play a taped-on-the-spot description with the actual sound effects as still pictures are shown on the air. By adroit selection of different stills sound motion-picture film may be simulated.

[9] Mosse and Whiting (eds.), *Television News Handbook* (Evanston, Illinois, 1953), p. 82.

Other stations have one or two 16 mm. motion-picture cameras which shoot silent film. The footage is usually processed at a commercial laboratory. The cameras are useful not only for news and sports coverage, but in the preparation of commercials. Film may be prepared for a sponsor who sells used cars to show different cars on his lot while the announcer describes over the film why individual models shown on the screen are "bargains."

Short features or documentaries may be prepared on film for use on all types of programs. The script of a film feature on Theodore Roosevelt's house follows. This unit originally appeared on a news and feature program. It is apparent, however, that the sequence could easily have been used on a daytime woman's program, as a program unit on a series dealing with activities around the community, on a series suggesting local "travel-tours," sponsored by a gasoline company, or included on a public-service series that surveys state historical spots and shrines.

EXAMPLE OF A FILM FEATURE

"Six O'clock Report" Feature, WCBS-TV, New York City, May 13, 1954, by John McGiffert, "Theodore Roosevelt House." [10]

WALLACE (live)

Some time next month we're going to have a new national shrine out Oyster Bay way, with President Eisenhower himself due to make a speech at the dedication. But getting the place in question ready to be a shrine is no easy job. It's calling for 500 thousand dollars' worth of sprucing up. So yesterday I took a run out to Oyster Bay to see how things are getting along.

MUSIC

FILM IN. 2 MIN. 45 SEC. SILENT
TIGER HEAD - PAN TO WOMAN
BRUSHING. 15 SEC.

.....This might make you think we're going to have a new national zoo....Fierce as he looks, though, this guy is just a placid member of the household.....Because the man to be honored is the late president Theodore Roosevelt.

CU TR PORTRAIT 3 SEC.

HOUSE. TREE and HOUSE. PAN.
ROOTS OF TREE. DRIVEWAY.
17 SEC.

And the shrine you'll soon be able to visit at 50 cents a head is Roosevelt's old home on Sagamore Hill....a 26-room, 70-year-old house that has taken a lot of perking up. The big

[10] Courtesy Columbia Broadcasting System.

outside jobs like re-roofing and re-painting were finished by the time I got there.

WOMAN ON PORCH. CU 8 SEC.

But the curator of Sagamore Hill, Mrs. Harold Kraft - who's standing right where President Eisenhower will stand to deliver his speech - still has a few outdoor chores to worry about.

FLAGPOLE. 4 SEC.

Like getting the big flag pole set up...

PAINTING CANNON. 4 SEC.

Making sure everything looks neat and trim....

STONE. 4 SEC.

including the grave of Teddy Roosevelt's favorite dogs...

HYDRANT. 4 SEC.

And seeing to it that the new water system is in good shape for protection from fire.

MAN AT DESK. CU PICTURE.
MAN UP AND OUT. CHAIR. 13 SEC.

Indoors, I found things busier. Mr. Howard C. Smith, an executive member of the Roosevelt Memorial Association, was working from a chair the late president brought to Sagamore Hill from the White House.

BEDROOM. CU DOLLS. 7 SEC.

Mrs. Kraft had just dusted the nursery, with its mementoes of T.R.'s six children

BED. ROUGH RIDER. 7 SEC.

She had polished up the massive bed of the famous sporting president, and was moving on to one of her special problems....

MONTAGE OF ANIMAL HEADS. 8 SEC.

Cleaning trophies of the chase - most of them bagged by the rough rider himself...Beasts everywhere...

LION PICTURE. PAN DOWN TO BATHTUB. 4 SEC.

And a picture of a beast even in this unlikely setting....

EMPTY ROOM. PORTRAIT. 7 SEC.

But the big north room is the real inner sanctum of this shrine to Theodore Roosevelt....

SWORDS AND PLAQUE. 7 SEC.

And Mrs. Kraft was getting the pieces set for exhibition - pieces like the samurai swords from the emperor of Japan...

And

SMALL ARMORED FIGURE.

The miniature warrior in armor from Admiral Togo.

MRS. K. AND MAN WITH PICTURES. WOMAN GETTING BOOKS FROM SHELVES. CU AT DESK. 23 SEC.

She also gave one of the workmen a glimpse that paying visitors will miss...Pictures of TR and Kaiser Wilhelm, too fragile to be displayed...Meanwhile, the librarian, Mrs. George Harer, was working on the 5,000 books in the Roosevelt collection - cataloguing the rare ones, the ones on wild life, the ones about the West, and early American travel.

TUSKS AND WOMAN. RUG CLEANING. WOMAN AND TUSKS. RUG. 19 SEC.

And finally, under the watchful eye of Mrs. Kraft, who was framed in a pair of elephant tusks sent to Theodore Roosevelt by Haile Selassie's predecessor as emperor of Abyssinia, I saw the cleaners going to work on the rug presented to Mrs. Roosevelt by the Shah of Persia.

HOUSE. 5 SEC. Film OUT.

Yes, it won't be long before it's ready - the shrine that the Roosevelt Memorial Association has been working for ever since their man died in 1919...A new chance to pay your respects to a national hero, at Oyster Bay, right here near New York.

Stations that engage in limited film production may also elect to do their own film processing. Small quantities of film, ranging from 50 to 200 feet, may be developed by use of an inexpensive manual "dishpan" method. Automatic machines which develop and process up to several hundreds of feet per minute are available to stations for $1,000 and more. A station will usually not install the equipment required to make extra prints, special photographic effects such as dissolves, wipes, fades, animation, superimposures, or color film. Film laboratories specializing in such services are utilized.

Film editing equipment is required whether processing is done on or off the premises. A minimum equipment list includes a viewer, a splicer, a footage counter, and a set of re-wind reels. Particular shots or sequences intended for broadcast may be selected from the rough footage, cut out, and spliced together. "Leader" must be spliced on to the first shot to be projected. This special strip of film is marked with a "test-pattern" design and large numerals indicating the seconds left until the start of the picture. The final three seconds are blank. The leader permits the video engineer to adjust the shading and enables the projectionist to cue up the film. During the final three seconds of blank film the picture is faded in. Thirty-six feet of 16 mm. film take one minute to project. Reference to a table of conversion enables the editor or writer to know how long a particular length of film will take on the air.

PARTIAL FILM CONVERSION TABLE

Time	16 mm. Film	Words of Copy (Approximate maximum— usually runs less)
1 second	24 frames	2
5 seconds	3 feet	11
10 "	6 "	23
15 "	9 "	35
20 "	12 "	46
30 "	18 "	70
1 minute	36 "	140
2 minutes	72 "	270
14:30	486 "	—
29:30	1062 "	—

Large metropolitan stations utilize film in a more extensive fashion. They not only add more still cameras, silent film cameras, specialized lenses, and more elaborate editing gear, but they usually purchase film sound-recording equipment. Generally, newsreel or simple documentary pick-ups are accomplished by the "single-system" sound camera which records the voice and picture on the same film while using only one camera. Lip sync, exact matching of lips and tongue action with words as heard is assured. Economy of operation is possible because one cameraman by himself can handle an assignment if time or budget requires that he do so. This system is also excellent for "deadline" shooting. Only the one strip of film needs to be developed. Speed and economy, however, are counterbalanced by two negative factors. First, it is difficult to do any editing. The mechanical design and operation of the camera requires that sound be recorded twenty-six frames ahead of the corresponding picture. Thus cutting and splicing different shots together will disturb lip sync if there is talking in either scene. Picture and audio will not match following such a splice. Second, since the one strip of film with both sound and picture has to be developed in the same chemical solution, some compromises have to be made in the formula used in the processing machine. This compromise results in some degree of deterioration in audio quality. However, most stations with their own film production units rely heavily on single-system sound cameras.

An alternate method of recording sound is by "double system." A film camera and separate sound-recording equipment are "locked together" by synchronizing devices. The sound is recorded either optically on a separate roll of film or on magnetic tape. If tape is used the sound is later transferred to film. The double system has greater flexibility in editing and gives higher audio fidelity. On the other hand, it requires more laboratory time and it is much more expensive because it uses more equipment and personnel in both filming and editing. Nevertheless, the superior quality of the results obtained and the flexibility of editing are of great importance to producers of feature films, documentaries, and commercials. Hollywood film studios use the double system exclusively.

The film stock used by station production units may be classified as "negative" or "reversal." When negative stock is employed, the original strip of film, following exposure and processing, remains negative; that is, the black-and-white values of the original scene are reversed. The negative is then used for making separate prints which are positive, black-and-white values of the original scene. These prints are then referred to as "release" prints. As many prints as needed may be made from the original negative. In films being produced for syndicated or theatrical distribution the original negative is retained in special storage with "dupe" (duplicate) negatives, made from a "fine-grain master positive" taken from the original negative, serving as the source for the many release prints. Because of the electronic characteristics of television equipment, it is possible for stations to project a strip of negative film and turn it into a positive picture for the home viewer. This eliminates one step in the film making process and is especially useful for the "rush" handling of news film. Except in such deadline operations, however, the negative is normally not run through a projection machine because of the danger that the negative may be scratched. If the negative is scratched, subsequent prints would show the same scratches.

The reversal stock is the type also widely used in amateur photography. The film is exposed in the camera and sent to a laboratory. After processing, the same piece of film is returned as a positive print. No negative exists. The photographer has only the one copy. If the positive print is damaged in any way the scenes are lost. The cost of a single print is lower than for the negative-positive method described above. Stations often do not desire extra prints. After one or a few showings the film is filed in the station's film library. When a film unit is shooting film for limited air use, economy of operation is desirable. Therefore stations and educational production centers may use a considerable amount of reversal stock. It should be noted, however, that it is possible for copies to be made from a print if no negative exists. First, a negative is made from the original print and then copies are printed in the usual manner.

Film stock used for kinescope recording may be direct positive stock, similar to reversal stock in that only one positive print results. When several duplicate prints are desired, negative stock is used.

The various stages and alternate methods in the filming process are summarized in the following chart. It should be emphasized that all stations and film production units do not follow standardized procedural steps. The chart illustrates some general methods followed.

STAGES IN FILM PROCESS

$\rightarrow$ refers to steps in processing
— — — refers to editing

16 mm. SILENT

Reversal stock $\rightarrow$ Release print
    or
Negative stock $\rightarrow$ Negative — — — $\rightarrow$ Release print

16 mm. SOUND

Single system
Reversal stock $\rightarrow$ Release print
    or
Negative stock $\rightarrow$ Negative — — — $\rightarrow$ Release print

Double system

Method A
Negative silent stock $\rightarrow$ Negative picture — — — $\searrow$
Negative sound stock $\rightarrow$ Negative sound — — — $\nearrow$ Release prints
   (Film track)
     or
Negative silent stock $\rightarrow$ Negative picture $\rightarrow$ Work print picture — —
Negative sound stock $\rightarrow$ Negative sound $\rightarrow$ Work print sound — —
   (Film track)
   — — edited negative picture $\searrow$
   — — edited negative sound $\nearrow$ Master positive $\rightarrow$ Dupe negative $\rightarrow$ Release prints

Method B
Negative silent stock $\rightarrow$ Negative picture — — — $\searrow$
Sound magnetic tape $\rightarrow$ Negative sound — — — $\nearrow$ Release prints
     or
Negative silent stock $\rightarrow$ Negative picture $\rightarrow$ Work print picture — —
Sound magnetic tape   (Tape is not processed at this stage)   — —
   — — edited negative picture $\searrow$
   — — edited magnetic tape $\nearrow$ Master positive $\rightarrow$ Dupe negative $\rightarrow$ Release prints

35 MM. SOUND FILM INTENDED FOR TV STATION USE AS 16 MM.

Negative silent stock (35 mm.) $\rightarrow$ Original negative picture (35 mm.)
                                   $\rightarrow$ work print picture (35 mm.) — —
Sound track $\rightarrow$ Original negative sound (35 mm.)
   35 mm. film or magnetic tape $\rightarrow$ work print sound (35 mm.) — —
                                   (If tape is used alternate
                                   approach is not to process tape here)
   — — edited negative picture (35 mm.) $\rightarrow$ Master positive picture (35 mm.) $\rightarrow$
   — — edited negative sound (35 mm.) $\rightarrow$ Master positive sound (35 mm.) $\rightarrow$
                                   (If tape is used it might be processed
                                   into film at this stage)
   $\rightarrow$ Dupe negative picture (16 mm.) $\searrow$
   $\rightarrow$ Dupe negative sound (16 mm.) $\nearrow$ Release prints

• PRODUCTION TECHNIQUES
BY PROFESSIONAL PRODUCERS •

Many of the black-and-white and color films made for television by professional producers do not differ materially in their method of production from the films made for theatrical release. Only one 35 mm. camera is used. One set is erected at a time and dressed with appropriate furniture and properties on a Hollywood or New York sound stage. All of the scenes in the film which take place on one set are shot before moving to another set. There is no continuity in filming the story according to the plot. Individual scenes are photographed separately. Each time the camera is moved to a different basic position the lights are relocated. It is not in techniques, but in time consumed in filming and editing that some of the chief differences exist between theatrical films and television films. Producers of syndicated films must meet the deadlines of weekly program releases, including rehearsals, filming, and editing. As a result, few special photographic effects such as elaborate montages are attempted. Even special hour films may take less than a week of actual shooting time. "A Christmas Carol," by Charles Dickens, starring Frederic March, was filmed for the holiday season as a CBS-TV color-film feature in only five days. Normal Hollywood scheduling would have required four weeks.[11]

The traditional one-camera technique has been modified by some television film producers not only because of the pressures to speed up production but also due to the desire of the performers to play before a live audience. Two or three film cameras are used and plot sequences are followed. The "I Love Lucy" series was perhaps the first major film situation comedy series to adopt this technique. Bleachers were installed in a motion-picture studio. Lighting was adjusted for overhead illumination to permit film camera movement and a clear view of action by the audience. Three 35 mm. film cameras mounted on movable platforms photograph the "I Love Lucy" program in approximately ninety minutes. As in live television, dialogue and live audience reactions are picked up simultaneously by overhead microphones and recorded on magnetic tape.

A typical weekly schedule might go as follows: Four days in sequence, such as Tuesday through Friday, are required for each half-hour program. The dialogue and action are rehearsed by the cast on the first two days of the sequence. Major script revisions may be incorporated as deemed necessary. On the third day several dry-runs in the studio permit the cast to become familiar with the sets in which the action takes place as they rehearse their movements. The program director and director of photography block out areas to be covered by the cameras, experiment with groupings and specific camera angles, and decide where lights should be located.

---

[11] Rufus Crater, "A Carol in Color," *Broadcasting-Telecasting,* December 20, 1954, pp. 35-38.

The cameramen assigned to each camera attend this rehearsal to become acquainted with the action and to discuss individual responsibilities. On the fourth day the sets are lighted, camera action is chalked on the studio floor, and the entire cast and technical crew run through the program several times on a stop-and-start basis. This period is climaxed by a dress rehearsal. There follows a brief discussion of any errors that took place during the dress rehearsal, and final script or action changes. A dinner break is taken by all. In the evening the audience is admitted and given a "warm-up" session in order to put it into a receptive mood for the antics of the characters. The program is presented and filmed in normal sequence scene by scene broken only by brief intermissions for re-positioning of the cameras on the different sets, and by costume and make-up changes. Re-takes are made in emergencies only. Working with such a tight schedule is disturbing to the serious director of photography. Karl Freund, who came into television with a distinguished career as a leading motion-picture cameraman, explains why: [12]

> I can't do photographic justice to the actors. No set ups . . . just get the story on film! In the movies I used to take forty-five minutes to an hour for a close up of Garbo . . I talk to Lucy and Desi about this but they say, "No, Karl, No." An audience stimulates them. The way they feel what's the good performing in front of electricians.

Not all companies which use the multiple-film camera technique shoot the programs in proper scene sequence or before an audience. Some use approximately the same weekly schedule but shoot film according to any sequence deemed most economical. The shooting may be spread over two days instead of being confined to one. With multiple cameras instead of one, considerable time is still saved because it is not necessary to stop frequently and to re-position the single camera and lights. When audience reactions are desired for variety or situation comedy programs, an edited work print of the program is projected on a large screen before an audience and the actual reactions to the program are recorded for synchronized insertion afterwards on film. Another method which has been attacked severely by many critics is to insert "canned" audience reactions available on film sound track from special-effects libraries. Any degree of response from a snicker to uproarious guffaws can be edited into the release prints.

Another production technique designed to approximate the spontaneity and flexibility possible in live television is the method used to film the Groucho Marx program, "You Bet Your Life." This program is edited for air use from an original one-hour quiz session before a live audience. Eight film cameras, placed in banks of two in four different locations, photograph the entire one hour without interruptions. While one camera in each bank is operating, its companion may be reloaded. A special control system and

[12] *New York Times,* August 23, 1953.

master recorder were designed to facilitate the follow-up editing and synchronizing work.

In a straight film operation the director cannot exactly see what is being photographed. In television production, however, the director can do this easily by referring to the video monitors. It was not surprising, therefore, that as television and film became more closely allied, some of the electronic aspects of television also were utilized in film production.

One example is the use of closed circuit television. A small vidicon TV camera is mounted side by side with each film camera. The televised picture can be distributed to remote viewing monitors for observation by the director. The areas of pick-up by the different lenses in television and film cameras are matched as closely as possible to give a similar field of view.

In 1955 the DuMont "Electronicam" and the Simon video-film camera developed with the co-operation of RCA were introduced. These cameras are single-unit television and film cameras which share an electronic viewfinder and a single lens and focusing system. It is possible with either system to telecast the scene and simultaneously to record the identical scene on film. Those who introduced this combination video-film camera predict its widespread adoption. Some time will be required before one can judge the validity of this forecast by Al Simon, who developed one of the new cameras:

> It isn't hard to foresee the video-film camera eventually replacing the image orthicon television cameras presently in use in the major network studios because, with this camera, it will be possible to make first-class film records of a show, replacing kinescopes. Where the camera is employed on TV Spectaculars, there will be recorded simultaneously a first-quality motion-picture color negative, from which excellent prints can be made for subsequent telecasting.[13]

EXAMPLE OF TELEVISION FILM
"Medic" [14]

Opening portion of "After the Darkness," Story No. 17.

```
         FADE IN:

    1.   STYNER - MED. SHOT
         He walks into a MED. CLOSE SHOT.  The background is not
         recognizable.
                             STYNER
                   My name's Konrad Styner.  I'm a Doctor of
                   Medicine.  Our story tonight has the title:
                   "After the Darkness."
                                      QUICK DISSOLVE:
```

[13] Al Simon, "The Video-Film Camera," *American Cinematographer*, March, 1955, pp. 140-142, 164-165.
[14] Courtesy of Medic TV Productions.

2.   CLOSE-UP - CENTER OF SHIELD

and It contains a gnarled staff with a single serpent twined
3.   around it. The figure of the staff and serpent is in
     relief, finely wrought in metal. It is executed in
     scrupulous detail.

                         VOICE
                    Guardian of birth . . .
                    Healer of the Sick . . .
                    Comforter of the Aged . . .

CAMERA STARTS TO PULL BACK SLOWLY revealing the entire
shield. It is a detailed piece of metalwork hanging
against a backdrop of rich drapery. The shield is marked
off in thirds, all sections equal. The upper right portion
contains the head of a lion. The upper left, the head of
an eagle. The lower third contains the hand of a woman.
All of the figures are in relief, thoroughly and finely
detailed. The lighting is low-key.

(NOTE: The symbolism of the three figures on the shield has
its basis in the ancient maxim, "...and the qualities of
the worthy physician are three: the eye of an eagle, the
heart of a lion, the hand of a woman.") CAMERA HOLDS on
the shield, TILTING UP slightly.

                         VOICE
                    To the Profession of Medicine
                    To the Men and Women Who Labor in its Cause ...
                    This story is dedicated.

The single word "MEDIC" is SUPERIMPOSED. The letters fill
the entire screen.
                                        FADE OUT:

FADE IN:

4.   DR. STYNER - MED. CLOSE SHOT
                         STYNER
                    Our presentation tonight...the field of oph-
                    thalmology...the science of the human eye.
                    The object in point:

                    The case in point: Sean Francis Gallagher.
                    He's thirty-one years old, unmarried. He plays
                    the piano for a living. The first five years
                    of his life were fairly normal, but at the age
                    of six a change took place and he was plunged
                    into a world of bright darkness. For twenty-
                    five years he's been living in that world.
                    In a few months it will come to a sudden end.

                                        DISSOLVE TO:

5.   INT. "OLD VIENNA" - MED. SHOT - THE BAR - NIGHT

The establishment is of the lower middle-class type, a
combination bar and self-service-cafe with steam table at
one end. At the opposite end on the "drinking side" of the
place there's a piano in one corner, a baby grand. A juke
box is also in evidence. EMMA KOWALSKI is standing behind
the bar at the moment drying a few glasses. The bartender,
BRUNO, is drawing a glass of tap beer for one of the customers at the bar. Generally the few customers are in

overalls, leather jackets, etc. SEAN is seated at the piano. He is playing the old English ballad, "Greensleeves." An elderly customer sitting at a table close to the piano is singing the lyrics. Sean's suit is rumpled, there are food stains down the front of his coat. His tie is loose, shirt unbuttoned at the neck. His hair could do with some combing. He holds a cigarette between his lips as he plays, the ashes spilling down the front of his coat. There is a half-finished drink on the piano in front of him. Because of the shadowed corner in which he sits his face is not discernible. As the song finishes, Emma glances up at the clock above the bar which reads a few minutes before two, then she turns and in a fairly loud voice addressed the few remaining customers. Her voice is fairly illustrative of her personality...rough but genial, warmly human.

> EMMA
> All right, that's eighty-six for everybody.
> Closing time.

6. EMMA - MED. CLOSE SHOT

As she finishes her chores behind the bar she glances toward Sean. Her face seems to soften a bit. Her expression and her attitude toward him is a strange mixture of compassion, warmth, motherliness and desire. Throughout the entire script this attitude is never resolved. It remains an enigma.

7. SEAN - MED. CLOSE SHOT

as he finishes the piano selection, picks up his drink and downs it. (NOTE: TECHNICAL ADVISOR) He stands up and reaches for his topcoat which has been flung over the back of a chair behind the piano. He starts to exit, carrying the coat over one arm. He also carries a can but it is just about completely covered. He weaves slightly to indicate that he's been drinking most of the night.

8. INT. BAR - MED. SHOT

As Sean crosses toward the exit, Emma comes up to him and touches him gently on the forearm as if to detain him.

> EMMA
> Sean, you're not gonna go out and get yourself
> in trouble again, are you?

> SEAN (flat)
> Good night, Emma.

He starts toward the exit, CAMERA PANNING with him. He half stumbles against a chair for no apparent reason. He curses under his breath, pushes the chair angrily aside. He takes the white cane from under his topcoat and we see it clearly for the first time. He makes his way uncertainly out the door.

9. EMMA - MED. CLOSE SHOT

as she reacts. Her face reflects deep concern as she half gestures, calling after him.

EMMA
Sean?

The door swings shut and Sean disappears. Emma's face is
wreathed in gloom.

DISSOLVE TO:

10. EXT. CITY STREET - MED. SHOT - SEAN - NIGHT

as he makes his way along the sidewalk, taking care to hug
the curbline for guidance. (NOTE - TECHNICAL ADVISOR:
PLEASE check on his manner of walking.)

11. EXT. THE CATHEDRAL - MED. LONG SHOT - SEAN

as he makes his way up to the street and pauses uncertainly
at the mouth of an alley which runs alongside the
cathedral.

12. SEAN - MED. SHOT

Despite his blindness he seems to know instinctively where
he is. He hesitates uncertainly then turns and makes his
way down the narrow alley which borders the cathedral.

13. EXT. SIDE ENTRANCE OF CHURCH - MED. SHOT - SEAN

The side doors are in the immediate right f.g. The lower
half of the doors are of heavy wood, the upper portion of
glass. Sean makes his way toward the CAMERA, moving up
and stopping at the entrance. He tries the door gently
but finds it locked. Feeling with his hands he determines
that the upper portion of the door is of glass. He pauses
a long moment, as if listening intently. Then he takes
his topcoat and wraps one sleeve around his fist, then
pauses again. With a short, hard jab he punches out the
lower portion of one of the panes of glass in the door.
He pauses again, listening very intently for any possible
reaction. Then he reaches in to unlatch the door.

14. INT. THE CATHEDRAL - MED. SHOT - THE SIDE DOOR - SEAN

as he enters. From his movements it's still fairly plain
that he's been drinking but nonetheless he moves slowly,
cautiously to avoid detection. The interior of the church
is bathed in deep shadows. One source of illumination
comes from a pair of vigil lights hung in the sanctuary.
They cast a pale, unreal light over the massive splendor
of the altar and the entire sanctuary. Another source of
light from off to one side is a bank of votive candles
which burn before the altar of the Blessed Virgin.

15. INT. CHURCH - MED. LONG SHOT - SEAN

CAMERA SHOOTING DOWN from the choir loft. Sean makes his
way unsteadily but fairly quietly down the aisle toward the
rear of the church.

16. SEAN - MED. SHOT

as he moves up to the door at the rear of the church leading to the choir loft, opens it and carefully makes his
way through the doorway. We gather through his movements
throughout this particular sequence that the darkness is
hardly a hindrance to him. He makes his way slowly but
steadily by the sense of touch, as if walking according to
a well-practiced formula.

17. INT. CHURCH - MED. SHOT - THE CHOIR LOFT

The organ console is prominent in the f.g. In the right
f.g. a good section of the rest of the church from this
POV is visible in the b.g. Sean enters the choir loft
through a side door. It is quite apparent from his movements it is the first time he's been up here. Cautiously,
with great concentration, he makes his way to the console
of the organ. He seems to recognize it for what it is at
the first touch and his expression and attitude mirrors a
sense of gratification and triumph. At this point his
bearing still displays the effects of the alcohol he's
consumed during the day. He fingers the console for a
moment to orient himself and when he is sure of his bear-
ings he allows his topcoat to slip from his arm to the
floor and he slides onto the bench of the organ. His
movements are instinctive, almost as if he has played
this same organ or others similar to it hundreds of times
before, as he uncovers the keyboard and switches on the
electric motor which operates the bellows. The expression
on his face is one of quiet but intense anticipation. He
rubs the palms of his hands on his trouser legs, then
starts to bring them up.

18. INT. CHURCH - MED. LONG SHOT - THE CHOIR LOFT

CAMERA SHOOTING UP toward the loft from the apse of the
church, approximately at a point directly in front of the
communion rail, as Sean begins to play and the first notes
of Bach's "Toccata and Fugue" thunder forth at full volume
from the organ.

19. EXT. THE RECTORY - MED. SHOT - FATHER MENDELSSOHN

He's dressed in his bathrobe and slippers. He exits to
the rectory and pauses briefly at a low flight of stairs
which lead to the entrance of the rectory. His attention
is centered o.s. toward the church from which issues the
sound of the pealing organ. His expression mirrors be-
wilderment. He starts quickly toward the church.

20. INT. CHURCH - MED. LONG SHOT - CHOIR LOFT

CAMERA AGAIN SHOOTING UP toward the loft from the apse of
the church (from the same angle as in Scene 18). Sean
continues to play. CAMERA PANS to the side entrance as
FATHER MENDELSSOHN enters and pauses just inside the doors.
He immediately glances up toward the choir loft. He starts
to make his way quickly down the aisle toward the rear of
the church and the door opening onto the stairway which
leads up to the choir loft. His expression and attitude
is the same. He's disturbed, angry.

21. STAIRWAY LANDING - MED. SHOT - FATHER MENDELSSOHN

as he moves into scene at the foot of the stairway which
leads up to the choir loft, CAMERA SHOOTING DOWN from
landing. His anger is now replaced by an expression of
wonderment. The priest's eyes are still directed upward,
his pace studied, slow. The magnificence of the music,
both in volume and in quality, seems to build to even
greater heights as the priest mounts the stairs to the
loft.

22. INT. CHURCH - MED. SHOT - THE CHOIR LOFT

CAMERA HOLDING on Sean in the immediate f.g. in the left hand side of the frame. In the right hand side of the frame in the b.g. we see Father Mendelssohn appear in the doorway. He pauses briefly then starts to cross slowly, quietly, coming toward the CAMERA. He stops half a dozen yards from the organ, simply standing there and listening, amazed, more than slightly overawed. The music builds to a thundering climax and comes to an end. Sean's shoulders slump a bit after the exertion. He wavers a bit uncertainly.

> FATHER MENDELSSOHN
> (calmly)
>
> Excellent. Very excellent.

Sean stiffens a bit, reacting, turning his head in the general direction of the priest's voice but not centering on him exactly. It's a fairly sobering thought, knowing that he's been caught in the act but Sean attempts to carry it off with jaunty casualness.

> SEAN
> An audience. Very encouraging. Did we attract a goodly number?

The priest starts to cross slowly to him, coming toward the CAMERA.

> FATHER MENDELSSOHN
> (as he crosses)
> Just one.

The priest stops beside the organ bench, Sean turning his head a bit in the direction of the sound, but still not centering directly on the priest.

> FATHER MENDELSSOHN
> (continuing)
> Three a.m. organ recitals never did draw very well in this town. Who are you?

> SEAN
> Sean Francis Patrick Aloysius Gallagher.

23. CLOSE-UP - SEAN

as he turns his face into the light and we realize he is blind. (NOTE: TECHNICAL ADVISOR: Check appearance of eyes for scarring.)

> SEAN
> I usually omit the Aloysius. It sounds too Irish. You say the eleven c'clock Mass on Sundays. Am I right?

24. MED. CLOSE SHOT - FATHER MENDELSSOHN

The priest realizes here that Sean is blind.

EXAMPLE OF STATION FILM DEPARTMENT
ORGANIZATION AND POLICIES

The National Association of Radio and Television Broadcasters published a *Film Manual* in 1955 for use of the television membership. Part II consisted of case histories. One of the five case histories follows: [15]

FILM POLICIES AND OPERATIONAL PROCEDURES

WSJS-TV

Winston-Salem, North Carolina

I. FILM PURCHASING

A. In negotiating film contracts with distributors, WSJS-TV uses the film contract provided by the National Television Film Council but will accept contracts applying basic provisions contained in the NTFC contract.
B. Policies. In addition, the station requires signatures on a rider amendment whereby the distributor warrants that all film sent to WSJS-TV will meet its physical and telecasting standards. In the event any film does not conform to these standards, the distributor, upon notification, agrees to make timely substitution and pays all transportation charges for the return of the unsatisfactory print by the station and the return of a physically satisfactory substitute print to the station.
    1. Re-runs. The station buys on a one or two-run basis, depending on the material under consideration and schedule availabilities.
    2. WSJS-TV insists on exclusivity in the market.
    3. No firm policy has been established regarding packages versus spot-buying. The station has used both methods. Cost plus number of top features always enters into the decision. In most cases, negotiating has eliminated unwanted subjects from so-called package deals. No cost formula has been evolved in purchasing film. Right is reserved to reject individual film and to edit film.

II. PERSONNEL

A. Total number.
    1. WSJS-TV maintains three separate sections—Film, Art, and Photography —within the Film Department.
    2. The Film Department has nine full-time employees. Four of these people devote all of their time to film duties, three others divide their time between film and other duties. One person devotes full-time to art work; another, full-time to photography.
B. Breakdown of full-time employees.
    1. Film Manager (1): Supervises over-all Film Department operation. Reports to Station Operations Manager.
    2. Film Technicians (5): Work on a rotating schedule in projection and editing rooms. One person devotes some time to art work. Responsible to Film Manager.
    3. Film Librarian (1): Receives, ships and catalogs film and slides. Main-

[15] *Film Manual*, NARTB (Washington, 1955), pp. 29-33. Courtesy of NARTB.

tains commercial film and slide files. Devotes some time to station musical activity. Reports to Traffic, Program and Film Managers.

4. Artist (1): Prepares art copy for slides and studio use. Responsible to Film Manager.
5. Photographer (1): Produces slides. Photographs and processes still and motion pictures of news, documentary and commercial subjects. Responsible to Film Manager.
6. Film Buyer: Film is purchased by the Program Manager, and is scheduled by that Department.

III. FILM EQUIPMENT

A. Total equipment in two editing rooms.
  1.   3 Splicers
     2 16-mm. screening projectors
     1 35-mm. slide screening projector
     3 16-mm. film timers
     3 pairs, 16-mm. rewinds
     1 16-mm. editing viewer
     1 Metal storage cabinet for program films
     36 Metal storage cabinets for film spot announcements
     1 Metal storage rack for reels, etc.
     1 Wall screen
     1 Portable screen
     6 Metal film racks
B. Total equipment for on-air.
  1.   2 16-mm. film projectors
     2 35-mm. slide projectors
     1 Balop (opaque-transparency) slide projector
     2 Film pick-up cameras (iconoscope)
C. Total equipment for darkroom and cameras.
  1. One film developing room with complete facilities for processing still and motion picture negative film.
  2. One darkroom with complete facilities for the production of still photographs and slides.
  3. Photographic equipment includes:
     1 16-mm. silent motion picture camera
     1 4x5 Speed Graphic camera
     1 Polaroid film adapter for Speed Graphic camera
     1 35-mm. Exakta camera
     1 35-mm. to 4x5 enlarger

IV. FILM FACILITIES

That part of the station's physical plant which is devoted to Film Department operations is divided into two groups. The darkroom, art department, and one editing and screening room are in one part of the building, while the on-air projection room, film library and office, and another editing room are grouped together elsewhere.

V. OPERATIONAL PROCEDURES AND PROGRAMMING

A. Scheduling:
  1. Film is scheduled by both Program and Commercial Sales Departments. When these film schedules are received by the Film Department, the necessary information about each film is entered on an inspection report

form, indicating program title, date and time scheduled, and film title. For example, the station runs *Big Town* on Monday night at 10:30 P.M. On the inspection-report form in the Program space, is entered "Big Town." In the Date space is entered "Monday, Jan. 10-55," and in the space for film title "Airplane Story—Big Town #114."

2. The film called "non-regular film" is handled the same way, with the same information being placed on the inspection-report form. This information indicates to the technicians exactly where to place the inspected film. Scheduling of this non-regular film is done both by Program and Commercial Sales Departments.

3. The station's projectionists pull and run commercial spots according to the log, which is made out by the Traffic Department from information furnished by the Commercial Sales Department.

B. Program Film:

1. All program film is delivered to the Film Library as soon as received and listed on the incoming log. It is then given a "quick-check" for preliminary determination of its general physical condition. Film passing this preliminary inspection is then logged on the individual report forms discussed above. Also on this form are spaces in which to indicate: total running time, total footage, segmented time and footage if film is so programmed, spaces in which to indicate the physical condition of the film, such as sprocket holes, sound track, splices, picture, sound, etc., date inspected, inspector and the date the completed inspection report is needed.

2. The film, together with its report form, is then assigned to a film technician who thoroughly checks the film; edits it, if indicated; makes necessary repairs; times and auditions it. The film is then placed in the ready film cabinet according to the day it is scheduled to run, and the completed report is placed in a loose-leaf binder for use by the Traffic Department. A file of these report forms is maintained for 30 days after show date. In the event of a question from the distributor about film condition, station has a complete record of its condition on arrival at this station.

3. Operational procedure for on-air projection at WSJS-TV calls for running programs and spots separately on the two film chains whenever possible, except when spot films occur within a program film. The first projectionist on duty in the morning is responsible for setting out the entire day's film run, according to the log. The projectionist on duty is responsible for the loading of the film and slide projectors. Video control is responsible for all film starts and the advancing of slides when the slide projectors are "in the light." The projectionist is responsible for all film projector stops, the lighting of the slide projectors, and advancing slides when the projectors are "dark." The projectionist on duty is also responsible for disassembly (when necessary), rewinding and return of commercials to the commercial spot file, and of program films to the "has run" rack for shipment.

C. Film Announcement Procedure:

1. Commercial spot announcements are handled much in the same manner as program film. The exception is that this film is routed to the commercial department immediately upon arrival at the station, since the scheduling of this film is determined by that department. As soon as the schedule of the film is "set," the film is forwarded to the Film Depart-

FILM INSPECTION REPORT FORM

WSJS-TV, Winston-Salem, North Carolina

FILM REPORT

Program_____　　Time Scheduled:

Date_____　　　_____

Film Title_____

Total Running Time_____

Total Footage_____

_____ Time_____ Footage_____

_____ Time_____ Footage_____

_____ Time_____ Footage_____

_____ Time_____ Footage_____

_____ Time_____ Footage_____

_____ Time_____ Footage_____

_____ Time_____ Footage_____

_____ Time_____ Footage_____

　　　　Total　　Time_____ Footage_____

Splices_____

Torn Sprockets_____

Picture_____

Sound_____

Inspected By_____

Date_____

　　Date Needed:_____

---

ment. The same inspection checks are performed and the same physical standards are imposed. Commercial spots are filed on 100-foot camera spool reels and are listed numerically in the station file. Running files, numerically and alphabetically, are kept on all spot film and slides. These numbers run consecutively, eliminating the possibility of confusion which might arise from the re-use of deleted film numbers. Duplicated commercial spot films are required on all films scheduled to run longer than "one time only."

2. Commercial programs and spot announcements are subject to "make-goods" if telecast was unsatisfactory by the station's normal operational standards. "Make-goods" are scheduled only after negotiation with client.

D. Still and Motion Picture Production:

1. WSJS-TV maintains facilities for the production and development of motion picture film for use on the air. Sixteen millimeter film is developed

as a negative, using Stineman reels and tanks. Station has one 200-foot reel and one 100-foot reel. Three hundred feet of film can be processed "ready-to-run" in approximately 45 minutes. Processing more than 300 feet of film entails a bit of a delay until the reels are dried.

The film is dried on a motor-driven, revolving squirrel-cage type dryer, which is suspended from an upper wall of the darkroom, in line with the incoming duct from the air conditioning system. It has a capacity of 500 feet and drying is accomplished in about 15 minutes. It is the station's own design and construction.

WSJS-TV's weekly average total of motion picture production, based on a 36-week period, is 1200 feet of motion picture film, divided as follows: 600 feet for news, 200 feet for documentary and 400 feet for commercial. For the same period, station averaged 43.2 (4x5 inch) still negatives; 21.6 of these for news, 8.4 for documentary and 13.2 for commercial. From these negatives was made an average of 32.4 (8x10-inch) prints for news, 42 for documentary and 83.1 for commercial and promotion. During this time, too, the film department produced an average of 14.7 (2x2-inch) slides per week, 8.8 of which were for commercial accounts. All of the photographic work is undertaken on a cost basis.

VI. SPECIFICATIONS

A. Slides:
  1. 35-mm. (2 x 2)
     Scanning area 29/32 x 1 & 7/32
     Safe viewing area 23/32 x 15/16
     Tape bound only
  2. Balop (opaques and transparencies)
     Over-all size 3¼ x 4
     Scanning area 2¼ x 3
     Safe viewing area 1⅞ x 2⅜
  3. ID's require that the commercial copy occupy three-quarters of the safe viewing area, leaving the upper right quarter of this area for station identification.
B. Film ID's:
  1. The shared-time ID announcement is identified as ten seconds. Actual timing of shared-time ID announcement:

1½	seconds 36 frames	Open
6	seconds	Commercial Audio
2	seconds	Station Identification Audio
½	second (12 frames)	Close

  2. The audio portion of the station identification will follow the audio portion of the commercial.
  3. The commercial copy will occupy three-quarters of the screen area, leaving the upper right quarter of the screen for station identification.

VII. ENGINEERING

A. On-Air equipment maintenance:
  1. Maintenance of the on-air film equipment is a cooperative effort by both film and engineering departments. All mechanical maintenance of the projection equipment is accomplished by the film department, while the electronic maintenance of the film cameras and projectors is performed

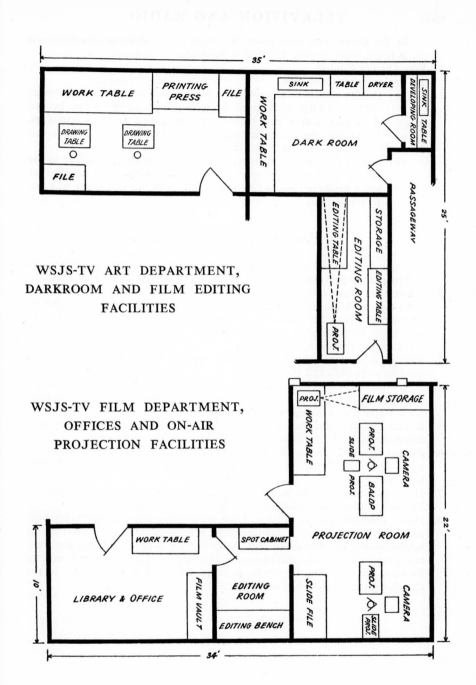

WSJS-TV ART DEPARTMENT, DARKROOM AND FILM EDITING FACILITIES

WSJS-TV FILM DEPARTMENT, OFFICES AND ON-AIR PROJECTION FACILITIES

by the engineering department. Constant check of the on-air operation is maintained by both film and engineering.
B. Film Quality Control.
 1. Preventive maintenance.
  (a) Quality control of all on-air film presentation begins with a thorough check of all film to be aired. Projection room equipment is checked daily and is kept under constant surveillance while in operation. Lamp and tube records are maintained daily.
 2. Most common causes of on-air film failure.
  (a) Station feels the most common source of on-air film failure is the film itself. Lack of proper film inspection, repair and handling of some prints is reflected by the condition of the film when received by the station.

Projects and Exercises

1. Examine the television station program schedules carried by newspapers and magazines and report on number and types of film used by the stations.
2. Select class representatives to visit station film departments. Request that these representatives observe the procedures followed in screening, choosing appropriate places for insertions of commercials, and checking film in and out. Have representative report on station equipment and staff used for shooting and processing its own film.
3. Tune in television stations and prepare reports on the editing techniques used on news reels and film features.
4. Screen representative nonentertainment films obtained from an audio-visual department. Discuss the techniques employed. Suggest alternate treatment for live television coverage of same subject.
5. Screen footage which has not been edited. Prepare individual editing run-down sheets listing the timing and order of each shot to be used.
6. Present recommendations for re-editing of "Theodore Roosevelt House" on page 588 to cut the script by one minute. What recommendations do you have if two or three minutes are to be cut?
7. Have someone demonstrate film camera operation and editing equipment. Practice loading and holding camera. Splice scrap footage.
8. Divide class into groups of three. Each group plans a two-minute voice over silent film feature. After a shooting script is roughed out, each person shoots approximately one minute of film. After the film is processed, edit the footage, prepare final script, and present the feature for class criticism. If no film facilities are available, distribute shooting scripts of group projects to the class for group analysis and discussion.

❋ 33 ❋

Broadcasting as a Career

"SHOULD I GO into radio?" "What about television?" These are questions frequently asked of any person on a station or network staff and of instructors in broadcasting. This chapter deals with those questions.

Television and radio have glamour. They are connected with "show business," hailed so much in song and described at such length in fiction. Show business is not all tinsel and spotlight. In spite of the publicity appearing in magazines and Sunday supplements, few unknowns are catapulted into stardom. It is usually a long, arduous, and grueling struggle before one attains any degree of financial success and security. For every leading actor, starring soloist, and recognized comic, there are hundreds in the shadows who have not "arrived." The statement by an executive of the American Federation of Television and Radio artists that 80 per cent of the union's membership of 15,000 make less than $2,000 a year from radio and television should be borne in mind by those thinking only of the performing positions and the "big time." [1]

However, the fulfillment of a creative desire, the opportunity for self-expression, the excitement of working in a dynamic medium of mass communication, the changing pattern of work in some positions, and the prestige of working in a spotlighted environment are the intangible factors that make television and radio so attractive to aspirants and often outweigh the more material factors.

Each individual should evaluate his abilities honestly, using any expert vocational guidance available to him. A glib "You have a nice voice on the telephone, you ought to be in radio!," or a casual "You photograph so nicely, why don't you go into television!" or an introspective "My, it would be thrilling, working in radio and television, I'd like that!" are not dependable evaluations. Examine and evaluate your experience, your talents, and your capabilities as you review the chapters concerned with the various areas and read the analysis which follows.

[1] *Broadcasting-Telecasting,* August 2, 1954, p. 73.

• THE RADIO AND TELEVISION INDUSTRIES •

Radio broadcasting has reached its peak and is no longer an expanding industry. Replacements are the primary source of employment. There are a small number of replacements as employees move over into television. Television is an expanding industry at present and should continue to be such for a few years. The investment involved in television precludes assigning responsible positions to untrained or casually employed persons. Work is so specialized that on-the-job training and experience is necessary. This means that an apprentice system is generally followed.

Two Procedures. Those who seek to enter commercial radio and television as a career, may elect one of two general procedures. One method is employment in the profession as soon as possible, going in on a very low level after high school and advancing through the years. Many have followed this method and succeeded. The second method is to take a college liberal arts education, including work in the fields of speech, art, drama, music, social sciences, home economics, agriculture, advertising, creative writing, and business, plus specialized work in broadcasting, photography and design. The broadcasting specialization, in many instances, should continue for an additional year beyond the bachelor's degree. The second method delays the beginning of actual work on the job, but most broadcasting executives prefer candidates with college educations. As one station executive phrased it: "Competition in the broadcasting business is too keen! You have to have people who can think, make decisions, judge wisely, and know a lot about a lot of things. College degrees don't guarantee that the people are like that but they are important indications."

The increasing number of colleges and universities with facilities for closed circuit television as well as equipment for radio enables more students to acquire on-the-job experience at educational institutions as well as at stations. Students who attend an institution where an educational television station or radio station exists often have opportunities to combine the preliminary apprenticeship in broadcasting with college work.

Announcing and Specialties. Announcing is a common method of entering the broadcasting field. Announcing in radio is almost entirely a male occupation. Very few women staff announcers are employed, although there are a substantial number of women commentators who handle homemaking programs. Explanations ranging from "custom" to "overpatronizing style" of delivery are given for the scarcity of staff announcing positions for women in radio. The irregular hours of work and the necessity for operating technical equipment are other important reasons. Although few regular announcing shifts in television are taken by women, the opportunities for TV staff employment as hostesses, demonstrators, interviewers, and commercial and program announcers appear to be on the increase. Several years ago weather forecasts, for example, were given almost exclusively by men;

now many women handle weather forecasts. Commercial announcing assignments may be taken by free-lance or part-time people who are employed for specific programs or series.

As announcers move up from small local stations to large stations, more emphasis is placed upon specialties, sports, fashions, quizzes, interviewing, news, popular music, agriculture, home economics, etc. A staff announcer in New York turned his hobby into a profitable vocation—sketching amusing and pertinent cartoons as he presented the weather report on television. A professional baseball player or a college sports star may be hired to handle play-by-play sports accounts.

It is often possible for announcers to move into management, production, or sales positions, instead of into specialized performing work, following the break-in period. Women in secretarial positions, traffic, or continuity, may be pressed into service in small stations as occasional commercial announcers or demonstrators or may be asked to handle women's or children's programs. If they give evidence of proficiency in these assignments they may transfer to staff positions in larger stations. Women who work in nontalent jobs in large stations and networks seldom have opportunities to move over into programming. Salaries for announcers at small stations may be very low, due to the large number of candidates who apply.

Acting. Careers in acting are limited almost entirely to work in New York City and Hollywood. Only a few stations originate dramas for radio or TV on a regular basis. Even with the increase of television and film work, the field is overcrowded. There are practically no staff positions, and very few long-term contracts. Fewer radio plays are presented as television has increased. There is great competition for the acting roles in television. Relatively few opportunities exist for the newcomer to break into acting. Producers and casting directors do not have the time or need to consider inexperienced people. They usually demand previous "credits," indicating considerable theatrical or film experience. Successful models may occasionally move from appearances as models to acting roles in commercials. For those who feel that they are qualified and determined to go ahead and try to become professional actors, it is recommended that they seek experience in college drama of all types, followed by stock, community theater, local TV and radio station jobs, films, and whatever on-Broadway or off-Broadway theatrical roles are available. Vocal instruction and training in dance are desirable in addition to work in acting. In addition to the casting directors at stations and networks, a great number of different program production firms, advertising agencies, and film producers must be approached for auditions and interviews. There is no central casting agency. Individual contacts must be made and renewed at several hundred locations in New York. The television actor in Hollywood also must compete with the aspiring motion-picture hopefuls. Some actors are represented by agents who receive approximately a 10-per-cent commission when above union scale stipends are received for television and radio work. Few agents, however, will take a chance on representing unknowns. Minimum fee scales are established by the respective trade unions, AFTRA (American Federation of Television and Radio Artists) for television and radio, and SAG (Screen Actors Guild) for film. It is wise for would-be actors who plan a career in New York or Hollywood to have enough funds for an entire year's subsistence. If this is not possible, one should seek part-time employment of a type that permits free daytime periods for "making the rounds."

Specialized Performance Areas. Solo and choral vocalists, solo or orchestral musicians, vaudeville artists, magicians, puppeteers, dancers, and comedians are needed and used in broadcasting. Talent, personality, and experience are the elements required to carve out a career as a performer. It is generally not the training in television techniques that is more important, but the background in the particular branch of show business. Working before a live audience is quite essential before attempting studio work. Supplemental training in acting or broadcast speech is desirable. Many performers are called upon to speak or act before the camera or on microphone.

Sound-Effects Technicians. There is very limited turnover among sound-effects technicians. There are few positions other than those in network centers. If a position exists in a station or film-production unit, it may lead into direction or production.

Script Writers. Station staff writers prepare all types of scripts from continuity, voice-over-film narration and interviews to commercial copy. This type of position is often the means of obtaining a foothold in broadcasting. Women may find opportunities for employment. Frequently this job is combined with that of traffic clerk or music librarian. Wide general knowledge, "a little about a lot," and more intensive information about music and advertising are useful, in addition to knowing how to write for the ear or eye. Ability to turn out an acceptable script while working under pressure of time is essential. Advancement calls for imagination and creativity. Fresh and interesting ways to present familiar material without resorting to "gimmicks" or tricks are needed. Advertising agency or network staff writers are specialists in commercial and continuity respectively.

Contract and Free-Lance Writers. These writers are employed for program series by stations, networks, independent package companies and production firms. Experience and specialized skills in the type of program being produced are needed by such writers. Some may develop particular aptitudes for writing children's programs, for thinking up stunts for quizzes, or for finding clever visual approaches to explain medical, deep scientific, or agricultural subjects. Some discover that they are good at interviewing program guests ahead of broadcast time and preparing questions for an MC or commentator to use. Some show amazing facility in scripting dialogue banter for a "name" personality and any guest stars appearing with him.

Comedy "gag"- or "situation"-writers are the highest paid, and suffer the greatest job mortality.

As the television industry grew, there was an increase in dramatic programs, both live and on film. More opportunities developed for writers of plays. However, production of such programs is restricted in the main to New York and Hollywood. It is not easy for the novice to first write, then sell a dramatic script—especially when he is away from the production centers and unavailable for personal consultations about re-writes. Those who choose television dramatic writing as a career must realize that it is "tough, time-consuming, frustrating and insecure," but on the other hand, "can be satisfying, lucrative and the kind of challenge that comes only with a creative job . . . the singular difference between the successful TV writer and the unsuccessful is just one word—*talent*." [2]

Producers may elect to seek out writers from fields other than broadcasting for special assignments. A "name" playwright may be signed for a special dramatic series. A journalist or feature magazine writer who is an "expert" in foreign affairs may be recruited for a documentary series in that area. Often a writer or editor experienced in broadcasting techniques, may be hired to perform any rewriting which is necessary to prepare such material for the air.

Newsmen. Networks usually hire their news editors from the ranks of working newspapermen. Newscasters on the networks may be former announcers who have shown special skills in delivering the news or men trained in journalism who have turned to broadcasting. Some stations, however, prefer that both news editors and newscasters have newspaper experience; others allow these positions to be filled by announcers. Students who have college courses in journalism and broadcasting may be able to secure positions on the news staffs of broadcasting stations directly upon graduation. Supplemental experience in operation of a tape recorder and film and press cameras is desirable.

Floor (Stage) Manager, Facilities Assistant, Stage Hand. Another common method to enter the broadcasting field at many stations is by obtaining a position at the "bottom" of the production ladder as a stage manager, facilities assistant, or stage hand. In large cities, union contracts may govern the hiring conditions for these positions. Many stations will select from applicants for these jobs those who appear to be potential candidates for assistant or associate directorships and then directorial positions. Background in technical areas of the theater or experience in television at institutions that provide such training is helpful. Few women are chosen to fill these jobs.

Directors. Few radio stations employ full-time directors. Some television stations promote their directors from within the ranks, others prefer to bring

[2] Rod Serling in *How to Write for Television,* William Kaufman, ed. (New York, 1955), p. 67.

in their directors from other stations or from the theater or film. Agency and free-lance directors at the national level are generally selected from the network staffs. A knowledge of television techniques is essential. A background in radio, theater, and film is desirable but many directors have been successful in television without much experience in film. It is recommended, however, that prospective directors seek opportunities to work with film because of the rapid increase in the production of films for all kinds of television programs.

Producers. Some stations use this term interchangeably with director. Some describe their employees as producer-directors. Generally the producer is the one who exercises administrative and budgetary supervision and who has responsibility for the concept, format, and quality of the series. Producers are often selected from the ranks of directors. Persons who have established a reputation in other branches of show business as producers may be employed at the local or network level. Program stars may decide to invest their earnings and become producers.

Unit Managers. In network television, the position of unit manager has been established on an important managerial level. The unit manager, working closely with the producer and the director, is responsible for obtaining all the physical elements required for production and for maintaining budgetary control.

Film. As the number of television stations increases, a sizeable number of positions in film handling or production should be available. Even the smallest station usually requires one full-time film director. Generally two or three assistants in the film department are needed to work with him. They check the film in and out, time, cut, splice, supervise processing, and handle projection. Some women are employed in station film departments. Many stations employ a still photographer or a small motion-picture crew to cover local sports and news events.

A comparable increase in opportunities for employment in the creative side of film production should accompany the growth of the television industry. Those who are interested in starting in these areas may discover that individual initiative is highly important. Not many institutions offer formal instruction in cinematography. However, camera clubs and film societies are becoming more common. The student who is seriously considering a career in film production should learn editing principles and how to use a camera. It may be possible to begin by selling footage to TV stations in the local area. Some news departments purchase free-lance film coverage of spot and feature news. An accumulation of such credits may lead to specific assignments.

Cameramen. There is no consistency within the industry as to whether cameramen are technicians and belong to the engineering department or whether they are a part of programming. The determining factor is usually the union contract in force. Some local stations hire inexperienced persons and give them on-the-job training. Frequently this position is combined with other responsibilities in the programming area.

Artists. Practically every TV station has at least a small art staff. The art director usually has specialized experience in commercial art. His training should include design and theatrical staging. Because the smaller stations are interested in employees who are competent in several areas, even limited experience in art may be helpful in obtaining a position at such stations. Lettering skills, cartooning or sketching abilities, and facility in construction of scale models may be put to use.

Production Assistants. This position may be held by women as well as by men. When this is true, the production assistant is often referred to as a "script girl." Usually such positions are found only at television stations in metropolitan centers that are very active in programming. The production assistant works with the director and handles details and paper work. The production assistant may be responsible for the following items: marking scripts and distributing copies to various production units, checking facilities lists, obtaining signed W2 forms (tax withholding forms) from talent, keeping rehearsal time sheets for subsequent payment, typing script revisions, clearance of music, notifying guests of rehearsal times, taking notes for the director during rehearsal, compiling master as-broadcast scripts for filing, and "going out for coffee." General experience in broadcasting, theater, or film and training in shorthand and typing are helpful.

Engineers. Technical qualifications and FCC regulations require special training and skills in broadcasting engineers. Employment is relatively steady and provides gradual advancement over long periods of time. Local radio stations may hire "combination" men—those who can announce and also possess a first class radiotelephone operator's license. Television stations use many more engineers than radio stations. Employers emphasize a thorough knowledge of electrical engineering and physics for those entrusted with supervisory responsibilities at the transmitter and studio. Many engineers are closely allied to the programming areas in TV when assigned as cameramen, lighting directors, microphone boom operators, switchers, and technical directors. In some stations engineers handle video engineering, but when union contracts permit, switching is usually handled by the director.

Office Personnel. The general requirements for office work are essentially the same for broadcasting as for any other business. This is an entering wedge for many who later move over into performance or administration. As noted earlier, women with secretarial training may find employment in a small station and become familiar with the needs and requirements of the organization. Any special aptitudes they show, such as preparation of commercial copy, demonstration, narration, interviewing, art, film, etc., may accelerate a move into programming or production. Positions such as facilities assistant, music librarian, film librarian, and traffic may be considered office positions, but they are closely integrated with programming. No specific experience in broadcasting may be required. They can lead through promotion directly into programming.

Promotion, Public Relations, Publicity. These positions may be combined in smaller organizations with office, program, or commercial positions. The ability to establish excellent relationships with local educational, governmental, civic, and club groups; to write effective publicity releases; to plan showmanlike promotion campaigns; and carry out merchandising programs is not easily come by. It is an extremely marketable skill. Many of those working in this area come into broadcasting from magazines and newspapers and public relations. Knowledge of audience research techniques is helpful. Those who occupy these positions may report to management of a station and are included in the commercial department. Women as well as men are selected for these positions.

Commercial Department. Training in business administration, advertising, bookkeeping, accounting, psychology and speech are desirable for positions in the commercial department. Knowledge of the program side is very useful. Not only time but programs are to be sold. Salesmen in many stations plan programs for clients, assist in selection of talent, and even write commercial copy. As in many businesses, the effective salesmen are among the highest-paid staff employees. Advancement into general administrative positions from the commercial department is a normal progression.

Agencies and Program Production Companies. Not all careers involving television and radio specialization are with stations and networks. Mention has been made of the advertising agency. The student who is interested in the program side alone often does not think of the advertising agency, yet many programs and all commercials are conceived, written, produced, and often directed by agency personnel. Those seeking employment as talent, writers and program production people for this work must apply to the agency. Agencies generally do not hire staff announcers, but they do employ copy writers, script editors, program supervisors, and producer-directors on a staff basis in their television and radio production departments. Students who plan to enter the business side of broadcasting may find more opportunities with advertising agencies than with stations. The American Association of Advertising Agencies gives annual aptitude examinations in the field of advertising. Results are made available for comparison with national scores and an estimate is given about the phases of advertising activity that seems best suited for the individual person. The test results may be used by applicants seeking positions in advertising agencies.

Many network programs and syndicated film series are produced by special companies. Some companies establish reputations as experts in religious or informational programming; others may work exclusively on musical or cartoon-type commercials; some may purchase the broadcasting rights to an author's works and develop an entire series; or one or several stars may form a production company. There are literally hundreds of such program-production companies. Generally these companies employ key people who have "credits" in the particular job classification. Employment may be remunerative but at the same time quite precarious. Short-term contracts with options for continued employment are the practice.

An entry into broadcasting by free-lance packaging of programming ideas for stations or program-production companies should not be overlooked. A program idea, script, and available talent may enable one person or a small group to enter into business.

Educational Radio and Television. The increased recognition of educational programming by school sytems, community groups and institutions of higher learning enables young people to combine specialization in broadcasting with courses and certification in the teaching profession. There are a substantial number of positions available in the areas of program development, promotion, evaluation, and research. Private businesses, social agencies, civic, labor and political organizations often employ persons who build informational broadcasts and films. Noncommercial stations and educational program production centers may have openings for those interested in a career in broadcasting. Some believe that the opportunities for creative expression that exist, and the personal satisfaction that comes about because of the content and purposes of educational programming, are strong motivating factors to lead one to select educational broadcasting instead of commercial work. Some approach educational broadcasting as an excellent means of learning fundamentals and developing skills which may be useful in commercial stations, networks, agencies and program production centers. Relatively more opportunities exist for women in educational television than in the commercial world of television and radio.

Glossary of Studio Terms

above-the-line. Talent elements in a television or radio show, including performers, writers, producers, directors, etc.

abstract set. A nonrepresentational setting using elements such as drapes, columns, steps, platforms, free-standing flats with various textures and geometrical forms, etc. Such a setting has no definite locale.

AD (Assistant Director). At television network headquarters, *Associate Director*.

ad lib. To depart from the prepared script with extemporaneous remarks or to proceed without any script or music. Pronounced ăd lib, not äd lib.

aspect-ratio. The ratio of width to height of the television picture transmitted— 4 to 3.

audio. Sound transmission as contrasted to video; radio frequency circuits, or power circuits.

back-timing. Timing the closing section prior to broadcast in order to establish the exact "clock" time when such section should begin on the actual broadcast in order to finish smoothly.

back-to-back. Consecutive programs originating from the same studio.

balance. Relative placement around microphones and level of volume projection of vocalists, musicians, actors, and sound effects according to desired artistic effects.

Balop. An opaque projector (reflected light instead of transparent light as in slide projectors). Derived from "Balopticon" manufactured by Bausch and Lomb.

barn door. Hinged metal flap for television lights. Used to prevent unwanted "spill" light.

BCU. Big close-up.

BG. Background.

beam. Area of effective microphone pick-up—varies according to type of microphone.

below-the-line. Production elements in a television show, including such items as technical facilities, staging services, studio usage, etc.

bend the needle. Sudden burst of volume making the needle on the VU meter shoot far past normal maximum peak.

bible. Reference book containing statements of station's or network's policies and regulations.

blast. Too much level, causing distortion.

blow-up. Enlargement of a particular portion of photograph or printed material for legible TV reception.

blue gag. Off-color material.

board. The control-room audio console. Also referred to as "panel" or "mixer."

board fade. Fading in or out of the program or any element by manipulation of the volume controls on the control-room console.

boom. (1) In radio, a microphone stand with horizontal arm permitting flexible adjustment of microphone position. (2) In television, more elaborate versions

619

for suspension of microphones out of camera range and elevation of cameras for overhead shots. These TV booms may be mounted on movable dollies and operated electrically.

bring it up. Order for increase in volume.

broad. A general source of light such as a scoop, fluorescent, or incandescent banks.

burn in. Image retention on camera tube following completion of shot. After several hundred hours of use the image orthicon tube tends to burn in if a shot is held for more than a few seconds, especially after shooting a title card, graphs, or advertising symbol.

busy. Anything too complicated or elaborate in design such as a "busy" background. Diverts attention away from desired focus of interest.

canned. Recorded or transcribed material.

cans. Head phones.

clambake. Ineffective performance due to unfortunate mistakes or poor showmanship.

clean it up. Order for additional rehearsal to smooth out rough spots.

clearance. Permission to use copyright material.

closed circuit. Point-to-point program feed. Contrasted to a "broadcast" presentation.

cold. Starting a broadcast with announcer or dialogue before program theme.

coming up. Program or portion of program about to begin.

contrast. The brightness relationships between different elements in picture being transmitted.

copy. Material to be read. Generally used to refer to announcer's material, either commercial credits or continuity.

corn, corny. Overly obvious or old and familiar material.

crawl. Device used to reveal program titles and credits. Motor or hand operation. Speed may be varied.

credits. Program personnel names—performers, writers, directors, producers, etc., who are given visual (and/or) aural recognition at opening and closing of program.

cross-fade. See *segue.*

cue. (1) Hand signal to performer. (2) Word signal in the script to start or stop an effect, speech, movement, or music. (3) Pre-established word signal for switching from one pick-up to another. (4) Station or network identification at the close of a program. (5) Music used for background mood music or bridges in dramatic programs. (6) "Cueing" records or transcriptions is to have them ready to play without delay when required.

cue sheet or *cue card.* Large cardboard sheets which contain lyrics, subject outline, or exact words of script. Held next to the camera for reference use by talent or speaker. Referred to also as "idiot sheets."

CU. Close-up.

cushion. Material near the end which may be used wholly, in part, or eliminated in order to complete the program on time.

cut. (1) To eliminate. (2) An individual selection or portion on a transcription.

Cyc. (Cyclorama). Neutral background, usually a light-colored, cloth backdrop stretched tight to eliminate wrinkles and folds. Frequently used for sky background.

definition. Distinctness, clarity of detail.

dead. (1) Insensitive side of a microphone. (2) A closed microphone or one which is not connected. (3) Possessing a high degree of sound absorbency.

(4) Element in a program which is not to be used.

depth of field. Distance to or from camera talent or object can move or be moved without becoming out of focus.

detail set. See *insert set*.

diffusor. Material (silk gauze or spun glass) used to soften a beam of light. Attached to the light by a metal-frame holder.

dissolve. Fade-in of picture from black or from the picture to black. Used for a transition from one camera to another with a slight overlapping of the two pictures.

dolly. Movable platform on which a camera or microphone is mounted.

dolly in, dolly out. Movement of camera in towards scene, movement away.

dress. Final rehearsal before performance. A run-through exactly as the program is to be presented.

dry-run. Program rehearsal without all of program personnel present such as a run-through without engineer, sound effects technicians, or camera men.

echo. Reverberation supplementing voice or music according to effect desired such as a cave or empty auditorium for speech and extra "brightness" or "life" for music. True echo, repetition of sound with a brief time lag, may be achieved electronically. Acoustical sound reflection, used more frequently, is accomplished by adding extra reverberation in an echo chamber. The echo chamber may be a separate room, tunnel, or labyrinth with a microphone at one end picking up the program coming out of a speaker at the other end. Additional open microphones in other parts of the studio may add reverberation without the use of an echo chamber.

ECU or *ETCU*. Extreme close-up.

ET. Electrical transcription. "Give ET" is to announce the program as being transcribed.

ETV. Educational television.

fade. Increase or decrease of audio or video volume. "Take a fade" is a direction to the actor to use a "physical" fade—moving away from or toward the microphone.

fader. Knob on audio or video amplifying equipment. In radio, generally means the volume controls on the control-room console. Referred to also as "pot." Technically a potentiometer or attenuator.

feed-back. Disturbing hum or whistle caused by a return of portion of an amplifier's output to its input as when a public address microphone is too close to its loud speaker.

FG. Foreground.

fill, filler. Material prepared in advance of broadcast for stretch purposes or to fill in dead spots during special events and sportscasts or emergencies.

film clip. Short length of film used within the program.

film loop. A length of film with ends spliced together. It may be projected continuously.

filter. Any device which changes the quality of transmitted sound by elimination of certain frequencies for telephone or "inner-voices" effects and the like. Usually accomplished electrically in the control room.

flexitron. Electronic device that can make the camera picture wave from side to side to create a special effect.

flip cards. Pieces of cardboard in the correct aspect ratio, containing credits, program titles, or commercial slogans. The cards may be pulled away one at a time, flipped up or flipped down to show material for camera pick-up.

fluff. An error or mistake in presentation by the performer or technician.

format. The arrangement of program elements in an established pattern.

frame-up. Camera direction to indicate need for correction of obvious error in composition.

45s. Records or transcriptions to be played at forty-five revolutions per minute.

free-lance. Nonstaff.

from the top. Order to start rehearsal from the very beginning of the musical number or script. May also refer to the start of a scene currently being rehearsed.

gain. Degree of amplification of an audio circuit.

gimmick. A new element or change in approach, arrangement, or emphasis in existing program format.

gizmo. A "catch-all" word to describe something for which no technical designation is known or when the speaker does not wish to use the correct term.

ike. The iconoscope camera.

in the mud. Low level of volume unsuitable for effective transmission.

inky. Small 150-watt spotlight often put on front of camera. Used for lighting eyes or face in a close-up. May be called an "inkie-dinky." Also used to refer to any incandescent light.

IO. Image orthicon tube. Also referred to as "eeymo" or "orth."

Insert set. Segment of a normal-sized set, such as two stools, a short section of a lunch counter, and a cash register representing a restaurant for a brief scene. Sometimes referred to as a "detail set."

kill. Eliminate or cut.

kine. Kinescope.

kinescope. (1) Cathode-ray receiving tube with fluorescent screen—either direct view or projection type. (2) Method for delayed telecast presentation by making a film from the monitor kinescope as the program is in progress.

lap. Camera direction calling for a superimposure. "Lap three" would mean that the switcher should super camera three over whatever picture is being transmitted.

leader. Blank film attached to beginning or end of film clip or reel. It is used to aid threading up the film in the projector. May be numbered to show the number of seconds remaining before the picture starts.

level. Amount of volume of transmitted sound.

limbo. A background which is "nothingness." No light reaches any part of the background.

live. (1) An open microphone. Also referred to as "hot." (2) Possessing a high degree of sound reflection. (3) Simultaneous performance and transmission for home reception.

log. A detailed chronological listing of a station's complete schedule.

logo. Symbol or trademark.

lose the light. Refers to the tally light. A camera direction indicating that the camera is no longer "hot." *i.e.,* "Move in for a close-up when you lose the light."

LS. Long shot.

master. (1) A complete and official script. (2) Authoritative schedule. (3) Transcription or record die kept on file and used to make duplications. (4) The fader on the control console with over-all regulation of volume.

MC. (1) Master of ceremonies. (2) Master control room.

MCU. Medium close-up.

MI. Move in (to cameraman).

mix. To manipulate the faders on the control-room console—blending two or more program elements according to desired balance.

mixer. (1) Speech amplifier having two or more inputs. (2) A studio engineer.

monitor. (1) To listen to or to view the program. (2) A TV kinescope for checking pictures before or during transmission. A "jeep monitor" used in the studio is movable.

MS. Medium shot.

nemo. A remote, a program originating away from the studio.

NI. Network identification.

noodle. Improvise on piano or other musical instrument.

off-mike. Location of performer or sound effect back from the microphone.

on-mike. Directly on the beam and near the microphone.

on-the-cuff. A performance without pay.

on-the-nose. Program starting, proceeding, or ending on time.

one shot. (1) A single appearance on a program series. (2) Close-up of one person in television.

open-end transcription. Transcribed program with allowance for local commercial copy at beginning, middle (possibly), and at close of the transcription.

orth. (1) Image orthicon camera. (2) Image orthicon tube.

PA. (1) Public-address system. (2) Press agent.

pan. Move camera horizontally to right or left to follow action or direct attention to another area or subject.

patch. To connect separate pieces of equipment by patch cords so as route the circuit as desired.

PAX. Private telephone system.

PB. Pull back (to cameraman).

PD. Material in the public domain—not protected by copyright and available for use without payment or permission.

peak. A meter reading indicating the relative volume of transmitted sound. In studio practice, "zero peaks" on the VU meter represent normal upper limits of volume without distortion.

pedestal up (down). Direction to camera man meaning to raise (or lower) the camera height.

pick-up. (1) The produced sound transmission due to relative placement of performers and microphones in a studio or from a remote. (2) A program origination location. (3) Transcription or phonograph arm.

pick it up. Direction to increase the tempo—to speed up performance.

pix. Picture.

PL. Private telephone line.

platter. Transcription or record.

play-back. To monitor a tape or disc recording immediately after it is made.

plug. Commercial announcement.

practical. Prop that is real or one which actually works, such as a practical door or window.

prerecorded. Method of recording speech or songs prior to telecast. Performer may then be free to dance or move freely about during play-back on the air. Lyrics or speech may be pantomimed in lip sync during the play-back.

presence. An "on-mike" pick-up which has effective intimacy.

prop. Physical materials of a set other than scenery and costume. Hand props are those handled by actors. Set dressing props are furniture and set decorations.

Q. Cue.

read-y. Mechanical or overly precise "word-by-word" reading style.

release. Direction to cameraman indicating that he is free to move to his next position.

ribbon. A velocity microphone.

ride gain. To regulate the volume level of transmitted sound. Extended to refer to the action of a studio engineer, regulation of levels, and mixing at the control-room console.

roll it. A cue for the start of film.

RP. Rear-screen projection. Stills or motion pictures projected on a large translucent screen provide a background for the scene.

RPM. Revolutions per minute.

salt-shaker. A Western Electric pressure-type microphone.

schmalz. An overly sweet manner of musical arrangements or presentation; a mawkish style of writing or delivery.

scoop. (1) Distortion (wow) due to the fader being turned up before the record or transcription attains regular speed. (2) General source of light, usually 500- to 2000-watt lamps. Parabolic shape. Used for base or fill light.

scratch. Groove noise on record or transcription which makes it unsuitable for broadcast if too intense. Referred to also as "fry."

scrim. Transparent gauze-like material used for special staging effects.

script. Complete written collection of all audio and video material and directions for the program as it is to be presented.

segue. (1) An overlapping of two elements as one fades in over another fading out. Sound effects, dialogue, or recorded music may be segued. Referred to as "cross fade." (2) In music, a transition from one number or theme to another.

set-up. (1) The relative physical location of performers, microphones, instruments and sound effects equipment in the studio. (2) To set up is to get ready technically for the program.

78s. Records to be played at seventy-eight revolutions per minute.

signature. Theme.

sneak. A very gradual fade in or out of music or sound so as to be unobtrusive.

soap opera. A daytime five-a-week serial.

SOF. Sound on film. Film which contains narration or dialogue.

sound truck. Movable cabinet with multiple turntables and attachments for playing recorded sound effects.

split screen. Electronic effect whereby portions of pictures from two cameras divide the screen. Frequently used for telephone scene. One part is at left—other at right.

spot. Spotlights. Source of specific and directional light. Used for key or modeling lighting, back lighting, accent lighting etc. Spots range from 250 to 2000 watts.

spread. (1) Time available for stretching a program or any portion of it. (2) In comedy or variety programs the time allotted for audience reactions such as applause and laughter as well as for ad libbing by performers.

stab. Short musical punctuation played with sharp attack. Also referred to as "sting."

stagger through. First rehearsal in studio with cameras.

stand by. (1) Order to get ready to begin. (2) A substitute program ready as a fill in case of an emergency.

stock footage. Scenes or sequences on film which are not limited to a specialized or one-time use but which may be used in different programs. Examples of scenes found on stock footage: Broadway, ocean liner, train passing in the night, storm, airplane view of New York, fields of waving grain, etc.

stretch. To slow down a performance.

strike. To pull down, dismantle, remove sets.

super imp. A superimposition in television—the use of two cameras at the same time, each with its own picture but transmitted as a single picture. More than two cameras may be used for special effects.

sync. Synchronization.

take. (1) A switching direction—"Ready One . . . Take One." (2) Picture or scene held by TV camera. (3) Such a scene so televised or filmed.

take five. Direction for a brief break or recess in rehearsal.

take it away. An engineering cue to start a program which is given over a telephone circuit with the identification of pick-up usually added to the cue such as "Take it away Central Park."

take a level. A prebroadcast test on microphone to determine balance and fader positions on the control-room console.

talk-back. Communication system permitting control-room personnel to talk to those in the studio.

tally light. Indicator light on a camera to show when it is "hot," on the air.

TC. Title card. May be extended to refer to any card or graphic.

TD. Technical director.

TelePrompter. A device mounted above the top lens on each camera, or on special stands which permits the performer to follow the script. Words are typed in extra large type on a continuous roll of paper. Speed of script exposure may be governed by pace of delivery by performer.

Telop. (1) An opaque projector. (2) A 3¼" x 4" opaque card used for titles, credits, and art work. Projected from film studio.

33s. (1) Transcriptions prepared for broadcasting and played at thirty-three-and-a-third revolutions per minute. (2) Long-playing microgroove records.

tight. A program which is so close to its allotted time that any spread might cause it to run over time.

tilt. Move camera vertically up or down.

time check. Synchronization of all clocks and watches involved in timing of a program.

truck. To move camera parallel to a piece of furniture or set background, or to move with a person crossing the set.

two-shot. Close-up of two persons in television.

VCU. Very extreme close-up. Also referred to as *XCU.*

V.I. Volume indicator. Refers to the VU meter on the control-room console which indicates electrically the volume of the sound being transmitted.

video. Visual portion of television transmission.

VO. Voice over. Live narration or dialogue presented during projection of silent film or action in the studio.

VU meter. A meter which indicates electrically the instantaneous volume of sound being transmitted. Readings by volume units (VU) in decibels from minus 20 to plus 3.

whodunit. Mystery melodrama.

winging a show. Directing a telecast without rehearsal.

wow. Speed variation resulting in distortion of a record or transcription at the start or during its playing. Referred to as "scoop" when coming at the start.

X/S. Over or across the shoulder shot.

zoom. Rapid change of camera pick-up effected electronically from long shot to close-up without losing focus.

Bibliography

Several useful bibliographies have been published in the field of radio and television. They are:

British Broadcasting: A Bibliography (London: BBC, 1954).

Broderick, Gertrude G. (ed.), *Radio and Television Bibliography* (Washington, 1952). This is a U. S. Government publication. It may be obtained by mailing fifteen cents to the Superintendent of Documents, U. S. Government Printing Office, Washington 25, D. C.

Cooper, Isabelle M., *Bibliography on Educational Broadcasting* (Chicago: University of Chicago Press, 1942). This is a bibliography on the historical, technical, and educational aspects of broadcasting.

Paulu, Burton, *A Radio and Television Bibliography* (Urbana, Illinois: National Association of Educational Broadcasters, 1952).

Rose, Oscar, (ed.), *Radio Broadcasting and Television* (New York: H. W. Wilson, 1947). This is an annotated listing of nearly one thousand books, articles, and pamphlets on radio and television, classified under a dozen subject headings.

Listings of current magazine articles on radio and television, accompanied by brief abstracts, appear regularly in the issues of the *Quarterly Journal of Speech*.

GENERAL

Ace, Goodman, *The Book of Little Knowledge* (New York: Simon & Schuster, 1955).

Archer, Gleason L., *Big Business and Radio* (New York: American Historical Society, 1939).

————, *History of Radio to 1926* (New York: American Historical Society, 1938).

Banning, W. P., *Commercial Broadcasting Pioneer* (Cambridge: Harvard University Press, 1947).

Barrett, Edward W., *Truth Is Our Weapon* (New York: Funk and Wagnalls, 1953).

BBC Handbook 1956 (London: BBC, 1956).

Beachcroft, T. O., *British Broadcasting* (London: Longmans, Green, 1946).

Brindze, Ruth, *Not To Be Broadcast* (New York: Vanguard, 1937).

Bryson, Lyman, *Time for Reason About Radio* (New York: George W. Stewart, 1948).

Cantril, Hadley, *The Invasion from Mars* (Princeton: Princeton University Press, 1940).

———— and Gordon W. Allport, *The Psychology of Radio* (New York: Harper, 1935).

Chafee, Zechariah, *Government and Mass Communications* (Chicago: University of Chicago Press, 1947), 2 vols.

Chappell, Matthew N. and C. E. Hooper, *Radio Audience Measurement* (New York: Stephen Daye, 1944).

Chase, Francis, *Sound and Fury* (New York: Harper, 1942).

Childs, Harwood L. and John B. Whitton, *Propaganda by Short Wave* (Princeton: Princeton University Press, 1942).

Coase, R. H., *British Broadcasting: A Study in Monopoly* (Cambridge: Harvard University Press, 1950).

Commission on Freedom of the Press, *A Free and Responsible Press* (Chicago: University of Chicago Press, 1947).

Crosby, John, *Out of the Blue* (New York: Simon & Schuster, 1952).

Day, Enid, *Radio Broadcasting for Retailers* (New York: Fairchild, 1947).

DeForest, Lee, *Father of Radio* (New York: Wilcox and Follett, 1950).

Dryer, Sherman, *Radio in Wartime* (New York: Greenberg, 1942).

Eckersley, P. P., *The Power Behind the Microphone* (London: Jonathan Cape, 1941).

Edelman, Murray, *The Licensing of Radio Services in the U. S.* (Urbana: University of Illinois Press, 1950).

Ernst, Morris L., *The First Freedom* (New York: Macmillan, 1946).

Evans, Jacob A., *Selling and Promoting Radio and Television* (New York: *Printer's Ink,* 1954).

Ewbank, Henry L. and Sherman P. Lawton, *Broadcasting: Radio and Television* (New York: Harper, 1952).

Federal Communications Commission, *An Economic Study of Standard Broadcasting* (Washington: Government Printing Office, 1947).

———, *Annual Reports* (Washington: Government Printing Office).

———, *Public Service Responsibility of Broadcast Licensees* (Washington: Government Printing Office, 1946).

———, *Report on Chain Broadcasting.* Commission Order No. 37, Docket No. 5060 (Washington: Government Printing Office, 1941).

Federal Council of Churches of Christ, *Broadcasting and the Public* (New York: Abingdon Press, 1938).

Friedrich, Carl J. and Jeanette Sayre, *The Development of the Control of Advertising on the Air* (Cambridge: Radiobroadcasting Research Project, 1940). (No. 1 in Studies in the Control of Radio.)

——— and Evelyn Sternberg, *Congress and the Control of Radiobroadcasting* (Cambridge: Radiobroadcasting Research Project, 1944). (No. 5 in Studies in the Control of Radio.)

Frost, S. E. Jr., *Is American Radio Democratic?* (Chicago: University of Chicago Press, 1937).

Garver, Robert I., *Successful Radio Advertising* (New York: Prentice-Hall, 1949).

Goldsmith, Alfred N. and Austin C. Lescarboura, *This Thing Called Broadcasting* (New York: Henry Holt, 1930).

Gordon, Lincoln, *The Public Corporation in Great Britain* (New York: Oxford University Press, 1938).

Gorham, Maurice, *Broadcasting and Television Since 1900* (London: Andrew Dakers, 1952).

Gorham, Maurice, *Sound and Fury: 21 Years in the BBC* (London: Percival Marshall and Co., 1948).

———, *Television* (New York: Macmillan, 1950).

Gross, Ben, *I Looked and I Listened* (New York: Random House, 1954).

Hearings before a Subcommittee of the Committee on Interstate and Foreign Commerce, United States Senate, 80th Congress, 1st Session, on S. 1333, a Bill to Amend the Communications Act of 1934, and for Other Purposes Washington: Government Printing Office, 1947).

Hearings before the U. S. Senate Interstate and Foreign Commerce Committee on S. 658 (1951); *Senate Report No. 44* (1951), The McFarland Bill (Washington: Government Printing Office, 1951).

Hearings before a Subcommittee of the Committee on Interstate and Foreign Commerce, House of Representatives, 82nd Congress, 2nd Session, on H. Res. 278 (1952). The Gathings Resolution (Washington: Government Printing Office, 1952).

Hearings before the Subcommittee to Investigate Juvenile Delinquency of the Committee on the Judiciary (1955), U. S. Senate (Washington: Government Printing Office, 1955).

Hearings before the Committee on Interstate and Foreign Commerce, U. S. Senate, on S. 2444 (1952). The Johnson-Case Bill (Washington: Government Printing Office, 1952).

Hearings before the Subcommittee on Communications of the Committee on Interstate and Foreign Commerce, 83rd Congress, U. S. Senate, on "The Status of UHF Television Stations and S. 3095" (Washington: Government Printing Office, 1954).

Hepner, Harry W., *Effective Advertising* (New York: McGraw-Hill, 1949).

Jones, Robert F., *Progress Report—Investigation of Television Networks and the UHF-VHF Problem.* U. S. Senate Committee on Interstate and Foreign Commerce, 84th Congress (Washington: Government Printing Office, 1955).

Kaplan, Milton A., *Radio and Poetry* (New York: Columbia University Press, 1949).

Kaufman, William I. and Robert Colodzin, *Your Career in Television* (New York: Merlin Press, 1950).

Kirby, Edward M. and Jack Harris, *Star-Spangled Radio* (Indianapolis: Bobbs-Merrill, 1946).

Klapper, Joseph T., *The Effects of Mass Media* (New York: Bureau of Applied Social Research, 1949).

Kris, Ernst and Hans Speier, *German Radio Propaganda* (New York: Oxford University Press, 1944).

Lambert, R. S., *Ariel and All His Quality: An Impression of the BBC from Within* (London: Gollancz, 1940).

Landry, Robert J., *This Fascinating Radio Business* (Indianapolis: Bobbs-Merrill, 1946).

———, *Who, What, Why Is Radio?* (New York: George W. Stewart, 1942).

Lazarsfeld, Paul F., *Radio and the Printed Page* (New York: Duell, Sloan & Pearce, 1940).

——— and Harry Field, *The People Look at Radio* (Chapel Hill: University of North Carolina Press, 1946).

——— and Patricia L. Kendall, *Radio Listening in America* (New York: Prentice-Hall, 1948).

——— and Frank N. Stanton, *Communications Research, 1948-1949* (New York: Harper, 1949).

Lazarsfeld, Paul F. and Frank N. Stanton, *Radio Research, 1941* (New York: Duell, Sloan & Pearce, 1941).

———, *Radio Research, 1942-1943* (New York: Duell, Sloan & Pearce, 1944).

Lerner, Daniel, *Sykewar: Psychological Warfare against Germany, D-Day to VE-Day* (New York: George W. Stewart, 1947).

Lewis, Howard T., "Radio," *Encyclopedia of Social Sciences,* XIII (New York: Macmillan, 1942).

Lindsley, Charles F., *Radio and Television Communication* (New York: Mc-Graw-Hill, 1952).

Mackey, David R., *Drama on the Air* (New York: Prentice-Hall, 1951).

Manvell, Roger, *The Crowded Air* (New York: Channel Press, 1953).

Marx, Herbert L. (ed.), *Television and Radio in American Life* (New York: H. W. Wilson, 1953).

McNicol, Donald, *Radio's Conquest of Space* (New York: Rinehart, 1946).

Merton, Robert K., *Mass Persuasion* (New York: Harper, 1946).

Midgley, Ned, *The Advertising and Business Side of Radio* (New York: Prentice-Hall, 1948).

Miller, Merle, *The Judges and the Judged* (New York: Doubleday, 1952).

Morris, Lloyd, *Not So Long Ago* (New York: Random House, 1949).

Moser, J. G. and Richard A. Lavine, *Radio and the Law* (Los Angeles: Parker, 1947).

Nielsen, A. C., *Television Audience Research for Great Britain* (Chicago: A. C. Nielsen, 1955).

Overseas Information Programs of the United States, Report of the Committee on Foreign Relations, U. S. Senate, 83rd Congress, 1st Session, Report No. 406 (Washington: Government Printing Office, 1953).

Parker, Everett C., Elinor Inman, and Ross Snyder, *Religious Radio* (New York: Harper, 1948).

————, D. W. Barry, and D. W. Smythe, *The Television-Radio Audience and Religion* (New York: Harper, 1955).

Phillips, David C. *et al., Introduction to Radio and Television* (New York: Ronald Press, 1954).

Plotkin, Harry M., *Memorandum—Television Network Regulation and the UHF Problem.* U. S. Senate Committee on Interstate and Foreign Commerce, 84th Congress (Washington: Government Printing Office, 1955).

Reinsch, J. Leonard, *Radio Station Management* (New York: Harper, 1948).

Reith, Sir John, *Into the Wind* (London: Hodder, 1949).

Report of the Broadcasting Committee, 1949 (London: H. M. Stationery Office, 1951).

Rolo, Charles J., *Radio Goes to War* (New York: G. P. Putnam's Sons, 1942).

Rose, C. B., *National Policy for Radio Broadcasting* (New York: Harper, 1940).

Royal Commission of Canada, *Report on National Development in the Arts, Letters and Sciences, 1949-1951* (Ottawa: The King's Printer, 1951).

Sandage, C. H., *Radio Advertising for Retailers* (Cambridge: Harvard University Press, 1945).

Schramm, Wilbur (ed.), *Mass Communications* (Urbana: University of Illinois Press, 1949).

Schramm, Wilbur, *The Process and Effects of Mass Communications* (Urbana: University of Illinois, 1954).

Seehafer, Eugene F. and J. W. Laemmar, *Successful Radio and Television Advertising* (New York: McGraw-Hill, 1951).

Seldes, Gilbert, *The Great Audience* (New York: Viking, 1950).

Shayon, Robert Lewis, *Television and Our Children* (New York: Longmans, Green, 1951).

Shurick, E. P. J., *The First Quarter-Century of American Broadcasting* (Kansas City: Midland, 1946).

Siepmann, Charles A., *Radio, Television, and Society* (New York: Oxford University Press, 1950).

———, *Radio in Wartime* (New York: Oxford University Press, 1942).

———, *Radio's Second Chance* (Boston: Little, Brown, 1946).

———, *The Radio Listener's Bill of Rights* (New York: Anti-Defamation League, 1948).

Sill, Jerome, *The Radio Station* (New York: George W. Stewart, 1946).

Smythe, Dallas W. and Angus Campbell, *Los Angeles Television May 23-29, 1952* (Urbana: University of Illinois, 1952).

Spingarn, Jerome, *Radio Is Yours*. Public Affairs Pamphlet 121 (New York, 1946).

Straight, Michael, *Trial by Television* (Boston: Beacon Press, 1954).

Summers, H. B. (ed.), *Radio Censorship* (New York: H. W. Wilson, 1939).

Thomson, Charles A. H., *Television and Presidential Politics* (Washington, The Brookings Institution, 1956).

Thurber, James, "Soapland," in *The Beast in Me and Other Animals* (New York: Harcourt, Brace, 1948).

True, Herbert (comp.), *Television Dictionary/Handbook for Sponsors* (New York: Sponsors Services, 1955).

UNESCO, *Report of the Commission on Technical Needs in Press, Radio, Film.* Following the Survey in Twelve War-Devastated Countries, Document 2C/8 (Paris, 1947).

———, *Report of the Commission on Technical Needs in Press, Film, Radio.* Following Surveys in Seventeen Countries, Publication 214 (Paris, 1948).

———, *Report Following Surveys in 14 Countries and Territories.* Publication 436 (Paris, 1949).

UNESCO, *Television: A World Survey* (New York: Columbia University Press, 1954).

———, *World Communications* (New York: Columbia University Press, 1950).

Waller, Judith C., *Radio: The Fifth Estate* (Boston: Houghton Mifflin, 1950).

Waples, Douglas (ed.), *Print, Radio and Film in a Democracy* (Chicago: University of Chicago Press, 1942).

White, Llewellyn, *The American Radio* (Chicago: University of Chicago Press, 1947).

——— and Robert D. Leigh, *Peoples Speaking to Peoples* (Chicago: University of Chicago Press, 1946).

Whiteside, Thomas, *The Relaxed Sell* (New York: Oxford University Press, 1954).

Williams, A. N., *Listening* (Denver: University of Denver Press, 1948).

Willis, Edgar E., *Foundations of Broadcasting: Radio and Television* (New York: Oxford University Press, 1951).

Wolfe, Charles H., *Modern Radio Advertising* (New York: *Printer's Ink,* 1949).

Wylie, Max, *Clear Channels: Television and the American People* (New York: Funk and Wagnalls, 1954).

EDUCATION

Advisory Committee on Educational Broadcasting, *Broadcasting to Schools.* A UNESCO Publication (New York: Columbia University Press, 1949).

Barr, Arvil S., Henry L. Ewbank, and Thomas C. McCormick (eds.), *Radio in the Classroom* (Madison: University of Wisconsin Press, 1942).

Callahan, Jennie Waugh, *Radio Workshop for Children* (New York: McGraw-Hill, 1948).

———, *Television in School, College, and Community* (New York: McGraw-Hill, 1953).

Clausse, Roger, *Education by Radio: School Broadcasting.* A UNESCO Publication (New York: Columbia University Press, 1949).

Cumming, William Kenneth, *This Is Educational Television* (1954).

Directory of College Courses in Radio and Television 1954-1955 (Washington: U. S. Office of Education, 1955).

Dunham, Franklin and R. R. Lowdermilk, *Television in Our Schools* (Washington: Government Printing Office, 1952).

Education on the Air (Columbus, Ohio: Ohio State University Press, 1930 to date).

French, Florence F., William B. Levenson and Vera C. Rockwell, *Radio English* (New York: McGraw-Hill, 1952).

Gordon, Dorothy, *All Children Listen* (New York: George W. Stewart, 1942).

Harrison, Margaret, *Radio in the Classroom* (New York: Prentice-Hall, 1937).

Henry, Nelson B. (ed.), *Mass Media and Education* (Chicago: University of Chicago Press, 1954).

Herzberg, Max J. (ed.), *Radio and English Teaching* (New York: D. Appleton-Century Co., 1941).

Hill, Frank Ernest, *Tune in for Education* (New York: National Committee on Education by Radio, 1942).

——— and W. E. Williams, *Radio's Listening Groups* (New York: Columbia University Press, 1941).

Hill, Harold E., *The National Association of Educational Broadcasters: A History* (Urbana, Ill.: National Association of Educational Broadcasters, 1954).

Lambert, Richard S., *Radio in Canadian Schools* (Toronto: School Aids and Text Book Publishing, 1949).

Levenson, William B. and Edward Stasheff, *Teaching Through Radio and Television* (New York: Rinehart, 1952).

Mabley, Jack, *What Educational TV Offers You,* Public Affairs Pamphlet 203 (New York, 1954).

Newsom, Carroll V. (ed.), *A Television Policy for Education* (Washington: American Council on Education, 1953).

O'Brien, Mae, *Children's Reactions to Radio Adaptations of Juvenile Books* (New York: King's Crown Press, Columbia University, 1950).

Palmer, Richard, *School Broadcasting in Britain* (London: BBC, 1947).

Poole, Lynn, *Science Via Television* (Baltimore: Johns Hopkins Press, 1950).

Sandage, Charles H., *Building Audiences for Educational Radio Programs* (Urbana: University of Illinois, 1951).

Siepmann, Charles A., *Television and Education in the United States.* A UNESCO Publication (New York: Columbia University Press, 1952).

Tyson, Levering (ed.), *Radio and Education* (Chicago: University of Chicago Press, 1931-1935).

Willey, Roy De Verl and Helen Ann Young, *Radio in Elementary Education* (Boston: Heath, 1948).

Williams, J. Grenfell, *Radio in Fundamental Education in Undeveloped Areas.* A UNESCO Publication (New York: Columbia University Press, 1950).

Witty, Paul and Harry Brecker, *Your Child and Radio, TV, Comics and Movies* (Chicago: Science Research Associates, 1952).

Woelfel, Norman and I. Keith Tyler, *Radio and the School* (Yonkers, N. Y.: World Book, 1945).

TECHNIQUES

Abbot, Waldo, *Handbook of Broadcasting* (New York: McGraw-Hill, 1950).

Adams, Charles, *Producing and Directing for Television* (New York: Henry Holt, 1953).

Allan, Doug, *How to Write for Television* (New York: Dutton, 1946).

Barnhart, Lyle D., *Radio and Television Announcing* (New York: Prentice-Hall, 1953).

Barnouw, Erik, *Handbook of Radio Writing* (Boston: Little, Brown, 1947).

———, *Handbook of Radio Production* (Boston: Little, Brown, 1949).

Batteson, John, *Movies for TV* (New York: Macmillan, 1951).

Bender, James F. (comp.), *NBC Handbook of Pronunciation* (New York: Crowell, 1943).

Bettinger, Hoyland, *Television Techniques.* Revised by Sol Cornberg (New York: Harper, 1955).

Bolen, Murray, *Fundamentals of Television* (Hollywood: Hollywood Radio Publishers, 1950).

Bretz, Rudy, *Techniques of Television Production* (New York: McGraw-Hill, 1953).

Brooks, William F., *Radio News Writing* (New York: McGraw-Hill, 1948).

Brown, Donald E. and John Paul Jones, *Radio and Television News* (New York: Rinehart, 1954).

Carlile, John S., *Production and Direction of Radio Programs* (New York: Prentice-Hall, 1939).

Charnley, Mitchell V., *News by Radio* (New York: Macmillan, 1948).

Chase, Gilbert, *Music in Radio Broadcasting* (New York: McGraw-Hill, 1946).

Chinn, Howard, *Television Broadcasting* (New York: McGraw-Hill, 1953).

Cowgill, Rome, *Fundamentals of Writing for Radio* (New York: Rinehart, 1949).

Creamer, Joseph and William B. Hoffman, *Radio Sound Effects* (New York: Ziff-Davis, 1945).

Crews, Albert, *Radio Production Directing* (Boston: Houghton Mifflin, 1944).

———, *Professional Radio Writing* (Boston: Houghton Mifflin, 1946).

Dimond, Sidney A. and Donald M. Anderson, *Radio and Television Workshop Manual* (New York: Prentice-Hall, 1952).

Duerr, Edwin, *Radio and Television Acting* (New York: Rinehart, 1950).

Gould, Samuel B. and Sidney A. Dimond, *Training the Local Announcer* (New York: Longmans, Green, 1950).

Greene, Robert S., *Television Writing* (New York: Harper, 1952).

Greet, W. Cabell, *World Words: Recommended Pronunciations* (New York: Columbia University Press, 1944).

Heath, Eric, *Writing for Television* (Los Angeles: American Book Institute, 1950).

Henneke, Ben G., *The Radio Announcer's Handbook* (New York: Rinehart, 1948).

Herman, Lewis, *A Practical Manual of Screen Playwriting for Theatre and Television Films* (Cleveland: World Publishing, 1952).

Herman, Lewis and Marguerite Shallet, *Manual of American Dialects for Radio, Stage, Screen, and Television* (Chicago: Ziff-Davis, 1947).

Hodapp, William, *The Television Actor's Manual* (New York: Appleton-Century-Crofts, 1955).

———, *The Television Manual* (New York: Farrar, Straus, and Young, 1953).

Hoffman, William G. and Ralph L. Rogers, *Effective Radio Speaking* (New York: McGraw-Hill, 1944).

Hotaling, Burton L., *A Manual of Radio News Writing* (Milwaukee: *The Milwaukee Journal,* 1947).

Hubbell, Richard W., *Television Programming and Production* (New York: Rinehart, 1950).

Joels, M. S., *Acting Is a Business: How to Get into Television and Radio* (New York: Hastings House, 1955).

Kaufman, William I., *How to Act for Television* (New York: Merlin Press, 1954).

———, *How to Write for Television* (New York: Hastings House, 1955).

Keith, Alice, *How to Speak and Write for Radio* (New York: Harper, 1944).

Kingson, Walter and Rome C. Cowgill, *Radio Drama Acting and Production* (New York: Rinehart, 1950).

Kingson, Walter, Rome Cowgill, and Ralph Levy, *Broadcasting Television and Radio* (New York: Prentice-Hall, 1955).

LaPrade, Ernest, *Broadcasting Music* (New York: Rinehart, 1947).

Livingston, Don, *Film and the Director* (New York: Macmillan, 1954).

McGill, Earl, *Radio Directing* (New York: McGraw-Hill, 1940).

McMahan, Harry W., *The Television Commercial* (New York: Hastings House, 1954).

Mosse, Baskett (ed.), *Television News Handbook* (Evanston, Ill.: Northwestern University, 1953).

O'Meara, Carroll, *Television Program Production* (New York: Ronald Press, 1955).

Poole, Lynn, *Science via Television* (Baltimore: Johns Hopkins Press, 1950).

Reisz, Karl, *The Technique of Film Editing: Basic Principles for TV* (New York: Farrar, Straus, and Young, 1953).

Roberts, Edward, *Television Writing and Selling* (Boston: *The Writer,* 1954).

Royal, John, *Television Production Problems* (New York: McGraw-Hill, 1948).

Seldes, Gilbert, *Writing for Television* (New York: Doubleday, 1952).

Settel, Irving, Norman Glenn, and Associates, *Television Advertising and Production Handbook* (New York: Crowell, 1953).

Skornia, Harry J., Robert H. Lee, and Fred Brewer, *Creative Broadcasting* (New York: Prentice-Hall, 1950).

Sposa, Louis, *Television Primer of Production and Direction* (New York: McGraw-Hill, 1947).

Stasheff, Edward and Rudy Bretz, *The Television Program* (New York: A. A. Wyn, 1951).

Tooley, Howard, *The Television Workshop* (Minneapolis: The Northwestern Press, 1953).

Turnbull, Robert B., *Radio and Television Sound Effects* (New York: Rinehart, 1951).

Wade, Robert J., *Designing for TV* (New York: Pelligrini and Cudahy, 1952).

———, *Staging TV Programs and Commercials* (New York: Hastings House, 1954).

Warren, Carl N., *Radio News Writing and Editing* (New York: Harper, 1947).

Weaver, Luther, *The Technique of Radio Writing* (New York: Prentice-Hall, 1948).

Weiss, Margaret R., *The TV Writer's Guide* (New York: Pellegrini and Cudahy, 1952).

White, Melvin R., *Beginning Television Production* (Minneapolis: Burgess Publishing Co., 1953).

White, Paul W., *News on the Air* (New York: Harcourt, Brace, 1947).

Wylie, Max, *Radio and Television Writing* (New York: Rinehart, 1950).

ANTHOLOGIES OF RADIO SCRIPTS

Barnouw, Erik (ed.), *Radio Drama in Action* (New York: Rinehart, 1945).

Benét, Stephen V., *They Burned the Books* (New York: Farrar & Rinehart, 1942).

————, *We Stand United and Other Radio Scripts* (Farrar & Rinehart, 1945).

Boyd, James (ed.), *The Free Company Presents* (New York: Dodd, Mead, 1941).

Corwin, Norman, *More by Corwin* (New York: Henry Holt, 1944).

————, *On a Note of Triumph* (New York: Simon & Schuster, 1945).

————, *This Is War* (New York: Dodd, Mead, 1942).

————, *Untitled and Other Radio Dramas* (New York: Henry Holt, 1947).

Coulter, Douglass (ed.), *Columbia Workshop Plays* (New York: Whittlesey House, 1939).

Erekson, R. B. and E. W. Ziebarth, *Six Classic Plays for Radio and How to Produce Them* (Minneapolis: Burgess Publishing, 1940).

Fitelson, H. Williams (ed.), *Theatre Guild on the Air* (New York: Rinehart, 1947).

Kozlenko, William (comp.), *100 Nonroyalty Radio Plays* (New York: Greenberg, 1941).

Lass, A. H., Earle L. McGill, and Donald Axelrod (eds.), *Plays from Radio* (Boston: Houghton Mifflin, 1948).

Let Freedom Ring! (Washington: Script and Transcription Exchange, U. S. Office of Education).

Liss, Joseph, *Radio's Best Plays* (New York: Greenberg, 1947).

MacLeish, Archibald, *Air Raid* (New York: Harcourt, Brace, 1939).

————, *The American Story* (New York: Duell, Sloan & Pearce, 1944).

Morris, James M., *Radio Workshop Plays* (New York: H. W. Wilson, 1943).

Oboler, Arch, *Fourteen Radio Plays* (New York: Random House, 1940).

————, *New Radio Plays* (New York: Random House, 1941).

————, *Oboler Omnibus* (New York: Duell, Sloan & Pearce, 1945).

————, *Plays for Americans* (New York: Farrar & Rinehart, 1941).

————, *This Freedom* (New York: Random House, 1942).

———— and Stephen Longstreet (ed.), *Free World Theatre* (New York: Random House, 1944).

Treasury Star Parade (New York: Farrar & Rinehart, 1942).

Watson, K. W., *Radio Plays for Children* (New York: H. W. Wilson, 1949).

Weiser, Norman S., *The Writer's Radio Theatre, 1940-41* (New York: Harper, 1941).

————, *The Writers' Radio Theatre* (New York: Harper, 1942).

Wishengrad, Morton, *The Eternal Light* (New York: Crown, 1947).

Wylie, Max, *Best Broadcasts of 1938-39* (New York: Whittlesey House, 1940).

————, *Best Broadcasts of 1939-40* (New York: Whittlesey House, 1940).

————, *Best Broadcasts of 1940-41* (New York: McGraw-Hill, 1942).

ANTHOLOGIES OF TELEVISION SCRIPTS

Bretz, Rudy and Edward Stasheff, *Television Scripts for Staging and Study* (New York: A. A. Wyn, 1953).

Chayefsky, Paddy, *Television Plays* (New York: Simon & Schuster, 1955).

Foote, Horton, *Harrison, Texas: Eight Television Plays* (New York: Harcourt, Brace, 1956).

Kaufman, William I., (ed.), *Best Television Plays of the Year*. Vols. I-III (New York: Merlin Press, 1951, 1952, 1953).

Rose, Reginald, *Six Television Plays* (New York: Simon & Schuster, 1956).

Settel, Irving (ed.), *Top TV Shows of the Year, 1954-55* (New York: Hastings House, 1955).

INDEX